Worlds of History

A Comparative Reader

Volume One: To 1550

Worlds of History

A Comparative Reader

Volume One: To 1550

Fourth Edition

Kevin Reilly

Raritan Valley College

Bedford/St. Martin's
Boston • New York

To those who taught me to think historically: Eugene Meehan, Donald Weinstein, and Peter Stearns; and to the memory of Warren Susman and Traian Stoianovich

For Bedford/St. Martin's

Publisher for History: Mary V. Dougherty
Executive Editor for History: Traci Mueller Crowell
Director of Development for History: Jane Knetzger
Senior Developmental Editor: Heidi L. Hood
Production Editor: Katherine Caruana
Production Supervisor: Jennifer Peterson
Executive Marketing Manager: Jenna Bookin Barry
Editorial Assistant: Jennifer Jovin
Copyeditor: Susan Zorn
Senior Art Director: Anna Palchik
Text Design: Janis Owens
Photo Research: Lisa Jelly Smith
Cover Design: Billy Boardman
Cover Art: Jean Froissart, *Masquerade at the French court,* 1393. HIP/Art Resource, N.Y.; *Dance scene,* Iran, 16th C.E. Réunion des Musées Nationaux/Art Resource, N.Y.
Cartography: Mapping Specialists, Ltd.
Composition: MPS Limited, A Macmillan Company
Printing and Binding: Haddon Craftsmen, Inc., an RR Donnelley & Sons Company

President: Joan E. Feinberg
Editorial Director: Denise B. Wydra
Director of Marketing: Karen R. Soeltz
Director of Editing, Design, and Production: Susan W. Brown
Assistant Director of Editing, Design, and Production: Elise S. Kaiser
Managing Editor: Elizabeth M. Schaaf

Library of Congress Control Number: 2010920450

5 4 3 2 1 0
f e d c b a

For information, write: Bedford/St. Martin's, 75 Arlington Street, Boston, MA 02116 (617-399-4000)

ISBN-10: 0-312-54987-3
ISBN-13: 978-0-312-54987-9

Preface

This new edition of *Worlds of History* offers affirmation of past success along with an opportunity to introduce some of the vast new scholarship that is bringing an ever receding past into sharper focus. The format, however, is the same that has worked to great acclaim in previous editions. Teaching introductory world history to college students for forty years has helped me appreciate three enduring truths that provide the framework for this book. The first is that any introductory history course must begin by engaging the students, as they sit before us in their remarkable diversity. The second is that the virtually infinite scope of the subject of world history can best be organized and presented topically and comparatively, thus addressing the interests of our students while respecting the integrity of the field. The third is that students need to learn to think historically, critically, and independently—goals that the study of history is ideally suited to realize. Adopters and reviewers have commented that this strategy has resulted in readings especially effective at piquing student interest and engaging students' minds. This new edition aims to maintain that high level of reader interest for today's students, who face an even greater number of calls on their attention. Accordingly, I have added controversial new studies (on, for instance, Judaism and Islam), a broader representation of new scholarship on sexuality, and a greater range of visual materials. The effort at making *Worlds of History* more accessible, however, has not dumbed it down. There are still more selections from the "great books," presented at greater length and with more annotation, than found elsewhere. I have also continued to carefully word selection introductions so that they cannot become an alternative to reading the source. Finally, I have continued to use the selections to show teachers and students how the study of history can not only teach broad trends and comparative experiences, but also develop what the Romans used to call "habits of mind" and what we today call "critical thinking skills."

The primary and secondary source selections in this reader address specific topics that I believe can impart a general understanding of world history while helping students develop critical thinking skills. The reader's format helps students (and instructors) make sense of the overwhelming richness and complexity of world history. As a framework, the reader has a **thematic and topical organization** that is also chronological, with each chapter focusing on a captivating topic within a particular time period. These topics are constructed to elucidate the major processes and themes most commonly taught in world history courses. Into these thematic chapters I've woven a **comparative approach**, examining two or more cultures at a time. In some chapters students can trace parallel developments in separate regions, such as the rise of ancient urban civilizations in Mesopotamia, Egypt, and Mexico in Volume One, or the advent of nationalism in Japan, India, and the Islamic world in Volume Two. In other cases students examine the enduring effects of contact and exchange between cultures, as in Volume One's chapter on Mongol and Viking raiding and settlements from the tenth to the fourteenth centuries, or Volume Two's chapter on the scientific revolution in Europe, the Ottoman Empire, the Americas, and Asia. To help students grapple with the diverse sources and cultures, a specific **critical thinking focus** in each chapter builds students' ability to analyze, synthesize, and interpret sources one step at a time.

A wealth of **pedagogical tools** helps students unlock the readings and hone their critical thinking skills. Each chapter begins with "Historical Context," an introduction to the chapter's topic that sets the stage for directed comparisons among the readings. A separate "Thinking Historically" section follows, which introduces a particular critical thinking skill—such as asking about author, audience, and agenda or distinguishing causes of change—that are designed to mine the chapter's selections. Headnotes preceding each selection provide additional context, while document-specific "Thinking Historically" paragraphs pose questions to encourage close analysis of the selections using the critical thinking skill introduced at the beginning of the chapter. **Explanatory gloss notes** and **pronunciation guides** throughout ensure comprehension of the readings. A set of "Reflections" that both summarizes and extends the chapter's lessons concludes each chapter.

To enrich the instructor's experience teaching with this reader, I have written an **instructor's resource manual** (*Editor's Notes for Worlds of History*). Available online at **bedfordstmartins.com/reilly/catalog** this manual provides the rationale for the selection and organization of the readings, suggestions for teaching with the documents, and information about additional resources, including films and Internet sites. In addition, all maps from the book are available in Make History at **bedfordstmartins.com/makehistory** where they can be downloaded for presentation.

■ NEW TO THIS EDITION

While I am continually testing selections in my own classroom, I appreciate input from readers and adopters, and I want to thank them for their many suggestions for exciting new chapters and selections. Having incorporated some of this feedback, I think those who have used the reader previously will find the fourth edition even more geographically and topically comprehensive, interesting, and accessible to students.

More than one-third of the new selections are on regions and topics from Latin America to Africa and on new theories on the Koran to women and science during the Enlightenment, which have allowed me to introduce fresh material into each volume. In addition, I have included five new chapters that explore the Chinese and Roman empires (Chapter 4); gender, sex, and love in the classical era (Chapter 5); the spread of Christianity, Buddhism, and Islam (Chapter 7); the Cold War and the Third World (Chapter 26); and the environment, population, and resources in the contemporary world (Chapter 27). With these new chapters I have also included five new "Thinking Historically" exercises: "Distinguishing Ideas from Actions and Understanding Their Relationship"; "Asking about Author, Audience, and Agenda"; "Understanding Continuity and Change"; "Finding a Point of View in Word Selection"; and "Evaluating Arguments."

Another exciting change to this edition is the inclusion of 20 percent more maps and images with more visuals acting as "documents," thereby increasing the reader's emphasis on the importance of nonwritten sources as historical evidence. Nine chapters now incorporate visual evidence, including Egyptian wall paintings in Chapter 2, Fayum portraits of women in Chapter 5, images of the Black Death in Chapter 12, new illustrations of medieval cities in Chapters 13, images of humans and the environment in Chapter 14, contrasting views of Amerindians and new illustrations of cross-Atlantic slavery in Chapter 16, new anatomical drawings on the Scientific Revolution in Chapter 19, Japanese images of Westernization in Chapter 23, and World War I propaganda posters, including new posters aimed at women on the home front, in Chapter 24.

Two more changes to this edition of *Worlds of History* have, I hope, made the reader text more accessible. First, I have expanded the popular explanatory gloss notes so students may read the documents with deeper appreciation. Second, due to favorable reception in the third edition, I have included more terms in the running pronunciation guide at the base of the page. This sounds out difficult-to-pronounce terms and names and should help students discuss the sources with greater confidence.

I am not a believer in change for its own sake; when I have a successful way of teaching a subject, I am not disposed to jettison it for something new. Consequently, many of my most satisfying changes are incremental: a better translation of a document, the addition of a newly discovered source, or additional questions to further inspire critical thinking. In some cases I have been able to further edit a useful source, retaining its muscle, but providing room for a precious new find. I begin each round of revision with the conviction that the book is already as good as it can get. And I end each round with the surprising discovery that it is much better than it was.

■ ACKNOWLEDGMENTS

A book like this cannot be written without the help and advice of a vast army of colleagues and friends. I consider myself enormously fortunate to have met and known such a large group of gifted and generous scholars. Some were especially helpful in the preparation of this new edition. They include W. Nathan Alexander, Troy University; Stanley Arnold, Northern Illinois University; Alan Barenberg, Columbus State University; Richard Bowler, Salisbury University; Michael Cardinal, Heartland Community College; Michael Clinton, Gwynedd-Mercy College; William D. Coleman, McMaster University; Clayton J. Drees, Virginia Wesleyan College; Paul Gillingham, University of North Carolina–Wilmington; Steven A. Glazer, Graceland University; Dale Griepenstroh, Chula Vista High School (CA); Gillian Hendershot, Grand Valley State University; Marianne Holdzkom, Southern Polytechnic State University; Megan Jones, University of Delaware; Dana Lightfoot, University of Texas at El Paso; Edward H. Lykens, Middle Tennessee State University; Eric Martin, Lewis-Clark State College; Thomas W. Maulucci, Jr., American International College; Eben Miller, Southern Maine Community College; Peter A. Ngwafu, Albany State University; Neal Palmer, Christian Brothers University; Elizabeth Peifer, Auburn University–Montgomery; Thomas Porter, North Carolina A&T State University; Dana Rabin, University of Illinois; Linda Rodish, Mesquite High School (AZ); Mary Louise Shell, Etowah High School (GA); George D. Sussman, LaGuardia Community College; Sarah Trembanis, Immaculata University; Jason Treter, National University; Julie Turner, Miami University of Ohio; Gary Vargas, Mt. San Jacinto College; Alfred Martin Wainwright, The University of Akron; Andrew Walzer, Los Angeles City College; Krista Webb, Woodstock High School (GA); James Whidden, Acadia University; Andrew Kier Wise, Daemen College; and Jack Zevin, Queens College.

Over the years I have benefited from the suggestions of innumerable friends and fellow world historians. Among them: Michael Adas, Rutgers University; Jerry Bentley, University of Hawai'i; David Berry, Essex County Community College; Edmund (Terry) Burke III, University of California–Santa Cruz; Catherine Clay, Shippensburg University; the late Philip Curtin, Johns Hopkins University; S. Ross Doughty, Ursinus College; Ross Dunn, San Diego State University; Marc Gilbert, Hawai'i Pacific University; Steve Gosch, University of Wisconsin–Eau Claire; Gregory Guzman, Bradley University; Brock Haussamen, Raritan Valley College; Allen Howard, Rutgers University; Sarah Hughes, Shippensburg University; Karen Jolly, University of Hawai'i; Stephen Kaufman, Raritan Valley College; Maghan Keita, Villanova University; Craig Lockard, University of Wisconsin–Green Bay; Pat Manning, University of Pittsburgh; Adam McKeown, Columbia University; John McNeill, Georgetown University; William H. McNeill, University of Chicago;

Gyan Prakash, Princeton University; Lauren Ristvet, University of Pennsylvania; Robert Rosen, University of California–Los Angeles; Heidi Roupp, Aspen High School; John Russell-Wood, Johns Hopkins University; Lynda Shaffer, Tufts University; Ira Spar, Ramapo College; Robert Strayer, California State University–Monterey Bay; Robert Tignor, Princeton University; and John Voll, Georgetown University.

I also want to thank the people at Bedford/St. Martin's. Joan Feinberg and Denise Wydra remained involved and helpful throughout, as did Mary Dougherty, Traci Mueller Crowell, and Jane Knetzger. Adrianne Hiltz provided invaluable help in reviewing the previous edition, and Jennifer Jovin coordinated the development of the instructor's manual, ensured the book's maps all appeared online in *Make History*, and provided invaluable behind-the-scenes support for the reader. I want to thank my production editor, Katherine Caruana, for overseeing the entire production process of design, copyediting, and page composition. I would also like to thank Susan Zorn for copyediting, Billy Boardman for the cover design, Kim Cevoli for designing promotional materials, and Jenna Bookin Barry for expertly marketing the book. Finally, my deepest appreciation goes to Senior Editor Louise Townsend for her editorial guidance through the first half of the revision and Senior Editor Heidi Hood for completing the process, challenging everything again, and forcing me to make it a better book than I had any right to expect.

None of this would have been possible if I had not been blessed in my own introduction to history and critical thinking at Rutgers in the 1960s with teachers I still aspire to emulate. Eugene Meehan taught me how to think and showed me that I could. Traian Stoianovich introduced me to the world and an endless range of historical inquiry. Warren Susman lit up a room with more life than I ever knew existed. Donald Weinstein guided me as a young teaching assistant to listen to students and talk with them rather than at them. And Peter Stearns showed me how important and exciting it could be to understand history by making comparisons. I dedicate this book to them.

Finally, I want to thank my own institution, Raritan Valley College, for nurturing my career, allowing me to teach whatever I wanted, and entrusting me with some of the best students one could encounter anywhere. I could not ask for anything more. Except, of course, a loving wife like Pearl.

Kevin Reilly

Introduction

Throughout both volumes of this reader you have a lesson in world history, which deals with a particular historical period and topic. Some of the topics are narrow and specific, covering events such as the Black Death and World War I in detail, while others are broad and general, such as the spread of universal religions and globalization.

As you learn about historical periods and topics, you will also be learning to explore history by analyzing primary and secondary sources systematically. The "Thinking Historically" exercises in each chapter encourage habits of mind that I associate with my own study of history. They are not necessarily intended to turn you into historians but, rather, to give you skills that will help you in all of your college courses and throughout your life. For example, the first chapter leads you to become more perceptive about time, the passage of time, measuring time, and the time between events, all of which are useful throughout life. Similarly, a number of chapters help you in various ways to distinguish between fact and opinion—an ability as necessary for work, on a jury, in the voting booth, and in discussions with friends as it is in the study of history.

World history is nothing less than everything ever done or imagined, so we cannot possibly cover it all; we are forced to choose among different places and times in our study of the global past. Our choices do include some particular moments in time, like the one in 111 C.E. in the first half of this reader, when the Roman governor of Bithynia consulted Emperor Trajan about proper treatment of Christians, but our attention will be directed toward much longer periods as well. And while we will visit particular places in time like Imperial Rome in the second century or Africa in the nineteenth century, typically we will study more than one place at a time by using a comparative approach.

Comparisons can be enormously useful in studying world history. When we compare cities globally in the religious origins of Christians and Buddhists, the raiding and trading of Vikings and Mongols, the scientific revolution in Europe and Japan, and the Cold War in Cuba and Afghanistan, we learn about the general and the specific at the same time. My hope is that by comparing some of the various worlds of history, a deeper and more nuanced understanding of our global past will emerge. With that understanding, we are better equipped to make sense of the world today and to confront whatever the future holds.

Contents

Preface   v

Introduction   xi

1. **Prehistory and the Origins of Patriarchy: Gathering, Agricultural, and Urban Societies, 20,000–1000 B.C.E. 1**

The agricultural revolution ten thousand years ago and the urban revolution five thousand years ago were probably the two most important events in human history. Did they "revolutionize" the power of women or begin the age of male domination? Thinking in "stages" can be more useful than thinking in years.

HISTORICAL CONTEXT 1

THINKING HISTORICALLY: Thinking about History in Stages 2

1. NATALIE ANGIER, Furs for Evening, But Cloth Was the Stone Age Standby 2

2. MARJORIE SHOSTAK, Nisa: The Life and Words of a !Kung Woman 9

3. MARGARET EHRENBERG, Women in Prehistory 15

4. RAMON A. GUTIERREZ, When Jesus Came, the Corn Mothers Went Away 22

5. CATHERINE CLAY, CHANDRIKA PAUL, AND CHRISTINE SENECAL, Women in the First Urban Communities (after 3500 B.C.E.) 29

6. An Assyrian Law and a Palace Decree 33

REFLECTIONS 35

2. The Urban Revolution and "Civilization": Mesopotamia, Egypt, and Mexico, 3500–1000 B.C.E. 37

The urban revolution created writing and interpretation, war and law, individual anonymity, money and taxes, paupers and kings. Did Mesopotamia, Egypt, and Mexico undergo the same development and changes? We have primary (written and visual) as well as secondary sources to find the answers.

HISTORICAL CONTEXT 37

THINKING HISTORICALLY: Distinguishing Primary and Secondary Sources 39

1. KEVIN REILLY, Cities and Civilization 40
2. The Epic of Gilgamesh 49
3. Hammurabi's Code 58
4. Advice to the Young Egyptian: "Be a Scribe" 62
5. Egyptian Book of the Dead 66
6. Images of Ancient Egypt 69
   Entering the Afterlife 70
   The Hall of Ma'at 71
7. JOHN NOBLE WILFORD, The Olmec: Mother Culture, or Only a Sister? 72

REFLECTIONS 77

3. Identity in Caste and Territorial Societies: Greece and India, 1000–300 B.C.E. 81

Ancient Greece and India developed with different ideas of society. Does who we are depend on where we are or who we know? While finding out, we explore the relationship between facts and opinions, sources and interpretations.

HISTORICAL CONTEXT 81

THINKING HISTORICALLY: Interpreting Primary Sources in Light of a Secondary Source 82

1. WILLIAM H. McNEILL, Greek and Indian Civilization 84
2. The Rig Veda: Sacrifice as Creation 91
3. The Upanishads: Karma and Reincarnation 93

4. The Upanishads: Brahman and Atman 94

5. The Bhagavad Gita: Caste and Self 96

6. ARISTOTLE, The Athenian Constitution: Territorial Sovereignty 102

7. THUCYDIDES, The Funeral Oration of Pericles 105

8. PLATO, The Republic 110

REFLECTIONS 120

4. Emperors and Philosophers: China and Rome, 300 B.C.E.–300 C.E. 122

Roughly two thousand years ago the Chinese Empire and the Roman Empire spanned Eurasia. In comparing these ancient empires, we seek to understand the relationship between emperors and philosophical ideas and, more generally, between power and knowledge. We ask how we understand the impact of ideas on actions and of actions on ideas.

HISTORICAL CONTEXT 122

THINKING HISTORICALLY: Distinguishing Ideas from Actions and Understanding Their Relationship 125

1. VALERIE HANSEN, The Creation of the Chinese Empire 126

2. SIMA QIAN, The First Emperor 133

3. CONFUCIUS, The Analects 138

4. HAN FEI, Legalism 140

5. LAOZI, Taoism: The Classic of the Way and the Power 144

6. REBECCA FLEMING, Rome: Knowledge and Empire 149

7. CICERO, On Government and Law 154

8. MARCUS AURELIUS, Meditations 158

REFLECTIONS 162

5. Gender, Sex, and Love in Classical Societies: India, China, and the Mediterranean, 500 B.C.E.–500 C.E. 164

The identities and experiences of women and men of the classical era varied from East Asia to the Mediterranean. Nevertheless, the predominance of patriarchy in all of these societies set certain limits to the possibilities for women and, in each case, shaped the way men and women related to each other. We can better understand the great works of the classical age (or any historical sources) by asking about their origins, reception, and intended purpose.

HISTORICAL CONTEXT *164*

THINKING HISTORICALLY: **Asking about Author, Audience, and Agenda** *165*

1. SARAH SHAVER HUGHES AND BRADY HUGHES, Women in the Classical Era *165*
2. BAN ZHAO, Lessons for Women *172*
3. VATSYANA, The Kama Sutra *177*
4. PLATO, The Symposium *182*
5. OVID, The Art of Love *186*
6. Portraits *192*
   Portrait of a Fayum Woman with Large Gold Necklace *193*
   Portrait of Fayum Woman with White Earrings *194*
   Portrait of "Ammonius from Antinoe," with Ankh *195*

REFLECTIONS *196*

6. From Tribal to Universal Religion: Hindu-Buddhist and Judeo-Christian Traditions, 600 B.C.E.–100 C.E. 198

Two religious traditions transformed themselves into universal religions at about the same time in two different parts of Asia as each became part of a more connected world. Their holy books reveal the changes as well as the desire to hold on to the tried and true.

HISTORICAL CONTEXT *198*

THINKING HISTORICALLY: **Detecting Change in Primary Sources** *199*

1. Hinduism: Svetasvatara Upanishad *200*
2. Buddhism: Gotama's Discovery *202*
3. Buddhism and Caste *207*
4. Mahayana Buddhism: The Lotus Sutra *209*
5. Judaism and the Bible: History, Laws, and Psalms *212*
6. Judaism and the Bible: Prophecy and the Apocalypse *223*
7. The Christian Bible: Jesus According to Matthew *228*
8. PAUL, Letters *231*

REFLECTIONS *234*

7. The Spread of Universal Religions: Afro-Eurasia, 100–1000 C.E. 236

Christianity, Buddhism, and later Islam spread far across Eurasia and Africa often along the same routes in the first thousand years of the Common Era. Perhaps Judaism did as well. What made these religions so expansive? How were they alike and different? Who converted whom? What did they change, and what did they leave the same?

HISTORICAL CONTEXT 236

THINKING HISTORICALLY: **Understanding Continuity and Change** 237

1. OFRI ILANI, Conversion and the Expansion of Judaism 239
2. Pliny Consults the Emperor Trajan 243
3. EUSEBIUS, Life of Constantine 246
4. Christianity in China: The Nestorian Monument 250
5. Buddhism in China: The Disposition of Error 254
6. Selections from the Koran 259
7. ALEXANDER STILLE, Scholars Are Quietly Offering New Theories of the Koran 267
8. Peace Terms with Jerusalem 272
9. The Epic of Sundiata 275

REFLECTIONS 277

8. Medieval Civilizations: European, Islamic, Chinese, and Maya Societies, 250–1250 280

By 1000 three great civilizations — European, Islamic, and Chinese — spanned Eurasia. Of the three, China and Islam were the strongest, Europe the weakest. Across the Atlantic, Mayan civilization gained cultural predominance even earlier. The similarities and differences can be best understood by looking separately at the social structure, economy, politics, and culture of each.

HISTORICAL CONTEXT 280

THINKING HISTORICALLY: **Distinguishing Social, Economic, Political, and Cultural Aspects of Civilizations** 281

1. Feudalism: An Oath of Homage and Fealty 281
2. The Magna Carta 284
3. Islam: Sayings Ascribed to the Prophet 289

4. Muhammad's Night Journey *291*

5. AL-TANUKHI, A Government Job *293*

6. ICHISADA MIYAZAKI, The Chinese Civil Service Exam System *296*

7. LIU TSUNG-YUAN, Camel Kuo the Gardener *303*

8. SIMON MARTIN AND NIKOLAI GRUBE, Chronicle of the Maya Kings and Queens *305*

REFLECTIONS *312*

9. Love, Sex, and Marriage: Medieval Europe and Asia, 400–1350 314

Love and marriage make the world go'round today, but not a thousand years ago. Love, sex, and marriage were also not always experienced in the same relationship, even ideally. These words meant different things to different people throughout Europe and Asia. We use cultural comparisons to find out more.

HISTORICAL CONTEXT *314*

THINKING HISTORICALLY: Analyzing Cultural Differences *315*

1. KEVIN REILLY, Love in Medieval Europe, India, and Japan *316*

2. ULRICH VON LIECHTENSTEIN, The Service of Ladies *324*

3. ANDREAS CAPELLANUS, The Art of Courtly Love *330*

4. KALIDASA, Shakuntala *335*

5. MURASAKI SHIKIBU, The Tale of Genji *338*

6. ZHOU DAGUAN, Sex in the City of Angkor *344*

REFLECTIONS *348*

10. The First Crusade: Muslims, Christians, and Jews during the First Crusade, 1095–1099 350

The First Crusade initiated a centuries-long struggle and dialogue between Christians and Muslims that would have a lasting impact on both. Wars are windows on cultures, but they also make moving narratives. Using the selections here, put together your own version of the story.

HISTORICAL CONTEXT *350*

THINKING HISTORICALLY: Analyzing and Writing Narrative *352*

1. FULCHER OF CHARTRES, Pope Urban at Clermont *353*

2. Chronicle of Solomon bar Simson *359*

3. ANNA COMNENA, The Alexiad *365*

4. FULCHER OF CHARTRES, The Siege of Antioch *370*

5. IBN AL-QALANISI, The Damascus Chronicle *373*

6. RAYMOND OF ST. GILES, COUNT OF TOULOUSE, The Capture of Jerusalem by the Crusaders *377*

7. IBN AL-ATHIR, The Conquest of Jerusalem *381*

8. Letter from a Jewish Pilgrim in Egypt *383*

REFLECTIONS *385*

11. Raiders of Steppe and Sea: Vikings and Mongols, Eurasia and the Atlantic, 900–1350 387

From the late ninth through the tenth century, waves of Viking ships attacked across Europe; a few centuries later, beginning in 1200, the Mongols swept across Eurasia, conquering all in their path and creating the largest empire the world had ever seen. What was the impact of these raiding peoples on settled societies and vice versa? In considering this question and the violent and destructive nature of these "barbarian" raids, we will consider the relationship of morality to history.

HISTORICAL CONTEXT *387*

THINKING HISTORICALLY: Distinguishing Historical Understanding from Moral Judgments *389*

1. GREGORY GUZMAN, Were the Barbarians a Negative or Positive Factor in Ancient and Medieval History? *391*

2. IBN FADLAN, The Viking Rus *398*

3. BARRY CUNLIFFE, The Western Vikings *403*

4. Eirik's Saga *410*

5. YVO OF NARBONA, The Mongols *413*

6. The Secret History of the Mongols *418*

7. JOHN OF PLANO CARPINI, History of the Mongols *425*

REFLECTIONS *430*

12. The Black Death: Afro-Eurasia, 1346–1350 432

The pandemic plague ravaged the population of Afro-Eurasia, killing about one-third of the population of Europe and Egypt. In this chapter, we examine the impact of the plague in various locales while also contemplating its causes and the relation between cause and effect.

HISTORICAL CONTEXT 432

THINKING HISTORICALLY: Considering Cause and Effect 432

1. MARK WHEELIS, Biological Warfare at the 1346 Siege of Caffa 433

2. GABRIELE DE' MUSSIS, Origins of the Black Death 441

3. GIOVANNI BOCCACCIO, The Plague in Florence: *From* the Decameron 447

4. Images of the Black Death 452

　　The Black Death, 1348 453

　　Flagellants, from a Fifteenth-Century Chronicle from Constance, Switzerland 454

　　The Burning of Jews in an Early Printed Woodcut 454

　　François de la Sarra, Tomb at La Sarraz, Switzerland, c. 1390 455

5. AHMAD AL-MAQRIZI, The Plague in Cairo 456

6. MICHAEL W. DOLS, The Comparative Communal Responses to the Black Death in Muslim and Christian Societies 459

REFLECTIONS 465

13. On Cities: European, Chinese, Islamic, and Mexican Cities, 1000–1550 467

What did increasing urbanization from the medieval period on mean for those who lived in cities and those who did not? Wandering through some of the great cities of medieval Europe, China, the Islamic world, and Mexico, we attempt to answer this question while also considering the validity and merits of one historian's famous comparative thesis about urbanization.

HISTORICAL CONTEXT 467

THINKING HISTORICALLY: Evaluating a Comparative Thesis 467

1. FERNAND BRAUDEL, Towns and Cities 468

2. GREGORIO DATI, Corporations and Community in Florence 479

3. Marco Polo, On the City of Hangchou *481*

4. S. D. Goitein, Cairo: An Islamic City in Light of the Geniza *487*

5. Bernal Díaz, Cities of Mexico *491*

6. Images of Medieval Cities *497*

City View of Florence, 1482 *498*

Cairo, 1549 *499*

A *Chinese City in* Along the River during the Qingming Festival *500*

Siena in Effects of Good Government *502*

Reflections *503*

14. Ecology, Technology, and Science: Europe, Asia, and Oceania, 500–1550 505

Since the Middle Ages, the most significant changes have occurred in the fields of ecology, technology, and science. In this chapter we read and assess three grand theories about the origins of our technological transformation and of our environmental problems, drawing on written and visual primary source evidence to develop our conclusions.

Historical Context *505*

Thinking Historically: Evaluating Grand Theories *506*

1. Lynn White Jr., The Historical Roots of Our Ecological Crisis *506*

2. Image from a Cistercian Manuscript, Twelfth Century *516*

3. Image from a French Calendar, Fifteenth Century *518*

4. Image of a Chinese *Feng-Shui* Master *520*

5. Image of European Surveying Instruments *522*

6. Lynda Norene Shaffer, Southernization *523*

7. Jared Diamond, Easter Island's End *535*

Reflections *543*

LIST OF MAPS

Map 2.1 Early Civilizations: Egypt and Mesopotamia *38*

Map 3.1 Indus River Valley, c. 500 B.C.E. *82*

Map 3.2 Archaic Greece, c. 750–500 B.C.E. *83*

Map 4.1 Imperial China, 210 B.C.E. and 120 C.E. *123*

Map 4.2 The Roman Empire, 264 B.C.E. and 117 C.E. *124*

Map 6.1 The Ancient Near East, 4000–1000 B.C.E. *214*

Map 7.1 The Spread of Early Christianity and Buddhism *238*

Map 7.2 The Expansion of Islam to 750 C.E. *260*

Map 10.1 The First Crusade, 1095–1099 *351*

Map 11.1 Viking Invasions and Voyages of the Ninth and Tenth Centuries *388*

Map 11.2 Mongol Invasions of the Thirteenth Century *390*

Map 12.1 Tentative Chronology of the Initial Spread of Plague in the Mid-Fourteenth Century *435*

1

Prehistory and the Origins of Patriarchy

Gathering, Agricultural, and Urban Societies, 20,000–1000 B.C.E.

■ HISTORICAL CONTEXT

Men control more of the world's income, wealth, and resources; enjoy more opportunities, freedoms, and positions of power; and exercise greater control over the bodies, wishes, and lives of others than do women. In most of the world, men dominate, parents prefer sons to daughters, and most people—even women—associate maleness with strength, energy, reason, science, and the important public sphere. A system of male rule—"patriarchy"—seems as old as humanity itself. But is it? This chapter will ask if patriarchy is natural or historical. If patriarchy did not always exist, did it have a historical beginning, middle, and, therefore, potentially a historical end? If patriarchy had human causes, can humans also create a more equal world?

The selections in this chapter span the three types of societies known to human history: hunting and gathering (the earliest human lifestyle), agricultural and pastoral (beginning about ten thousand years ago), and urban (beginning about five thousand years ago). Thus, we can speak of the agricultural revolution (8000 B.C.E.) and the urban revolution (3000 B.C.E.) as two of the most important changes in human history. These events drastically transformed the way people earned a living and led to increased populations, greater productivity, and radically changed lifestyles.

How did the lives of men and women change with these revolutions? How did the relationships between men and women change? As people settled in agricultural villages, and later in cities, economic and social differences between groups became more marked. Did differences between the sexes increase as well? Did men and women have relatively equal power before the development of agriculture and the rise of cities? Did patriarchy originate as part of the transition from agricultural to urban society, or did men always have more power?

■ THINKING HISTORICALLY

Thinking about History in Stages

To answer these questions, one must think of early human history in broad periods or stages. However, history does not develop in neat compartments, one clearly distinguished from the other. Historians must organize and analyze disparate events and developments that occur over time to make sense of them. This chapter follows a widely accepted division of early history into the hunting-gathering, agricultural-pastoral, and urban stages. You might reflect on how this system of structuring the past makes history more intelligible; you might also consider the shortcomings of such a system. What challenges to the idea of historical stages do the readings in the chapter pose? On balance, does organizing history into stages make it easier or more difficult to understand complex changes, such as evolving gender roles?

1

NATALIE ANGIER

Furs for Evening, But Cloth Was the Stone Age Standby

The female "Venus" statues discussed in the following article date back over 20,000 years and are the earliest sculptures of humans. Archaeologists have long considered them symbols of fertility, given their exaggerated depiction of the female anatomy. As *New York Times* science writer Natalie Angier reports, some archaeologists have recently begun to reinterpret these "Venuses," emphasizing the detailed clothing and reconsidering what these costumes might reveal about the role of women in hunting and gathering societies. What conclusions do archaeologists draw from these new interpretations? What conclusions might you draw from these statues about the roles of women and their relative status in prehistoric society?

Source: Natalie Angier, "Furs for Evening, But Cloth Was the Stone Age Standby," *New York Times*, December 15, 1999, p. F1.

THINKING HISTORICALLY

Grouping prehistory into the hunting-gathering, agricultural-pastoral, and urban stages emphasizes how early people sustained themselves. Archaeologists and historians also divide prehistory into eras defined by the tools that humans developed. They also call the age of hunters and gatherers the Old Stone Age, or Paleolithic Era, because of the rough stone tools and arrow points that humans fashioned in this period. The age of agriculture is called the New Stone Age, or Neolithic Era, because of the use of more sophisticated stone tools. The urban age is often called the Bronze Age because city people began to smelt tin and copper to make bronze tools. Angier's article asks us to reconsider the importance of these designations by highlighting what Dr. Elizabeth Wayland Barber has termed the "string revolution." What is the string revolution, and what was its significance? According to Angier, how might the string revolution prompt us to reconsider stages of prehistory?

Ah, the poor Stone Age woman of our kitschy imagination. When she isn't getting bonked over the head with a club and dragged across the cave floor by her matted hair, she's hunched over a fire, poking at a roasting mammoth thigh while her husband retreats to his cave studio to immortalize the mammoth hunt in fresco. Or she's Raquel Welch, saber-toothed sex kitten, or Wilma Flintstone, the original Soccer Mom. But whatever her form, her garb is the same: some sort of animal pelt, cut nasty, brutish, and short.

Now, according to three anthropologists, it is time to toss such hidebound clichés of Paleolithic woman on the midden heap of prehistory. In a new analysis of the renowned "Venus" figurines, the handsize statuettes of female bodies carved from 27,000 to 20,000 years ago, the researchers have found evidence that the women of the so-called upper Paleolithic era were far more accomplished, economically powerful, and sartorially gifted than previously believed.

As the researchers see it, subtle but intricate details on a number of the figurines offer the most compelling evidence yet that Paleolithic women had already mastered a revolutionary skill long thought to have arisen much later in human history: the ability to weave plant fibers into cloth, rope, nets, and baskets.

And with a flair for textile production came a novel approach to adorning and flaunting the human form. Far from being restricted to a wardrobe of what Dr. Olga Soffer, one of the researchers, calls "smelly animal hides," Paleolithic people knew how to create fine fabrics that very likely resembled linen. They designed string skirts, slung low on the hips or belted up on the waist, which artfully revealed at least as much as

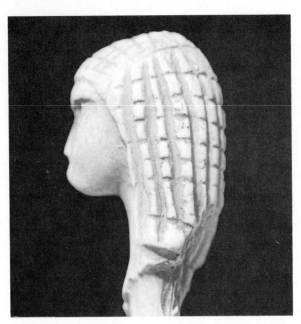

Figure 1.1   The Venus of Brassempouy, France.
Source: Steve Holland, University of Illinois.

they concealed. They wove elaborate caps and snoods for the head, and bandeaux for the chest—a series of straps that amounted to a cupless brassiere. [See Figure 1.1.]

"Some of the textiles they had must have been incredibly fine, comparable to something from Donna Karan or Calvin Klein," said Dr. Soffer, an archaeologist with the University of Illinois in Urbana-Champaign.

Archaeologists and anthropologists have long been fascinated by the Venus figurines and have theorized endlessly about their origin and purpose. But nearly all of that speculation has centered on the exaggerated body parts of some of the figurines: the huge breasts, the bulging thighs and bellies, the well-defined vulvas. Hence, researchers have suggested that the figurines were fertility fetishes, or prehistoric erotica, or gynecology primers.

"Because they have emotionally charged thingies like breasts and buttocks, the Venus figurines have been the subject of more spilled ink than anything I know of," Dr. Soffer said. "There are as many opinions on them as there are people in the field."

In their new report, which will be published in the spring in the journal *Current Anthropology*, Dr. Soffer and her colleagues, Dr. James M. Adovasio and Dr. David C. Hyland of the Mercyhurst Archaeological Institute at Mercyhurst College in Erie, Pa., point out that voluptuous

Figure 1.2   The Venus of Kostenki (Russia), wearing a woven bandeau.

Source: Bill Wiegand, University of Illinois.

body parts notwithstanding, a number of the figurines are shown wearing items of clothing. And when they zeroed in on the details of those carved garments, the researchers saw proof of considerable textile craftsmanship, an intimate knowledge of how fabric is woven.

"Scholars have been looking at these things for years, but unfortunately, their minds have been elsewhere," Dr. Adovasio said. "Most of them didn't recognize the clothing as clothing. If they noticed anything at all, they misinterpreted what they saw, writing off the bandeaux, for example, as tattoos or body art." [See Figure 1.2.]

Scrutinizing the famed Venus of Willendorf, for example, which was discovered in lower Austria in 1908, the researchers paid particular attention to the statuette's head. The Venus has no face to speak of, but detailed coils surround its scalp. Most scholars have interpreted the coils as a kind of paleo-coiffure, but Dr. Adovasio, an authority on textiles and basketry, recognized the plaiting as what he called a "radially sewn piece of headgear with vertical stem stitches."

Willendorf's haberdashery "might have looked like one of those woven hats you see on Jamaicans on the streets of New York," he said, adding, "These were cool things."[See Figure 1.3.]

Figure 1.3   The Venus of Willendorf.
Source: Visual Arts Library (London)/Alamy.

On the Venus of Lespugue, an approximately 25,000-year-old figurine from southwestern France, the anthropologists noticed a "remarkable" degree of detail lavished on the rendering of a string skirt, with the tightness and angle of each individual twist of the fibers carefully delineated. The skirt is attached to a low-slung hip belt and tapers in the back to a tail, the edges of its hem deliberately frayed.

"That skirt is to die for," said Dr. Soffer, who, before she turned to archaeology, was in the fashion business. "Though maybe it's an acquired taste."

To get an idea of what such an outfit might have looked like, she said, imagine a hula dancer wrapping a 1930s-style beaded curtain around her waist. "We're not talking protection from the elements here," Dr. Soffer said. "This would have been ritual wear, if it was worn at all, a way of communicating with higher powers."

Other anthropologists point out that string skirts, which appear in Bronze-Age artifacts and are mentioned by Homer, may have been worn at the equivalent of a debutantes' ball, to advertise a girl's coming of age. In some parts of Eastern Europe, the skirts still survive as lacy elements of folk costumes.

The researchers presented their results earlier this month at a meeting on the importance of perishables in prehistory that was held at the University of Florida in Gainesville. "One of the most common reactions we heard was, 'How could we have missed that stuff all these years?'" Dr. Adovasio said.

Dr. Margaret W. Conkey, a professor of anthropology at the University of California at Berkeley, and co-editor, with Joan Gero, of *Engendering Archaeology* (Blackwell Publishers, 1991) said, "They're helping us to look at old materials in new ways, to which I say bravo!"

Not all scholars had been blinded by the Venusian morphology. Dr. Elizabeth Wayland Barber, a professor of archaeology and linguistics at Occidental College in Los Angeles, included in her 1991 volume *Prehistoric Textiles* a chapter arguing that some Venus figurines were wearing string skirts. The recent work from Dr. Soffer and her colleagues extends and amplifies on Dr. Barber's original observations.

The new work also underscores the often neglected importance of what Dr. Barber has termed the "string revolution." Archaeologists have long emphasized the invention of stone and metal tools in furthering the evolution of human culture. Even the names given to various periods in human history and prehistory are based on heavyweight tools: the word *Paleolithic*—the period extending from about 750,000 years ago to 15,000 years ago—essentially means "Old Stone Age." And duly thudding and clanking after the Paleolithic period were the Mesolithic and Neolithic, or Middle and New Stone Age, the Bronze Age, the Iron Age, the Industrial Age.

But at least as central to the course of human affairs as the invention of stone tools was the realization that plant products could be exploited for purposes other than eating. The fact that some of the Venus figurines are shown wearing string skirts, said Dr. Barber, "means that the people who made them must also have known how to make twisted string."

With the invention of string and the power to weave, people could construct elaborate yet lightweight containers in which to carry, store, and cook food. They could fashion baby slings to secure an infant snugly against its mother's body, thereby freeing up the woman to work and wander. They could braid nets, the better to catch prey animals without the risk of hand-to-tooth combat. They could lash together wooden logs or planks to build a boat.

"The string revolution was a profound event in human history," Dr. Adovasio said. "When people started to fool around with plants and plant byproducts, that opened vast new avenues of human progress."

In the new report, the researchers argue that women are likely to have been the primary weavers and textile experts of prehistory, and may have even initiated the string revolution in the first place—although men undoubtedly did their share of weaving when it came to making hunting and fishing nets, for example. They base that conclusion on modern crosscultural studies, which have found that women constitute the great bulk of the world's weavers, basketry makers, and all-round mistresses of plant goods.

But while vast changes in manufacturing took the luster off the textile business long ago, with the result that such "women's work" is now accorded low status and sweatshop wages, the researchers argue that weaving and other forms of fiber craft once commanded great prestige. By their estimate, the detailing of the stitches shown on some of the Venus figurines was intended to flaunt the value and beauty of the original spinsters' skills. Why else would anybody have bothered etching the stitchery in a permanent medium, if not to boast, whoa! Check out these wefts!

"It's made immortal in stone," Dr. Soffer said. "You don't carve something like this unless it's very important."

The detailing of the Venusian garb also raises the intriguing possibility that the famed little sculptures, which rank right up there with the Lascaux cave paintings in the pantheon of Western art, were hewn by women—moonlighting seamstresses, to be precise. "It's always assumed that the carvers were men, a bunch of guys sitting around making their zaftig Barbie dolls," Dr. Soffer said. "But maybe that wasn't the case, or not always the case. With some of these figurines, the person carving them clearly knew weaving. So either that person was a weaver herself, or he was living with her. He's got an adviser."

Durable though the Venus figurines are, Dr. Adovasio and his coworkers are far more interested in what their carved detailing says about the role of perishables in prehistory. "The vast bulk of what humans made was made in media that hasn't survived," Dr. Adovasio said. Experts estimate the ratio of perishable objects to durable objects generated in the average culture is about 20 to 1.

"We're reconstructing the past based on 5 percent of what was used," Dr. Soffer said.

Because many of the items that have endured over the millennia are things like arrowheads and spear points, archaeologists studying the Paleolithic era have generally focused on the ways and means of that noble savage, a.k.a. Man the Hunter, to the exclusion of other members of the tribe.

"To this day, in Paleolithic studies we hear about Man the Hunter doing such boldly wonderful things as thrusting spears into woolly mammoths, or battling it out with other men," Dr. Adovasio said. "We've emphasized the activities of a small segment of the population—healthy young men—at the total absence of females, old people of either sex, and children. We've glorified one aspect of Paleolithic life ways at the expense of all the other things that made that life way successful."

Textiles are particularly fleeting. The oldest examples of fabric yet discovered are some carbonate-encrusted swatches from France that are about 18,000 years old, while pieces of cordage and string dating back 19,000 years have been unearthed in the Near East, many thousands of years after the string and textile revolution began.

In an effort to study ancient textiles in the absence of textiles, Dr. Soffer, Dr. Adovasio, and Dr. Hyland have sought indirect signs of textile manufacture. They have pored over thousands of ancient fragments of fired and unfired clay, and have found impressions of early textiles on a number of them, the oldest dating to 29,000 B.C.E. But the researchers believe that textile manufacture far predates this time period, for the sophistication of the stitchery rules out its being, as Dr. Soffer put it, "what you take home from Crafts 101." Dr. Adovasio estimates that weaving and cord-making probably goes back to the year 40,000 B.C.E. "at a minimum," and possibly much further.

Long before people had settled down into towns with domesticated plants and animals, then, while they were still foragers and wanderers, they had, in a sense, tamed nature. The likeliest sort of plants from which they extracted fibers were nettles. "Nettle in folk tales and mythology is said to have magic properties," Dr. Soffer said. "In one story by the Brothers Grimm, a girl whose two brothers have been turned into swans has to weave them nettle shirts by midnight to make them human again." The nettles stung her fingers, but she kept on weaving.

But what didn't make it into Grimms' was that when the girl was done with the shirts, she took out a chisel, and carved herself a Venus figurine.

2

MARJORIE SHOSTAK

Nisa: The Life and Words of a !Kung Woman

Marjorie Shostak, a writer and photographer, interviewed Nisa, a woman of the hunting-gathering !Kung people of the Kalahari Desert of southern Africa. (The exclamation point at the beginning of !Kung indicates one of the clicking sounds used in their language.) From these interviews, which took place between 1969 and 1971, Shostak compiled Nisa's story in Nisa's own words.

As you read Nisa's account of her early adulthood, consider how it is similar to, and how it is different from, that of a young woman

Source: Marjorie Shostak, *Nisa: The Life and Words of a !Kung Woman* (Cambridge: Harvard University Press, 1981), 51, 56–59, 61–62, 89–90, 132–38.

growing up today in modern society. If Nisa is typical of women in her world, do !Kung women have more or less authority, prestige, or power than women in your own society?

Finally, what does Nisa's story tell us about women in hunting-gathering societies?

THINKING HISTORICALLY

Keep in mind that Nisa exists in the late twentieth century. When we think of stages of history, we are abstracting the human past in a way that vastly oversimplifies what happened but allows us to draw important conclusions. We know hunting and gathering did not end ten thousand years ago when agriculture first began. Hunters and gatherers still live in the world today—in places like the Arctic, the Amazon, and the Kalahari. That is why we use Nisa's account, which we are lucky to have. We have no vivid first-person accounts from those ancient hunters and gatherers—writing was not invented until the first cities developed five thousand years ago. So we generalize from Nisa's experience because we know that in some ways her life is like that of our hunting-gathering ancestors. But there are ways in which it is not. At the very least, the hunters and gatherers in the world today have been pushed by farmers and city people into the most remote parts of the globe—like the Kalahari Desert.

Using a contemporary of ours, like Nisa, as a kind of representative of our most distant ancestors is clearly a strange thing to do. Does it work? What precautions should we take when using a contemporary account as evidence of life in the Paleolithic Era?

One time, my father went hunting with some other men and they took dogs with them. First they saw a baby wildebeest and killed it. Then, they went after the mother wildebeest and killed that too. They also killed a warthog.

As they were coming back, I saw them and shouted out, "Ho, ho, Daddy's bringing home meat! Daddy's coming home with meat!" My mother said, "You're talking nonsense. Your father hasn't even come home yet." Then she turned to where I was looking and said, "Eh-hey, daughter! Your father certainly has killed something. He *is* coming with meat."

I remember another time when my father's younger brother traveled from far away to come and live with us. The day before he arrived he killed an eland. He left it in the bush and continued on to our village. When he arrived, only mother and I were there. He greeted us and asked where his brother was. Mother said, "Eh, he went to look at some tracks he had seen near a porcupine hole. He'll be back when the sun sets." We sat together the rest of the day. When the sun was low in the sky, my father came back. My uncle said, "Yesterday, as I was coming here, there was an eland—perhaps it was just a small one—but I spent a long time tracking it and finally killed it in the thicket beyond the dry water pan. Why don't we get the meat and bring it back to the village?" We packed some things, left others hanging in the trees, and went to where the eland had died. It was a huge animal with plenty of fat. We lived there while they skinned the animal and the meat into strips to dry. A few days later we started home, the men carrying the meat on sticks and the women carrying it in their karosses.

At first my mother carried me on her shoulder. After a long way, she set me down and I started to cry. She was angry, "You're a big girl. You know how to walk." It was true that I was fairly big by then, but I still wanted to be carried. My older brother said, "Stop yelling at her, she's already crying," and he picked me up and carried me. After a long time walking, he also put me down. Eventually, we arrived back at the village.

We lived, eating meat; lived and lived. Then, it was finished. . . .

When adults talked to me, I listened. When I was still a young girl with no breasts, they told me that when a young woman grows up, her parents give her a husband and she continues to grow up next to him.

When they first talked to me about it, I said, "What kind of thing am I that I should take a husband? When I grow, I won't marry. I'll just lie by myself. If I married, what would I be doing it for?"

My father said, "You don't know what you're saying. I, I am your father and am old; your mother is old, too. When you marry, you will gather food and give it to your husband to eat. He also will do things for you. If you refuse, who will give you food? Who will give you things to wear?"

I said, "There's no question about it, I won't take a husband. Why should I? As I am now, I'm still a child and won't marry." I said to my mother, "You say you have a man for me to marry? Why don't you take him and set him beside Daddy? You marry him and let them be co-husbands. What have I done that you're telling me I should marry?"

My mother said, "Nonsense. When I tell you I'm going to give you a husband, why do you say you want me to marry him? Why are you talking to me like this?"

I said, "Because I'm only a child. When I grow up and you tell me to take a husband, I'll agree. But I haven't passed through my childhood yet and I won't marry!" . . .

When I still had no breasts, when my genitals still weren't developed, when my chest was without anything on it, that was when a man named Bo came from a distant area and people started talking about marriage. Was I not almost a young woman?

One day, my parents and his parents began building our marriage hut. The day we were married, they carried me to it and set me down inside. I cried and cried and cried. Later, I ran back to my parents' hut, lay down beside my little brother, and slept, a deep sleep like death.

The next night, Nukha, an older woman, took me into the hut and stayed with me. She lay down between Bo and myself, because young girls who are still children are afraid of their husbands. So, it is our custom for an older woman to come into the young girl's hut to teach her not to be afraid. The woman is supposed to help the girl learn to like her husband. Once the couple is living nicely together and getting along, the older woman leaves them beside each other.

That's what Nukha was supposed to do. Even the people who saw her come into the hut with me thought she would lay me down and that once I fell asleep, she would leave and go home to her husband.

But Nukha had within her clever deceit. My heart refused Bo because I was a child, but Nukha, she liked him. That was why, when she laid me down in the hut with my husband, she was also laying me down with her lover. She put me in front and Bo was behind. We stayed like that for a very long time. As soon as I was asleep, they started to make love. But as Bo made love to Nukha, they knocked into me. I kept waking up as they bumped me, again and again.

I thought, "I'm just a child. I don't understand about such things. What are people doing when they move around like that? How come Nukha took me into my marriage hut and laid me down beside my husband, but when I started to cry, she changed places with me and lay down next to him? Is he hers? How come he belongs to her yet Mommy and Daddy said I should marry him?"

I lay there, thinking my thoughts. Before dawn broke, Nukha got up and went back to her husband. I lay there, sleeping, and when it started getting light, I went back to my mother's hut.

The next night, when darkness sat, Nukha came for me again. I cried, "He's your man! Yesterday you took me and brought me inside the hut, but after we all lay there, he was with you! Why are you now bringing me to someone who is yours?" She said, "That's not true, he's not mine. He's *your* husband. Now, go to your hut and sit there. Later, we'll lie down."

She brought me to the hut, but once inside, I cried and cried and cried. I was still crying when Nukha lay down with us. After we had been lying there for a very long time, Bo started to make love to her again. I thought, "What is this? What am I? Am I supposed to watch this? Don't they see me? Do they think I'm only a baby?" Later, I got up and told them I had to urinate. I passed by them and went to lie down in mother's hut and stayed there until morning broke.

That day, I went gathering with my mother and father. As we were collecting mongongo nuts and klaru roots, my mother said, "Nisa, as you are, you're already a young woman. Yet, when you go into your marriage hut to lie down, you get up, come back, and lie down with me. Do you think I have married you? No, I'm the one who gave birth to you. Now, take this man as your husband, this strong man who will get food, for you and for me to eat. Is your father the only one who can find food? A husband kills things and gives them to you; a husband works on things that become your things; a husband gets meat that is food for you to eat. Now, you have a husband, Bo; he has married you."

I said, "Mommy, let me stay with you. When night sits, let me sleep next to you. What have you done to me that I'm only a child, yet the first husband you give me belongs to Nukha?" My mother said, "Why are you saying that? Nukha's husband is not your husband. Her husband sits elsewhere, in another hut."

I said, "Well . . . the other night when she took me and put me into the hut, she laid me down in front of her; Bo slept behind. But later, they woke me up, moving around the way they did. It was the same last night. Again, I slept in front and Bo behind and again, they kept bumping into me. I'm not sure exactly what they were doing, but that's why tonight, when night sits, I want to stay with you and sleep next to you. Don't take me over there again."

My mother said, "Yo! My daughter! They were moving about?" I said, "Mm. They woke me while I was sleeping. That's why I got up and came back to you." She said, "Yo! How horny that Bo is! He's screwing Nukha! You are going to leave that man, that's the only thing I will agree to now."

My father said, "I don't like what you've told us. You're only a child, Nisa, and adults are the ones responsible for arranging your marriage. But when an adult gives a husband and that husband makes love to someone else, then that adult hasn't done well. I understand what you have told us and I say that Bo has deceived me. Therefore, when Nukha comes for you tonight, I will refuse to let you go. I will say, 'My daughter won't go into her marriage hut because you, Nukha, you have already taken him for a husband.'"

We continued to talk on our way back. When we arrived at the village, I sat down with my parents. Bo walked over to our marriage hut, then Nukha went over to him. I sat and watched as they talked. I thought, "Those two, they were screwing! That's why they kept bumping into me!"

I sat with Mother and Father while we ate. When evening came, Nukha walked over to us. "Nisa, come, let me take you to your hut." I said, "I won't go." She said, "Get up. Let me take you over there. It's your hut. How come you're already married but today you won't make your hut your home?"

That's when my mother, drinking anger, went over to Nukha and said, "As I'm standing here, I want you to tell me something. Nisa is a child who fears her husband. Yet, when you took her to her hut, you and her husband had sex together. Don't you know her husband should be trying to help bring her up? But that isn't something either of you are thinking about!"

Nukha didn't say anything, but the fire in my mother's words burned. My mother began to yell, cursing her, "Horny, that's what you are! You're no longer going to take Nisa to her husband. And, if you ever have sex with him again, I'll crack your face open. You horny woman! You'd screw your own father!"

That's when my father said, "No, don't do all the talking. You're a woman yet, how come you didn't ask me? I am a man and I will do the talking now. You, you just listen to what I say. Nisa is my child. I also gave birth to her. Now, you are a woman and will be quiet because I am a man."

Then he said, "Nukha, I'm going to tell you something. I am Gau and today I'm going to pull my talk from inside myself and give it to you. We came together here for this marriage, but now something very bad has happened, something I do not agree to at all. Nisa is no longer going to go from here, where I am sitting, to that hut over there, that hut which you have already made your own. She is no longer going to look for anything for herself near that hut."

He continued, "Because, when I agree to give a man to my daughter, then he is only for my daughter. Nisa is a child and her husband isn't there for two to share. So go, take that man, he's already yours. Today my daughter will sit with me; she will sit here and sleep here. Tomorrow I will take her and we will move away. What you have already done to this marriage is the way it will remain."

Nukha didn't say anything. She left and went to the hut without me. Bo said, "Where's Nisa? Why are you empty, returning here alone?" Nukha said, "Nisa's father refused to let her go. She told him that you had made love to me and that's what he just now told me. I don't know what to do about this, but I won't go back to their hut again." Bo said, "I have no use for that kind of talk. Get the girl and come back with her." She said, "I'm not going to Gau's hut. We're finished with that talk now. And when I say I'm finished, I'm saying I won't go back there again."

She left and walked over to her own hut. When her husband saw her, he said, "So, you and Bo are lovers! Nisa said that when you took her to Bo, the two of you . . . how exactly *did* Bo reward you for your help?" But Nukha said, "No, I don't like Bo and he's not my lover. Nisa is just a child and it is just a child's talk she is talking."

Bo walked over to us. He tried to talk but my father said, "You, be quiet. I'm the one who's going to talk about this." So Bo didn't say anything more, and my father talked until it was finished.

The next morning, very early, my father, mother, and aunt packed our things and we all left. We slept in the mongongo groves that night and traveled on until we reached another water hole where we continued to live.

We lived and lived and nothing more happened for a while. After a long time had passed, Bo strung together some trade beads made of wood, put them into a sack with food, and traveled the long distance to the water hole where we were living.

It was late afternoon; the sun had almost left the sky. I had been out gathering with my mother, and we were coming back from the bush. We arrived in the village and my mother saw them, "Eh-hey, Bo's over there. What's he doing here? I long ago refused him. I didn't ask him to come back. I wonder what he thinks he's going to take away from here?"

We put down our gatherings and sat. We greeted Bo and his relatives—his mother, his aunt, Nukha, and Nukha's mother. Bo's mother said, "We have come because we want to take Nisa back with us." Bo said, "I'm again asking for your child. I want to take her back with me."

My father said, "No, I only just took her from you. That was the end. I won't take her and then give her again. Maybe you didn't hear me the first time? I already told you that I refused. Bo is Nukha's husband and my daughter won't be with him again. An adult woman does not make love to the man who marries Nisa."

Then he said, "Today, Nisa will just continue to live with us. Some day, another man will come and marry her. If she stays healthy and her eyes stand strong, if God doesn't kill her and she doesn't die, if God stands beside her and helps, then we will find another man to give to her."

That night, when darkness set, we all slept. I slept beside mother. When morning broke, Bo took Nukha, her mother, and the others and they left. I stayed behind. They were gone, finally gone.

We continued to stay at that water hole, eating things, doing things, and just living. No one talked further about giving me another husband, and we just lived and lived and lived.

3

MARGARET EHRENBERG

Women in Prehistory

British anthropologist Margaret Ehrenberg argues here that women were likely the first farmers as well as the originators of many of the innovations of the agricultural revolution. What evidence does she offer? What was the importance of the agricultural revolution? When and how, according to Ehrenberg, did men take over?

Source: Margaret Ehrenberg, *Women in Prehistory* (Norman: University of Oklahoma Press, 1989), 77–81, 99–100, 103–7.

THINKING HISTORICALLY

In this selection much of the author's evidence is anthropological or ethnographic (rather than archaeological). That is, it comes from our contemporary world, not from digging up the past. How does the use of this kind of evidence depend on the idea of historical stages? From the standpoint of women, was the agricultural revolution a single stage of history, or should we think of it as two stages? If so, what were those stages?

From the point of view of the lives of women, the Neolithic period is perhaps the most important phase of prehistory. . . . It is likely that at the end of the Palaeolithic and Mesolithic, women enjoyed equality with men. They probably collected as much, if not more, of the food eaten by the community and derived equal status from their contribution. But by about four thousand years ago, in the Bronze Age, many of the gender roles and behaviour typical of the world today had probably been established. The implication is that the crucial changes must have taken place during the Neolithic period. . . .

The discovery of farming techniques has usually been assumed to have been made by men, but it is in fact very much more likely to have been made by women. On the basis of anthropological evidence for societies still living traditional foraging lifestyles and those living by simple, non-mechanised farming, taken in conjunction with direct archaeological evidence, it seems probable that it was women who made the first observations of plant behaviour, and worked out, presumably by long trial and error, how to grow and tend crops.

This transition from foraging to farming, which marks the change from the Palaeolithic and Mesolithic or Old and Middle Stone Ages to the period known to archaeologists as the Neolithic or New Stone Age, seems to have taken place initially in south-west Asia some time after 10,000 BC. By 6000 BC farming was well established throughout that part of the world. . . .

How and why did this change to agriculture take place, and, more particularly, what can we say about the role of women in this process?

. . . Foraging societies still living in the world today . . . gather and hunt food in a way similar to Palaeolithic societies before the invention of agriculture; among these people there is a regularly recurring pattern of food procurement. . . . Women are mainly concerned with gathering plant food, which provides the bulk of the diet of nearly all foragers, while men spend much time hunting animals. Although animal products form an important source of proteins in the diet, meat actually makes up a relatively small proportion of the food intake of these societies. We can also study other groups of people in places such as New Guinea and parts of Africa who still grow crops and keep animals with the aid of only the very simplest technology, in much the same way as we may imagine Neolithic societies would have done. These societies do not use ploughs or artificial irrigation, and they keep few, if any, animals. To distinguish them from people using more mechanised agricultural technologies, anthropologists usually call this type of farming horticulture, and the people using it horticultural societies. . . .

Although present-day horticulturalists live in a wide variety of places around the world, many remarkably regular patterns of behaviour can be observed, and this gives us some degree of confidence in using their lifestyles as a model for the Neolithic, particularly if some of the behaviour patterns can be seen to be reflected in evidence from archaeological sites.

Studies of the roles of women in different types of agricultural communities show a remarkably consistent pattern. In societies where plough agriculture is practised and animals are kept on a significant scale, most of the agricultural work is done by men, with women playing no direct part, or only a very subsidiary role. On the other hand, in horticultural societies, in which hoes or digging sticks are used for making holes or drills in which to plant roots or seeds, women are usually almost wholly responsible for agricultural production. A study of 104 horticultural societies existing today showed that in 50 per cent of them women were exclusively responsible for agriculture, in 33 per cent women and men shared various tasks, and in only 17 per cent were men wholly responsible for farming, and this is after decades or even centuries of contact with societies whose ideology would encourage men to take on greater roles in production. Horticultural societies are still widespread, mainly within the Tropics, in many parts of Africa, central America and Asia. The typical pattern in these areas is one of shifting cultivation, where patches of land are worked for a few years, and then when soil fertility declines another plot is cleared and cultivated. Although men often help to clear the plots of trees and undergrowth, women usually hoe, sow, tend and harvest the crops. Studies carried out early this century suggest that this pattern of cultivation was more common then than it is today. It also seems very likely that it was even more typical before most parts of the world had contact with European traders and missionaries, with their preconceived ideas about what it was right and proper for women and men to do. . . .

The Secondary Products Revolution, or the Great Male Takeover Bid

In an earlier section it was argued that women almost certainly "invented" or worked out the principles of farming as well as many of the concomitant skills and tools which go to make crop agriculture possible and profitable. As principal food providers they were probably respected and had equal status with men. But between then and now, in all but the most traditional hunter-gatherer and horticultural societies, the status of women has been drastically reduced, and in many areas farming has become a predominantly male preserve. Why the change, and when did it happen? Two facts are certain: Firstly, by the time of the earliest written records, everywhere in Europe farming was primarily a male occupation, and men owned the farmland and the tools. Secondly, in those areas of the world where women are still the main agricultural producers, most of the farming is concerned with crop production, and if animals are kept at all, it is usually on a small farmyard scale, rather than as large herds or flocks. The change to male dominance in agriculture, therefore, took place at some time between the first stages of the Neolithic period and the advent of written records, and may be related to the changing role of animals within the farming economies of prehistoric Europe. It also seems likely that such a drastic shift in lifestyle, whether it took place gradually over millennia or as a sudden "revolution," would have been associated with other changes within society. Anthropologists have shown that in present-day societies a significant (though not 100 per cent) correlation exists between plough agriculture and patrilineal descent and land ownership in the same way as there is a correlation between non-plough agriculture and the heavy involvement, and consequent enhanced status, of women. We can look for evidence of this shift in the archaeological record: for example, changes in family structure, wealth or ownership patterns may show up in settlement sites or in burials. . . .

The crucial changes in farming practice are thought to have taken place around 3000 BC, in the later Neolithic period. This would have been some five millennia after the introduction of farming in the Near East, and similar economic shifts can be detected in many areas of Europe at about the same time. Andrew Sherratt has suggested that although domesticated animals were kept during the early Neolithic, they were used only as a source of meat; the consumption of milk or milk products was probably not significant, nor were the animals used for pulling ploughs or carts. All these innovations came later and not only revolutionised agricultural productivity, but also reduced the amount of labour involved in farming. Moreover, the greater importance of domesticated animals and their products would have reduced the necessity for hunting wild animals. As the balance of work changed from part hunting, part crop cultivation and tending a small number of animals to an economy dependent

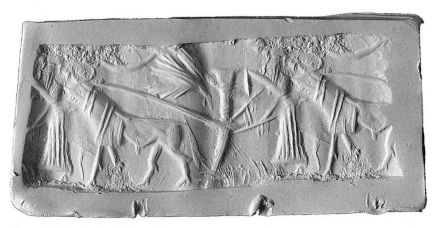

Figure 1.4 Men leading and guiding a two-handled plough, depicted on a cylinder seal from Mesopotamia, late third millennium BC.

Source: Oxford Ashmolean Museum, AN1969.346.

on mixed farming, so the roles and duties of women and men may have shifted. Let us examine the evidence and arguments. . . .

Both carts and ploughs first appear in depictions on clay tablets and cylinder seals in Mesopotamia, around the beginning of the fourth millennium BC, and both seem to have spread to Europe fairly rapidly over 500 years or so. One of the earliest depictions of ploughing [Figure 1.4] shows an ox drawing a two-handled plough with a sowing funnel, a device used for sowing seed deeply in the soil and often associated with areas where irrigation is needed. Most significantly the two individuals involved, one guiding the animal from the front, the other guiding the plough, both appear to be men with beards. Early depictions of ploughs in Egypt, from Old Kingdom tombs, also show them being used by men. . . .

In areas of the world where plough agriculture and the herding of animals are the predominant form of farming, men universally play the major role in agricultural tasks. Women either take no part in farming or only a small one. They may sometimes contribute to harvesting, or to the care of domestic animals, if these are kept only in small numbers. An important distinction exists today between Africa, where horticulture predominates, and Asia, where plough agriculture is far more common and where domesticated animals are kept. Even in those areas of Asia, for example, where women are involved to some extent in aspects of plough agriculture, they work fewer hours than men; whereas in Africa, where farming is predominantly carried out without the use of the plough, and primarily by women, they do far more work than men. The other main difference between these two farming regimes is that social and economic stratification is a far more significant factor, with greater extremes of poverty and wealth and of land ownership amongst the Asian plough agriculturalists than amongst the African hoe agriculturalists or horticulturalists. . . .

Patterns of social organisation in horticultural societies today are quite different from those of intensive agriculturalists: these seem to be linked to the balance of agricultural tasks and to their allocation to each sex. One of the greatest differences is in the position of women. This reinforces the theory that it was in the later Neolithic, when men began to take over most agricultural work, that the social status of women declined.

. . . It is likely that most of the tending of animals was done by men. Large-scale herding often takes place some way from the farm or settlement, as fresh grazing land is continually sought. Raiding by neighbouring tribes seems to be an endemic part of most cattle herding—almost a variation on hunting! This has been seen as the origin of warfare, when for the first time people owned a resource which it was both worthwhile and fairly easy to steal.

Secondly, the invention of plough agriculture, too, would probably have resulted in farming becoming predominantly a male activity, while on the basis of ethnographic analogy, at least, women would probably have spent more time in food preparation, child-rearing and textile and perhaps other craft production.

Thirdly, although less land is needed for the same amount of production, plough agriculture is far more labour-intensive than hoe agriculture: where land is poor, ploughing makes agriculture possible. In some areas of prehistoric Europe it had the effect of making large tracts of lighter, sandy soil available, but in other areas it may have allowed an increase in population where there was a real or perceived shortage of land. In the earliest phases of the Neolithic, land shortages would certainly not have been a problem, as witnessed by the rapid population spread discussed in an earlier section. However, in the later Neolithic there may have been a shortage of land perceived to be suitable for agriculture. Women would therefore have been expected to produce more children and thus more labourers. This would have been seen as their major role. Moreover, male children might have been valued most highly, as future farm workers. Women, meanwhile, would have become less valued by men in their own right: as more time was spent in pregnancy and the care of very young infants, so less time could be spent on farming activities. As men took over many of their tasks, they no longer contributed so much to the daily production of food, which had been a crucial factor in maintaining the equal status they had previously enjoyed.

Fourthly, another social change which might have been an indirect result of the secondary products revolution was the switch from matrilocal residence and matrilineal descent to patrilocal residence and patrilineal descent. There is a very strong ethnographic correlation between male-dominated farming and patrilineal descent and patrilocal residence. A male farmer will teach his sons the necessary skills and expect them to tend his land and animals. In a matrilineal system his sister's sons, rather than his own sons, inherit these herds, land and equipment on his death. This is not in the male interest if men are the main agriculturalists. When women were involved in the land-based tasks, they would have learnt the basic skills from their mothers, so it would have been more obvious for them also to inherit their land and equipment. However, it also seems that individual land ownership is less common amongst hoe agriculturalists, and, by definition, less equipment is used. Therefore, at least in terms of material goods, far less is typically at stake in matrilineal than in patrilineal systems.

Finally, the development of agriculture brought with it a large increase, not only in the number of related tasks, including several which are very time-consuming, but also in the range of material possessions such as farming and food-preparation tools and storage vessels. Two consequences would have resulted. On the one hand, this may be seen as the spur to the development of craft specialisation, as some individuals concentrated on the production of one particular item, which they would exchange for other products or services. At first this could have been in addition to normal farming tasks, but increasingly some people might have found that they could acquire enough food and other necessities by producing only their specialised article. In this way exchange must have become more common, and more sophisticated. On the other hand these material possessions, as well as the domesticated animals themselves, would have constituted considerable wealth, which could be accumulated and handed on from one generation to the next. . . .

The wealthy can become powerful by lending to poorer families in return for services, such as farm labour, or support in combat against other groups. By this means the rich are able to become more wealthy, while the poorer become indebted to other families, and have to produce more and more, or spend time on tasks other than directly for their own subsistence. So the vicious circle develops, and it is easy to see how from this point permanent hierarchies not only of wealth, but of power and status come about, in a way which is impossible in forager societies. This is also the context in which a society can begin to think of people, as well as material possessions and land, as objects of value and exchange. A child could be given as labour to a family to whom the child's parents were indebted, or a woman given to work or to produce extra children.

How such fundamental changes actually took place is not clear, even if we assume they were a gradual process in each community. The full consequences which have just been discussed would have developed very slowly, even over millennia, and are difficult to pinpoint chronologically. In any case, as women were increasingly relegated to secondary tasks, by the end of the Neolithic period they had fewer personal resources with which to assert their status. Presumably, as with so many innovations even in the modern world, the social and economic consequences of seemingly minor innovations would not have been apparent until it was too late to return to former *mores*. The discovery of agriculture, which at the beginning of the Neolithic had been such a positive step by women, was by the end of the period to have had unforeseen, and unfortunate, consequences for them.

4

RAMON A. GUTIERREZ

When Jesus Came, the Corn Mothers Went Away

Agriculture originated in the Western Hemisphere between seven and ten thousand years ago, independently of the slightly earlier Neolithic revolution in Eurasia. Evidence of corn cultivation has been found on the Yucatan Peninsula of Mexico, dating from 7000 B.C.E. From there it spread north and south, reaching modern New Mexico sometime between 1500 and 1000 B.C.E. Native Americans had a smaller range of edible plants to domesticate than those available to the peoples of Eurasia, but the combination of corn, beans, and squash as staples provided all of the necessary ingredients for a healthy diet. This brief selection comes from a history of the Spanish cultural conquest of New Mexico. Gutierrez begins by recounting a Pueblo myth of origins. He then describes the actual workings of Pueblo society around 1500 C.E. What did it mean to be a man or a woman in Pueblo society? Who had more power or greater status in that society? What were the sources of that power or status? In what ways was the impact of agriculture on gender similar to, and different from, what occurred in the Eastern Hemisphere?

THINKING HISTORICALLY

What can this society from five hundred years ago tell us about the agricultural revolution ten thousand years ago? The title of the book from which this selection is drawn suggests that women's prestige was undermined by the Spanish conquest and Christianity. But the previous selection argues that different changes disempowered women in Eurasia much earlier. What were those changes, and why did they not occur in the society of the Pueblo?

Source: Ramon A. Gutierrez, *When Jesus Came, the Corn Mothers Went Away: Marriage, Sexuality and Power in New Mexico, 1500–1846* (Stanford, CA: Stanford University Press, 1991), 3–5, 13–18.

In the beginning two females were born underneath the earth at a place called Shipapu. In total darkness Tsichtinako (Thought Woman) nursed the sisters, taught them language and gave them each a basket that their father Uchtsiti had sent them containing the seeds and fetishes of all the plants and animals that were to exist in the world. Tsichtinako told the sisters to plant the four pine tree seeds they had in their basket and then to use the trees to ascend to the light. One grew so tall that it pushed a hole through the earth. Before the sisters climbed up the tree from the underworld, Thought Woman taught them how to praise the Sun with prayer and song. Every morning as the Sun rose, they would thank him for bringing them to the light by offering with outstretched hands sacred cornmeal and pollen. To the tones of the creation song, they would blow the offering to the sky, asking for long life, happiness, and success in all their endeavors.

When the sisters reached the earth's surface it was soft, spongy, and not yet ripe. So they waited for the Sun to appear. When it rose, the six directions of the cosmos were revealed to them: the four cardinal points, the earth below, and the four skies above. The sisters prayed to the Sun, and as they did, Thought Woman named one of the girls Iatiku and made her Mother of the Corn clan; the other she named Nautsiti, Mother of the Sun clan.

"Why were we created?" they asked. Thought Woman answered, "Your father Uchtsiti made the world by throwing a clot of his blood into space, which by his power grew into the earth. He planted you within it so that you would bring to life all the things in your baskets in order that the world be complete for you to rule over it."

When the first day ended, the girls slept. They awoke before dawn to greet the Sun with a prayer on their lips and an offering of cornmeal and pollen. When Sun rose and gave them warmth, the sisters were very happy. Tsichtinako then took several seeds from their baskets and showed the sisters how to plant corn. With a dig stick she poked holes into Mother Earth and deposited seeds in her womb. The corn germinated and grew. When its ears were ripe and plump, Thought Woman showed them how to pick it, how to collect its pollen, and how to mill its kernels into the meal they would offer their father daily.

That night a flash of brilliant red light fell from the sky and when it touched the earth, it exploded into fire. "Your father Sun gives you fire to cook your food and to keep you warm," explained Thought Woman. "The fire's tongues will stay alive if fed branches from the pine tree that gave you passage from the underworld." From that day forward, Iatiku and Nautsiti had fire with which to cook corn. They flavored the corn with the salt they found in their baskets and ate to their hearts' content.

Next, Thought Woman taught the sisters how to give life to the animal fetishes in their baskets so that the animals would give them life in return. Mice, rats, moles, and prairie dogs were created and were given grasses on which to forage and multiply. The sisters cast pebbles in various directions and from these emerged mountains, plains, mesas, and canyons. From the seeds they next strewed about, pine, cedar, oak, and walnut trees grew and underneath them beans and squash sprouted and yielded their fruit. Rabbits, antelope, bison, and deer were dispatched to the open plains. To the mountains went the elk with their predators the lions, wolves, wildcats, and bears. Eagle, hawk, and turkey were cast into the sky, but turkey fell back to earth and never learned to fly. In the earth's waters fish, water snakes, and turtles were placed, and there they flourished and multiplied. Now Thought Woman told the sisters to kill an animal. "Roast meat and corn together and flavor it with salt," she instructed. "Before you eat, always pray and offer morsels of these to your father Uchtsiti who created the world and lives in the fourth sky above."

Tsichtinako cautioned Iatiku and Nautsiti to handle their baskets carefully. At first they did. But as they were giving life to the snakes one fetish fell out of a basket unnoticed and came to life of its own power as the serpent Pishuni. Pishuni bred selfishness and competitiveness between the sisters. Soon Nautsiti became sullen and refused to associate with Iatiku. When this occurred, Pishuni asked Nautsiti: "Why are you lonely and unhappy? If you want what will make you happy, I can tell you what to do. If you bore someone like yourself, you would no longer be lonely. Tsichtinako wants to hold back this happiness from you," he said. . . . Nautsiti believed Pishuni and agreed to meet him near a rainbow. On a rock near the specified rainbow, Nautsiti lay on her back, and as she did drops of rain entered her body. From this rain she conceived and bore twin sons. Father Sun had strictly forbidden the sisters to bear children, and when he learned that Nautsiti had, he took Thought Woman away.

When Nautsiti's sons grew up, the sisters separated. Nautsiti departed East with her favorite child; Iatiku remained with Tiamuni, the son Nautsiti disliked. Iatiku and Tiamuni eventually married and had many daughters to whom they gave clan names representing all the things that their father had given them at emergence: Sky, Water, Fire, and Corn. . . .

The Pueblo Indians viewed the relations between the sexes as relatively balanced. Women and men each had their own forms of wealth and power, which created independent but mutually interdependent spheres of action. The corn fetish[1] every child was given at birth and the flint arrowhead with which boys were endowed symbolized these relations and expressed the basic preoccupations of a people living in a semi-arid environment. Corn and flint were food and water, but they were also the cosmic principles of femininity and masculinity. Female and male combined as corn seeds and rain combined to perpetuate life. Corn plants without rain would shrivel and die; water without corn was no life at all. The ear

---

[1] An object believed to have the magical power to protect or assist the one to whom it belongs. [Ed.]

of corn infants received represented the Corn Mothers that had given life to all humans, plants, and animals. At Acoma Pueblo this corn fetish is still called Iatiku, because it contains her heart and breath. For this reason too the Hopi called this corn fetish "mother." "Corn is my heart, it will be to [you] . . . as milk from my breasts," Zia's Corn Mother told her people. Individuals kept this corn fetish throughout their entire lives, for if crops failed its perfect seeds held the promise of a new crop cycle.

If the corn ear represented the feminine generative powers latent in seeds, the earth, and women, the flint arrowhead represented the masculine germinative forces of the sky. Father Sun gave men flint arrowheads to bring forth rain, to harness heat, and to use as a weapon in the hunt. The noise emitted by striking together two pieces of flint resembled the thunder and lightning that accompanied rain. Rain fertilized seeds as men fertilized their women. Without rain or semen life could not continue. The flint arrowhead was the sign of the hunter and warrior. Sun gave his sons, the Twin War Gods, arrowheads with which to give and take away life. From flint too came fire. When men struck flint and created that gift Sun gave them at the beginning of time, they transformed that which was raw into that which was cooked. To the Pueblo Indians flint, rain, semen, and hunting were to male as corn, earth, and childbearing were to female. This idea is conveyed in the Hopi word *posumi*, which means both corn seed and nubile woman. We see this too in the ceremony Zuñi women perform to celebrate the sex of their babies. Over a girl's vulva the women place a large seed-filled gourd and pray that her sexual parts grow large and her fruit abundant. The boy's penis is sprinkled with water, and the women pray that it remains small. Men became very angry when they saw this ritual, for through it women asserted that their life-bearing capacity was immense in comparison to that of men. Men vigorously contested this claim in their rituals to vivify the earth, sporting large artificial penises to show women that their fructifying powers were really more immense, "singing about the penis being the thing that made the women happy."

The natal home was the primary unit of affiliation in Pueblo society. Everyone belonged to a home. Humans, animals, deities, and even the natural forces were believed to each have a home within which they lived. In the sixteenth century the Pueblos were matrilineal, anchoring maternity to matrilocal households. "The houses belong to the women, they being the ones who build them," observed Espinosa in 1601.

The household was preeminently a female domain of love and ritual. Women joined together to fashion houses out of the entrails of Mother Earth, setting her stones in charcoal ash and dirt mortar, assiduously building those multistoried edifices they still call home. Though houses were clustered together in hive-like compounds, each had its own entrance, a hearth for heat and cooking, sleeping rooms, and a room for the storage of seeds, sacred fetishes, and religious objects. The interior walls of a house were whitewashed and decorated with the clan's eponym. Reed mats for sleeping, pottery utensils for cooking and storage, and a mill stone for grinding corn were basic furnishings. When a household outgrew its space, usually when daughters married, adjacent rooms were added as vertical or horizontal extensions to the hearth.

Towns were an aggregation of households. Each town contained anywhere from 50 to 500 houses grouped around a central plaza in which several kivas[2] stood. Houses rarely had ground floor entrances; they were usually entered by ascending moveable ladders that connected the various terrace levels of a housing compound. This was supremely a defensive architectural design. If enemies attacked, town residents climbed up to the highest terrace, removed the ladders to the lower ones, and from these heights, pelted outsiders with arrows and stones. From these heights, too, women protected their homes, rallying assistance with smoke signals or by "lifting their hands to their mouths and letting out a loud cry which could be heard far away."

The role men played in the construction of homes was rather limited. "The women mix the plaster and erect the walls; the men bring the [roof and support] timbers and set them in place," observed Pedro de Castañeda in 1540. Timber came from distant mountains outside of the town—the province of men and gods. Women owned the domestic hearth, exercised authority over those that lived within it, and at death passed on the edifice to their daughters. The female household head was custodian of its rights and possessions: the agricultural plots their husbands and sons worked, all food and seed reserves, and the sacred fetishes and ritual objects of the clan. The implication of these facts for domestic politics was clear to Fray Alonso de Benavides in 1634: "[The woman] always commands and is the mistress of the house, and not the husband."

The typical household unit consisted of a grandmother and her husband, her sisters and their husbands, her daughters and their husbands, various young children, and perhaps an orphan, slave, or stray. Women were attached to their natal dwelling throughout their lives, said Hernán Gallegos in 1582, and did "not leave except when permitted by their mothers." Men moved from house to house according to their stage of life. During childhood boys lived with their mothers, and at adolescence they moved into a kiva to learn male magical lore. When they had mastered these skills, and were deemed worthy of marriage by their kin, they took up residence in their wife's home. A man nonetheless remained tied to his maternal home throughout his life. For important ceremonial events, men returned to their maternal households. When this occurred the household became a matrilineage. Matrilineages that acknowledged descent from a common ancestor, usually through ownership of a similar animal or spirit fetish, formed larger, primarily religious aggregations known as clans.

---

[2] Pueblo Indian ceremonial structures that are usually round and partly underground. [Ed.]

When a child was born, the umbilical cord was buried — inside the household underneath the grinding stone if it belonged to a girl, outside in a cornfield if it belonged to a boy. This natal practice nicely delineated the sexual division of space and labor. The house and compound were female space invested with descendent earth-bound symbols. In the household women gave men their love and their bodies. They bore children, reared them, and engaged in that ritual activity that was at the core of kinship — feeding. Women fed their children, their mothers and grandmothers, their brothers and maternal uncles, and their husbands. Kinship was reckoned through genealogical principles — born of blood and substance. But just as importantly, kinship was created through feeding, what the Puebloans call "adoption." Any life or spirit form was transformed into kin through feeding. Thus women regularly fed the sun and prepared food for the katsina.[3] They fed the household animal fetishes and the scalps of enemy dead to assure that they remained content. Before hunters carried the carcass of an animal into the pueblo, the women fed it, and by so doing adopted it into a household. This feeding assured that the animal's spirit would not haunt the hunter. When foreign chiefs and caciques were feasted, the social exchange of food that signified peace was accomplished through the role of women's feeding.

Large portions of a woman's day were spent preparing meals for her household. Corn, beans, and squash were the main staples of the diet. Corn was the most important and symbolic of these. It was boiled whole, toasted on the cob, or dried and ground into a fine powder easily cooked as bread or gruel. Every day a woman and her daughters knelt before metates,[4] grinding corn to feed their gods, their fetishes, and their kin. . . .

After feeding, the activity of greatest cultural import to Pueblo women was sexual intercourse. Women were empowered through their sexuality. Through sex women bore the children who would offer them labor and respect in old age. Through sex women incorporated husbands into their maternal households and expected labor and respect from them. Through sex women domesticated the wild malevolent spirits of nature and transformed them into beneficent household gods. Accordingly, then, sexuality was deemed essential for the peaceful continuation of life.

Female sexuality was theirs to give and withhold. In marriage a woman gave her husband her love and her body because of the labor he gave her mother, and because of all the marriage-validating gifts that had been given on her behalf to her in-laws. When women gave the gift of their body to men with whom no obligational ties existed, they expected

---

[3] A Pueblo doll representing a spirit, often the spirit of a deceased who has become a rain maker. These dolls vary from clay scultures to painted wooden figures wearing animal masks, feathers, and ceremonial clothing (about eight inches high). [Ed.]

[4] Stones used for grinding corn. [Ed.]

something in return, such as blankets, meat, salt, and hides. For a man to enjoy a woman's body without giving her a gift in return was for him to become indebted to her in a bond of obligation.

Erotic behavior in its myriad forms (heterosexuality, homosexuality, bisexuality) knew no boundaries of sex or age. Many of the great gods—the Zuñi Awonawilona, the Navajo First Man/First Woman, the Hopi Kawasaitaka katsina—were bisexual, combining the potentialities of male and female into one—a combination equally revered among humans. If the Indians sang of sex, copulated openly, staged orgiastic rituals, and named landmarks "Clitoris Spring," "Girl's Breast Point," "Buttocks-Vagina," and "Shove Penis," it was because the natural world around them was full of sexuality.

Sexuality was equated with fertility, regeneration, and the holy by the Pueblo Indians, a pattern Mircea Eliade[5] has found to be common to many societies. Humanity was dependent on sexuality for its continuation. The Acoma Indians say they were conceived when Pishuni, the serpentine deity of water, entered Nautsiti's body as rain. At the beginning of time, too, Thought Woman taught the Corn Mothers that maize would give them life if planted deep within Mother Earth's womb. When the clouds (men) poured down their rain (semen) the seeds (women) would germinate and come to life. The reader will recall that this is why a boy's penis was sprinkled with water at birth and a girl's vulva was covered with a seed-filled gourd.

Modesty and shame were not sentiments the Pueblo Indians knew in relationship to their bodies. Before European contact they wore little clothing and were "entirely naked except for the covering of their privy parts." Women wore what resembled "table napkins, with fringes and a tassel at each corner, tying them around the hips." Most men left their genitals totally exposed; some tied their penis "near the prepuce with a maguey fiber" to protect it from evil spirits.

Sexual intercourse was the symbol of cosmic harmony for the Pueblo Indians because it united in balance all the masculine forces of the sky with all the feminine forces of the earth. The solstitial rituals that renewed the union between Nautsiti and Pishuni from which the Acoma Indians were born culminated in sexual intercourse. Whenever the katsina[6] visited, these Cloud-Beings brought fructifying rain so that seeds germinated, animals multiplied, and cosmic peace prevailed. What better way to celebrate fertility than by copulating with the katsina? And this is precisely what always happened, said Fray Nicolas de Chávez in 1660: "men and women have sexual intercourse in bestial fashion."

Society was made whole through libidinous female sexuality. Through intercourse, outsiders (men from other towns or clans) became insiders (household and community members). . . .

---

[5] Renowned religious historian. [Ed.]

[6] In this case, the katsina is probably an actual shaman or person who was believed to be able to communicate with the spirit world. [Ed.]

CATHERINE CLAY, CHANDRIKA PAUL, AND CHRISTINE SENECAL

Women in the First Urban Communities (after 3500 B.C.E.)

This selection comes from a text on women in world history. Since world history is full of patriarchal, or male-dominated, societies, one of the thorniest problems is to determine just how widespread patriarchy was. Against the commonly held assumption that patriarchy has always existed, that it is universal or natural, we have seen that male domination was not common in most hunting-gathering and early agricultural societies—that is, throughout most of human history. When and how did it come about? What is the answer given in this selection? What kind of evidence best supports the author's conclusion?

THINKING HISTORICALLY

As already mentioned, one of the earliest, and still widely accepted, stage theories of human history posits three important stages: hunter-gatherer, agricultural-pastoral, and city-based or urban. Archaeologists use the corresponding terms of Paleolithic (Old Stone Age), Neolithic (New Stone Age), and Bronze Age. This reading suggests other developments of the urban or Bronze Age that might be better descriptions of the "third" stage than cities or bronze: states, plow agriculture, stratified, slave, and literate and writing-based societies. How does each of these new developments affect the lives of women? If you were to divide only women's history into two, three, or four stages, what would they be?

The world's first cities emerged in Eurasia around 3500 BCE. Fostered by the spread of villages, the urban centers of this continent grew up along major river systems—an environment conducive to planting and harvesting crops with relatively predictable patterns. There were four major regions where urban civilizations developed: in the Fertile Crescent along the Tigris and Euphrates* Rivers (also known as Mesopotamia, "the land between the two rivers"), along the Nile in Egypt, along the Indus River in modern Pakistan, and along the Yellow and Yangtze† Rivers in China.

---

* TY gruhs and yu FRAY teez

† yang zuh

Note: Pronunciations of difficult-to-pronounce terms will be given throughout the book. The emphasis goes on the syllables appearing in all capitals. [Ed.]

Source: Catherine Clay, Chandrika Paul, and Christine Senecal, *Envisioning Women in World History* (New York: McGraw-Hill, 2009), 20–23.

Eurasia's urban centers brought rapid changes in the organization of populations. Institutional patriarchy probably developed alongside the state, tribute extraction, social stratification, and slavery. The state, especially, was a political institution that organized, disciplined, and enslaved numerous inhabitants in order to provide security and order for itself. Law codes to promote universal standards of behavior, irrigation projects to ensure food supply, and extensive military defense were now possible and deemed necessary. Of course, in order to manage this type of society, institutional governments were needed, and the leaders who ran these growing states exercised a disproportionate share of power. State power transformed everything.

At the same time the world's first urban political institutions were taking shape, a disparity of wealth also grew in urban centers. Gaps between the haves and the have-nots of society appeared in heretofore unseen proportions. Slavery and the slave trade, essential to ancient Eurasian civilizations, are first in evidence. Some have argued that men's control and exchange of women's sexuality and reproductive capacity generally became the basis of private property in Mesopotamia between 3100 and 600 BCE. This affected not only female slaves and concubines but also the daughters of elite and free men. A bride's father, representing his family, exchanged her reproductive capacity for wealth and household goods and sometimes less tangible objects, such as status and/or influence. Sometimes payments were made in installments, and after a marriage, when her first child was born, the balance of bridewealth or dowry payments became due. This overall disparity in status, wealth, and power spelled a worsening of women's position.

Another explanation for the worsening of women's position and the emergence of patriarchy focuses on demography and technology, beginning with burgeoning populations of village communities, which, as discussed above, encouraged women's fertility to supply the needed workforce. Populous urban centers could no longer practice *hoe* agriculture, but often needed intensive *plow* agriculture to feed everyone. With more children, urban women had less time for heavier agricultural work and the long, intensive hours needed for cultivation. Women of plow-using cultures may have preferred and chosen to work around the house and to perform lighter agricultural work. This scenario resulted in a gradual loss of women's social power and prestige—sometimes through their own choices that made sense to them at the time, but that accelerated men's control over economic activity and social resources. Ultimately, then, when the communities began using plows and more laborious, intensive methods of cultivation (and the groups prospered materially), women's status changed.

Women's experience in the first urban centers was marked by a general devaluation of their social freedoms, a denial of their claims to the results of their labor, and sometimes even a reshaping of their religious expression. This decline did not affect all women's communities in the same way or at the same time. We notice this in the great variety of women's experiences across Eurasia in all four of the earliest urban areas.

Women and Society in the Earliest Civilizations

Although some villages had begun to experience greater social stratification by 3500 BCE, the difference between the powerful and the powerless was not nearly as marked as it was in the earliest cities. The increased wealth possessed by a small proportion of the urban population led to a growing interest in keeping wealth and power within familial units. And it led in many ways to the constriction of women's lives, whether slave, concubine, free, or elite.

The social experience of many women was shaped by the flourishing Eurasian slave trade. In Mesopotamia as early as 2300 BCE, inscriptions for "slave girl" appear earlier than those translating as "slave male." Female slaves in Mesopotamia often originated as captives of raids and were more plentiful than male slaves. They also seem to have been valued more than male slaves. In Syria, the reward for the return of fleeing females was double that for male fugitive slaves. Enslaved women lived under a wide range of conditions, from the relative comfort of high-level slaves important in the domestic realm, such as concubines (unfree females purchased for reproduction) to female slaves used for their brute physical labor. Thus, although many enslaved women held very low positions in society, the status of some was not as low as slaves in other time periods. For instance, a second-generation slave was often valued more than one that had been recently captured. Furthermore, female slaves could upon occasion be freed from their servitude. In Babylon around 1750 BCE, slave concubines were frequently freed after the demise of their masters. Additionally, the children of freewomen and male slaves were considered to be of free status there. High slave mortality and these legal paths to slave freedom made slave raiding for new supplies a constant imperative.

The situation of free and elite women was shaped by family control. Ensuring the lineage of a family meant keeping ever-closer tabs on women's morality, which could include preserving a woman's virginity until marriage and ensuring that she had only her husband for a sexual partner. This would guarantee that the paternity of family members would be unquestioned. Even a woman's reputation could be of critical interest to her family. We see this in practices such as veiling and seclusion, which marked women's high familial social standing and reputation for chastity (meaning virginity when single and fidelity in marriage), and actually prevented her from any sexual contact with males other than her husband.

As mentioned above, the decrease in women's social influence did not strike equally in all places. For instance, little evidence points to women's morality being constrained in the cities of Harappa and Mohenjo Daro in the Indus River Valley around 2500 BCE. The thousands of written sources from this civilization have yet to be deciphered, and thus it would be hazardous to assume that women's social position never declined there, and yet archaeological evidence suggests that the gap between the haves and the have-nots might not have been terribly significant to the urban population. The façades of the residential buildings in those cities were relatively similar, even though some families possessed much larger store-rooms than others. This evidence therefore suggests that maintaining a family's wealth and power, and the corresponding demotion that meant for women, was not as marked there. . . . Similarly, in the less urbanized Egyptian civilization, evidence suggests that women held positions of relative social equality and enjoyed freedom of movement unlike in other ancient societies. Given geographic barriers protecting them from warlike neighbors, Nile and Indus River civilizations were more militarily secure generally than civilizations in Mesopotamia and East Asia, and this may have resulted in fewer constraints on women.

Insight from Law Codes

We can see the inferior social position of urban women in law codes. Although legal texts from Mesopotamia often reflected social guidelines rather than actual practice, they nevertheless give critical insight to the way a society's most powerful people intended to govern. For example, in one Mesopotamian city in 2000 BCE, the murder of a woman was a capital offense. But by the time of Hammurabi‡ (d. 1750 BCE), a Babylonian ruler and famous lawmaker in Mesopotamia, killing a common woman only resulted in a fine according to the law code. (There was a stronger punishment if an elite woman were the victim.)

We can also see the uneven treatment of urban women in the law and practices surrounding marriage and divorce. For instance, wives' positions in Mesopotamia differed from city to city even within the same time frame. Whereas one law code from the urban civilization of Sumer made it legal for a new bride to refuse intercourse without punishment, later, a woman could be drowned if she refused to consummate her marriage.

---

‡ ha muh RAH bee

By 2500 BCE a law allowed a man to break his wife's teeth with a burnt brick if she disagreed with him. Divorce laws from Mesopotamian civilizations show that, although women experienced new inequities and constraints, they continued to enjoy some protections also. The cases compiled by the Babylonian ruler Hammurabi about 1700 BCE forbade women from divorcing, yet allowed men to terminate their marriages. Nevertheless, even Hammurabi's law code required divorced men to support their former spouses and any children they had together.

6

An Assyrian Law and a Palace Decree

This selection consists of two official documents from a Mesopotamian city-based empire of about 1100 B.C.E., known today as the Middle Assyrian Empire because it followed the early Assyrian period (twentieth to fifteenth century B.C.E.) and preceded the Neo-Assyrian era (tenth to seventh century B.C.E.). Archaeologists working in Syria and Iraq continue to unearth many laws from all Assyrian eras.

The first document is only one of many laws, and sections are missing. Nevertheless, it provides a rare window onto one urban society at the end of the second millennium B.C.E. What does it tell you about the role of women in this place at this time? What does it tell you about the attitudes of men toward women? What do you think was the purpose of passing this law?

The second document was a palace regulation meant to apply only to a select group of men and women, not the entire Assyrian society. What does this decree tell you about the lives of men and women in the palace? How were matters at the palace similar to, and different from, those of the larger society?

THINKING HISTORICALLY

No one or two documents can stand for an entire civilization, much less an urban "stage" of history. Nevertheless, what elements of this urban society would have been absent in hunting-gathering or early agricultural society? What aspects of city society seem to encourage patriarchal ideas and behavior?

Source: Martha T. Roth, *Law Collections from Mesopotamia and Asia Minor*, 2nd ed. (Atlanta: Scholar's Press, 1997), 167–68 and 205–6.

Law

Wives of a man, or [widows], or any [Assyrian] women who go out into the main thoroughfare [shall not have] their heads [bare]. Daughters of a man . . . [with] either a . . . -cloth or garments or . . . shall be veiled, . . . their heads. . . . When they go about . . . in the main thoroughfare during the daytime, they shall be veiled. A concubine who goes about in the main thoroughfare with her mistress is to be veiled. A married *qadiltu-* woman[1] is to be veiled (when she goes about) in the main thoroughfare, but an unmarried one is to leave her head bare in the main thoroughfare, she shall not veil herself. A prostitute shall not be veiled, her head shall be bare. Whoever sees a veiled prostitute shall seize her, secure witnesses, and bring her to the palace entrance. They shall not take away her jewelry, but he who has seized her takes her clothing; they shall strike her 50 blows with rods; they shall pour hot pitch over her head. And if a man should see a veiled prostitute and release her, and does not bring her to the palace entrance, they shall strike the man 50 blows with rods; the one who informs against him shall take his clothing; they shall pierce his ears, thread them on a cord, tie it at his back; he shall perform the king's service for one full month. Slave women shall not be veiled, and he who should see a veiled slave woman shall seize her and bring her to the palace entrance; they shall cut off her ears; he who seizes her shall take her clothing.

Palace Decree of Tiglath-Pileser I
(r. 1114–1076 B.C.E.)

Tiglath-pileser, king of the universe, king of Assyria, son of Ashur-rēsa-ishi, himself also king of Assyria, issued a decree for the palace commander of the Inner City, the palace herald, the chief of the water sprinklers of the Processional Residence, the physician of the Inner Quarters, and the administrator of all the palaces of the entire extent of the country:

Royal court attendants or dedicatees of the palace personnel who have access to the palace shall not enter the palace without an inspection; if he is not (properly) castrated, they shall turn him into a (castrated) court attendant for a second time.

If either the palace commander of the Inner City, or the palace herald, or the chief of the water sprinklers of the Processional Residence, or the physician of the Inner Quarters, or the administrator of all the palaces of the entire expanse of the country allows an uncastrated court attendant to enter into the palace, and he is later discovered, they shall amputate one foot of each of these officials.

---

[1] A class of templewomen. [Ed.]

■ REFLECTIONS

A historical stage is a specific example of a larger process that historians call *periodization*. Dividing history into periods is one way historians make the past comprehensible. Without periodization, history would be a vast, unwieldy continuum, lacking points of reference and intelligibility.

One of the earliest forms of historical periodization—years of reign—was a natural system of record keeping in the ancient cities dominated by kings. Each kingdom had its own list of kings, and each marked the current date by numbering the years of the king's reign. Some ancient societies periodized their history according to the years of rule of local officials or priesthoods. In the ancient Roman Republic, time was figured according to the terms of the elected consuls. The ancient Greeks used four-year periods called Olympiads, beginning with the first Olympic games in 776 B.C.E.

The ancient Greeks did not use "B.C." or "B.C.E.," of course. The periodization of world history into B.C. ("before Christ") and A.D. (*anno Domini*, "the Year of Our Lord" or "after Christ") did not come until the sixth century A.D., when a Christian monk hit upon a way to center Christ as the major turning point in history. We use a variant of this system in this text, when designating events "B.C.E." for "before the common era" or "C.E." for "of the common era." This translation of "B.C." and "A.D." avoids the Christian bias of the older system but preserves the simplicity of this common dating system, one used worldwide by most people today—even many non-Christians—because of its convenience.

All systems of periodization implicitly claim to designate important transitions in the past. The B.C. periodization inscribed the Christian belief that Christ's life, death, and resurrection fundamentally changed world history. Muslims count the years from a year one A.H. (*anno Hegire*, designating the year of the Prophet Muhammad's escape from Mecca to Medina) in 622 A.D. of the Christian calendar, and Jews date the years from a biblical year one.

Millennia, centuries, and decades are useful periods for societies that count by tens. Although such multiples are only mathematical, some historians use them for rough periodization, to distinguish between the 1950s and the 1960s or between the eighteenth and nineteenth centuries, for example, as if there were a genuine and important transition between one period and the other. Sometimes historians "stretch" the boundaries of centuries or decades to account for earlier or later changes. For example, some historians speak of "the long nineteenth century," embracing the period from the French Revolution in 1789 to the First World War in 1914, on the grounds that peoples' lives were transformed in 1789 rather than in 1800 and in 1914 rather than in 1900. Similarly, the "sixties," as a term for American society and culture during the Vietnam War era, often means the period from about 1963 to about 1975, since civil rights and antiwar activity became significant a few years after the beginning of the decade and the war continued until 1975.

Characterizing and defining a decade or century in chronological terms is only one method of periodization, however. Processes can also be periodized, as we saw in this chapter. All of world history can be divided into three periods: hunting-gathering, agricultural-pastoral, and urban. These are overlapping and continuing periods, and we can date only the beginning of the agricultural-pastoral and the urban periods, at about ten thousand and five thousand years ago, respectively. Further, we found it useful to divide the agricultural-pastoral period into two parts: early hoe agriculture or horticulture, when women still played a primary role, and later plow agriculture and the pastoral "secondary products revolution," when men's work predominated. Thus, our effort to understand the origins of patriarchy benefited from a four-stage periodization in which patriarchy began in an advanced agricultural-pastoral society and subsequent urban societies. These periods began at different times in different places: generally earliest in the Middle East and later in the Americas. In fact, we saw evidence that a full patriarchy did not come to the less urbanized parts of the Americas until it was brought by the European Christians. Not until then did people of the Americas know plow agriculture and draft animals (though large cities had been made possible by irrigation systems, stimulating the development of patriarchies in Mexico and Peru). To note how processes like plow agriculture or cities change people's lives (so much that we see a new stage of history) is not to say that all societies must take the same route. There may be different historical processes that lead to the same stage, as either plows or irrigation may produce enough food for cities (and lead to patriarchies). All societies do not go through all the same stages. Some today remain at a nonurban stage (making it possible to extrapolate about the past using recent information from anthropologists). Still, some historical processes—the adoption of new technologies or ways of life—can be so powerful that they effect changes almost everywhere. Can you think of other examples of such stage-making processes besides those mentioned in this chapter?

You might also get a sense of how the historian goes about periodizing and a feeling for its value if you periodize something you know a lot about—your own life, for instance. Think of the most important change or changes in your life. How have these changes divided your life into certain periods? Outline your autobiography by marking these periods as parts or chapters of the story of your life so far. To gain a sense of how periodization is imposed on reality and how arbitrary this structuring of the past can be, imagine how a parent or good friend would periodize your life. Would it be different from the way you did it? How and why? How might you periodize your life ten or twenty years from now? How would you have done it five years ago?

2

The Urban Revolution and "Civilization"

Mesopotamia, Egypt, and Mexico, 3500–1000 B.C.E.

■ HISTORICAL CONTEXT

The urban revolution that began approximately five thousand years ago produced a vast complex of new inventions, institutions, and ideas in the cities that dominated surrounding farms and pastures. The first selection in this chapter surveys the wide range of innovations in these earliest civilizations.

The term *civilization* has to be used cautiously. Especially when the idea of civilization is used as part of a stage theory of human history, we tend to assume that technological advancement means moral advancement. For instance, one hundred years ago scholars described ancient history as the progression from "savagery" to "barbarism" to "civilization."

It would be a shame to throw out the word *civilization* because it has been written more often with an axe than with a pen. The fact remains that the ancient cities created new ways of life for better or worse that were radically different from the world of agricultural villages. If we discard the word *civilization* as too overburdened with prejudice, we will have to find another one to describe that complex of changes. The term *civilization* comes from the Latin root word for city, *civitas*, from which we also get *civic*, *civilian*, and *citizen*. But, as the first reading argues, cities also created social classes, institutionalized inequalities, and calls to arms; most civilizations created soldiers as well as civilians.

37

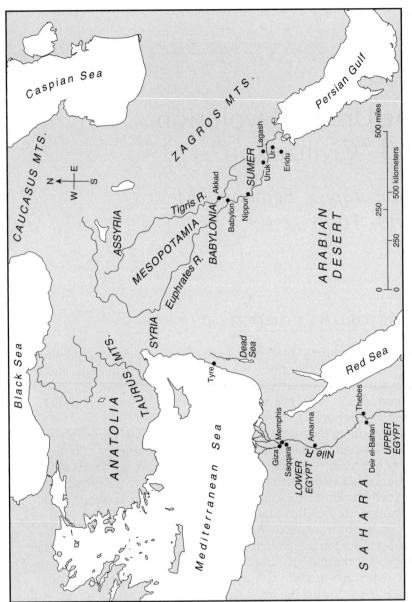

Map 2.1 Early Civilizations: Egypt and Mesopotamia.

The earliest cities, the small city-states on the Tigris and Euphrates* in ancient Sumer, included King Gilgamesh's Uruk, which is recounted in the second reading. Later cities, like Hammurabi's† Babylon, united Sumerian city-states and upriver pastoral kingdoms into giant empires (see Map 2.1). The third reading presents excerpts from Hammurabi's law code.

The ancient Egyptian empire depended less on cities than on the power of the king or pharaoh, but life along the Nile was magnified in the pharaoh's residence city and in his future home in the City of the Dead.

As you examine these selections, consider the overall transformation of the urban revolution in both Mesopotamia and Egypt. Note also the differences between Mesopotamian and Egyptian civilizations. Finally, how was the urban revolution in Mexico similar to, and different from, that in Egypt and Mesopotamia?

■ THINKING HISTORICALLY

Distinguishing Primary and Secondary Sources

For some historians, the "age of cities" is the beginning of history because cities invented writing. The period before city building and the creation of writing systems thus is often called "prehistory."

Our knowledge of ancient cities is enormously enhanced by ancient writings, art, and artifacts, which we call primary sources. These include literature, law codes, and inscriptions but also sculpture, murals, building remains, tools, and weapons—indeed, virtually anything from the time and place being studied. Secondary sources differ: They are written after the fact. History books or historical interpretations are called secondary sources because they rely on primary sources for information. Historians read, study, and interpret primary sources to compose secondary sources. In this chapter you will read both primary and secondary sources to help you learn ways to discern sources and extrapolate information from them.

---

* TY gruhs and yu FRAY teez
† ha muh RAH bee

1

KEVIN REILLY

Cities and Civilization

This selection from a college textbook is an obvious secondary source. You know it is a secondary source because it was written long after the events described by a modern historian—me.

This selection does two things. First, it explores the wide range of changes brought about by the urban revolution, from particulars like writing and money and metallurgy to abstractions like social class, visual acuity, and anonymity. After you read the selection, you might make a list of all the inventions and new phenomena of cities. You will likely be surprised by the great number of ideas, institutions, and activities that originated in the first cities. You might also find it interesting to place pluses and minuses next to the items on your list to help you determine whether "civilization" (city life) was, on balance, beneficial or harmful.

Second, the selection compares the "civilizations" of Mesopotamia and Egypt. According to the selection, what are the chief differences between Mesopotamian and Egyptian civilization? What accounts for these differences?

THINKING HISTORICALLY

To get a feel for the differences between a primary source and a secondary source, try to determine what primary sources might lead to some of these interpretations. Choose a sentence or two that appear specific enough to be based on a primary source. What kind of source could lead to such an interpretation? Conversely, find interpretations in this selection that *could not possibly* derive from a primary source and ask yourself, why not? Finally, consider what kind of non-written sources and evidence inform this account.

The Urban Revolution: Civilization and Class

The full-scale urban revolution occurred not in the rain-watered lands that first turned some villages into cities, but in the potentially more productive river valleys of Mesopotamia around 3500 B.C.E. Situated along the Tigris and Euphrates rivers, large villages like Eridu, Erech,

---

Source: Kevin Reilly, *The West and the World: A History of Civilization*, 2nd ed. (New York: Harper & Row, 1989), 48–54, 56, 58, 60.

Lagash, Kish, and later Ur and Babylon built irrigation systems that increased farm production enormously. Settlements like these were able to support five thousand, even ten thousand people, and still allow something like 10 percent of the inhabitants to work full-time at nonfarming occupations.

A change of this scale was a revolution, certainly the most important revolution in human living since the invention of agriculture five thousand years earlier. The urban revolution was prepared by a whole series of technological inventions in agricultural society. Between 6000 and 3000 B.C.E. people not only learned how to harness the power of oxen and the wind with the plow, the wheeled cart, and the sailboat; they also discovered the physical properties of metals, learned how to smelt copper and bronze, and began to work out a calendar based on the movements of the sun. River valleys like those of the Tigris and Euphrates were muddy swamps that had to be drained and irrigated to take advantage of the rich soil deposits. The dry land had literally to be built by teams of organized workers.

Therefore, cities required an organizational revolution that was every bit as important as the technological one. This was accomplished under the direction of the new class of rulers and managers—probably from the grasslands—who often treated the emerging cities as a conquered province. The work of irrigation itself allowed the rulers ample opportunity to coerce the inhabitants of these new cities. Rain knows no social distinctions. Irrigated water must be controlled and channeled.

It is no wonder then that the first cities gave us our first kings and our first class societies. In Mesopotamia, along the Nile of Egypt, in China, and later in Middle America the king is usually described as the founder of cities. These kings were able to endow their control with religious sanction. In Egypt and America the king was god. In Mesopotamia a new class of priests carried out the needs of the king's religion of control.

In some cities the new priesthood would appoint the king. In others, the priests were merely his lieutenants. When they were most loyal, their religion served to deify the king. The teachings of the new class of Mesopotamian priests, for instance, were that their god had created the people solely to work for the king and make his life easier. But even when the priesthood attempted to wrest some of the king's power from him, the priests taught the people to accept the divided society, which benefited king and priesthood as providers of a natural god-given order. The priesthood, after all, was responsible for measuring time, bounding space, and predicting seasonal events. The mastery of people was easy for those who controlled time and space.

The priesthood was only one of the new classes that insured the respectability of the warrior-chieftain turned king. Other palace intellectuals—scribes (or writers), doctors, magicians, and diviners—also struggled to maintain the king's prestige and manage his kingdom. This new class was rewarded, as were the priests, with leisure, status, and magnificent buildings, all of which further exalted the majesty of the king and his city.

Beneath the king, the priesthood, and the new class of intellectuals-managers was another new class charged with maintaining the king's law and order. Soldiers and police were also inventions of the first cities. Like the surrounding city wall, the king's military guard served a double function: It provided defense from outside attack and an obstacle to internal rebellion.

That these were the most important classes of city society can be seen from the physical remains of the first cities. The archeologist's spade has uncovered the monumental buildings of these classes in virtually all of the first cities. The palace, the temple, and the citadel (or fort) are, indeed, the monuments that distinguish cities from villages. Further, the size of these buildings and the permanency of their construction (compared with the small, cheaply built homes of the farmers) attest to the fundamental class divisions of city society.

Civilization: Security and Variety

The most obvious achievements of the first civilizations are the monuments—the pyramids, temples, palaces, statues, and treasures—that were created for the new ruling class of kings, nobles, priests, and their officials. But civilized life is much more than the capacity to create monuments.

Civilized life is secure life. At the most basic level this means security from the sudden destruction that village communities might suffer. Civilized life gives the feeling of permanence. It offers regularity, stability, order, even routine. Plans can be made. Expectations can be realized. People can be expected to act predictably, according to the rules.

The first cities were able to attain stability with walls that shielded the inhabitants from nomads and armies, with the first codes of law that defined human relationships, with police and officials who enforced the laws, and with institutions that functioned beyond the lives of their particular members. City life offered considerably more permanence and security than village life.

Civilization involves more than security, however. A city that provided only order would be more like a prison than a civilization. The first cities provided something that the best-ordered villages lacked. They provided far greater variety: More races and ethnic groups were speaking more languages, engaged in more occupations, and living a greater variety of lifestyles. The abundance of choice, the opportunities for new sensations, new experiences, knowledge—these have always been the appeals of city life. The opportunities for growth and enrichment were far greater than the possibilities of plow and pasture life.

Security plus variety equals creativity. At least the possibility of a more creative, expressive life was available in the protected, semipermanent city enclosures that drew, like magnets, foreign traders and diplomats, new ideas about gods and nature, strange foods and customs, and the magicians, ministers, and mercenaries of the king's court. Civilization is the enriched life that this dynamic urban setting permitted and the human creativity and opportunity that it encouraged. At the very least, cities made even the most common slave think and feel a greater range of things than the tightly knit, clannish agricultural village allowed. That was (and still is) the root of innovation and creativity—of civilization itself.

The variety of people and the complexity of city life required new and more general means of communication. The villager knew everyone personally. Cities brought together people who often did not even speak the same language. Not only law codes but written language itself became a way to bridge the many gaps of human variety. Cities invented writing so that strangers could communicate, and so that those communications could become permanent—remembered publicly, officially recorded. [Writer and philosopher Ralph Waldo] Emerson was right when he said that the city lives by memory, but it was the official memory that enabled the city to carry on its business or religion beyond the lifetime of the village elders. Written symbols that everyone could recognize became the basis of laws, invention, education, taxes, accounting, contracts, and obligations. In short, writing and records made it possible for each generation to begin on the shoulders of its ancestors. Village life and knowledge often seemed to start from scratch. Thus, cities cultivated not only memory and the past, but hope and the future as well. City civilizations invented not only history and record keeping but also prophecy and social planning.

Writing was one city invention that made more general communication possible. Money was another. Money made it possible to deal with anyone just as an agreed-upon public language did. Unnecessary in the village climate of mutual obligations, money was essential in the city society of strangers. Such general media of communication as writing and money vastly increased the number of things that could be said and thought, bought and sold. As a consequence, city life was more impersonal than village life, but also more dynamic and more exciting.

The "Eye" and "I"

[Communication theorist] Marshall McLuhan has written that "civilization gave the barbarian an eye for an ear." We might add that civilization also gave an "I" for an "us." City life made the "eye" and the "I" more important than they had been in the village. The invention of writing made knowledge more visual. The eye had to be trained to recognize the minute differences in letters and words. Eyes took in a greater abundance of detail: laws, prices, the strange cloak of the foreigner, the odd type of shoes made by the new craftsworker from who-knows-where, the colors of the fruit and vegetable market, and elaborate painting in the temple, as well as the written word. In the village one learned by listening. In the city seeing was believing. In the new city courts of law an "eyewitness account" was believed to be more reliable than "hearsay evidence." In some villages even today, the heard and the spoken are thought more reliable than the written and the seen. In the city, even spoken language took on the uniformity and absence of emotion that is unavoidable in the written word. Perhaps emotions themselves became less violent. "Civilized" is always used to mean emotional restraint, control of the more violent passions, and a greater understanding, even tolerance, of the different and foreign.

Perhaps empathy (the capacity to put yourself in someone else's shoes) increased in cities—so full of so many different others that had to be understood. When a Turkish villager was recently asked, "What would you do if you were president of your country?" he stammered: "My God! How can you ask such a thing? How can I . . . I cannot . . . president of Turkey . . . master of the whole world?" He was completely unable to imagine himself as president. It was as removed from his experience as if he were master of the world. Similarly, a Lebanese villager who was asked what he would do if he were editor of a newspaper accused the interviewer of ridiculing him, and frantically waved the interviewer on to another question. Such a life was beyond his comprehension. It was too foreign to imagine. The very variety of city life must have increased the capacity of the lowest commoner to imagine, empathize, sympathize, and criticize.

The oral culture of the village reinforced the accepted by saying and singing it almost monotonously. The elders, the storytellers, and the minstrels must have had prodigious memories. But their stories changed only gradually and slightly. The spoken word was sacred. To say it differently was to change the truth. The written culture of cities taught "point of *view*." An urban individual did not have to remember everything. That was done permanently on paper. Knowledge became a recognition of different interpretations and the capacity to look up things. The awareness of variety meant the possibility of criticism, analysis, and an ever-newer synthesis. It is no wonder that the technical and scientific knowledge of cities increased at a geometric rate compared with the knowledge of villages. The multiplication of knowledge was implicit in the city's demand to recognize difference and variety. Civilization has come to mean that ever-expanding body of knowledge and skill. Its finest achievements have been that knowledge, its writing, and its visual art. The city and civilization (like the child) are to be seen and not heard.

It may seem strange to say that the impersonal life of cities contributed greatly to the development of personality—the "I" as well as the "eye." Village life was in a sense much more personal. Everything was taken personally. Villagers deal with each other not as "the blacksmith," "the baker," "that guy who owes me a goat," or "that no-good bum." They do not even "deal" with each other. They know each other by name and family. They love, hate, support, and murder each other because of who they are, because of personal feelings, because of personal and family responsibility. They have full, varied relationships with each member of the village. They do not merely buy salt from this person, talk about the weather with this other person, and discuss personal matters with only this other person. They share too much with each other to divide up their relationships in that way.

City life is a life of separated, partial relationships. In a city you do not know about the butcher's life, wife, kids, and problems. You do not care. You are in a hurry. You have too many other things to do. You might discuss the weather—but while he's cutting. You came to buy meat. Many urban relationships are like that. There are many business, trading, or "dealing" relationships because there are simply too many people to know them all as relatives.

The impersonality of city life is a shame in a way. (It makes it easier to get mugged by someone who does not even hate you.) But the luxurious variety of impersonal relationships (at least some of the time) provides the freedom for the individual personality to emerge. Maybe that is why people have often dreamed of leaving family and friends (usually for a city) in the hope of "finding themselves." Certainly, the camaraderie and community of village life had a darker side of surveillance and conformity. When everything was known about everyone, it was difficult for the individual to find his or her individuality. Family ties and village custom were often obstacles to asserting self-identity. The city offered its inhabitants a huge variety of possible relationships and personal identities. The urban inhabitant was freer than his village cousin to choose friends, lovers, associates, occupation, housing, and lifestyle. The city was full of choices that the village could not afford or condone. The village probably provided more security in being like everyone else and doing what was expected. But the city provided the variety of possibilities that could allow the individual to follow the "inner self" and cultivate inner gardens.

The class divisions of city society made it difficult for commoners to achieve an effective or creative individuality. But the wealthy and powerful—especially the king—were able to develop models of individuality and personality that were revolutionary. No one before had ever achieved such a sense of the self, and the model of the king's power and freedom became a goal for the rest of the society. The luxury, leisure, and opportunity of the king was a revolutionary force. In contrast to a village elder, the king could do whatever he wanted. Recognizing that, more and more city inhabitants asked, "Why can't we?" City revolutions have continually extended class privilege and opportunities ever since.

Once a society has achieved a level of abundance, once it can offer the technological means, the educational opportunities, the creative outlets necessary for everyone to lead meaningful, happy, healthy lives, then classes may be a hindrance. Class divisions were, however, a definite stimulus to productivity and creativity in the early city civilizations. The democratic villagers preferred stability to improvement. As a result, their horizons were severely limited. They died early, lived precipitously, and suffered without much hope. The rulers of the first cities discovered the possibilities of leisure, creation, and the good life. They invented heaven and utopia—first for themselves. Only very gradually has the invention of civilization, of human potential, sifted down to those beneath the ruling class. In many cases, luxury, leisure, freedom, and opportunity are still the monopolies of the elite. But once the powerful have exploited the poor enough to establish their own paradise on earth and their own immortality after death, the poor also have broader horizons and plans.

Mesopotamian and Egyptian Civilizations: A Tale of Two Rivers

Experts disagree as to whether Mesopotamian or Egyptian civilization is older. Mesopotamian influence in Egypt was considerable enough to suggest slightly earlier origins, but both had evolved distinct civilizations by 3000 B.C.E. Indeed, the difference between the two civilizations attests to the existence of multiple routes to civilized life. In both cases, river valleys provided the necessary water and silt for an agricultural surplus large enough to support classes of specialists who did not have to farm. But the differing nature of the rivers had much to do with the different types of civilization that evolved.

The Egyptians were blessed with the easier and more reliable of the two rivers. The Nile overflowed its banks predictably every year on the parched ground in the summer after August 15, well after the harvest had been gathered, depositing its rich sediment, and withdrawing by early October, leaving little salt or marsh, in time for the sowing of winter crops. Later sowings for summer crops required only simple canals that tapped the river upstream and the natural drainage of the Nile Valley. Further, transportation on the Nile was simplified by the fact that the prevailing winds blew from the north, while the river flowed from the south, making navigation a matter of using sails upstream and dispensing with them coming downstream.

The Euphrates offered none of these advantages as it cut its way through Mesopotamia. The Euphrates flowed high above the flood plain (unlike the neighboring Tigris) so that its waters could be used, but it flooded suddenly and without warning in the late spring, after the summer crops had been sown and before the winter crops could be harvested. Thus, the flooding of the Euphrates offered no natural irrigation. Its waters were needed at other times, and its flooding was destructive. Canals were necessary to drain off water for irrigation when the river was low, and these canals had to be adequately blocked, and the banks reinforced, when the river flooded. Further, since the Euphrates was not as easily navigable as the Nile, the main canals had to serve as major transportation arteries as well.

In Mesopotamia the flood was the enemy. The Mesopotamian deities who ruled the waters, Nin-Girsu and Tiamat, were feared. The forces of nature were often evil. Life was a struggle. In Egypt, on the other hand, life was viewed as a cooperation with nature. Even the Egyptian god of the flood, Hapi, was a helpful deity, who provided the people's daily bread. Egyptian priests and philosophers were much more at ease with their world than were their Mesopotamian counterparts. And, partly because of their different experiences with their rivers, the Mesopotamians developed a civilization based on cities, while the Egyptians did not. From the first Sumerian city-states on the lower Euphrates to the later northern Mesopotamian capital of Babylon, civilization was the product and expression of city life. Egyptian civilization, in contrast, was the creation of the pharaoh's court rather than of cities. Beyond the court, which was moved from one location to another, Egypt remained a country of peasant villages.

A prime reason for Egypt's lack of urbanization was the ease of farming on the banks of the Nile. Canal irrigation was a relatively simple process that did not demand much organization. Small market towns were sufficient for the needs of the countryside. They housed artisans, shopkeepers, the priests of the local temple, and the agents of the pharaoh, but they never swelled with a large middle class and never developed large-scale industry or commerce.

In Sumer, and later in Mesopotamia, the enormous task of fighting the Euphrates required a complex social organization with immediate local needs. Only communal labor could build and maintain the network of subsidiary canals for irrigation and drainage. Constant supervision was necessary to keep the canals free of silt, to remove salt deposits, to maintain the riverbanks at flood-time, and to prevent any farmer from monopolizing the water in periods of drought. Life on the Euphrates required cooperative work and responsibility that never ceased. It encouraged absolute, administrative control over an area larger than the village, and it fostered participation and loyalty to an irrigated area smaller than the imperial state. The city-state was the political answer to the economic problems of Sumer and Mesopotamia.

The religious practices in the Euphrates Valley reflected and supported city organization. Residents of each local area worshiped the local god while recognizing the existence of other local gods in a larger Sumerian, and eventually Mesopotamian, pantheon of gods. The priests of the local temple supervised canal work, the collection of taxes, and the storage of written records, as well as the proper maintenance of religious rituals. Thus, religious loyalty reinforced civic loyalty. Peasant and middle-class Sumerians thought of themselves as citizens of their particular city, worshipers of their particular city god, subjects of their particular god's earthly representative, but not as Sumerian nationals. By contrast, the Egyptian peasant was always an Egyptian, a subject of the pharaoh, but never a citizen.

The local, civic orientation of Mesopotamian cities can be seen in the physical structure of the capital city of Sumer, the city of Ur. Like other cities on the Euphrates, Ur was surrounded by a wall. It was dominated by the temple of Nannar, the moon-god who owned the city, and the palace complex beneath the temple. The residential areas were situated outside of the sacred Temenos, or temple compound, but within the walls, between the river and the main canal. The well-excavated remains of Ur of the seventeenth century B.C.E. show a residential street plan that looks like many Middle Eastern cities of today. A highly congested area of winding alleys and broad streets sheltered one- and two-story houses of merchants, shopkeepers, tradespeople, and occasional priests and scribes that suggest a large, relatively prosperous middle class. Most houses were built around a central courtyard that offered shade throughout the day, with mud-brick, often even plastered, outside walls that protected a number of interior rooms from the sun and the eyes of the tax inspector. The remains of seventeenth-century Ur show both the variety and the density of modern city life. There are specialized districts throughout the city. Certain trades have their special quarters: a bakers' square, probably special areas for the dyers, tanners, potters, and metalworkers. But life is mixed together as well. Subsidiary gods have temples outside the Temenos. Small and large houses are jumbled next to each other. There seems to be a slum area near the Temenos, but there are small houses for workers, tenant farmers, and the poor throughout the city. And no shop or urban professional is more than a short walking distance away. The entire size of the walled city was an oval that extended three-quarters of a mile long and a half a mile wide.

A well-excavated Egyptian city from roughly the same period (the fourteenth century B.C.E.) offers some striking contrasts. Akhetaton, or Tell el Amarna, Pharaoh Akhenaton's capital on the Nile, was not enclosed by walls or canals. It merely straggled down the eastern bank of the Nile for five miles and faded into the desert. Without the need for extensive irrigation or protection, Tell el Amarna shows little of the crowded, vital density of Ur. Its layout lacks any sense of urgency. The

North Palace of the pharaoh is a mile and a half north of the temple complex and offices, which are three and a half miles from the official pleasure garden. The palaces of the court nobility and the large residences of the court's officials front one of the two main roads that parallel the river, or they are situated at random. There is plenty of physical space (and social space) between these and the bunched villages of workers' houses. The remains suggest very little in the way of a middle class or a merchant or professional class beyond the pharaoh's specialists and retainers. Life for the wealthy was, judging from the housing, more luxurious than at Ur, but for the majority of the population, city life was less rich. In many ways, the pharaoh's court at Tell el Amarna was not a city at all.

2

The Epic of Gilgamesh

The Epic of Gilgamesh is the earliest story written in any language. It also serves as a primary source for the study of ancient Mesopotamia—the land between the two great rivers, the Tigris and Euphrates.

Gilgamesh was an ancient king of Sumer who lived about 2700 B.C.E. Since *The Epic* comes from a thousand years later, we can assume Sumerians kept telling this tale about King Gilgamesh for some time before it was written down. In Sumer, writing was initially used by temple priests to keep track of property and taxes. Soon, however, writing was used to preserve stories and to celebrate kings.

The more you know about the Sumerian people, the more information you will be able to mine from your source. In the previous secondary selection, you read some historical background that will help you make sense of this story. Look in *The Epic* for evidence of the urban revolution discussed in the previous selection. What is the meaning of the story of the taming of Enkidu by the harlot? Does Enkidu also tame Gilgamesh? What two worlds do Enkidu and Gilgamesh represent?

Do the authors or listeners of *The Epic* think city life is better than life in the country? According to *The Epic*, what are the advantages of the city? What problems does it have?

What does the story of the flood tell you about life in ancient Mesopotamia? Would you expect the ancient Egyptians to tell a similar story?

Source: *The Epic of Gilgamesh*, trans. N. K. Sandars (London: Penguin Books, 1972), 61–69, 108–13.

THINKING HISTORICALLY

Reading a primary source differs markedly from reading a secondary source. Primary sources were not written with you or me in mind. It is safe to say that the author of *The Epic of Gilgamesh* never even imagined our existence. For this reason, primary sources are a bit difficult to access. Reading a primary source usually requires some intensive work. You have to keep asking yourself, why was this story told? How would a story like this help or teach people at that time? That is, you must put yourself in the shoes of the original teller and listener.

Primary sources offer us a piece of the past. No historian is in your way explaining things. With your unique perspective, you have an advantage over the intended audience: You can ask questions about the source that the author and original audience never imagined or, possibly, would not have dared ask.

Ask a question for which this primary source can provide an answer, then find the answer.

Prologue: Gilgamesh King in Uruk

I will proclaim to the world the deeds of Gilgamesh. This was the man to whom all things were known; this was the king who knew the countries of the world. He was wise, he saw mysteries and knew secret things, he brought us a tale of the days before the flood. He went on a long journey, was weary, worn-out with labor; returning he rested, he engraved on a stone the whole story.

When the gods created Gilgamesh they gave him a perfect body. Shamash the glorious sun endowed him with beauty, Adad the god of the storm endowed him with courage, the great gods made his beauty perfect, surpassing all others, terrifying like a great wild bull. Two thirds they made him god and one third man.

In Uruk he built walls, a great rampart, and the temple of blessed Eanna for the god of the firmament Anu, and for Ishtar the goddess of love. Look at it still today: the outer wall where the cornice runs, it shines with the brilliance of copper; and the inner wall, it has no equal. Touch the threshold; it is ancient. Approach Eanna the dwelling of Ishtar, our lady of love and war, the like of which no latter-day king, no man alive can equal. Climb upon the wall of Uruk; walk along it, I say; regard the foundation terrace and examine the masonry; is it not burnt brick and good? The seven sages laid the foundations.

The Coming of Enkidu

Gilgamesh went abroad in the world, but he met with none who could withstand his arms till he came to Uruk. But the men of Uruk muttered in their houses, "Gilgamesh sounds the tocsin for his amusement, his arrogance has no bounds by day or night. No son is left with his father, for Gilgamesh takes from all, even the children; yet the king should be a shepherd to his people. His lust leaves no virgin to her lover, neither the warrior's daughter nor the wife of the noble; yet this is the shepherd of the city, wise, comely, and resolute."

The gods heard their lament, the gods of heaven cried to the Lord of Uruk, to Anu the god of Uruk: "A goddess made him, strong as a savage bull, none can withstand his arms. No son is left with his father, for Gilgamesh takes them all; and is this the king, the shepherd of his people? His lust leaves no virgin to her lover, neither the warrior's daughter nor the wife of the noble." When Anu had heard their lamentation the gods cried to Aruru, the goddess of creation, "You made him, O Aruru, now create his equal; let it be as like him as his own reflection, his second self, stormy head for stormy heart. Let them contend together and leave Uruk in quiet."

So the goddess conceived an image in her mind, and it was of the stuff of Anu of the firmament. She dipped her hands in water and pinched off clay, she let it fall in the wilderness, and noble Enkidu* was created. There was virtue in him of the god of war, of Ninurta himself. His body was rough; he had long hair like a woman's; it waved like the hair of Nisaba, the goddess of corn. His body was covered with matted hair like Samuqan's, the god of cattle. He was innocent of mankind; he knew nothing of cultivated land.

Enkidu ate grass in the hills with the gazelle and lurked with wild beasts at the water-holes; he had joy of the water with the herds of wild game. But there was a trapper who met him one day face to face at the drinking-hole, for the wild game had entered his territory. On three days he met him face to face, and the trapper was frozen with fear. He went back to his house with the game that he had caught, and he was dumb, benumbed with terror. His face was altered like that of one who has made a long journey. With awe in his heart he spoke to his father: "Father, there is a man, unlike any other, who comes down from the hills. He is the strongest in the world, he is like an immortal from heaven. He ranges over the hills with wild beasts and eats grass; he ranges through your land and comes down to the wells. I am afraid and dare not go near him. He fills in the pits which I dig and tears up my traps set for the game; he helps the beasts to escape and now they slip through my fingers."

* EHN kee doo

His father opened his mouth and said to the trapper, "My son, in Uruk lives Gilgamesh; no one has ever prevailed against him, he is strong as a star from heaven. Go to Uruk, find Gilgamesh, extol the strength of this wild man. Ask him to give you a harlot, a wanton from the temple of love; return with her, and let her woman's power overpower this man. When next he comes down to drink at the wells she will be there, stripped naked; and when he sees her beckoning he will embrace her, and then the wild beasts will reject him."

So the trapper set out on his journey to Uruk and addressed himself to Gilgamesh saying, "A man unlike any other is roaming now in the pastures; he is as strong as a star from heaven and I am afraid to approach him. He helps the wild game to escape; he fills in my pits and pulls up my traps." Gilgamesh said, "Trapper, go back, take with you a harlot, a child of pleasure. At the drinking-hole she will strip, and when he sees her beckoning he will embrace her and the game of the wilderness will surely reject him."

Now the trapper returned, taking the harlot with him. After a three days' journey they came to the drinking-hole, and there they sat down; the harlot and the trapper sat facing one another and waited for the game to come. For the first day and for the second day the two sat waiting, but on the third day the herds came; they came down to drink and Enkidu was with them. The small wild creatures of the plains were glad of the water, and Enkidu with them, who ate grass with the gazelle and was born in the hills; and she saw him; the savage man, come from far-off in the hills. The trapper spoke to her: "There he is. Now, woman, make your breasts bare, have no shame, do not delay but welcome his love. Let him see you naked, let him possess your body. When he comes near uncover yourself and lie with him; teach him, the savage man, your woman's art, for when he murmurs love to you the wild beasts that shared his life in the hills will reject him."

She was not ashamed to take him, she made herself naked and welcomed his eagerness; as he lay on her murmuring love she taught him the woman's art. For six days and seven nights they lay together, for Enkidu had forgotten his home in the hills; but when he was satisfied he went back to the wild beasts. Then, when the gazelle saw him, they bolted away; when the wild creatures saw him they fled. Enkidu would have followed, but his body was bound as though with a cord, his knees gave way when he started to run, his swiftness was gone. And now the wild creatures had all fled away; Enkidu was grown weak, for wisdom was in him, and the thoughts of a man were in his heart. So he returned and sat down at the woman's feet, and listened intently to what she said. "You are wise, Enkidu, and now you have become like a god. Why do you want to run wild with the beasts in the hills? Come with me. I will take you to strong-walled Uruk, to the blessed temple of Ishtar and of Anu, of love and of heaven: there Gilgamesh lives, who is very strong, and like a wild bull he lords it over men."

When she had spoken Enkidu was pleased; he longed for a comrade, for one who would understand his heart. "Come, woman, and take me to that holy temple, to the house of Anu and of Ishtar, and to the place where Gilgamesh lords it over people. I will challenge him boldly, I will cry out aloud in Uruk, 'I am the strongest here, I have come to change the old order, I am he who was born in the hills, I am he who is strongest of all.'"

She said, "Let us go, and let him see your face. I know very well where Gilgamesh is in great Uruk. O Enkidu, there all the people are dressed in their gorgeous robes, every day is holiday, the young men and the girls are wonderful to see. How sweet they smell! All the great ones are roused from their beds. O Enkidu, you who love life, I will show you Gilgamesh, a man of many moods; you shall look at him well in his radiant manhood. His body is perfect in strength and maturity; he never rests by night or day. He is stronger than you, so leave your boasting. Shamash the glorious sun has given favors to Gilgamesh, and Anu of the heavens, and Enlil, and Ea the wise has given him deep understanding. I tell you, even before you have left the wilderness, Gilgamesh will know in his dreams that you are coming."

Now Gilgamesh got up to tell his dream to his mother, Ninsun, one of the wise gods. "Mother, last night I had a dream. I was full of joy, the young heroes were round me and I walked through the night under the stars of the firmament, and one, a meteor of the stuff of Anu, fell down from heaven. I tried to lift it but it proved too heavy. All the people of Uruk came round to see it, the common people jostled and the nobles thronged to kiss its feet; and to me its attraction was like the love of woman. They helped me, I braced my forehead and I raised it with thongs and brought it to you, and you yourself pronounced it my brother."

Then Ninsun, who is well-beloved and wise, said to Gilgamesh, "This star of heaven which descended like a meteor from the sky; which you tried to lift, but found too heavy, when you tried to move it it would not budge, and so you brought it to my feet; I made it for you, a goad and spur, and you were drawn as though to a woman. This is the strong comrade, the one who brings help to his friend in his need. He is the strongest of wild creatures, the stuff of Anu; born in the grasslands and the wild hills reared him; when you see him you will be glad; you will love him as a woman and he will never forsake you. This is the meaning of the dream."

Gilgamesh said, "Mother, I dreamed a second dream. In the streets of strong-walled Uruk there lay an axe; the shape of it was strange and the people thronged round. I saw it and was glad. I bent down, deeply drawn towards it; I loved it like a woman and wore it at my side." Ninsun answered, "That axe, which you saw, which drew you so powerfully like love of a woman, that is the comrade whom I give you, and he will come in his strength like one of the host of heaven. He is the brave companion who rescues his friend in necessity." Gilgamesh said to his mother, "A friend, a counsellor has come to me from Enlil, and now I shall befriend and counsel him." So Gilgamesh told his dreams; and the harlot retold them to Enkidu.

And now she said to Enkidu, "When I look at you you have become like a god. Why do you yearn to run wild again with the beasts in the hills? Get up from the ground, the bed of a shepherd." He listened to her words with care. It was good advice that she gave. She divided her clothing in two and with the one half she clothed him and with the other herself; and holding his hand she led him like a child to the sheepfolds, into the shepherds' tents. There all the shepherds crowded round to see him, they put down bread in front of him, but Enkidu could only suck the milk of wild animals. He fumbled and gaped, at a loss what to do or how he should eat the bread and drink the strong wine. Then the woman said, "Enkidu, eat bread, it is the staff of life; drink the wine, it is the custom of the land." So he ate till he was full and drank strong wine, seven goblets. He became merry, his heart exulted and his face shone. He rubbed down the matted hair of his body and anointed himself with oil. Enkidu had become a man; but when he had put on man's clothing he appeared like a bridegroom. He took arms to hunt the lion so that the shepherds could rest at night. He caught wolves and lions and the herdsmen lay down in peace; for Enkidu was their watchman, that strong man who had no rival.

He was merry living with the shepherds, till one day lifting his eyes he saw a man approaching. He said to the harlot, "Woman, fetch that man here. Why has he come? I wish to know his name." She went and called the man saying, "Sir, where are you going on this weary journey?" The man answered, saying to Enkidu, "Gilgamesh has gone into the marriage-house and shut out the people. He does strange things in Uruk, the city of great streets. At the roll of the drum work begins for the men, and work for the women. Gilgamesh the king is about to celebrate marriage with the Queen of Love, and he still demands to be first with the bride, the king to be first and the husband to follow, for that was ordained by the gods from his birth, from the time the umbilical cord was cut. But now the drums roll for the choice of the bride and the city groans." At these words Enkidu turned white in the face. "I will go to the place where Gilgamesh lords it over the people, I will challenge him boldly, and I will cry aloud in Uruk, 'I have come to change the old order, for I am the strongest here.'"

Now Enkidu strode in front and the woman followed behind. He entered Uruk, that great market, and all the folk thronged round him where he stood in the street in strong-walled Uruk. The people jostled; speaking of him they said, "He is the spit of Gilgamesh." "He is shorter." "He is bigger of bone." "This is the one who was reared on the milk of wild beasts. His is the greatest strength." The men rejoiced: "Now

Gilgamesh has met his match. This great one, this hero whose beauty is like a god, he is a match even for Gilgamesh."

In Uruk the bridal bed was made, fit for the goddess of love. The bride waited for the bridegroom, but in the night Gilgamesh got up and came to the house. Then Enkidu stepped out, he stood in the street and blocked the way. Mighty Gilgamesh came on and Enkidu met him at the gate. He put out his foot and prevented Gilgamesh from entering the house, so they grappled, holding each other like bulls. They broke the doorposts and the walls shook, they snorted like bulls locked together. They shattered the doorposts and the walls shook. Gilgamesh bent his knee with his foot planted on the ground and with a turn Enkidu was thrown. Then immediately his fury died. When Enkidu was thrown he said to Gilgamesh, "There is not another like you in the world. Ninsun, who is as strong as a wild ox in the byre, she was the mother who bore you, and now you are raised above all men, and Enlil has given you the kingship, for your strength surpasses the strength of men." So Enkidu and Gilgamesh embraced and their friendship was sealed.

The Story of the Flood

[Utnapishtim, the old man, tells the story to Gilgamesh.]

"You know the city Shurrupak, it stands on the banks of Euphrates? That city grew old and the gods that were in it were old. There was Anu, lord of the firmament, their father, and warrior Enlil their counsellor, Ninurta the helper, and Ennugi watcher over canals; and with them also was Ea. In those days the world teemed, the people multiplied, the world bellowed like a wild bull, and the great god was aroused by the clamour. Enlil heard the clamour and he said to the gods in council, 'The uproar of mankind is intolerable and sleep is no longer possible by reason of the babel.' So the gods agreed to exterminate mankind. Enlil did this, but Ea because of his oath warned me in a dream. He whispered their words to my house of reeds, 'Reed-house, reed-house! Wall, O wall, hearken reed-house, wall reflect; O man of Shurrupak, son of Ubara-Tutu; tear down your house and build a boat, abandon possessions and look for life, despise worldly goods and save your soul alive. Tear down your house, I say, and build a boat. These are the measurements of the barque as you shall build her: let her beam equal her length, let her deck be roofed like the vault that covers the abyss; then take up into the boat the seed of all living creatures.'

"When I had understood I said to my lord, 'Behold, what you have commanded I will honour and perform, but how shall I answer the people, the city, the elders?' Then Ea opened his mouth and said to me, his servant, 'Tell them this: I have learnt that Enlil is wrathful against me, I dare no longer walk in his land nor live in his city; I will go down to the Gulf to dwell with Ea my lord. But on you he will rain down abundance, rare fish and shy wild-fowl, a rich harvest-tide. In the evening the rider of the storm will bring you wheat in torrents.'

"In the first light of dawn all my household gathered round me, the children brought pitch and the men whatever was necessary. On the fifth day I laid the keel and the ribs, then I made fast the planking. The ground-space was one acre, each side of the deck measured one hundred and twenty cubits, making a square. I built six decks below, seven in all, I divided them into nine sections with bulkheads between. I drove in wedges where needed, I saw to the punt-poles, and laid in supplies. The carriers brought oil in baskets, I poured pitch into the furnace and asphalt and oil; more oil was consumed in caulking, and more again the master of the boat took into his stores. I slaughtered bullocks for the people and every day I killed sheep. I gave the shipwrights wine to drink as though it were river water, raw wine and red wine and oil and white wine. There was feasting then as there is at the time of the New Year's festival; I myself anointed my head. On the seventh day the boat was complete.

"Then was the launching full of difficulty; there was shifting of ballast above and below till two thirds was submerged. I loaded into her all that I had of gold and of living things, my family, my kin, the beast of the field both wild and tame, and all the craftsmen. I sent them on board, for the time that Shamash had ordained was already fulfilled when he said 'In the evening, when the rider of the storm sends down the destroying rain, enter the boat and batten her down.' The time was fulfilled, the evening came, the rider of the storm sent down the rain. I looked out at the weather and it was terrible, so I too boarded the boat and battened her down. All was now complete, the battening and the caulking; so I handed the tiller to Puzur-Amurri the steersman, with the navigation and the care of the whole boat.

"With the first light of dawn a black cloud came from the horizon; it thundered within where Adad, lord of the storm, was riding. In front over hill and plain Shullat and Hanish, heralds of the storm, led on. Then the gods of the abyss rose up; Nergal pulled out the dams of the nether waters, Ninurta the war-lord threw down the dykes, and the seven judges of hell, the Annunaki, raised their torches, lighting the land with their livid flame. A stupor of despair went up to heaven when the god of the storm turned daylight to darkness, when he smashed the land like a cup. One whole day the tempest raged, gathering fury as it went, it poured over the people like the tides of battle; a man could not see his brother nor the people be seen from heaven. Even the gods were terrified at the flood, they fled to the highest heaven, the firmament of Anu; they crouched against the walls, cowering like curs. . . .

"For six days and six nights the winds blew, torrent and tempest and flood overwhelmed the world, tempest and flood raged together like warring hosts. When the seventh day dawned the storm from the south subsided, the sea grew calm, the flood was stilled; I looked at the face of the world and there was silence, all mankind was turned to clay. The surface of the sea stretched as flat as a roof-top; I opened a hatch and the light fell on my face. Then I bowed low, I sat down and I wept, the tears streamed down my face, for on every side was the waste of water. I looked for land in vain, but fourteen leagues distant there appeared a mountain, and there the boat grounded; on the mountain of Nisir the boat held fast, she held fast and did not budge. One day she held, and a second day on the mountain of Nisir she held fast and did not budge. A third day, and a fourth day she held fast on the mountain and did not budge; a fifth day and a sixth day she held fast on the mountain. When the seventh day dawned I loosed a dove and let her go. She flew away, but finding no resting-place she returned. Then I loosed a swallow, and she flew away but finding no resting-place she returned. I loosed a raven, she saw that the waters had retreated, she ate, she flew around, she cawed, and she did not come back. Then I threw everything open to the four winds, I made a sacrifice and poured out a libation on the mountain top. Seven and again seven cauldrons I set up on their stands, I heaped up wood and cane and cedar and myrtle. When the gods smelled the sweet savour, they gathered like flies over the sacrifice. Then, at last, Ishtar also came, she lifted her necklace with the jewels of heaven that once Anu had made to please her. 'O you gods here present, by the lapis lazuli round my neck I shall remember these days as I remember the jewels of my throat; these last days I shall not forget. Let all the gods gather round the sacrifice, except Enlil. He shall not approach this offering, for without reflection he brought the flood; he consigned my people to destruction.'

"When Enlil had come, when he saw the boat, he was wrath and swelled with anger at the gods, the host of heaven, 'Has any of these mortals escaped? Not one was to have survived the destruction.' Then the god of the wells and canals Ninurta opened his mouth and said to the warrior Enlil, 'Who is there of the gods that devise without Ea? It is Ea alone who knows all things.' Then Ea opened his mouth and spoke to warrior Enlil, 'Wisest of gods, hero Enlil, how could you so senselessly bring down the flood?

    Lay upon the sinner his sin,
    Lay upon the transgressor his transgression,
    Punish him a little when he breaks loose,
    Do not drive him too hard or he perishes;
    Would that a lion had ravaged mankind
    Rather than the flood,
    Would that a wolf had ravaged mankind
    Rather than the flood,
    Would that famine had wasted the world
    Rather than the flood,
    Would that pestilence had wasted mankind
    Rather than the flood.

It was not I that revealed the secret of the gods; the wise man learned it in a dream. Now take your counsel what shall be done with him.'

"Then Enlil went up into the boat, he took me by the hand and my wife and made us enter the boat and kneel down on either side, he standing between us. He touched our foreheads to bless us saying, 'In time past Utnapishtim was a mortal man; henceforth he and his wife shall live in the distance at the mouth of the rivers.' Thus it was that the gods took me and placed me here to live in the distance, at the mouth of the rivers."

3

Hammurabi's Code

King Hammurabi of Babylon conquered the entire area of Mesopotamia (including Sumer) between 1793 and 1750 B.C.E. His law code provides us with a rare insight into the daily life of ancient urban society.

Law codes give us an idea of a people's sense of justice and notions of proper punishment. This selection includes only parts of Hammurabi's Code, so we cannot conclude that if something is not mentioned here it was not a matter of legal concern. We can, however, deduce much about Babylonian society from the laws mentioned in this selection.

What do these laws tell us about class divisions or social distinctions in Babylonian society? What can we learn from these laws about the roles of women and men? Which laws or punishments seem unusual today? What does that difference suggest to you about ancient Babylon compared to modern society?

THINKING HISTORICALLY

As a primary source, law codes are extremely useful. They zero in on a society's main concerns, revealing minutiae of daily life in great detail. But, for a number of reasons, law codes cannot be viewed as a precise reflection of society.

We cannot assume, for instance, that all of Hammurabi's laws were strictly followed or enforced, nor can we assume that for our own society. If there was a law against something, we can safely assume that some people obeyed it and some people did not. (That is, if no one engaged in the behavior, there would be no need for the law.) Therefore, law codes suggest a broad range of behaviors in a society.

While laws tell us something about the concerns of the society that produces them, we cannot presume that all members of society

Source: Martha T. Roth, *Law Collections from Mesopotamia and Asia Minor*, 2nd ed. (Atlanta: Scholar's Press, 1997), 82–128 (selections as numbered).

share the same concerns. Recall that, especially in ancient society, laws were written by the literate, powerful few. What evidence do you see of the upper-class composition of Babylonian law in this code?

Finally, if an ancient law seems similar to our own, we cannot assume that the law reflects motives, intents, or goals similar to our own laws. Laws must be considered within the context of the society in which they were created. Notice, for instance, the laws in Hammurabi's Code that may seem, by our standards, intended to protect women. On closer examination, what appears to be their goal?

Property and Theft[1]

6. If a man steals valuables belonging to the god or to the palace, that man shall be killed, and also he who receives the stolen goods from him shall be killed.

8. If a man steals an ox, a sheep, a donkey, a pig, or a boat — if it belongs either to the god or to the palace, he shall give thirtyfold; if it belongs to a commoner, he shall replace it tenfold; if the thief does not have anything to give, he shall be killed.

14. If a man should kidnap the young child of another man, he shall be killed.

15. If a man should enable a palace slave, a palace slave woman, a commoner's slave, or a commoner's slave woman to leave through the main city-gate, he shall be killed.

17. If a man seizes a fugitive slave or a slave woman in the open country and leads him back to his owner, the slave owner shall give him 2 shekels of silver.

21. If a man breaks into a house, they shall kill him and hang him in front of that very breach.

22. If a man commits a robbery and is then seized, that man shall be killed.

24. If a life (is lost during the robbery), the city and the governor shall weigh and deliver to his kinsmen 60 shekels of silver.

Economics and Contracts

48. If a man has a debt lodged against him, and the storm god Adad devastates his field or a flood sweeps away his crops, or there is no grain grown in the field due to insufficient water — in that year he will not

---

[1] Topical headings added by the editor of this volume are in neither the original nor translated source. [Ed.]

repay grain to his creditor; he shall suspend performance of his contract and he will not give interest payments for that year.

53. If a man neglects to reinforce the embankment of (the irrigation canal of) his field and does not reinforce its embankment and allows the water to carry away the common irrigated area, the man in whose embankment the breach opened shall replace the grain whose loss he caused.

59. If a man cuts down a tree in another man's date orchard without the permission of the owner of the orchard, he shall weigh and deliver 30 shekels of silver.

117. If an obligation is outstanding against a man and he sells or gives into debt service his wife, his son, or his daughter, they shall perform service in the house of their buyer of the one who holds them in debt service for three years; their release shall be secured in the fourth year.

Family and Marriage

128. If a man marries a wife but does not draw up a formal contract for her, that woman is not a wife.

129. If a man's wife should be seized lying with another male, they shall bind them and cast them into the water; if the wife's master allows his wife to live, then the king shall allow his subject (i.e., the other male) to live.

130. If a man pins down another man's virgin wife who is still residing in her father's house, and they seize him lying with her, that man shall be killed; that woman shall be released.

142. If a woman repudiates her husband, and declares, "You will not have marital relations with me" — her circumstances shall be investigated by the authorities of her city quarter, and if she is circumspect and without fault, but her husband is wayward and disparages her greatly, that woman will not be subject to any penalty; she shall take her dowry and she shall depart for her father's house.

143. If she is not circumspect but is wayward, squanders her household possessions, and disparages her husband, they shall cast that woman into the water.

155. If a man selects a bride for his son and his son carnally knows her, after which he himself then lies with her and they seize him in the act, they shall bind that man and cast him into the water.

156. If a man selects a bride for his son and his son does not yet carnally know her, he shall weigh and deliver to her 30 shekels of silver; moreover, he shall restore to her whatever she brought from her father's house, and a husband of her choice shall marry her.

Assault and Personal Injury

195. If a child should strike his father, they shall cut off his hand.

196. If an *awīlu* [highest class] should blind the eye of another *awīlu*, they shall blind his eye.

197. If he should break the bone of another *awīlu*, they shall break his bone.

198. If he should blind the eye of a commoner or break the bone of a commoner, he shall weigh and deliver 60 shekels of silver.

199. If he should blind the eye of an *awīlu*'s slave or break the bone of an *awīlu*'s slave, he shall weigh and deliver one half of his value (in silver).

200. If an *awīlu* should knock out the tooth of another *awīlu* of his own rank, they shall knock out his tooth.

201. If he should knock out the tooth of a commoner, he shall weigh and deliver 20 shekels of silver.

202. If an *awīlu* should strike the cheek of an *awīlu* who is of status higher than his own, he shall be flogged in the public assembly with 60 stripes of an ox whip.

Responsibility and Liability

229. If a builder constructs a house for a man but does not make his work sound, and the house that he constructs collapses and causes the death of the householder, that builder shall be killed.

230. If it should cause the death of a son of the householder, they shall kill a son of that builder.

231. If it should cause the death of a slave of the householder, he shall give to the householder a slave of comparable value for the slave.

232. If it should cause the loss of property, he shall replace anything that is lost; moreover, because he did not make sound the house which he constructed and it collapsed, he shall construct (anew) the house which collapsed at his own expense.

251. If a man's ox is a known gorer, and the authorities of his city quarter notify him that it is a known gorer, but he does not blunt its horns or control his ox, and that ox gores to death a member of the *awīlu* class, he (the owner) shall give 30 shekels of silver.

252. If it is a man's slave (who is fatally gored), he shall give 20 shekels of silver.

Advice to the Young Egyptian: "Be a Scribe"

Writing was a hallmark of the urban revolution five thousand years ago. Egyptian society, like Mesopotamian, prospered through written laws, records, and knowledge. Urban societies required many occupations that had not existed in the agricultural village, but foremost among these was the writer, or scribe. Sometimes a priest, often an official, the scribe, by virtue of his ability to read and write, provided the glue that held complex societies together.

Excavations of ancient Egypt have unearthed many papyri like these from the 20th Dynasty (twelfth century B.C.E.) that urge young Egyptians to become scribes. Because these papyri often contain spelling mistakes and other errors, archaeologists have concluded they are probably writing exercises for future scribes. How would the assignment to copy these paragraphs help train writers in ancient Egypt? What do these papyri tell you about the life of the scribe in ancient Egypt?

THINKING HISTORICALLY

These paragraphs tell us about other occupations besides that of the scribe. What, according to the papyri, were some of the other occupations common in ancient Egypt? How accurate do you think the descriptions of these occupations are? This document is sometimes called "the satire on the trades." Why would it be called that? How might you use this document to argue that Egyptian society was reasonably fair and egalitarian for the ancient world? How might you use this document to argue that Egyptian society was a deeply divided class society? Which do you think it was?

All Occupations Are Bad Except That of the Scribe

See for yourself with your own eye. The occupations lie before you.

The washerman's day is going up, going down. All his limbs are weak, (from) whitening his neighbors' clothes every day, from washing their linen.

The maker of pots is smeared with soil, like one whose relations have died. His hands, his feet are full of clay; he is like one who lives in the bog.

Source: Miriam Lichtheim, *Ancient Egyptian Literature: A Book of Readings,* vol. 2, *The New Kingdom* (Berkeley: University of California Press, 1976), 169–72.

The cobbler mingles with vats. His odor is penetrating. His hands are red with madder,[1] like one who is smeared with blood. He looks behind him for the kite, like one whose flesh is exposed.

The watchman prepares garlands and polishes vase-stands. He spends a night of toil just as one on whom the sun shines.

The merchants travel downstream and upstream. They are as busy as can be, carrying goods from one town to another. They supply him who has wants. But the tax collectors carry off the gold, that most precious of metals.

The ships' crews from every house (of commerce), they receive their loads. They depart from Egypt for Syria, and each man's god is with him. (But) not one of them says: "We shall see Egypt again!"

The carpenter who is in the shipyard carries the timber and stacks it. If he gives today the output of yesterday, woe to his limbs! The shipwright stands behind him to tell him evil things.

His outworker who is in the fields, his is the toughest of all the jobs. He spends the day loaded with his tools, tied to his tool-box. When he returns home at night, he is loaded with the tool-box and the timbers, his drinking mug, and his whetstones.

The scribe, he alone, records the output of all of them. Take note of it!

The Misfortunes of the Peasant

Let me also expound to you the situation of the peasant, that other tough occupation. [Comes] the inundation and soaks him . . . he attends to his equipment. By day he cuts his farming tools; by night he twists rope. Even his midday hour he spends on farm labor. He equips himself to go to the field as if he were a warrior. The dried field lies before him; he goes out to get his team. When he has been after the herdsman for many days, he gets his team and comes back with it. He makes for it a place in the field. Comes dawn, he goes to make a start and does not find it in its place. He spends three days searching for it; he finds it in the bog. He finds no hides on them; the jackals have chewed them. He comes out, his garment in his hand, to beg for himself a team.

When he reaches his field he finds [it] "broken up." He spends time cultivating, and the snake is after him. It finishes off the seed as it is cast to the ground. He does not see a green blade. He does three plowings with borrowed grain. His wife has gone down to the merchants and found nothing for "barter." Now the scribe lands on the shore. He surveys the harvest. Attendants are behind him with staffs,

[1] A plant used to make red dye. [Ed.]

Nubians with clubs. One says (to him): "Give grain." "There is none." He is beaten savagely. He is bound, thrown in the well, submerged head down. His wife is bound in his presence. His children are in fetters. His neighbors abandon them and flee. When it's over, there's no grain.

If you have any sense, be a scribe. If you have learned about the peasant, you will not be able to be one. Take note of it!

Be a Scribe

The scribe of the army and commander of the cattle of the house of Amun, Nebmare-nakht, speaks to the scribe Wenemdiamun, as follows. Be a scribe! Your body will be sleek; your hand will be soft. You will not flicker like a flame, like one whose body is feeble. For there is not the bone of a man in you. You are tall and thin. If you lifted a load to carry it, you would stagger, your legs would tremble. You are lacking in strength; you are weak in all your limbs; you are poor in body.

Set your sight on being a scribe; a fine profession that suits you. You call for one; a thousand answer you. You stride freely on the road. You will not be like a hired ox. You are in front of others.

I spend the day instructing you. You do not listen! Your heart is like an [empty] room. My teachings are not in it. Take their ["meaning"] to yourself!

The marsh thicket is before you each day, as a nestling is after its mother. You follow the path of pleasure; you make friends with revellers. You have made your home in the brewery, as one who thirsts for beer. You sit in the parlor with an idler. You hold the writings in contempt. You visit the whore. Do not do these things! What are they for? They are of no use. Take note of it!

The Scribe Does Not Suffer Like the Soldier

Furthermore, look, I instruct you to make you sound; to make you hold the palette freely. To make you become one whom the king trusts; to make you gain entrance to treasury and granary. To make you receive the shipload at the gate of the granary. To make you issue the offerings on feast days. You are dressed in fine clothes; you own horses. Your boat is on the river; you are supplied with attendants. You stride about inspecting. A mansion is built in your town. You have a powerful office, given you by the king. Male and female slaves are about you.

Those who are in the fields grasp your hand, on plots that you have made. Look, I make you into a staff of life! Put the writings in your heart, and you will be protected from all kinds of toil. You will become a worthy official.

Do you not recall the (fate of) the unskilled man? His name is not known. He is ever burdened [like an ass carrying] in front of the scribe who knows what he is about.

Come, [let me tell] you the woes of the soldier, and how many are his superiors: the general, the troop-commander, the officer who leads, the standard-bearer, the lieutenant, the scribe, the commander of fifty, and the garrison-captain. They go in and out in the halls of the palace, saying: "Get laborers!" He is awakened at any hour. One is after him as (after) a donkey. He toils until the Aten sets in his darkness of night. He is hungry, his belly hurts; he is dead while yet alive. When he receives the grain-ration, having been released from duty, it is not good for grinding.

He is called up for Syria. He may not rest. There are no clothes, no sandals. The weapons of war are assembled at the fortress of Sile. His march is uphill through mountains. He drinks water every third day; it is smelly and tastes of salt. His body is ravaged by illness. The enemy comes, surrounds him with missiles, and life recedes from him. He is told: "Quick, forward, valiant soldier! Win for yourself a good name!" He does not know what he is about. His body is weak, his legs fail him. When victory is won, the captives are handed over to his majesty, to be taken to Egypt. The foreign woman faints on the march; she hangs herself [on] the soldier's neck. His knapsack drops, another grabs it while he is burdened with the woman. His wife and children are in their village; he dies and does not reach it. If he comes out alive, he is worn out from marching. Be he at large, be he detained, the soldier suffers. If he leaps and joins the deserters, all his people are imprisoned. He dies on the edge of the desert, and there is none to perpetuate his name. He suffers in death as in life. A big sack is brought for him; he does not know his resting place.

Be a scribe, and be spared from soldiering! You call and one says: "Here I am." You are safe from torments. Every man seeks to raise himself up. Take note of it!

Egyptian Book of the Dead

This document is one of the many funerary texts found in Egyptian tombs, evidently composed to help the deceased pass through the obstacles to the afterlife. (We see illustrations of this journey or process in selection 6.) These texts included magic spells, incantations, hymns, meditations, and guides that were written on papyrus, the wooden coffin, or the walls of the tomb; they were collectively called "Book of the Dead," first by tomb robbers and then by archaeologists. This particular document, sometimes called Chapter 125 or the "Negative Confession," tells the deceased what to say to pass judgment. What does this text tell you about Egyptian ideas of death?

THINKING HISTORICALLY

Like Hammurabi's Code or the Ten Commandments, this guide for the deceased tells us what people did, as well as what they tried not to do. Better than a guide to actual behavior, it helps us understand a particular set of ideals. How are these ideals similar to, or different from, those of Hammurabi's Code or the Ten Commandments? Do you see any signs in this document that it was composed for a particular group or class of people?

[The dead will say:]
Homage to you, Great God, the Lord of the double
    Ma'at*(Truth)!
I have come to you, my Lord,
I have brought myself here to behold your beauties.
I know you, and I know your name,
And I know the names of the two and forty gods,
Who live with you in the Hall of the Two Truths,[1]

* muh AHT
[1] Truth and righteousness or truth and right.

Source: Adapted from *Book of the Dead*, Chapter 125, introduction. http://www.wsu.edu/~dee/EGYPT/BOD125.HTM. ©1996, Richard Hooker.

Who imprison the sinners, and feed upon their blood,
On the day when the lives of men are judged in the presence
   of Osiris.
In truth, you are "The Twin Sisters with Two Eyes,"[2] and
   "The Daughters of the Two Truths."
In truth, I now come to you, and I have brought Ma'at to you,
And I have destroyed wickedness for you.
I have committed no evil upon men.
I have not oppressed the members of my family.
I have not wrought evil in the place of right and truth.
I have had no knowledge of useless men.
I have brought about no evil.
I did not rise in the morning and expect more than was
   due to me.
I have not brought my name forward to be praised.
I have not oppressed servants.
I have not scorned any god.
I have not defrauded the poor of their property.
I have not done what the gods abominate.
I have not caused harm to be done to a servant by his master.
I have not caused pain.
I have caused no man to hunger.
I have made no one weep.
I have not killed.
I have not given the order to kill.
I have not inflicted pain on anyone.
I have not stolen the drink left for the gods in the temples.
I have not stolen the cakes left for the gods in the temples.
I have not stolen the cakes left for the dead in the temples.
I have not fornicated.
I have not polluted myself.[3]
I have not diminished the bushel when I've sold it.
I have not added to or stolen land.
I have not encroached on the land of others.
I have not added weights to the scales to cheat buyers.

---

[2] Another way of saying the double truth or truth and righteousness.

[3] Another translation of these two statements is "I have not penetrated the penetrater of a penetrater; I have not masturbated" (from http://www.digitalegypt.ucl.ac.uk/literature/religious/bd125a.html; Copyright © 2003 University College London).

I have not misread the scales to cheat buyers.
I have not stolen milk from the mouths of children.
I have not driven cattle from their pastures.
I have not captured the birds of the preserves of the gods.
I have not caught fish with bait made of like fish.[4]
I have not held back the water when it should flow.
I have not diverted the running water in a canal.
I have not put out a fire when it should burn.
I have not violated the times when meat should be offered to
    the gods.
I have not driven off the cattle from the property of the gods.
I have not stopped a god in his procession through the temple.
I am pure.
I am pure.
I am pure.
I am pure.
My purity is the purity the great *Bennu* (heron)[5] in
    Heracleopolis.
Behold, I am the nose of the God of Breath,[6] who gives life to
    the people,
On the day of completing the Eye of Ra[7] in Heliopolis,[8]
On the last day of the second month of winter,
In the presence of the pharaoh of this land.
I have seen the Eye of Horus when it was full in Heliopolis!
Therefore, let no evil befall me in this land
In this Hall of the Two Truths,
Because I know the names of all the gods within it,
And all the followers of the great God.

---

[4] Another translation reads, "I have not caught fish in their pools" (University College
London).

[5] Another translation is *phoenix*, suggesting a mythical fire-bird that rises from its ashes.

[6] Osiris.

[7] Ra is the sun-god.

[8] The city of the sun.

Images of Ancient Egypt

Thanks to the preservative dry climate and the ancient Egyptian interest in illustrating books of papyrus and painting the interiors of pyramids, temples, and tombs, we have excellent visual primary sources
on the daily life of ancient Egypt. These two images are from a papyrus called Hunefer's *Book of the Dead*. Hunefer was a royal official of
the thirteenth century B.C.E. Like other wealthy or powerful Egyptians,
Hunefer had a version of the *Book of the Dead*, with all its prayers and
incantations, prepared especially for him.

In Figure 2.1, Hunefer's mummy is prepared to enter the afterlife.
His wife and daughter dab their heads with dirt. Three priests administer the rituals. The priest on the far left, dressed in a leopard skin,
burns incense and readies the food offerings. Two others prepare the
important ceremony of opening the mummy's mouth so that it can
breathe and eat. Anubis, the jackal-headed god of death, holds the
mummy. Behind him we can read an enlarged version of Hunefer's
tombstone, which will be placed in front of his tomb, a miniature
image of which we see on the far right.

In Figure 2.2 we see Hunefer led by Anubis, about to be judged. In
the center of the frame Hunefer's heart is weighed against a feather. If
his heart is lighter than the feather he will be admitted to the presence of Osiris and enter the afterlife. If not, his heart will be devoured
by the demon Ammut, whose crocodile head is turned to the ibis-
headed god Thoth, standing to the right of the scales and writing the
verdict. In that case, his existence will end forever. Fortunately,
Hunefer's artist assures him of a happy ending. Thoth conducts
Hunefer to Osiris seated on a throne, behind his four sons standing
on a lotus leaf and in front of his wife, the goddess Isis, and her sister. What do these images tell you about Egyptian society? How do
they compare to your own ideas of death?

THINKING HISTORICALLY

Reading primary sources, whether they be words or images, is always
tricky. Unlike secondary sources, they were not written, painted, or
left for us. The assumptions and intentions of the writer or artist may
be very different from our own, and so we may misunderstand the
meaning or purpose of a work.

Entering an Egyptian tomb today, one cannot help being overwhelmed by the beauty of the paintings. Their vitality can be

Source: *Book of the Dead* of Hunefer, Thebes, Egypt, 19th Dynasty, around 1275 B.C.E.

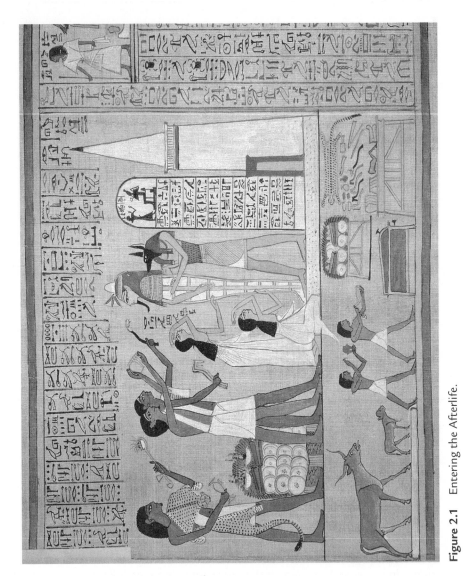

Figure 2.1 Entering the Afterlife.

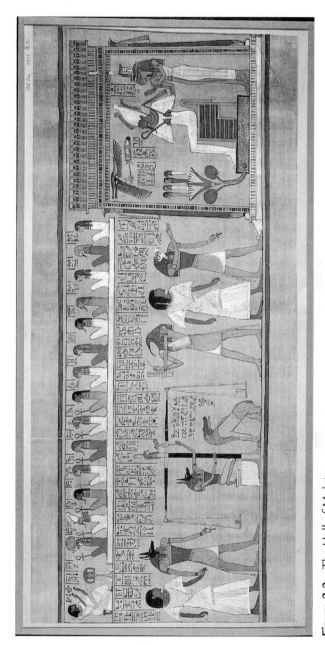

Figure 2.2 The Hall of Ma'at.

breathtaking. To the modern viewer, especially in museums where paintings and papyrus are torn from their original setting, they appear to us as beautiful works of art. And so they are. But for the ancient Egyptians, these images were more than representations, more than art. They were the things depicted. The food that was displayed was food for the deceased in the afterlife; the people painted on the walls were there to provide and serve. The pictures were intended to be more vital than we can imagine. Are visual images more or less reliable as primary sources than written words? What do visuals add to our understanding? How might they mislead us?

Images are different from written words in another way. You are able to make sense of these images from Hunefer's *Book of the Dead* because primary and secondary texts enable us to provide a summary of the story behind them. But the Egyptian artist and viewer knew that story, and hundreds of subplots, by heart. Imagine "reading" the images the way an ancient Egyptian viewer would have. Would the difference between your modern interpretation and the Egyptian viewer's interpretation be similar to the difference between seeing a movie and reading the book? And if "the book" was the wisdom of the ages as everyone knew it, and images could be real, what sort of movie would that be?

7

JOHN NOBLE WILFORD

The Olmec: Mother Culture, or Only a Sister?

The complex of city culture developed a bit later in the Americas, but already by 1000 B.C.E. the Olmec in what is today Mexico had created many of the elements of city life. Which elements of this revolution do you see in this description of Olmec civilization? What is the issue debated in this article? What evidence does Blomster use to make his case? What kind of evidence would lead you to dismiss Blomster's claims?

THINKING HISTORICALLY

This is clearly a secondary source, written by a science writer for the *New York Times*. Newspapers (like textbooks) are sometimes even called tertiary (or third-level) sources: They may be based on some

Source: John Noble Wilford, "Mother Culture, or Only a Sister?" *New York Times*, March 15, 2005.

primary sources, but they are often based mainly on secondary sources, that is, the work of historians. In fact, this article is an amalgam of the interpretations of various historians. Most are quoted interviews, but what printed secondary source is referred to in the article?

Olmec writing has not been deciphered, and archaeologists have only recently discovered a group of Olmec symbols similar to those used by the Maya much later. What, then, are the primary sources available for historians of the Olmec? What primary sources were used by the authors referred to here?

On a coastal flood plain etched by rivers flowing through swamps and alongside fields of maize [corn] and beans, the people archaeologists call the Olmecs lived in a society of emergent complexity. It was more than 3,000 years ago along the Gulf of Mexico around Veracruz.

The Olmecs, mobilized by ambitious rulers and fortified by a pantheon of gods, moved a veritable mountain of earth to create a plateau above the plain, and there planted a city, the ruins of which are known today as San Lorenzo. They left behind palace remnants, distinctive pottery and art with anthropomorphic jaguar motifs. Most impressive were Olmec sculptures: colossal stone heads with thick lips and staring eyes that are assumed to be monuments to revered rulers.

Figure 2.3   An Olmec Stone Head Monument.
Source: Jeanne White/PhotoResearchers, Inc.

The Olmecs are widely regarded as creators of the first civilization in Mesoamerica, the area encompassing much of Mexico and Central America, and a cultural wellspring of later societies, notably the Maya. Some scholars think the Olmec civilization was the first anywhere in America, though doubt has been cast by recent discoveries in Peru.

Archaeologists have split sharply over how much influence the Olmecs had on contemporary and subsequent Mesoamerican cultures. Were Olmecs the "mother" culture? Or were they one among "sister" cultures whose interactions through the region produced shared attributes of religion, art, political structure and hierarchical society?

Last month, the simmering pot of mother-sister controversy was stirred anew by Dr. Jeffrey P. Blomster, an Olmec archaeologist at George Washington University. In a report in the journal *Science,* he and other researchers described evidence of the widespread export of Olmec ceramics that they said supported "Olmec priority in the creation and spread of the first unified style and iconographic system in Mesoamerica."

Dr. Blomster's team analyzed the chemistry of 725 pieces of pottery decorated with symbols and designs in the Olmec style and collected throughout the region. The researchers compared the composition of the ceramics with local clays. They determined that most of these were not imitations of the Olmec style made by local potters. In a significant number of pots, the clay matched the chemistry of material found around San Lorenzo.

"The evidence is overwhelming that San Lorenzo, the first Olmec capital, was doing the exporting," Dr. Blomster said. "The Olmecs were disseminating their culture and it was something of great interest to others."

The research, he added, showed that San Lorenzo did not appear to be importing artifacts emblematic of other cultures or that regional contemporaries were exchanging such material with one another. The city on the artificial plateau seemed to be the hub of regional culture and central, he said, to understanding the origin and development of complex society in Mesoamerica.

Dr. Richard A. Diehl of the University of Alabama wrote in *Science* that the findings "provide powerful support for the mother-culture school," adding, "San Lorenzo thus dominated in the commercial relationships and attendant spread of Olmec iconography and belief systems."

But Dr. Diehl, a proponent of the mother school and the author of "The Olmec," published last year, said in an interview that the "connections we are seeing may not have lasted more than a generation, perhaps the time of a particular ruler, and at most, not more than a century or century and a half."

The Blomster research dealt with pottery from the latter half of the early formative period of Mesoamerican culture, which extended from

Figure 2.4   A Relief Sculpture of a Man Carrying a Child, Brought from the Ruins of La Venta to Villahermosa, Mexico.

Source: Danny Lehman/Corbis.

1500 to 900 B.C. The last centuries of this period were the time of San Lorenzo's ascendance, but afterward the city was largely abandoned and the Olmec hub gravitated to La Venta, nearby in what is now the state of Tabasco. . . .

Proponents of the sister school are not letting the interpretation of the new research go unchallenged. . . .

Dr. [Susan D.] Gillespie [University of Florida] acknowledged that the Olmecs established a vibrant culture and that their accomplishments were extraordinary. She also agreed that they were innovative and that their leaders presided over a political system capable of mobilizing labor for public works. It was no easy task raising an artificial plateau or hauling heavy blocks of basalt 40 miles to San Lorenzo from volcanic fields and fashioning them into the stone heads that stand as high as 10 feet.

Olmecs also contributed games with rubber balls, which became popular and fiercely played by later regional cultures. The Aztecs, much later, used the name in their own language for "rubber people" — Olmec — to describe the culture that was by then long vanished but not forgotten. No one knows what the ancient Olmecs called themselves.

"But others in the area were doing things equally complex, though different," Dr. Gillespie said. "Other areas were also taking steps on their own toward the development of Mesoamerican civilization."

That, and an active interchange of ideas and beliefs among various neighboring societies, is the essence of the argument advanced by sister-culture proponents. They further contend that the concept of the Olmecs as a mother culture grew out of 19th-century ethnocentrism, in which the construction of stone sculptures is a sign of civilization because that is a hallmark of early Western civilizations.

Many of these archaeologists have concentrated their research and excavations on non-Olmec areas with evidence of ancient complex societies, like the Valley of Oaxaca, the central basin of Mexico and the Pacific coastal sites of Chiapas in southwestern Mexico. Dr. Gillespie, though, has studied Olmec workshops that were operating in the culture's heyday, mainly producing stone artifacts thought to be altar thrones.

Dr. Blomster cited recent excavations by Dr. Ann Cyphers of the National University of Mexico that "emphasize the higher sociopolitical level that the Olmecs achieved relative to contemporaneous groups in Mesoamerica," a view contrary to the sister-culture position. Dr. Cyphers said the rulers of San Lorenzo appear to have lived in a palace with huge basalt columns and sculptures, while leaders in the adjacent Valley of Oaxaca had places not much better than the wattle-and-daub huts of commoners.

Dr. Michael D. Coe, an archaeologist at Yale who is an authority on the Olmec and the Maya cultures, sides more with the mother-culture school, saying that "much of the complex culture in Mesoamerica has an Olmec origin."

In the new edition of his book "The Maya," Dr. Coe writes that during four centuries of San Lorenzo's prime, ending about 900 B.C., "Olmec influence emanating from this area was found throughout Mesoamerica, with the curious exception of the Maya domain—perhaps because there were few Maya populations at that time sufficiently large to have interested the expanding Olmecs."

But early Olmec rulers were aware of the territory where the Maya eventually established imposing cities. Three years ago, scientists reported finding a rich lode of jadite, including huge boulders of it, in the jungles of Guatemala. Traces of ancient mining were uncovered, and some of the outcroppings were of blue jade, the prized gemstone Olmec artists used for carving delicate human forms and scary masks.

Archaeologists said the discovery not only solved a mystery of the origin of Olmec jade, but also showed that the Olmecs exerted wide influence over the region, either directly or by trade through intermediaries.

The Olmec influence on the Maya began to show up in artifacts, starting before 100 B.C. By then, Dr. Coe and other scholars said, Olmec art, religion, rubber-ball games and the ceremonial dress of rulers had clearly found its way to Maya cities. . . .

The classic maize god of the Maya, scholars say, appears to be a clear descendant of a similar Olmec god. A Maya wall painting in San Bartolo, Guatemala, shows a resurrected maize god surrounded by figures offering him gifts of tamales and water. "The deity's head is purely Olmec," Dr. Coe said.

The assumption is that aspects of Olmec culture reached the Maya indirectly, probably through what is known as the Izapa civilization in the territory extending from the Gulf Coast across to the Pacific Coast of Chiapas, in Mexico, and of Guatemala. The city known as Izapa is the site of imposing temple mounds in Chiapas, a place where the Olmec sculpture and Maya painting and glyphs seemed to converge. . . .

. . . [T]here was so far no archaeological evidence suggesting that the Olmecs conquered or proselytized its neighboring societies. Neither is there a clear picture of what happened to San Lorenzo.

Nothing in the ruins or later legends points to conquest by an invading army. More likely, some scientists think, the city was abandoned by the ninth century B.C. because of natural catastrophe: the rivers they depended on probably changed course, the result of silt and tectonic shifts in the coastal landscape.

La Venta, the new capital, came to an equally mysterious end around 400 B.C., and it was not long until the Olmecs lapsed into decline. Pockets of the culture persisted in Tres Zapotes, near the former capitals, and scattered communities in southern Mexico.

By the time the first major civilization of Mesoamerica was disappearing, the Olmecs blending into other societies, it apparently had reached out far enough in trade and influence to pass on a legacy of politics, art and religion to the up-and-coming Maya. A few mother-culture archaeologists, citing the new research, liken the relationship of the Olmecs to the Maya to the Greeks and Romans of Western civilization.

■ REFLECTIONS

To focus our subject in a brief chapter, we have concentrated on Mesopotamia and Egypt almost exclusively. This enabled us to observe the beginnings of the urban revolution in Mesopotamia and one of the most spectacular and best preserved of ancient civilizations in Egypt. The city-states of Mesopotamia and the territorial state of Egypt were the two extremes of ancient civilization. City-states packed most people tightly within their walls. Eighty percent of Mesopotamians lived within city walls by 2800 B.C.E. By contrast, less than 10 percent of Egyptians lived in cities—if we can call their unwalled settlements, palace compounds, and pyramid construction sites "cities" at all. The lesser role of cities in Egypt has led some historians to drop the term *urban revolution* for *the rise of civilization.* Other historians, objecting to the moralistic implications of the term *civilization,* prefer *the rise of complex societies. Complex* is not a very precise term, but it would refer to the appearance of social classes; the mixing of different populations; a multilayered governmental structure with rulers, officials, and ordinary people; and numerous specialists who are not full-time farmers or herders. More specifically, we might include kings, priests, writing, wheels, monumental building, markets, and money.

Our addition of the Olmec broadens our lens somewhat, though not nearly as much as historians used to think. Archaeologists have found evidence of increasingly earlier dating of Mexican cities and a process of state building similar to that of Eurasia. It used to be said that the civilizations of the Americas developed without wheels—until wheels were found on childrens' toys. Historians also used to say that these American civilizations lacked writing, but recent scholars have learned to "translate" the images and symbols of Middle-American paintings and the knotted color strings of Andean civilization in South America. Although not river-valley civilizations, American cities were also built on irrigated agriculture. Although most lacked bronze and viable beasts of burden, the American cities served as magnets of trade and luxury and beacons of law and spirituality.

If we broaden our view to include the "complex societies" of South Asia and China as well as the Americas, similar types of cities pop up like mushrooms after a spring rain. Along the Indus River in Pakistan dozens of small and midsize cities formed independent clones of Harappa and Mohenjo-Daro. These numerous cities seem to have enjoyed the independence of city-states, linked more by culture and trade than by powerful kings or large armies. A vast web of such cities is still being excavated, stretching from Iran to India and from the coast of East Africa to southern Russia. In China, by contrast, vast territorial states integrated dozens of cities along river valleys and trade routes and throughout the interior, creating a cultural and political unity more like Egypt than Mesopotamia. Thus, a larger lens raises more questions than we have allowed in our brief examination of Mesopotamia and Egypt. How important were such "urban inventions" as kings, soldiers, warfare, wheels, and writing if they did not exist everywhere cities were created? Furthermore, how important were cities in the creation of the complex lives we have lived for the last five thousand years?

We might also ask the larger question: Has the urban revolution improved our lives? The belief that it has lies behind the use of the word *civilization*. Though the root of the word is the same as *city*, *civil*, and *civilian*, the word *civilization* came into the modern vocabulary of historians and social scientists in the nineteenth century. At this time anthropologists were working to distinguish stages of history and to illustrate the differences between what were then called "primitive" peoples and people of the modern world whom anthropologists considered "civilized." Thus, they contended there had been three stages of history that could be summarized, in chronological order, as savagery, barbarism, and civilization. By the early twentieth century, in the work of the great prehistorian V. Gordon Childe, these terms stood for hunting-gathering, agricultural, and urban societies.

The belief that the world of the anthropologists and the "moderns" of the nineteenth and twentieth centuries was more civilized than the preurban world that they studied was more than a bit presumptuous. But this presumption continues today, in the popular mythology of "country bumpkins" who lack the manners and savoir-faire of their city cousins. Interestingly, it was also the assumption of the earliest founders of cities. *The Epic of Gilgamesh* tells of the need of the city to tame the wild Enkidu so that he can take his place in

. . . ramparted Uruk,
Where fellows are resplendent in holiday clothing,
Where every day is set for celebration.

There are many reasons to be skeptical of the so-called achievements of city life: increased inequality, suppression of women, slavery, organized warfare, conscription, heavy taxation, forced labor, to name some of the most obvious. But our museums are full of the art and artifacts that testify to what the ancients meant by "civilization." The pyramids of Egypt and of Mexico and the ziggurats of Mesopotamia are among the wonders of the world. Does it matter that the great pyramids of Egypt were built from the forced labor of thousands to provide a resting place for a single person and that people were entombed alive in order to serve him? We can view the pyramids today as a remarkable achievement of engineering and organization while still condemning the manner of their execution. We can admire the art in the tombs, thrill to the revealing detail of ancient Egyptian life, marvel at the persistence of vivid colors mixed almost five thousand years ago, and treasure the art for what it reveals of the world of its creators, while we still detest its purpose.

We can do this because these monuments have become something different for us than what they were for the ancients. They have become testaments to human achievement, regardless of the cost. These ancient city-based societies were the first in which humans produced abundant works of art and architecture, which still astound us in their range, scope, and design.

The significance of the urban revolution was that it produced things that lasted beyond their utility or meaning—thanks to new techniques in cutting and hauling stone; baking brick, tile, and glass; and smelting tin, copper, and bronze—as a legacy for future generations. Even three thousand years ago, Egyptian engineers studied the ancient pyramids to understand a very distant past, 1,500 years before, and to learn, adapt, revive, or revise ancient techniques. In short, the achievement of the urban revolution is that it made knowledge cumulative, so that each generation could stand on the shoulders of its predecessors.

3

Identity in Caste and Territorial Societies

Greece and India, 1000–300 B.C.E.

■ HISTORICAL CONTEXT

Both India and Greece developed ancient city-based civilizations within a thousand years of the urban revolution. In India that civilization was concentrated on the Indus River Valley in what is today Pakistan. (See Map 3.1.) In Greece the Minoan civilization on the island of Crete was followed by the Mycenaean civilization on the mainland. (See Map 3.2.) But both ancient Indian and ancient Greek civilizations were transformed by new peoples from the grasslands of Eurasia, who settled in both areas between 1500 and 1000 B.C.E. Called by later generations the Aryans in India and the Dorians in Greece, these pastoral peoples arrived with horses, different customs, and new technologies. The Aryans came with chariots (as had the early Mycenaeans), while the Dorians, somewhat later, brought iron tools and weapons.

Despite the similar origins of the newcomers and the similar urban experience of the lands in which they settled, Aryan India and Dorian Greece developed in significantly different ways. As William H. McNeill writes in the first selection, by the year 500 B.C.E. Indian and Greek civilizations had found entirely different ways of organizing and administering their societies. And these differences had profound effects on the subsequent history of Indian and European society.

■ THINKING HISTORICALLY

Interpreting Primary Sources in Light of a Secondary Source

In Chapter 2, we distinguished between primary and secondary sources. Similarly, we begin here with a secondary source, or an interpretation. We then turn, as we did in the last chapter, to a series of primary sources. But whereas the last chapter focused on recognizing and distinguishing primary from secondary sources, here we concentrate on the relationship of the primary sources to the secondary interpretation—how one affects our reading of the other.

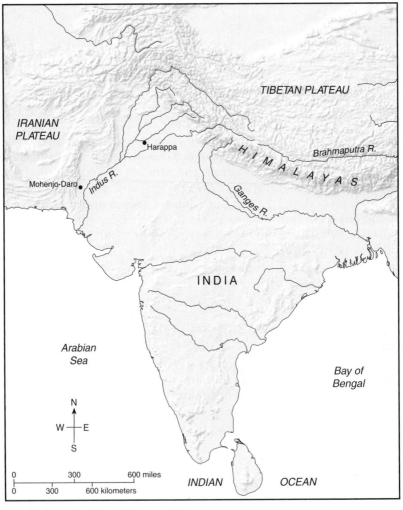

Map 3.1   Indus River Valley, c. 500 B.C.E.

In this chapter, the primary sources were chosen to illustrate points made in the introductory interpretation. This provides an opportunity to understand the interpretation in some detail and with some degree of subtlety. The primary sources do not give you enough material to argue that McNeill is right or wrong, but you will be able to flesh out some of the meaning of his interpretation. You might also reflect more generally on the relationship of sources and interpretations. You will be asked how particular sources support or even contradict the interpretation. You will consider the relevance of sources for other interpretations, and you will imagine what sort of sources you might seek for evidence.

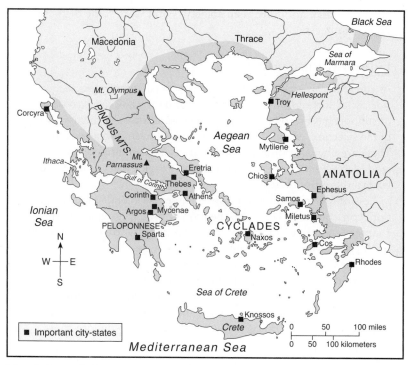

Map 3.2   Archaic Greece, c. 750–500 B.C.E.

1

WILLIAM H. McNEILL
Greek and Indian Civilization

William H. McNeill is one of the leading world historians in the
United States. In this selection from his college textbook *A World
History*, he compares the different ways in which Indian and Greek
civilizations of the classical age (by around 500 B.C.E.) organized
themselves. He distinguishes between Indian *caste* and Greek
territorial sovereignty. These concepts are complex but useful in
distinguishing between two of the basic ways societies organize
and identify themselves. As you read, try to define what each
term means. McNeill argues that caste and territorial sovereignty
had enormously different effects on the subsequent development of Indian and European society. What were some of these
different effects?

THINKING HISTORICALLY

As you read this secondary source or historical interpretation, consider what sort of primary sources might have led McNeill to this view
or support his interpretation. Notice especially that in the first half
of the selection, McNeill mentions specific ancient Indian writings:
These are obvious primary sources for his interpretation. Not having
read McNeill's primary sources, can you imagine what in them would
lead to this interpretation?

Less of McNeill's interpretation of Greece is included in this selection; consequently, there is no mention of primary sources. In this
chapter, you will read a number of Greek primary sources, but at this
point can you speculate about what types of sources would demonstrate the Greek idea of territorial sovereignty?

Keep in mind that caste and territorial sovereignty are
modern terms not known or used by the ancients; therefore, you
will not find them in the primary sources that follow. What words
might the ancient Indians or Greeks have used to denote these
concepts?

Source: William H. McNeill, *A World History*, 2nd ed. (New York: Oxford University Press,
1971), 78–83, 88, 90, 95, 99–100.

Caste

A modern caste is a group of persons who will eat with one another and intermarry, while excluding others from these two intimacies. In addition, members of any particular caste must bear some distinguishing mark, so that everyone will know who belongs and who does not belong to it. Definite rules for how to behave in the presence of members of other castes also become necessary in situations where such contacts are frequent. When an entire society comes to be organized on these principles, any group of strangers or intruders automatically becomes another caste, for the exclusive habits of the rest of the population inevitably thrust the newcomers in upon themselves when it comes to eating and marrying. A large caste may easily break into smaller groupings as a result of some dispute, or through mere geographical separation over a period of time. New castes can form around new occupations. Wanderers and displaced individuals who find a new niche in society are automatically compelled to eat together and marry one another by the caste-bound habits of their neighbors.

How or when Indian society came to be organized along these lines remains unclear. Perhaps the Indus civilization itself was built upon something like the caste principle. Or perhaps the antipathy between Aryan invaders and the dark-skinned people whom they attacked lay at the root of the caste system of later India. But whatever the origins of caste, three features of Indian thought and feeling were mobilized to sustain the caste principle in later times. One of these was the idea of ceremonial purity. Fear of contaminating oneself by contact with a member of a lower, "unclean" caste gave Brahmans and others near the top of the pyramid strong reasons for limiting their association with low-caste persons.

From the other end of the scale, too, the poor and humble had strong reasons for clinging to caste. All but the most miserable and marginal could look down upon somebody, a not unimportant psychological feature of the system. In addition, the humbler castes were often groups that had only recently emerged from primitive forest life. They naturally sought to maintain their peculiar customs and habits, even in the context of urban or mixed village life, where men of different backgrounds and different castes lived side by side. Other civilized societies usually persuaded or compelled newcomers to surrender their peculiar ways, and assimilated them in the course of a few generations to the civilized population as a whole. In India, on the contrary, such groups were able to retain their separate identities indefinitely by preserving their own peculiar customs within the caste framework, generation after generation.

The third factor sustaining the caste principle was theoretical: the doctrine of reincarnation and of "varna." The latter declared that all men were naturally divided into four castes: the Brahmans who prayed, the Kshatriyas* who fought, the Vaisyas† who worked, and the Sudras who performed unclean tasks. Official doctrine classified the first three castes as Aryan, the last as non-Aryan, and put much stress on caste rank, from Brahmans at the top to Sudras at the bottom. Reality never corresponded even remotely to this theory. There were hundreds if not thousands of castes in India, rather than the four recognized in Brahmanical teaching. But apparent injustices and anomalies disappeared when the doctrine of reincarnation was combined with the doctrine of varna. The idea of reincarnation, indeed, gave logical explanation and justification to the system by explaining caste as a divinely established institution, hereditary from father to son, and designed to reward and punish souls for their actions in former lives. This undoubtedly helped to stabilize the confused reality. A man of unblemished life, born into the lowest caste, could hope for rebirth higher up the ladder. Conversely, a man of high caste who failed to conform to proper standards could expect rebirth in a lower caste. A man even risked reincarnation as a worm or beetle, if his misbehavior deserved such a punishment.

Clearly, the caste system as observed today did not exist in ancient India. Yet modern castes are the outgrowth of patterns of social organization that are as old as the oldest records. Early Buddhist stories, for instance, reveal many episodes turning upon caste distinctions, and passages in the *Rig Veda*‡ and other ancient writings imply caste-like practices and attitudes. By 500 B.C.E. we can at least be sure that the seeds from which the modern caste organization of society grew had already sprouted luxuriantly on Indian soil.

Caste lessened the significance of political, territorial administration. Everyone identified himself first and foremost with his caste. But a caste ordinarily lacked both definite internal administration and distinct territorial boundaries. Instead, members of a particular caste mingled with men of other castes, observing the necessary precautions to prevent contamination of one by the other. No king or ruler could command the undivided loyalty of people who felt themselves to belong to a caste rather than to a state. Indeed, to all ordinary caste members, rulers, officials, soldiers, and tax collectors were likely to seem mere troublesome outsiders, to be neglected whenever possible and obeyed only as far as necessary. The fragile character

---

* KSHAH tree uh
† VYS yuh
‡ rihg VAY dah

of most Indian states resulted in large part from this fact. A striking absence of information about war and government is characteristic of all early Indian history; and this, too, presumably reflects Indian peoples' characteristic emotional disengagement from the state and from politics. . . .

The Vedas and Brahmanas

Our knowledge of Aryan religion derives from the Vedas. The Vedas, used as handbooks of religious ritual, consist of songs that were recited aloud during sacrifices, together with other passages instructing the priests what to do during the ceremony. In course of time, the language of the Vedas became more or less unintelligible, even to priests. A great effort was thereupon made to preserve details of accent and pronunciation, by insisting on exact memorization of texts from master to pupil across the generations. Every jot and tittle of the inherited verses was felt to matter, since a misplaced line or mispronounced word could nullify a whole sacrifice and might even provoke divine displeasure.

Preoccupation with correctness of detail speedily shifted emphasis from the gods of the Aryan pantheon to the act of worship and invocation itself. Aryan priests may also have learned about magical powers claimed by priests of the Indus civilization. At any rate, some Brahmans began to argue that by performing rituals correctly they could actually compel the gods to grant what was asked of them. Indeed, proper sacrifice and invocation created the world of gods and men anew, and stabilized afresh the critical relation between natural and supernatural reality. In such a view, the importance and personalities of the separate gods shrank to triviality, while the power and skill of the priesthood was greatly magnified. These extravagant priestly claims were freely put forward in texts called Brahmanas. These were cast in the form of commentaries on the Vedas, purportedly explaining what the older texts really meant, but often changing meanings in the process.

The Upanishads and Mysticism

Priestly claims to exercise authority over gods and men were never widely accepted in ancient India. Chiefs and warriors might be a bit wary of priestly magic, but they were not eager to cede to the priests the primacy claimed by the Brahmanas. Humbler ranks of society also objected to priestly presumption. This is proved by the fact that a rival type of piety took hold in India and soon came to constitute the most distinctive element in the whole religious tradition of the land. Another body of oral literature, the Upanishads,* constitutes our evidence of this religious development. The Upanishads are not systematic treatises nor do they agree in all details. Yet they do express a general consensus on important points.

First of all, the Upanishads conceive the end of religious life in a radically new way. Instead of seeking riches, health, and long life, a wise and holy man strives merely to escape the endless round of rebirth. Success allows his soul to dissolve into the All from whence it had come, triumphantly transcending the suffering, pain, and imperfection of existence.

In the second place, holiness and release from the cycle of rebirths were attained not by obedience to priests nor by observance of ceremonies. The truly holy man had no need of intermediaries and, for that matter, no need of gods. Instead, by a process of self-discipline, meditation, asceticism, and withdrawal from the ordinary concerns of daily life, the successful religious athlete might attain a mystic vision of Truth—a vision which left the seer purged and happy. The nature and content of the mystic vision could never be expressed in words. It revealed Truth by achieving an identity between the individual soul and the Soul of the universe. Such an experience, surpassing human understanding and ordinary language, constituted a foretaste of the ultimate bliss of self-annihilation in the All, which was the final goal of wise and holy life. . . .

While India worked its way toward the definition of a new and distinctive civilization on one flank of the ancient Middle East, on its other flank another new civilization was also emerging: the Greek. The principal stages of early Greek history closely resemble what we know or can surmise about Indian development. But the end product differed fundamentally. The Greeks put political organization into territorial states above all other bases of human association, and attempted to explain the world and man not in terms of mystic illumination but through laws of nature. Thus despite a similar start, when fierce "tamers of horses"—like those of whom Homer[1] later sang—overran priest-led agricultural societies, the Indian and Greek styles of civilization diverged strikingly by 500 B.C.E. . . .

The self-governing city-states created by Greeks on the coast of Asia Minor had . . . great . . . importance in world history. For by inventing the city-state or *polis* (hence our word "politics"), the Greeks of Ionia established the prototype from which the whole Western world derived its penchant for political organization into territorially defined

---

* oo PAH nee shahdz
[1] Greek poet c. 800 B.C.E.; author of *The Iliad* and *The Odyssey*. [Ed.]

sovereign units, i.e., into states. The supremacy of territoriality over all other forms of human association is neither natural nor inevitable, as the Indian caste principle may remind us. . . .

Dominance of the Polis in Greek Culture

So powerful and compelling was the psychological pull of the polis that almost every aspect of Greek cultural activity was speedily caught up in and—as it were—digested by the new master institution of Greek civilization. Religion, art, literature, philosophy, took shape or acquired a new accent through their relationship with the all-engulfing object of the citizens' affection. . . .

Despite the general success of the polis ordering of things, a few individuals fretted over the logical inconsistencies of Greek religion and traditional world view. As trade developed, opportunities to learn about the wisdom of the East multiplied. Inquiring Greeks soon discovered that among the priestly experts of the Middle East there was no agreement about such fundamental questions as how the world was created or why the planets periodically checked their forward movement through the heavens and went backward for a while before resuming their former motion. It was in Ionia that men first confronted this sort of question systematically enough to bother recording their views. These, the first philosophers, sought to explain the phenomena of the world by imaginative exercise of their power of reason. Finding conflicting and unsupported stories about the gods to be unsatisfactory, they took the drastic step of omitting the gods entirely, and boldly substituted natural law instead as the ruling force of the universe. To be sure, the Ionian philosophers did not agree among themselves when they sought to describe how the laws of nature worked, and their naive efforts to explain an ever wider range of phenomena did not meet with much success.

Nevertheless, their attempts at using speculative reason to explain the nature of things marked a major turning point in human intellectual development. The Ionian concept of a universe ruled not by the whim of some divine personality but by an impersonal and unchangeable law has never since been forgotten. Throughout the subsequent history of European and Middle Eastern thought, this distinctively Greek view of the nature of things stood in persistent and fruitful tension with the older, Middle Eastern theistic explanation of the universe. Particular thinkers, reluctant to abandon either position entirely, have sought to reconcile the omnipotence of the divine will with the unchangeability of natural law by means of the most various arguments. Since, however, the two views are as logically incompatible with one another as were the myths from which the Ionian philosophers started, no formulation or reconciliation ever attained lasting and universal consent. Men always had to start over again to reshape for themselves a more satisfactory metaphysic and theology. Here, therefore, lay a growing point for all subsequent European thought which has not yet been exhausted.

Indeed, the recent successes of natural science seem to have vindicated the Ionian concept of natural law in ways and with a complexity that would have utterly amazed Thales* (d. c. 546 B.C.E.) or any of his successors, who merely voiced what turned out to be amazingly lucky guesses. How did they do it? It seems plausible to suggest that the Ionians hit upon the notion of natural law by simply projecting the tight little world of the polis upon the universe. For it was a fact that the polis was regulated by law, not by the personal will or whim of a ruler. If such invisible abstractions could govern human behavior and confine it to certain roughly predictable paths of action, why could not similar laws control the natural world? To such a question, it appears, the Ionians gave an affirmative answer, and in doing so gave a distinctive cast to all subsequent Greek and European thought.

Limitations of the Polis

It would be a mistake to leave the impression that all facets of Greek life fitted smoothly and easily into the polis frame. The busy public world left scant room for the inwardness of personal experience. Striving for purification, for salvation, for holiness, which found such ample expression in the Indian cultural setting, was almost excluded. Yet the Greeks were not immune from such impulses. Through the ancient mystery religions, as well as through such an association as the "Order" founded by Pythagoras,† the famous mathematician and mystic (d. c. 507 B.C.E.), they sought to meet these needs. But when such efforts took organized form, a fundamental incompatibility between the claims of the polis to the unqualified loyalty of every citizen and the pursuit of personal holiness quickly became apparent. This was illustrated by the stormy history of the Pythagorean Order. Either the organized seekers after holiness captured the polis, as happened for a while in the city of Croton in southern Italy, or the magistrates of the polis persecuted the Order, as happened in Pythagoras' old age. There seemed no workable ground of compromise in this, the earliest recorded instance of conflict between church and state in Western history.

* THAY leez
† py THAG uhr ahs

The fundamental difference between Greek and Indian institutions as shaped by about 500 B.C.E. was made apparent by this episode. The loose federation of cultures allowed by the caste principle in India experienced no difficulty at all in accommodating organized seekers after holiness such as the communities of Buddhist monks. By contrast, the exclusive claim upon the citizens' time, effort, and affection which had been staked out by the Greek polis allowed no sort of corporate rival.

Enormous energies were tapped by the polis. A wider segment of the total population was engaged in cultural and political action than had been possible in any earlier civilized society, and the brilliant flowering of classical Greek civilization was the consequence. Yet the very intensity of the political tie excluded ranges of activity and sensitivity that were not compatible with a territorial organization of human groupings, and sowed seeds of civil strife between the Greek cities which soon proved disastrous. But every achievement involves a surrender of alternatives: It is merely that the Greek achievement, by its very magnitude, casts an unusually clear light upon what it also excluded.

2

The Rig Veda: Sacrifice as Creation

As McNeill discusses in the previous selection, the Vedas are the writings of the ancient Brahman priests in India. They cover a wide variety of religious subjects and concerns: ritual, sacrifice, hymns, healing, incantations, allegories, philosophy, and the problems of everyday life. In general, the earliest Vedas (like the Rig Veda) focus more on the specifics of ritual and sacrifice, reflecting the needs and instructions of the priests during the Aryan conquest. The last of the Vedas (like the Upanishads) are more philosophical and speculative.

This selection is from the Rig Veda. What happened when Purusha was sacrificed? What is the meaning of this first sacrifice? How does this story support the role of priests?

THINKING HISTORICALLY

Consider how this primary source supports the division of Indian society into castes, as McNeill discusses in the previous selection. How does this story suggest that the people who wrote the Rig Veda

Source: "Rig Veda," 10.90, in *Sources of Indian Tradition*, 2nd ed., ed. and rev. Ainslie T. Embree (New York: Columbia University Press, 1988), 18–19.

thought the division of society into four castes was pretty basic?
Can you deduce from this source which of the four castes was most
likely the originator of the story? Does this support anything else that
McNeill said in his interpretation?

Thousand-headed Purusha, thousand-eyed, thousand-footed—he, having pervaded the earth on all sides, still extends ten fingers beyond it.

Purusha alone is all this—whatever has been and whatever is going
to be. Further, he is the lord of immortality and also of what grows on
account of food.

Such is his greatness; greater, indeed, than this is Purusha. All
creatures constitute but one-quarter of him, his three-quarters are the
immortal in the heaven.

With his three-quarters did Purusha rise up; one-quarter of him
again remains here. With it did he variously spread out on all sides over
what eats and what eats not.

From him was Virāj born, from Virāj the evolved Purusha. He, being
born, projected himself behind the earth as also before it.

When the gods performed the sacrifice with Purusha as the oblation,
then the spring was its clarified butter, the summer the sacrificial fuel,
and the autumn the oblation.

The sacrificial victim, namely, Purusha, born at the very beginning,
they sprinkled with sacred water upon the sacrificial grass. With him as
oblation, the gods performed the sacrifice, and also the Sādhyas [a class
of semidivine beings] and the rishis [ancient seers].

From that wholly offered sacrificial oblation were born the verses
[ṛc] and the sacred chants; from it were born the meters [chandas]; the
sacrificial formula was born from it.

From it horses were born and also those animals who have double
rows [i.e., upper and lower] of teeth; cows were born from it, from it
were born goats and sheep.

When they divided Purusha, in how many different portions did they
arrange him? What became of his mouth, what of his two arms? What
were his two thighs and his two feet called?

His mouth became the brāhman; his two arms were made into the
rajanya; his two thighs the vaishyas; from his two feet the shūdra was
born.

The moon was born from the mind, from the eye the sun was born;
from the mouth Indra and Agni, from the breath [prāna] the wind [vāyu]
was born.

From the navel was the atmosphere created, from the head the
heaven issued forth; from the two feet was born the earth and the

quarters (the cardinal directions) from the ear. Thus did they fashion the worlds.

Seven were the enclosing sticks in this sacrifice, thrice seven were the fire-sticks made when the gods, performing the sacrifice, bound down Purusha, the sacrificial victim.

With this sacrificial oblation did the gods offer the sacrifice. These were the first norms [*dharma*] of sacrifice. These greatnesses reached to the sky wherein live the ancient Sādhyas and gods.

3

The Upanishads: Karma and Reincarnation

The idea of karma (cause and effect, appropriate consequences) appears in the earliest Upanishads. Karma meant: "As you sow, so shall you reap." Good karma would be enhanced; bad karma would lead to more bad karma. The universe was a system of complete justice in which all people got what they deserved. The idea that the soul might be reborn in another body may have been an even older idea, but in the Upanishads it combined easily with the idea of karma. That a good soul was reborn in a higher life, or a bad soul in a lower, was perhaps a more material, less subtle, version of the justice of karma. The idea of reincarnation, or the transmigration of souls, united justice with caste.

What effect would these ideas have on people? In what ways would these ideas aid people in gaining a sense of power over their lives? How might these ideas be tools of control? What does "morality" mean in this tradition?

THINKING HISTORICALLY

How does the idea of karma presented in this primary source support McNeill's interpretation of the importance of the caste system in India? Would the idea of reincarnation make caste organization stronger or weaker?

Source: *Brihad Aranyaka*, IV:4:5–6, in *The Thirteen Principal Upanishads*, ed. and trans. R. E. Hume (Bombay: Oxford University Press, 1954), 140–41. *Chandogya*, V:10:7, in Hume, quoted in *The Hindu Tradition: Readings in Oriental Thought*, ed. Ainslie T. Embree (New York: Vintage, 1966, copyright renewed 1994), 62–63.

According as one acts, according as one conducts himself, so does he become. The doer of good becomes good. The doer of evil becomes evil. One becomes virtuous by virtuous action, bad by bad action.

But people say: "A person is made not of acts, but of desires only." In reply to this I say: As is his desire, such is his resolve; as is his resolve, such the action he performs; what action (*karma*) he performs, that he procures for himself.

On this point there is this verse:—

Where one's mind is attached—the inner self
Goes thereto with action, being attached to it alone.

> *Obtaining the end of his action,*
> *Whatever he does in this world,*
> *He comes again from that world*
> *To this world of action.*

—So the man who desires.

Now the man who does not desire.—He who is without desire, who is freed from desire, whose desire is satisfied, whose desire is the Soul—his breaths do not depart. Being very Brahman, he goes to Brahman.

Accordingly, those who are of pleasant conduct here—the prospect is, indeed, that they will enter a pleasant womb, either the womb of a Brahman, or the womb of a Kshatriya, or the womb of a Vaishya. But those who are of stinking conduct here—the prospect is, indeed, that they will enter a stinking womb, either the womb of a dog, or the womb of a swine, or the womb of an outcaste (*candāla*).

4

The Upanishads: Brahman and Atman

In this selection *Brahman* does not refer to priests or to a specific god. In the late Vedas, or Upanishads, Brahman is all divinity, and all is Brahman. Even the individual soul or *atman* can be one with the universal Brahman, "as the Father of Svetaketu demonstrates to his son through the examples of a banyan tree and salt water." How would ideas like these challenge the caste system?

Source: *Chandogya Upanishad*, in *The Upanishads*, trans. Juan Mascaro (Harmondsworth: Penguin Press, 1965), 113–14.

McNeill suggests that the Upanishads expressed a religious vision
that challenged the power of priests, sacrifice, and caste. How does
this selection from the Upanishads support that interpretation?

Great is the Gayatri, the most sacred verse of the Vedas; but how much
greater is the Infinity of Brahman! A quarter of his being is this whole vast
universe: the other three quarters are his heaven of Immortality. (3.12.5)

There is a Light that shines beyond all things on earth, beyond us all,
beyond the heavens, beyond the highest, the very highest heavens. This
is the Light that shines in our heart. (3.13.7)

All this universe is in the truth Brahman. He is the beginning and
end and life of all. As such, in silence, give unto him adoration.

Man in truth is made of faith. As his faith is in this life, so he becomes in the beyond: with faith and vision let him work.

There is a Spirit that is mind and life, light and truth and vast spaces.
He contains all works and desires and all perfumes and all tastes. He
enfolds the whole universe, and in silence is loving to all.

This is the Spirit that is in my heart, smaller than a grain of rice, or a
grain of barley, or a grain of mustard-seed, or a grain of canary-seed, or
the kernel of a grain of canary-seed. This is the Spirit that is in my heart,
greater than the earth, greater than the sky, greater than heaven itself,
greater than all these worlds.

He contains all works and desires and all perfumes and all tastes. He
enfolds the whole universe and in silence is loving to all. This is the Spirit
that is in my heart, this is Brahman. (3.14)

"Bring me a fruit from this banyan tree."

"Here it is, father."

"Break it."

"It is broken, Sir."

"What do you see in it?"

"Very small seeds, Sir."

"Break one of them, my son."

"It is broken, Sir."

"What do you see in it?"

"Nothing at all, Sir."

Then his father spoke to him: "My son, from the very essence in the
seed which you cannot see comes in truth this vast banyan tree.

Believe me, my son, an invisible and subtle essence is the Spirit of the whole universe. That is Reality. That is Atman. THOU ART THAT."

"Explain more to me, father," said Svetaketu.

"So be it, my son.

Place this salt in water and come to me tomorrow morning."

Svetaketu did as he was commanded, and in the morning his father said to him: "Bring me the salt you put into the water last night."

Svetaketu looked into the water, but could not find it, for it had dissolved.

His father then said: "Taste the water from this side. How is it?"

"It is salt."

"Taste it from the middle. How is it?"

"It is salt."

"Taste it from that side. How is it?"

"It is salt."

"Look for the salt again and come again to me."

The son did so, saying: "I cannot see the salt. I only see water."

His father then said: "In the same way, O my son, you cannot see the Spirit. But in truth he is here.

An invisible and subtle essence is the Spirit of the whole universe. That is Reality. That is Truth. THOU ART THAT." (6.12–14)

5

The Bhagavad Gita: Caste and Self

The *Bhagavad Gita** is the best-known work in Hindu religious literature. It is part of a larger epic called the *Mahabharata*,[†] a story of two feuding families that may have had its origins in India as early as 1500 B.C.E. The *Bhagavad Gita* is a philosophical interlude that interrupts the story just before the great battle between the two families. It poses some fundamental questions about the nature of life, death, and proper religious behavior. It begins as the leader of one of the battling armies, Arjuna, asks why he should fight his friends and relatives on the other side. The answer comes from none other than the god Krishna, who has taken the form of Arjuna's charioteer.

* BUH guh vahd GEE tuh
† mah hah BAH rah tah

Source: *Bhagavad Gita*, trans. Barbara Stoler Miller (New York: Bantam Books, 1986), 31–34, 52, 86–87.

What is Krishna's answer? What will happen to the people Arjuna kills? What will happen to Arjuna? What would happen to Arjuna if he refused to fight the battle? What does this selection tell you about Hindu ideas of life, death, and the self?

THINKING HISTORICALLY

In some ways this work reconciles the conflict in the Upanishads between caste and *atman*. Performing the *dharma*, or duty, of caste is seen as a liberating act. Would the acceptance of this story support or challenge the caste system? Does this primary source support McNeill's interpretation of Indian society?

Lord Krishna

You grieve for those beyond grief,
and you speak words of insight;
but learned men do not grieve
for the dead or the living.

Never have I not existed,
nor you, nor these kings;
and never in the future
shall we cease to exist.

Just as the embodied self
enters childhood, youth, and old age,
so does it enter another body;
this does not confound a steadfast man.

Contacts with matter make us feel
heat and cold, pleasure and pain.
Arjuna, you must learn to endure
fleeting things—they come and go!

When these cannot torment a man,
when suffering and joy are equal
for him and he has courage,
he is fit for immortality.

Nothing of nonbeing comes to be,
nor does being cease to exist;
the boundary between these two
is seen by men who see reality.

Indestructible is the presence
that pervades all this;
no one can destroy
this unchanging reality.

Our bodies are known to end,
but the embodied self is enduring,
indestructible, and immeasurable;
therefore, Arjuna, fight the battle!

He who thinks this self a killer
and he who thinks it killed,
both fail to understand;
it does not kill, nor is it killed.

It is not born,
it does not die;
having been,
it will never not be;
unborn, enduring,
constant, and primordial,
it is not killed
when the body is killed.

Arjuna, when a man knows the self
to be indestructible, enduring, unborn,
unchanging, how does he kill
or cause anyone to kill?

As a man discards
worn-out clothes
to put on new
and different ones,
so the embodied self
discards
its worn-out bodies
to take on other new ones.

Weapons do not cut it,
fire does not burn it,
waters do not wet it,
wind does not wither it.

It cannot be cut or burned;
it cannot be wet or withered;
it is enduring, all-pervasive,
fixed, immovable, and timeless.

It is called unmanifest,
inconceivable, and immutable;
since you know that to be so,
you should not grieve!

If you think of its birth
and death as ever-recurring,
then too, Great Warrior,
you have no cause to grieve!

Death is certain for anyone born,
and birth is certain for the dead;
since the cycle is inevitable,
you have no cause to grieve!

Creatures are unmanifest in origin,
manifest in the midst of life,
and unmanifest again in the end.
Since this is so, why do you lament!

Rarely someone
sees it,
rarely another
speaks it,
rarely anyone
hears it—
even hearing it,
no one really knows it.

The self embodied in the body
of every being is indestructible;
you have no cause to grieve
for all these creatures, Arjuna!

Look to your own duty;
do not tremble before it;
nothing is better for a warrior
than a battle of sacred duty.

The doors of heaven open
for warriors who rejoice
to have a battle like this
thrust on them by chance.

If you fail to wage this war
of sacred duty,
you will abandon your own duty
and fame only to gain evil.

People will tell
of your undying shame,
and for a man of honor
shame is worse than death.

[In this next passage from the *Bhagavad Gita*, Krishna reveals a deeper meaning to his message to Arjuna. Not only must Arjuna act like a warrior because that is his caste, but he must also act without regard to the consequences of his action. What does Krishna seem to mean by this? How does one do "nothing at all even when he engages in action"?]

Abandoning attachment to fruits
of action, always content, independent,
he does nothing at all
even when he engages in action.

He incurs no guilt if he has no hope,
restrains his thought and himself,
abandons possessions,
and performs actions with his body only.

Content with whatever comes by chance,
beyond dualities, free from envy,
impartial to failure and success,
he is not bound even when he acts.

When a man is unattached and free,
his reason deep in knowledge,
acting only in sacrifice,
his action is wholly dissolved.

When devoted men sacrifice
to other deities with faith,
they sacrifice to me, Arjuna,
however aberrant the rites.

I am the enjoyer
and the lord of all sacrifices;
they do not know me in reality,
and so they fail.

Votaries of the gods go to the gods,
ancestor-worshippers go to the ancestors,
those who propitiate ghosts go to them,
and my worshippers go to me.

The leaf or flower or fruit or water
that he offers with devotion,
I take from the man of self-restraint
in response to his devotion.

Whatever you do—what you take,
what you offer, what you give,
what penances you perform—
do as an offering to me, Arjuna!

You will be freed from the bonds of action,
from the fruit of fortune and misfortune;
armed with the discipline of renunciation,
your self liberated, you will join me.

I am impartial to all creatures,
and no one is hateful or dear to me;
but men devoted to me are in me,
and I am within them.

If he is devoted solely to me,
even a violent criminal
must be deemed a man of virtue,
for his resolve is right.

His spirit quickens to sacred duty,
and he finds eternal peace;
Arjuna, know that no one
devoted to me is lost.

If they rely on me, Arjuna,
women, commoners, men of low rank,
even men born in the womb of evil,
reach the highest way.

How easy it is then for holy priests
and devoted royal sages—
in this transient world of sorrow,
devote yourself to me!

Keep me in your mind and devotion,
sacrifice to me, bow to me,
discipline yourself toward me,
and you will reach me!

6

ARISTOTLE

The Athenian Constitution: Territorial Sovereignty

The process of establishing political authority based on the territorial state was not achieved at one particular moment in history. Much of Greek history (indeed, much of world history since the Greeks) witnessed the struggle of territorial authority over family, blood, and kinship ties.

The process of replacing kinship and tribal alliances with a territorial "politics of place" can, however, be seen in the constitutional reforms attributed to the Athenian noble Cleisthenes* in 508 B.C.E. Cleisthenes was not a democrat; his reform of Athenian politics was probably intended to win popular support for himself in his struggle with other noble families. But the inadvertent results of his reforms were to establish the necessary basis for democracy: a territorial state in which commoners as citizens had a stake in government. A description of those reforms is contained in a document called "The Athenian Constitution," discovered in Egypt only a hundred years ago and thought to have been written by the philosopher Aristotle (384–322 B.C.E.) around 330 B.C.E.

Modern scholars doubt that Cleisthenes created the *demes*† (local neighborhoods) that were the basis of his reforms. Some existed earlier. But by making the *demes* the root of political organization, he undoubtedly undercut the power of dominant families. As *demes* were given real authority, power shifted from relatives to residents. Also, as

* KLYS thuh neez
† deems

Source: Aristotle, "The Athenian Constitution," in *Aristotle, Politics, and the Athenian Constitution*, trans. John Warrington (London: David Campbell Publishers, 1959).

Cleisthenes expanded the number of citizens, the *deme* structure became more "*deme*-ocratic."

Notice how the constitutional reform combined a sense of local, residential identity with citizenship in a larger city-state by tying city, country, and coastal *demes* together in each new "tribe." Why were these new tribes less "tribal" than the old ones? What would be the modern equivalent of these new tribes? Was democracy possible without a shift from kinship to territorial or civic identity? Was it inevitable?

THINKING HISTORICALLY

Territorial sovereignty is something we take for granted. It means the law of the land. Regardless of the beliefs of our parents or ancestors, we obey the law of the territory. In the United States, we are bound to observe the law of the nation and the law of the state and municipal ordinances. We do not take our own family law with us when we move from one town or state or country to another. When we go to Japan, we are bound by Japanese law, even if we are not Japanese. In the modern world, sovereignty, ultimate authority, is tied to territory. Because this is so obvious to us in modern society, it is difficult to imagine that this was not always the case.

Historians have to acknowledge that things they and their societies take for granted may not have always existed; rather, they have developed throughout history. McNeill's interpretation of the essential difference between India and Greece makes such a leap. Many people have pointed out the unique Athenian invention of democracy. But McNeill recognized that the Athenians invented democracy because they had already invented something more fundamental — territorial sovereignty, politics, government, citizenship. How does "The Athenian Constitution" support McNeill's interpretation?

The overthrow of the Peisistratid tyranny left the city split into two actions under Isagoras and Cleisthenes respectively. The former, a son of Tisander, had supported the tyrants; the latter was an Alcmaeonid. Cleisthenes, defeated in the political clubs, won over the people by offering citizen rights to the masses. Thereupon Isagoras, who had fallen behind in the race for power, once more invoked the help of his friend Cleomenes and persuaded him to exorcise the pollution; that is, to expel the Alcmaeonidae, who were believed still to be accursed. Cleisthenes accordingly withdrew from Attica with a small band of adherents, while Cleomenes proceeded to drive out seven hundred Athenian families. The Spartan next attempted to dissolve the Council and to set up Isagoras with three hundred of his supporters as the sovereign authority. The

Council, however, resisted; the populace flew to arms; and Cleomenes with Isagoras and all their forces took refuge in the Acropolis, to which the people laid siege and blockaded them for two days. On the third day it was agreed that Cleomenes and his followers should withdraw. Cleisthenes and his fellow exiles were recalled.

The people were now in control, and Cleisthenes, their leader, was recognized as head of the popular party. This was not surprising; for the Alcmaeonidae were largely responsible for the overthrow of the tyrants, with whom they had been in conflict during most of their rule.

. . . The people, therefore, had every grounds for confidence in Cleisthenes. Accordingly, three years after the destruction of the tyranny, in the archonship of Isagoras, he used his influence as leader of the popular party to carry out a number of reforms. (A) He divided the population into ten tribes instead of the old four. His purpose here was to intermix the members of the tribes so that more persons might have civic rights; and hence the advice "not to notice the tribes," which was tendered to those who would examine the lists of the clans. (B) He increased the membership of the Council from 400 to 500, each tribe now contributing fifty instead of one hundred as before. His reason for not organizing the people into *twelve* tribes was to avoid the necessity of using the existing division into trittyes, which would have meant failing to regroup the population on a satisfactory basis. (C) He divided the country into thirty portions—ten urban and suburban, ten coastal, and ten inland—each containing a certain number of demes. These portions he called trittyes, and assigned three of them by lot to each tribe in such a way that each should have one portion in each of the three localities just mentioned. Furthermore, those who lived in any given deme were to be reckoned fellow demesmen. This arrangement was intended to protect new citizens from being shown up as such by the habitual use of family names. Men were to be officially described by the names of their demes; and it is thus that Athenians still speak of one another. Demes had now supplanted the old naucraries,[1] and Cleisthenes therefore appointed Demarchs whose duties were identical with those of the former Naucrari. He named some of the demes from their localities, and others from their supposed founders; for certain areas no longer corresponded to named localities. On the other hand, he allowed everyone to retain his family and clan and religious rites according to ancestral custom. He also gave the ten tribes names which the Delphic oracle had chosen out of one hundred selected national heroes.

---

[1] Forty-eight subdivisions of the old four tribes, each responsible for one galley of the Athenian navy. [Ed.]

7

THUCYDIDES
The Funeral Oration of Pericles

The most famous statement of Greek loyalty to the city-state is the following account of the funeral speech of the Athenian statesman Pericles in the classic *History of the Peloponnesian War* by the ancient historian Thucydides.* The speech eulogized the Athenian soldiers who had died in the war against Sparta in 431 B.C.E.

Notice the high value placed on loyalty to Athens and service to the state. Here is the origin of patriotism. Pericles also insists that Athens is a democratic city-state. He praises Athenian freedom as well as public service. Could there be a conflict between personal freedom and public service? If so, how would Pericles resolve such a conflict? You might also notice that Pericles is praising Athenian citizen-soldiers who died defending not their home but the empire. Could there be a conflict between Athenian democracy and the ambitious empire?

THINKING HISTORICALLY

Are the sentiments that Pericles expresses a consequence of territorial sovereignty? Could such sentiments be expressed in defense of caste? Notice how Pericles speaks of ancestors, family, and parents. Do his words suggest any potential conflict between family ties and loyalty to the state? How is Pericles able to convince his audience of the priority of the state over kinship ties? How does this primary source provide evidence for McNeill's interpretation?

I will speak first of our ancestors, for it is right and seemly that now, when we are lamenting the dead, a tribute should be paid to their memory. There has never been a time when they did not inhabit this land, which by their valour they have handed down from generation to generation, and we have received from them a free state. But if they were worthy of praise, still more were our fathers, who added to their inheritance, and after many a struggle transmitted to us their sons this great empire. And we ourselves assembled here today, who are still

* thoo SIH duh deez

Source: *The History of Thucydides*, Book II, trans. Benjamin Jowett (New York: Tandy-Thomas, 1909).

most of us in the vigour of life, have carried the work of improvement further, and have richly endowed our city with all things, so that she is sufficient for herself both in peace and war. Of the military exploits by which our various possessions were acquired, or of the energy with which we or our fathers drove back the tide of war, Hellenic or Barbarian [non-Greek], I will not speak: for the tale would be long and is familiar to you. But before I praise the dead, I should like to point out by what principles of action we rose to power, and under what institutions and through what manner of life our empire became great. For I conceive that such thoughts are not unsuited to the occasion, and that this numerous assembly of citizens and strangers may profitably listen to them.

Our form of government does not enter into rivalry with the institutions of others. We do not copy our neighbours, but are an example to them. It is true that we are called a democracy, for the administration is in the hands of the many and not of the few. But while the law secures equal justice to all alike in their private disputes, the claim of excellence is also recognised; and when a citizen is in any way distinguished, he is preferred to the public service, not as a matter of privilege, but as the reward of merit. Neither is poverty a bar, but a man may benefit his country whatever be the obscurity of his condition. There is no exclusiveness in our public life, and in our private intercourse we are not suspicious of one another, nor angry with our neighbour if he does what he likes; we do not put on sour looks at him which, though harmless, are not pleasant. While we are thus unconstrained in our private intercourse, a spirit of reverence pervades our public acts; we are prevented from doing wrong by respect for the authorities and for the laws, having an especial regard to those which are ordained for the protection of the injured as well as to those unwritten laws which bring upon the transgressor of them the reprobation of the general sentiment.

And we have not forgotten to provide for our weary spirits many relaxations from toil; we have regular games and sacrifices throughout the year; our homes are beautiful and elegant; and the delight which we daily feel in all these things helps to banish melancholy. Because of the greatness of our city the fruits of the whole earth flow in upon us; so that we enjoy the goods of other countries as freely as of our own.

Then, again, our military training is in many respects superior to that of our adversaries. Our city is thrown open to the world, and we never expel a foreigner or prevent him from seeing or learning anything of which the secret if revealed to an enemy might profit him. We rely not upon management or trickery, but upon our own hearts and hands. And in the matter of education, whereas they from early youth are always undergoing laborious exercises which are to make them brave, we live at ease, and yet are equally ready to face the perils which they face. And here is the proof. . . .

If then we prefer to meet danger with a light heart but without laborious training, and with a courage which is gained by habit and not enforced by law, are we not greatly the gainers? Since we do not anticipate the pain, although, when the hour comes, we can be as brave as those who never allow themselves to rest; and thus too our city is equally admirable in peace and in war. For we are lovers of the beautiful, yet simple in our tastes, and we cultivate the mind without loss of manliness. Wealth we employ, not for talk and ostentation, but when there is a real use for it. To avow poverty with us is no disgrace; the true disgrace is in doing nothing to avoid it. An Athenian citizen does not neglect the state because he takes care of his own household; and even those of us who are engaged in business have a very fair idea of politics. We alone regard a man who takes no interest in public affairs, not as a harmless, but as a useless character; and if few of us are originators, we are all sound judges of policy. The great impediment to action is, in our opinion, not discussion, but the want of that knowledge which is gained by discussion preparatory to action. For we have a peculiar power of thinking before we act and of acting too, whereas other men are courageous from ignorance but hesitate upon reflection. And they are surely to be esteemed the bravest spirits who, having the clearest sense both of the pains and pleasures of life, do not on that account shrink from danger. In doing good, again, we are unlike others; we make our friends by conferring, not by receiving favours. Now he who confers a favour is the firmer friend, because he would fain by kindness keep alive the memory of an obligation; but the recipient is colder in his feelings, because he knows that in requiting another's generosity he will not be winning gratitude but only paying a debt. We alone do good to our neighbours, not upon a calculation of interest, but in the confidence of freedom and in a frank and fearless spirit.

To sum up: I say that Athens is the school of Hellas, and that the individual Athenian in his own person seems to have the power of adapting himself to the most varied forms of action with the utmost versatility and grace. This is no passing and idle word, but truth and fact; and the assertion is verified by the position to which these qualities have raised the state. For in the hour of trial Athens alone among her contemporaries is superior to the report of her. No enemy who comes against her is indignant at the reverses which he sustains at the hands of such a city; no subject complains that his masters are unworthy of him. And we shall assuredly not be without witnesses; there are mighty monuments of our power which will make us the wonder of this and of succeeding ages; we shall not need the praises of Homer or of any other panegyrist whose poetry may please for the moment, although his representation of the facts will not bear the light of day. For we have compelled every land and every sea to open a path for our valour, and have everywhere planted eternal memorials of our friendship and of our enmity. Such is the city of whose sake these men nobly fought and died; they could not bear the thought that she might be taken from them; and every one of us who survive should gladly toil on her behalf.

I have dwelt upon the greatness of Athens because I want to show you that we are contending for a higher prize than those who enjoy none of these privileges, and to establish by manifest proof the merit of these men whom I am now commemorating. Their loftiest praise has been already spoken. For in magnifying the city I have magnified them, and men like them whose virtues made her glorious. And of how few Hellenes can it be said as of them, that their deeds when weighed in the balance have been found equal to their fame! . . . They resigned to hope their unknown chance of happiness; but in the fact of death they resolved to rely upon themselves alone. And when the moment came they were minded to resist and suffer, rather than to fly and save their lives; they ran away from the word of dishonour, but on the battlefield their feet stood fast, and in an instant, at the height of their fortune, they passed away from the scene, not of their fear, but of their glory.

Such was the end of these men; they were worthy of Athens, and the living need not desire to have a more heroic spirit, although they may pray for a less fatal issue. The value of such a spirit is not to be expressed in words. Any one can discourse to you forever about the advantages of a brave defence, which you know already. But instead of listening to him I would have you day by day fix your eyes upon the greatness of Athens, until you become filled with the love of her; and when you are impressed by the spectacle of her glory, reflect that this empire has been acquired by men who knew their duty and had the courage to do it, who in the hour of conflict had the fear of dishonour always present to them, and who, if ever they failed in an enterprise, would not allow their virtues to be lost to their country, but freely gave their lives to her as the fairest offering which they could present at her feast. The sacrifice which they collectively made was individually repaid to them; for they received again each one of himself a praise which grows not old, and the noblest of all sepulchres—I speak not of that in which their remains are laid, but of that in which their glory survives, and is proclaimed always and on every fitting occasion both in word and deed. For the whole earth is the sepulchre of famous men; not only are they commemorated by columns and inscriptions in their own country, but in foreign lands there dwells also an unwritten memorial of them, graven not on stone but in the hearts of men. Make them your examples, and, esteeming courage to be freedom and freedom to be happiness, do not weigh too nicely the perils of war. The unfortunate who has no hope of a change for the better has less reason to throw away his life than the prosperous who, if he survives, is always liable to a change for the worse, and to whom any accidental fall makes the most serious difference. To a man of spirit, cowardice and disaster coming together are far more bitter than death striking him unperceived at a time when he is full of courage and animated by the general hope.

Wherefore I do not now commiserate the parents of the dead who stand here; I would rather comfort them. You know that your life has been passed amid manifold vicissitudes; and that they may be deemed fortunate who have gained most honour, whether an honourable death like theirs, or an honourable sorrow like yours, and whose days have been so ordered that the term of their happiness is likewise the term of their life. I know how hard it is to make you feel this, when the good fortune of others will too often remind you of the gladness which once lightened your hearts. And sorrow is felt at the want of those blessings, not which a man never knew, but which were a part of his life before they were taken from him. Some of you are of an age at which they may hope to have other children, and they ought to bear their sorrow better; not only will the children who may hereafter be born make them forget their own lost ones, but the city will be doubly a gainer. She will not be left desolate, and she will be safer. For a man's counsel cannot have equal weight or worth, when he alone has no children to risk in the general danger. To those of you who have passed their prime, I say: Congratulate yourselves that you have been happy during the greater part of your days; remember that your life of sorrow will not last long, and be comforted by the glory of those who are gone. For the love of honour alone is ever young, and not riches, as some say, but honour is the delight of men when they are old and useless.

To you who are the sons and brothers of the departed, I see that the struggle to emulate them will be an arduous one. For all men praise the dead, and, however pre-eminent your virtue may be, hardly will you be thought, I do not say to equal, but even to approach them. The living have their rivals and detractors, but when a man is out of the way, the honour and good-will which he receives is unalloyed. And, if I am to speak of womanly virtues to those of you who will henceforth be widows, let me sum them up in one short admonition: To a woman not to show more weakness than is natural to her sex is a great glory, and not to be talked about for good or for evil among men.

I have paid the required tribute, in obedience to the law, making use of such fitting words as I had. The tribute of deeds has been paid in part; for the dead have been honourably interred, and it remains only that their children should be maintained at the public charge until they are grown up; this is the solid prize with which, as with a garland, Athens crowns her sons living and dead, after a struggle like theirs. For where the rewards of virtue are greatest, there the noblest citizens are enlisted in the service of the state. And now, when you have duly lamented, everyone his own dead, you may depart.

PLATO

The Republic

This selection is from one of the world's most famous books of philosophy. Two events dominated the early life of Plato (428–348 B.C.E.), turning him away from the public life he was expected to lead. Plato was born in the shadow of the Peloponnesian War, which ended with the defeat of Athens in his twenty-third year. Disillusioned with the postwar governments, especially the democracy that condemned his teacher Socrates in 399 B.C.E., Plato forsook the political arena for a life of contemplation.

Plato's philosophical books, called dialogues because of the way they develop ideas from discussion and debate, follow Plato's teacher Socrates around the city-state of Athens. Often they begin, like *The Republic*, with a view of Socrates and other Athenian citizens enjoying the public spaces and festivals of the city. Notice in this introduction how territorial sovereignty creates public places and public activities.

THINKING HISTORICALLY

Plato was neither a democrat nor politically active. Nevertheless, his life and his philosophy exemplify a commitment to the world of what McNeill calls "territorial sovereignty."

A primary source can support a particular viewpoint by espousing it, as Plato espouses the benefits of living in a territorial state or thinking about government. But a source can also provide clues about the society from which it comes. What clues in Plato's text show that his life and the lives of the people around him are shaped by the city-state?

Chapter 1

SOCRATES. I walked down to the Piraeus yesterday with Glaucon, the son of Ariston, to make my prayers to the goddess. As this was the first celebration of her festival, I wished also to see how the ceremony would be conducted. The Thracians, I thought, made as fine a show in the procession as our own people, though they did well enough. The

Source: Plato, *The Republic of Plato*, trans. F. M. Cornford (London: Oxford University Press, 1941), 2–3, 177–79, 227–35.

prayers and the spectacle were over, and we were leaving to go back to the city, when from some way off Polemarchus, the son of Cephalus, caught sight of us starting homewards and sent his slave running to ask us to wait for him. The boy caught my garment from behind and gave me the message.

I turned around and asked where his master was.

There, he answered; coming up behind. Please wait.

Very well, said Glaucon; we will.

A minute later Polemarchus joined us, with Glaucon's brother, Adeimantus, and Niceratus, the son of Nicias, and some others who must have been at the procession.

Socrates, said Polemarchus, I do believe you are starting back to town and leaving us.

You have guessed right, I answered.

Well, he said, you see what a large party we are?

I do.

Unless you are more than a match for us, then, you must stay here.

Isn't there another alternative? said I; we might convince you that you must let us go.

How will you convince us, if we refuse to listen?

We cannot, said Glaucon.

Well, we shall refuse; make up your minds to that.

Here Adeimantus interposed: Don't you even know that in the evening there is going to be a torch-race on horseback in honour of the goddess?

On horseback! I exclaimed; that is something new. How will they do it? Are the riders going to race with torches and hand them on to one another?

Just so, said Polemarchus. Besides, there will be a festival lasting all night, which will be worth seeing. We will go out after dinner and look on. We shall find plenty of young men there and we can have a talk. So please stay, and don't disappoint us.

It looks as if we had better stay, said Glaucon.

Well, said I, if you think so, we will.

Accordingly, we went home with Polemarchus.

[At the home of Polemarchus, the participants meet a number of other old friends. After the usual greetings and gossip, the discussion begins in response to Socrates' question, "What is justice?"

Each of the participants poses an idea of justice that Socrates challenges. Then Socrates outlines an ideal state that would be based on absolute justice. In the following selection he is asked how this ideal could ever come about.

Aside from the specifics of Socrates' argument, notice the way in which public issues, for Socrates, are passionate personal concerns.]

Chapter 18

But really, Socrates, Glaucon continued, if you are allowed to go on like this, I am afraid you will forget all about the question you thrust aside some time ago; whether a society so constituted can ever come into existence, and if so, how. No doubt, if it did exist, all manner of good things would come about. I can even add some that you have passed over. Men who acknowledged one another as fathers, sons, or brothers and always used those names among themselves would never desert one another; so they would fight with unequalled bravery. And if their womenfolk went out with them to war, either in the ranks or drawn up in the rear to intimidate the enemy and act as a reserve in case of need, I am sure all this would make them invincible. At home, too, I can see many advantages you have not mentioned. But, since I admit that our commonwealth would have all these merits and any number more, if once it came into existence, you need not describe it in further detail. All we have now to do is to convince ourselves that it can be brought into being and how.

This is a very sudden onslaught, said I; you have no mercy on my shillyshallying. Perhaps you do not realize that, after I have barely escaped the first two waves, the third, which you are now bringing down upon me, is the most formidable of all. When you have seen what it is like and heard my reply, you will be ready to excuse the very natural fears which made me shrink from putting forward such a paradox for discussion.

The more you talk like that, he said, the less we shall be willing to let you off from telling us how this constitution can come into existence; so you had better waste no more time.

Well, said I, let me begin by reminding you that what brought us to this point was our inquiry into the nature of justice and injustice.

True; but what of that?

Merely this: suppose we do find out what justice is, are we going to demand that a man who is just shall have a character which exactly corresponds in every respect to the ideal of justice? Or shall we be satisfied if he comes as near to the ideal as possible and has in him a larger measure of that quality than the rest of the world?

That will satisfy me.

If so, when we set out to discover the essential nature of justice and injustice and what a perfectly just and a perfectly unjust man would be like, supposing them to exist, our purpose was to use them as ideal patterns: we were to observe the degree of happiness or unhappiness that each exhibited, and to draw the necessary inference that our own destiny would be like that of the one we most resembled. We did not set out to show that these ideals could exist in fact.

That is true.

Then suppose a painter had drawn an ideally beautiful figure complete to the last touch, would you think any the worse of him, if he could not show that a person as beautiful as that could exist?

No, I should not.

Well, we have been constructing in discourse the pattern of an ideal state. Is our theory any the worse, if we cannot prove it possible that a state so organized should be actually founded?

Surely not.

That, then, is the truth of the matter. But if, for your satisfaction, I am to do my best to show under what conditions our ideal would have the best chance of being realized, I must ask you once more to admit that the same principle applies here. Can theory ever be fully realized in practice? Is it not in the nature of things that action should come less close to truth than thought? People may not think so; but do you agree or not?

I do.

Then you must not insist upon my showing that this construction we have traced in thought could be reproduced in fact down to the last detail. You must admit that we shall have found a way to meet your demand for realization, if we can discover how a state might be constituted in the closest accordance with our description. Will not that content you? It would be enough for me.

And for me too.

Then our next attempt, it seems, must be to point out what defect in the working of existing states prevents them from being so organized, and what is the least change that would effect a transformation into this type of government—a single change if possible, or perhaps two; at any rate let us make the changes as few and insignificant as may be.

By all means.

Well, there is one change which, as I believe we can show, would bring about this revolution—not a small change, certainly, nor an easy one, but possible.

What is it?

I have now to confront what we called the third and greatest wave. But I must state my paradox, even though the wave should break in laughter over my head and drown me in ignominy. Now mark what I am going to say.

Go on.

Unless either philosophers become kings in their countries or those who are now called kings and rulers come to be sufficiently inspired with a genuine desire for wisdom; unless, that is to say, political power and philosophy meet together, while the many natures who now go their several ways in the one or the other direction are forcibly debarred from doing so, there can be no rest from troubles, my dear Glaucon, for states, nor yet, as I believe, for all mankind; nor can this commonwealth which we have imagined ever till then see the light of day and grow to its full stature. This it was that I have so long hung back from saying; I knew what a paradox it would be, because it is hard to see that there is no other way of happiness either for the state or for the individual.

Socrates, exclaimed Glaucon, after delivering yourself of such a pronouncement as that, you must expect a whole multitude of by no means contemptible assailants to fling off their coats, snatch up the handiest weapon, and make a rush at you, breathing fire and slaughter. If you cannot find arguments to beat them off and make your escape, you will learn what it means to be the target of scorn and derision.

Well, it was you who got me into this trouble.

Yes, and a good thing too. However, I will not leave you in the lurch. You shall have my friendly encouragement for what it is worth; and perhaps you may find me more complaisant than some would be in answering your questions. With such backing you must try to convince the unbelievers.

I will, now that I have such a powerful ally.

[In arguing that philosophers should be kings, Plato (or Socrates) was parting ways with the democratic tradition of Athens. Like other conservative Athenians, he seems to have believed that democracy degenerated into mob rule. The root of this antidemocratic philosophy was the belief that the mass of people was horribly ignorant and only the rare philosopher had true understanding. Plato expressed this idea in one of the most famous passages in the history of philosophy: the parable of the cave.]

Next, said I, here is a parable to illustrate the degrees in which our nature may be enlightened or unenlightened. Imagine the condition of men living in a sort of cavernous chamber underground, with an entrance open to the light and a long passage all down the cave. Here they have been from childhood, chained by the leg and also by the neck, so that they cannot move and can see only what is in front of them, because the chains will not let them turn their heads. At some distance higher up is the light of a fire burning behind them; and between the prisoners and the fire is a track with a parapet built along it, like the screen at a puppet-show, which hides the performers while they show their puppets over the top.

I see, said he.

Now behind this parapet imagine persons carrying along various artificial objects, including figures of men and animals in wood or stone or other materials, which project above the parapet. Naturally, some of these persons will be talking, others silent.

It is a strange picture, he said, and a strange sort of prisoners.

Like ourselves, I replied; for in the first place prisoners so confined would have seen nothing of themselves or of one another, except the shadows thrown by the firelight on the wall of the Cave facing them, would they?

Not if all their lives they had been prevented from moving their heads.

And they would have seen as little of the objects carried past.

Of course.

Now, if they could talk to one another, would they not suppose that their words referred only to those passing shadows which they saw?

Necessarily.

And suppose their prison had an echo from the wall facing them? When one of the people crossing behind them spoke, they could only suppose that the sound came from the shadow passing before their eyes.

No doubt.

In every way, then, such prisoners would recognize as reality nothing but the shadows of those artificial objects.

Inevitably.

Now consider what would happen if their release from the chains and the healing of their unwisdom should come about in this way. Suppose one of them was set free and forced suddenly to stand up, turn his head, and walk with eyes lifted to the light; all these movements would be painful, and he would be too dazzled to make out the objects whose shadows he had been used to see. What do you think he would say, if someone told him that what he had formerly seen was meaningless illusion, but now, being somewhat nearer to reality and turned towards more real objects, he was getting a truer view? Suppose further that he were shown the various objects being carried by and were made to say, in reply to questions, what each of them was. Would he not be perplexed and believe the objects now shown him to be not so real as what he formerly saw?

Yes, not nearly so real.

And if he were forced to look at the firelight itself, would not his eyes ache, so that he would try to escape and turn back to the things which he could see distinctly, convinced that they really were clearer than these other objects now being shown to him?

Yes.

And suppose someone were to drag him away forcibly up the steep and rugged ascent and not let him go until he had hauled him out into the sunlight, would he not suffer pain and vexation at such treatment, and, when he had come out into the light, find his eyes so full of its radiance that he could not see a single one of the things that he was now told were real?

Certainly he would not see them all at once.

He would need, then, to grow accustomed before he could see things in that upper world. At first it would be easiest to make out shadows, and then the images of men and things reflected in water, and later on the things themselves. After that, it would be easier to watch the heavenly bodies and the sky itself by night, looking at the light of the moon and stars rather than the Sun and the Sun's light in the daytime.

Yes, surely.

Last of all, he would be able to look at the Sun and contemplate its nature, not as it appears when reflected in water or any alien medium, but as it is in itself in its own domain.

No doubt.

And now he would begin to draw the conclusion that it is the Sun that produces the seasons and the course of the year and controls everything in the visible world, and moreover is in a way the cause of all that he and his companions used to see.

Clearly he would come at last to that conclusion.

Then if he called to mind his fellow prisoners and what passed for wisdom in his former dwelling-place, he would surely think himself happy in the change and be sorry for them. They may have had a practice of honouring and commending one another, with prizes for the man who had the keenest eye for the passing shadows and the best memory for the order in which they followed or accompanied one another, so that he could make a good guess as to which was going to come next. Would our released prisoner be likely to covet those prizes or to envy the men exalted to honour and power in the Cave? Would he not feel like Homer's Achilles, that he would far sooner "be on earth as a hired servant in the house of a landless man" or endure anything rather than go back to his old beliefs and live in the old way?

Yes, he would prefer any fate to such a life.

Now imagine what would happen if he went down again to take his former seat in the Cave. Coming suddenly out of the sunlight, his eyes would be filled with darkness. He might be required once more to deliver his opinion on those shadows, in competition with the prisoners who had never been released, while his eyesight was still dim and unsteady; and it might take some time to become used to the darkness. They would laugh at him and say that he had gone up only to come back with his sight ruined; it was worth no one's while even to attempt the ascent. If they could lay hands on the man who was trying to set them free and lead them up, they would kill him.

Yes, they would.

Every feature in this parable, my dear Glaucon, is meant to fit our earlier analysis. The prison dwelling corresponds to the region revealed to us through the sense of sight, and the firelight within it to the power of the Sun. The ascent to see the things in the upper world you may take as standing for the upward journey of the soul into the region of the intelligible; then you will be in possession of what I surmise, since that is what you wish to be told. Heaven knows whether it is true; but this, at any rate, is how it appears to me. In the world of knowledge, the last thing to be perceived and only with great difficulty is the essential Form of Goodness. Once it is perceived, the conclusion must follow that, for all things, this is the cause of whatever is right and good; in the visible world it gives birth to light and to the lord of light, while it is itself sovereign in the intelligible world and the parent of intelligence and truth. Without having had a vision of this Form no one can act with wisdom, either in his own life or in matters of state.

So far as I can understand, I share your belief.

Then you may also agree that it is no wonder if those who have reached their height are reluctant to manage the affairs of men. Their souls long to spend all their time in that upper world—naturally enough, if here once more our parable holds true. Nor, again, is it at all strange that one who comes from the contemplation of divine things to the miseries of human life should appear awkward and ridiculous when, with eyes still dazed and not yet accustomed to the darkness, he is compelled, in a law court or elsewhere, to dispute about the shadows of justice or the images that cast those shadows, and to wrangle over the notions of what is right in the minds of men who have never beheld Justice itself.

It is not at all strange.

No; a sensible man will remember that the eyes may be confused in two ways—by a change from light to darkness or from darkness to light; and he will recognize that the same thing happens to the soul. When he sees it troubled and unable to discern anything clearly, instead of laughing thoughtlessly, he will ask whether, coming from a brighter existence, its unaccustomed vision is obscured by the darkness, in which case he will think its condition enviable and its life a happy one; or whether, emerging from the depths of ignorance, it is dazzled by excess of light. If so, he will rather feel sorry for it; or, if he were inclined to laugh, that would be less ridiculous than to laugh at the soul which has come down from the light.

That is a fair statement.

If this is true, then, we must conclude that education is not what it is said to be by some, who profess to put knowledge into a soul which does not possess it, as if they could put sight into blind eyes. On the contrary, our own account signifies that the soul of every man does possess the power of learning the truth and the organ to see it with; and that, just as one might have to turn the whole body round in order that the eye should see light instead of darkness, so the entire soul must be turned away from this changing world, until its eye can bear to contemplate reality and that supreme splendour which we have called the Good. Hence there may well be an art whose aim would be to effect this very thing, the conversion of the soul, in the readiest way; not to put the power of sight into the soul's eye, which already has it, but to ensure that, instead of looking in the wrong direction, it is turned the way it ought to be.

Yes, it may well be so.

It looks, then, as though wisdom were different from those ordinary virtues, as they are called, which are not far removed from bodily qualities, in that they can be produced by habituation and exercise in a soul which has not possessed them from the first. Wisdom, it seems, is certainly the virtue of some diviner faculty, which never loses its power, though its use for good or harm depends on the direction towards which it is turned. You must have noticed in dishonest men with a reputation for sagacity the shrewd glance of a narrow intelligence piercing the objects to which it is directed. There is nothing wrong with their power of vision, but it has been forced into the service of evil, so that the keener its sight, the more harm it works.

Quite true.

And yet if the growth of a nature like this had been pruned from earliest childhood, cleared of those clinging overgrowths which come of gluttony and all luxurious pleasure and, like leaden weights charged with affinity to this mortal world, hang upon the soul, bending its vision downwards; if, freed from these, the soul were turned round towards true reality, then this same power in these very men would see the truth as keenly as the objects it is turned to now.

Yes, very likely.

Is it not also likely, or indeed certain after what has been said, that a state can never be properly governed either by the uneducated who know nothing of truth or by men who are allowed to spend all their days in the pursuit of culture? The ignorant have no single mark before their eyes at which they must aim in all the conduct of their own lives and of affairs of state; and the others will not engage in action if they can help it, dreaming that, while still alive, they have been translated to the Islands of the Blest.

Quite true.

It is for us, then, as founders of a commonwealth, to bring compulsion to bear on the noblest natures. They must be made to climb the ascent to the vision of Goodness, which we called the highest object of knowledge; and, when they have looked upon it long enough, they must not be allowed, as they now are, to remain on the heights, refusing to come down again to the prisoners or to take any part in their labours and rewards, however much or little these may be worth.

Shall we not be doing them an injustice, if we force on them a worse life than they might have?

You have forgotten again, my friend, that the law is not concerned to make any one class specially happy, but to ensure the welfare of the commonwealth as a whole. By persuasion or constraint it will unite the citizens in harmony, making them share whatever benefits each class can contribute to the common good; and its purpose in forming men of that spirit was not that each should be left to go his own way, but that they should be instrumental in binding the community into one.

True, I had forgotten.

You will see, then, Glaucon, that there will be no real injustice in compelling our philosophers to watch over and care for the other citizens. We can fairly tell them that their compeers in other states may quite reasonably refuse to collaborate: there they have sprung up, like a self-sown plant, in despite of their country's institutions; no one has fostered their growth, and they cannot be expected to show gratitude for a care they have never received. "But," we shall say, "it is not so with you. We have brought you into existence for your country's sake as well as for your own, to be like leaders and king-bees in a hive; you have been better and more thoroughly educated than those others and hence you are more capable of playing your part both as men of thought and as men of action. You must go down, then, each in his turn, to live with the rest and let your eyes grow accustomed to the darkness. You will then see a thousand times better than those who live there always; you will recognize every image for what it is and know what it represents, because you have seen justice, beauty, and goodness in their reality; and so you and we shall find life in our commonwealth no mere dream, as it is in most existing states, where men live fighting one another about shadows and quarrelling for power, as if that were a great prize; whereas in truth government can be at its best and free from dissension only where the destined rulers are least desirous of holding office."

Quite true.

Then will our pupils refuse to listen and to take their turns at sharing in the work of the community, though they may live together for most of their time in a purer air?

No; it is a fair demand, and they are fair-minded men. No doubt, unlike any ruler of the present day, they will think of holding power as an unavoidable necessity.

Yes, my friend; for the truth is that you can have a well-governed society only if you can discover for your future rulers a better way of life than being in office; then only will power be in the hands of men who are rich, not in gold, but in the wealth that brings happiness, a good and wise life. All goes wrong when, starved for lack of anything good in their own lives, men turn to public affairs hoping to snatch from thence the happiness they hunger for. They set about fighting for power, and this internecine conflict ruins them and their country. The life of true philosophy is the only one that looks down upon offices of state; and access to power must be confined to men who are not in love with it; otherwise rivals will start fighting. So whom else can you compel to undertake the guardianship of the commonwealth, if not those who, besides understanding best the principles of government, enjoy a nobler life than the politician's and look for rewards of a different kind?

There is indeed no other choice.

■ REFLECTIONS

Caste and territorial sovereignty were alternate but equally effective systems of social organization in the ancient world. Both worked. Both allocated jobs and rewards, arranged marriages and created families, ensured the peace and fought wars. Neither was necessarily more just, tyrannical, expensive, or arbitrary. Yet each system created its own complex world of ideas and behavior.

Caste and territorial sovereignty were not the only bases for identity in the ancient world. In many societies, a person's identity was based on family ties of a different sort than caste. In China, the family lineage, constituting many generations of relatives, was particularly important. Almost every society in human history organized itself around families to a certain extent, and most societies also had a sense of multiple family units called clans or tribes. The Indian caste system was only one variant of these multifamily systems, and some non-Indian societies had divisions resembling castes.

Family, clan, and tribe are still important determinants of identity in the modern world. In some societies, the authority of a tribal leader, clan elder, or family patriarch rivals that of the state. Nevertheless, the modern world is made up of states. We live according to the law of the land, not that of kinship. In the United States, one obeys the laws of the United States, regardless of who one knows. If the police pull you over for driving through a red light, you do not say that your father gave you permission or your uncle ordered you to drive through red lights. In the territory of the United States, you obey the laws of the United States and the particular state in which you find yourself. When a citizen of the United States goes to Canada, he or she must obey the laws of Canada. This is the world of states, of territorial sovereignty.

One of the major transitions in human history in the last five thousand years has been the rise of territorial sovereignty and the supplanting of the authority of the law of the state over the rule of family, clan, tribe, and caste. This is what developed in ancient Greece twenty-five hundred years ago. It did not occur completely and finally with Cleisthenes or even with the rise of Greek democracy in the fifth century B.C.E. Tribal alliances reasserted themselves periodically in Greece and elsewhere, in the Middle Ages and in modern society. The establishment of territorial sovereignty and ultimately of civil society, where political parties replaced tribes, was gradual and interrupted and is still continuing. Aristotle tells us that after Cleisthenes, Greeks took new surnames based on their new civic "tribes." That would have ended the rule of the old family-based tribes, but we know the old tribal names did not disappear. A thorough transition would mean that political parties would express entirely civic goals without a trace of tribal identity, but that too is a process that still continues. In modern Ireland, for instance, one of the political parties, Finn Gael, means literally the tribe of the Gael. In the wake of the U.S. invasion of Iraq in 2003, many Americans have learned how difficult it is to impose a system of territorial sovereignty on a society where tribal identities are strong.

India today is also a modern state in which the law of the land applies to all regardless of caste, family, or tribe. In fact, recent Indian governments have outlawed discrimination based on caste and created affirmative action programs on behalf of Dahlits, the outcastes or untouchables. Nevertheless, Indian newspapers still run matrimonial ads that specify caste, though international Web sites often do not.

Modern society encourages us to be many things. Family and caste can still play a role. Religion, ethnicity, national origin, even race are given an importance in modern society that was often absent or irrelevant in ancient societies. But with the civic society produced by territorial sovereignty comes not only citizenship but also a range of chosen identities based on career, education, job, hobbies, friends, and a wide range of living possibilities. These choices can sometimes overwhelm. Sometimes the indelibility of family, caste, or birth can seem a comfort. But over the long term of history, the range and choice of identities seem likely to increase, and more and more of them will likely be voluntary rather than stamped on the birth certificate.

4

Emperors and Philosophers

China and Rome, 300 B.C.E.—300 C.E.

The Chinese and Roman empires of the classical era were similar in many ways. They were roughly contemporaneous. The Chinese Empire began under the Qin dynasty in 221 B.C.E. and continued in revised form through the Han dynasty until 220 C.E. Rome also reached imperial dimensions after 200 B.C.E., recognizing its first emperor in 27 B.C.E. Like China, the Roman Empire was shaken by invading nomads after 200 C.E. Both empires ruled at least fifty million people over an area of one and a half million square miles. (See Maps 4.1 and 4.2.) Both managed to field and maintain enormous armies and tax, govern, and keep the peace for hundreds of years. How did these empires rule and administer such vast areas for so long? In this chapter we explore the management of both empires by studying the actions of emperors and their governments. We examine the longevity of the empires by reflecting on the interplay of ideas and actions. Beyond their emperors, armies, and administrators, the success of the empires was achieved by spreading ideas and cultural traditions that united their subjects and gave legitimacy to their rule. In turn, new ideas and information gathered from expansion into new lands further enriched these empires.

The Greek philosopher Plato famously argued that philosophers would make the best kings. He wanted philosophers to be kings because he believed that only they could grasp the True, the Good, and the Virtuous and thereby create the ideal society.

No philosopher — or anyone else — has ever created a perfect government or governed perfectly. But the period that this chapter covers, from 300 B.C.E. to 300 C.E., was one that witnessed both startling innovations in philosophical thought and the emergence of powerful

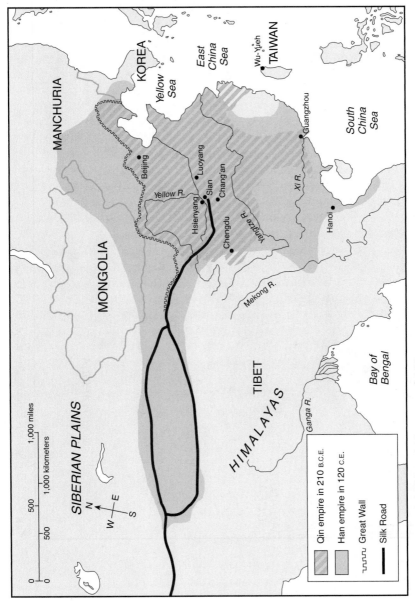

Map 4.1 Imperial China, 210 B.C.E. and 120 C.E.

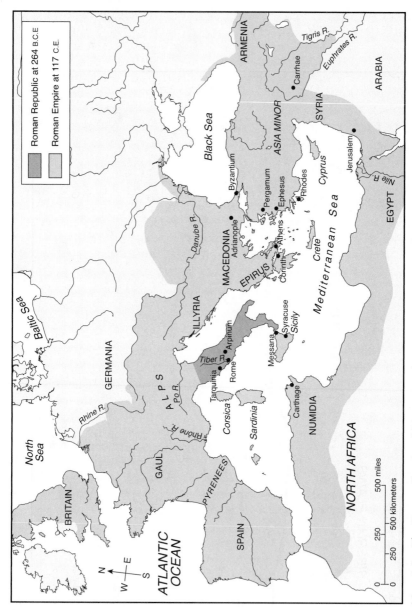

Map 4.2 The Roman Empire, 264 B.C.E. and 117 C.E.

and sweeping empires on both sides of Eurasia. The Chinese and Roman empires were each larger than any the world had ever seen. (The only previous empire that came close was that of Alexander the Great, which lasted only during the conqueror's lifetime, just before our period.) The exact role philosophy played in the rise of these great empires is open to question. Even before 300 B.C.E., the great rulers of China and Rome employed philosophers as tutors and advisors; most famously, Philip of Macedon employed the philosopher Aristotle to tutor his son Alexander the Great. Rulers also frequently recruited the best military and scientific minds to aid them in the pursuit of their goals. But in this period of the Roman and Chinese empires, global ambitions and global ideas collided and colluded to a degree never known before. We will explore this meeting of the minds and clashing of heads in this chapter.

■ THINKING HISTORICALLY

Distinguishing Ideas from Actions and Understanding Their Relationship

We all know that ideas are different from actions. Historians traditionally divide themselves between those who concentrate on ideas (intellectual and cultural historians) and those whose primary focus is on actions (social, political, diplomatic, and economic historians). It is important not to confuse ideas and actions.

It is even more important to understand how ideas and actions are related. It is obvious that many historical actions are products of ideas. You will read of Chinese and Roman emperors who have ideas, or accept ideas of advisors, and then act according to those ideas. But we also know that some actions follow from greed, ambition, or other emotions, rather than ideas. Not every action by an emperor, or anyone else, is thoughtful. In addition, some actions generate new ideas: A defeat in battle leads to the contemplation of peace; the capture of foreign prisoners opens the victors to the spread of foreign ideas. Thus, we will not only distinguish ideas and actions, but we will also consider how they are related.

1

VALERIE HANSEN

The Creation of the Chinese Empire

The author of this selection, a modern historian of China, explains
how the Qin (Chin) state organized to defeat the other states of
the Warring States period (476–221 B.C.E.) and establish a Chinese
Empire in 221 B.C.E. Hansen suggests that the Legalist philosophers
Han Fei and Lord Shang were particularly instrumental in aiding the
first emperor to mold Qin strength and dominance. What was the
philosophy of the Legalists? How did Legalism differ from Confucian
philosophy?

THINKING HISTORICALLY

Notice how the author discusses the influence of the Legalists,
sometimes citing their philosophical and political ideas and sometimes focusing on their actions as advisors. This is because many of
them played both roles. How did political ideas get translated into
actions, according to this account? Why was Legalism instrumental
in strengthening the Qin state? What role did Confucian philosophy
play in this process of Chinese state building? If you were a state
builder, why might you prefer the ideas of a Lord Shang or Han Fei to
the ideas of Confucius? What was Liu Bang's attitude toward Legalism and Confucianism, and why was his view better suited to the
longer-term interests of the Han dynasty? How, according to
Hansen's account, were Chinese political ideas translated into
political action?

In 221 B.C.E., the Warring States period came to a sudden end when
the kingdom of Qin defeated all its competitor kingdoms and unified
the empire—roughly two-thirds of the area of modern China—for the
first time. The Qin ruler then crowned himself China's first emperor.
Indeed, the English word for China (which came via Latin and Sanskrit)
derives from the name of the uniting dynasty, the Qin. The Qin were
able to conquer their rivals not because of any new technologies but
because they found a new way to organize their state. To draw a modern analogy, one could say that the armies of the regional kingdoms
all fought with the same hardware—crossbows, bronze weapons,
and armor—but that the Qin had the advantage of new software—
namely a bureaucracy organized on the basis of merit. The Qin founder

Source: Valerie Hansen, *The Open Empire: A History of China to 1600* (New York:
W. W. Norton, 2000), 97, 99–104, 112–15.

followed the teachings of Legalist ministers who advocated the abolition of all privileges of the nobility.

In twentieth-century America, the word *bureaucracy* carries largely negative connotations of inefficiency. In third-century B.C.E. China, however, bureaucracy provided a new form of government far more efficient than the aristocratic rule of the Warring States period. The Qin ruler used this new type of government to build a powerful fighting machine. The state created by the Qin survived for a mere fourteen years, but its immediate successor, the Han dynasty, ruled China for the next four hundred years. Although the Han founders denounced the rule of the Qin as brutal, the Han dynasty took over many Qin-dynasty organizational techniques. One of the greatest challenges for the modern analyst is to assess the accomplishments of the Qin dynasty without being blinded by overly critical Han-dynasty sources. . . .

With the founding of the empire, Chinese society assumed the contours it would retain for the next two thousand years. During the Warring States period, social commentators envisioned a society of two classes: the privileged aristocracy and the laboring masses. But after 221 B.C.E., observers ranked society into four groups: scholars, peasants, artisans, and merchants. . . . This ranking reflected Legalist prejudices in favor of producers, namely peasants and artisans, over merchants, whom they felt manufactured nothing and so contributed little of value to the economy. Of course, merchants had much more money and much more freedom than did peasants, and most cultivators would have gladly switched places with any merchant. . . .

The Legalist State

The philosophers of the Warring States, most notably Xunzi, had remarked on the unusual strength and Legalist policies of the state of Qin at the turn of the third century B.C.E. In an age that prized eloquence, the Legalist thinker Han Fei (280–233 B.C.E.) stuttered, so he wrote directly to his ruler about his philosophy of government. In doing so, he became the first thinker to record his own ideas — unlike earlier thinkers whose students compiled their teachings after their deaths, often in a question-and-answer format. . . . The ruler was to remain detached from the everyday business of government; if he applied an unbending standard to judge his officials and his people, his kingdom would become stronger than its rivals.

Although the Chinese term for Legalist, *fajia*, literally means "law experts," Legalist thinkers did not advocate rule of law in the modern Western sense. They did not believe in a law that could be used to challenge their rule. Instead, they believed in a law that treated all men equally. Only the systematic application of the law, Legalists felt, could control people, whose essential nature was evil.

The Architect of Qin Success: Shang Yang's Reforms

In 359 B.C.E., a powerful prime minister named Shang Yang initiated a series of reforms to build a strong Legalist state. These are described in a book bearing the name *The Book of Lord Shang*, which was written after his death. Since the seventh century B.C.E., the Qin kingdom had occupied the former homeland the Zhou dynasty abandoned when it moved to Luoyang, but it did not rise up above its rivals until Shang Yang's term in office. His policies strengthened the fiscal basis of the Qin state, enabling it to finance a fighting force far stronger than that of any other contemporary state.

Legalist teachings differed from all other Warring States–period philosophies in their disdain for the past, voiced in this passage from *The Book of Lord Shang*:

> Former generations did not follow the same doctrines, so what antiquity should one imitate? The emperors and kings did not copy one another, so what rites should one follow? . . . As rites and laws were fixed in accordance with what was opportune, regulations and orders were all expedient, and weapons, armor, implements, and equipment were all practical.

This skepticism about the past allowed Legalists to reject all that the Confucians valued, especially ritual, which Legalists viewed as a series of expensive and pointless ceremonies.

Sima Qian's *Records of the Grand Historian* gives a detailed description of the measures Shang Yang took to reorganize the Qin state: "He commanded that the people be divided into tens and fives." The registration of individual households marked the culmination of a trend taking place in other kingdoms of the Warring States period. By abolishing all intermediaries between cultivators and the state, the Legalists extended the earlier attempts of Warring States–period rulers to establish a direct link between subject and ruler.

As part of this reform, Minister Shang established population registers to record who lived together in different households.

> He commanded that . . . they supervise each other and be mutually liable. Anyone who failed to report criminal activity would be chopped in two at the waist, while those who reported it would receive the same reward as that for obtaining the head of an enemy.

The registers listed the members of groups of five and ten who bore mutual responsibility should anyone in their group commit a crime. Once a man reached sixteen or seventeen years of age and a height of

1.5 meters (5 feet), he was obliged to perform military service, fulfill his labor obligations, and pay taxes on his land. Because the Legalists drew no distinction between the army and society, they expected all men to serve in the army.

Minister Shang is credited with establishing private ownership of land. In fact, land continued to be viewed as the property of the ruler, but the link between land ownership and military service provided people with a stronger claim to the land than when they had worked on estates in earlier ages. The institution of the population registers marked a sharp break with the past, with officials keeping detailed records of their subjects for the first time. These registers shaped popular consciousness as well, because many people thought the gods kept a set of parallel registers on which they recorded each person's allotted life span.

"Any family that had more than two adult males who did not divide the household would pay a double military tax," continued Historian Sima Qian. This clause documents the deep antipathy of the Legalists toward cherished Confucian beliefs. Where Confucians advocated that sons live together in harmony with their parents, Legalists required that an extended family break apart into separate households, a trend that may have been occurring anyway.

"Those who had achievements in the army would receive an increase in rank in proportion to their accomplishments." This simple statement represented a startling departure from past practice. The entire population of the Qin state was divided into twenty different ranks, each with its own perquisites in the form of permitted clothing, land, slaves, or housing. All hereditary titles—even those of the royal family—were dropped in favor of this new ranking based strictly on performance. The Legalists did not subscribe to the Confucian belief that only gentlemen should serve as officials or even that one should reward virtue. They felt instead that strict standards of personal achievement should replace subjective judgment and hereditary privilege. In the army, for example, soldiers gained promotions strictly on the basis of how many severed heads they submitted. Those who submitted more heads rose faster than those who submitted fewer heads. "Those who devoted themselves to the fundamental enterprises and through their farming and weaving contributed much grain and cloth would be freed from tax and corvee." Here, the historian Sima Qian summarizes the economic thinking of the Legalists. Because all farmers also served as soldiers, the agricultural sector provided the lifeblood of the state. The farmer-soldiers of the Qin staffed the Qin armies, completed all the public works, and produced the food for everyone in the state. Anyone who did not produce food must, then, play a less important role in society. This rigid blueprint of the economy minimized the importance of merchants and scholars.

"He collected the small district towns together into large counties and established officials for them." Minister Shang Yang divided society into a series of interlocking units, the smallest of which was the groups of five or ten households. These units formed larger units of counties (*xian*), which provided the population with the services of local government. County officials organized the army, carried out public works, collected taxes, and administered justice. The Qin state reached up from the county to the center, and it reached down to the very lowest unit of land, an individual's fields.

"For the fields he opened up the footpaths and set up boundaries." Although the meaning of "opened up" is not clear, it is likely that the Qin eliminated the grid paths through agricultural land. Later historians thought these reforms made the sale of land possible. "He equalized the military levies and land tax and standardized the measures of capacity, weight, and length," continues Sima. The standardizing impulse extended to different measures of weight and length, which varied from place to place.

The Qin first implemented these measures within their own borders, but in 316 B.C.E., the Qin state began a series of conquests that accelerated under the leadership of young King Zheng (259–210 B.C.E.), who came to the throne in 246 B.C.E. at the age of thirteen. In 237 B.C.E., when the king turned twenty-two, he took power into his own hands and led his kingdom through fifteen years of all-out war that culminated in the unification of China in 221 B.C.E.

China's First Emperor

. . . As part of his effort to unify China, the Qin ruler required that the six defeated kings move to his capital accompanied by the noble families of their kingdoms. The title he took, *Shi Huangdi*, literally meant First August Emperor. *Di* ("emperor," "highest deity") contrasted with the word *wang* ("king") that earlier regional rulers, including the founders of the Zhou, had used to refer to themselves.

Once he had assumed his new title, the Qin emperor implemented various policies to shore up his power. He toured his empire five times between 220 and 210 B.C.E., in an effort to show himself to his people and to make offerings to the spirits. In line with Shang Yang's teachings, the First August Emperor emphasized farming as the mainstay of the economy. He unified all measures and imposed a standard currency on the empire. A circular coin with a square in the middle replaced the different monies of the Warring States period, which had taken the shape of knives, shovels, or shells. This new currency had the advantage that it could be threaded together to form strings, which became the major unit of accounting in subsequent periods. In addition to implementing a unified system of units for length and volume, the new dynasty also specified a national standard gauge for vehicles so that roads could be a uniform width and carts could travel freely throughout the empire.

After unifying the empire, the Qin divided all the territory under its control into regional units called commanderies (the initial thirty-six were increased to forty-two), and the commanderies were further subdivided into counties. The administrative structure of the commanderies replicated that of the central government. Governmental functions were divided into three: civil matters having to do with taxation and the registration of the population, military affairs, and the supervision of governmental officials. The top officials in the central government were the chancellor, who headed the bureaucracy; the imperial secretary, who drafted the emperor's orders; and the grand commandant, who was in charge of the military. Similarly, each commandery had three main officials; first, the administrator who collected taxes, updated population registers, and heard legal disputes; next, an oversight official who ensured that the administrator followed all imperial regulations and laws; finally, a commandant who recruited and trained the militia. The law of avoidance, which held that no official could serve in his home area, was already in effect at the time, but clerks were recruited locally.

Perhaps the most striking standardization was that of the script. Scribes in earlier centuries had used Large Seal script to write, and many regional variants of the same character had come into use in the years of the coexisting Warring States. The Qin reformers introduced a new, simpler script called Small Seal script, and they discouraged the use of different variants for the same character. (The Small Seal script they used was largely abandoned in the succeeding dynasty, when it was replaced by the characters in use today.) Because the Qin forbade any writing in regional or popular variants, the rulers ensured that linguistic unity would continue even when the empire was no longer unified. Chinese characters continued to be used without significant change until the introduction of simplified characters after 1949. . . .

The Founding of the Han Dynasty

The absence of peasant uprisings during his reign suggests that the Qin emperor must have enjoyed a measure of popularity with his subjects. As soon as he died and his unpopular second son succeeded him, many of the former regional states broke away once again. The rebels may initially have hoped to restore the emperor's first son to power while leaving the Qin dynasty in place. As the situation at court deteriorated, the rebels, who included both bona fide peasants and low-ranking officials, began to denounce the cruelty of the Qin and to call for the founding of a new dynasty. The rebel who would defeat all his rivals to become the founder of the Han, Liu Bang (reigned 206–195 B.C.E.) was one of only two emperors born into a commoner family. (The other founded the Ming dynasty.) The Grand Historian Sima Qian describes him as a man whose oafish ways antagonized everyone he met, but also as a man whom local innkeepers allowed to drink for free since their receipts unaccountably went up whenever he was around. During the years of the Qin, he passed an examination and won a low-level appointment as a neighborhood head who supervised one thousand households.

As he sought to increase his popular support, Liu Bang attacked the Qin for its brutal laws. When his forces won the decisive battle and entered the Qin capital, he proclaimed an agreement with the assembled leaders of the community:

> You elders have long suffered under the harsh laws of Qin. . . . I make an agreement with you that the law shall consist of only three sections: He who kills others shall die; he who harms others or steals from them shall incur appropriate punishment. For the rest, all other Qin laws should be abolished.

So Liu Bang pledged, but in fact he retained most of the Qin laws. His service as a neighborhood head gave him some experience with the Qin legal system, whose careful procedures must have impressed him. Sima Qian described the early Han legal reforms saying, "When Han arose it lopped off the harsh corners of the Qin code and retreated to an easy roundness, whittled away the embellishments and achieved simplicity." As his comment suggests, the early Han rulers modified rather than eliminated the Qin legal system. They allowed those who had been found guilty to pay fines rather than be subject to stipulated punishments, the most gruesome of which they canceled.

One major departure from Qin policies concerned the treatment of the nobility. Where the Qin emperor had required all the nobility of the vanquished kingdoms to reside in his capital, the Han founder created a new nobility. He gave nine of his brothers and sons the title of king and the lands necessary to sustain them, and named one hundred fifty of his most important followers to the rank of marquis. Two-thirds of his territory remained in the hands of his sons and other relatives. Only one-third of his empire, the crucial western half containing the capital, remained under direct administration. We should remember that the core of the Han-dynasty empire lay in the region around Changan, or the modern city of Xian in the province of Shaanxi, while the coastal areas and much of south China remained backwaters largely populated by non-Chinese peoples.

As with their Qin predecessors, the Han-dynasty government at both the central and local levels had three major divisions: one branch supervised the collection of taxes, one the army, and the third, government officials. The central authorities presided over some one hundred commanderies, which were in turn divided into fifteen hundred counties. Local authorities were in charge of registering the population, collecting taxes, maintaining waterways, and dispensing justice. Local officials also recommended literate men of good character for government positions.

After Liu Bang had defeated his rivals and assumed the title of emperor, he asked prominent Confucians to design new rituals for his court. He hoped to create an aura around himself that would discourage his former drinking companions from being too familiar. Although occasionally willing to take the advice of ritual specialists, the future emperor did not slavishly follow all of Confucius's teachings. At one point in the struggle to gain power, his main rival Xiang Yu (233–202 B.C.E.) captured Liu Bang's father and threatened to boil him alive unless the son surrendered. Liu Bang replied that because he and Xiang Yu had taken an oath of brotherhood, his father was also Xiang Yu's father. As he put it, "My father is your father too. If you insist on boiling your own father, I hope you will be kind enough to send me a cup of the soup." Shockingly to Confucians, he did not allow familial ties, even the all-important bond between parent and child, to interfere with his ambition to rule the empire. (Xiang Yu subsequently adhered to the terms of his oath and freed the father.) . . .

2

SIMA QIAN
The First Emperor

Sima Qian (145–86 B.C.E.) was Grand Historian of China during the Han dynasty. Pursuing the profession of his father, he traveled throughout China collecting historical records and devoted himself to writing the general history of the empire. In 99 B.C.E., he advised the Han emperor Wudi to pardon an unsuccessful general, a request the emperor interpreted as treasonous. Wudi imprisoned Sima Qian and issued a death sentence, which could be commuted only by castration, a fate Sima Qian accepted in order to finish the work his father had inspired. In this selection from the *Historical Records* he recounts how the First Emperor established the Qin dynasty. He also relates the events of the First Emperor's thirty-third and thirty-fourth years.

Source: Sima Qian, *Historical Records*, trans. Raymond Dawson (Oxford: Oxford University Press, 1994), 64–65, 65–66, 75–77.

Our selection begins with King Zheng of Qin's victory over the other kings and princes. King Zheng is faced with the problem of how to control the rival kings, princes, and feudal lords. What solution is proposed by his advisors? In what ways did King Zheng as First Emperor end feudalism (decentralized authorities based on family and personal ties) and create a uniform administration? In what ways were his actions similar to those that were taken in Greece after 500 B.C.E. (according to Aristotle in the reading in Chapter 3)? At the banquet in the thirty-fourth year of his reign, what is the disagreement between the Confucian Chunyu Yue and the Legalist chief minister Li Si?

THINKING HISTORICALLY

How would you describe the role of philosophers, especially Legalists and Confucians, during the reign of the First Emperor? What accounts for the differing influences of the two schools of philosophy? Sima Qian tells us of an effort by the Legalist chief minister Li Si in the First Emperor's thirty-fourth year to nullify the influence of Confucian philosophers. Why did the Legalists oppose Confucian philosophy?

. . . Chief Minister Wang Wan, Imperial Secretary Feng Jie, Superintendent of Trials Li Si, and others all said: "In days of old the territory of the Five Emperors was 1,000 *li*[1] square, and beyond this was the territory of the feudal princes and of the barbarians. Some of the feudal princes came to court and some did not, for the Son of Heaven was unable to exercise control. Now Your Majesty[2] has raised a righteous army to punish the oppressors and bring peace and order to all under Heaven, so that everywhere within the seas has become our provinces and districts and the laws and ordinances have as a result become unified. This is something which has never once existed from remote antiquity onwards, and which the Five Emperors did not attain. Your servants have carefully discussed this with the scholars of broad learning and, as in antiquity there was the Heavenly August, the Earthly August, and the Supreme August, and the Supreme August was the most highly honoured, so your servants, risking death, submit a venerable title, and propose that the King should become "the Supreme August." His commands should be "edicts," his orders should be "decrees," and the Son of Heaven should refer to himself as "the mysterious one." The King said: "Omit the word 'supreme' and write 'august' and pick out the title of 'emperor' used from remote antiquity, so that the title will be 'August Emperor.' The rest shall be as you suggest." And an edict was

---

[1] One *li* is about a third of a mile. [Ed.]
[2] "Son of Heaven" and "Your Majesty" were titles taken by the emperor. [Ed.]

issued saying that it should be done. King Zhuangxiang was to be post-humously honoured as "the Supreme August on High.". . .

The Chief Minister Wang Wan and others said: "The states are newly defeated and the territories of Yan, Qi, and Chu are distant, so if we do not establish kings for them there will be no means of bring-ing order to them. We beg to set up your sons in authority, but it is up to the Supreme One alone to favour us with his agreement." The First Emperor handed down their suggestion to the ministers, and they all thought this would be expedient. But the Superintendent of Trials Li Si advised: "Only after an extremely large number of sons and younger brothers and people of the same surname had been enfeoffed[3] by King Wen and King Wu did they win the adherence of the distant, and then they attacked and smote each other and behaved like enemies. And when the feudal states wrought vengeance on each other more and more, the Zhou Son of Heaven was incapable of preventing them. Now all within the seas has been unified thanks to Your Majesty's divine power, and everywhere has been turned into provinces and districts. And if your sons and the successful officials are richly rewarded from the public revenues, that will be quite sufficient to secure easy control. If there is no dissension throughout the Empire, then this is the technique for securing tranquility. To establish feudal states would not be expedient." The First Emperor said: "It is because of the existence of marquises and kings that all under Heaven has shared in suffering from unceasing hostilities. When, thanks to the ancestral temples, all under Heaven has for the first time been brought to order, if states are reintroduced, this will mean the establishment of armies, and it would surely be difficult to seek peace in those places. The advice of the Superintendent of Trials is right."

So the Empire was divided into thirty-six provinces, and a governor and army commander and an inspector were established for each. The people were renamed "the black-headed people," and there were great celebrations. The weapons from all under Heaven were gathered in and collected together at Xianyang and were melted down to make bells and stands and twelve statues of men made of metal, each 1,000 piculs in weight,[4] to be set up in the courts and palaces. All weights and measures were placed under a unified system, and the axle length of carriages was standardized. For writings they standardized the characters.[5] . . .

---

[3] Placed in a feudal relationship of personal dependence on the king. [Ed.]

[4] A huge weight, since a picul is what a man can carry.

[5] In this version of the reforms the text speaks of the standardization of the script rather than of bureaucratic practice. The standardization of the axle length of carriages may appear bizarre or possibly a concession to numerology, but it may have seemed prudent to have wheel-ruts a standard size, especially in [the soft soil of] loess country.

[The following takes place much later in the reign of the First Emperor.]

In the thirty-third year men who had once absconded, or who were useless sons-in-law, or were traders were sent forth to capture the territory of Luliang. Guilin, Xiang province, and Nanhai were created and convicts were sent to garrison them. In the north-west the Xiongnu were driven back. The area from Yuzhong eastwards along the Yellow River was attached to the Yin Mountains, making forty-four districts, and walls were built along the river as frontier defences. Then Meng Tian was sent across the Yellow River to take Gaoque, Mount Tao, and Beijia. Outposts were built in order to repel the Rong people. And convicts were transported to populate the newly established districts. As a result of a prohibition they could not offer sacrifices. The Morning Star appeared in the west. In the thirty-fourth year judicial officials who had behaved improperly were banished either to build the Great Wall or go to the territory of Southern Yue.

The First Emperor arranged a banquet in the palace at Xianyang, and the seventy scholars of broad learning came into his presence to wish him long life. The Chief Administrator of these scholars, Zhou Qingchen, came forward to offer eulogies, saying: "At another time Qin territory did not exceed 1,000 *li*, but now thanks to Your Majesty's divine power and brilliant sagacity the area within the seas has been restored to order and the barbarian tribes driven off. Wherever the sun and moon shine no one does not offer his submission. The feudal states have been made into provinces and districts, individuals are contented and pleased with themselves, and there is no worry about war and conflict, and this will be handed down for 10,000 generations. Since high antiquity Your Majesty's authority and virtue have not been matched."

The First Emperor was pleased. Then the scholar of broad learning Chunyu Yue, a man of Qi, stepped forward and said: "Your servant has heard that the fact that the Yin and Zhou reigned for more than 1,000 years was because they enfeoffed their sons and younger brothers and successful officials to provide branches and supports for themselves. Now although Your Majesty possesses all within the seas, your sons and younger brothers are private individuals; and ultimately if you have such subordinates as Tian Chang or the six ministers, if there is no one to offer support and assistance, how will you rescue each other? That an enterprise can survive for long if it is not modelled on antiquity is not anything I have heard about. Now Qingchen is also flattering you to your face so as to aggravate Your Majesty's mistakes. This is not behaving like a loyal subject."

When the First Emperor passed down his comments Chief Minister Li Si said: "The Five Emperors did not repeat each other and the Three Dynasties did not copy each other, yet each enjoyed good government. It is not that they were going against each other, but because times change. Now Your Majesty has created a great enterprise and constructed an achievement which will last for 10,000 generations, which is certainly not something which a foolish Confucian would understand. Moreover what Yue is referring to is just the activities of the Three Dynasties, but they are surely not worth being taken as precedents. In other times the feudal lords were in competition with each other to give a generous welcome to itinerant men of learning. But now all under Heaven has been restored to order and the laws and ordinances derive from a single source. The common people at home put their effort into farming and handicrafts, and the public servants on the other hand study the laws and prohibitions. Now all the scholars do not take the present as a model but study antiquity, and thus they reject the present generation and throw the black-headed people into confusion. As chief minister, your servant Li Si speaks out at risk of death: in antiquity all under Heaven was divided and in chaos, and nobody could unify it, and it was for this reason that the feudal lords became active together, and in their utterances all spoke of the past to injure the present, and they made a display of empty verbiage in order to throw the truth into confusion. People approved what they had learnt in private in order to reject what their superiors had laid down. Now the August Emperor has unified and taken possession of all under Heaven. You have distinguished white from black and established a single focus of adulation. But those who have studied privately collaborate with each other to reject the laws and teachings, and when people hear ordinances promulgated everyone criticizes them in accordance with his own studies. Indoors they mentally reject them and outside they make criticisms in the byways. They brag to their sovereign in order to make a reputation. Disagreement they regard as noble, and they encourage all the lower orders to fabricate slander. If such things are not prohibited, then above the sovereign's power will decline, and below factions will form. To prohibit this would be expedient.

"Your servant requests that the records of the historians apart from those of Qin should all be burnt. Apart from those copies which the scholars of broad learning are responsible for in their official capacity, anyone in all under Heaven who dares to possess and hide away the *Songs*, the *Documents*,[6] and the sayings of the hundred schools, should hand them all over to a governor or commandant and they should be indiscriminately burnt. If there is anyone who dares to mention the

---

[6] *Songs* and *Documents* were two of the five Confucian Classics. [Ed.]

Songs or *Documents* in private conversation, he should be executed. Those who, using the old, reject the new will be wiped out together with their clans. Officers who see and become aware of such cases but do not report them should be convicted of the same crime with them. If thirty days after the ordinance has been promulgated the books are not burnt, then the culprit should be branded and sent to do forced labour on the walls. There should be exemption for books concerned with medicine, pharmacy, divination by tortoiseshell and milfoil, the sowing of crops, and the planting of trees. If anyone intends to make a study of the laws and ordinances, he should take the law officers as teachers." This proposal was sanctioned by decree.

3

CONFUCIUS

The Analects

Confucius (551–479 B.C.E.), China's most renowned thinker, was an independent teacher and political advisor in the feudal period that preceded the founding of the Qin Empire. His *Analects*, a collection of sayings or teachings compiled by his students, touch on all of his major concerns: filial piety (or respects of sons for fathers), virtuous conduct, governance by good example, tradition, rites, music, and dance. The teachings of Confucius came to form the bedrock of Chinese culture and have also profoundly influenced the cultures of Japan, Korea, and Vietnam. His ideas, however, were not always popular. In fact, as revealed in the previous selection, the Qin Legalists harshly criticized Confucian ideas and convinced the First Emperor to burn the Confucian Classics. The debate between the Confucians and Legalists continued through the brief Qin dynasty (221–207 B.C.E.) and into the Han dynasty (206 B.C.E.–220 C.E.). As the early efforts at state building were followed by the needs of continuity and long-term maintenance, the Confucians won out. In 140 B.C.E., the Han emperor Wu created a Confucian academy and selected imperial administrators partly on the basis of their knowledge of the Confucian Classics. Confucianism became a kind of state religion under the Han.

Source: *The Analects of Confucius*, trans. Arthur Waley (London: George Allen & Unwin, 1938). Confucius, *The Analects* (New York: A.A. Knopf, Everyman's Library, 2001), 76, 80, 84, 155, 157, 158, 163, 164.

From this brief selection of writings attributed to Confucius, how would you characterize his philosophy? Why might Confucian philosophy displease people who are creating an empire but appeal to those securely in power?

THINKING HISTORICALLY

Confucius was a teacher who believed his ideas might change the world but would not likely be put into practice by intellectuals. How did Confucius imagine his ideas would be put into effect? What kind of person did Confucius want to influence? If you were emperor, how would you institute the ideas of Confucius? How is Confucius both a man of ideas and a man of action? What did Confucius think about the relationship between ideas and action?

On Government by Moral Force

I, 5. The Master [Confucius] said, "A country of a thousand war-chariots cannot be administered unless the ruler attends strictly to business, punctually observes his promises, is economical in expenditure, shows affection toward his subjects in general, and uses the labour of the peasantry only at the proper times of year."

II, 3. The Master said, "Govern the people by regulations, keep order among them by chastisements, and they will flee from you, and lose all self-respect. Govern them by moral force, keep order among them by ritual and they will keep their self-respect and come to you of their own accord."

XII, 11. Duke Ching of Ch'i asked Master K'ung [Confucius] about government. Master K'ung replied saying, "Let the prince be a prince, the minister a minister, the father a father and the son a son." The Duke said, "How true! For indeed when the prince is not a prince, the minister not a minister, the father not a father, the son not a son, one may have a dish of millet in front of one and yet not know if one will live to eat it."

XII, 19. Chi L'ang-tzu asked Master K'ung about government, saying, "Suppose I were to slay those who have not the Way in order to help on those who have the Way, what would you think of it?" Master K'ung replied saying, "You are there to rule, not to slay. If you desire what is good, the people will at once be good. The essence of the gentleman is that of wind; the essence of small people is that of grass. And when a wind passes over the grass, it cannot choose but bend."

XIII, 6. The Master said, "If the ruler himself is upright, all will go well even though he does not give orders. But if he himself is not upright, even though he gives orders, they will not be obeyed."

XIII, 10. The Master said, "If only someone were to make use of me, even for a single year, I could do a great deal; and in three years I could finish off the whole work."

XIII, 11. The Master said, "'Only if the right sort of people had charge of a country for a hundred years would it become really possible to stop cruelty and do away with slaughter.' How true the saying is!"

On Public Opinion

II, 19. Duke Ai asked, "What can I do in order to get the support of the common people?" Master K'ung replied, "If you 'raise up the straight and set them on top of the crooked,' the commoners will support you. But if you raise the crooked and set them on top of the straight, the commoners will not support you."

II, 20. Chi L'ang-tzu asked whether there were any form of encouragement by which he could induce the common people to be respectful and loyal. The Master said, "Approach them with dignity, and they will respect you. Show piety towards your parents and kindness toward your children, and they will be loyal to you. Promote those who are worthy, train those who are incompetent; that is the best form of encouragement."

XII, 7. Tzu-kung asked about government. The Master said, "Sufficient food, sufficient weapons, and the confidence of the common people." Tzu-kung said, "Suppose you had no choice but to dispense with one of these three, which would you forgo?" The Master said, "Weapons." Tzu-kung said, "Suppose you were forced to dispense with one of the two that were left, which would you forgo?" The Master said, "Food. For from of old death has been the lot of all men; but a people that no longer trusts its rulers is lost indeed."

4

HAN FEI

Legalism

Han Fei (280–233 B.C.E.) was the leading philosopher of Legalism during the Qin dynasty. Along with Li Si, the Legalist minister of the Qin (mentioned by Sima Qian), both of whom studied with a leading Confucian scholar of the time, Han Fei turned against Confucian assumptions about human nature and Confucian ideas of governance. A son of a noble family from the enemy state of Han, Han Fei fell

Source: *Sources of Chinese Tradition*, comp. William Theodore de Bary et al. (New York: Columbia University Press, 1963), 1:127–29, 133–35.

under suspicion as an advisor of the Qin king Zheng, who became First Emperor. His rival Li Si had him arrested and poisoned. The following was taken from the *Han Fei Tzu* (*Master Han Fei*), as his collected political essays have become known. What Confucian ideas did Han Fei reject, and what alternatives did he propose? How might Han Fei be a better state builder than Confucius?

THINKING HISTORICALLY

In his life and work, Han Fei challenges some of our expectations about the relationship between ideas and politics. He seems to oppose the efforts of "literati" or other intellectuals to direct governments, and yet he is an intellectual with his own ideas of how it should be done. He prefers laws to "those who practice humanity and righteousness." Are these ideas contradictory? If so, how do you reconcile them? If a ruler thoroughly put Han Fei's ideas into action, what would the Legalist state be like? Compare Han Fei's ideas with the actions of the First Emperor.

A final irony raises another question about the relationship between ideas, intentions, and actions. That irony is that Han Fei wrote for the defense of the Han state against the Qin, but his ideas drew the attention of King Zheng of Qin, who adopted them and then jailed the author. The question is what, if anything, the historian should make of unintended consequences. And to add one more twist: Sima Qian tells us that Han Fei took to writing down his ideas because as a stutterer no king would listen to him. This raises all sorts of questions that cannot be answered: Would the Han king have been more receptive to Han Fei's writing than talking? Would it have mattered if China had been unified by the Han rather than the Qin? Would Legalism have been less of a force if Han Fei had not stuttered?

When the sage rules the state, he does not count on people doing good of themselves, but employs such measures as will keep them from doing any evil. If he counts on people doing good of themselves, there will not be enough such people to be numbered by the tens in the whole country. But if he employs such measures as will keep them from doing evil, then the entire state can be brought up to a uniform standard. Inasmuch as the administrator has to consider the many but disregard the few, he does not busy himself with morals but with laws.

Evidently, if one should have to count on arrows which are straight of themselves, there would not be any arrows in a hundred generations; if one should only count on pieces of wood which are circular of themselves, there would not be any wheels in a thousand generations. Though in a hundred generations there is neither an arrow that is straight of itself nor a wheel that is circular of itself, yet people in every generation ride carts and shoot birds. Why is that? It is because the tools for straightening and bending are used. Though without the use of such tools there might happen to be an arrow straight of itself or a wheel circular of itself, the skilled carpenter will not prize it. Why? Because it is not just one person who wishes to ride, or just one shot that the archers wish to shoot. Similarly, though without the use of rewards and punishments there might happen to be an individual good of himself, the intelligent ruler will not prize him. The reason is that the law of the state must not be sidetracked and government is not for one man. Therefore, the capable prince will not be swayed by occasional virtue, but will pursue a course that will assure certainty. . . .

Now, when witches and priests pray for people, they say: "May you live as long as one thousand and ten thousand years!" Even as the sounds, "one thousand and ten thousand years," are dinning upon one's ears, there is no sign that even a single day has been added to the age of any man. That is the reason why people despise witches and priests. Likewise, when the Confucianists of the present day counsel the rulers they do not discuss the way to bring about order now, but exalt the achievement of good order in the past. They neither study affairs pertaining to law and government nor observe the realities of vice and wickedness, but all exalt the reputed glories of remote antiquity and the achievements of the ancient kings. Sugar-coating their speech, the Confucianists say: "If you listen to our words, you will be able to become the leader of all feudal lords." Such people are but witches and priests among the itinerant counselors, and are not to be accepted by rulers with principles. Therefore, the intelligent ruler upholds solid facts and discards useless frills. He does not speak about deeds of humanity and righteousness, and he does not listen to the words of learned men.

Those who are ignorant about government insistently say: "Win the hearts of the people." If order could be procured by winning the hearts of the people, then even the wise ministers Yi Yin and Kuan Chung would be of no use. For all that the ruler would need to do would be just to listen to the people. Actually, the intelligence of the people is not to be relied upon any more than the mind of a baby. If the baby does not have his head shaved, his sores will recur; if he does not have his boil cut open, his illness will go from bad to worse. However, in order to shave his head or open the boil someone has to hold the baby while the affectionate mother is performing the work, and yet he keeps crying and yelling incessantly. The baby does not understand that suffering a small pain is the way to obtain a great benefit.

Now, the sovereign urges the tillage of land and the cultivation of pastures for the purpose of increasing production for the people, but they think the sovereign is cruel. The sovereign regulates penalties and increases punishments for the purpose of repressing the wicked, but the people think the sovereign is severe. Again, he levies taxes in cash and in grain to fill up the granaries and treasuries in order to relieve famine and provide for the army, but they think the sovereign is greedy. Finally, he insists upon universal military training without personal favoritism, and urges his forces to fight hard in order to take the enemy captive, but the people think the sovereign is violent. These four measures are methods for attaining order and maintaining peace, but the people are too ignorant to appreciate them. . . .

The literati by means of letters upset laws; the cavaliers[1] by means of their prowess transgress prohibitions. Yet the ruler treats them both with decorum. This is actually the cause of all the disorder. Every departure from the law ought to be apprehended, and yet scholars are nevertheless taken into office on account of their literary learning. Again, the transgression of every prohibition ought to be censured, and yet cavaliers are patronized because of their readiness to draw the sword. Thus, those whom the law reproves turn out to be those whom the ruler employs, and those whom the magistrates suppress are those whom the sovereign patronizes. Thus legal standard and personal inclination as well as ruler and ministers are sharply opposed to each other and all fixed standards are lost. Then, even if there were ten Yellow Emperors,[2] they would not be able to establish any order. Therefore, those who practice humanity and righteousness should not be upheld, for if upheld, they would hinder concrete accomplishments. Again, those who specialize in refinement and learning should not be employed, for if employed, they would disturb the laws. There was in Ch'u an upright man named Kung, who, when his father stole a sheep, reported it to the authorities. The magistrate said: "Put him to death," as he thought the man was faithful to the ruler but disloyal to his father. So the man was apprehended and convicted. From this we can see that the faithful subject of the ruler was an outrageous son to his father. Again, there was a man of Lu who followed his ruler to war, fought three battles, and ran away three times. Confucius interrogated him. The man replied: "I have an old father. Should I die, nobody would take care of him." Confucius regarded him as virtuous in filial piety, commended and exalted him. From this we can see that the dutiful son of the father was a rebellious subject to

---

[1] Horse-mounted soldiers, knights. [Ed.]
[2] Legendary Chinese ruler and culture hero. [Ed.]

the ruler. Naturally, following the censure of the honest man by the magistrate, no more culprits in Ch'u were reported to the authorities; and following the reward of the runaway by Confucius, the people of Lu were prone to surrender and run away. The interests of superior and subordinate being so different, it would be hopeless for any ruler to try to exalt the deeds of private individuals and, at the same time, to promote the public welfare of the state. . . .

Today one cannot count even ten men of devotion and faithfulness, yet official posts in the country are counted by the hundreds. If only men of devotion and faithfulness were appointed to office, there would be an insufficiency of candidates, and in that case guardians of order would be few, while disturbers of peace would be many. Therefore the way of the enlightened sovereign consists in making laws uniform and not depending upon the wisdom of men, in making statecraft firm and not yearning after faithful persons, so that the laws do not fail to function and the multitude of officials will commit neither villainy nor deception. . . .

5

LAOZI

Taoism: The Classic of the Way and the Power

The formation of the Chinese Empire in Qin and early Han times centered on the conflict between Confucian and Legalist schools of thought. But there was an earlier Chinese philosophy that resurfaced throughout Chinese history, called Taoism or Daoism.

Laozi (or Lao Tze), meaning Old Master, is the name given to an actual or mythical philosopher said to live at some point between the sixth and fourth centuries B.C.E. This selection of Taoist (or Daoist) writings from what is called the *Tao Te Ching* (or *Daodejing*) — *The Classic of the Way and the Power* — contains some of the writings ascribed to Laozi. Originating perhaps as proverbs, fragments of this larger work have been found in a Chinese tomb dating to 300 B.C.E. But there is little mention of the *Tao Te Ching* before the Han dynasty, when it began to invite the variety of interpretations and legions of devotees

Source: Arthur Waley, *The Way and Its Power: A Study of the* Tao Te Ching *and Its Place in Chinese Thought* (London: Allen & Unwin, 1934), http://home.pages.at/onkellotus/TTK/English_Waley_TTK.html.

that it has charmed over the ages. How would you characterize the philosophy of the *Tao Te Ching*? How would you compare it with that of Confucius and Han Fei?

THINKING HISTORICALLY

The *Tao Te Ching* has been interpreted as both opposing authority and supporting absolute power. How might either of these interpretations be drawn from the text? What would you expect a Taoist emperor to do? Compare the Taoist idea of thoughtless action with the Confucian idea of ritual and the Legalist idea of law.

4

The Way is like an empty vessel
That yet may be drawn from
Without ever needing to be filled.
It is bottomless; the very progenitor of all things in the world.
In it all sharpness is blunted,
All tangles untied,
All glare tempered,
All dust soothed.
It is like a deep pool that never dries.
Was it too the child of something else?
We cannot tell.
But as a substanceless image it existed before the Ancestor.[1]

9

Stretch a bow to the very full,
And you will wish you had stopped in time;
Temper a sword-edge to its very sharpest,
And you will find it soon grows dull.
When bronze and jade fill your hall
It can no longer be guarded.
Wealth and place breed insolence.
That brings ruin in its train.
When your work is done, then withdraw!
Such is Heaven's Way.

---

[1] Before all origins. [Ed.]

11

We put thirty spokes together and call it a wheel;
But it is on the space where there is nothing
That the usefulness of the wheel depends.
We turn clay to make a vessel;
But it is on the space where there is nothing
That the usefulness of the vessel depends.
We pierce doors and windows to make a house;
And it is on these spaces where there is nothing
That the usefulness of the house depends.
Therefore just as we take advantage of what is,
We should recognize the usefulness of what is not.

19

Banish wisdom, discard knowledge,
And the people will be benefited a hundredfold.
Banish human kindness, discard morality,
And the people will be dutiful and compassionate.
Banish skill, discard profit,
And thieves and robbers will disappear.
If when these three things are done they find life too plain and
    unadorned,
Then let them have accessories;
Give them Simplicity to look at, the Uncarved Block to hold,
Give them selflessness and fewness of desires.
Banish learning, and there will be no more grieving.

30

He who by Tao purposes to help a ruler of men
Will oppose all conquest by force of arms;
For such things are wont to rebound.
Where armies are, thorn and brambles grow.
The raising of a great host
Is followed by a year of dearth.
Therefore a good general effects his purpose and then stops; he
    does not take further advantage of his victory.
Fulfills his purpose and does not glory in what he has done;
Fulfills his purpose and does not boast of what he has done;
Fulfills his purpose, but takes no pride in what he has done;
Fulfills his purpose, but only as a step that could not be avoided.
Fulfills his purpose, but without violence;

For what has a time of vigour also has a time of decay.
This is against Tao,
And what is against Tao will soon perish.

46

When there is Tao in the empire
The galloping steeds are turned back to fertilize the ground by their
    droppings.
When there is not Tao in the empire
War horses will be reared even on the sacred mounds below the
    city walls.
(No lure is greater than to possess what others want),
No disaster greater than not to be content with what one has,
No presage of evil greater than men should be wanting to get more.
Truly:
"He who has once known the contentment that comes simply
    through being content,
Will never again be otherwise than contented."

57

"Kingdoms can only be governed if rules are kept;
Battles can only be won if rules are broken."
But the adherence of all under heaven can only be won by
    letting-alone.
How do I know that it is so?
By this.
The more prohibitions there are, the more ritual avoidances,
The poorer the people will be.
The more "sharp weapons" there are,
The more benighted will the whole land grow.
The more cunning craftsmen there are,
The more pernicious contrivances will be invented.
The more laws are promulgated,
The more thieves and bandits there will be.
Therefore a sage has said:
So long as I "do nothing" the people will of themselves be
    transformed.
So long as I love quietude, the people will of themselves go straight.
So long as I act only by inactivity the people will of themselves
    become prosperous.
So long as I have no wants
The people will of themselves return to the "state of the Uncarved
    Block."

66

How did the great rivers and seas get their kingship
Over the hundred lesser streams?
Through the merit of being lower than they;
That was how they got their kingship.
Therefore the Sage
In order to be above the people
Must speak as though he were lower than the people.
In order to guide them
He must put himself behind them.
Only thus can the Sage be on top and the people not be crushed by
    his weight.
Only thus can he guide, and the people not be led into harm
Indeed in this way everything under heaven will into harm be
    pushed by him
And will not find his guidance irksome.
This he does by not striving;
And because he does not strive, none can contend with him.

78

Nothing under heaven is softer or more yielding than water;
But when it attacks things hard and resistant there is not one of
    them that can prevail.
For they can find no way of altering it.

That the yielding conquers the resistant
And the soft conquers the hard is a fact known by all men,
Yet utilized by none.

Yet it is in reference to this that the Sage said
"Only he who has accepted the dirt of the country can be lord of
    its soil shrines;
Only he who takes upon himself the evils of the country
Can become a king among those that dwell under heaven."
Straight words seem crooked.

6

REBECCA FLEMING
Rome: Knowledge and Empire

The Roman Empire did not begin like the Chinese Empire with a
Legalist attack on feudalism; nor did it begin with the replacement
of tribal sovereignty with territorial sovereignty. Rome and most of
the other cities, states, and kingdoms that were integrated into the
Roman Empire had already established state-based systems of territorial sovereignty. Like the Qin, the Roman Empire began in conquest, but the Romans began with the conquest of Greek colonies
and city-states, which already had long traditions of government by
laws, traditions that shaped Roman ideas of government. The lawyers, judges, and politicians who built the Roman Empire were not
trained in Legalist philosophy. The Roman Empire was formed by
lawyers, judges, and politicians who had read Greek philosophy for
generations. Still, the stereotype is that Romans were more practical
thinkers than philosophers — with a few important exceptions, like
the legal thinker Cicero and the Stoic philosopher Marcus Aurelius.
We will turn to them shortly.

   Through historian Rebecca Fleming's article we introduce a different take on the relationship between ideas and actions. Fleming
asks not about how ideas influenced the actions of emperors but
how the existence of the empire itself, and the actions taken to create the empire, changed ideas. According to the author, how did
the existence of empire — at least in the Roman case — change what
the philosophers knew? Further, how did the Roman Empire change
what Romans thought could be known? How did their new model of
knowledge resemble the empire itself?

THINKING HISTORICALLY

Compare Fleming's historical writing with Hansen's in the first selection. Notice Fleming's absence of "So-and-so did such-and-such"
sentences. Whereas Hansen attributes many actions to the ideas of
particular people, Fleming does not do this at all. Her difference in
style has nothing to do with the difference between Roman and Chinese history. It has everything to do with the different questions she
asks. To see this, try to imagine how you might use the information
in this selection if you asked about "the relationship of emperors and
philosophers." This would be practically impossible because despite
the fact that Fleming mentions emperors and philosophers by name,

---

Source: Rebecca Fleming, "Knowledge and Empire," in *Cambridge Illustrated History of the
Roman World*, ed. Greg Woolf (Cambridge: Cambridge University Press, 2003), 234–37.

she is not interested in how thinkers influenced actors. Consequently, she offers no detail about specific exchanges. Rather, she is interested in the more abstract question of how empires affected knowledge. This opens up a different way of thinking about ideas in history—on a scale where individual thoughts and actions are subsumed under larger movements. How might you use the material in this selection to argue the reverse of what Fleming is arguing? That is, without focusing on individual decision makers, how might you argue that a new kind of thinking contributed to the expansion of the Roman Empire?

You might also consider how this way of thinking could be applied to the study of the Chinese empires. For example, do you think the expansion of the Chinese empire would have led to the same sorts of new knowledge that developed in the Roman Empire? What factors in China might have led to either a similar or different result?

As historians of modern European empires have stressed, colonial expansion is intimately bound up with the expansion of knowledge. Knowledge both enables conquest and is produced by it; knowledge is captured along with territories and peoples, and generated in the process of acquiring and establishing domination. Like these other new domains, it too must be ordered and organised, brought into line with the wider systems of imperial rule and productively managed—though these moves may be met with resistance and evasion.

So, in the eighteenth and nineteenth centuries, for instance, disciplines like botany, zoology, ethnography and geography all greatly expanded along with the European empires that needed and sustained them. Empires depended not only on the information these disciplines produced (which facilitated conquest, settlement and the exploitation of colonial resources), but also on their ideological support, on the legitimacy they provided by linking imperial expansion with the expansion of knowledge. In the classical world too, the conquests of Alexander the Great, which extended from Asia Minor and Egypt to the Hindu Kush, led to an explosion in knowledge—about the world, its lands, peoples, plants, animals and minerals; about the human body, diseases and cures; about the structure of the cosmos itself, and more mundane mechanics—and to various moves to systematise that knowledge. The Hellenistic period saw, amongst its multitudinous intellectual developments, the creation of various literary corpora and canons,[1] the solidification of several recognised bodies of knowledge. Many of these

---

[1] Works and standards. [Ed.]

developments were, moreover, promoted and fostered by the ruling dynasties that succeeded Alexander. The most ambitious and expansive patrons were the early Ptolemies, as they strove to make Alexandria the new cultural capital of the now much larger Greek world and not just of their Egyptian empire; but all Hellenistic monarchs gathered at least some men of learning and imagination at their courts, for this kind of patronage became an integral part of their power.

The Roman Empire is no exception to this rule of expanding imperial knowledge. Nonetheless, it is a very particular case, most notably because of the ways in which the specific aims, methods and conditions of Roman empire-building combined to create a rather different set of attitudes to the cultures of the conquered than those that characterised either their Greek predecessors or later European successors. In particular, the long and complex relationship between Greece and Rome . . . had a part to play here. For, as the Romans made increasing military advances across the Hellenistic world, they subjugated people in whose culture they had already, in some senses, invested as the dominant cultural currency of the ancient Mediterranean, and they opened up vistas of knowledge unmatched by Roman traditions of learning. But Rome did, nonetheless, conquer the Greeks, and demonstrated clearly not only military superiority over the defeated but also the moral and religious superiority with which Roman martial prowess was bound up. The question was how would Roman power assert itself over such lofty cultural terrain, and establish a Roman Empire of knowledge alongside its political dominion.

Pompey and Mithridates

The specific conditions of the encounter between Roman power and Greek learning can be seen in an episode from the end of Rome's wars with its great enemy, Mithridates VI Eupator, King of Pontus, a key set of conflicts both in Rome's military conquest of the East and in the development of Roman relations with its cultures. Mithridates was a monarch who, following the examples of Alexander the Great and the successor dynasties, took his role as intellectual patron very seriously. The outstanding botanist Crateuas, amongst others, was associated with his court and the king himself took a direct interest in scientific research: most famously in the field of poisons and their antidotes, but in a number of related areas also. A highly successful military conqueror in his own right, Mithridates collected information and objects from all over his vast realm, and consolidated and organised them around himself like his other dominions—as the great Roman general Pompey discovered after finally defeating him in 63 BC. Amongst the extensive royal booty were treatises on the medicinal properties of plants and on toxicology, together with examples of the plants in question and various other items of natural historical interest, perhaps including a whole zoo.

Pompey, like other Romans, also found Alexander an attractive model, as heroic conqueror and empire builder, and like Alexander he was accompanied on his Eastern campaigns by Greek friends (and freedmen) who would record not just his military achievements, but also the territories traversed, their peoples, flora and fauna. He was, therefore, already committed to the value and importance of his enemy's scientific activities, but no less committed to Roman victory and rule. His response to these discoveries was, therefore, both respectful and assertive. Mithridates's achievements were recognised, but stripped from him and stamped with the mark of Roman (and Pompey's) authority. Pompey ordered his freedman Lenaeus to translate the medical treatises into Latin, and he arranged for a number of the more valuable and spectacular specimens in the collections to be transported to Rome. There, some (for example, a prized ebony tree) were carried in his triumph, some (the more exotic animals) ended up in the arena, and Mithridates's collection of precious stones was deposited on the Capitol. Knowledge had been captured along with the kingdom, its natural resources and plentiful populations; all were now—thanks to Pompey—subject to Roman power. Rome's expanded dominion in all these respects was variously demonstrated: through the encompassing of Greek medical and botanical texts as well as the more public displays of the triumph, games and temple.

By the end of the Mithridatic wars, Rome had acquired a vastly increased amount of Greek knowledge. This knowledge was accumulated in literary form in the libraries of great nobles like Marcus Licinius Lucullus; in the personal form of Greek scholars and teachers—slave, freed and free—who now made the imperial capital their home in much greater numbers; and in the form of more material booty. The encounter between Greek learning and Roman power was accordingly intensified, on both sides. Roman attempts to get to grips with this new intellectual territory became more systematic, as did Greek responses to the redrawn political map of their world.

The Birth of the Roman Encyclopaedia

The first attempt at overall mastery, and Roman recasting, of the Greek learned tradition was made by Marcus Terrentius Varro, the dominant figure in Latin intellectual life at the end of the Republic. A man who pursued a successful political and military career as well as a life of letters, Varro increased the scope of Latin literature in many directions, giving virtually all aspects of Roman life, customs and history a literary manifestation. He was supported in his efforts initially by Pompey, and then by a clement Julius Caesar. In much of this enterprise he was applying Greek methods—of subject definition and structure, research and presentation—to Roman materials, as also had (for all his anti-Greek rhetoric) Cato the Elder in the previous century. Indeed, in writing the treatise *On Agriculture* and in some of his historical ventures, Varro was following very directly in Cato's footsteps; but he went much further, exceeding previous Latin models in many ways, his literary horizons expanding with Rome's imperial boundaries.

A key work, not just of expansion but also of consolidation and organisation, was Varro's nine-book *Disciplinae*, written in the 30s BC. It is now unfortunately lost, but the influence of this endeavour is manifest from the large number of references to it found in the surviving literature. From these it is also possible to reconstruct the overall shape and structure of the work, as well as to recover at least some of the content. The *Disciplinae* aimed to encompass all the disciplines, or arts—that is, recognised bodies of knowledge and skills—that a Roman gentleman ought to master (though not in a professional sense, for it would of course be demeaning for a member of the Roman elite to make a living from any of these arts). But these were accomplishments that not only demonstrated a high degree of cultural formation, as befitted a rising imperial ruling class, but would also prove useful in the general business of being a Roman aristocrat. The disciplines that Varro considered vital in this respect were: grammar, rhetoric and dialectic (that is, roughly, an understanding of language, persuasion and argument), geometry, arithmetic, astronomy and musical theory (the mathematical subjects), and also medicine and architecture. The first seven topics broadly constituted the Greek *enkyklios paideia*, the general education from which more specialised, or advanced, teaching might follow. Medicine and architecture usually came into the more specialist category (and the most characteristic "advanced" subject was philosophy, which Varro largely left to Cicero).

So, while Varro adopted Greek definitions of, and organisational approaches to, the disciplines, his selection of topics and coverage of them all within a single encyclopaedia is distinctive, and Roman as well as Greek sources and traditions provided his material. Indeed, if his extant treatise *On Agriculture* is anything to go by, the net was cast wider than that. For he counts the work of Mago the Carthaginian, originally written in his native Punic but abridged and adapted into Greek, as the most authoritative on the subject (Mago's work had also been translated into Latin). There was, then, a gathering up of useful knowledge, of whatever origin, using Greek models but Roman judgement; and the imposition of a unified order, as in the Empire itself.

CICERO

On Government and Law

Marcus Tullius Cicero (106–43 B.C.E.) was the leading Roman philosopher, orator, and statesman during the turbulent last years of the
Roman Republic. As a lawyer and champion of the Roman constitution,
Cicero fought against tyranny and political corruption, yet he opposed
the assassins of Julius Caesar, and in the subsequent civil war he supported Caesar's adopted son, Octavian, against Mark Anthony, a move
that ultimately cost him his life. Cicero died before Octavian emerged
victorious to declare himself Augustus and replace the republic with the
empire. Despite his support of Octavian, all of Cicero's writings point
toward opposition to the creation of an emperor. Nevertheless, Cicero
happily served a Senate that governed a territorial empire.

Whether we date the end of the republic and the beginning of the
empire from the declaration of Julius Caesar as permanent dictator in
42 B.C.E. or of Octavian as Augustus in 27 B.C.E., much of the Mediterranean world had long since fallen under the control of Roman
armies, laws, administrators, and tax collectors. The territorial empire
preceded the official emperor by at least a hundred years.

In these selections from his *Treatise on the Commonwealth* and his
Treatise on the Laws, Cicero asserts political ideas that have become syn-
onymous with Greco-Roman tradition. What is the value of patriotism
or civic duty for Cicero? What are the advantages and disadvantages
of the three principal kinds of constitutions, according to Cicero, and
what kind of constitution does he propose? Compare Cicero's attitude
toward kings and emperors with his attitude toward empires. What,
according to Cicero, is the difference between natural law and civic law?

How are Cicero's ideas similar to, or different from, classical
Chinese ideas about governance and law? How is the Roman idea
of law that is expressed here different from that of the Chinese
Legalists? How is Cicero's idea of natural law similar to, or different
from, those of Laozi or Confucius?

THINKING HISTORICALLY

Cicero was both a philosopher and a politician. In fact, in addition to
being the most noted philosopher of his age, he also held the republic's highest office, the consulship, in 63 B.C.E. Yet three years later, he

Source: *The Political Works of Marcus Tullius Cicero: Comprising His Treatise on the Commonwealth; and His Treatise on the Laws*, trans. Francis Barham, Esq. (London: Edmund
Spettigue, 1841–42), vol. 1, bks. 1 and 3; vol. 2, bk. 1. The Online Library of Liberty, A project of Liberty Fund, Inc., http://oll.libertyfund.org/title/545/83321 and http://oll.libertyfund.org/
title/546/83295 (accessed August 4, 2009).

declined to join Caesar in an alliance that he feared would bring down the republic. What did Cicero see as the proper relationship between philosophers and political action? Compare his ideas about philosophers and power with those of the Chinese philosophers you have read.

In the previous selection, Fleming pointed out that "knowledge both enables conquest and is produced by it." What knowledge might Cicero have gained by serving as a provincial administrator, lawyer, and then consul of a large empire? What, if any, of Cicero's ideas expressed here would more likely develop in a large empire than in a small kingdom?

Patriotism and Civic Duty

This only I insist on—so great is the necessity of patriotism which nature has implanted in man, so great is the ambition to defend the safety of our country, that its energy has continually overcome all the blandishments of pleasure and repose.

Nor is it sufficient to possess this virtue as an art, unless we reduce it to practice. An art, indeed, though not exercised, may still be retained in knowledge; but all virtue consists in its proper use and action. Now the noblest use of virtue is the government of the Commonwealth, and the realization of all those patriotic theories which are discussed in the schools. For nothing is spoken by philosophers, so far as they speak wisely, which has not been discovered and confirmed by those who established the laws of states. . . .

It is reported of Xenocrates,[1] one of the sublimest philosophers, when someone asked him what his disciples learned, that he replied, "they do that of their own accord, which they might be compelled to do by law." . . .

To virtuous, brave, and magnanimous men, there could be a no better reason for seeking a life in government than this, that we should not be subjected to scoundrels, nor suffer the commonwealth to be distracted by them, lest we should discover, too late, when we desire to save her, that we are without the power. . . .

Monarchy, Aristocracy, and Democracy

Every people . . . must be regulated by a certain authority, in order to be permanent.

---

[1] zen OK rahtees   Greek philosopher and follower of Plato, 396–314 B.C.E. [Ed.]

This intelligent authority should always refer itself to that grand first principle which constituted the Commonwealth. It must be deposited in the hands of one monarch; be entrusted to the administration of certain delegated rulers; or be undertaken by the whole multitude. When the direction of all depends on one monarch, we call this individual a king, and this form of political constitution, a kingdom. When it is in the power of privileged delegates, the state is said to be ruled by an aristocracy; and when the people are all in all, they call it a democracy, or popular constitution. If the tie of social affection, which originally united men in political associations for the sake of public interest, maintains its force, each of these forms of government is, I will not say perfect, nor, in my opinion, essentially good, but tolerable and susceptible of preference. For whether it be a just and wise king, or a selection of the most eminent citizens, or even the mixed populace; (though this is the least commendable) either may, saving the interference of crime and cupidity, form a constitution sufficiently secure.

In a monarchy, the other members of the state are often too much deprived of public counsel and jurisdiction; and under the rule of an aristocracy, the multitude can hardly possess its due share of liberty, since it is allowed no public deliberation or influence. And when all things are carried by a democracy, although it be just and moderate, its very equality is a culpable leveling, since it allows no gradations of dignity. . . .

There is a fourth kind of government, therefore, which, in my opinion is preferable to all these; it is that *mixed and moderated government,* which is composed of the three particular forms I have before noticed. . . .

I wish to establish in a Commonwealth, a royal and preeminent chief. Another portion of power should be deposited in the hands of the aristocracy, and certain things should be reserved to the judgment and wish of the multitude. This mixed constitution, in the first place, possesses that great equality, without which men cannot long maintain their freedom,—and it offers a great stability, unlike the particular separate and isolated forms, which easily fall into their contraries; so that a king is succeeded by a despot,—an aristocracy by a faction,—a democracy by a mob and a hubbub; and all these forms are frequently sacrificed to new revolutions. In this *united and mixed constitution,* however, which I take the liberty of recommending, similar disasters cannot happen without the greatest vices in public men. For there can be little to occasion revolution in a state, in which every person is firmly established in his appropriate rank, and there are but few modes of corruption into which he can fall. . . .

Philosophers and Politicians

There exists this general difference between these two classes of great men, namely philosophers and politicians, that among the former, the development of the principles of nature is the subject of their study and eloquence; and among the latter, national laws and institutions form the principal topics of investigation.

In honor of our country we may assert that she has produced within herself a great number, I will not say, of sages, (since philosophy is so jealous of this name) but of men worthy of the highest celebrity, because by them the precepts and discoveries of the sages have been carried out into actual practice.

If you consider that there have existed and still exist, many great and glorious empires, and if you acknowledge that the noblest master-piece of genius in the world is the establishment of a durable state and commonwealth, reckoning but a single legislator for each empire, the number of these political legislators will appear very numerous. To be convinced of this, we have only to turn our eyes on Italy, Latium, the Sabines, the Volscians, the Samnites, the Etrurians, and then direct our attention to the Greeks, Assyrians, Persians, and Carthaginians.[2] . . .

Natural Law and Civil Law

What nation is there, in which kindness, benignity, gratitude, and mindfulness of benefits are not recommended? What nation in which arrogance, malice, cruelty, and unthankfulness, are not reprobated and detested! This uniformity of opinions, invincibly demonstrates that mankind was intended to compose one fraternal association. And to affect this, the faculty of reason must be improved till it instructs us in all the arts of well-living. . . .

It follows, then, in the line of our argument, *that nature made us just that we might participate our goods with each other, and supply each others' wants.* You observe in this discussion whenever I speak of nature, I mean *nature in its genuine purity*, and not in the corrupt state which is displayed by the depravity of evil custom, which is so great, that the natural and innate flame of virtue is often almost extinguished and stifled by the antagonist vices, which are accumulated around it. . . .

It is therefore an absurd extravagance in some philosophers to assert that all things are necessarily just, which are established by the civil laws and the institutions of the people. Are then the laws of tyrants just, simply because they are laws? If the thirty tyrants of Athens imposed certain laws on the Athenians, and if these Athenians were delighted with these tyrannical laws, are we therefore bound to consider these laws as just? For my own part, I do not think such laws deserve any greater estimation

---

[2] Cicero argues that the existence of many great empires is proof that there have been many great empire makers (legislators): five in Italy alone, in addition to the others mentioned. [Ed.]

than that passed during our own interregnum, which ordained, that the dictator should be empowered to put to death with impunity, whatever citizens he pleased, without hearing them in their own defense. . . .

If the will of the people, the decrees of the senate, the adjudications of magistrates, were sufficient to establish justice, the only question would be how to gain suffrages, and to win over the votes of the majority, in order that corruption and spoliation, and the falsification of wills, should become lawful. But if the opinions and suffrages of foolish men had sufficient weight to outbalance the nature of things, might they not determine among them, that what is essentially bad and pernicious should henceforth pass for good and beneficial? Or why should not a law able to enforce injustice, take the place of equity? Would not this same law be able to change evil into good, and good into evil?

As far as we are concerned, we have no other rule capable of distinguishing between a good or a bad law, than our natural conscience and reason. These, however, enable us to separate justice from injustice, and to discriminate between the honest and the scandalous. For common sense has impressed in our minds the first principles of things, and has given us a general acquaintance with them, by which we connect with Virtue every honorable and excellent quality, and with Vice all that is abominable and disgraceful.

8

MARCUS AURELIUS
Meditations

Marcus Aurelius (121–180 C.E.) was both a Roman emperor (161–180 C.E.) and a philosopher. In fact, he is ranked highly in both areas. He is numbered the last of the "five good emperors," a line of emperors that began in 96 C.E. and included Trajan (see selection 2 in Chapter 7) and Hadrian. According to the great historian Edward Gibbon, this was an era in which "the Roman Empire was governed by absolute power, under the guidance of wisdom and virtue."[1]

[1] Edward Gibbon, *The Decline and Fall of the Roman Empire* (New York: Everyman's Library, 1993), vol. 1, chap. 3, p. 90.

Source: Marcus Aurelius, *Meditations*, trans. George Long, bk. 2, *The Internet Classics Archive*, http://classics.mit.edu/Antoninus/meditations.2.two.html.

Although much of his reign was taken up with wars, Marcus Aurelius also initiated legal reform on behalf of slaves, minors, and widows. As a philosopher, he was an adherent of Stoicism, a set of beliefs aptly summarized in this selection from his *Meditations*, written about 167 C.E. Stoicism originated in Greece in the third century B.C.E. Stoics believed that negative emotions were the result of poor judgment and that wisdom made one immune to pain or misfortune. Compare these ideas to Chinese Taoism or Confucianism. Compare the ways these philosophies functioned politically in the two empires.

THINKING HISTORICALLY

The *Meditations* is full of personal injunctions in which the emperor tells himself how he should act. In keeping with his Stoic convictions, Marcus Aurelius calls for the mind to regulate the body. Thus it would seem he meant to lead a very controlled and contemplative life. And yet, to be the emperor was to be the most important actor in the Roman world. Were contradictions inevitable? The historian Dio Cassius tells us that Marcus Aurelius treated his enemies humanely, but the historian also relates stories of the emperor's desire to exterminate an entire enemy people. Sculptural reliefs show the emperor both granting clemency and supervising the execution of conquered German prisoners. How might Marcus Aurelius have reconciled his ideas and his actions to produce such varying results? What advice to an emperor would follow from the ideas in the *Meditations*?

The years after 165 C.E. were particularly difficult for the emperor and the empire. Roman forces had just defeated the Parthian army, only to return to their homes with a pandemic disease (possibly smallpox or measles) that lasted until about 180 C.E., claiming the lives of as many as five million people, including Marcus's co-emperor and eventually Marcus Aurelius himself. How might these events have influenced the emperor's philosophy as recorded in the *Meditations*?

Begin the morning by saying to thyself, I shall meet with the busybody, the ungrateful, arrogant, deceitful, envious, unsocial. All these things happen to them by reason of their ignorance of what is good and evil. But I who have seen the nature of the good that it is beautiful, and of the bad that it is ugly, and the nature of him who does wrong, that it is akin to me, not only of the same blood or seed, but that it participates in the same intelligence and the same portion of the divinity, I can neither be injured by any of them, for no one can fix on me what is ugly, nor can I be angry with my kinsman, nor hate him, for we are made for co-operation, like feet, like hands, like eyelids, like the rows of the upper and lower teeth. To act against one another then is contrary to nature; and it is acting against one another to be vexed and to turn away.

Whatever this is that I am, it is a little flesh and breath, and the ruling part. Throw away thy books; no longer distract thyself: it is not allowed; but as if thou wast now dying, despise the flesh; it is blood and bones and a network, a contexture of nerves, veins, and arteries. See the breath also, what kind of a thing it is, air, and not always the same, but every moment sent out and again sucked in. The third then is the ruling part: consider thus: Thou art an old man; no longer let this be a slave, no longer be pulled by the strings like a puppet to unsocial movements, no longer either be dissatisfied with thy present lot, or shrink from the future. . . .

Every moment think steadily as a Roman and a man to do what thou hast in hand with perfect and simple dignity, and feeling of affection, and freedom, and justice; and to give thyself relief from all other thoughts. And thou wilt give thyself relief, if thou doest every act of thy life as if it were the last, laying aside all carelessness and passionate aversion from the commands of reason, and all hypocrisy, and self-love, and discontent with the portion which has been given to thee. Thou seest how few the things are, the which if a man lays hold of, he is able to live a life which flows in quiet, and is like the existence of the gods; for the gods on their part will require nothing more from him who observes these things.

Do wrong to thyself, do wrong to thyself, my soul; but thou wilt no longer have the opportunity of honoring thyself. Every man's life is sufficient. But thine is nearly finished, though thy soul reverences not itself but places thy felicity in the souls of others. . . .

How quickly all things disappear, in the universe the bodies themselves, but in time the remembrance of them; what is the nature of all sensible things, and particularly those which attract with the bait of pleasure or terrify by pain, or are noised abroad by vapoury fame; how worthless, and contemptible, and sordid, and perishable, and dead they are. . . .

Though thou shouldst be going to live three thousand years, and as many times ten thousand years, still remember that no man loses any other life than this which he now lives, nor lives any other than this which he now loses. The longest and shortest are thus brought to the same. For the present is the same to all, though that which perishes is not the same; and so that which is lost appears to be a mere moment. For a man cannot lose either the past or the future: for what a man has not, how can anyone take this from him? These two things then thou must bear in mind; the one, that all things from eternity are of like forms and come round in a circle, and that it makes no difference whether a man shall see the same things during a hundred years or two hundred, or an infinite time; and the second, that the longest liver and he who will die soonest lose just the same. For the present is the only thing of which a man can be deprived, if it is true that this is the only thing which he has, and that a man cannot lose a thing if he has it not. . . .

The soul of man does violence to itself, first of all, when it becomes an abscess and, as it were, a tumour on the universe, so far as it can. For to be vexed at anything which happens is a separation of ourselves from nature, in some part of which the natures of all other things are contained. In the next place, the soul does violence to itself when it turns away from any man, or even moves towards him with the intention of injuring, such as are the souls of those who are angry. In the third place, the soul does violence to itself when it is overpowered by pleasure or by pain. Fourthly, when it plays a part, and does or says anything insincerely and untruly. Fifthly, when it allows any act of its own and any movement to be without an aim, and does anything thoughtlessly and without considering what it is, it being right that even the smallest things be done with reference to an end; and the end of rational animals is to follow the reason and the law of the most ancient city and polity.

Of human life the time is a point, and the substance is in a flux, and the perception dull, and the composition of the whole body subject to putrefaction, and the soul a whirl, and fortune hard to divine, and fame a thing devoid of judgment. And, to say all in a word, everything which belongs to the body is a stream, and what belongs to the soul is a dream and vapor, and life is a warfare and a stranger's sojourn, and after-fame is oblivion. What then is that which is able to conduct a man? One thing and only one, philosophy. But this consists in keeping the daemon[2] within a man free from violence and unharmed, superior to pains and pleasures, doing nothing without purpose, nor yet falsely and with hypocrisy, not feeling the need of another man's doing or not doing anything; and besides, accepting all that happens, and all that is allotted, as coming from thence, wherever it is, from whence he himself came; and, finally, waiting for death with a cheerful mind, as being nothing else than a dissolution of the elements of which every living being is compounded. But if there is no harm to the elements themselves in each continually changing into another, why should a man have any apprehension about the change and dissolution of all the elements? For it is according to nature, and nothing is evil which is according to nature.

[2] Spirit. [Ed.]

■ REFLECTIONS

Legalism, Confucianism, Taoism, and Stoicism are very different philosophies. We have noticed some similarities between Taoism and Stoicism, and we could also find similarities between Chinese Legalism and Roman emphasis on law. But all of these philosophies, those modeled on nature and those stressing law, have a common element that might have been new in the age of empires. That element is their universality. Empires invariably expanded the range of human awareness from the local to the general. The Chinese emperor fashioned himself the Son of Heaven, his realm the center of the world. Similarly, Roman emperors imagined that they governed the entire civilized world. If all under heaven was to conform to the will of a single ruler, there had to be rules or reasons that governed all peoples regardless of their local deities, myths, and customs. Nature herself provided one model of a system that encompassed the entire world. Both Taoists and Stoics found comfort in the sure rhythms of nature. Both confronted the discrepancies between the ways of nature and the actions of men.

This was the age, after the second century B.C.E., of the Silk Roads that connected the Chinese and Roman empires by way of Central Asia and India. Chinese Buddhists traveled to India to find the roots of their faith and brought back caravans of sacred scrolls. Hoards of Roman coins have been found in southern India, once traded in exchange for Indian spices. Roman senators complained that the cost of fashionable Chinese silks was draining the Roman treasury. People knew they were living in a world that extended beyond even their empire. In an age of empires and global trade routes, the import and export of universal philosophies, viable for all peoples, challenged and sometimes influenced local beliefs, folk customs, and provincial cultures.

Does this mean that ideas follow actions more than they cause them? It would be hard to find a way of measuring that. Individuals certainly experience the feeling of acting according to their ideas. In retrospect, some ideas might seem to owe much to events, particularly the larger events like devastating plagues or globalization. The big philosophical and religious systems may develop to fit particular social systems, but they are still voiced and put into action by particular individuals.

Historians have long debated the primacy of ideas versus actions. This is not the place to hazard an answer to an eternal debate. In some ways, one's position depends on one's view of individual capacity, or people's power to realize their ideas and dreams. Most of the philosophies we have studied here took a dim view of human capacity. Neither Confucians nor Legalists placed any faith in the actions of untutored or undirected individuals. Stoics demanded an almost superhuman willpower, but for resignation to existing situations. Only the Taoists imagined that the world would flow smoothly if people were left to their own devices, without guiding ideas. The people would prosper, Laozi thought, if only they could "banish wisdom, discard knowledge." He likely meant the seemingly useless knowledge of Confucian bureaucrats and sages, but he proposes no alternative beyond "actionless activity."

We live in an age that places greater hope in the power of ideas and human capacity. Ours is also an age more suspicious of imperial politics but more eager to universalize our truths. Though none of us has the influence of a Confucius or the power of a Marcus Aurelius, collectively we can influence our governments more directly than the subjects of ancient empires. In a democratic society it is even a responsibility.

5

Gender, Sex, and Love in Classical Societies

India, China, and the Mediterranean, 500 B.C.E.–500 C.E.

■ HISTORICAL CONTEXT

In the first chapter we saw how male-dominated societies or patriarchies developed, or at the very least strengthened and consolidated, in the wake of plow agriculture, irrigation, and city and state building, beginning about five thousand years ago. In some areas of the world—the Americas, sub-Saharan Africa, and Southeast Asia—patriarchies emerged later or remained less vigorous. Between 500 B.C.E. and 500 C.E. patriarchies flourished in the core areas of early city-societies or "civilizations" in the Mediterranean, India, and China. Historians call this period "classical" because it witnessed the florescence of a number of cultural traditions that are still honored as formative, among them Confucianism, Buddhism, Christianity, and Greco-Roman philosophy. The last chapter illuminated the importance of such philosophical traditions as Confucianism, Taoism, Legalism, and Stoicism in the period. The next chapter will explore the impact of the great religious traditions of Hinduism, Buddhism, Judaism, and Christianity—all of which were founded or took recognizable form in this period.

This chapter asks about the relationships of men and women in this age of cultural flowering and increasing gender discrimination. What did it mean to be a man or a woman in the classical era? What was the impact of these classical traditions on gender identity? How was being a woman or a man different, and how was it similar, across these classical civilizations? Was it also the classical formative period of our own identities, ideas, and feelings? Or was it ancient history?

164

■ THINKING HISTORICALLY

Asking about Author, Audience, and Agenda

Historical sources, from the simplest laundry list to the most sophisticated work of art, are made by someone for someone to serve a
particular purpose. In other words, each has an author, an audience,
and an agenda. The better we understand who created a source, its
intended reader or viewer, and the reasons it was created, the better we
can make sense of the source and the society or culture in which it was
produced. In many cases much of this information is not available to
us, at least not in the detail we would like. But there are often clues in
the source itself that enable us to determine the author, audience, and
agenda. In this chapter we will interrogate the sources themselves to
find this information.

1

SARAH SHAVER HUGHES AND BRADY HUGHES

Women in the Classical Era

Sarah and Brady Hughes are modern historians. This selection is part
of their essay on the history of women in the ancient world written for
a book on the history of women. They write here of the classical era
in India, China, Greece, and Rome. All of these were patriarchal societies, but how were they different? The authors also mention Greek
Hellenistic society and pre-Roman Etruscan society. How do these two
societies round out your understanding of women between 500 B.C.E.
and 500 C.E.? What seem to be the conditions or causes that
improved the status of women in some societies and in some periods?

THINKING HISTORICALLY

The authors, audience, and agenda in this selection are fairly
transparent because it is a secondary source written by modern
historians. The authors do not reveal anything of themselves, but
their writing is matter-of-fact and dispassionate and shows an effort

Source: Sarah Shaver Hughes and Brady Hughes, "Women in Ancient Civilizations," in
Women's History in Global Perspective, ed. Bonnie G. Smith (Urbana: University of Illinois
Press, published with the American Historical Association, 2005), 2:26–30, 36–39.

to be thorough. All of this is appropriate in an informative essay written for a college-level audience. Note that this essay is part of a book published with the American Historical Association, the national organization of history teachers and scholars. The original essay carried a considerable number of footnotes (68 notes for a 35-page article), and it lacked the pronunciation and explanatory notes included with this reprinting. Does this suggest a work aimed at scholars, teachers, or students? Does the essay argue a point of scholarship, or does it summarize the scholarly work of others? What other clues in the reading indicate the intended audience and the purpose or agenda of the article?

India

... Women's rights deteriorated after the Vedic* period (1600–800 B.C.E.). No one has been able to prove why this happened. Scholarly interest has focused on women's exclusion from performing Hindu rituals, which was in effect by 500 B.C.E. . . . Julia Leslie[1] thinks that women's exclusion resulted from intentional mistranslation of the Vedas[2] by male scholars, as the rituals became more complicated and as the requirement for property ownership was more rigorously enforced at a time when women could not own property.

The falling age of marriage for Indian women is another illustration of their loss of rights. In 400 B.C.E. about sixteen years was a normal age for a bride at marriage; between 400 B.C.E. and 100 C.E. it fell to pre-puberty; and after 100 C.E. pre-puberty was favored. These child marriages also affected women's religious roles. Because girls married before they could finish their education, they were not qualified to perform ritual sacrifices. Furthermore, wives' legal rights eroded. As child wives, they were treated as minors. Then their minority status lengthened until they were lifetime minors as wards of their husbands. Finally, women were prohibited any independence and were always under men's control: their fathers, husbands, or sons. By 100 C.E. Hindu texts defined women with negative characteristics, stating, for example, that women would be promiscuous unless controlled by male relatives. While Indian women were losing their independence, Indian men continued to glorify

---

*VAY dihk

[1] Leslie, "Essence and Existence: Women and Religion in Ancient Indian Text," in *Women's Religious Experience*, ed. Pat Holden (Totawa: Barnes and Noble Books, 1983). Dr. Isobel Julia Leslie (1948–2004), philosopher, historian, and novelist of Indian culture, wrote widely on women in India. [Ed.]

[2] The Vedas (see Chapter 3) were the writings of ancient Indian Hinduism, usually dated as above between 1600 and 800 B.C.E. in origins, though extant texts were written later. [Ed.]

their wives and mothers. A wife was the essence of the home, a man was not complete without a wife, and sons were expected to respect their mothers more than their fathers. As Romila Thapar sums up these contradictions, "The symbol of the woman in Indian culture has been a curious intermeshing of low legal status, ritual contempt, sophisticated sexual partnership, and deification."

One of the causes for this deterioration of women's rights and independence was the increasing rigidity of Hinduism under the influence of the Brahmans.[3] By 600 B.C.E. sects were springing up that opposed Brahman power and ostentatiously omitted some of the Hindu essentials, such as priests, rituals and ceremonies, animal sacrifices, and even caste distinctions.[4] Jainism and Buddhism are two of the sects that have survived. They were especially attractive to women. Jainism, the older religion, gained prominence with the efforts of its last prophet, Mahavira, who lived at the end of the sixth century B.C.E. Jains sought to live without passion and to act "correctly." One could achieve liberation only by living within a monastery or nunnery. Women who sought to join a nunnery found that the Jains had no membership restrictions. Many women entered and found new and exciting roles that were for the first time open to them. . . .

Mahavira's contemporary, Gautama Siddhartha* (the Buddha), began the religion that eventually spread throughout Asia. Among studies of Buddhist women, the early years have been a focus of interest. While Buddhism had no priests, it relied on celibate monks, who were initially homeless, except in the monsoon season, and had to beg for their necessities as they spread their ideas. The Buddha was reluctant to allow women to become nuns. He refused even the women in his family who sought to become nuns until he was reminded repeatedly by his aunt and his disciple Ananda of his stated principle that anyone could attain enlightenment. The Buddha then reluctantly accepted women followers, and they, like monks, eventually lived in their own self-governing celibate monasteries. . . .

China

. . . For Chinese women the ideas of Confucius (551–479 B.C.E.) have been most influential. There is little mention of women in his *Analects*. His neo-Confucian interpreters corrected this omission, however. They made explicit men's desire for a woman's subordination to her family, her husband, and her sons. For example, Lieh Nu Chuan (also known

---

*GAW tah moh   sih DAHR thah

[3] Brahmans were priests of the Hindu religion. Because the Vedas enshrined priests as the highest caste, early Hinduism is sometimes called Brahminism. *Brahman* is also used to mean the totality of the divine (God). [Ed.]

[4] Some of these "Hindu essentials" may have actually become Hindu essentials in the Brahman encounter with Buddhism and Jainism after 600 B.C.E. [Ed.]

as Liu Hsiang, 80–87 B.C.E.) wrote *The Biographies of Eminent Chinese Women*, in which he included 125 biographies of women from the peasant class to the emperor's wife, taken from prehistoric legends to the early years of the Han dynasty.

Although the purpose of these biographical sketches was to provide moral instruction in the passive ideals of Confucian womanhood, translator Albert Richard O'Hara's analysis of the women's actions reveals their influence on events that were important to them. The traditional Chinese interpretation of the genre is evident in one of the best known biographies, that of the widowed mother of Mencius (Meng K'o, or Meng-tzu), whose stern supervision and self-sacrifice were shown to have shaped her son's character and philosophy. This tale drives home the point that a woman's highest ambitions should be fulfilled indirectly through the talents of her sons. Pan Chao,[5] a female scholar in the first century C.E., wrote *The Seven Feminine Virtues* as a Confucian manual for girls' behavior. Its prescriptions of humility, meekness, modesty, and hard work continued to be copied by generations of young women until the twentieth century. . . .

Occasionally, imperial women seized power to govern when acting as regent for an underage emperor. Usually regents exercised this power cautiously behind the scenes because there was much opposition to women's open governance. Two famous empresses ruled openly, however, and sought to transfer royal descent to their own natal families. The first, Empress Lu, violated every canon of Confucian femininity. The widow of Gaodi, the first Han emperor (ruled 202–195 B.C.E.), Empress Lu acted swiftly and brutally to eliminate competitors at court during the near-fifteen years of her rule as regent for her son, her grandson, and another adopted infant grandson. By retaining power until her death in 181 B.C.E., she expected that her own nephews would succeed her. Instead, a civil war over the succession ended the period of peaceful prosperity, low taxes, and lessened punishment for crimes that had made her reign popular with the Chinese people. . . .

Greece

Classical Greece has long been admired for its political theories, philosophy, science, and the arts. Until recently, Greek social history was largely ignored. Slavery, homosexuality, and subordination of women are topics once dismissed as insignificant but now recognized as important to understanding the culture. In the classical period there were actually many "Greeces," with distinct societies developing in the citystates of Athens, Sparta, and Thebes. Gender patterns varied considerably among these cities. Sparta's aristocratic women, for example, were often left alone to acquire wealth

---

[5] Ban Zhao in selection 2 in this chapter. [Ed.]

and some autonomy when their mercenary husbands soldiered elsewhere. To some Athenian men such as Aristotle, Spartan women were thought to be despicable, licentious, greedy, and the reason for Sparta's decline.

Aristotle and other Athenian men dominate the discourse from classical Greece. Their male descriptions tell how Athenian society secluded elite women, denigrated and exploited them, and made them the legal dependents of men. Because no women's writings survive, only indirect evidence suggests how Athenian wives escaped their lives of hard work in the isolated, dark rooms that their husbands imagined necessary to preserve their chastity. But as drawn on vases, groups of Athenian women read to one another, spun and wove, shared child care, or talked. Women are shown in public processions and getting water from wells. Bits of documentary records show respectable married women earning their livings as wet nurses, farm workers, and retail vendors. Most records reveal the lives of privileged women, yet many Athenian women were slaves. Exposure of unwanted female babies was one internal source of slaves, for the rescuer of such an infant became her owner. Athenian enslavement of females was exceptional in its celebration of prostitution in literary and artistic records. One explanation for the large number of slave sex workers may be the Athenians' desire to attract sailors and merchants to their port.

Research on women in the Hellenistic period concentrates on Greek women living in Egypt. These women were much more assertive and influential than their sisters in either contemporary Greece or later Rome. Women in the ruling Ptolemaic[6] family often actually ruled Egypt, some as regents, others as queens. Cleopatra VII (69–30 B.C.E.), one of the best-known women in ancient history, guided her country from a tributary position in the Roman Empire into a partnership with Marc Antony that might have led to Egypt's domination of the eastern Mediterranean. Non-elite women had unusual freedom. They owned property (including land), participated in commerce, produced textiles, were educated, and enjoyed careers as artists, poets, and farmers. But some women were slaves. . . .

Rome

As late as the sixth century B.C.E., Rome was dominated by its northern neighbors, the Etruscans. Although no body of Etruscan literature exists, scholars have sought evidence of women's lives from inscriptions and art found in their tombs. Upper-class Etruscan women were more autonomous and privileged than contemporary Greek women. Paintings of husbands

---

[6] The ruling family of Egypt, descended from Alexander the Great's general, Ptolemy, who took power in 323 B.C.E. The Ptolemies ruled for three hundred years until the Roman conquest. The last of the Ptolemies was Cleopatra VII, who ruled briefly with Marc Antony but was conquered by Octavian in 30 B.C.E. and committed suicide. [Ed.]

and wives feasting together horrified Greek males, who only allowed prostitutes to attend their banquets. Etruscan women were not restricted to their homes as Greek women were and attended the games at gymnasiums. In Italy, all women left votive statues of women in sacred places, probably as a fertility offering, but only Etruscan statues included a nursing child, suggesting an affection for children that paralleled the affectionate touching between couples occasionally shown in their art. Finally, Etruscan women had personal names, in contrast to Greek women, who were known first as their fathers' daughters and later as their husbands' wives.

The Romans did not duplicate the autonomy of women in Etruscan society. Roman women legally were constrained within a highly patriarchal agricultural system organized around clans. A father could kill or sell his children into slavery without fear of legal action. Husbands could kill their wives if they were caught in adultery. Women did not speak in public meetings. They could not buy and sell property without their male relatives' approval. Legally treated as minors, women were first the responsibility of their fathers, then of their husbands, and finally of appointed guardians. Rome was a warrior society and a male republic. Men even dominated the state religion, with the exception of the six Vestal Virgins who served as priestesses. Roman society remained staunchly male until conquests brought wealth to Italy in the second century B.C.E. Changes that accompanied the booty of empire gave women a measure of economic and marital independence that is illustrated by the loosening of legal restrictions against women's property ownership.

The paterfamilias, the oldest male in the family, had complete *manus* (legal control) over his children. In marriage, manus passed from the paterfamilias to the new husband. Among other things, that meant the husband then controlled all of his wife's property. Before the first century B.C.E. some Roman marriages were made without transferring manus to the husband; the wife and her property would remain under her father's control, whose approval was theoretically required for the daughter to buy or sell property. Susan Treggiari explains how this enabled many women to gain control over their property:

> Given ancient expectation of life, it is probable that many women were fatherless for a relatively long period of their married lives. The pattern . . . for the middle ranks of Roman society is that girls married in their late teens and men in their mid- to late twenties. If expectation of life at birth is put between twenty and thirty, then 46 percent of fifteen-year-olds had no father left alive. The percentage grows to 59 percent of twenty-year-olds and 70 percent of twenty-five-year-olds. So there is about a 50 percent chance that a woman was already fatherless at the time of her first marriage.

Upon a father's death, manus was transferred to a guardian, and women began to choose as their guardians men who agreed with them.

By the later years of the Roman Republic, therefore, many women bought and sold land as they pleased. Rome's expansion contributed to this change as it fueled a growing market in real and personal property.

In the third century B.C.E., Rome began two centuries of conquests that eventually placed most of the land surrounding the Mediterranean under Roman administration or in the hands of client states. Roman wives farmed while citizen-soldiers of the Republic were on campaigns, sometimes for more than a decade. Successful wars enriched a Roman elite who accumulated estates worked by male and female slaves as small farmers sold their lands and moved to the city with their wives and children. Elite Romans, both men and women, possessed large estates, luxurious urban houses, much rental property, and many slaves. By 50 B.C.E., Rome had a population of approximately one million. Slaves poured into Italy after successful campaigns, when the defeated enemy was enslaved. As the Romans conquered country after country, they brutalized the captured women, enslaving many. Ruling queens in subdued countries were inevitably replaced with either indigenous male elites or Roman officials. Queen Boudicca of Britain, for example, led a revolt that ended in her death in the first century C.E. Queen Zenobia of Palmyra's invasion of the empire in the third century C.E. was so well organized that Roman authors praised her. Cleopatra of Egypt committed suicide when her plan to make Egypt a regional partner of Rome failed.

Roman women did not publicly speak in the Forum (where men debated civic affairs), with the notable exception of Hortensia in 43 B.C.E. She was the spokesperson for a demonstration of wealthy women who protested taxation without representation for civil wars they did not support. Elite women usually indirectly influenced political decisions through networks of politicians' wives. During the civil wars of the first century B.C.E., wives of some tyrants even made temporary political decisions. On a wider scale, middle-class and elite women took advantage of the turmoil at the end of the Republic[7] to acquire businesses, as analysis of Pompeii[8] shows. Prostitution flowered in Rome with the inflow of slaves, both male and female. A small part of the elite lived in the self-indulgent luxury that became famous in literature. In a brief period of two generations at the end of the first century B.C.E., Roman elite women eschewed children and family responsibilities for a glamorous and self-absorbed life of parties and lovers. In this period men and women were openly adulterous. This "café society" flourished in the chaos of civil wars that nearly destroyed the prestige of the elite and killed or exiled many of them.

[7] In the second half of the first century B.C.E. [Ed.]

[8] The city of Pompeii was buried in the ashes caused by the eruption of Mount Vesuvius (near modern Naples) in 79 C.E. Because of its instant burial, it is a rich source of information and artifacts from the period. [Ed.]

This era of chaos ended during the reign of the emperor Augustus (ruled 27 B.C.E.–14 C.E.), who sought to stabilize Roman society in part by reducing women's freedoms. Women were criticized for adultery, wearing too much makeup, having immodest dress and conduct, and especially for refusing to have children. Augustus procured laws that intended to remove control of marriage and reproduction from the family and allow the state to regulate marriage and reproduction. He attempted to penalize women between the ages of twenty and fifty and men over the age of twenty-five who did not marry and have children by denying them the right to inherit wealth. Furthermore, women were not to be released from male guardianship until they had three children. The Augustan laws made the state the regulator of private behavior and attempted to raise the birthrate of citizens while accepting some of the social changes that had modified the patriarchal society of the old Roman Republic. Augustus sought political support from conservative males by decreasing the autonomy of women who had less political influence than men.

2

BAN ZHAO

Lessons for Women

The teachings of Confucius (561–479 B.C.E.) provided the Chinese and other Asian peoples with ideals of private and public conduct. Confucius's teachings emphasized the importance of filial piety, or the duty of children to serve and obey their parents, as well as to exercise restraint and treat others as one would like to be treated (see selection 3 in Chapter 4 for excerpts from Confucius's *Analects*). Ban Zhao* (45–116 C.E.) (Pan Chao in the previous selection) was the leading female Confucian scholar of classical China. Born into a literary family and educated by her mother, she was married at the age of fourteen. After her husband's death she finished writing her brother's history of the Han dynasty and served as imperial historian to Emperor Han Hedi (r. 88–105 C.E.) and as an advisor to the Empress-Dowager Deng.

Ban Zhao is best remembered, however, for her *Lessons for Women*, which she wrote to fill a gap in Confucian literature. With their

*bahn ZHOW

Source: *Pan Chao: Foremost Woman Scholar of China*, trans. Nancy Lee Swann (New York: Century Co., 1932), 82–90.

emphasis on the responsibilities of the son to the father and on the moral example of a good ruler, the writings of Confucius virtually ignored women. Ban Zhao sought to rectify that oversight by applying Confucian principles to the moral instruction of women. What does this piece say about the roles of both men and women? In what ways would Ban Zhao's *Lessons* support Chinese patriarchy? In what ways might they challenge the patriarchy or make it less oppressive for women?

THINKING HISTORICALLY

The author of this primary source provides an unusual bounty of personal autobiographical information in the first section. But why might the modern reader find much of this self-description unconvincing? Similarly, there is a discrepancy between the author's description of her audience and purpose in writing and the modern reader's idea of her audience and agenda. In fact, the introduction (above) and a line by the Hugheses in the previous selection tell you what historians think of the likely audience and agenda for Ban Zhao. What is this discrepancy between the author's presentation and what historians know to be her audience and agenda? How do these discrepancies actually help us better understand the author and, perhaps, Chinese or Confucian classical culture?

I, the unworthy writer, am unsophisticated, unenlightened, and by nature unintelligent, but I am fortunate both to have received not a little favor from my scholarly Father, and to have had a cultured mother and instructresses upon whom to rely for a literary education as well as for training in good manners. More than forty years have passed since at the age of fourteen I took up the dustpan and the broom in the Cao family.[1] During this time with trembling heart I feared constantly that I might disgrace my parents, and that I might multiply difficulties for both the women and the men of my husband's family. Day and night I was distressed in heart, but I labored without confessing weariness. Now and hereafter, however, I know how to escape from such fears.

Being careless, and by nature stupid, I taught and trained my children without system. Consequently I fear that my son Gu may bring disgrace upon the Imperial Dynasty by whose Holy Grace he has unprecedentedly received the extraordinary privilege of wearing the Gold and the Purple,[2] a privilege for the attainment of which by my son, I a humble subject never even hoped. Nevertheless, now that he is a man and able to plan his own life, I need not again have concern for him. But

[1] Her husband's family. [Ed.]
[2] Gold seal and purple robe were symbols of high nobility. [Ed.]

I do grieve that you, my daughters, just now at the age for marriage, have not at this time had gradual training and advice; that you still have not learned the proper customs for married women. I fear that by failure in good manners in other families you will humiliate both your ancestors and your clan. I am now seriously ill, life is uncertain. As I have thought of you all in so untrained a state, I have been uneasy many a time for you. At hours of leisure I have composed . . . these instructions under the title, "Lessons for Women." In order that you may have something wherewith to benefit your persons, I wish every one of you, my daughters each to write out a copy for yourself.

From this time on every one of you strive to practice these lessons.

Humility

On the third day after the birth of a girl the ancients observed three customs: first to place the baby below the bed; second to give her a potsherd[3] with which to play; and third to announce her birth to her ancestors by an offering. Now to lay the baby below the bed plainly indicated that she is lowly and weak, and should regard it as her primary duty to humble herself before others. To give her potsherds with which to play indubitably signified that she should practice labor and consider it her primary duty to be industrious. To announce her birth before her ancestors clearly meant that she ought to esteem as her primary duty the continuation of the observance of worship in the home.

These three ancient customs epitomize woman's ordinary way of life and the teachings of the traditional ceremonial rites and regulations. Let a woman modestly yield to others; let her respect others; let her put others first, herself last. Should she do something good, let her not mention it; should she do something bad let her not deny it. Let her bear disgrace; let her even endure when others speak or do evil to her. Always let her seem to tremble and to fear. When a woman follows such maxims as these then she may be said to humble herself before others.

Let a woman retire late to bed, but rise early to duties; let her not dread tasks by day or by night. Let her not refuse to perform domestic duties whether easy or difficult. That which must be done, let her finish completely, tidily, and systematically. When a woman follows such rules as these, then she may be said to be industrious.

Let a woman be correct in manner and upright in character in order to serve her husband. Let her live in purity and quietness of spirit, and attend to her own affairs. Let her love not gossip and silly laughter.

---

[3] A piece of broken pottery. [Ed.]

Let her cleanse and purify and arrange in order the wine and the food for the offerings to the ancestors. When a woman observes such principles as these, then she may be said to continue ancestral worship.

No woman who observes these three fundamentals of life has ever had a bad reputation or has fallen into disgrace. If a woman fails to observe them, how can her name be honored; how can she but bring disgrace upon herself?

Husband and Wife

The Way of husband and wife is intimately connected with Yin and Yang and relates the individual to gods and ancestors. Truly it is the great principle of Heaven and Earth, and the great basis of human relationships. Therefore the "Rites"[4] honor union of man and woman; and in the "Book of Poetry"[5] the "First Ode" manifests the principle of marriage. For these reasons the relationship cannot but be an important one.

If a husband be unworthy, then he possesses nothing by which to control his wife. If a wife be unworthy, then she possesses nothing with which to serve her husband. If a husband does not control his wife, then the rules of conduct manifesting his authority are abandoned and broken. If a wife does not serve her husband, then the proper relationship between men and women and the natural order of things are neglected and destroyed. As a matter of fact the purpose of these two[6] is the same. . . .

Respect and Caution

As Yin and Yang are not of the same nature, so man and woman have different characteristics. The distinctive quality of the Yang is rigidity; the function of the Yin is yielding. Man is honored for strength; a woman is beautiful on account of her gentleness. Hence there arose the common saying: "A man though born like a wolf may, it is feared, become a weak monstrosity; a woman though born like a mouse may, it is feared, become a tiger."

Now for self-culture nothing equals respect for others. To counteract firmness nothing equals compliance. Consequently it can be said that the Way of respect and acquiescence is woman's most important principle of conduct. So respect may be defined as nothing other than holding on to

[4] *The Classic of Rites*, one of the five classics of the Confucian canon, believed to be written by Confucius, though the current text dates from the Han dynasty. [Ed.]

[5] *The Classic of Odes*. Also declared one of five classics in the Han dynasty, the *Book of Odes* or *Songs* contains poems from as early as 1000 B.C.E. in the Zhou dynasty, presumed to be edited by Confucius. [Ed.]

[6] The controlling of women by men, and the serving of men by women. [Ed.]

that which is permanent; and acquiescence nothing other than being liberal and generous. Those who are steadfast in devotion know that they should stay in their proper places; those who are liberal and generous esteem others, and honor and serve them.

If husband and wife have the habit of staying together, never leaving one another, and following each other around within the limited space of their own rooms, then they will lust after and take liberties with one another. From such action improper language will arise between the two. This kind of discussion may lead to licentiousness. But of licentiousness will be born a heart of disrespect to the husband. Such a result comes from not knowing that one should stay in one's proper place.

Furthermore, affairs may be either crooked or straight; words may be either right or wrong. Straightforwardness cannot but lead to quarreling; crookedness cannot but lead to accusation. If there are really accusations and quarrels, then undoubtedly there will be angry affairs. Such a result comes from not esteeming others, and not honoring and serving them.

If wives suppress not contempt for husbands, then it follows that such wives rebuke and scold their husbands. If husbands stop not short of anger, then they are certain to beat their wives. The correct relationship between husband and wife is based upon harmony and intimacy, and conjugal love is grounded in proper union. Should actual blows be dealt, how could matrimonial relationship be preserved? Should sharp words be spoken, how could conjugal love exist? If love and proper relationship both be destroyed, then husband and wife are divided.

Womanly Qualifications

A woman ought to have four qualifications: (1) womanly virtue; (2) womanly words; (3) womanly bearing; and (4) womanly work. Now what is called womanly virtue need not be brilliant ability, exceptionally different from others. Womanly words need be neither clever in debate nor keen in conversation. Womanly appearance requires neither a pretty nor a perfect face and form. Womanly work need not be work done more skillfully than that of others.

To guard carefully her chastity; to control circumspectly her behavior; in every motion to exhibit modesty; and to model each act on the best usage, this is womanly virtue.

To choose her words with care; to avoid vulgar language; to speak at appropriate times; and not to weary others with much conversation, may be called the characteristics of womanly words.

To wash and scrub filth away; to keep clothes and ornaments fresh and clean; to wash the head and bathe the body regularly, and to keep the person free from disgraceful filth, may be called the characteristics of womanly bearing.

With whole-hearted devotion to sew and to weave; to love not gossip and silly laughter; in cleanliness and order to prepare the wine and food for serving guests, may be called the characteristics of womanly work.

These four qualifications characterize the greatest virtue of a woman. No woman can afford to be without them. In fact they are very easy to possess if a woman only treasures them in her heart. The ancients had a saying: "Is love afar off? If I desire love, then love is at hand!" So can it be said of these qualifications.

3

VATSYANA

The Kama Sutra

We know next to nothing about the author of this classic Indian book on *kama* (love, sex, or sensual experience), written between the fourth and sixth centuries C.E. in the Gupta period (280–550 C.E.).[1] What seems to be the importance of *kama* in this culture? What does this selection tell you about Indian culture and society, particularly about men, women, and the way they interacted? What does it tell you about sexuality and religion in classical India?

THINKING HISTORICALLY

Vatsyana does not directly tell us anything about himself. Assuming, however, that the translation is faithful to the original, how would you characterize the author's tone and style?

Vatsyana does give us some idea of his intended audience and his purpose in composing the *Kama Sutra*. In fact, he is at pains to answer the objections of some who question his entire enterprise. How would you characterize his intended audience and agenda? For what kind of people did he write, and what do you think he hoped to accomplish? At the end of the book—a section not included here—the author writes: "The Kama Sutra was composed, according to the precepts of Holy Writ, for the benefit of the world, by Vatsyayana, while leading the life of a religious student, and wholly engaged in the contemplation of the Deity." Does that statement change your idea of the author, his audience, or his agenda in writing the work?

[1] The Gupta period was a period not only of cultural flowering, but also of political expansion. The Gupta Empire covered most of north and central India.

Source: Mallanaga Vatsyana, *The Kama Sutra*, trans. Sir Richard F. Burton (1883), *Internet Sacred Texts Archive*, http://www.sacred-texts.com/sex/kama/kama101.htm.

Chapter II
On the Acquisition of Dharma, Artha and Kama

Man, the period of whose life is one hundred years, should practice Dharma, Artha and Kama[2] at different times and in such a manner that they may harmonize together and not clash in any way. He should acquire learning in his childhood, in his youth and middle age he should attend to Artha and Kama, and in his old age he should perform Dharma, and thus seek to gain Moksha, i.e. release from further transmigration.[3] Or, on account of the uncertainty of life, he may practice them at times when they are enjoined to be practiced. But one thing is to be noted, he should lead the life of a religious student until he finishes his education.

Dharma is obedience to the command of the Shastra or Holy Writ of the Hindus to do certain things, such as the performance of sacrifices, which are not generally done, because they do not belong to this world, and produce no visible effect; and not to do other things, such as eating meat, which is often done because it belongs to this world, and has visible effects.

Dharma should be learnt from the Shruti (Holy Writ), and from those conversant with it.

Artha is the acquisition of arts, land, gold, cattle, wealth, equipages and friends. It is, further, the protection of what is acquired, and the increase of what is protected.

Artha should be learnt from the king's officers, and from merchants who may be versed in the ways of commerce.

Kama is the enjoyment of appropriate objects by the five senses of hearing, feeling, seeing, tasting and smelling, assisted by the mind together with the soul. The ingredient in this is a peculiar contact between the organ of sense and its object, and the consciousness of pleasure which arises from that contact is called Kama.

Kama is to be learnt from the Kama Sutra (aphorisms on love) and from the practice of citizens.

When all the three, viz. Dharma, Artha and Kama, come together, the former is better than the one which follows it, i.e. Dharma is better than Artha, and Artha is better than Kama. But Artha should always be first practiced by the king for the livelihood of men is to be obtained from it only. Again, Kama being the occupation of public women, they should prefer it to the other two, and these are exceptions to the general rule.

---

[2] Defined further on in the paragraph, but roughly mean religious duty, wealth, and sensual experience, respectively. [Ed.]

[3] The Hindu idea of the transmigration of souls held that a soul was reincarnated (born again) in another body after death. [Ed.]

Objection 1

Some learned men say that as Dharma is connected with things not belonging to this world, it is appropriately treated in a book; and so also is Artha, because it is practiced only by the application of proper means, and a knowledge of those means can only be obtained by study and from books. But Kama being a thing which is practiced even by the brute creation, and which is to be found everywhere, does not want any work on the subject.

Answer

This is not so. Sexual intercourse being a thing dependent on man and woman requires the application of proper means by them, and those means are to be learnt from the Kama Shastra.[4] The non-application of proper means, which we see in the brute creation, is caused by their being unrestrained, and by the females among them only being fit for sexual intercourse at certain seasons and no more, and by their intercourse not being preceded by thought of any kind.

Objection 2

The Lokayatikas[5] say: Religious ordinances should not be observed, for they bear a future fruit, and at the same time it is also doubtful whether they will bear any fruit at all. What foolish person will give away that which is in his own hands into the hands of another? Moreover, it is better to have a pigeon today than a peacock tomorrow; and a copper coin which we have the certainty of obtaining, is better than a gold coin, the possession of which is doubtful.

Answer

It is not so. 1st. Holy Writ, which ordains the practice of Dharma, does not admit of a doubt.

2nd. Sacrifices such as those made for the destruction of enemies, or for the fall of rain, are seen to bear fruit.

3rd. The sun, moon, stars, planets and other heavenly bodies appear to work intentionally for the good of the world.

---

[4] A holy (or philosophical) book on Kama like this one, the *Kama Sutra*. [Ed.]
[5] Materialist philosophers who opposed Brahmanism since at least the sixth century B.C.E. [Ed.]

4th. The existence of this world is affected by the observance of the rules respecting the four classes of men and their four stages of life.[6]

5th. We see that seed is thrown into the ground with the hope of future crops.

Vatsyayana is therefore of opinion that the ordinances of religion must be obeyed. . . .

Chapter III
On the Arts and Sciences to be Studied

Man should study the Kama Sutra and the arts and sciences subordinate thereto, in addition to the study of the arts and sciences contained in Dharma and Artha. Even young maids should study this Kama Sutra along with its arts and sciences before marriage, and after it they should continue to do so with the consent of their husbands.

Here some learned men object, and say that females, not being allowed to study any science, should not study the Kama Sutra.

But Vatsyayana is of the opinion that this objection does not hold good, for women already know the practice of Kama Sutra, and that practice is derived from the Kama Shastra, or the science of Kama itself. Moreover, it is not only in this but in many other cases that, though the practice of a science is known to all, only a few persons are acquainted with the rules and laws on which the science is based. Thus . . . persons do the duties required of them on auspicious days, which are fixed by astrology, though they are not acquainted with the science of astrology. . . . And similarly the people of the most distant provinces obey the laws of the kingdom from practice, and because there is a king over them, and without further reason. And from experience we find that some women, such as daughters of princes and their ministers, and public women, are actually versed in the Kama Shastra.

A female, therefore, should learn the Kama Shastra, or at least a part of it, by studying its practice from some confidential friend. She should study alone in private the sixty-four practices that form a part of the Kama Shastra. Her teacher should be one of the following persons: the daughter of a nurse brought up with her and already married, or a female friend who can be trusted in everything, or the sister of her mother (i.e. her aunt), or an old female servant, or a female beggar who may have formerly lived in the family, or her own sister who can always be trusted. . . .

---

[6] The four classes or castes are Brahman priests, Kshatriya warriors, Vaishya merchants, and Shudra workers; the four stages of life are student, householder, retired man, and holy man renouncing life. [Ed.]

Chapter IV
The Life of a Citizen

Having acquired learning, a man, with the wealth that he may have gained by gift, conquest, purchase, deposit,[7] or inheritance from his ancestors, should become a householder, and pass the life of a citizen. He should take a house in a city, or large village, or in the vicinity of good men, or in a place which is the resort of many persons. This abode should be situated near some water, and divided into different compartments for different purposes. It should be surrounded by a garden, and also contain two rooms, an outer and an inner one. The inner room should be occupied by the females, while the outer room, balmy with rich perfumes, should contain a bed, soft, agreeable to the sight, covered with a clean white cloth, low in the middle part, having garlands and bunches of flowers upon it, and a canopy above it, and two pillows, one at the top, another at the bottom. . . .

Social Gatherings

When men of the same age, disposition and talents, fond of the same diversions and with the same degree of education, sit together in company with public women,[8] or in an assembly of citizens, or at the abode of one among themselves, and engage in agreeable discourse with each other, such is called a Sitting in company or a social gathering. The subjects of discourse are to be the completion of verses half composed by others, and the testing the knowledge of one another in the various arts. The women who may be the most beautiful, who may like the same things that the men like, and who may have power to attract the minds of others, are here done homage to.

Going to Gardens or Picnics

In the forenoon, men having dressed themselves should go to gardens on horseback, accompanied by public women and followed by servants. And having done there all the duties of the day, and passed the time in various agreeable diversions, such as the fighting of quails, cocks and rams, and other spectacles, they should return home in the afternoon in the same manner, bringing with them bunches of flowers, etc. . . .

---

[7] Brahmans receive gifts; Kshatriyas win conquests; Vaishyas earn purchases or deposits. [Ed.]

[8] Courtesans. [Ed.]

Chapter V
About the Kinds of Women Resorted to by the Citizens, and of Friends and Messengers

When Kama is practiced by men of the four castes according to the rules of the Holy Writ (i.e. by lawful marriage) with virgins of their own caste, it then becomes a means of acquiring lawful progeny and good fame, and it is not also opposed to the customs of the world. On the contrary the practice of Kama with women of the higher castes, and with those previously enjoyed by others, even though they be of the same caste, is prohibited. But the practice of Kama with women of the lower castes, with women excommunicated from their own caste, with public women, and with women twice married, is neither enjoined nor prohibited. The object of practicing Kama with such women is pleasure only.

4

PLATO

The Symposium

Plato (428–348 B.C.E.) is certainly the most widely read and most influential philosopher of classical Greece. The twentieth-century Platonist A. N. Whitehead famously wrote that all of European philosophy consisted of footnotes to Plato.[1] When we speak of Plato, however, we also mean Socrates, Plato's teacher. In fact, since Plato's writings consist almost entirely of dialogues (discussions) in which Plato is absent but Socrates asks questions and elicits answers and then spells out his own ideas, we have no way of distinguishing the ideas of Plato from those of Socrates. We credit Plato, however, since he is the author of these thirty-five dialogues as well as thirteen letters and was the founder of the Athenian Academy of philosophy.

The Symposium, one of the better-known dialogues, was written about 385 B.C.E. The subject is a symposium or drinking party in which the participants eat, drink, and discuss some philosophical topic—in this case, the meaning of love. This selection contains two views of love before Socrates speaks. What are those views, and what

[1] Alfred North Whitehead, *Process and Reality* (New York: Free Press, 1979), 39.

Source: Plato, *Symposium*, trans. Benjamin Jowett, http://www.ellopos.net/elpenor/greek-texts/ancient-Greece/plato/plato-symposium.asp.

do they tell you about the Greek society of the time — particularly about sexuality and gender? What finally does Socrates say about love? What does his speech tell you about Greek ideas of men, women, love, and sex?

THINKING HISTORICALLY

This dialogue, like the others, is a sort of play with its own author, audience, and agenda. Whose voice is telling the story? What kind of people make up the "audience" of the dinner party? Why have these men come together to discuss this topic? What different agenda might they have had? Of course, even the intended audience of Plato's written dialogue is very much larger than a few men talking. For whom do you think he wrote this? What might have been his purpose? Finally, whose ideas are these? If we know little of the biography of Plato, other than that he was the author of these works and the founder of the Athenian Academy, we know less about Socrates. Indeed, in some dialogues Socrates raises questions as to whether or not he expresses his own ideas. How does he suggest that his ideas may not even be his own in this dialogue?

Regarding audience and agenda, we might assume that the dialogues were to be used for teaching purposes at the Academy, but we have no evidence for that assumption either. To what degree do these uncertainties limit our understanding of classical Greek society and culture? Despite these uncertainties, what can we say — from the internal evidence of the dialogue itself — about the likely audience and agenda of this work?

[Our selection begins as the participants have just finished dinner.]

Then, said Eryximachus, as you are all agreed that drinking is to be voluntary, and that there is to be no compulsion, I move, in the next place, that the flute-girl, who has just made her appearance, be told to go away and play to herself, or, if she likes, to the women who are within. Today let us have conversation instead; and, if you will allow me, I will tell you what sort of conversation. . . .

I think that at the present moment we who are here assembled cannot do better than honor the god Love. If you agree with me, there will be no lack of conversation; for I mean to propose that each of us in turn, going from left to right, shall make a speech in honor of Love. Let him give us the best which he can; and Phaedrus, because he is sitting first on the left hand, and because he is the father of the thought,[2] shall begin. . . .

---

[2] Phaedrus had earlier suggested the topic. [Ed.]

[Phaedrus:]

Numerous are the witnesses who acknowledge Love to be the eldest of the gods. And not only is he the eldest, he is also the source of the greatest benefits to us. For I know not any greater blessing to a young man who is beginning life than a virtuous lover or to the lover than a beloved youth.[3] For the principle which ought to be the guide of men who would nobly live at principle, I say, neither kindred, nor honor, nor wealth, nor any other motive is able to implant so well as love. Of what am I speaking? Of the sense of honor and dishonor, without which neither states nor individuals ever do any good or great work. And I say that a lover who is detected in doing any dishonorable act, or submitting through cowardice when any dishonor is done to him by another, will be more pained at being detected by his beloved than at being seen by his father, or by his companions, or by anyone else. The beloved too, when he is found in any disgraceful situation, has the same feeling about his lover. And if there were only some way of contriving that a state or an army should be made up of lovers and their loves, they would be the very best governors of their own city, abstaining from all dishonor, and emulating one another in honor; and when fighting at each other's side, although a mere handful, they would overcome the world. . . .

[Pausanias:]

If there were only one Love, then what you said would be well enough; but since there are more Loves than one, [we] should have begun by determining which of them was to be the theme of our praises. I will amend this defect; and first of all I would tell you which Love is deserving of praise, and then try to hymn the praiseworthy one in a manner worthy of him. For we all know that Love is inseparable from Aphrodite,[4] and if there were only one Aphrodite there would be only one Love; but as there are two goddesses there must be two Loves.

And am I not right in asserting that there are two goddesses? The elder one, having no mother, who is called the heavenly Aphrodite . . . and the Love who is her fellow-worker is rightly called common, as the other love is called heavenly.[5] . . . The Love who is the offspring of the common Aphrodite is essentially common, and has no discrimination, being such as the meaner sort of men feel, and is apt to be of women as well as of youths, and is of the body rather than of the soul; the most

---

[3] Note that this only concerns men and boys. [Ed.]

[4] The Greek goddess of love and beauty. [Ed.]

[5] Pausanias makes this distinction to account for two Aphrodite origin myths at the time. One is the story of an Aphrodite born in sea foam from her father's discarded genitals — this is the heavenly Aphrodite. Another myth concerns an Aphrodite of common birth. The first accounts for homosexual love, the second for the love between a husband and wife. [Ed.]

foolish beings are the objects of this love which desires only to gain an end, but never thinks of accomplishing the end nobly, and therefore does good and evil quite indiscriminately. The goddess who is his mother is far younger than the other, and she was born of the union of the male and female, and partakes of both.

But the offspring of the heavenly Aphrodite is derived from a mother in whose birth the female has no part: She is from the male only; this is that love which is of youths, and the goddess being older, there is nothing of wantonness in her. Those who are inspired by this love turn to the male, and delight in him who is the more valiant and intelligent nature; any one may recognize the pure enthusiasts in the very character of their attachments. For they love not boys, but intelligent beings whose reason is beginning to be developed, much about the time at which their beards begin to grow. And in choosing young men to be their companions, they mean to be faithful to them, and pass their whole life in company with them, not to take them in their inexperience, and deceive them, and play the fool with them, or run away from one to another of them. But the love of young boys should be forbidden by law,[6] because their future is uncertain; they may turn out good or bad, either in body or soul, and much noble enthusiasm may be thrown away upon them; in this matter the good are a law to themselves, and the coarser sort of lovers ought to be restrained by force; as we restrain or attempt to restrain them from fixing their affections on women of free birth. These are the persons who bring a reproach on love; and some have been led to deny the lawfulness of such attachments because they see the impropriety and evil of them; for surely nothing that is decorously and lawfully done can justly be censured. . . .

[Finally, it is the turn of Socrates:]

And now, taking my leave of you, I would rehearse a tale of love which I heard from Diotima of Mantineia, a woman wise in this and in many other kinds of knowledge, who in the days of old, when the Athenians offered sacrifice before the coming of the plague, delayed the disease ten years. She was my instructress in the art of love, and I shall repeat to you what she said to me. . . . "Love," she said, "may be described generally as the love of the everlasting possession of the good." "That is most true" [I agreed]. "Then if this be the nature of love, can you tell me further," she said, "what is the manner of the pursuit? What are they doing who show all this eagerness and heat which is called love? And what is the object which they have in view? Answer me." "Nay, Diotima," I replied, "if I had known, I should not have wondered at your wisdom, neither should I have come to learn from you about this very matter." "Well,"

---

[6] Such love is only appropriate when expressed toward *ephebos* (boys entering manhood, roughly eighteen to twenty years old). It should be against the law if boys are younger. [Ed.]

she said, "I will teach you: The object which they have in view is birth in beauty, whether of body or, soul. . . . And this is the reason why, when the hour of conception arrives, and the teeming nature is full, there is such a flutter and ecstasy about beauty whose approach is the alleviation of the pain of travail. For love, Socrates, is not, as you imagine, the love of the beautiful only." "What then?" "The love of generation and of birth in beauty." "Yes," I said. "Yes, indeed," she replied. "But why of generation?" "Because to the mortal creature, generation is a sort of eternity and immortality," she replied; "and if, as has been already admitted, love is of the everlasting possession of the good, all men will necessarily desire immortality together with good: Wherefore love is of immortality." . . .

". . . [T]he essence of beauty, . . . my dear Socrates, . . . is that life above all others which man should live, in the contemplation of beauty absolute; a beauty which if you once beheld, you would see not to be after the measure of gold, and garments, and fair boys and youths, whose presence now entrances you; and you and many a one would be content to live seeing them only and conversing with them without meat or drink, if that were possible—you only want to look at them and to be with them. But what if man had eyes to see the true beauty—the divine beauty, I mean, pure and clear and unalloyed, not clogged with the pollutions of mortality and all the colors and vanities of human life—thither looking, and holding converse with the true beauty simple and divine? Remember how in that communion only, beholding beauty with the eye of the mind, he will be enabled to bring forth, not images of beauty, but realities (for he has hold not of an image but of a reality), and bringing forth and nourishing true virtue to become the friend of God and be immortal, if mortal man may. . . ."

5

OVID

The Art of Love

Ovid (43 B.C.E.–17 C.E.) was one of the leading poets of the culturally rich age of Augustus, the first emperor. Born into a wealthy family, he socialized in imperial circles and practiced law until he gave it up to write poetry. His first major work, *Amores* (Loves), told love stories of the gods and of his own personal life, having been married three

Source: Ovid, *The Art of Love*, trans. A. S. Kline, *Poetry in Translation*, http://www .poetryintranslation.com/klineasartoflove.htm.

times and divorced twice by the age of thirty. Later, in 1 B.C.E., he began publishing the three volumes of his *Ars Amatoria* (Art of Love), the playful guide to seduction included here. Despite the publication of his more respectable poems about the changing forms of gods and nature, *The Metamorphoses*, Ovid was identified with his poems on love and sexuality at a time when Augustus sought to put an end to the loose morality of Roman nobility, including members of his own family. Because of his poetry and a mistake "more serious than murder," he later wrote, Ovid was exiled by Augustus in 8 C.E. to the coast of the Black Sea, where he lived the last decade of his life, pining for the culture and excitement of Rome.

What does this selection tell you about how men and women could behave in Roman society? What does Ovid think of love? How is Ovid's idea of love different from Plato's? Compare Ovid's *Art of Love* with Vatsyana's *Kama Sutra*. What does this selection suggest about the differences in attitudes toward sexuality between Roman society and Greek, Indian, or Chinese society?

THINKING HISTORCALLY

The author appears loud, front, and center in these poems. How would you characterize his voice? He is also fairly explicit about his audience (or audiences), and he suggests various motivations for writing. How would you describe the social class of his intended audience? How does the shift in audience in Book III change your assessment of Ovid's motives? What other reasons might have made him write these poems?

Book I
Part I: His Task

Should anyone here not know the art of love,
read this, and learn by reading how to love.
By art the boat's set gliding, with oar and sail,
by art the chariot's swift: love's ruled by art.

. . .

I sing of safe love, permissible intrigue,
and there'll be nothing sinful in my song.
Now the first task for you who come as a raw recruit
is to find out who you might wish to love.
The next task is to make sure that she likes you:
the third, to see to it that the love will last.
That's my aim, that's the ground my chariot will cover:
that's the post my thundering wheels will scrape.

Part II: How to Find Her

While you're still free, and can roam on a loose rein,
pick one to whom you could say: "You alone please me."
She won't come falling for you out of thin air:
the right girl has to be searched for: use your eyes.

. . .

If you'd catch them very young and not yet grown,
real child-brides will come before your eyes:
if it's young girls you want, thousands will please you.
You'll be forced to be unsure of your desires:
if you delight greatly in older wiser years,
here too, believe me, there's an even greater crowd.

. . .

Part IV: Or at the Theatre

But hunt for them, especially, at the tiered theatre:
that place is the most fruitful for your needs.
There you'll find one to love, or one you can play with,
one to be with just once, or one you might wish to keep.
As ants return home often in long processions,
carrying their favourite food in their mouths,
or as the bees buzz through the flowers and thyme,
among their pastures and fragrant chosen meadows,
so our fashionable ladies crowd to the famous shows:
my choice is often constrained by such richness.
They come to see, they come to be seen as well:
the place is fatal to chaste modesty.

. . .

Part V: Or at the Races, or the Circus

Don't forget the races, those noble stallions:
the Circus holds room for a vast obliging crowd.
No need here for fingers to give secret messages,
nor a nod of the head to tell you she accepts:
You can sit by your lady: nothing's forbidden,
press your thigh to hers, as you can do, all the time:
and it's good the rows force you close, even if you don't like it,
since the girl is touched through the rules of the place.
Now find your reason for friendly conversation,
and first of all engage in casual talk.
Make earnest enquiry whose those horses are:
and rush to back her favourite, whatever it is.
When the crowded procession of ivory gods goes by,

you clap fervently for Lady Venus[1]:
if by chance a speck of dust falls in the girl's lap,
as it may, let it be flicked away by your fingers:
and if there's nothing, flick away the nothing:
let anything be a reason for you to serve her.
If her skirt is trailing too near the ground,
lift it, and raise it carefully from the dusty earth:
Straightaway, the prize for service, if she allows it,
is that your eyes catch a glimpse of her legs.

. . .

Part IX: How to Win Her

So far, riding her unequal wheels, the Muse has taught you
where you might choose your love, where to set your nets.
Now I'll undertake to tell you what pleases her,
by what arts she's caught, itself a work of highest art.

. . .

Part X: First Secure the Maid

But to get to know your desired-one's maid
is your first care: she'll smooth your way.
See if she's close to her mistress's thoughts,
and has plenty of true knowledge of her secret jests.
Corrupt her with promises, and with prayers:
you'll easily get what you want, if she wishes.
She'll tell the time (the doctors would know it too)
when her mistress's mind is receptive, fit for love.
Her mind will be fit for love when she luxuriates
in fertility,[2] like the crop on some rich soil.

. . .

Part XVII: Tears, Kisses, and Take the Lead

And tears help: tears will move a stone:
let her see your damp cheeks if you can.
If tears (they don't always come at the right time)
fail you, touch your eyes with a wet hand.
What wise man doesn't mingle tears with kisses?
Though she might not give, take what isn't given.
Perhaps she'll struggle, and then say "you're wicked":

---

[1] Roman goddess of love; origins in Latin goddess of vegetation and Greek Aphrodite. [Ed.]

[2] Recent studies confirm increased desire at the point of ovulation, but Ovid knew only the Roman (and general ancient) association of women and earth, passion and flowering. [Ed.]

struggling she still wants, herself, to be conquered.
Only, take care her lips aren't bruised by snatching,
and that she can't complain that you were harsh.

. . .

Book II
Part XX: The Task's Complete . . . But Now . . .

. . .

I've given you weapons: Vulcan[3] gave Achilles his:
excel with the gifts you're given, as he excelled.
But whoever overcomes an Amazon[4] with my sword,
write on the spoils "Ovid was my master."
Behold, you tender girls ask for rules for yourselves:
well yours then will be the next task for my pen!

Book III
Part I: It's Time to Teach You Girls

I've given the Greeks arms, against Amazons: arms remain,
to give to you Penthesilea,[5] and your Amazon troop.
Go equal to the fight: let them win, those who are favoured
by Venus, and her Boy, who flies through all the world.
It's not fair for armed men to battle with naked girls:
that would be shameful, men, even if you win.
Someone will say: "Why add venom to the snake,
and betray the sheepfold to the rabid she-wolf?"
Beware of loading the crime of the many onto the few:
let the merits of each separate girl be seen.

. . .

Only playful passions will be learnt from me:
I'll teach girls the ways of being loved.
Women don't brandish flames or cruel bows:
I rarely see men harmed by their weapons.
Men often cheat: it's seldom tender girls,
and, if you check, they're rarely accused of fraud.

. . .

What destroyed you all, I ask? Not knowing how to love:
your art was lacking: love lasts long through art.
You still might lack it now: but, before my eyes,
stood Venus herself, and ordered me to teach you.

[3] Roman god of fire; forged the shield of the warrior Achilles. [Ed.]
[4] Mythic tribe of warrior women. [Ed.]
[5] In Greek mythology Penthesilea was queen of the Amazons (the warrior women). [Ed.]

She said to me, then: "What have the poor girls done,
an unarmed crowd betrayed to well-armed men?
Two books of *their* tricks have been composed:
let this lot too be instructed by your warnings." ...

. . .

Part IV: Make-Up, but in Private

How near I was to warning you, no rankness of the wild goat
under your armpits, no legs bristling with harsh hair!
But I'm not teaching girls from the Caucasian hills,
or those who drink your waters, Mysian Caicus.[6]
So why remind you not to let your teeth get blackened,
by being lazy, and to wash your face each morning in water?
You know how to acquire whiteness with a layer of powder:
she who doesn't blush by blood, indeed, blushes by art.
You make good the naked edges of your eyebrows,
and hide your natural cheeks with little patches.

. . .

Still, don't let your lover find cosmetic bottles ...

. . .

Part XIV: Use Jealousy and Fear

Let all be betrayed: I've unbarred the gates to the enemy:
and let my loyalty be to treacherous betrayal.
What's easily given nourishes love poorly:
mingle the odd rejection with welcome fun.
Let him lie before the door, crying: "Cruel entrance!,"
pleading very humbly, threatening a lot too.
We can't stand sweetness: bitterness renews our taste:

. . .

Also when the lover you've just caught falls into the net,
let him think that only he has access to your room.
Later let him sense a rival, the bed's shared pact:
remove these arts, and love grows old.
The horse runs swiftly from the starting gate,
when he has others to pass, and others follow.
Wrongs relight the dying fires, as you wish:
See (I confess!), I don't love unless I'm hurt.

---

[6] Caucasian hills and Mysian Caicus suggest unrefined people from wild areas: the rugged
mountains of the Caucusus and the swirling waters of the Caicus River in Roman Asia (northwest Turkey). [Ed.]

Part XVIII: And So to Bed

To have been taught more is shameful: but kindly Venus
said: "What's shameful is my particular concern."
Let each girl know herself: adopt a reliable posture
for her body: one layout's not suitable for all.
She who's known for her face, lie there face upwards:
let her back be seen, she whose back delights.

　　　　　. . .

Woman, feel love, melted to your very bones,
and let both delight equally in the thing.
Don't leave out seductive coos and delightful murmurings,
don't let wild words be silent in the middle of your games.
You too whom nature denies sexual feeling,
pretend to sweet delight with artful sounds.
Unhappy girl, for whom that sluggish place is numb,
which man and woman equally should enjoy.
Only beware when you feign it, lest it shows:
create belief in your movements and your eyes.
When you like it, show it with cries and panting breath:
Ah! I blush, that part has its own secret signs.
She who asks fondly for a gift after love's delights,
can't want her request to carry any weight.
Don't let light into the room through all the windows:
it's fitting for much of your body to be concealed.

The game is done: time to descend, you swans,
you who bent your necks beneath my yoke.
As once the boys, so now my crowd of girls
inscribe on your trophies "Ovid was my master."

6

Portraits

Some of the most vivid and best-preserved images of women from
antiquity come from the Fayum region of Egypt and date from the
first century B.C.E. to the third century C.E. These are the beautifully
painted and distinctive mummy portraits of inhabitants of Hellenistic
and Roman Egypt, portraits usually painted while the subjects were
alive and interred with them after death. The practice of painting
tomb portraits in encaustic (that is, with hot pigmented wax)
on wooden panels was a fairly common one in the region, and

Egypt's extremely dry climate ensured the survival of many of these ancient works.

Figures 5.1 and 5.2 show portraits of women buried in Fayum, while Figure 5.3 depicts one "Ammonius from Antinoe," a young man from a town near Fayum. We do not know their ethnic background, although it is likely that they were either Roman settlers in Egypt or descendants of Egypt's Hellenistic rulers and colonists from Macedonia after Alexander the Great conquered Egypt. What clues *do* these visual sources offer about their subjects?

Figure 5.1   Portrait of a Fayum Woman with Large Gold Necklace.

Source: The Detroit Institute of Arts, USA, Gift of Julius H. Haass/The Bridgeman Art Library International.

Figure 5.2   Portrait of Fayum Woman with White Earrings.

Source: Louvre, Paris, France, Lauros/Giraudon/The Bridgeman Art Library International.

Sarah and Brady Hughes argue in their selection that Greek women living in Egypt during the Hellenistic period "were much more assertive . . . than their sisters in either contemporary Greece or later Rome" (see page 169) and that even "non-elite women had unusual freedom. They owned property (including land), participated in commerce, produced textiles, were educated, and enjoyed careers as artists, poets, and farmers." Do Figures 5.1 and 5.2 appear to support this argument? Why or why not?

Figure 5.3 Portrait of "Ammonius from Antinoe," with Ankh.

Source: Visual Arts Library (London)/Alamy.

THINKING HISTORICALLY

Consider these images, individually and collectively. How would you describe the subjects' expressions? Content? Anxious? Serene? Fatalistic? Sad? What, if anything, can each tell us about the historical moment in which they were created? What are their limitations as evidence about their subjects? Can these portraits tell us anything meaningful about those who sat for them?

The practice of painting the face of the deceased on a shroud, panel, or actual sarcophagus goes back to the time of the ancient pharaohs. Ammonius is holding an ankh, the ancient Egyptian hieroglyph that symbolized life force and eternal life, and one often carried as a good luck charm or amulet by the Hellenistic and Roman inhabitants of Egypt. Who was the audience for these portraits?

■ REFLECTIONS

Over thirty years ago the historian Di Joan Kelly-Gadol ignited the study of women's history with an essay that asked: "Did Women Have a Renaissance?" Questioning whether the great eras in men's history were also great eras for women, she found that men's achievements often came at the expense of women. We have seen how the urban revolution fit this pattern. The rise of cities, the creation of territorial states, the invention of writing, and the development of complex societies, all beginning about five thousand years ago, accompanied the development of patriarchal institutions and ideas. Similarly, the rise of classical cultures, cities, and states about twenty-five hundred years ago seems to have cemented patriarchy. The great religious and philosophical traditions of the classical era emerged with the new states. Some, like Chinese Legalism, voiced support for the new order; others, like Confucianism, evoked an older feudal order that was fading. In China neither the statist nor feudal philosophy brought relief to women, though in the hand of someone like Ban Zhao, Confucianism might be shaped to strengthen the bonds between husband and wife as well as the more traditional male-centered bonds. Indian state building of the classical age similarly pitted a renewed patriarchal Brahmanism against emerging Buddhist and other reforming movements for greater social equality. But by the time of the Gupta era, patriarchal Brahmanism had won the day, creating a world for the upper-caste Hindu male secure enough to not require the sexual repression of all women. The upper-class Greek classical patriarchy enjoyed similar assurances.

History is a method of investigation as well as a subject matter. Historians use various methods, some of which we have included in our "Thinking Historically" sections. But beyond these, history is a general method as well. Historians historicize. We make things historical that were previously thought to have no history. We find that some aspects of life that were generally thought to be eternal or unchanging actually have changed over the course of time. They have a history. This chapter shows how ideas of love and gender are historical rather than always and everywhere the same. To see that different cultures have developed or emphasized different ideas of love is not to rule out any role for biology or human nature, but it is to recognize that our emotions are also learned, perhaps more than we thought.

In addition to love, we have learned to historicize gender identity. Male and female stereotypes that held sway into the mid-twentieth century have long been undermined by historical studies of gender, psychological studies, sensitivity training, and public law. We recognize that personality traits stereotypically thought to be "masculine" or "feminine" can be learned or genetically not coded to a male or female anatomy. In this and previous chapters we have also historicized sexuality to the degree that we have seen different ideas about sex and the sacred, and different customs related to sex in different societies. Homosexuality raises the possibility of a more sweeping historicizing of sexuality. Is it possible that the percentage of homosexuals or heterosexuals in society also varies historically? Is same-sex or opposite-sex preference also historical? Are we taught to be "gay" or "straight"? These questions are prompted, of course, by our study of classical Greece, mainly Athens, and, for that matter, a small class of intellectuals in that city-state. Their influence very likely goes far beyond their numbers. We have no way of knowing if Athens contained a higher proportion of homosexuals or bisexuals than other societies. In fact, these may be the wrong questions. It may be that *heterosexuality* and *homosexuality* are also historical constructs. These modern words and the concepts they entail, based as they are on post-Greek religious traditions (Judaic, Christian, and Islamic) that oppose and moralize the difference, may miss what the Greeks meant and felt. For them, these liaisons had more to do with education than lifestyle, they were often more spiritual than physical, and physical penetration had more to do with social standing than gender. For most of these Greeks, it would make more sense to speak of *bisexuality* rather than *homosexuality*, except that bisexuality implies a combination of two extremes they probably did not see. The world has been constantly changing, and so too have the words we use to describe it.

6

From Tribal to Universal Religion

Hindu-Buddhist and Judeo-Christian Traditions, 600 B.C.E.—100 C.E.

■ HISTORICAL CONTEXT

From 1000 B.C.E. to 100 C.E. two major religious traditions, one centered in the Middle East and the other in northern India, split into at least four major religious traditions, so large that today they are embraced by a majority of the inhabitants of the world. Both of the two original traditions, Hinduism and Judaism, were in 1000 B.C.E. highly restricted in membership. Neither sought converts but instead ministered to members of their own tribe and castes. This chapter explores how these two essentially inward-looking religions created universal religions, open to all. It is a story not only of the emergence of Christianity and Buddhism but also of the development of modern Judaic and Hindu religions.

Remarkably, both of these traditions moved from tribal to universal religions; even more remarkable are the common elements, given their different routes along that path. While Hinduism cultivated a psychological approach to spiritual enlightenment out of a religion based on caste, Brahman priests, and offerings to innumerable deities, Judaism developed an abiding faith in a universal historical providence after the repeated conquest of a local temple administered by a tribal priesthood. In both transitions, traditions of sacrifice, ritual, worldly prosperity, and inherited status diminished, to be replaced by ideas of universal salvation from this world.

Understanding how religions change or evolve is especially difficult because of the tendency of religious adherents to emphasize the timelessness of their truths. Fortunately, religious commitment and belief do not require a denial of historical change. Indeed, many adherents have found strength in all manifestations of the sacred—the specific and historical as well as the universal and eternal.

Whether motives are primarily religious or secular, however, the historical study of religion offers a useful window on understanding large-scale changes in human behavior. Since religions tend to conserve, repeat, and enshrine, change is more gradual than in many other aspects of human thought and behavior: fashion, say, or technology. Thus, when religions develop radically new ideas or institutions, we can learn much about human resistance and innovation by studying the circumstances.

As you read the selections in this chapter, notice over the course of the first millennium B.C.E. how both core religions created new faiths and reformed the old. Notice also the fundamentally different ways these two great religious traditions changed. Finally, observe how the later offspring religions, Buddhism and Christianity, preached ideas that were already current, but not dominant, in the "parental" traditions.

■ THINKING HISTORICALLY

Detecting Change in Primary Sources

Because religions typically prefer conservation over innovation, changes are often grafted onto old formulations. Historians who want to understand when and how change occurred must sometimes look at primary sources to uncover new ideas and ways of doing things that have been assimilated into the tradition.

The easiest way to see change in primary sources is to compare a number of them composed in different historical periods. However, sometimes we are able to see examples of change in a single document. A written source may, for instance, originate in more than one oral account, and the writer may combine them both even though one is later than the other and they represent different ideas. A manuscript might also pick up errors or updates as it is rewritten for the next generation. We will see examples of both of these changes and others in the documents in this chapter.

1

Hinduism: Svetasvatara Upanishad

In Chapter 3 selections from the Hindu Vedas* and Upanishads†
help introduce some basic ideas in Hinduism: the belief that animals
and human castes were created out of the primal sacrifice of the god
Purusha in the Vedas, the complementary ideas of karma and reincarnation in the Upanishads, and, lastly, the identification of Brahman
and *atman* (God and self), also in the Upanishads.

Take a look at the same selections again to understand the changing
nature of Hinduism from the earliest Vedas to the latest Upanishads.
For example, we see in Chapter 3, selection 2, the interest of the
authors of the Vedas in defining and justifying caste differences and
the supremacy of the Brahman priests as masters of sacrifice, prayers,
rituals, and sacred hymns.

The authors of the Upanishads were less interested in sacrifice and
priestly rituals and more absorbed by philosophical questions. Thus,
Chapter 3, selection 3, on karma and reincarnation, spells out the
idea of justice and a philosophy of nature that reflects the interests of
a later settled society. Finally, selection 4 on the identity of Brahman
and *atman* reflects an even more meditative Upanishad that virtually
ignores the role of priests. This meditative tradition may have existed
in early Hinduism, but there is far more evidence of its expression in
the Upanishads (after 800 B.C.E.) than in the earlier Vedas.

The *Svetasvatara*‡ Upanishad selection included here reflects an
additional step along the path from the religion of priests, sacrifice,
and caste obligation to individualized spirituality. Here the idea of
the transmigration of souls from one body to another in an endless
cycle of reincarnations — an idea that developed after the Vedas — is
challenged by the idea that the individual who seeks Brahman might
break out of the wheel of life. How would this idea of escaping reincarnation diminish the power of Brahman priests? How does it mini-
mize the importance of caste and karma?

THINKING HISTORICALLY

Recognizing changes in the Hindu tradition is more difficult than in the
Judaic tradition. The literature of Judaism is full of historical references:
names of historical figures and even dates. Hindu sacred literature, as

* VAY duhz
† oo PAH nee shahdz
‡ sveh tah SVAH tah ruh

Source: *Svetasvatara* Upanishad in *The Upanishads: The Breath of the Eternal*, trans. Swami
Prabhavananda and Frederick Manchester (Hollywood: The Vedanta Society of Southern
California, 1948; New York: Mentor Books, 1957), 118–21.

you can tell from this brief introduction, shows virtually no interest in historical names and dates. Because time in India was conceived as cyclical, rather than linear, and the cycles of the Indian time scheme were immense, determining the exact time an event occurred was less important in Hindu thought than understanding its eternal meaning.

Consequently, our analysis of the changes in Hinduism is more logical than chronological. We can therefore speak of a long-term historical process even though we cannot date each step.

The oldest of the thirteen universally recognized Upanishads, all of which were composed between 800 and 400 B.C.E., are the Brihad Aranyaka and the Chandogya (from which selections 3 and 4 in Chapter 3 are taken). The *Svetasvatara* is one of the last of the thirteen, composed closer to 400 B.C.E. What is the idea of time suggested by this Upanishad?

This vast universe is a wheel. Upon it are all creatures that are subject to birth, death, and rebirth. Round and round it turns, and never stops. It is the wheel of Brahman. As long as the individual self thinks it is separate from Brahman, it revolves upon the wheel in bondage to the laws of birth, death, and rebirth. But when through the grace of Brahman it realizes its identity with him, it revolves upon the wheel no longer. It achieves immortality.

He who is realized by transcending the world of cause and effect, in deep contemplation, is expressly declared by the scriptures to be the Supreme Brahman. He is the substance, all else the shadow. He is the imperishable. The knowers of Brahman know him as the one reality behind all that seems. For this reason they are devoted to him. Absorbed in him, they attain freedom from the wheel of birth, death, and rebirth.

The Lord supports this universe, which is made up of the perishable and the imperishable, the manifest and the unmanifest. The individual soul, forgetful of the Lord, attaches itself to pleasure and thus is bound. When it comes to the Lord, it is freed from all its fetters.

Mind and matter, master and servant—both have existed from beginningless time. The Maya which unites them has also existed from beginningless time. When all three—mind, matter, and Maya—are known as one with Brahman, then is it realized that the Self is infinite and has no part in action. Then is it revealed that the Self is all.

Matter is perishable. The Lord, the destroyer of ignorance, is imperishable, immortal. He is the one God, the Lord of the perishable and of all souls. By meditating on him, by uniting oneself with him, by identifying oneself with him, one ceases to be ignorant.

Know God, and all fetters will be loosed. Ignorance will vanish. Birth, death, and rebirth will be no more. Meditate upon him and transcend physical consciousness. Thus will you reach union with the lord of the universe. Thus will you become identified with him who is One without a second. In him all your desires will find fulfillment.

The truth is that you are always united with the Lord. But you must *know* this. Nothing further is there to know. Meditate, and you will realize that mind, matter, and Maya (the power which unites mind and matter) are but three aspects of Brahman, the one reality.

Fire, though present in the firesticks, is not perceived until one stick is rubbed against another. The Self is like that fire: It is realized in the body by meditation on the sacred syllable OM.[1]

Let your body be the stick that is rubbed, the sacred syllable OM the stick that is rubbed against it. Thus shall you realize God, who is hidden within the body as fire is hidden within the wood.

Like oil in sesame seeds, butter in cream, water in the river bed, fire in tinder, the Self dwells within the soul. Realize him through truthfulness and meditation.

Like butter in cream is the Self in everything. Knowledge of the Self is gained through meditation. The Self is Brahman. By Brahman is all ignorance destroyed.

To realize God, first control the outgoing senses and harness the mind. Then meditate upon the light in the heart of the fire—meditate, that is, upon pure consciousness as distinct from the ordinary consciousness of the intellect. Thus the Self, the Inner Reality, may be seen behind physical appearance.

[1] Sacred symbol for God and the sound chanted in meditation. [Ed.]

2

Buddhism: Gotama's Discovery

Gotama Siddhartha* (c. 563–483 B.C.E.), known to history as the Buddha, was the son of a Hindu Kshatriya prince in northern India. This selection tells a traditional story about his youth. Because his father was warned by "Brahman soothsayers" that young Gotama would leave his home to live among the seekers in the forest, his father kept the boy distracted in the palace, the sufferings of people outside hidden from him. This selection begins when the prince, or *rāja*, finally agrees to let Gotama tour outside the palace.

*GAH tah mah   sih DAHR thah

Source: "The Life of Gotama the Buddha," trans. E. H. Brewster, in Clarence H. Hamilton, *Buddhism* (1926; reprint, New York: The Bobbs-Merrill Company, 1952), 6–11.

What does Gotama discover? What seems to be the meaning of these discoveries for him? How is his subsequent thought or behavior similar to that of other Hindus in the era? How is the message of this story similar to the lessons of the Upanishads?

THINKING HISTORICALLY

None of the stories we have of the Buddha was written during his lifetime. For some four hundred years, stories of the Buddha were passed by word of mouth before they were put into writing. Can you see any signs in this story that it was memorized and told orally? When the stories were finally written down, some were no doubt more faithful to the Buddha's actual words and experience than others. What elements in this story would most likely reflect the historical experience of Gotama? What parts of the story would most likely be added later by people who worshiped the Buddha?

Now the young lord Gotama, when many days had passed by, bade his charioteer make ready the state carriages, saying: "Get ready the carriages, good charioteer, and let us go through the park to inspect the pleasaunce."[1] "Yes, my lord," replied the charioteer, and harnessed the state carriages and sent word to Gotama: "The carriages are ready, my lord; do now what you deem fit." Then Gotama mounted a state carriage and drove out in state into the park.

Now the young lord saw, as he was driving to the park, an aged man as bent as a roof gable, decrepit, leaning on a staff, tottering as he walked, afflicted and long past his prime. And seeing him Gotama said: "That man, good charioteer, what has he done, that his hair is not like that of other men, nor his body?"

"He is what is called an aged man, my lord."

"But why is he called aged?"

"He is called aged, my lord, because he has not much longer to live."

"But then, good charioteer, am I too subject to old age, one who has not got past old age?"

"You, my lord, and we too, we all are of a kind to grow old; we have not got past old age."

"Why then, good charioteer, enough of the park for today. Drive me back hence to my rooms."

[1] A garden. [Ed.]

"Yea, my lord," answered the charioteer, and drove him back. And he, going to his rooms, sat brooding sorrowful and depressed, thinking, "Shame then verily be upon this thing called birth, since to one born old age shows itself like that!"

Thereupon the rāja sent for the charioteer and asked him: "Well, good charioteer, did the boy take pleasure in the park? Was he pleased with it?"

"No, my lord, he was not."

"What then did he see on his drive?"

(And the charioteer told the rāja all.)

Then the rāja thought thus: We must not have Gotama declining to rule. We must not have him going forth from the house into the homeless state. We must not let what the brāhman soothsayers spoke of come true.

So, that these things might not come to pass, he let the youth be still more surrounded by sensuous pleasures. And thus Gotama continued to live amidst the pleasures of sense.

Now after many days had passed by, the young lord again bade his charioteer make ready and drove forth as once before. . . .

And Gotama saw, as he was driving to the park, a sick man, suffering and very ill, fallen and weltering in his own water, by some being lifted up, by others being dressed. Seeing this, Gotama asked: "That man, good charioteer, what has he done that his eyes are not like others' eyes, nor his voice like the voice of other men?"

"He is what is called ill, my lord."

"But what is meant by ill?"

"It means, my lord, that he will hardly recover from his illness."

"But am I too, then, good charioteer, subject to fall ill; have I not got out of reach of illness?"

"You, my lord, and we too, we are all subject to fall ill; we have not got beyond the reach of illness."

"Why then, good charioteer, enough of the park for today. Drive me back hence to my rooms." "Yea, my lord," answered the charioteer, and drove him back. And he, going to his rooms, sat brooding sorrowful and depressed, thinking: Shame then verily be upon this thing called birth, since to one born decay shows itself like that, disease shows itself like that.

Thereupon the rāja sent for the charioteer and asked him: "Well, good charioteer, did the young lord take pleasure in the park and was he pleased with it?"

"No, my lord, he was not."

"What did he see then on his drive?"

(And the charioteer told the rāja all.)

Then the rāja thought thus: We must not have Gotama declining to rule; we must not have him going forth from the house to the homeless state; we must not let what the brāhman soothsayers spoke of come true.

So, that these things might not come to pass, he let the young man be still more abundantly surrounded by sensuous pleasures. And thus Gotama continued to live amidst the pleasures of sense.

Now once again, after many days . . . the young lord Gotama . . . drove forth.

And he saw, as he was driving to the park, a great concourse of people clad in garments of different colours constructing a funeral pyre. And seeing this he asked his charioteer: "Why now are all those people come together in garments of different colours, and making that pile?"

"It is because someone, my lord, has ended his days."

"Then drive the carriage close to him who has ended his days."

"Yea, my lord," answered the charioteer, and did so. And Gotama saw the corpse of him who had ended his days and asked: "What, good charioteer, is ending one's days?"

"It means, my lord, that neither mother, nor father, nor other kinsfolk will now see him, nor will he see them."

"But am I too then subject to death, have I not got beyond reach of death? Will neither the rāja, nor the ranee, nor any other of my kin see me more, or shall I again see them?"

"You, my lord, and we too, we are all subject to death; we have not passed beyond the reach of death. Neither the rāja, nor the ranee, nor any other of your kin will see you any more, nor will you see them."

"Why then, good charioteer, enough of the park for today. Drive me back hence to my rooms."

"Yea, my lord," replied the charioteer, and drove him back.

And he, going to his rooms, sat brooding sorrowful and depressed, thinking: Shame verily be upon this thing called birth, since to one born the decay of life, since disease, since death shows itself like that!

Thereupon the rāja questioned the charioteer as before and as before let Gotama be still more surrounded by sensuous enjoyment. And thus he continued to live amidst the pleasures of sense.

Now once again, after many days . . . the lord Gotama . . . drove forth.

And he saw, as he was driving to the park, a shaven-headed man, a recluse, wearing the yellow robe. And seeing him he asked the charioteer, "That man, good charioteer, what has he done that his head is unlike other men's heads and his clothes too are unlike those of others?"

"That is what they call a recluse, because, my lord, he is one who has gone forth."

"What is that, 'to have gone forth'?"

"To have gone forth, my lord, means being thorough in the religious life, thorough in the peaceful life, thorough in good action, thorough in meritorious conduct, thorough in harmlessness, thorough in kindness to all creatures."

"Excellent indeed, friend charioteer, is what they call a recluse, since so thorough is his conduct in all those respects, wherefore drive me up to that forthgone man."

"Yea, my lord," replied the charioteer and drove up to the recluse. Then Gotama addressed him, saying, "You master, what have you done that your head is not as other men's heads, nor your clothes as those of other men?"

"I, my lord, am one who has gone forth."

"What, master, does that mean?"

"It means, my lord, being thorough in the religious life, thorough in the peaceful life, thorough in good actions, thorough in meritorious conduct, thorough in harmlessness, thorough in kindness to all creatures."

"Excellently indeed, master, are you said to have gone forth since so thorough is your conduct in all those respects." Then the lord Gotama bade his charioteer, saying: "Come then, good charioteer, do you take the carriage and drive it back hence to my rooms. But I will even here cut off my hair, and don the yellow robe, and go forth from the house into the homeless state."

"Yea, my lord," replied the charioteer, and drove back. But the prince Gotama, there and then cutting off his hair and donning the yellow robe, went forth from the house into the homeless state.

Now at Kapilavatthu, the rāja's seat, a great number of persons, some eighty-four thousand souls, heard of what prince Gotama had done and thought: Surely this is no ordinary religious rule, this is no common going forth, in that prince Gotama himself has had his head shaved and has donned the yellow robe and has gone forth from the house into the homeless state. If prince Gotama has done this, why then should not we also? And they all had their heads shaved and donned the yellow robes; and in imitation of the Bodhisat [Buddha][2] they went forth from the house into the homeless state. So the Bodhisat went forth from the house into the homeless state. So the Bodhisat went up on his rounds through the villages, towns, and cities accompanied by that multitude.

Now there arose in the mind of Gotama the Bodhisat, when he was meditating in seclusion, this thought: That indeed is not suitable for me that I should live beset. 'Twere better were I to dwell alone, far from the crowd.

So after a time he dwelt alone, away from the crowd. Those eighty-four thousand recluses went one way, and the Bodhisat went another way.

Now there arose in the mind of Gotama the Bodhisat, when he had gone to his place and was meditating in seclusion, this thought: Verily, this world had fallen upon trouble—one is born, and grows old, and dies, and falls from one state, and springs up in another. And from the suffering, moreover, no one knows of any way to escape, even from decay and death. O, when shall a way of escape from this suffering be made known—from decay and from death?

---

[2] Here the author clearly means the Buddha, but the term *Bodhisat* or *Bodhisattva* came to designate a kind of Buddhist saint who helped others achieve salvation in the later Mahayana school of Buddhism. [Ed.]

3

Buddhism and Caste

This story, part of the Buddhist canon that was written between one hundred and four hundred years after his death, tells of a confrontation between the Buddha and Brahmans, members of the Hindu priestly caste. Such an encounter would have been common as Brahmans and Buddhists confronted each other during the Maurya Empire (321–184 B.C.E.), which included the great Buddhist convert, King Ashoka (304–232 B.C.E.). (A Brahman reaction set in during the following Shunga dynasty, and Buddhism almost vanished from India.) How would you expect most Brahmans to react to the Buddha's opposition to caste? Would some Brahmans be persuaded by the Buddha's arguments? How and why might Buddhism have a wider appeal than Hinduism?

THINKING HISTORICALLY

What signs do you see in the document that it was not written during the lifetime of the Buddha? Notice the mention of Greece and the dialogue style of this selection. If, as some scholars have suggested, there may be Greek influence here, which Greek writer would they be referring to (see Chapter 3)? How might this Greek influence help us find an approximate date for this writing?

Once when the Lord was staying at Sāvatthī there were five hundred brāhmans from various countries in the city . . . and they thought: "This ascetic Gautama preaches that all four classes are pure. Who can refute him?"

At that time there was a young brāhman named Assalāyana in the city . . . a youth of sixteen, thoroughly versed in the Vedas . . . and in all brāhmanic learning. "He can do it!" thought the brāhmans, and so they asked him to try; surrounded by a crowd of brāhmans, he went to the Lord, and, after greeting him, sat down and said:

"Brāhmans maintain that only they are the highest class, and the others are below them. They are white, the others black; only they are pure, and not the others. Only they are the true sons of Brahmā, born from his mouth, born of Brahmā, creations of Brahmā, heirs of Brahmā. Now what does the worthy Gautama say to that?"

"Do the brāhmans really maintain this, Assalāyana, when they're born of women just like anyone else, of brāhman women who have their periods and conceive, give birth and nurse their children, just like any other women?"

Source: *The Buddhist Tradition in India, China and Japan*, ed. William Theodore de Bary (New York: Random House, 1969), 49–51.

"For all you say, this is what they think. . . ."

"Have you ever heard that in the lands of the Greeks and Kambojas and other peoples on the borders there are only two classes, masters and slaves, and a master can become a slave and vice versa?"

"Yes, I've heard so."

"And what strength or support does that fact give to the brāhmans' claim?"

"Nevertheless, that is what they think."

"Again if a man is a murderer, a thief, or an adulterer, or commits other grave sins, when his body breaks up on death does he pass on to purgatory if he's a kshatriya,[1] vaishya,[2] or shūdra,[3] but not if he's a brāhman?"

"No, Gautama. In such a case the same fate is in store for all men, whatever their class."

"And if he avoids grave sin, will he go to heaven if he's a brāhman, but not if he's a man of the lower classes?"

"No, Gautama. In such a case the same reward awaits all men, whatever their class."

"And is a brāhman capable of developing a mind of love without hate or ill-will, but not a man of the other classes?"

"No, Gautama. All four classes are capable of doing so."

"Can only a brāhman go down to a river and wash away dust and dirt, and not men of the other classes?"

"No, Gautama, all four classes can."

"Now suppose a king were to gather together a hundred men of different classes and to order the brāhmans and kshatriyas to take kindling wood of sāl, pine, lotus, or sandal, and light fires, while the lowclass folk did the same with common wood. What do you think would happen? Would the fires of the high-born men blaze up brightly . . . and those of the humble fail?"

"No, Gautama. It would be alike with high and lowly. . . . Every fire would blaze with the same bright flame." . . .

"Suppose there are two young brāhman brothers, one a scholar and the other uneducated. Which of them would be served first at memorial feasts, festivals, and sacrifices, or when entertained as guests?"

"The scholar, of course; for what great benefit would accrue from entertaining the uneducated one?"

"But suppose the scholar is ill-behaved and wicked, while the uneducated one is well-behaved and virtuous?"

"Then the uneducated one would be served first, for what great benefit would accrue from entertaining an ill-behaved and wicked man?"

---

[1] KSHAH tree uh   Warrior. [Ed.]

[2] VYS yuh   Free peasant, artisan, or producer. [Ed.]

[3] SHOO druh   Serf. [Ed.]

"First, Assalāyana, you based your claim on birth, then you gave up birth for learning, and finally you have come round to my way of thinking, that all four classes are equally pure!"

At this Assalāyana sat silent . . . his shoulders hunched, his eyes cast down, thoughtful in mind, and with no answer at hand.

4

Mahayana Buddhism: The Lotus Sutra

Written in India in the first or early second century c.e., the Lotus Sutra became one of the favorite Buddhist scriptures in China, Japan, and other Mahayana Buddhist countries. This very brief section from the sutra tells of the Buddha's death ("passing into extinction" or nirvana). The goal of all Buddhists, like the Buddha himself, was a state of consciousness called *bodhi* (enlightenment, or awakening) that brought a release from the suffering of the world and the attainment of ultimate peace, called nirvana. After the Buddha achieved this state, two Buddhist schools developed concerning the issue of how others might attain nirvana. One, the Theravada, said you had to emulate the hard, ascetic life of the Buddha. Another, the Mahayana, said it was easier and open to everyone because you could pray for help.

Mahayana Buddhism developed alongside but in opposition to Theravada (or Orthodox) Buddhism in its home in India. Theravada Buddhism (still practiced in Southeast Asia) was the more exacting and orthodox form of Buddhism; it encouraged all young men to emulate the Buddha by becoming monks, practicing rigorous discipline begging for their food, and studying the classic texts. Mahayana Buddhism means "the Greater Vehicle" because it could appeal to a greater range of people. Central to Mahayana Buddhism is the idea of a Bodhisattva—a Buddha-type who is capable of achieving nirvana but who, instead, helps others reach enlightenment. Thus, one can pray to a Bodhisattva to achieve salvation. Mahayana Buddhism spread through China and North Asia, offering a less demanding avenue to salvation than Theravada Buddhism, because instead of renouncing the everyday world and becoming a monk or a nun, one could continue a normal life while worshiping at temples and making offerings to the Buddha and various Bodhisattvas.

Source: *The Lotus Sutra*, translated by the Buddhist Text Translation Society, Mahayana Buddhists sutras in English at http://www.cttbusa.org/lotus/lotus1_1.asp.

Which ideas of this sutra make Buddhism more universal or offer "salvation" to a broader audience than monks, nuns, and other religious specialists?

THINKING HISTORICALLY

Some words and ideas in this document are "pre-Buddha" and some are "post-Buddha." That is, some words and ideas could be found in a Hindu text before the Buddha was born. Others seem to come from a world after the Buddha has died. Which words or ideas fit into one or the other of these categories? How can you distinguish between what might have happened at the time of the Buddha's death and what was probably added some time later? How are the ideas expressed in this sutra different from the ideas attributed to the Buddha in previous selections from this chapter? What might account for these differences? How did the early Buddhists who composed this sutra transform the Buddha as seeker of enlightenment into the Buddha as object of worship?

I recall that in ages past,
Limitless, countless aeons ago,
There appeared a Buddha, one honored among people
By the name of Brightness of Sun-Moon-Lamp,
That World Honored One[1] proclaimed the Dharma,[2]
Taking limitless living beings across,
Causing countless millions of Bodhisattvas
To enter the wisdom of the Buddhas.

Before that Buddha had left home,
The eight royal sons born to him,
Seeing the Great Sage leave his home,
Also followed him to practice Brahman conduct.

The Buddha then spoke a Great Vehicle[3]
Sutra by the name of Limitless Principles;
Amidst the assembly, and for their sake,
He set it forth in extensive detail.
When the Buddha had finished speaking the Sutra,
Seated in the Dharma-seat,

[1] The Buddha. [Ed.]
[2] The Law. [Ed.]
[3] *Mahayana* literally means "Great Vehicle." [Ed.]

He sat in full lotus[4] and entered the Samadhi[5]
Called the Station of Limitless Principles.
From the heavens fell a rain of Mandarava flowers,[6]
And heavenly drums of themselves did sound,
While all the gods, dragons, ghosts and spirits,
Made offerings to the Honored One;
And, within all the Buddha lands,
There occurred a mighty trembling.
The light emitted from between the Buddha's brows
Manifested all these rare events.

The light illumined to the east
Eighteen thousand Buddha lands,
Revealing the places of living beings'
Karmic retributions of birth and death.
Seen, too, were Buddha lands adorned
With a multitude of gems,
The color of lapis lazuli[7] and crystal,
Illumined by the Buddha's light.
Seen as well were gods and people,
Dragons, spirits, and Yaksha[8] Hordes,
Gandharvas and Kinnaras,[9]
Each making offering to the Buddha. . . .

The Buddha, having spoken The Dharma Flower[10]
And caused the assembly to rejoice,
Later, on that very day,
Announced to the host of gods and humans;
"The meaning of the real mark of all Dharmas
Has already been spoken for all of you,
And now at midnight, I
shall enter into Nirvana.
You should single-heartedly advance with vigor,
And avoid laxness, for
Buddhas are difficult indeed to meet,
Encountered but once in a million aeons."

[4] Yoga position on folded legs. [Ed.]
[5] Highest state of consciousness reached in meditation. [Ed.]
[6] Bright scarlet flowers associated with the story of an Indian princess. [Ed.]
[7] Rare blue stone. [Ed.]
[8] Indian nature spirits, often tree spirits, imagined in human form. [Ed.]
[9] Ancient tribal peoples or music spirits. [Ed.]
[10] The words that lead to the flowering of the Law; the Buddha's last words; sometimes refers to this Lotus Sutra itself. [Ed.]

All of the disciples of the World Honored One
Hearing of the Buddha's entry into Nirvana,
Each harbored grief and anguish,
"Why must the Buddha take extinction so soon?"
The sagely Lord, the Dharma King,
Then comforted the limitless multitude:
"After my passage into extinction,
None of you should worry or fear,
For the Bodhisattva Virtue Treasury,[11]
With respect to the non-outflow mark of reality,[12]
In heart has penetrated it totally;
He will next become a Buddha,
By the name of Pure Body, and
Will also save uncounted multitudes.

That night the Buddha passed into extinction,
As a flame dies once its fuel has been consumed.
The Sharira[13] were divided up,
And limitless stupas[14] built.
The Bhikshus and Bhikshuni,[15]
Their number like the Ganges' sands,
Redoubled their vigor in advancing
In their quest for the unsurpassed path.

[11] The name of the first Bodhisattva. [Ed.]
[12] He understands the true reality. [Ed.]
[13] The bones of the Buddha after cremation. [Ed.]
[14] Temples, usually built over a bone or other relic of the Buddha. [Ed.]
[15] Ordained nuns and monks. [Ed.]

5

Judaism and the Bible: History, Laws, and Psalms

Just as the caste-based Hinduism of ancient Aryan tribes gave rise
to universal Buddhism after 500 B.C.E., so did the Judaism of the
Hebrew tribe of Abraham give birth to universalist Christianity. Judaism was already an ancient religion by the time of Jesus and the birth
of Christianity. It traced its roots back (perhaps two thousand years)

Source: Gen. 1:1–31, 2:1–25, 17:1–14; Exod. 19:1–9, 20:1–18; Lev. 1:1–9; Ps. 23:1–6; Amos 5:21–24. All biblical selections are from the New International Version.

to Abraham himself, who, according to tradition, made a contract (or covenant) with God to worship him and him alone.

This commitment to one god, and one god only, was a development unique to the history of Judaism. The worship of various ancestral and nature spirits was common practice among hunting-gathering and agricultural peoples. Early cities added numerous local protectors and, in some cases, a pantheon of deities presented in myth and legend. The Bronze Age empires were probably the first to imagine a single ruler of the heavens — an obvious parallel to the role of the emperor on Earth. The Egyptians for a brief moment (around 1300 B.C.E.) preached the singularity of god, in this case the sun god Aton, but that was soon renounced. Persian Zoroastrianism imagined competing gods of light and darkness, each supreme in his realm, an idea that was to leave its mark in Persian-occupied Jerusalem. But the idea of a single creator of the universe — and no other gods — was new to the ancient Hebrews.

Since such a belief was unusual, the descendants of Abraham had difficulty accepting it. In their wanderings throughout the land of the Tigris and Euphrates rivers, from Abraham's native Ur to Egypt (see Map 6.1), the Jews came into contact with many different religious beliefs; some were even tempted by foreign gods. However, by around 1300 B.C.E., Abraham's descendants had escaped Egyptian domination, crossed the Red Sea, and with the help of Moses renewed their covenant with God in the Ten Commandments. Even then, stories were told of Jews who worshiped the Golden Calf and other idols and of the displeasure of the God of Abraham. "I am a jealous God," he told his people. "You shall have no other gods before me."

Such is the story told in the books of the Hebrew Bible,[1] written after the Jews settled in Jerusalem and the surrounding area sometime after 1000 B.C.E. The Hebrew Bible not only recounts the story of the people of Abraham but also takes its story back ages before the patriarch, stretching back to the beginning of the world and forward to the period of Jewish kingdoms after 900 B.C.E., when Kings Saul, David, and Solomon ruled large parts of what is today Israel, Palestine, and Jordan. The Hebrew Bible included their histories, the laws of the two Jewish kingdoms Judah and Israel, and various other writings (songs, poetry called psalms, philosophy, and stories of prophecy).

As you read these first selections from the Bible (Genesis, Exodus, Leviticus, Psalms, Amos), note how they are similar to, and different from, the Vedas and Upanishads of Hinduism. How, for instance, is the Bible's story of the beginning of the world different from the

---

[1] *Hebrew Bible* refers to the books in the Bible that were written in Hebrew. Christians call these books the Old Testament. The first five books of the Bible are called the Torah by Jews. [Ed.]

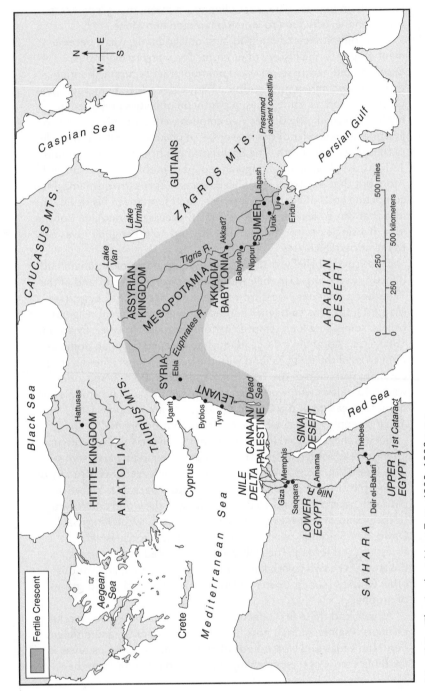

Map 6.1 The Ancient Near East, 4000–1000 B.C.E.

Hindus' creation story of the sacrifice of Purusha? Why might an understanding of history be more important to the Jews than it was to the Hindus? Compare the role of morality in the religion of Jews and Hindus. In what sense is the morality of Judaism universal and that of Hinduism caste based? How is the Judaic emphasis on morality also different from Buddhist ideas?

THINKING HISTORICALLY

Since the books of the Hebrew Bible were composed over a long period of time, from about 900 B.C.E. to about 165 B.C.E., we might expect to see changes in emphasis, especially since this period was such a tumultuous one in Jewish history. The immediate descendants of Abraham were a nomadic pastoral people—shepherds, Psalm 23 reminds us—though this beautiful psalm attributed to King David was written in an urban, monarchal stage of Jewish history. Leviticus, too, echoes an earlier pastoral life when animal sacrifice, and the worship by shepherds generally, was still practiced.

When did morality replace sacrifice as the sign of respect to the God of Abraham? Was it around 1300 B.C.E., the traditional date for the reception by Moses of the Ten Commandments? Or is the existence of Leviticus, perhaps five hundred years later, a sign that sacrifice was still practiced? The sentiments of Amos (783–743 B.C.E.) suggest that the Jews later rejected not only animal sacrifice but also moral obedience that was not truly felt.

When did monotheism (the belief in one god) become unequivocal, unquestioned? Since this was a new idea, there must have been a time when it wasn't held. Some scholars see signs of an earlier polytheism (belief in many gods) in the book of Genesis itself. For instance, in Genesis 3:5 we find "ye shall be as gods," and Genesis 3:22 reads "And the Lord God said: Behold the man has become like one of us."

Certainly the beginning of Genesis is no-nonsense monotheism, majestically so: "In the beginning God created the heavens and the earth." But scholars have pointed out that this opening is followed by another story of origin, beginning at Chapter 2, Verse 4, that not only tells the story over again, but does so without the intense declarative monotheism. They date this document at about 850 B.C.E. and the section from 1:1 to 2:3 at about 650 B.C.E. Compare the language in Genesis 1 to 2:3 with the section that begins at 2:4. Which selection from Genesis seems more idealized, which more like a report? Which version would probably be closer to the oral storytelling tradition? Which reflects the style of a sophisticated, urban, philosophical culture? Which term is more monotheistic: *God* or *Lord God*?

If we can see increased emphasis on monotheism from 850 to 650 B.C.E., we might also see in these selections the transition from the religion of a tribe of shepherds to that of a political kingdom. What evidence do you see that a pastoral religion of animal sacrifice became a religion of law, or even internalized morality?

Finally, notice that there is no heaven here—no afterlife. God promised Abraham land and prosperity. The ideas of a last judgment, heaven and hell, and salvation became important in Christianity, but we will explore the development of these ideas in Judaism in the second century B.C.E.

Genesis 1

The Beginning

1 In the beginning God created the heavens and the earth.

2 Now the earth was formless and empty, darkness was over the surface of the deep, and the Spirit of God was hovering over the waters.

3 And God said, "Let there be light," and there was light. 4 God saw that the light was good, and He separated the light from the darkness. 5 God called the light "day," and the darkness he called "night." And there was evening, and there was morning—the first day.

6 And God said, "Let there be an expanse between the waters to separate water from water." 7 So God made the expanse and separated the water under the expanse from the water above it. And it was so. 8 God called the expanse "sky." And there was evening, and there was morning—the second day.

9 And God said, "Let the water under the sky be gathered to one place, and let dry ground appear." And it was so. 10 God called the dry ground "land," and the gathered waters he called "seas." And God saw that it was good.

11 Then God said, "Let the land produce vegetation: seed-bearing plants and trees on the land that bear fruit with seed in it, according to their various kinds." And it was so. 12 The land produced vegetation: plants bearing seed according to their kinds and trees bearing fruit with seed in it according to their kinds. And God saw that it was good. 13 And there was evening, and there was morning—the third day.

14 And God said, "Let there be lights in the expanse of the sky to separate the day from the night, and let them serve as signs to mark seasons and days and years, 15 and let them be lights in the expanse of the sky to give light on the earth." And it was so. 16 God made two great lights—the greater light to govern the day and the lesser light to govern the night. He also made the stars. 17 God set them in the expanse of the sky to give light on the earth, 18 to govern the day and the night, and to

separate light from darkness. And God saw that it was good. 19 And there was evening, and there was morning—the fourth day.

20 And God said, "Let the water teem with living creatures, and let birds fly above the earth across the expanse of the sky." 21 So God created the great creatures of the sea and every living and moving thing with which the water teems, according to their kinds, and every winged bird according to its kind. And God saw that it was good. 22 God blessed them and said, "Be fruitful and increase in number and fill the water in the seas, and let the birds increase on the earth." 23 And there was evening, and there was morning—the fifth day.

24 And God said, "Let the land produce living creatures according to their kinds: livestock, creatures that move along the ground, and wild animals, each according to its kind." And it was so. 25 God made the wild animals according to their kinds, the livestock according to their kinds, and all the creatures that move along the ground according to their kinds. And God saw that it was good.

26 Then God said, "Let us make man in our image, in our likeness, and let them rule over the fish of the sea and the birds of the air, over the livestock, over all the earth, and over all the creatures that move along the ground."

27 So God created man in his own image,
in the image of God he created him;
male and female he created them.

28 God blessed them and said to them, "Be fruitful and increase in number; fill the earth and subdue it. Rule over the fish of the sea and the birds of the air and over every living creature that moves on the ground."

29 Then God said, "I give you every seed-bearing plant on the face of the whole earth and every tree that has fruit with seed in it. They will be yours for food. 30 And to all the beasts of the earth and all the birds of the air and all the creatures that move on the ground—everything that has the breath of life in it—I give every green plant for food." And it was so.

31 God saw all that he had made, and it was very good. And there was evening, and there was morning—the sixth day.

Genesis 2

1 Thus the heavens and the earth were completed in all their vast array.

2 By the seventh day God had finished the work he had been doing; so on the seventh day he rested from all his work. 3 And God blessed the seventh day and made it holy, because on it he rested from all the work of creating that he had done.

Adam and Eve

4 This is the account of the heavens and the earth when they were created.

When the LORD God made the earth and the heavens—5 and no shrub of the field had yet appeared on the earth and no plant of the field had yet sprung up, for the LORD God had not sent rain on the earth and there was no man to work the ground, 6 but streams came up from the earth and watered the whole surface of the ground—7 the LORD God formed the man from the dust of the ground and breathed into his nostrils the breath of life, and the man became a living being.

8 Now the LORD God had planted a garden in the east, in Eden; and there he put the man he had formed. 9 And the LORD God made all kinds of trees grow out of the ground—trees that were pleasing to the eye and good for food. In the middle of the garden were the tree of life and the tree of the knowledge of good and evil.

10 A river watering the garden flowed from Eden; from there it was separated into four headwaters. 11 The name of the first is the Pishon; it winds through the entire land of Havilah, where there is gold. 12 (The gold of that land is good; aromatic resin and onyx are also there.) 13 The name of the second river is the Gihon; it winds through the entire land of Cush. 14 The name of the third river is the Tigris; it runs along the east side of Asshur. And the fourth river is the Euphrates.

15 The LORD God took the man and put him in the Garden of Eden to work it and take care of it. 16 And the LORD God commanded the man, "You are free to eat from any tree in the garden; 17 but you must not eat from the tree of the knowledge of good and evil, for when you eat of it you will surely die."

18 The LORD God said, "It is not good for the man to be alone. I will make a helper suitable for him."

19 Now the LORD God had formed out of the ground all the beasts of the field and all the birds of the air. He brought them to the man to see what he would name them; and whatever the man called each living creature, that was its name. 20 So the man gave names to all the livestock, the birds of the air and all the beasts of the field.

But for Adam no suitable helper was found. 21 So the LORD God caused the man to fall into a deep sleep; and while he was sleeping, he took one of the man's ribs and closed up the place with flesh. 22 Then the LORD God made a woman from the rib he had taken out of the man, and he brought her to the man.

23 The man said,

"This is now bone of my bones
and flesh of my flesh;
she shall be called 'woman,'
for she was taken out of man."

24 For this reason a man will leave his father and mother and be united to his wife, and they will become one flesh.

25 The man and his wife were both naked, and they felt no shame.

Genesis 17

The Covenant of the Circumcision

1 When Abram was ninety-nine years old, the LORD appeared to him and said, "I am God Almighty; walk before me and be blameless. 2 I will confirm my covenant between me and you and will greatly increase your numbers."

3 Abram fell facedown, and God said to him, 4 "As for me, this is my covenant with you: You will be the father of many nations. 5 No longer will you be called Abram; your name will be Abraham, for I have made you a father of many nations. 6 I will make you very fruitful; I will make nations of you, and kings will come from you. 7 I will establish my covenant as an everlasting covenant between me and you and your descendants after you for the generations to come, to be your God and the God of your descendants after you. 8 The whole land of Canaan, where you are now an alien, I will give as an everlasting possession to you and your descendants after you; and I will be their God."

9 Then God said to Abraham, "As for you, you must keep my covenant, you and your descendants after you for the generations to come. 10 This is my covenant with you and your descendants after you, the covenant you are to keep: Every male among you shall be circumcised. 11 You are to undergo circumcision, and it will be the sign of the covenant between me and you. 12 For the generations to come every male among you who is eight days old must be circumcised, including those born in your household or bought with money from a foreigner—those who are not your offspring. 13 Whether born in your household or bought with your money, they must be circumcised. My covenant in your flesh is to be an everlasting covenant. 14 Any uncircumcised male, who has not been circumcised in the flesh, will be cut off from his people; he has broken my covenant. . . ."

Exodus 19

At Mount Sinai

1 In the third month after the Israelites left Egypt—on the very day—they came to the Desert of Sinai. 2 After they set out from Rephidim, they entered the Desert of Sinai, and Israel camped there in the desert in front of the mountain.

3 Then Moses went up to God, and the LORD called to him from the mountain and said, "This is what you are to say to the house of Jacob and what you are to tell the people of Israel: 4 'You yourselves have seen what I did to Egypt, and how I carried you on eagles' wings and brought you to myself. 5 Now if you obey me fully and keep my covenant, then out of all nations you will be my treasured possession. Although the whole earth is mine, 6 you will be for me a kingdom of priests and a holy nation.' These are the words you are to speak to the Israelites."

7 So Moses went back and summoned the elders of the people and set before them all the words the LORD had commanded him to speak. 8 The people all responded together, "We will do everything the LORD has said." So Moses brought their answer back to the LORD.

9 The LORD said to Moses, "I am going to come to you in a dense cloud, so that the people will hear me speaking with you and will always put their trust in you." Then Moses told the LORD what the people had said.

Exodus 20

The Ten Commandments

1 And God spoke all these words:

2 "I am the LORD your God, who brought you out of Egypt, out of the land of slavery.

3 "You shall have no other gods before me.

4 "You shall not make for yourself an idol in the form of anything in heaven above or on the earth beneath or in the waters below. 5 You shall not bow down to them or worship them; for I, the LORD your God, am a jealous God, punishing the children for the sin of the fathers to the third and fourth generation of those who hate me, 6 but showing love to a thousand [generations] of those who love me and keep my commandments.

7 "You shall not misuse the name of the LORD your God, for the LORD will not hold anyone guiltless who misuses his name.

8 "Remember the Sabbath day by keeping it holy. 9 Six days you shall labor and do all your work, 10 but the seventh day is a Sabbath to the LORD your God. On it you shall not do any work, neither you, nor your son or daughter, nor your manservant or maidservant, nor your animals, nor the alien within your gates. 11 For in six days the LORD made the heavens and the earth, the sea, and all that is in them, but he rested on the seventh day. Therefore the LORD blessed the Sabbath day and made it holy.

12 "Honor your father and your mother, so that you may live long in the land the LORD your God is giving you.

13 "You shall not murder.

14 "You shall not commit adultery.

15 "You shall not steal.

16 "You shall not give false testimony against your neighbor.

17 "You shall not covet your neighbor's house. You shall not covet your neighbor's wife, or his manservant or maidservant, his ox or donkey, or anything that belongs to your neighbor."

18 When the people saw the thunder and lightning and heard the trumpet and saw the mountain in smoke, they trembled with fear.

Leviticus 1

The Burnt Offering

1 The LORD called to Moses and spoke to him from the Tent of Meeting. He said, 2 "Speak to the Israelites and say to them: 'When any of you brings an offering to the LORD, bring as your offering an animal from either the herd or the flock.

3 "'If the offering is a burnt offering from the herd, he is to offer a male without defect. He must present it at the entrance to the Tent of Meeting so that it will be acceptable to the LORD. 4 He is to lay his hand on the head of the burnt offering, and it will be accepted on his behalf to make atonement for him. 5 He is to slaughter the young bull before the LORD, and then Aaron's sons the priests shall bring the blood and sprinkle it against the altar on all sides at the entrance to the Tent of Meeting. 6 He is to skin the burnt offering and cut it into pieces. 7 The sons of Aaron the priest are to put fire on the altar and arrange wood on the fire. 8 Then Aaron's sons the priests shall arrange the pieces, including the head and the fat, on the burning wood that is on the altar. 9 He is to wash the inner parts and the legs with water, and the priest is to burn all of it on the altar. It is a burnt offering, an offering made by fire, an aroma pleasing to the LORD. . . .'"

Psalm 23

A Psalm of David

1 The LORD is my shepherd, I shall not be in want.

2 He makes me lie down in green pastures,
   he leads me beside quiet waters,

3 he restores my soul.
   He guides me in paths of righteousness
   for his name's sake.

4 Even though I walk
  through the valley of the shadow of death,[1]
  I will fear no evil,
  for you are with me;
  your rod and your staff,
  they comfort me.

5 You prepare a table before me
  in the presence of my enemies.
  You anoint my head with oil;
  my cup overflows.

6 Surely goodness and love will follow me
  all the days of my life,
  and I will dwell in the house of the LORD
  forever.

Amos 5

21 "I hate, I despise your religious feasts;
   I cannot stand your assemblies.

22 Even though you bring me burnt offerings and grain offerings,
   I will not accept them.
   Though you bring choice fellowship offerings,
   I will have no regard for them.

23 Away with the noise of your songs!
   I will not listen to the music of your harps.

24 But let justice roll on like a river,
   righteousness like a never-failing stream!"

[1] Or *through the darkest valley*. [Ed.]

Judaism and the Bible: Prophecy and the Apocalypse

The golden days of Jewish kings were not to last. Powerful empires rose up to challenge and dominate the Jews: the Assyrians in 800 B.C.E., the Babylonians around 600 B.C.E., then the Medes, the Persians, the armies of Alexander the Great, his successor states — ruled by his generals and their descendants — and then the Romans after 64 B.C.E. The Babylonians were among the worst of the invaders. They conquered Jerusalem, destroyed the temple, and brought Jews as hostages to Babylon. In 538 B.C.E. Cyrus, king of the Persians, allowed Jews to return to Jerusalem and even rebuild the temple. But the Jews never regained their kingdom or independence (except for brief periods), and the Greek Seleucid* rulers after Alexander proved to be intolerant of non-Greek forms of worship.

Ironically, it was during this period of conquest and dispersal that Judaism began to develop the elements of a universal religion. The Babylonian destruction of the temple and population transfer made the religion of Yahweh less dependent on place. Virtually all religions of the ancient world were bound to a particular place, usually the sacred temple where the god was thought to reside. Judaism remained a religion of the descendants of Abraham and his son Israel, and the period after 600 B.C.E. was one of intense cultivation of that identity. But much of the Hebrew Bible was composed in exile, as a way of recalling a common history, reaffirming a common identity, and predicting a common destiny. The prophets foresaw a brighter future or explained how the violation of the covenant had brought God's wrath on the people.

One of the great prophets of the exile and the postexile period was Daniel, described as one of the young men who was brought to Babylon by Nebuchadnezzar,† conqueror of Jerusalem in 586 B.C.E. The Book of Daniel begins by recounting that conquest. In Babylon Nebuchadnezzar asked Daniel to reveal the meaning of a dream. You will read his response below.

Daniel is the first to foretell of an apocalyptic end to history and the first to envision personal immortality. Previous prophets had predicted a new independent kingdom of Judah or God's punishment of his people, but Daniel prophesied that God would come down to reign on Earth forever, judging the living and the dead for all eternity.

*sel OO sihd
†neh boo kuhd NEH zur

Source: Dan. 2:31–45, 11:28–45, 12:1–13. New International Version.

These ideas—an end to history, the Last Judgment, the Kingdom of God, eternal life or damnation—became more important later in Christianity than in Judaism, where these notions never entered the mainstream. But their appearance in Daniel shows the way in which Judaic ideas became more universal over the course of the first millennium B.C.E. Why would Daniel's ideas open the Judaic tradition to non-Jews or people not descended from Abraham? How would Daniel's prophecy affect his contemporaries? How would it affect you?

THINKING HISTORICALLY

When did the idea of an afterlife enter Judaism? To answer this question we have to date the Book of Daniel, which is a bit more complex than it would seem. As mentioned, the book is presented as the prophecy of a Daniel who was taken from Jerusalem to Babylon around 586 B.C.E. But the author of the book knows considerably more about the period toward the end of his prophecy (180–165 B.C.E.) than about the third to sixth century B.C.E. This discrepancy and the use of second-century Hebrew and Aramaic have led biblical scholars to conclude that the Book of Daniel is prophecy after the fact, or a book of history presented as prophecy. Detailed footnotes have been added to this selection to show that the author's references to very specific events of the second century, especially the time of Antiochus IV (r. 175–163 B.C.E.), would have been easily recognized by a contemporary audience. So the author lived sometime in this period. He recounts the unhappy story of the conquests of the Jews by successive empires: from the Babylonian (627–550 B.C.E.) and Median (612–550 B.C.E.) to the Persian (550–330 B.C.E.) to the Greek under Alexander (330–323 B.C.E.) to the Seleucids (Alexander's successors), including Antiochus (312–63 B.C.E.). This is the meaning of the gold, silver, bronze, iron, and clay ages. When the author then speaks of the signs of the last days, he distinctly sees the acts of Antiochus IV as the turning point that will bring about God's eternal kingdom. Antiochus pressured the Jews to accept Greek gods. In 168 B.C.E. he polluted the temple in Jerusalem by slaughtering pigs on the altar and then erecting a statue of the Greek god Zeus. This is the event that the author predicts will bring on God's last judgment. Many Jews must have felt that the desecration of the holy temple was such a world-changing event. In fact, the acts of Antiochus also sparked a Jewish revolt under the Macabees, who eventually defeated Antiochus in 163 B.C.E. and restored an independent Jewish state.

What would be the purpose of presenting this prophecy? What would be the advantage of presenting it as the writing of someone who had lived hundreds of years earlier? How can we know that the Book of Daniel was written after 165 but before 163 B.C.E.? When and why would the author of the Book of Daniel have predicted that the end of the world would occur 1,290 days (about 3½ years) after an event in 168 B.C.E.? When and why would the author have written, "Blessed is the one who waits . . . 1,335 days"?

Daniel 2 [Daniel Interprets the Dream of Nebuchadnezzar]

31 "You looked, O king, and there before you stood a large statue—an enormous, dazzling statue, awesome in appearance. 32 The head of the statue was made of pure gold, its chest and arms of silver, its belly and thighs of bronze, 33 its legs of iron, its feet partly of iron and partly of baked clay. 34 While you were watching, a rock was cut out, but not by human hands. It struck the statue on its feet of iron and clay and smashed them. 35 Then the iron, the clay, the bronze, the silver and the gold were broken to pieces at the same time and became like chaff on a threshing floor in the summer. The wind swept them away without leaving a trace. But the rock that struck the statue became a huge mountain and filled the whole earth.

36 "This was the dream, and now we will interpret it to the king. 37 You, O king, are the king of kings. The God of heaven has given you dominion and power and might and glory; 38 in your hands he has placed mankind and the beasts of the field and the birds of the air. Wherever they live, he has made you ruler over them all. You are that head of gold.

39 "After you, another kingdom[1] will rise, inferior to yours. Next, a third kingdom, one of bronze,[2] will rule over the whole earth. 40 Finally, there will be a fourth kingdom,[3] strong as iron—for iron breaks and smashes everything—and as iron breaks things to pieces, so it will crush and break all the others. 41 Just as you saw that the feet and toes were partly of baked clay and partly of iron, so this will be a divided kingdom;[4] yet it will have some of the strength of iron in it, even as you saw iron mixed with clay. 42 As the toes were partly iron and partly clay, so this kingdom will be partly strong and partly brittle. 43 And just as you saw the iron mixed with baked clay, so the people will be a mixture[5] and will not remain united, any more than iron mixes with clay.

---

[1] Media, or the Mede Empire; Iranians who shared rule with Neo-Babylonians (Chaldeans) and were seen as successors in the Middle East to 550 B.C.E. [Ed.]

[2] Persia, 550–330 B.C.E. [Ed.]

[3] Greek empire of Alexander the Great, 330–323 B.C.E. [Ed.]

[4] The Middle Eastern portion of Alexander's empire was divided after his death in 323 B.C.E. by his generals: Seleucus in Palestine and Syria and Ptolemy in Egypt. The kingdom of the Seleucids (iron) was stronger than that of the Ptolemies (clay). These two dynasties lasted until conquered by Rome and Persian Parthia. [Ed.]

[5] Probably refers to mixing of peoples and cultures in Alexander's and his successors' empire. [Ed.]

44 "In the time of those kings, the God of heaven will set up a kingdom that will never be destroyed, nor will it be left to another people. It will crush all those kingdoms and bring them to an end, but it will itself endure forever. 45 This is the meaning of the vision of the rock cut out of a mountain, but not by human hands—a rock that broke the iron, the bronze, the clay, the silver and the gold to pieces.

"The great God has shown the king what will take place in the future. The dream is true and the interpretation is trustworthy."

Daniel 11 [Daniel Sees the End of the Age of Iron and Clay]

28 "The king[6] of the North will return to his own country[7] with great wealth, but his heart will be set against the holy covenant.[8] He will take action against it and then return to his own country.

29 "At the appointed time he will invade the South again,[9] but this time the outcome will be different from what it was before. 30 Ships of the western coastlands[10] will oppose him, and he will lose heart. Then he will turn back and vent his fury against the holy covenant. He will return and show favor to those who forsake[11] the holy covenant.

31 "His armed forces will rise up to desecrate the temple fortress and will abolish the daily sacrifice. Then they will set up the abomination that causes desolation.[12] 32 With flattery he will corrupt those who have violated the covenant, but the people who know their God will firmly resist him.

33 "Those who are wise will instruct many, though for a time they will fall by the sword or be burned or captured or plundered. 34 When they fall, they will receive a little help,[13] and many who are not sincere will join them.[14] 35 Some of the wise will stumble, so that they may be refined, purified and made spotless until the time of the end, for it will still come at the appointed time.

---

[6] Antiochus IV, the Seleucid emperor from 175 to 164 B.C.E., ruled Palestine, Syria, and Alexander's eastern empire, which included Jerusalem. [Ed.]

[7] Antiochus IV returned to Jerusalem after his first war with Egypt, 170 B.C.E. [Ed.]

[8] Antiochus stole temple treasures and massacred many Jews, 169 B.C.E. [Ed.]

[9] The second war of Antiochus IV with Egypt in 168 B.C.E. was not successful. [Ed.]

[10] Cyprus. Here it means ships of Romans, generally, who blocked him. [Ed.]

[11] Jews like Jason the high priest, who favored Greek customs. [Ed.]

[12] The army of Antiochus broke down the temple walls, desecrated the interior, and installed Greek statues. [Ed.]

[13] While many Jews chose martyrdom, some received the help of Judas Maccabeus, leader of the opposition to Antiochus. [Ed.]

[14] Some of the followers of Judas Maccabeus were insincere. [Ed.]

The King Who Exalts Himself

36 "The king will do as he pleases. He will exalt and magnify himself above every god[15] and will say unheard-of things against the God of gods. He will be successful until the time of wrath is completed, for what has been determined must take place. 37 He will show no regard for the gods of his fathers or for the one desired by women, nor will he regard any god, but will exalt himself above them all. 38 Instead of them, he will honor a god of fortresses; a god unknown to his fathers he will honor with gold and silver, with precious stones and costly gifts. 39 He will attack the mightiest fortresses with the help of a foreign god and will greatly honor those who acknowledge him. He will make them rulers over many people and will distribute the land at a price.

40 "At the time of the end the king of the South[16] will engage him in battle, and the king of the North will storm out against him with chariots and cavalry and a great fleet of ships. He will invade many countries and sweep through them like a flood. 41 He will also invade the Beautiful Land. Many countries will fall, but Edom, Moab and the leaders of Ammon will be delivered from his hand. 42 He will extend his power over many countries; Egypt will not escape. 43 He will gain control of the treasures of gold and silver and all the riches of Egypt, with the Libyans and Nubians in submission. 44 But reports from the east and the north[17] will alarm him, and he will set out in a great rage to destroy and annihilate many. 45 He will pitch his royal tents between the seas at the beautiful holy mountain.[18] Yet he will come to his end,[19] and no one will help him."

Daniel 12

The End Times

1 "At that time Michael,[20] the great prince who protects your people, will arise. There will be a time of distress such as has not happened from the beginning of nations until then. But at that time your people—everyone whose name is found written in the book—will be delivered. 2 Multitudes who sleep in the dust of the earth will awake: some to everlasting life, others to shame and everlasting contempt. 3 Those who are wise will shine like the brightness of the heavens, and

---

[15] Antiochus had himself declared "Epiphanes," or God Manifest. [Ed.]

[16] Ptolemy VI Philometor (Egypt) initiated the third Egyptian war, against Antiochus. [Ed.]

[17] Antiochus spent his last year in war with Armenia and Parthia (Persia). [Ed.]

[18] In Palestine. [Ed.]

[19] Antiochus IV died at Tabae in Persia in 163 B.C.E. [Ed.]

[20] Protective angel of Israel. [Ed.]

those who lead many to righteousness, like the stars for ever and ever. 4 But you, Daniel, close up and seal the words of the scroll until the time of the end. Many will go here and there to increase knowledge."

5 Then I, Daniel, looked, and there before me stood two others, one on this bank of the river and one on the opposite bank. 6 One of them said to the man clothed in linen, who was above the waters of the river, "How long will it be before these astonishing things are fulfilled?"

7 The man clothed in linen, who was above the waters of the river, lifted his right hand and his left hand toward heaven, and I heard him swear by him who lives forever, saying, "It will be for a time, times and half a time. When the power of the holy people has been finally broken, all these things will be completed."

8 I heard, but I did not understand. So I asked, "My lord, what will the outcome of all this be?"

9 He replied, "Go your way, Daniel, because the words are closed up and sealed until the time of the end. 10 Many will be purified, made spotless and refined, but the wicked will continue to be wicked. None of the wicked will understand, but those who are wise will understand.

11 "From the time that the daily sacrifice is abolished and the abomination that causes desolation is set up, there will be 1,290 days. 12 Blessed is the one who waits for and reaches the end of the 1,335 days.

13 "As for you, go your way till the end. You will rest, and then at the end of the days you will rise to receive your allotted inheritance."

7

The Christian Bible: Jesus According to Matthew

The ideas first enunciated in Daniel — the coming end of the world or the Kingdom of God, the Last Judgment, individual immortality or life after death — were to become central to the branch of Judaism that produced Christianity. Along with Judaic monotheism and the insistence of the prophets (like Amos) on internalized morality, the idea of personal responsibility and eternal salvation or damnation gave Christianity an appeal that would eventually reach far beyond the children of Abraham.

In this selection from the Christian New Testament, the evangelist Matthew recounts Jesus speaking of the apocalypse with a note of urgency. Like Daniel, Jesus speaks of the signs that the end is at hand.

Source: Matt. 24:1–41. New International Version.

Yet, in the same chapter, sometimes in the same paragraph, Matthew recounts Jesus telling his listeners that there is plenty of time before the end.

What accounts for this apparent contradiction? If you were in the audience listening to Jesus, which idea would motivate you more — that the end of the world is rapidly approaching or that it is generations away? If you were taking notes for the daily newspaper, which message would get the headline? If you were writing a history of Jesus for future generations, which message would you emphasize?

THINKING HISTORICALLY

Matthew wrote his gospel about forty years after Jesus died. If he had been among those who heard Jesus speak, he took a long time to write it down. It is more likely that the author of this gospel is a second-generation evangelist, drawing on an earlier source, now lost. He may have had access to an earlier eyewitness account or to a collection of sayings of Jesus.

We know that Matthew updated the words of Jesus for the benefit of those Christians living after 70 C.E. Notice, for example, Matthew's reference to Daniel in 24:15: Jesus tells his listeners that when they see the abomination of the temple of which Daniel spoke, they should flee into the mountains to prepare for the end. But we know today that Daniel was speaking of the desecration of the temple by Antiochus IV in 168 B.C.E. Matthew, unaware of the historical context of Daniel and writing after the Roman destruction of the temple in 70 C.E., believed that Roman destruction was the event Daniel was predicting. So Matthew updates the message of Jesus for future generations by including the temple destruction for the readers of his gospel ("let the reader understand"). This is one of the ways we know that Matthew's text was written after 70 C.E. Jesus would not have referred to an event that was for his audience forty years into the future and expect his audience to understand his reference. In addition to the Daniel reference, which parts of this selection are most likely the written updates of Matthew? Which statements are most likely the actual spoken words of Jesus?

Matthew 24

Signs of the End of the Age

1 Jesus left the temple and was walking away when his disciples came up to him to call his attention to its buildings. 2 "Do you see all these things?" he asked. "I tell you the truth, not one stone here will be left on another; every one will be thrown down."

3 As Jesus was sitting on the Mount of Olives, the disciples came to him privately. "Tell us," they said, "when will this happen, and what will be the sign of your coming and of the end of the age?"

4 Jesus answered: "Watch out that no one deceives you. 5 For many will come in my name, claiming, 'I am the Christ,' and will deceive many. 6 You will hear of wars and rumors of wars, but see to it that you are not alarmed. Such things must happen, but the end is still to come. 7 Nation will rise against nation, and kingdom against kingdom. There will be famines and earthquakes in various places. 8 All these are the beginning of birth pains.

9 "Then you will be handed over to be persecuted and put to death, and you will be hated by all nations because of me. 10 At that time many will turn away from the faith and will betray and hate each other, 11 and many false prophets will appear and deceive many people. 12 Because of the increase of wickedness, the love of most will grow cold, 13 but he who stands firm to the end will be saved. 14 And this gospel of the kingdom will be preached in the whole world as a testimony to all nations, and then the end will come.

15 "So when you see standing in the holy place 'the abomination that causes desolation,' spoken of through the prophet Daniel—let the reader understand—16 then let those who are in Judea flee to the mountains. 17 Let no one on the roof of his house go down to take anything out of the house. 18 Let no one in the field go back to get his cloak. 19 How dreadful it will be in those days for pregnant women and nursing mothers! 20 Pray that your flight will not take place in winter or on the Sabbath. 21 For then there will be great distress, unequaled from the beginning of the world until now—and never to be equaled again. 22 If those days had not been cut short, no one would survive, but for the sake of the elect those days will be shortened. 23 At that time if anyone says to you, 'Look, here is the Christ!' or, 'There he is!' do not believe it. 24 For false Christs and false prophets will appear and perform great signs and miracles to deceive even the elect—if that were possible. 25 See, I have told you ahead of time.

26 "So if anyone tells you, 'There he is, out in the desert,' do not go out; or, 'Here he is, in the inner rooms,' do not believe it. 27 For as lightning that comes from the east is visible even in the west, so will be the coming of the Son of Man. 28 Wherever there is a carcass, there the vultures will gather.

29 "Immediately after the distress of those days

'the sun will be darkened,
and the moon will not give its light;
the stars will fall from the sky,
and the heavenly bodies will be shaken.'

30 "At that time the sign of the Son of Man will appear in the sky, and all the nations of the earth will mourn. They will see the Son of Man

coming on the clouds of the sky, with power and great glory. 31And he will send his angels with a loud trumpet call, and they will gather his elect from the four winds, from one end of the heavens to the other.

32 "Now learn this lesson from the fig tree: As soon as its twigs get tender and its leaves come out, you know that summer is near. 33 Even so, when you see all these things, you know that it is near, right at the door. 34 I tell you the truth, this generation will certainly not pass away until all these things have happened. 35 Heaven and earth will pass away, but my words will never pass away.

The Day and Hour Unknown

36 "No one knows about that day or hour, not even the angels in heaven, nor the Son, but only the Father. 37 As it was in the days of Noah, so it will be at the coming of the Son of Man. 38 For in the days before the flood, people were eating and drinking, marrying and giving in marriage, up to the day Noah entered the ark; 39 and they knew nothing about what would happen until the flood came and took them all away. That is how it will be at the coming of the Son of Man. 40 Two men will be in the field; one will be taken and the other left. 41 Two women will be grinding with a hand mill; one will be taken and the other left."

8

Paul, Letters

Paul of Tarsus (d. c. 65 C.E.), born with the name Saul in a Jewish community in what is today southeastern Turkey, was educated in the Hellenistic Greek culture of his time. As a young man, according to his testimony, he persecuted the followers of Jesus until, about the year 33, on the road to Damascus he was thrown from his horse, blinded, and reprimanded by God for his actions. From then on, Paul became the most vigorous missionary of Jesus, traveling throughout the Mediterranean converting nonbelievers and corresponding with communities of fellow followers. In contrast to the followers of Jesus in Jerusalem, Paul spread his gospel to others who were neither Jewish nor had known Jesus, believing that the message of the life, death, and resurrection of Jesus transcended any particular national community. In these selections from his letters to communities of Jesus followers throughout the Mediterranean, Paul emphasizes certain

Source: Rom. 2:25–29; 1 Cor. 15:1–8; Eph. 1:1–10, 2:1–10. New International Version.

ideas that opened up the religion to non-Jews and aided its spread to new communities. What are these ideas? How would these new ideas or emphases make the early church of Jesus universal in its appeal and potential membership?

THINKING HISTORICALLY

As a Jew, Paul would have been familiar with the Hebrew Bible in Greek translation, though it had not yet been codified in its present form. He would also have had access to stories about Jesus, though the gospels that we have in Greek had not yet been written. How different is Paul's message about Jesus from the message that later appeared in the gospel according to Matthew? How similar is it? Is Paul more interested in presenting the message *of* Jesus or the message *about* Jesus?

Romans 2

25 Circumcision has value if you observe the law, but if you break the law, you have become as though you had not been circumcised. 26 If those who are not circumcised keep the law's requirements, will they not be regarded as though they were circumcised? 27 The one who is not circumcised physically and yet obeys the law will condemn you who, even though you have the written code and circumcision, are a lawbreaker.

28 A man is not a Jew if he is only one outwardly, nor is circumcision merely outward and physical. 29 No, a man is a Jew if he is one inwardly; and circumcision is circumcision of the heart, by the Spirit, not by the written code. Such a man's praise is not from men, but from God.

1 Corinthians 15

The Resurrection of Christ

1 Now, brothers, I want to remind you of the gospel I preached to you, which you received and on which you have taken your stand. 2 By this gospel you are saved, if you hold firmly to the word I preached to you. Otherwise, you have believed in vain.

3 For what I received I passed on to you as of first importance: that Christ died for our sins according to the Scriptures, 4 that he was buried, that he was raised on the third day according to the Scriptures, 5 and that he appeared to Peter, and then to the Twelve. 6 After that, he appeared to more than five hundred of the brothers at the same time, most

of whom are still living, though some have fallen asleep. 7 Then he appeared to James, then to all the apostles, 8 and last of all he appeared to me also, as to one abnormally born.[1]

Ephesians 1

1 Paul, an apostle of Christ Jesus by the will of God,
  To the saints in Ephesus, the faithful in Christ Jesus:
2 Grace and peace to you from God our Father and the Lord Jesus Christ.

Spiritual Blessings in Christ

3 Praise be to the God and Father of our Lord Jesus Christ, who has blessed us in the heavenly realms with every spiritual blessing in Christ. 4 For he chose us in him before the creation of the world to be holy and blameless in his sight. In love 5 he predestined us to be adopted as his sons through Jesus Christ, in accordance with his pleasure and will—6 to the praise of his glorious grace, which he has freely given us in the One he loves. 7 In him we have redemption through his blood, the forgiveness of sins, in accordance with the riches of God's grace 8 that he lavished on us with all wisdom and understanding. 9 And he made known to us the mystery of his will according to his good pleasure, which he purposed in Christ, 10 to be put into effect when the times will have reached their fulfillment—to bring all things in heaven and on earth together under one head, even Christ. . . .

Ephesians 2

Made Alive in Christ

1 As for you, you were dead in your transgressions and sins, 2 in which you used to live when you followed the ways of this world and of the ruler of the kingdom of the air, the spirit who is now at work in those who are disobedient. 3 All of us also lived among them at one time, gratifying the cravings of our sinful nature and following its desires and thoughts. Like the rest, we were by nature objects of wrath. 4 But because of his great love for us, God, who is rich in mercy, 5 made us alive with Christ even when we were dead in transgressions—it is by grace you have been saved. 6 And God raised us up with Christ and seated us

---

[1] Refers to vision on road to Damascus after death of Jesus—an event out of normal time. [Ed.]

with him in the heavenly realms in Christ Jesus, 7 in order that in the coming ages he might show the incomparable riches of his grace, expressed in his kindness to us in Christ Jesus. 8 For it is by grace you have been saved, through faith—and this not from yourselves, it is the gift of God—9 not by works, so that no one can boast. 10 For we are God's workmanship, created in Christ Jesus to do good works, which God prepared in advance for us to do.

■ REFLECTIONS

The layers of revision are etched more sharply in the book of Daniel in the Hebrew Bible and Matthew in the New Testament of the Bible than in the Hindu and Buddhist documents because dates, chronology, and time sequences were far more important to the Judeo-Christian tradition. It was, and is, a tradition committed to the belief that God works in time; that there is a beginning, middle, and end to things; and that it is crucially important for humans to know where they are in the providential timeline. A modern skeptic might be bothered by the way the author or authors of Daniel turn history into prophecy. But for the Jews of the 160s B.C.E., the need to get the dates right and be ready for the end of days was far more important than checking who predicted what when.

Ironically, the precise prophecy of Daniel transcended its historical moorings when it was used by the author of Matthew in an effort to update the prophecy of Jesus, and it has been used regularly by every generation since with a different "king of the south" and new supporting cast. But if the Judeo-Christian tradition has left a legacy of apocalyptic warnings and millennial musings, it has also given us the interest and the tools that have shaped this chapter. The need to date, to find the actual words, to peel away the layers of rust that obfuscate an authentic past—that is a fine legacy indeed.

We have seen how Hinduism produced Buddhism and how Judaism generated Christianity, but neither Hinduism nor Judaism ended two thousand years ago. In fact, both "parental" religions underwent profound changes as well. Both became more universal, less dependent on particular places or people, and less limited to caste, region, or tribe.

We saw in the Upanishads how, around 500 B.C.E., Hinduism became almost monotheistic in its worship of Brahman. Similarly, about three hundred years later, Hindu devotional cults that centered on two of the other deities of the Hindu pantheon (Vishnu—especially in his incarnation as Krishna—and Shiva) developed. Reread the last eight stanzas of the *Bhagavad Gita* (written about 200 B.C.E.) in

Chapter 3 to see how the worship of Vishnu/Krishna became enormously appealing to masses of Indian people.

At about the time of Jesus, Judaism also underwent a transformation that has continued until this day. A process that began with the destruction of the first temple and the captivity in Babylon in the sixth century B.C.E. — the development of a Judaism independent of a particular temple or place — was revived after the Romans destroyed the second temple in 70 C.E. The Roman conquest created a more global Judaism than the Babylonian conquest. Judaism became a religion of rabbis (teachers) rather than of temple priests and guardians. So great was this transformation of Judaism that one might argue, with Alan Segal in *Rebecca's Children*, that "the time of Jesus marks the birth of not one but two great religions in the West, Judaism and Christianity. . . . So great is the contrast between previous Jewish religious systems and rabbinism."[1]

---

[1] Alan F. Segal, *Rebecca's Children: Judaism and Christianity in the Roman World* (Cambridge: Harvard University Press, 1986), 1.

7.

The Spread of Universal Religions

Afro-Eurasia, 100–1000 c.e.

■ HISTORICAL CONTEXT

From their beginnings, Buddhism and Christianity were less tribal and more universal than their parental religions, Hinduism and Judaism, because they offered universal salvation to their followers. The teachings of Jesus and the Buddha emphasized personal religious experience over the dictates of caste, ancestry, and formal law, making their ideas more likely to spread beyond their cultures of origin. Both religions, however, had relatively small followings at the deaths of their founders. How, then, did they win millions of converts within the next few hundred years? Similarly, how did Islam, founded in 622, spread from the Arabian peninsula to embrace the Berbers of North Africa, the Visigoths of Spain, Syrians, Persians, Turks, Central Asians, Indians, and even the western Chinese by 750? What was happening throughout Eurasia that explained these successes? In this chapter we explore how both an array of powerful and charismatic individuals and specific economic, political, and social conditions helped to broaden the appeal of the salvation religions and find larger audiences for their gospels.

The previous chapter explored the rise of universal religions. Paul of Tarsus almost singlehandedly separated Jesus from his Jewish roots, presenting him as the Son of God who was sacrificed for the sins of humankind, not just a prophet or messiah (king) of the Jewish people. Similarly, Mahayana Buddhists taught that Buddha was more than a teacher and spiritual guide whom one could imitate; he was a savior, responsive to prayer and worship. In addition, the devout could appeal to numerous Christian saints or Buddhist Bodhisattvas for help in achieving salvation.

236

Religious leaders weren't the only ones spreading faith; merchants and traders (occupations of the Prophet Muhammad) also played a crucial role. The spread of universal faiths and common cultures over great distances owed much to the expansive roads and maritime transport of the Roman and Chinese empires, as well as the Persian, Central Asian, and Indian states in between (see Map 7.1 on p. 238). But it was also a product of the Silk Road, or Roads, that connected China with Rome by land and sea after 100 B.C.E. The expansion of the great religious traditions was the work of merchants as well as monks; statues of gods traveled in camel caravans, and holy images were carried on rolls of silk.

Contact alone, however, is not enough to explain why people converted to Christianity, Buddhism, and Islam. The appeals to salvation beyond this world testified to difficult times. Nomadic pastoral peoples undermined the stability of empires already weakened by public debt, class antagonisms, dwindling crop yields, and disease. Populations declined from 200 to 800 C.E. and did not reach earlier levels again until about 1000 C.E. in Europe and China. People sought spiritual reassurance as well as economic alliances that would protect them in uncertain times. When those in power adopted new religions, it often benefited others to follow their lead, and thus a network of influence for new religious movements was secured.

■ THINKING HISTORICALLY

Understanding Continuity and Change

Thinking historically involves thinking about the way things do and do not change over time. In this chapter we will be looking at Christianity, Buddhism, and Islam as they expand, and we will ask how they bring change to the regions, people, and customs where they make converts. We will also ask how the religions themselves change as they expand. Only when we can see exactly what has changed, and what has remained constant, can we begin to understand the causes of change.

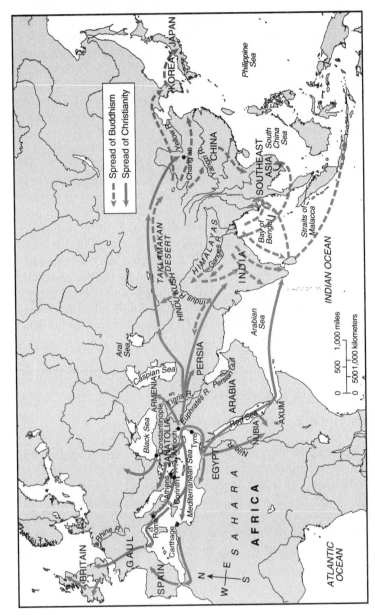

Map 7.1 The Spread of Early Christianity and Buddhism.

1

OFRI ILANI

Conversion and the Expansion of Judaism

It is a common belief that Judaism is a religion into which one is born. Conversions are infrequent and not even encouraged by some orthodox groups. We saw in the last chapter that Judaism was indeed an inherited national religion for the people of ancient Palestine. But in the Hellenistic period (after Alexander the Great and his successors spread Greek culture throughout the Middle East), some schools of Judaism embraced a more global view of their place in the world. We saw different manifestations of such universalism in the teachings of Daniel, Jesus, and, especially, Paul. But maybe Paul was neither as unique nor such a break with Judaism as is usually maintained.

In this selection from *Haaretz*, an Israeli newspaper, we are asked to consider the possibility that Christianity was not the only branch of Judaism that converted large numbers of people in the centuries after the Roman Empire. What is the argument of Shlomo Sand? What is his evidence? What do you think of his conclusion?

THINKING HISTORICALLY

Sand makes a number of startling claims for both continuity and change. What claims of change does he make for the Jewish people and for the Jewish religion? What claim of continuity does he make for the people of Palestine?

Of all the national heroes who have arisen from among the Jewish people over the generations, fate has not been kind to Dahia al-Kahina, a leader of the Berbers in the Aures Mountains.[1] Although she was a proud Jewess, few Israelis have ever heard the name of this warrior-queen who, in the seventh century C.E., united a number of Berber tribes and pushed back the Muslim army that invaded North Africa. It is possible that the reason for this is that al-Kahina was the daughter of a Berber tribe that had converted to Judaism, apparently several generations before she was born, sometime around the 6th century C.E.

According to the Tel Aviv University historian, Prof. Shlomo Sand, author of "Matai ve'ech humtza ha'am hayehudi?" ("When and How the Jewish People Was Invented?"; Resling, in Hebrew), the queen's tribe

---

[1] High mountain range in what is today eastern Algeria and northwestern Tunisia. [Ed.]

Source: Ofri Ilani, "Shattering a National Mythology," *Haaretz*, March 21, 2008. http://www.haaretz.com/hasen/spages/966952.html.

and other local tribes that converted to Judaism are the main sources from which Spanish Jewry sprang. This claim that the Jews of North Africa originated in indigenous tribes that became Jewish—and not in communities exiled from Jerusalem—is just one element of the far-reaching argument set forth in Sand's new book.

In this work, the author attempts to prove that the Jews now living in Israel and other places in the world are not at all descendants of the ancient people who inhabited the Kingdom of Judea during the First and Second Temple period. Their origins, according to him, are in varied peoples that converted to Judaism during the course of history, in different corners of the Mediterranean Basin and the adjacent regions. Not only are the North African Jews for the most part descendants of pagans who converted to Judaism, but so are the Jews of Yemen (remnants of the Himyar Kingdom in the Arab Peninsula, who converted to Judaism in the fourth century) and the Ashkenazi Jews of Eastern Europe (refugees from the Kingdom of the Khazars, who converted in the eighth century). . . .

According to Sand, the description of the Jews as a wandering and self-isolating nation of exiles, "who wandered across seas and continents, reached the ends of the earth and finally, with the advent of Zionism, made a U-turn and returned en masse to their orphaned homeland," is nothing but "national mythology." Like other national movements in Europe, which sought out a splendid Golden Age, through which they invented a heroic past—for example, classical Greece or the Teutonic tribes—to prove they have existed since the beginnings of history, "so, too, the first buds of Jewish nationalism blossomed in the direction of the strong light that has its source in the mythical Kingdom of David."

So when, in fact, was the Jewish people invented, in Sand's view? At a certain stage in the 19th century, intellectuals of Jewish origin in Germany, influenced by the folk character of German nationalism, took upon themselves the task of inventing a people "retrospectively," out of a thirst to create a modern Jewish people. From historian Heinrich Graetz on, Jewish historians began to draw the history of Judaism as the history of a nation that had been a kingdom, became a wandering people and ultimately turned around and went back to its birthplace. . . .

Inventing the Diaspora

"After being forcibly exiled from their land, the people remained faithful to it throughout their Dispersion and never ceased to pray and hope for their return to it and for the restoration in it of their political freedom"—thus states the preamble to the Israeli Declaration of Independence. This is also the quotation that opens the third chapter of

Sand's book, entitled "The Invention of the Diaspora." Sand argues that the Jewish people's exile from its land never happened.

"The supreme paradigm of exile was needed in order to construct a long-range memory in which an imagined and exiled nation-race was posited as the direct continuation of 'the people of the Bible' that preceded it," Sand explains. Under the influence of other historians who have dealt with the same issue in recent years, he argues that the exile of the Jewish people is originally a Christian myth that depicted that event as divine punishment imposed on the Jews for having rejected the Christian gospel.

"I started looking in research studies about the exile from the land—a constitutive event in Jewish history, almost like the Holocaust. But to my astonishment I discovered that it has no literature. The reason is that no one exiled the people of the country. The Romans did not exile peoples and they could not have done so even if they had wanted to. They did not have trains and trucks to deport entire populations. That kind of logistics did not exist until the 20th century. From this, in effect, the whole book was born: in the realization that Judaic society was not dispersed and was not exiled."

If the people was not exiled, are you saying that in fact the real descendants of the inhabitants of the Kingdom of Judah are the Palestinians?

"No population remains pure over a period of thousands of years. But the chances that the Palestinians are descendants of the ancient Judaic people are much greater than the chances that you or I are its descendents. The first Zionists, up until the Arab Revolt [1936–39], knew that there had been no exiling, and that the Palestinians were descended from the inhabitants of the land. They knew that farmers don't leave until they are expelled. Even Yitzhak Ben-Zvi, the second president of the State of Israel, wrote in 1929 that, 'the vast majority of the peasant farmers do not have their origins in the Arab conquerors, but rather, before then, in the Jewish farmers who were numerous and a majority in the building of the land.'"

And how did millions of Jews appear around the Mediterranean Sea?

"The people did not spread, but the Jewish religion spread. Judaism was a converting religion. Contrary to popular opinion, in early Judaism there was a great thirst to convert others. The Hasmoneans[2] were the first to begin to produce large numbers of Jews through mass conversion, under the influence of Hellenism. The conversions between the Hasmonean Revolt [163 B.C.E.] and Bar Kochba's

---

[2] The Hasmoneans were an independent Jewish state in the second to first century B.C.E., beginning with the successful revolt of the Macabees in 167 B.C.E. and ending with Roman conquest. [Ed.]

rebellion [133 C.E.][3] are what prepared the ground for the subsequent, wide-spread dissemination of Christianity. After the victory of Christianity in the fourth century, the momentum of conversion was stopped in the Christian world, and there was a steep drop in the number of Jews. Presumably many of the Jews who appeared around the Mediterranean became Christians. But then Judaism started to permeate other regions—pagan regions, for example, such as Yemen and North Africa. Had Judaism not continued to advance at that stage and had it not continued to convert people in the pagan world, we would have remained a completely marginal religion, if we survived at all."

How did you come to the conclusion that the Jews of North Africa were originally Berbers who converted?

"I asked myself how such large Jewish communities appeared in Spain. And then I saw that Tariq ibn Ziyad, the supreme commander of the Muslims who conquered Spain, was a Berber, and most of his soldiers were Berbers. Dahia al-Kahina's Jewish Berber kingdom had been defeated only 15 years earlier. And the truth is there are a number of Christian sources that say many of the conquerors of Spain were Jewish converts. The deep-rooted source of the large Jewish community in Spain was those Berber soldiers who converted to Judaism."

Sand argues that the most crucial demographic addition to the Jewish population of the world came in the wake of the conversion of the kingdom of Khazaria—a huge empire that arose in the Middle Ages on the steppes along the Volga River, which at its height ruled over an area that stretched from the Georgia of today to Kiev. In the eighth century, the kings of the Khazars adopted the Jewish religion and made Hebrew the written language of the kingdom. From the 10th century the kingdom weakened; in the 13th century it was utterly defeated by Mongol invaders, and the fate of its Jewish inhabitants remains unclear.

Sand revives the hypothesis, which was already suggested by historians in the 19th and 20th centuries, according to which the Judaized Khazars constituted the main origins of the Jewish communities in Eastern Europe.

"At the beginning of the 20th century there is a tremendous concentration of Jews in Eastern Europe—three million Jews in Poland alone," he says. "The Zionist historiography claims that their origins are in the earlier Jewish community in Germany, but they do not succeed in explaining how a small number of Jews who came from Mainz and Worms could have founded the Yiddish people of Eastern Europe. The Jews of Eastern Europe are a mixture of Khazars and Slavs who were pushed eastward."

---

[3] The Bar Kochba rebellion was another Jewish war against the Romans; it was successful for two years. Afterward the Romans banned Jews (and Christians) from Jerusalem, but not from the rest of Judea. [Ed.]

"Degree of Perversion"

If the Jews of Eastern Europe did not come from Germany, why did they speak Yiddish, which is a Germanic language?

"The Jews were a class of people dependent on the German bourgeoisie in the East, and thus they adopted German words. Here I base myself on the research of linguist Paul Wechsler of Tel Aviv University, who has demonstrated that there is no etymological connection between the German Jewish language of the Middle Ages and Yiddish. As far back as 1828, the Ribal (Rabbi Isaac Ber Levinson) said that the ancient language of the Jews was not Yiddish. Even Ben Zion Dinur, the father of Israeli historiography, was not hesitant about describing the Khazars as the origin of the Jews in Eastern Europe, and describes Khazaria as 'the mother of the diasporas' in Eastern Europe. But more or less since 1967, anyone who talks about the Khazars as the ancestors of the Jews of Eastern Europe is considered naive and moonstruck."

2

Pliny Consults the Emperor Trajan

The inhabitants of an average city of the ancient Mediterranean worshiped dozens of gods, though usually one was thought to be a special guardian of the populace and a protector of the state. Cities of the Roman Empire added deities and cults from conquered and distant territories, creating a bewildering array. General tolerance prevailed. No one cared which gods an individual worshiped. Only Rome, as the capital of the empire, might require worship of a state god, including, at times, the emperor himself. But aside from this matter of loyalty to the state, one's religious convictions were one's own affair.

Christians ran afoul of the law and communal practice not only by refusing the demonstration of loyalty to the state but also by aggressively denying the validity of all other gods — an attitude that many found distasteful.

Like the Jews, Christians were alternately persecuted and ignored. Roman oppression broke out when Nero blamed Christians for the great fire in Rome in 64 C.E. but then abated under the moderate rule of Trajan.

Source: Pliny, Letters 10:96–97, in *Pliny Secundus: Letters and Panegyricus*, Loeb Classical Library, trans. Betty Radice (Cambridge: Harvard University Press, 1959), 2:285, 287, 289, 291, 293.

A brief correspondence between Pliny,* serving as governor of Bithynia (in modern Turkey), and the Emperor Trajan† from about the year 111 c.e. has survived, throwing light on official Roman policy toward Christians of that era. What does Pliny's letter to Trajan tell you about official Roman policy? What do you think of Trajan's answer?

THINKING HISTORICALLY

Pliny asks a question we sometimes hear in other versions today: How effective is aggressive prosecution of Christians (even persecution or torture) in changing behavior? Does he think on balance that aggressive prosecution works? What kinds of change does he hope it will bring? What did the Emperor Trajan think? What idea of change and continuity did Trajan express by referring to "the spirit of our age"?

Pliny to the Emperor Trajan

It is my custom to refer all my difficulties to you, Sir, for no one is better able to resolve my doubts and to inform my ignorance.

I have never been present at an examination of Christians. Consequently, I do not know the nature or the extent of the punishments usually meted out to them, nor the grounds for starting an investigation and how far it should be pressed. Nor am I at all sure whether any distinction should be made between them on the grounds of age, or if young people and adults should be treated alike; whether a pardon ought to be granted to anyone retracting his beliefs, or if he has once professed Christianity, he shall gain nothing by renouncing it; and whether it is the mere name of Christian which is punishable, even if innocent of crime, or rather the crimes associated with the name.

For the moment this is the line I have taken with all persons brought before me on the charge of being Christians. I have asked them in person if they are Christians, and if they admit it, I repeat the question a second and third time, with a warning of the punishment awaiting them. If they persist, I order them to be led away for execution; for, whatever the nature of their admission, I am convinced that their stubbornness and unshakeable obstinacy ought not to go unpunished. There have been others similarly fanatical who are Roman citizens. I have entered them on the list of persons to be sent to Rome for trial.

* PLIH nee
† TRAY juhn

Now that I have begun to deal with this problem, as so often happens, the charges are becoming more widespread and increasing in variety. An anonymous pamphlet has been circulated which contains the names of a number of accused persons. Among these I considered that I should dismiss any who denied that they were or ever had been Christians when they had repeated after me a formula of invocation to the gods and had made offerings of wine and incense to your statue (which I had ordered to be brought into court for this purpose along with the images of the gods), and furthermore had reviled the name of Christ: none of which things, I understand, any genuine Christian can be induced to do.

Others, whose names were given to me by an informer, first admitted the charge and then denied it; they said that they had ceased to be Christians two or more years previously, and some of them even twenty years ago. They all did reverence to your statue and the images of the gods in the same way as the others, and reviled the name of Christ. They also declared that the sum total of their guilt or error amounted to no more than this: They had met regularly before dawn on a fixed day to chant verses alternately among themselves in honour of Christ as if to a god, and also to bind themselves by oath, not for any criminal purpose, but to abstain from theft, robbery and adultery, to commit no breach of trust and not to deny a deposit when called upon to restore it. After this ceremony it had been their custom to disperse and reassemble later to take food of an ordinary, harmless kind; but they had in fact given up this practice since my edict, issued on your instructions, which banned all political societies. This made me decide it was all the more necessary to extract the truth by torture from two slave-women, whom they call deaconesses. I found nothing but a degenerate sort of cult carried to extravagant lengths.

I have therefore postponed any further examination and hastened to consult you. The question seems to me to be worthy of your consideration, especially in view of the number of persons endangered; for a great many individuals of every age and class, both men and women, are being brought to trial, and this is likely to continue. It is not only the towns, but villages and rural districts too which are infected through contact with this wretched cult. I think though that it is still possible for it to be checked and directed to better ends, for there is no doubt that people have begun to throng the temples which had been almost entirely deserted for a long time; the sacred rites which had been allowed to lapse are being performed again, and flesh of sacrificial victims is on sale everywhere, though up till recently scarcely anyone could be found to buy it. It is easy to infer from this that a great many people could be reformed if they were given an opportunity to repent.

Trajan to Pliny

You have followed the right course of procedure, my dear Pliny, in your examination of the cases of persons charged with being Christians, for it is impossible to lay down a general rule to a fixed formula. These people must not be hunted out; if they are brought before you and the charge against them is proved, they must be punished, but in the case of anyone who denies that he is a Christian, and makes it clear that he is not by offering prayers to our gods, he is to be pardoned as a result of his repentance however suspect his past conduct may be. But pamphlets circulated anonymously must play no part in any accusation. They create the worst sort of precedent and are quite out of keeping with the spirit of our age.

3

EUSEBIUS

Life of Constantine

If Christians were persecuted by Roman officials and emperors, and despised by the thoughtful and powerful elite of Roman society, how then did Christianity ever succeed?

Part of the answer lies in the location of these Christians. They were more concentrated in urban than rural areas (the Latin word *pagan* meant "rural" before it meant "unchristian") and managed to gain significant advocates among the powerful elite.

Perhaps the most powerful urban, elite advocate for Christianity was the Roman emperor Constantine (288–337 C.E.). The emperor's historian Eusebius* (260–339 C.E.) recognized both the importance of the emperor and the role of the empire in the success of Christianity in winning the Roman Empire:

> At the same time one universal power, the Roman Empire arose and flourished, while the enduring and implacable hatred of nation against nation was now removed; and as the knowledge of one god and one way of religion and salvation, even the doctrine of Christ, was made known to all mankind; so at the same

*yoo SAY bee uhs

Source: P. Schaff and H. Wace, eds., *The Library of Nicene and Post-Nicene Fathers*, vol. I, *Church History, Life of Constantine, Oration in Praise of Constantine* (New York: The Christian Literature Company, 1890), 489–91.

time the entire dominion of the Roman Empire being invested in a single sovereign, profound peace reigned throughout the world. And thus, by the express appointment of the same God, two roots of blessing, the Roman Empire and the doctrine of Christian piety, sprang up together for the benefit of men.[1]

Prior to his rule as emperor, Constantine ruled the imperial lands of Gaul and Britain as a Caesar. In 312 C.E., Constantine (r. 306–337) was about to invade Italy and try to gain the throne of the western empire by defeating Maxentius, who ruled Rome. In his *Life of Constantine*, Eusebius, who knew the emperor, tells a story about events prior to the invasion that must have circulated at the time to explain Constantine's support of Christianity. What reasons does Eusebius give for Constantine's adoption of Christianity? What does this story suggest about Constantine's knowledge of Christianity before his conversion? What does it suggest about the way people chose religions at this time?

THINKING HISTORICALLY

We think of conversion as a transforming experience. However, a close reading of this selection shows little change in Constantine himself. Other sources confirm this. Constantine continued the gladiator displays that had been so offensive to Christians, left memorials to other deities, and ruled brutally. But if adopting Christianity was more of a political than spiritual mission for Constantine, he nevertheless carried it out forcefully. He styled himself an Old Testament King David, rebuilt Jerusalem, unified the eastern and western halves of the Roman Empire (which had been split under the previous emperor for administrative purposes), and commandeered the church by holding councils, persecuting "heresies," and enforcing a uniform dogma that transformed the church from a marginalized cult protest to prominence in the governance of the empire. How was the Christianity that Constantine embraced different from that known to Paul or Pliny?

Being convinced, however, that he needed some more powerful aid than his military forces could afford him, on account of the wicked and magical enchantments which were so diligently practiced by the tyrant [Maxentius], he sought Divine assistance, deeming the possession of

---

[1] Eusebius, *Oration in Praise of Constantine*, xv, 4. [Ed.]

arms and a numerous soldiery of secondary importance, but believing the cooperating power of Deity invincible and not to be shaken. He considered, therefore, on what God he might rely for protection and assistance. While engaged in this enquiry, the thought occurred to him, that, of the many emperors who had preceded him, those who had rested their hopes in a multitude of gods, and served them with sacrifices and offerings, had in the first place been deceived by flattering predictions, and oracles which promised them all prosperity, and at last had met with an unhappy end, while not one of their gods had stood by to warn them of the impending wrath of heaven; while one alone [Constantine's father][2] who had pursued an entirely opposite course, who had condemned their error, and honored the Supreme God during his whole life, had found him to be the Saviour and Protector of his empire, and the Giver of every good thing. Reflecting on this, and well weighing the fact that they who had trusted in many gods had also fallen by manifold forms of death, without leaving behind them either family or offspring, stock, name, or memorial among men: while the God of his father had given to him, on the other hand, manifestations of his power and very many tokens: and considering farther that those who had already taken arms against the tyrant, and had marched to the battle-field under the protection of a multitude of gods, had met with a dishonorable end (for one of them had shamefully retreated from the contest without a blow, and the other, being slain in the midst of his own troops, became, as it were, the mere sport of death); reviewing, I say, all these considerations, he judged it to be folly indeed to join in the idle worship of those who were no gods, and after such convincing evidence, to err from the truth; and therefore felt it incumbent on him to honor his father's God alone.

Accordingly he called on Him with earnest prayer and supplications that he would reveal to him who He was, and stretch forth His right hand to help him in his present difficulties. And while he was thus praying with fervent entreaty, a most marvelous sign appeared to him from heaven, the account of which it might have been hard to believe had it been related by any other person. But since the victorious emperor himself long afterwards declared it to the writer of this history, when he was honored with his acquaintance and society, and confirmed his statement by an oath, who could hesitate to accredit the relation, especially since the testimony of after-time has established its truth? He said that about noon, when the day was already

---

[2] Eusebius claims that Constantine's father, Constantius, was a Christian, though he appeared to be pagan. [Ed.]

beginning to decline, he saw with his own eyes the trophy of a cross of light in the heavens, above the sun, and bearing the inscription, CONQUER BY THIS. At this sight he himself was struck with amazement, and his whole army also, which followed him on this expedition, and witnessed the miracle.

He said, moreover, that he doubted within himself what the import of this apparition could be. And while he continued to ponder and reason on its meaning, night suddenly came on; then in his sleep the Christ of God appeared to him with the same sign which he had seen in the heavens, and commanded him to make a likeness of that sign which he had seen in the heavens, and to use it as a safeguard in all engagements with his enemies.

At the dawn of day he arose, and communicated the marvel to his friends: and then, calling together the workers in gold and precious stones, he sat in the midst of them, and described to them the figure of the sign he had seen, bidding them represent it in gold and precious stones. And this representation I myself have had an opportunity of seeing. . . .

The emperor constantly made use of this sign of salvation as a safeguard against every adverse and hostile power, and commanded that others similar to it should be carried at the head of all his armies.

These things were done shortly afterwards. But at the time above specified, being struck with amazement at the extraordinary vision, and resolving to worship no other God save Him who had appeared to him, he sent for those who were acquainted with the mysteries of His doctrines, and enquired who that God was, and what was intended by the sign of the vision he had seen.

They affirmed that He was God, the only begotten Son of the one and only God: that the sign which had appeared was the symbol of immortality, and the trophy of that victory over death which He had gained in time past when sojourning on earth. They taught him also the causes of His advent, and explained to him the true account of His incarnation. Thus he was instructed in these matters, and was impressed with wonder at the divine manifestation which had been presented to his sight. Comparing, therefore, the heavenly vision with the interpretation given, he found his judgment confirmed; and, in the persuasion that the knowledge of these things had been imparted to him by Divine teaching, he determined thenceforth to devote himself to the reading of the inspired writings.

4

Christianity in China:
The Nestorian Monument

This selection is part of an inscription found on a ten-foot stone in China. It was inscribed in Aramaic and Chinese in 781 by Nestorian Christian missionaries in China who came from Syria. In Syria, Nestorian Christian beliefs were not very different from those of other Christians. They believed that Jesus had both a human and divine nature but emphasized the human side of Jesus more than other Christians. From Syria, Nestorians brought Christianity to Persia and Central Asia, reaching China by at least 635. What does the emperor's proclamation suggest about the way Christianity came to China? Why did the emperor support it?

THINKING HISTORICALLY

How is the message of this inscription different from that of Jesus, Paul, or other early Christians (see Chapter 6)? What words or ideas in this document show the influence of Confucian or Daoist thought? What expected Christian words or ideas are missing from this document? What do these changes tell you about Christianity in China? What seems to have remained constant, and what seems to have changed?

"Behold the unchangeably true and invisible, who existed through all eternity without origin; the far-seeing perfect intelligence, whose mysterious existence is everlasting; operating on primordial substance he created the universe, being more excellent than all holy intelligences, inasmuch as he is the source of all that is honorable. This is our eternal true lord God, triune[1] and mysterious in substance. He appointed the cross as the means

---

[1] The idea of the Trinity, that God consisted of three persons—Father, Son, and Holy Spirit—became orthodox in the fourth century, after the Council at Nicaea (325) declared that the Father and Son were of the same substance. Ironically, this council defeated the Arian emphasis on the humanity of Jesus, which was closer to the view of Nestorian Christianity. The Council of Nicaea was called by Constantine to unify Christian belief; Nicaea (modern Iznik, Turkey) was the capital of Bithnia, where Pliny governed, attempted urban renewal, and met Christians in the first century. [Ed.]

Source: Charles F. Horne, ed., *The Sacred Books and Early Literature of the East*, vol. XII, *Medieval China* (New York: Parke, Austin, & Lipscomb, 1917), 381–92. Modernized by Jerome S. Arkenberg. Internet East Asian History Sourcebook. http://www.fordham.edu/halsall/eastasia/781nestorian.html.

for determining the four cardinal points,[2] he moved the original spirit, and produced the two principles of nature;[3] the somber void[4] was changed, and heaven and earth were opened out; the sun and moon revolved, and day and night commenced; having perfected all inferior objects, he then made the first man; upon him he bestowed an excellent disposition, giving him in charge the government of all created beings; man, acting out the original principles of his nature, was pure and unostentatious;[5] his unsullied and expansive mind was free from the least inordinate desire; until Satan introduced the seeds of falsehood,[6] to deteriorate his purity of principle; the opening thus commenced in his virtue gradually enlarged, and by this crevice in his nature was obscured and rendered vicious; hence three hundred and sixty-five sects followed each other in continuous track,[7] inventing every species of doctrinal complexity; while some pointed to material objects as the source of their faith,[8] others reduced all to vacancy, even to the annihilation of the two primeval principles,[9] some sought to call down blessings by prayers and supplications,[10] while others by an assumption of excellence held themselves up as superior to their fellows;[11] their intellects and thoughts continually wavering, their minds and affections incessantly on the move, they never obtained their vast desires, but being exhausted and distressed they revolved in their own heated atmosphere; till by an accumulation of obscurity they lost their path, and after long groping in darkness they were unable to return. Thereupon, our Trinity being divided in nature, the illustrious and honorable Messiah,[12] veiling his true dignity, appeared in the world as a man; angelic powers promulgated the glad tidings, a virgin gave birth to the Holy One in Syria; a bright star announced the felicitous event, and Persians observing the splendor came to present tribute; the ancient dispensation, as declared by the twenty-four holy men [the writers of the

[2] The Chinese character for the number 10 is a cross. So this could be translated as "he appointed the Chinese figure for 10 as the means for determining the four cardinal points" of the compass: north, east, south, and west. One translator suggests that this is a whimsical way of saying that this God created all the universe; that is, he is not just a god of a mountain or stream. [Ed.]

[3] Probably refers to the Nestorian idea that the two natures of Christ, human and divine, were conjoined. A church council at Ephesus in 431 held that they became one nature, causing some Nestorians to split and move eastward. The Chinese may have thought of two natures as yin and yang. [Ed.]

[4] This void may be closer to Daoism or Buddhism. [Ed.]

[5] Compare this sentence to Genesis. [Ed.]

[6] May refer to the temptation of Adam. [Ed.]

[7] May refer to mankind cast out of paradise. [Ed.]

[8] Possibly a criticism of the Buddhist idea of the world as maya, or illusion. [Ed.]

[9] May refer to the Daoist idea of emptiness. [Ed.]

[10] May refer to ancestor worship. [Ed.]

[11] May refer to Confucians. [Ed.]

[12] "Second Person of the Trinity" may be a better translation, since there is no Chinese for "Messiah." [Ed.]

Old Testament], was then fulfilled, and he laid down great principles for the government of families and kingdoms; he established the new religion of the silent[13] operation of the pure spirit of the Triune; he rendered virtue subservient to direct faith; he fixed the extent of the eight boundaries,[14] thus completing the truth and freeing it from dross; he opened the gate of the three constant principles,[15] introducing life and destroying death; he suspended the bright sun[16] to invade the chambers of darkness, and the falsehoods of the devil were thereupon defeated; he set in motion the vessel of mercy[17] by which to ascend to the bright mansions, whereupon rational beings were then released, having thus completed the manifestation of his power, in clear day he ascended to his true station.[18]

Twenty-seven sacred books [the number in the New Testament] have been left, which disseminate intelligence by unfolding the original transforming principles. By the rule for admission, it is the custom to apply the water of baptism,[19] to wash away all superficial show and to cleanse and purify the neophytes. As a seal, they hold the cross, whose influence is reflected in every direction, uniting all without distinction. As they strike the wood, the fame of their benevolence is diffused abroad; worshiping toward the east, they hasten on the way to life and glory; they preserve the beard to symbolize their outward actions, they shave the crown to indicate the absence of inward affections; they do not keep slaves, but put noble and mean all on an equality; they do not amass wealth, but cast all their property into the common stock; they fast, in order to perfect themselves by self-inspection; they submit to restraints, in order to strengthen themselves by silent watchfulness; seven times a day they have worship and praise for the benefit of the living and the dead; once in seven days they sacrifice, to cleanse the heart and return to purity.

It is difficult to find a name to express the excellence of the true and unchangeable doctrine; but as its meritorious operations are manifestly displayed, by accommodation it is named the Illustrious Religion.[20] Now without holy men,[21] principles cannot become expanded; without

---

[13] Recalls the Daoist idea that the sage conveys wisdom without words. [Ed.]

[14] Perhaps the eight beatitudes in Matthew ("Blessed are the . . . ," etc.), as opposed to the Buddha's eight-fold path. [Ed.]

[15] Some translate this as three virtues: faith, hope, and charity. Followers of Persian Manichaenism would understand it as the three Permanences of the Almighty: his Light, Strength, and Goodness. [Ed.]

[16] Possible reference to crucifixion (though, if so, very veiled). Probable intent is that followers will recognize meaning but nonbelievers won't be put off by the idea of a God who was executed and died. [Ed.]

[17] Christ's death on the cross, like the sacrifice of a Bodhisattva (a vessel of mercy). [Ed.]

[18] Reference to Christ asending into heaven. [Ed.]

[19] Baptism, or immersion in water as a rite of purification, was practiced in Judaism, but in early Christianity it became associated with being a Christian. [Ed.]

[20] This sentence is full of phrases from the *Tao Te Ching*. [Ed.]

[21] Some translators prefer "ruler" to "holy men," suggesting that this was a flattering call for the Chinese emperor to help spread the religion. [Ed.]

principles, holy men cannot become magnified; but with holy men and right principles, united as the two parts of a signet, the world becomes civilized and enlightened.

In the time of the accomplished Emperor Tai-tsung, the illustrious and magnificent founder of the dynasty, among the enlightened and holy men who arrived was the most-virtuous Olopun,[22] from the country of Syria. Observing the azure clouds, he bore the true sacred books; beholding the direction of the winds,[23] he braved difficulties and dangers. In the year of our Lord 635 he arrived at Chang-an; the Emperor sent his Prime Minister, Duke Fang Hiuen-ling; who, carrying the official staff to the west border, conducted his guest into the interior; the sacred books were translated in the imperial library, the sovereign investigated the subject in his private apartments; when becoming deeply impressed with the rectitude and truth of the religion, he gave special orders for its dissemination.

In the seventh month of the year A.D. 638 the following imperial proclamation was issued:

"Right principles have no invariable name, holy men have no invariable station; instruction is established in accordance with the locality, with the object of benefiting the people at large. The greatly virtuous Olopun, of the kingdom of Syria, has brought his sacred books and images from that distant part, and has presented them at our chief capital. Having examined the principles of this religion, we find them to be purely excellent and natural; investigating its originating source, we find it has taken its rise from the establishment of important truths; its ritual is free from perplexing expressions, its principles will survive when the framework is forgot; it is beneficial to all creatures; it is advantageous to mankind. Let it be published throughout the Empire, and let the proper authority build a Syrian church in the capital in the I-ning May,[24] which shall be governed by twenty-one priests. When the virtue of the Chau Dynasty declined, the rider on the azure ox ascended to the west;[25] the principles of the great Tang becoming resplendent, the Illustrious breezes have come to fan the East."

Orders were then issued to the authorities to have a true portrait of the Emperor taken; when it was transferred to the wall of the church, the

---

[22] Identified as Raban in some translations, the Nestorian monk who brought Christianity. [Ed.]

[23] Reference (not translated here) to the sound of winds in musical tubes refers to the Chinese form of divination. [Ed.]

[24] I-ning quarter of Chang-an was west where Persian and Central Asian merchants were concentrated. [Ed.]

[25] Evokes story told of Lao Tze riding an ox into the west at the end of his life. The point of this sentence, which was probably not part of the imperial proclamation, is that the Nestorian faith prospered after the end of the dynasty. [Ed.]

dazzling splendor of the celestial visage irradiated the Illustrious portals. The sacred traces emitted a felicitous influence, and shed a perpetual splendor over the holy precincts. According to the Illustrated Memoir of the Western Regions, and the historical books of the Han and Wei dynasties, the kingdom of Syria reaches south to the Coral Sea; on the north it joins the Gem Mountains; on the west it extends toward the borders of the immortals and the flowery forests; on the east it lies open to the violent winds and tideless waters. The country produces fire-proof cloth,[26] life-restoring incense,[27] bright moon-pearls,[28] and night-luster gems. Brigands and robbers are unknown, but the people enjoy happiness and peace. None but Illustrious laws prevail; none but the virtuous are raised to sovereign power. The land is broad and ample, and its literary productions are perspicuous and clear. . . .

[The following is in Syriac at the foot of the stone.]

"In the year of the Greeks one thousand and ninety-two [781 c.e.], the Lord Jazedbuzid, Priest and Vicar-episcopal of Cumdan the royal city, son of the enlightened Mailas, Priest of Balkh a city of Turkestan, set up this tablet, whereon is inscribed the Dispensation of our Redeemer, and the preaching of the apostolic missionaries to the King of China."

---

[26] Probably asbestos. [Ed.]
[27] Probably a balsam said to revive plague victims; used medicinally and in mummification. [Ed.]
[28] Likely oysters. [Ed.]

5

Buddhism in China: The Disposition of Error

When Buddhist monks traveled from India to China, they came to a culture with different philosophical and religious traditions. In China, ancestor worship, which did not exist for Indians who believed in reincarnation, was a very important religious tradition. The leading Chinese philosopher Confucius said very little about religion but stressed the need for respect: sons to fathers (filial piety), wives to husbands,

---

Source: Hung-ming Chi, in Taishō daizōkyō, LII, 1–7, quoted in William Theodore de Bary, ed., *The Buddhist Tradition in India, China and Japan* (New York: Random House, 1969), 132–37.

children to parents, students to teachers, youngsters to elders, everyone to the emperor, the living to the deceased. More spiritual and meditative was the religion developed by the followers of a contemporary of Confucius, Lao Tze,* whose *Dao De Jing* (The Book of the Way) prescribed the peace that came from an acceptance of natural flows and rhythms. "Practice nonaction" was the Daoist method.

The Disposition of Error is a Buddhist guide for converting the Chinese. While the author and date are uncertain, this kind of tract was common under the Southern Dynasties (420–589 C.E.). The author uses a frequently-asked-questions (FAQ) format that enables us to see what the Chinese — mainly Confucian — objections were to Buddhism, as well as what they considered good Buddhist answers.

What were the main Chinese objections to Buddhism? Why were Buddhist ideas of death and rebirth such a stumbling block for Chinese Confucians? Were Confucian ideas about care of the body and hair only superficial concerns, or did they reflect basic differences between Confucianism and Buddhism? What did the Buddhists expect to be the main appeal of their religion?

THINKING HISTORICALLY

This Buddhist missionary's guide to converting the Chinese offers a unique window on both the continuities of Chinese tradition and the possibilities of change. We can see continuities in those Chinese beliefs and styles that the Buddhist monks accept, adopt, or attempt to work within. Note the style of presentation in this guide, for instance. Compare it to the *Analects* of Confucius and the Buddhist documents you have read. Is an FAQ format closer to Confucian or Buddhist style? Note also the different ways in which Confucian and Buddhist documents refer to an authority to solve a problem. Does this document follow Confucian or Buddhist style?

Why Is Buddhism Not Mentioned in the Chinese Classics?

The questioner said: If the way of the Buddha is the greatest and most venerable of ways, why did Yao, Shun, the Duke of Chou, and Confucius not practice it? In the Five Classics one sees no mention of it. You, sir, are fond of the *Book of Odes* and the *Book of History*, and you take pleasure in rites and music. Why, then, do you love the way of the Buddha and rejoice in outlandish arts? Can they exceed the Classics and

*low TSAY

commentaries and beautify the accomplishments of the sages? Permit me the liberty, sir, of advising you to reject them.

Mou Tzu said: All written works need not necessarily be the words of Confucius, and all medicine does not necessarily consist of the formulae of [the famous physician] P'ien-ch'üeh. What accords with principle is to be followed, what heals the sick is good. The gentleman-scholar draws widely on all forms of good, and thereby benefits his character. Tzu-kung [a disciple of Confucius] said, "Did the Master have a permanent teacher?" Yao served Yin Shou, Shun served Wuch'eng, the Duke of Chou learned from Lü Wang, and Confucius learned from Lao Tzu. And none of these teachers is mentioned in the Five Classics. Although these four teachers were sages, to compare them to the Buddha would be like comparing a white deer to a unicorn, or a swallow to a phoenix. Yao, Shun, the Duke of Chou, and Confucius learned even from such teachers as these. How much less, then, may one reject the Buddha, whose distinguishing marks are extraordinary and whose superhuman powers know no bounds! How may one reject him and refuse to learn from him? The records and teachings of the Five Classics do not contain everything. Even if the Buddha is not mentioned in them, what occasion is there for suspicion?

Why Do Buddhist Monks Do Injury to Their Bodies?

The questioner said: The *Classic of Filial Piety* says, "Our torso, limbs, hair, and skin we receive from our fathers and mothers. We dare not do them injury." When Tseng Tzu was about to die, he bared his hands and feet.[1] But now the monks shave their heads. How this violates the sayings of the sages and is out of keeping with the way of the filially pious! . . .

Mou Tzu said: . . . Confucius has said, "He with whom one may follow a course is not necessarily he with whom one may weigh its merits." This is what is meant by doing what is best at the time. Furthermore, the *Classic of Filial Piety* says, "The kings of yore possessed the ultimate virtue and the essential Way." T'ai-po cut his hair short and tattooed his body, thus following of his own accord the customs of Wu and Yüeh and going against the spirit of the "torso, limbs, hair, and skin" passage.[2] And yet Confucius praised him, saying that his might well be called the ultimate virtue.

[1] To show he had preserved them intact from all harm.

[2] Uncle of King Wen of the Chou who retired to the barbarian land of Wu and cut his hair and tattooed his body in barbarian fashion, thus yielding his claim to the throne to King Wen.

Why Do Monks Not Marry?

The questioner said: Now of felicities there is none greater than the continuation of one's line, of unfilial conduct there is none worse than childlessness. The monks forsake wife and children, reject property and wealth. Some do not marry all their lives. How opposed this conduct is to felicity and filial piety! . . .

Mou Tzu said: . . . Wives, children, and property are the luxuries of the world, but simple living and inaction are the wonders of the Way. Lao Tzu has said, "Of reputation and life, which is dearer? Of life and property, which is worth more?" . . . Hsü Yu and Ch'ao-fu dwelt in a tree. Po I and Shu Ch'i starved in Shou-yang, but Confucius praised their worth, saying, "They sought to act in accordance with humanity and they succeeded in acting so." One does not hear of their being illspoken of because they were childless and propertyless. The monk practices the Way and substitutes that for the pleasures of disporting himself in the world. He accumulates goodness and wisdom in exchange for the joys of wife and children.

Death and Rebirth

The questioner said: The Buddhists say that after a man dies he will be reborn. I do not believe in the truth of these words. . . .

Mou Tzu said: . . . The spirit never perishes. Only the body decays. The body is like the roots and leaves of the five grains, the spirit is like the seeds and kernels of the five grains. When the roots and leaves come forth they inevitably die. But do the seeds and kernels perish? Only the body of one who has achieved the Way perishes. . . .

Someone said: If one follows the Way one dies. If one does not follow the Way one dies. What difference is there?

Mou Tzu said: You are the sort of person who, having not a single day of goodness, yet seeks a lifetime of fame. If one has the Way, even if one dies one's soul goes to an abode of happiness. If one does not have the Way, when one is dead one's soul suffers misfortune.

Why Should a Chinese Allow Himself to Be Influenced by Indian Ways?

The questioner said: Confucius said, "The barbarians with a ruler are not so good as the Chinese without one." Mencius criticized Ch'en Hsiang for rejecting his own education to adopt the ways of [the foreign teacher] Hsü Hsing, saying, "I have heard of using what is Chinese to change what is barbarian, but I have never heard of using what is barbarian to change what is Chinese." You, sir, at the age of twenty learned the way of Yao, Shun, Confucius, and the Duke of Chou. But now you have rejected them, and instead have taken up the arts of the barbarians. Is this not a great error?

Mou Tzu said: . . . What Confucius said was meant to rectify the way of the world, and what Mencius said was meant to deplore one-sidedness. Of old, when Confucius was thinking of taking residence among the nine barbarian nations, he said, "If a gentleman-scholar dwells in their midst, what baseness can there be among them?" . . . The Commentary says, "The north polar star is in the center of heaven and to the north of man." From this one can see that the land of China is not necessarily situated under the center of heaven. According to the Buddhist scriptures, above, below, and all around, all beings containing blood belong to the Buddha-clan. Therefore I revere and study these scriptures. Why should I reject the Way of Yao, Shun, Confucius, and the Duke of Chou? Gold and jade do not harm each other, crystal and amber do not cheapen each other. You say that another is in error when it is you yourself who err.

Why Must a Monk Renounce Worldly Pleasures?

The questioner said: Of those who live in the world, there is none who does not love wealth and position and hate poverty and baseness, none who does not enjoy pleasure and idleness and shrink from labor and fatigue. . . . But now the monks wear red cloth, they eat one meal a day, they bottle up the six emotions, and thus they live out their lives. What value is there in such an existence?

Mou Tzu said: Wealth and rank are what man desires, but if he cannot obtain them in a moral way, he should not enjoy them. Poverty and meanness are what man hates, but if he can only avoid them by departing from the Way, he should not avoid them. Lao Tzu has said, "The five colors make men's eyes blind, the five sounds make men's ears deaf, the five flavors dull the palate, chasing about and hunting make men's minds mad, possessions difficult to acquire bring men's conduct to an impasse. The sage acts for his belly, not for his eyes." Can these words possibly be vain? Liu-hsia Hui would not exchange his way of life for the rank of the three highest princes of the realm. Tuankan Mu would not exchange his for the wealth of Prince Wen of Wei. . . . All of them followed their ideas, and cared for nothing more. Is there no value in such an existence?

Does Buddhism Have No Recipe for Immortality?

The questioner said: The Taoists say that Yao, Shun, the Duke of Chou, and Confucius and his seventy-two disciples did not die, but became immortals. The Buddhists say that men must all die, and that none can escape. What does this mean?

Mou Tzu said: Talk of immortality is superstitious and unfounded; it is not the word of the sages. Lao Tzu says, "Even Heaven and earth cannot be eternal. How much the less can man!" Confucius says, "The wise man leaves the world, but humanity and filial piety last forever." I have observed the six arts and examined the commentaries and records. According to them, Yao died, Shun had his [death place at] Mount Ts'ang-wu, Yü has his tomb on K'uai-chi, Po I and Shu Ch'i have their grave in Shou-yang. King Wen died before he could chastise Chou, King Wu died without waiting for King Ch'eng to grow up. We read of the Duke of Chou that he was reburied, and of Confucius that [shortly before his death] he dreamed of two pillars. [As for the disciples of Confucius], Po-yü died before his father, of Tzu Lu it is said that his flesh was chopped up and pickled.

6

Selections from the Koran

In the centuries following the expansion of Christianity and Buddhism, a new monotheistic salvation religion, Islam, originated in Arabia and spread rapidly among Arab polytheists as well as many Jews and Christians along ancient trade routes (see Map 7.2). The new faith centered on the Koran (or Qu'ran), which is said by Islamic believers, or Muslims, to be the word of God as spoken by the Angel Gabriel to the Prophet Muhammad about 610. Muhammad then recited these words so that others could memorize them or write them down. After Muhammad's death (632), these writings and memories were gathered together to form the Koran (literally "Recitation").

The chapters (or *surahs*) of the Koran, 114 in all, are organized primarily by length, with the longest, which tended to be the most recent, first. This means that the earliest pieces, which are among the shortest, are found at the end of the book. We begin with the first, an exception to this length rule, *surah* 1, "The Opening," followed in rough chronology by a few of the earliest *surahs*: numbers 99, 109, and 112. We conclude with excerpts from the later *surahs*, number 2, "The Cow,"[1] and number 4, "Women." What beliefs do these *surahs*

---

[1] The title "The Cow" refers to verses 67–73 in *surah* 2 of the Koran (not included here), which tell of a dispute between Moses and the Israelites. After Moses tells the Israelites that God wants them to sacrifice a cow, they hesitate by asking a number of questions as to what kind of cow. The Muslim meaning is that one should submit to God, not debate his commands. [Ed.]

Source: Chapters 1, 91, 109, and 112: *Approaching the Qu'ran: The Early Revelations*, trans. Michael Sells (Ashland, OR: White Cloud Press, 1999), 42, 108, 128, 136. Chapters 2 and 4: *The New On-Line Translation of the Qur'an*, the Noor Foundation, http://islamusa.org/.

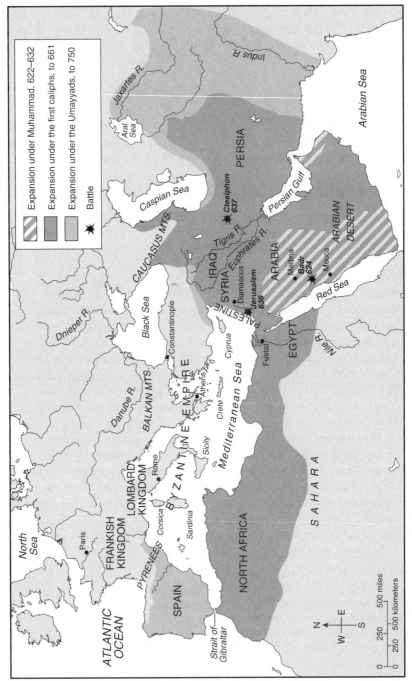

Map 7.2 The Expansion of Islam to 750 C.E.

convey? How are they similar to, and different from, the beliefs of Judaism and Christianity? Which messages of the Koran would be effective in aiding the expansion of the religion?

THINKING HISTORICALLY

The early *surahs* (those with higher numbers) almost certainly reflect the concerns of early Islam. What are these concerns? The later *surahs* (such as 2 and 4) were probably written after Muhammad, threatened by the ruling tribes, had fled Mecca and taken control of the government of Medina. They may even have been written after Muhammad's death when his successors struggled with problems of governance. Judging from these later chapters, what kinds of issues most concerned leaders of the Muslim community? How did the message or emphasis change from the early to the later *surahs*? What would account for such a change?

Surah 1
The Opening

In the name of God
   the Compassionate the Caring
Praise be to God
   lord sustainer of the worlds
the Compassionate the Caring
master of the day of reckoning
To you we turn to worship
   and to you we turn in time of need
Guide us along the road straight
the road of those to whom you are giving
   not those with anger upon them
   not those who have lost the way

Surah 99
The Quaking

In the Name of God the Compassionate the Caring

   When the earth is shaken, quaking
   When the earth bears forth her burdens
   And someone says "What is with her?"
   At that time she will tell her news

As her lord revealed her
At that time people will straggle forth
   to be shown what they have done
Whoever does a mote's weight good will see it
Whoever does a mote's weight wrong will see it

Surah 109
Those Who Reject the Faith

In the Name of God the Compassionate the Caring

Say: You who reject the faith
I do not worship what you worship
and you do not worship what I worship
I am not a worshipper of what you worship
You are not a worshipper of what I worship
A reckoning for you and a reckoning for me

Surah 112
Sincerity / Unity

In the Name of God the Compassionate the Caring

Version 1
   Say he is God, one
   God forever
   Not begetting, unbegotten,
     and having as an equal none

Version 2
   Say he is God, one
   God the refuge
   Not begetting, unbegotten,
     and having as an equal none

Version 3
   Say he is God, one
   God the rock
   Not begetting, unbegotten,
     and having as an equal none

Surah 2
The Cow

Section 22

177. It is not the sole virtue that you turn your faces to the east or the west but true virtue is theirs, who believe in Allâh, the Last Day, the angels, the Book, and in the Prophets, and who give away their wealth (and substance) out of love for Him, to the near of kin, the orphans, the needy, the wayfarer and to those who ask (in charity) and in ransoming the slaves; and who observe the Prayer, who go on presenting the *Zakât* (the purifying alms) and those who always fulfill their pledges and agreements when they have made one, and those who are patiently persevering in adversity and distress and (steadfast) in times of war. It is these who have proved truthful (in their promises and in their faith) and it is these who are strictly guarded against evil.

178. O you who believe! equitable retaliation has been ordained for you in (the matter of) the slain. (Everyone shall pay for his own crime), the freeman (murderer) for the freeman (murdered), and the slave (murderer) for the slave (murdered), and the female (murderer) for the female (murdered), but who has been granted any remission by his (aggrieved) brother (or family) then pursuing (of the matter) shall be done with equity and fairness, and the payment (of the blood money) to him (the heir) should be made in a handsome manner. This is an alleviation from your Lord and a mercy. But he who exceeds the limits after this (commandment), for him is a grievous punishment.

179. O people of pure and clear wisdom! your very life lies in (the law of) equitable retaliation, (you have been so commanded) so that you may enjoy security.

180. It has been prescribed for you at the time of death to any one of you, that if the (dying) person is leaving considerable wealth behind, to make a will to his parents and the near of kin to act with equity and fairness. This is an obligation incumbent on those who guard against evil.

181. He who alters it (the will) after he has heard it, (should know that) it is those that alter it who shall bear the burden of sin. Allâh indeed is All-Hearing, All-Knowing.

182. If anyone apprehends that the testator is partial or follows a sinful course there will be no blame on him provided he sets things right (and so brings about reconciliation) between them (the parties concerned under the will). Surely, Allâh is Great Protector, Ever Merciful.

Section 23

183. O you who believe! you are bound to observe fasting as those before you (followers of the Prophets) were bound, so that you may guard against evil.

184. (You are required to fast) for a prescribed number of days. But if anyone of you is sick or is on a journey he shall fast (to make up) the prescribed number in other days. And for those who are able to fast is an expiation (as thanksgiving) the feeding of a poor person (daily for the days of fasting). And he who volunteers (extra) good, (will find that) it is even better for him. And that you observe fasting is better for you, if you only know.

185. The (lunar) month of *Ramadzân* is that in which the Qur'ân (started to be) revealed as a guidance for the whole of mankind with its clear evidences (providing comprehensive) guidance and the Discrimination (between right and wrong). Therefore he who shall witness the month, should fast (for full month) during it, but he who is sick or is on a journey shall fast (to make up) the prescribed number in other days. Allâh wishes facility for you and does not wish hardship for you. (This facility is given to you) that you may complete the number (of required fasts) and you may exalt the greatness of Allâh for His having guided you, and that you may render thanks (to Him). . . .

187. (Though during Fasting you must abstain from all the urges of nature including the sexual urge) it is made lawful for you on the nights of the fasts to approach and lie with your wives (for sexual relationship). They are (a sort of) garment for you and you are (a sort of) garment for them. Allâh knows that you have been doing injustice to yourselves (by restricting conjugal relations with your wives even at night), so He turned to you with mercy and provided you relief; now enjoy their company (at night during *Ramadzân*) and seek what Allâh has ordained for you. Eat and drink till the white streak of the dawn becomes distinct to you from the black streak (of the darkness), then complete the fast till nightfall. And you shall not lie with them (your wives) while you perform *I'tikâf* (while you are secluding in the mosque for prayer and devotion to God). These are the limits (imposed) by Allâh so do not approach these (limits). Thus does Allâh explain His commandments for people that they may become secure against evil. . . .

Section 24

190. And fight in the cause of Allâh those who fight and persecute you, but commit no aggression. Surely, Allâh does not love the aggressors.

191. And slay them (the aggressors against whom fighting is made incumbent) when and where you get the better of them, in disciplinary way, and turn them out whence they have turned you out. (Killing is bad but) lawlessness is even worse than carnage. But do not fight them in the precincts of *Masjid al-Harâm* (the Holy Mosque at Makkah) unless they fight you therein. Should they attack you (there) then slay them. This indeed is the recompense of such disbelievers.

192. But if they desist (from aggression) then, behold, Allâh is indeed Great Protector, Ever Merciful.

193. And fight them until persecution is no more and religion is (freely professed) for Allâh. But if they desist (from hostilities) then (remember) there is no punishment except against the unjust (who still persist in persecution). . . .

195. And spend in the cause of Allâh and do not cast yourselves into ruin with your own hands, and do good to others, and verily Allâh loves the doers of good to others.

196. Accomplish the _Hajj_* (the Greater Pilgrimage to Makkah) and the _'Umrah_ (the minor pilgrimage) for the sake of Allâh. But if you are kept back, then (offer) whatever sacrifice is easily available, and do not shave your heads (as is prescribed for the Pilgrims) till the offering reaches its destination (in time, or place). And whosoever of you is sick and has an ailment of his head (necessitating shaving before time) then he should make an expiation either by fasting or alms-giving or by making a sacrifice. When you are in peaceful conditions then he, who would avail himself of the _'Umrah_ (a visit to the _Ka'bah_ or a minor _Hajj_) together with the _Hajj_ (the Greater Pilgrimage and thus performs _Tammattu'_) should make whatever offering is easily available; and whosoever finds none (for an offering) should fast for three days during (the days of) the pilgrimage and (for) seven (days) when he returns (home) — these are ten complete (days of fasting in all). This is for him whose family does not reside near the _Masjid al-Harâm_ (the Holy Mosque at Makkah). Take Allâh as a shield, and know that Allâh is Severe in retribution (if you neglect your duties).

Section 25

197. The months of performing the _Hajj_ are well Known; so whoever undertakes to perform the _Hajj_ in them (should remember that) there is (to be) no obscenity, nor abusing, nor any wrangling during the (time of) _Hajj_. And whatever good you do Allâh knows it. And take provisions for yourselves. Surely, the good of taking provision is guarding (yourselves) against the evil (of committing sin and begging). Take Me alone as (your) shield, O people of pure and clear wisdom!

198. There is no blame on you that you seek munificence from your Lord (by trading during the time of _Hajj_). When you pour forth (in large numbers) from 'Arafât then glorify Allâh (with still more praises) near _Mash'aral-Harâm_ (Holy Mosque in _Muzdalifah_), and remember Him (with gratitude) as He has guided you, though formerly you were certainly amongst the astray. . . .

*HAH juh

Surah 4
Women

Section 1

1. O you people! take as a shield your Lord Who created you from a single being. The same stock from which He created the man He created his spouse, and through them both He caused to spread a large number of men and women. O people! regard Allâh with reverence in Whose name you appeal to one another, and (be regardful to) the ties of relationship (particularly from the female side). Verily, Allâh ever keeps watch over you.

2. And give the orphans their property and substitute not (your) worthless things for (their) good ones, nor consume their property mingling it along with your own property, for this indeed is a great sin.

3. And if (you wish to marry them and) you fear that you will not be able to do justice to the orphan girls then (marry them not, rather) marry of women (other than these) as may be agreeable to you, (you may marry) two or three or four (provided you do justice to them), but if you fear that you will not be able to deal (with all of them) equitably then (confine yourselves only to) one, or (you may marry) that whom your right hands possess (your female captives of war). That is the best way to avoid doing injustice.

4. And give the women their dowers unasked, willingly and as agreed gift. But if they be pleased to remit you a portion thereof, of their own free will, then take it with grace and pleasure.

Section 2

11. Allâh prescribes (the following) law (of inheritance) for your children. For male is the equal of the portion of two females; but if they be all females (two or) more than two, for them is two thirds of what he (the deceased) has left; and if there be only one, for her is the half and for his parents, for each one of the two is a sixth of what he has left, if he (the deceased) has a child; but if he has no child and his parents only be his heirs, then for the mother is one third (and the rest two thirds is for the father); but if there be (in addition to his parents) his brothers (and sisters) then there is one sixth for the mother after (the payment of) any bequest he may have bequeathed or (still more important) of any debt (bequests made by the testator and his debts shall however be satisfied first). Your fathers and your children, you do not know which of them deserve better to benefit from you. (This) fixing (of portions) is from Allâh. Surely, Allâh is All-Knowing, All-Wise.

12. And for you is half of that which your wives leave behind, if they have no child; but if they have a child, then for you is one fourth of what they leave behind, after (the payment of) any bequest they may have

bequeathed or (still more important) of any (of their) debt. And for them (your wives) is one fourth of what you leave behind if you have no child; but if you leave a child, then, for them is an eighth of what you leave after (the payment of) any bequest you have bequeathed or (still more important) of any debt. And if there be a man or a woman whose heritage is to be divided and he (or she—the deceased) has no child and he (or she) has (left behind) a brother or a sister then for each one of the twain is a sixth; but if they be more than one then they are (equal) sharers in one third after the payment of any bequest bequeathed or (still more important) of any debt (provided such bequest made by the testator and the debt) shall be without (any intent of) being harmful (to the interests of the heirs). This is an injunction from Allâh, and Allâh is All-Knowing, Most Forbearing.

13. These are the limits (of the law imposed) by Allâh, and who obeys Allâh and His Messenger He will admit them into Gardens served with running streams; therein they shall abide for ever; and that is a great achievement.

14. But whoso disobeys Allâh and His Messenger and transgresses the limits imposed by Him He will make him enter Fire where he shall abide long, and for him is a humiliating punishment.

15. As to those of your women who commit sexual perversity, call in four of you to witness against them, and if they bear witness then confine them to their houses, until death overtakes them or Allâh makes for them a way out.

16. And if two of your males commit the same (act of indecency), then punish them both, so if they repent and amend (keeping their conduct good) then turn aside from them, verily Allâh is Oft-Returning (with compassion), Ever Merciful.

7

ALEXANDER STILLE

Scholars Are Quietly Offering New Theories of the Koran

This article from the *New York Times* recounts a recent development in the scholarship of early Islam, a faith that begins with the Koran (or Qu'ran). Some scholars argue that the Koran is both older and younger than previously thought. What are the reasons for these new interpretations? A review article like this provides little of the

Source: Alexander Stille, "Scholars Are Quietly Offering New Theories of the Koran," *New York Times*, March 2, 2002, p. 1.

evidence, but in addition to reading any of the books mentioned, what sort of evidence would you look for to decide if you agree or disagree?

THINKING HISTORICALLY

If you accepted any of these new theories about the Koran, what new continuities would be implied? How might you think differently about religious change in the medieval Middle East?

To Muslims the Koran is the very word of God, who spoke through the Angel Gabriel to Muhammad: "This book is not to be doubted," the Koran declares unequivocally at its beginning. Scholars and writers in Islamic countries who have ignored that warning have sometimes found themselves the target of death threats and violence, sending a chill through universities around the world.

Yet despite the fear, a handful of experts have been quietly investigating the origins of the Koran, offering radically new theories about the text's meaning and the rise of Islam.

Christoph Luxenberg, a scholar of ancient Semitic languages in Germany, argues that the Koran has been misread and mistranslated for centuries. His work, based on the earliest copies of the Koran, maintains that parts of Islam's holy book are derived from pre-existing Christian Aramaic texts that were misinterpreted by later Islamic scholars who prepared the editions of the Koran commonly read today.

So, for example, the virgins who are supposedly awaiting good Islamic martyrs as their reward in paradise are in reality "white raisins" of crystal clarity rather than fair maidens.

Christoph Luxenberg, however, is a pseudonym, and his scholarly tome "The Syro-Aramaic Reading of the Koran" had trouble finding a publisher, although it is considered a major new work by several leading scholars in the field. Verlag Das Arabische Buch in Berlin ultimately published the book.

The caution is not surprising. Salman Rushdie's "Satanic Verses" received a fatwa because it appeared to mock Muhammad. The Egyptian novelist Naguib Mahfouz was stabbed because one of his books was thought to be irreligious. And when the Arab scholar Suliman Bashear argued that Islam developed as a religion gradually rather than emerging fully formed from the mouth of the Prophet, he was injured after being thrown from a second-story window by his students at the University of Nablus in the West Bank. Even many broad-minded liberal Muslims become upset when the historical veracity and authenticity of the Koran is questioned.

The reverberations have affected non-Muslim scholars in Western countries. "Between fear and political correctness, it's not possible to say anything other than sugary nonsense about Islam," said one scholar at an American university who asked not to be named, referring to the threatened violence as well as the widespread reluctance on United States college campuses to criticize other cultures.

While scriptural interpretation may seem like a remote and innocuous activity, close textual study of Jewish and Christian scripture played no small role in loosening the Church's domination on the intellectual and cultural life of Europe, and paving the way for unfettered secular thought. "The Muslims have the benefit of hindsight of the European experience, and they know very well that once you start questioning the holy scriptures, you don't know where it will stop," the scholar explained.

The touchiness about questioning the Koran predates the latest rise of Islamic militancy. As long ago as 1977, John Wansbrough of the School of Oriental and African Studies in London wrote that subjecting the Koran to "analysis by the instruments and techniques of biblical criticism is virtually unknown."

Mr. Wansbrough insisted that the text of the Koran appeared to be a composite of different voices or texts compiled over dozens if not hundreds of years. After all, scholars agree that there is no evidence of the Koran until 691 — 59 years after Muhammad's death — when the Dome of the Rock mosque in Jerusalem was built, carrying several Koranic inscriptions.

These inscriptions differ to some degree from the version of the Koran that has been handed down through the centuries, suggesting, scholars say, that the Koran may have still been evolving in the last decade of the seventh century. Moreover, much of what we know as Islam — the lives and sayings of the Prophet — is based on texts from between 130 and 300 years after Muhammad's death.

In 1977 two other scholars from the School for Oriental and African Studies at London University — Patricia Crone (a professor of history at the Institute for Advanced Study in Princeton) and Michael Cook (a professor of Near Eastern history at Princeton University) — suggested a radically new approach in their book "Hagarism: The Making of the Islamic World."

Since there are no Arabic chronicles from the first century of Islam, the two looked at several non-Muslim, seventh-century accounts that suggested Muhammad was perceived not as the founder of a new religion but as a preacher in the Old Testament tradition, hailing the coming of a Messiah. Many of the early documents refer to the followers of Muhammad as "hagarenes," and the "tribe of Ishmael," in other words as descendants of Hagar, the servant girl that the Jewish patriarch Abraham used to father his son Ishmael.

In its earliest form, Ms. Crone and Mr. Cook argued, the followers of Muhammad may have seen themselves as retaking their place in the Holy Land alongside their Jewish cousins. (And many Jews appear to have welcomed the Arabs as liberators when they entered Jerusalem in 638.)

The idea that Jewish messianism animated the early followers of the Prophet is not widely accepted in the field, but "Hagarism" is credited with opening up the field. "Crone and Cook came up with some very interesting revisionist ideas," says Fred M. Donner of the University of Chicago and author of the recent book "Narratives of Islamic Origins: The Beginnings of Islamic Historical Writing." "I think in trying to reconstruct what happened, they went off the deep end, but they were asking the right questions."

The revisionist school of early Islam has quietly picked up momentum in the last few years as historians began to apply rational standards of proof to this material.

Mr. Cook and Ms. Crone have revised some of their early hypotheses while sticking to others. "We were certainly wrong about quite a lot of things," Ms. Crone said. "But I stick to the basic point we made: that Islamic history did not arise as the classic tradition says it does."

Ms. Crone insists that the Koran and the Islamic tradition present a fundamental paradox. The Koran is a text soaked in monotheistic thinking, filled with stories and references to Abraham, Isaac, Joseph and Jesus, and yet the official history insists that Muhammad, an illiterate camel merchant, received the revelation in Mecca, a remote, sparsely populated part of Arabia, far from the centers of monotheistic thought, in an environment of idol-worshiping Arab Bedouins. Unless one accepts the idea of the angel Gabriel, Ms. Crone says, historians must somehow explain how all these monotheistic stories and ideas found their way into the Koran.

"There are only two possibilities," Ms. Crone said. "Either there had to be substantial numbers of Jews and Christians in Mecca or the Koran had to have been composed somewhere else."

Indeed, many scholars who are not revisionists agree that Islam must be placed back into the wider historical context of the religions of the Middle East rather than seeing it as the spontaneous product of the pristine Arabian desert. "I think there is increasing acceptance, even on the part of many Muslims, that Islam emerged out of the wider monotheistic soup of the Middle East," says Roy Mottahedeh, a professor of Islamic history at Harvard University.

Scholars like Mr. Luxenberg and Gerd-R. Puin, who teaches at Saarland University in Germany, have returned to the earliest known copies of the Koran in order to grasp what it says about the document's origins and composition. Mr. Luxenberg explains these copies are written without vowels and diacritical dots that modern Arabic uses to make it clear what letter is intended. In the eighth and ninth centuries, more than a century after the death of Muhammad, Islamic commentators added diacritical marks to clear up the ambiguities of the text, giving precise meanings to passages based on what they considered to be their proper context. Mr. Luxenberg's radical theory is that many of the text's difficulties can be clarified when it is seen as closely related to Aramaic, the language group of most Middle Eastern Jews and Christians at the time.

For example, the famous passage about the virgins is based on the word hur, which is an adjective in the feminine plural meaning simply "white." Islamic tradition insists the term hur stands for "houri," which means virgin, but Mr. Luxenberg insists that this is a forced misreading of the text. In both ancient Aramaic and in at least one respected dictionary of early Arabic, hur means "white raisin."

Mr. Luxenberg has traced the passages dealing with paradise to a Christian text called Hymns of Paradise by a fourth-century author. Mr. Luxenberg said the word paradise was derived from the Aramaic word for garden and all the descriptions of paradise described it as a garden of flowing waters, abundant fruits and white raisins, a prized delicacy in the ancient Near East. In this context, white raisins, mentioned often as hur, Mr. Luxenberg said, makes more sense than a reward of sexual favors.

In many cases, the differences can be quite significant. Mr. Puin points out that in the early archaic copies of the Koran, it is impossible to distinguish between the words "to fight" and "to kill." In many cases, he said, Islamic exegetes [interpreters] added diacritical marks that yielded the harsher meaning, perhaps reflecting a period in which the Islamic Empire was often at war.

A return to the earliest Koran, Mr. Puin and others suggest, might lead to a more tolerant brand of Islam, as well as one that is more conscious of its close ties to both Judaism and Christianity.

"It is serious and exciting work," Ms. Crone said of Mr. Luxenberg's work. Jane McAuliffe, a professor of Islamic studies at Georgetown University, has asked Mr. Luxenberg to contribute an essay to the Encyclopedia of the Koran, which she is editing.

Mr. Puin would love to see a "critical edition" of the Koran produced, one based on recent philological work, but, he says, "the word critical is misunderstood in the Islamic world — it is seen as criticizing or attacking the text."

Some Muslim authors have begun to publish skeptical, revisionist work on the Koran as well. Several new volumes of revisionist scholarship, "The Origins of the Koran," and "The Quest for the Historical Muhammad," have been edited by a former Muslim who writes under the pen name Ibn Warraq. Mr. Warraq, who heads a group called the Institute for the Secularization of Islamic Society, makes no bones about having a political agenda. "Biblical scholarship has made people less dogmatic, more open," he said, "and I hope that happens to Muslim society as well."

But many Muslims find the tone and claims of revisionism offensive. "I think the broader implications of some of the revisionist scholarship is to say that the Koran is not an authentic book, that it was fabricated 150 years later," says Ebrahim Moosa, a professor of religious studies at Duke University, as well as a Muslim cleric whose liberal theological leanings earned him the animosity of fundamentalists in South Africa, which he left after his house was firebombed.

Andrew Rippin, an Islamicist at the University of Victoria in British Columbia, Canada, says that freedom of speech in the Islamic world is more likely to evolve from within the Islamic interpretative tradition than from outside attacks on it. Approaches to the Koran that are now branded as heretical—interpreting the text metaphorically rather than literally—were widely practiced in mainstream Islam a thousand years ago.

"When I teach the history of the interpretation it is eye-opening to students the amount of independent thought and diversity of interpretation that existed in the early centuries of Islam," Mr. Rippin says. "It was only in more recent centuries that there was a need for limiting interpretation."

8

Peace Terms with Jerusalem

The early expansion of Islam was far more rapid and more forceful than the expansion of Christianity and Buddhism. By 636, Arab armies had conquered many of the lands previously held by the Byzantine and Persian empires. Merchants and holy men would spread the faith even further afield at a later stage. But by 750 an Arab-dominated Muslim government controlled North Africa, the Arabian peninsula, and significant portions of Eurasia from the Strait of Gibraltar to the western borders of India and China. (See Map 7.2 on page 260.)

Source: "Peace Terms with Jerusalem (636)," in *Islam from the Prophet Muhammad to the Conquest of Constantinople*, ed. and trans. Bernard Lewis, vol. I, *Politics and War* (New York: Harper & Row, 1974), 235–36. Originally published in Al Tabari, *Tarik al-Rusulcwa'l muluk*, vol. I (Leiden: Brill), 2405–6.

How much of this early expansion was military conquest and how much religious conversion? To help us answer this question, we look at an early peace treaty after the conquest of Jerusalem from the Byzantine Empire (known then as the Roman Empire, but ruled from Constantinople).

As the Arabian force for Judeo-Christian monotheism, Muslims had a strong sentimental attachment to Jerusalem. In the first years of the faith, Muhammad and his followers prayed facing Jerusalem, Al Quds (the Holy City, as it is still called in Arabic). In 624, after only modest Jewish conversions, Mecca was substituted as the *qibla* or direction to face for prayer. At the time of Muhammad's death (632), his followers controlled most of Arabia. His successor (or *caliph*), Abu Bakr (r. 632–634), regained control of the tribes that tried to withdraw from the alliance after the Prophet's death and turned to the conquest of Iraq and Syria. The second caliph, Umar (r. 634–644), negotiated the surrender of the Byzantine forces that controlled Jerusalem after the defeat of Byzantine armies in 636. This document, written by the caliph and directed to the Christian community of Jerusalem, set the terms for continued Christian presence in the city. Many of these terms were continuations of past practice. One of the terms included *jizya*, which was a tax or tribute that non-Muslims paid Muslim governments for protection. This document also reinstates the expulsion of Jews from Jerusalem, a policy first instated under Roman administration and later continued under the Byzantine Christian administration, though Umar later allowed Jews to reside in the city.

Other Muslim sources tell us that the inhabitants of Jerusalem appealed to Umar to take control of Jerusalem. What evidence do you see in these terms that would make that story plausible? What would both sides, Muslim and Christian, seem to gain by these terms?

THINKING HISTORICALLY

If this peace treaty were observed as written, what would have changed in Jerusalem? What would have remained the same? Are these changes mainly religious or political? To what extent, if any, does Muslim control of Jerusalem suggest Jewish or Christian conversions to Islam?

In the name of God the Merciful and the Compassionate.

This is the safe-conduct accorded by the servant of God Umar, the Commander of the Faithful, to the people of Aelia [Jerusalem].[1]

He accords them safe-conduct for their persons, their property, their churches, their crosses, their sound and their sick, and the rest of their worship.

Their churches shall neither be used as dwellings nor destroyed. They shall not suffer any impairment, nor shall their dependencies, their crosses, nor any of their property.

No constraint shall be exercised against them in religion nor shall any harm be done to any among them.

No Jew shall live with them in Aelia.

The people of Aelia must pay the *jizya*[2] in the same way as the people of other cities.

They must expel the Romans[3] and the brigands from the city. Those who leave shall have safe-conduct for their persons and property until they reach safety. Those who stay shall have safe-conduct and must pay the *jizya* like the people of Aelia.

Those of the people of Aelia who wish to remove their persons and effects and depart with the Romans and abandon their churches and their crosses shall have safe-conduct for their persons, their churches, and their crosses, until they reach safety.

The country people who were already in the city before the killing of so-and-so may, as they wish, remain and pay the *jizya* the same way as the people of Aelia or leave with the Romans or return to their families. Nothing shall be taken from them until they have gathered their harvest.

This document is placed under the surety of God and the protection [*dhimma*] of the Prophet, the Caliphs and the believers, on condition that the inhabitants of Aelia pay the *jizya* that is due from them.

Witnessed by Khālid ibn al-Wald, 'Amr ibn al-Āṣ, 'Abd al-Raḥmān ibn 'Awf, Muāwiya ibn Abī Sufyān, the last of whom wrote this document in the year 15 [636].

---

[1] Aelia Capitolina was the name given to Jerusalem by Roman emperor Hadrian after he suppressed the second Jewish revolt in 132–135 (the first revolt was 66–70). He also expelled Jews from the city and banned them from living there. The Christian Byzantines continued this policy. Thus, this was a concession to Christians. Umar later let the Jews return to Jerusalem. In the seventh century one could be both a Jew and a Muslim. [Ed.]

[2] A tax on non-Muslims in return for exemption from the *zakat* tax on Muslims and military service. [Ed.]

[3] Byzantine soldiers and officials. [Ed.]

9

The Epic of Sundiata

This is a brief selection from one of the great epics of West Africa. In a culture without a system of written notation, stories like this were told by griots — specialists with prodigious memories. Most of these griots worked in the courts of kings, learning, like their fathers before them, to tell the story of their patron's family. The *Epic of Sundiata* is the account of one of the great families of the Mande people. The *Epic* centers on Sundiata Keita (c. 1217–1255), who founded the Mali Empire. Our selection is drawn from the story of Maghan Konfara, Sundiata's father, and tells of his conversion to Islam. It begins with the declaration of a visitor, Manjan Bereté, after Maghan Konfara has asked to marry his sister. What does this story add to your understanding of religious conversions and the spread of salvation religions?

THINKING HISTORICALLY

A single conversion would seem to bring far less change than the conquest of a city. Yet, as we have seen, the conversion of a king might have consequences as profound as the conquest of a kingdom. What sort of changes would you expect to occur after this conversion? We are also used to thinking of religious conversion as a momentous change for the individual who experiences it, not the casual affair depicted here. What, if anything, does this story tell you about the history of internal or psychological change?

[The visitor declares:]

"We are Bereté.
It was our ancestor who planted a date farm for the Prophet
        at Mecca
That was the beginning of our family identity.
When the date farm was planted for the Prophet,
He blessed our ancestor.
He said everyone should leave us alone:
Bè anu to yè, and that is why they call us Bereté.
No man of Manden will tell you
That we originated the Bereté family identity.
It was the Prophet who said we should be set apart,
That nobody's foolishness should trouble us.

Source: *Sunjata: A West African Epic of the Mande Peoples*, trans. David C. Conrad and narrated by Djanka Tassey Condé (Indianapolis, IN: Hackett, 2004), 17–19 (lines 420–93).

Bè anu to yè, everyone should leave us alone.
Thus we became the Bereté.
From that time up to today,
We have not done anything other than the Prophet's business.
This place[1] has already become impious
Because of your lack of attention to Islam.
So how can I give you my little sister?
I did not come from Farisi[2] for that purpose,
So I will not give you my little sister."
"Aaah," said Simbon,[3] "Give her to me.
If you want wealth, I will give you wealth."
(You heard it?)
"If you not give her to me,
I will take her for myself,
Because you are not in your home, you are in my home."
When Manjan Bereté was told this, he said,
"If you take my sister for yourself, I will go back to Farisi.
I will go and get Suraka[4] warriors to come and destroy Manden
If you take my little sister by force."
Simbon said, "You just do that.
If you go back to Farisi to get warriors,
You might come and destroy Manden.
But by then your sister will be pregnant,
I will have a child by then.
Even if I die, it will still be my child."
(You heard it?)
He said, "I have taken her."
He took her.
"If you call for wealth, I will give you wealth.
If you call for the sword, I will agree to that.
I have the power, you have no power, you are in my place."

Manjan Bereté packed up his books and went back to Farisi.
He went and told his fathers and brothers,
"The Mande *mansa*[5] that I went to visit,
He has used his chiefly power to take my little sister from me."
His fathers and brothers said, "Ah, Manjan Bereté,
Your youth has betrayed you.

[1] Maghan Konfara's place, Konfara, Farakoro, or more generally the land of the Mande (modern southwest Mali). [Ed.]
[2] Fars, Persia. [Ed.]
[3] Speaks for Maghan Konfara. [Ed.]
[4] Arab, Moor, or North African warriors. [Ed.]
[5] King.

You carry the sacred book.
Go back and tell the Mande people,
Tell Simbon,
That if he is in love with your younger sister,
You will give him both her and the book.
Tell him 'If you convert, and become another like me,
So that we can proselytize together,
I will give you my younger sister,
But if you refuse to convert, I will go for my warriors.'
If he does not convert, come back and we will give you warriors.
If he agrees to convert, that is what you went for."

Manjan Bereté returned to Farakoro.
After he explained to Simbon,
Maghan Konfara said, "What your father said,
That your youth betrayed you, is true.
If you had done what he said in the first place,
You would not have returned to Farisi.
All I want is a child, no matter what the cost.
I agree to what you propose.
Since you have requested that I convert,
I agree."
They shaved his head, and together they read the Koran.
After reading the Koran,
Manjan Bereté gave his little sister to Maghan Konfara.

■ REFLECTIONS

The expansion of the great universal religions continued well beyond 1000. In fact, it continues today. We live in a world of about two hundred nation-states, but two-thirds of the world's people follow only three religions: Christianity, Islam, and Buddhism. We return to the question that opened this chapter: What enabled these particular religions to convert so many?

We noted here, and in the previous chapter, that many of the religions of this period were book or text based. The Bible and Koran were said by many to be given by God. The stories of the Buddha also took on an aura of authority that must have enhanced their appeal. Most people could not read or write, of course, but the great religions created writing-based bureaucracies, educators, and thinkers who ensured the dissemination of the sacred scripture, eternal truths, and revered tales. The stories of the life of Jesus were carved into the walls of the Christian churches, etched into the colored glass of the windows, and told and reenacted in the religious rite of the Eucharist, which celebrated the last supper of Jesus. Statues of the Buddha of every size and description were carved and placed for worship in temples throughout Asia. Five times a day, the Muslim call to prayer reverberated from the minarets that spiked the skyline from Morocco to Malacca, and from Tashkent to Timbuktu. One did not have to be able to read in order to pray.

The learned devised, collected, or correlated these texts, often insisting they were the words of the founder, spoken by God or engraved in stone. Then they and their successors explained and interpreted them, often turning intractable prose into metaphor, amending failed prophecies, and inventing myths to suit current politics.

Our readings suggest that the decision to adopt a particular religion was often more political than theological. Kings and emperors made the decision, often with the same degree of calculation whether they were defending state cults, like Trajan, embracing radical challenges, like Constantine, or simply negotiating a marriage, like Sundiata's father. Universal religions and imperial systems fit well together because it was easier for the emir or emperor to work with a unified set of religious values and only universal religions allowed new converts. Example and influence probably played a greater role than conquest. The spread of Islam was the most obvious conquest in this period (as Christianity was later), but the image of Muslims forcing others to convert or die was largely a projection of later Christian crusaders. Recent historical research reveals a rapid military conquest by traditional Arab raiding armies followed later by a gradual process of conversion. Many conquered people, like the Jews of Jerusalem, viewed the Arab armies as liberators. In general, Arab rule was remote and indirect. Normally, the Arabs left earlier structures in control, sometimes making the collection of tribute more efficient, even more lenient. Arab Muslim conquerors were not highly motivated in winning converts because mass conversions would limit the *jizya*, the head tax that only non-Muslims paid. A study by the historian Richard Bulliet shows that Iranians adopted Muslim names (a sign of conversion) gradually a hundred years after the conquest of 648 and that the number of Iranian Muslims increased over the next few hundred years at rates that can be charted on a standard bell curve, the same way any new style or technology rises and then levels off close to saturation.

Distinguishing change and continuity is a historical skill useful in understanding any historical document, period, process, or place. It helps us pose questions, not give simplistic answers like "religion x was continuous, but religion y changed." Everything changes to some degree. It is relative change or constancy that we are after. How fast, how sudden, what specifically changed, and what continued pretty much as before? And what can we learn from asking these questions?

If Judaism was a universal religion that converted large populations from North Africa to Central Asia in the years after the fall of Rome, then its continuity, like that of the other universal religions, is in belief and tradition, not ethnicity or place. If the continuity of Islam stretches back to Aramaic Christianity and a more widespread Judaism than previously thought, then it makes sense to think of a Judeo-Christian-Islamic tradition, to recognize the apocalyptic theme that pulses through it, and to see the continuity between Islam and Nestorian Christianity, as well as the seal of a new prophecy. On the other hand, a post-Nestorian Christianity in Tang China that neither mentions Jesus nor explains the symbolism of the cross, but instead speaks in the metaphors of the Dao, may tell us more about the continuity of Chinese cultural traditions than of Christianity. Lessons like these are not only interesting in their own right. They might have also been useful for later generations of empire builders, colonial settlers, missionaries, and diplomats.

8

Medieval Civilizations

European, Islamic, Chinese, and Maya Societies, 250–1250

■ HISTORICAL CONTEXT

In the centuries after 200 C.E., an influx of nomadic peoples from the grasslands of Eurasia into the Roman and Han Chinese empires brought an end to the classical civilizations. In their wake, three distinct civilizations developed: European Christian, Islamic (after 622), and Chinese. Of the three, the Chinese was most like its preceding classical civilization; in some ways the Sui dynasty (589–618) revived the institutions of the Han. The greatest change occurred in Western Europe, especially the former urban areas of the Roman Empire, some of which virtually disappeared. The area from Byzantium to the Indus River was radically transformed by the rise of Islam, but a foreign observer might have been struck more by the continuity of urban growth and material progress than by the change of faith in Western Asia from the classical to Muslim period.

In any case, these three worlds of Eurasia in the Middle Ages were vastly different from each other. A goal of this chapter is to explore some of those differences.

We extend the comparative framework by looking at the contemporary Maya of the Americas as well. The Maya were also successors to an earlier classical civilization, the Olmec (see Chapter 2, selection 7). They too expanded over a vast area, in Mexico and Central America, in a fairly brief time, and Maya culture exerted an enormous influence over later American peoples.

■ THINKING HISTORICALLY

Distinguishing Social, Economic, Political, and Cultural Aspects of Civilizations

Comparing civilizations is a daunting undertaking; there are so many variables one must keep in mind. Consequently, when historians compare civilizations, or any social system, they first break them down into parts. Most commonly, historians distinguish between the political, economic, social, and cultural features of a system. The political refers to how a society or civilization is governed, the economic to how it supports itself, the social to how it organizes population groups, including families, and the cultural to how it explains and represents itself, including its religion.

In this chapter, you are asked to be systematic in distinguishing among these features for each of the four civilizations. We will break them down to compare each part—for example, European and Chinese politics, Muslim and Chinese culture—but also to see how the parts of each civilization make a whole: for example, how Chinese politics and Chinese culture fit together.

1

Feudalism: An Oath of Homage and Fealty

This primary source is from France, selected to illustrate one of the important institutions of Europe in the Middle Ages: feudalism. This document from the year 1110 details the mutual obligation between a feudal lord and his vassal. In this case, the feudal lord is a religious institution, the monastery of St. Mary of Grasse. Acting for the monastery and its lands is the abbot, Leo. The vassal (dependent) works the properties of the monastery in trust and pledges homage and fealty (submission and loyalty) to the lord. The vassal in this document is Bernard Atton, viscount of Carcassonne.*

* cahr cas OHN

Source: "Charter of Homage and Fealty of the Viscount of Carcassone, 1110," in *Translations and Reprints from the Original Sources of European History*, ed. D. C. Munro, vol. 4, bk. 3 (Philadelphia: University of Pennsylvania Press, 1897), 18–20.

What exactly does the viscount of Carcassonne promise to do? What is Leo the abbot's responsibility on behalf of the monastery? How new or old does this agreement appear to be? What else does this document tell you about the relationship of lords and vassals in European feudalism?

THINKING HISTORICALLY

Using the distinctions suggested in the chapter introduction, how would you characterize this agreement? In short, is it an economic, political, social, or cultural agreement? Because it obviously has more than one of these elements, how might you argue for each of the four characterizations?

What would be the closest equivalent to this sort of agreement today? Would you characterize the modern equivalent as economic, political, social, or cultural?

In the name of the Lord, I, Bernard Atton, Viscount of Carcassonne, in the presence of my sons, Roger and Trencavel, and of Peter Roger of Barbazan, and William Hugo, and Raymond Mantellini, and Peter de Vietry, nobles, and of many other honorable men, who had come to the monastery of St. Mary of Grasse, to the honor of the festival of the august St. Mary; since lord Leo, abbot of the said monastery, has asked me, in the presence of all those above mentioned, to acknowledge to him the fealty and homage for the castles, manors, and places which the patrons, my ancestors, held from him and his predecessors and from the said monastery as a fief,[1] and which I ought to hold as they held, I have made to the lord abbot Leo acknowledgment and homage as I ought to do.

Therefore, let all present and to come know that I the said Bernard Atton, lord and viscount of Carcassonne, acknowledge verily to thee my lord Leo, by the grace of God, abbot of St. Mary of Grasse, and to thy successors that I hold and ought to hold as a fief, in Carcassonne, the following: . . . Moreover, I acknowledge that I hold from thee and from the said monastery as a fief the castle of Termes in Narbonne; and in Minerve the castle of Ventaion, and the manors of Cassanolles, and of Ferral and Aiohars; and in Le Rogès, the little village of Longville; for each and all of which I make homage and fealty with hands and with mouth to thee my said lord abbot Leo and to thy successors, and I swear upon these four gospels of God that I will always be a faithful vassal to thee and to thy successors and to St. Mary of Grasse in all things in which a vassal is required to be faithful to his lord, and I will defend

---

[1] Property held in trust as part of a feudal contract. [Ed.]

thee, my lord, and all thy successors, and the said monastery and the monks present and to come and the castles and manors and all your men and their possessions against all malefactors and invaders, at my request and that of my successors at my own cost; and I will give to thee power over all the castles and manors above described, in peace and in war, whenever they shall be claimed by thee or by thy successors.

Moreover I acknowledge that, as a recognition of the above fiefs, I and my successors ought to come to the said monastery, at our own expense, as often as a new abbot shall have been made, and there do homage and return to him the power over all the fiefs described above. And when the abbot shall mount his horse I and my heirs, viscounts of Carcassonne, and our successors ought to hold the stirrup for the honor of the dominion of St. Mary of Grasse; and to him and all who come with him, to as many as two hundred beasts, we should make the abbot's purveyance in the borough of St. Michael of Carcassonne, the first time he enters Carcassonne, with the best fish and meat and with eggs and cheese, honorably according to his will, and pay the expense of the shoeing of the horses, and for straw and fodder as the season shall require.

And if I or my sons or their successors do not observe to thee or to thy successors each and all the things declared above, and should come against these things, we wish that all the aforesaid fiefs should by that very fact be handed over to thee and to the said monastery of St. Mary of Grasse and to thy successors.

I, therefore, the aforesaid lord Leo, by the grace of God, abbot of St. Mary of Grasse, receive thy homage and fealty for all the fiefs of castles and manors and places which are described above; in the way and with the agreements and understandings written above; and likewise I concede to thee and thy heirs and their successors, the viscounts of Carcassonne, all the castles and manors and places aforesaid, as a fief, along with this present charter, divided through the alphabet.[2] And I promise to thee and thy heirs and successors, viscounts of Carcassonne, under the religion of my order, that I will be a good and faithful lord concerning all those things described above.

Moreover, I, the aforesaid viscount, acknowledge that the little villages of [twelve are listed] with the farmhouse of Mathus and the chateaux of Villalauro and Claromont, with the little villages of St. Stephen of Surlac, and of Upper and Lower Agrifolio, ought to belong to the said monastery, and whoever holds anything there holds from the same monastery, as we have seen and have heard read in the privileges and charters of the monastery, and as was there written.

---

[2] Completely, without exception. [Ed.]

Made in the year of the Incarnation of the Lord 1110, in the reign of Louis. Seal of [the witnesses named in paragraph one, Bernard Atton and abbot Leo] who has accepted this acknowledgment of the homage of the said viscount.

And I, the monk John, have written this charter at the command of the said lord Bernard Atton, viscount of Carcassonne and of his sons, on the day and year given above, in the presence and witness of all those named above.

2

The Magna Carta

The Magna Carta was a contract between King John of England and his nobles (or "liegemen") in which the king agreed to recognize certain rights and liberties of the nobility. In return the nobles accepted certain obligations to the king. According to this excerpt, what were some of these rights and obligations? Can you tell from these provisions what some of the nobles' complaints had been? Did the signing of this agreement in 1215 improve the position of the common people, women, or foreigners? What does the document tell you about English society in the early thirteenth century?

THINKING HISTORICALLY

This is obviously a political document, as it details the mutual obligations of King John and his nobles, the barons. But in addition to political matters, it covers a number of issues that might be considered economic, social, and cultural. Which items would you characterize as falling into one of those categories?

What does the Magna Carta have in common with the European document on feudalism? What does this commonality tell you about European society in the Middle Ages?

John, by the grace of God, King of England, Lord of Ireland, Duke of Normandy and Aquitaine, and Count of Anjou: To the Archbishops, Bishops, Abbots, Earls, Barons, Justiciaries, Foresters, Sheriffs, Reeves,

Source: "Magna Carta," trans. E. P. Cheney, in *Translations and Reprints from the Original Sources of European History*, ed. D. C. Munro, vol. 1, bk. 6 (Philadelphia: University of Pennsylvania Press, 1897), 6–15, passim.

Ministers, and all Bailiffs and others, his faithful subjects, Greeting. Know ye that in the presence of God, and for the health of Our soul, and the souls of Our ancestors and heirs, to the honor of God, and the exaltation of Holy Church, and amendment of Our Kingdom, by the advice of Our reverend Fathers, Stephen, Archbishop of Canterbury, Primate of all England, and Cardinal of the Holy Roman Church; Henry, Archbishop of Dublin; William of London, Peter of Winchester, Jocelin of Bath and Glastonbury, Hugh of Lincoln, Walter of Worcester, William of Coventry, and Benedict of Rochester, Bishops; Master Pandulph, the Pope's subdeacon and familiar; Brother Aymeric, Master of the Knights of the Temple in England; and the noble persons, [17 named] . . . , and others, Our liegemen:

1. We have, in the first place, granted to God, and by this Our present Charter confirmed for Us and Our heirs forever — That the English Church shall be free and enjoy her rights in their integrity and her liberties untouched. And that We will this so to be observed appears from the fact that We of Our own free will, before the outbreak of the dissensions between Us and Our barons,[1] granted, confirmed, and procured to be confirmed by Pope Innocent III the freedom of elections, which if considered most important and necessary to the English Church, which Charter We will both keep Ourself and will it to be kept with good faith by Our heirs forever. We have also granted to all the free men of Our kingdom, for Us and Our heirs forever, all the liberties underwritten, to have and to hold to them and their heirs of Us and Our heirs.

2. If any of Our earls, barons, or others who hold of Us in chief by knight's service shall die, and at the time of his death his heir shall be of full age and owe a relief[2] he shall have his inheritance by ancient relief; to wit, the heir or heirs of an earl of an entire earl's barony, £100; the heir or heirs of a baron of an entire barony, £100; the heir or heirs of a knight of an entire knight's fee, 100s. at the most; and he that owes less shall give less, according to the ancient custom of fees.

3. If, however, any such heir shall be under age and in ward, he shall, when he comes of age, have his inheritance without relief or fine.

4. The guardian of the land of any heir thus under age shall take therefrom only reasonable issues, customs, and services, without destruction or waste of men or property; and if We shall have committed the wardship of any such land to the sheriff or any other person answerable to Us for the issues thereof, and he commit destruction or waste, We will take an amends from him, and the land shall be committed to two lawful and discreet men of that fee, who shall be answerable for the

---

[1] John wanted more taxes and military service from his barons (his vassals), especially after losing family lands in France. In 1215, the barons rebelled and entered London, forcing King John to agree to the Charter. [Ed.]

[2] A form of tax. [Ed.]

issues to Us or to whomsoever We shall have assigned them. And if We shall give or sell the wardship of any such land to anyone, and he commit destruction or waste upon it, he shall lose the wardship, which shall be committed to two lawful and discreet men of that fee, who shall, in like manner, be answerable unto Us as has been aforesaid.

5. The guardian, so long as he shall have the custody of the land, shall keep up and maintain the houses, parks, fishponds, pools, mills, and other things pertaining thereto, out of the issues of the same, and shall restore the whole to the heir when he comes of age, stocked with ploughs and tillage, according as the season may require and the issues of the land can reasonably bear.

6. Heirs shall be married without loss of station, and the marriage shall be made known to the heir's nearest of kin before it be contracted.

7. A widow, after the death of her husband, shall immediately and without difficulty have her marriage portion and inheritance. She shall not give anything for her marriage portion, dower, or inheritance which she and her husband held on the day of his death, and she may remain in her husband's house for forty days after his death, within which time her dower shall be assigned to her.

8. No widow shall be compelled to marry so long as she has a mind to live without a husband, provided, however, that she give security that she will not marry without Our assent, if she holds of Us,[3] or that of the lord of whom she holds, if she holds of another.

9. Neither We nor Our bailiffs shall seize any land or rent for any debt so long as the debtor's chattels are sufficient to discharge the same; nor shall the debtor's sureties be distrained so long as the debtor is able to pay the debt. If the debtor fails to pay, not having the means to pay, then the sureties shall answer the debt, and, if they desire, they shall hold the debtor's lands and rents until they have received satisfaction of the debt which they have paid for him, unless the debtor can show that he has discharged his obligation to them.

10. If anyone who has borrowed from the Jews any sum of money, great or small, dies before the debt has been paid, the heir shall pay no interest on the debt so long as he remains under age, of whomsoever he may hold. If the debt shall fall into Our hands, We will take only the principal sum named in the bond. . . .

13. The City of London shall have all her ancient liberties and free customs,[4] both by land and water. Moreover, We will and grant that all other cities, boroughs, towns, and ports shall have their liberties and free customs.

---

[3] Is dependent on us (the king); is vassal of. [Ed.]
[4] Free of paying custom fees to the king. [Ed.]

14. For obtaining the common counsel of the kingdom concerning the assessment of aids (other than in the three cases aforesaid) or of scutage,[5] We will cause to be summoned, severally by Our letters, the archbishops, bishops, abbots, earls, and great barons; We will also cause to be summoned, generally, by Our sheriffs and bailiffs, all those who hold lands directly of Us, to meet on a fixed day, but with at least forty days' notice, and at a fixed place. In all letters of such summons We will explain the cause thereof. The summons being thus made, the business shall proceed on the day appointed, according to the advice of those who shall be present, even though not all the persons summoned have come. . . .

16. No man shall be compelled to perform more service for a knight's fee or other free tenement[6] than is due therefrom.

17. Common Pleas shall not follow Our Court, but shall be held in some certain place. . . .

20. A free man shall be amerced[7] for a small fault only according to the measure thereof, and for a great crime according to its magnitude, saving his position; and in like manner a merchant saving his trade, and a villein saving his tillage, if they should fall under Our mercy. None of these amercements shall be imposed except by the oath of honest men of the neighborhood.

21. Earls and barons shall be amerced only by their peers, and only in proportion to the measure of the offense.

22. No amercement shall be imposed upon a clerk's[8] lay property, except after the manner of the other persons aforesaid, and without regard to the value of his ecclesiastical benefice.[9]

23. No village or person shall be compelled to build bridges over rivers except those bound by ancient custom and law to do so. . . .

28. No constable or other of Our bailiffs shall take corn or other chattels of any man without immediate payment, unless the seller voluntarily consents to postponement of payment.

29. No constable shall compel any knight to give money in lieu of castle-guard when the knight is willing to perform it in person or (if reasonable cause prevents him from performing it himself) by some other fit man. Further, if We lead or send him into military service, he shall be quit of castle-guard for the time he shall remain in service by Our command.

[5] A tax paid to avoid military service. [Ed.]
[6] Property; gift from the king. [Ed.]
[7] Fined. [Ed.]
[8] Clergyman. [Ed.]
[9] Church property or office of value. [Ed.]

30. No sheriff or other of Our bailiffs, or any other man, shall take the horses or carts of any free man for carriage without the owner's consent.

31. Neither We nor Our bailiffs will take another man's wood for Our castles or for any other purpose without the owner's consent. . . .

35. There shall be one measure of wine throughout Our kingdom, and one of ale, and one measure of corn, to wit, the London quarter, and one breadth of dyed cloth, russets, and haberjets[10] to wit, two cells within the selvages.[11] As with measure so shall it also be with weights. . . .

38. In the future no bailiff shall upon his own unsupported accusation put any man to trial without producing credible witnesses to the truth of the accusation.

39. No free man shall be taken, imprisoned, disseised,[12] outlawed, banished, or in any way destroyed, nor will We proceed against or prosecute him, except by the lawful judgment of his peers and by the law of the land.

40. To no one will We sell, to none will We deny or delay, right or justice.

41. All merchants shall have safe conduct to go and come out of and into England, and to stay in and travel through England by land and water for purposes of buying and selling, free of illegal tolls, in accordance with ancient and just customs, except, in time of war, such merchants as are of a country at war with Us. If any such be found in Our dominion at the outbreak of war, they shall be attached, without injury to their persons or goods, until it be known to Us or Our Chief Justiciary how Our merchants are being treated in the country at war with Us, and if Our merchants be safe there, then theirs shall be safe with Us.

42. In the future it shall be lawful (except for a short period in time of war, for the common benefit of the realm) for anyone to leave and return to Our kingdom safely and securely by land and water, saving his fealty to Us. Excepted are those who have been imprisoned or outlawed according to the law of the land, people of the country at war with Us, and merchants, who shall be dealt with as aforesaid. . . .

52. If anyone has been disseised or deprived by Us, without the legal judgment of his peers, of lands, castles, liberties, or rights, We will immediately restore the same, and if any dispute shall arise thereupon, the matter shall be decided by judgment of the twenty-five barons mentioned below in the clause for securing the peace. With regard to all those things, however, of which any man was disseised or deprived,

---

[10] Types of cloth. [Ed.]

[11] Cells . . . selvages: a measurement standard for woven cloth. [Ed.]

[12] Dispossessed. [Ed.]

without legal judgment of his peers, by King Henry Our Father or Our Brother King Richard,[13] and which remain in Our warranty, We shall have respite during the term commonly allowed to the Crusaders, except as to those matters on which a plea had arisen, or an inquisition had been taken by Our command, prior to Our taking the Cross. Immediately after Our return from Our pilgrimage, or if by chance We should remain behind from it, We will at once do full justice.

[13] King John reigned 1199–1216; he succeeded his brother King Richard, who had succeeded their father, King Henry II. [Ed.]

3

Islam: Sayings Ascribed to the Prophet

Islamic civilization originated in the seventh century to the south and west of European Christian civilization in Arabia, from where it expanded into North Africa and Spain, sub-Saharan Africa, the Middle East, and beyond. For Muslims the Prophet Muhammad (c. 570–632) was the last of a long line of spiritual visionaries who knew God, but like Abraham, Moses, and Jesus, he was only human. The Koran, on the other hand, was the direct word of God; no other writing was comparable. Nevertheless, when Muslims engaged in politics, considered laws, or studied social, economic, cultural, or other issues, they could also refer to a body of writing called *hadiths*: sayings, stories, and anecdotes related to the Prophet that were gathered by Muhammad's contemporaries. The hadiths described the decisions, acts, and the statements of the Prophet of Islam, who was the religion's first governor. What likely effect would the sayings included here have on the thinking of a devout Muslim in the aftermath of the Prophet's death? What likely Muslim attitude toward government and rebellion would come out of readings like these?

THINKING HISTORICALLY

What are the topics of these particular *hadiths*? Would you classify them as social, economic, political, or cultural? If this selection were all you had to construct a Muslim idea of government, what would it be? How are these political ideas different from those in medieval Europe?

Source: Al-Muttaqi, *Kanz al'Ummal*, quoted in *Islam from the Prophet Muhammad to the Capture of Constantinople*, ed. and trans. Bernard Lewis (New York: Harper, 1974), 1:150–51.

I charge the Caliph[1] after me to fear God, and I commend the community of the Muslims to him, to respect the great among them and have pity on the small, to honor the learned among them, not to strike them and humiliate them, not to oppress them and drive them to unbelief, not to close his doors to them and allow the strong to devour the weak.

The Imams[2] are of Quraysh;[3] the godly among them rulers of the godly, and the wicked among them rulers of the wicked. If Quraysh gives a crop-nosed Ethiopian slave authority over you, hear him and obey him as long as he does not force any of you to choose between his Islam and his neck. And if he does force anyone to choose between his Islam and his neck, let him offer his neck.

> Hear and obey, even if a shaggy-headed black slave is appointed
>   over you.
> Whosoever shall try to divide my community, strike off his head.
> If allegiance is sworn to two Caliphs, kill the other.

He who sees in his ruler something he disapproves should be patient, for if anyone separates himself from the community, even by a span, and dies, he dies the death of a pagan.

Obey your rulers, whatever happens. If their commands accord with the revelation I brought you, they will be rewarded for it, and you will be rewarded for obeying them; if their commands are not in accord with what I brought you, they are responsible and you are absolved. When you meet God, you will say, "Lord God! No evil." And He will say, "No evil!" And you will say, "Lord God! Thou didst send us Prophets, and we obeyed them by Thy leave; and Thou didst appoint over us Caliphs, and we obeyed them by Thy leave; and Thou didst place over us rulers, and we obeyed them for Thy sake." And He will say, "You speak truth. They are responsible, and you are absolved."

If you have rulers over you who ordain prayer and the alms tax and the Holy War for God, then God forbids you to revile them and allows you to pray behind them.

If anyone comes out against my community when they are united and seeks to divide them, kill him, whoever he may be.

He who dies without an Imam dies the death of a pagan, and he who throws off his obedience will have no defense on the Day of Judgment.

Do not revile the Sultan,[4] for he is God's shadow on God's earth. Obedience is the duty of the Muslim man, whether he like it or not, as

---

[1] KAY lihf Successor to the prophet; supreme authority. [Ed.]

[2] A leader, especially in prayer; clergyman. [Ed.]

[3] An aristocratic trading clan of Mecca; hostile to Muhammad, but after his death regained prominence. That religious leaders come from Quraysh was agreed after victory of the Meccan faction in 661. [Ed.]

[4] Ruler of a Muslim country; king. [Ed.]

long as he is not ordered to commit a sin. If he is ordered to commit a sin, he does not have to obey.

The nearer a man is to government, the further he is from God; the more followers he has, the more devils; the greater his wealth, the more exacting his reckoning.

He who commends a Sultan in what God condemns has left the religion of God.

4

Muhammad's Night Journey

The Night Journey is a *hadith* that tells of the Prophet Muhammad, summoned by the angel Gabriel, traveling by air from Mecca to Paradise, or Heaven. There he meets many of the patriarchs and prophets of the Bible, including Adam, Abraham, Moses, and Jesus. What does the following part of the story suggest about early Muslim attitudes toward Jews and Judaism?

THINKING HISTORICALLY

How would you classify this story? Is it a piece of social, economic, political, or cultural history? How might it fit into more than one of these categories?

Then the Prophet ascended to the seventh heaven, and that is where our Messenger saw Prophet *Ibrahim.*[1] Prophet *Ibrahim* is the best of the prophets after our prophet, *Muhammad.* The Prophet saw Prophet *Ibrahim* with his back against *al-Bayt al-Ma^mur.*[2] To the inhabitants of the skies, *al-Bayt al-Ma^mur* is like the *Ka^bah*[3] is to us, the inhabitants of the earth. Every day 70,000 angels go there; then exit from it, and never return. The next day another 70,000 angels go, come

[1] Abraham. [Ed.]

[2] House of God and his angels; holy house; "inhabited" house; house with memory of God. [Ed.]

[3] The cube structure that is the sacred center of the mosque in Mecca, toward which Muslims pray and aspire to walk around in a haj, or pilgrimage. [Ed.]

Source: Miracle of Al-Isra and Al-Miraj at http://www.geocities.com/islamicmiracles/miracle_of_al.htm. Provided by info@islamicmiracles.cjb.net.

out, and never return. This will continue until the Day of Judgment. In this, there is an indication as to the greatness of the numbers of the angels—their numbers are far more than the numbers of the humans and the *jinns*[4] together.

In the seventh heaven, Prophet *Muḥammad* saw *Sidrat al-Muntaha*[5]—a very big tree of *sidr*.[6] Each of the fruits of this tree is as large as a big jar. The leaves of this tree are similar to the ears of the elephants. *Sidrat al-Muntaha* is an extremely beautiful tree. It is visited by butterflies made of gold. When these butterflies gather on this tree, its beauty is beyond description.

Then the Prophet ascended to what is beyond the seven skies; he entered Paradise. He saw examples of the inhabitants of Paradise and how their situation would be. He saw most of the inhabitants of Paradise are the poor people. . . .

Then the Prophet ascended beyond Paradise. He reached a place where he heard the creaking of the pens used by the angels who are copying from the Preserved Tablet.[7] It is at that location Prophet *Muḥammad* heard the *Kalam* of *Allah*,[8] which is an attribute of the Self of *Allah*. He heard the *Kalam* of *Allah* which does not resemble our speech—so it is not something that occurs bit after bit. It is not letter after letter or a word that comes after another word. Rather, it is an attribute of *Allah* which is eternal and everlasting. It does not resemble our attributes. The *Kalam* of *Allah* has neither silence nor interruptions. It is an attribute of *Allah*, and it does not resemble the attributes of the creation.

The Prophet understood several things from hearing this *Kalam* of *Allah*. He understood the obligation of the five Obligatory Prayers. At first, *Allah* obligated fifty prayers. When Prophet *Muḥammad* encountered *Musa*,[9] *Musa* told him to make supplication *(du^a')* to his Lord to ease the obligation of fifty (50) prayers, because his nation could not handle that. *Musa* said, "I have experience with the people of Israel, and I know your nation cannot bear that." So the Prophet asked his Lord to lessen these prayers for his people. Five prayers were eliminated. Once again, *Musa* told the Prophet to ask *Allah* to lessen the number of prayers. *Allah* did. Nine times the Prophet made supplication to *Allah* to lessen these prayers—until these prayers were lessened to five Obligatory Prayers. So Prophet *Musa* was a great benefit to us. Had we been obligated to pray fifty prayers a day, this would have been a difficult matter for us.

---

[4] Genies, spirits. [Ed.]

[5] The lotus tree of the furthest boundary, beyond which no mortal can pass. [Ed.]

[6] The sidr tree is mentioned in the Bible; native to Arabia, its flowers, fruit, leaves, and "honey" are used for medicinal purposes. [Ed.]

[7] The Koran. [Ed.]

[8] Voice of God; transcendent tongue of God. [Ed.]

[9] Moses. [Ed.]

5

AL-TANUKHI

A Government Job

Al-Tanukhi* (d. 994) was a judge in Baghdad, the capital of the Abbasid Caliphate. In this selection, he relates the story of his great-uncle Abu Qasim's† response when he asked him why he gave up a government job. What does Abu Qasim's story tell you about the job of government officials in Muslim Baghdad in the tenth century? How was government in Muslim Baghdad different from government in Europe in that period? How were ideas of government different in these two civilizations?

THINKING HISTORICALLY

This story concerns a political post, but in what ways is the story an economic one as well? Would you say the lesson of the story is political, economic, or religious?

How did you come to repent of being in Government service, Abu Qasim? I once asked, What was the cause?

This was the cause, said my great-uncle. Abu Ali Jubbai (the great Rationalist theologian) used to stay with me when he came to Ahwaz. I was Clerk to the Ahwaz municipality as well as deputy Finance Minister, so that all business used to pass through my hands. I really ran the whole place. Once a year, when the Land Tax collections began, Abu Ali Jubbai used to come to Ahwaz to arrange to have the taxes due from certain persons, who over the years had come to regard themselves as his dependents, added to the Land Tax on his own private estate at Jubba. Everybody treated him with the highest honor and respect whenever he came to town. As a rule he would only stay with me; and I used to settle his business with the Governor. The Governor, of course, was not always a friend of mine, nor was he always a man who realized Abu Ali's position, or else the amount at which his assessment was fixed would have

* ahl tah NOO kee
† ah BOO kah SEEM

Source: Judge Muhassin Tanukhi, "Resurrections of Loquacity or Table-talk (10th century)," in Eric Schroeder, *Muhammad's People: A Tale by Anthology* (Portland, ME: Bond Wheelwright Company, 1955), 566–68.

been even lower than it was. But he would always remit at least half or a third of the tax due from him.

Returning to Jubba, Abu Ali never kept for himself any of the money which in an ordinary case would have been taken in taxes from an estate like his. He used to deduct from the gross amount the sum he was to pay to Government, and then distribute the remainder among the members of his religious following, stipulating in return that each of them should entertain for a whole year one of the poor students who attended his lectures; the actual expense these students put them to was small, not a fifth of the amount due which Abu Ali's high standing had sufficed to get remitted. Then he would go to his own house, and there take out of the revenues of his estate a full tithe, which he used to give in alms among the poor people of his village, Pool, where he maintained his disciples. And he did all this every year.

On one occasion, he was staying with me at the usual season, I had done what he wanted in the matter of his Land Tax, and we were sitting talking in the evening.

Abu Ali, I said to him, are you afraid of the consequences for me in the Hereafter of the profession I am following?

How could I but be anxious, Abu Qasim? he replied. For be sure of this: if you should die employed as you now are, you will never breathe the fragrance of the Garden.

Why not? I asked. How am I guilty? I am only an accountant— I act merely as a copyist, an employee of the Treasury. It may be that somebody will come to me with a grievance, some man whose Land Tax has been unduly raised; and if I reduce it for him and set matters straight, he is only too glad to give me a present. At times perhaps I may appropriate something which really belongs to the Sovereign; but it only represents a share in the booty of the Muslims, to which I have a right.

Abu Qasim, he rejoined, *GOD IS NOT DECEIVED.* Tell me this: is it not you who appoints the land surveyors and sends them out to make their surveys, which are supposed to be accurate? And don't they go out into the country, and raise the acreage figures by ten or twenty per cent, with pen on paper, and then hand in these falsifications of theirs, and do you not make up your assessment registers on the basis of these same falsifications? And then hand over these registers to the Collector's officer, and tell him that unless he produces so much money at the Collector's Office within so many days his hands will be nailed to his feet?

Yes, I admitted.

And then the officer sets out with his escort of soldiers, horse and foot, his despatch riders and speed-up men, and flogs and cuffs and fetters? and all the time he is acting on your instructions. For if you bid him let a man off, or give him time, he does that; whereas if you give no such permission he is merciless until the man pays up.

Yes, said I.

And then the money is deposited at the Collector's Office, and the receipt forms are issued to him from your office, with your mark on them?

Yes, said I.

Then what part of the whole business, asked Abu Ali, is not of your undertaking? What part are you not answerable for? Beware of God, or you are lost. Give up your Government job. Provide for your future.

From such exhortations, from such grave warnings he would not desist until at last I burst into tears.

You are not more highly favored, he then said, nor more highly placed than Ja'far ibn Harb was: he held high office at court, his privileges and rank were almost those of a Vizier; and he was also an orthodox Believer, and a famous scholar, the author of more than one book which is still read. And yet Ja'far, when he was in office, and riding one day in a superb cavalcade, on the very crest of pomp and circumstance, suddenly heard a man reading the verse: *IS NOT THE HOUR YET COME WHEN ALL WHO TRULY BELIEVE MUST BE BROKEN AND CONTRITE OF HEART AT THE VERY MENTION OF GOD AND OF TRUTH REVEALED?* Ay, the hour is come! Ja'far exclaimed. Over and over again he said it, weeping. And he dismounted, and stripped off his dress, and waded into Tigris until the water came up to his neck. Nor did he come out again until he had given away everything he owned to atone for wrongs he had done, in reparations, pious foundations, and alms, doing everything that his system of Belief demanded, or that he thought his duty. Some passer-by, who saw him standing in the water and was told his story, gave him a shirt and a pair of breeches to cover his coming out; and he put them on. He gave himself to study and devotion from then until his death.

After a moment, Abu Ali said to me: Go, and do thou likewise, Abu Qasim. But if you cannot bring yourself to go the whole way, at least repent of being an official.

What Jubbai said made a great impression on me. I resolved that I would repent, that I would give up my job. For some time I conducted my affairs with this in view; and when I saw an opportunity of getting out of Government service, I repented, my mind made up that I would never take public office again.

6

ICHISADA MIYAZAKI

The Chinese Civil Service Exam System

The Chinese civil service examination system originated in the seventh century, making it the first in the world. As a device for ensuring government by the brightest young men, regardless of class or social standing, it may also be viewed as one of the world's earliest efforts at creating a meritocracy (a rule based on merit). For the most part, however, only sons of the moderately wealthy and ambitious could afford the time to study and take the exams.

This selection consists of two sections from a book by a noted modern Japanese historian of China. The first section concerns the elaborate early preparations for the exams. The second section presents an evaluation of the system.

What did young boys have to learn? In what ways was their education different from your own? What effects did the examination system have on the goals and values of young people?

THINKING HISTORICALLY

The Chinese examination system was primarily a political system, a way for the emperor to rule most effectively, employing the most talented administrators. In what sense did this system make China more "democratic" or egalitarian than the political systems of Western Europe or the Muslim world? In what sense was it less so? Did it become more or less democratic over the course of Chinese history? How did its purpose change from the Tang (T'ang) dynasty (618–907) to the Song (Sung) dynasty (960–1279)?

Like any political system, the civil service system had a major impact on other aspects of life — social, economic, and cultural. How did it affect Chinese society, families, class differences, boys and girls? What were the economic effects of the system? How did it influence Chinese cultural values, ideas, and education?

Judging from this excerpt and your readings about Western Europe and the Islamic world, what was the single most important difference between Chinese and Western European civilizations? Between Chinese and Muslim civilizations?

Source: Ichisada Miyazaki, *China's Examination Hell*, trans. Conrad Schirokauer (New York: Weatherhill, 1976), 13–17, 111–16, passim.

Preparing for the Examinations

Competition for a chance to take the civil service examinations began, if we may be allowed to exaggerate only a little, even before birth. On the back of many a woman's copper mirror the five-character formula "Five Sons Pass the Examinations" expressed her heart's desire to bear five successful sons. Girls, since they could not take the examinations and become officials but merely ran up dowry expenses, were no asset to a family; a man who had no sons was considered to be childless. People said that thieves warned each other not to enter a household with five or more girls because there would be nothing to steal in it. The luckless parents of girls hoped to make up for such misfortune in the generation of their grandchildren by sending their daughters into marriage equipped with those auspicious mirrors. . . .

If, indeed, a boy was born the whole family rejoiced, but if a girl arrived everyone was dejected. On the third day after her birth it was the custom to place a girl on the floor beneath her bed, and to make her grasp a tile and a pebble so that even then she would begin to form a lifelong habit of submission and an acquaintance with hardship. In contrast, in early times when a boy was born arrows were shot from an exorcising bow in the four directions of the compass and straight up and down. In later times, when literary accomplishments had become more important than the martial arts, this practice was replaced by the custom of scattering coins for servants and others to pick up as gifts. Frequently the words "First-place Graduate" were cast on those coins, to signify the highest dreams of the family and indeed of the entire clan.

It was thought best for a boy to start upon his studies as early as possible. From the very beginning he was instructed almost entirely in the classics, since mathematics could be left to merchants, while science and technology were relegated to the working class. A potential grand official must study the Four Books, the Five Classics, and other Confucian works, and, further, he must know how to compose poems and write essays. For the most part, questions in civil service examinations did not go beyond these areas of competence.

When he was just a little more than three years old, a boy's education began at home, under the supervision of his mother or some other suitable person. Even at this early stage the child's home environment exerted a great effect upon his development. In cultivated families, where books were stacked high against the walls, the baby sitter taught the boy his first characters while playing. As far as possible these were characters written with only a few strokes. . . .

After he had learned in this way to hold the brush and to write a number of characters, he usually started on the *Primer of One Thousand Characters*. This is a poem that begins:

> Heaven is dark, earth is yellow,
> The universe vast and boundless . . .

It consists of a total of two hundred and fifty lines, and since no character is repeated, it provided the student with a foundation of a thousand basic ideograms.

Upon completing the *Primer*, a very bright boy, who could memorize one thing after another without difficulty, would go on to a history text called *Meng Ch'iu* (*The Beginner's Search*) and then proceed to the Four Books and the Five Classics normally studied in school. If rumors of such a prodigy reached the capital, a special "tough examination" was held, but often such a precocious boy merely served as a plaything for adults and did not accomplish much in later life. Youth examinations were popular during the Sung dynasty, but declined and finally were eliminated when people realized how much harm they did to the boys.

Formal education began at about seven years of age (or eight, counting in Chinese style). Boys from families that could afford the expense were sent to a temple, village, communal, or private school staffed by former officials who had lost their positions, or by old scholars who had repeatedly failed the examinations as the years slipped by. Sons of rich men and powerful officials often were taught at home by a family tutor in an elegant small room located in a detached building, which stood in a courtyard planted with trees and shrubs, in order to create an atmosphere conducive to study.

A class usually consisted of eight or nine students. Instruction centered on the Four Books, beginning with the *Analects*, and the process of learning was almost entirely a matter of sheer memorization. With their books open before them, the students would parrot the teacher, phrase by phrase, as he read out the text. Inattentive students, or those who amused themselves by playing with toys hidden in their sleeves, would be scolded by the teacher or hit on the palms and thighs with his fan-shaped "warning ruler." The high regard for discipline was reflected in the saying, "If education is not strict, it shows that the teacher is lazy."

Students who had learned how to read a passage would return to their seats and review what they had just been taught. After reciting it a hundred times, fifty times while looking at the book and fifty with the book face down, even the least gifted would have memorized it. . . .

Along with the literary curriculum, the boys were taught proper conduct, such as when to use honorific terms, how to bow to superiors and to equals, and so forth—. . . .

It was usual for a boy to enter school at the age of eight and to complete the general classical education at fifteen. The heart of the curriculum was the classics. If we count the number of characters in the classics that the boys were required to learn by heart, we get the following figures:

Analects	11,705
Mencius	34,685
Book of Changes	24,107
Book of Documents	25,700
Book of Poetry	39,234
Book of Rites	99,010
Tso Chuan	196,845

The total number of characters a student had to learn, then, was 431,286.

. . . [But] of course, those were not 431,286 *different* characters: Most of the ideographs would have been used many times in the several texts. Even so, the task of having to memorize textual material amounting to more than 400,000 characters is enough to make one reel. They required exactly six years of memorizing, at the rate of two hundred characters a day.

After the students had memorized a book, they read commentaries, which often were several times the length of the original text, and practiced answering questions involving passages selected as examination topics. On top of all this, other classical, historical, and literary works had to be scanned, and some literary works had to be examined carefully, since the students were required to write poems and essays modeled upon them. Anyone not very vigorous mentally might well become sick of it all halfway through the course.

Moreover, the boys were at an age when the urge to play is strongest, and they suffered bitterly when they were confined all day in a classroom as though under detention. Parents and teachers, therefore, supported a lad, urging him on to "become a great man!" From ancient times, many poems were composed on the theme, "If you study while young, you will get ahead.". . .

Nonetheless, in all times and places students find shortcuts to learning. Despite repeated official and private injunctions to study the Four Books and Five Classics honestly, rapid-study methods were devised with the sole purpose of preparing candidates for the examinations. Because not very many places in the classics were suitable as subjects for examination questions, similar passages and problems were often repeated. Aware of this, publishers compiled collections of examination answers, and a candidate who, relying on these compilations, guessed successfully during the course of his own examinations could obtain a good rating without having worked very hard. But if he guessed wrong he faced unmitigated disaster because, unprepared, he would have submitted so bad a paper that the officials could only shake their heads and fail him. Reports from perturbed officials caused the government to issue frequent prohibitions of the publication of such collections of model answers, but since it was a profitable business with a steady demand, ways of issuing them surreptitiously were arranged, and time and again the prohibitions rapidly became mere empty formalities.

An Evaluation of the Examination System

. . . The purpose of instituting the examinations, some fourteen hundred years ago under the Sui[1] rulers, was to strike a blow against government by the hereditary aristocracy, which had prevailed until then, and to establish in its place an imperial autocracy. The period of disunion[2] lasting from the third to the sixth century was the golden age of the Chinese aristocracy: during that time it controlled political offices in central and local governments. . . .

The important point in China, as in Japan, was that the power of the aristocracy seriously constrained the emperor's power to appoint officials. He could not employ men simply on the basis of their ability, since any imperial initiative to depart from the traditional personnel policy evoked a sharp counterattack from the aristocratic officials. This was the situation when the Sui emperor, exploiting the fact that he had reestablished order and that his authority was at its height, ended the power of the aristocracy to become officials merely by virtue of family status. He achieved this revolution when he enacted the examination system (and provided that only its graduates were to be considered qualified to hold government office), kept at hand a reserve of such officials, and made it a rule to use only them to fill vacancies in central and local government as they occurred. This was the origin of the examination system.

The Sui dynasty was soon replaced by the T'ang, which for the most part continued the policies of its predecessor. Actually, as the T'ang was in the process of winning control over China, a new group of aristocrats appeared who hoped to transmit their privileges to their descendants. To deal with this problem the emperor used the examination system and favored its *chin-shih*[3] trying to place them in important posts so that he could run the government as he wished. The consequence was

[1] Sui dynasty, 581–616. [Ed.]
[2] Between end of Han (220 C.E.) and rise of Sui (581 C.E.); a period of competing warlords. [Ed.]
[3] Highest degree winners. [Ed.]

strife between the aristocrats and the *chin-shih*, with the contest gradually turning in favor of the latter. Since those who gained office simply through their parentage were not highly regarded, either by the imperial government or by society at large, career-minded aristocrats, too, seem to have found it necessary to enter officialdom through the examination system. Their acceptance of this hard fact meant a real defeat for the aristocracy.

The T'ang can be regarded as a period of transition from the aristocratic government inherited from the time of the Six Dynasties to the purely bureaucratic government of future regimes. The examination system made a large contribution to what was certainly a great advance for China's society, and in this respect its immense significance in Chinese history cannot be denied. Furthermore, that change was begun fourteen hundred years ago, at about the time when in Europe the feudal system had scarcely been formed. In comparison, the examination system was immeasurably progressive, containing as it did a superb idea the equal of which could not be found anywhere else in the world at that time.

This is not to say that the T'ang examination system was without defects. First, the number of those who passed through it was extremely small. In part this was an inevitable result of the limited diffusion of China's literary culture at a time when printing had not yet become practical and hand-copied books were still both rare and expensive, thus restricting the number of men able to pursue scholarly studies. Furthermore, because the historical and economic roots of the new bureaucratic system were still shallow, matters did not always go smoothly and sometimes there were harsh factional conflicts among officials. The development of those conflicts indicates that they were caused by the examination system itself and constituted a second serious defect.

As has been indicated, a master-disciple relationship between the examiner and the men he passed was established, much like that between a political leader and his henchmen, while the men who passed the examination in the same year considered one another as classmates and helped one another forever after. When such combinations became too strong, factions were born.

These two defects of the examination system were eliminated during the Sung regime. For one thing, the number of men who were granted degrees suddenly rose, indicating a similar rise in the number of candidates. This was made possible by the increase in productive power and the consequent accumulation of wealth, which was the underlying reason that Chinese society changed so greatly from the T'ang period to the Sung. A new class appeared in China, comparable to the bourgeoisie [that appeared later] in early modern Europe. In China this newly risen class concentrated hard on scholarship, and with the custom of this group, publishers prospered mightily. The classic books of Buddhism and Confucianism were printed; the collected writings of contemporaries and their discourses and essays on current topics were published; and the government issued an official gazette, so that in a sense China entered upon an age of mass communications. As a result learning was so widespread that candidates for the examinations came from virtually every part of the land, and the government could freely pick the best among them to form a reserve of officials.

In the Sung dynasty the system of conducting the examinations every three years was established. Since about three hundred men were selected each time, the government obtained an average of one hundred men a year who were qualified for the highest government positions. Thus the most important positions in government were occupied by *chin-shih*, and no longer were there conflicts between men who differed in their preparatory backgrounds, such as those between *chin-shih* and non–*chin-shih* that had arisen in the T'ang period. . . .

The position of the emperor in the political system changed greatly from T'ang times to Sung. No longer did the emperor consult on matters of high state policy with two or three great ministers deep in the interior of the palace, far removed from actual administrators. Now he was an autocrat, directly supervising all important departments of government and giving instructions about every aspect of government. Even minor matters of personnel needed imperial sanction. Now the emperor resembled the pivot of a fan, without which the various ribs of government would fall apart and be scattered. The creation of the palace examination as the final examination, given directly under the emperor's personal supervision, went hand in hand with this change in his function in the nation's political machinery and was a necessary step in the strengthening of imperial autocracy.

Thus, the examination system changed, along with Chinese society as a whole. Created to meet an essential need, it changed in response to that society's demand. It was most effective in those early stages when, first in the T'ang period, it was used by the emperor to suppress the power of the aristocracy, and then later, in the Sung period, when the cooperation of young officials with the *chin-shih* was essential for the establishment of imperial autocracy. Therefore, in the early Sung years *chin-shih* enjoyed very rapid promotion; this was especially true of the first-place *chin-shih*, not a few of whom rose to the position of chief councilor in fewer than ten years.

7

LIU TSUNG-YUAN

Camel Kuo the Gardener

Liu Tsung-yuan* (773–819) was one of the great writers of the Tang
dynasty (618–907). He was especially loved for his scenes of nature,
a topic he uses here for an allegory about government. What is the
message of the allegory?

THINKING HISTORICALLY

Are the ideas of government expressed here more like those
of Confucius or Laozi (see Chapter 4)? How do you think Liu
Tsung-yuan felt about the civil service system?

How does this view of government differ from that of Western
European or Muslim societies? In what sense is it more typically
Chinese?

Whatever name Camel Kuo may have had to begin with is not known.
But he was a hunchback and walked in his bumpy way with his face to
the ground, very like a camel, and so that was what the country folk
called him. When Camel Kuo heard them he said, "Excellent. Just the
right name for me." —And he forthwith discarded his real name and
himself adopted "Camel" also.

He lived at Feng-lo, to the west of Ch'ang-an. Camel was a grower of
trees by profession; and all the great and wealthy residents of Ch'ang-an
who planted trees for their enjoyment or lived off the sale of their fruit
would compete for the favour of his services. It was a matter of observation that when Camel Kuo had planted a tree, even though it was
uprooted from elsewhere, there was never a one but lived, and grew
strong and glossy, and fruited early and abundantly. Other growers,
however they spied on him and tried to imitate his methods, never could
achieve his success.

Once, when questioned on the point, Camel replied: "I cannot make
a tree live for ever or flourish. What I *can* do is comply with the nature
of the tree so that it takes the way of its kind. When a tree is planted its
roots should have room to breathe, its base should be firmed, the soil it

* lee OU tsung WAHN

Source: Liu Tsung-yuan, "Camel Kuo the Gardener," in *Anthology of Chinese Literature*, ed.
and trans. Cyril Birch (New York: Grove Press, 1965), 258–59.

is in should be old, and the fence around it should be close. When you have it this way, then you must neither disturb it nor worry about it, but go away and not come back. If you care for it like this when you plant it, and neglect it like this *after* you have planted it, then its nature will be fulfilled and it will take the way of its kind. And so all *I* do is avoid harming its growth—I have no power to make it grow; I avoid hindering the fruiting—I have no power to bring it forward or make it more abundant.

"With other growers it is not the same. They coil up the roots and they use fresh soil. They firm the base either too much or not enough. Or if they manage to avoid these faults, then they dote too fondly and worry too anxiously. They inspect the tree every morning and cosset it every night; they cannot walk away from it without turning back for another look. The worst of them will even scrape off the bark to see if it is still living, or shake the roots to test whether they are holding fast. And with all this the tree gets further every day from what a tree should be. This is not mothering but smothering, not affection but affliction. This is why they cannot rival my results: what other skill can I claim?"

"Would it be possible to apply this philosophy of yours to the art of government?" asked the questioner.

"My only art is the growing of trees," said Camel Kuo in answer. "Government is not my business. But living here in the country I have seen officials who go to a lot of trouble issuing orders as though they were deeply concerned for the people; yet all they achieve is an increase of misfortune. Morning and evening runners come yelling, 'Orders from the government: plough at once! Sow right away! Harvest inspection! Spin your silk! Weave your cloth! Raise your children! Feed your livestock!' Drums roll for assembly, blocks are struck to summon us. And we the common people miss our meals to receive the officials and still cannot find the time: how then can we expect to prosper our livelihood and find peace in our lives? This is why we are sick and weary; and in this state of affairs I suppose there may be some resemblance to my profession?"

"Wonderful!" was the delighted cry of the man who had questioned him. "The art I sought was of cultivating trees; the art I found was of cultivating men. Let this be passed on as a lesson to all in office!"

8

SIMON MARTIN AND NIKOLAI GRUBE
Chronicle of the Maya Kings and Queens

In this secondary account, two experts in the study of Maya civilization describe the culture and politics of the Maya during that society's classical era (250–900 C.E.). Maya civilization originated after 2000 B.C.E., partly under the influence of the earlier Olmec (see Chapter 2, document 7) in the Yucatan Peninsula of Mexico. By the time of the classical period, Maya cities could be found from Guatemala to central Mexico, and the influence of Maya civilization extended north into what became the southern United States.

Regarding politics, how large, powerful, centralized, or independent were Maya states? What were the basic power units, and how extensive were they? Why is this difficult to answer for the Maya? Do the authors think the Maya state was more like China, or more like Europe in this respect? In what ways was Maya civilization similar to all three major civilizations of Eurasia? In what ways was it different from each?

THINKING HISTORICALLY

The first part of this selection discusses Maya culture, and the second Maya politics. Yet as clear as these categories are, most elements of Maya life (or of any other peoples) can be classified in other categories. Corn, for example, was clearly economic, but how did it also play a cultural role in Maya society? We think of ball games as social events, but how in Maya society were they also political? The institution of an "overking" was political, but how might it also have been social, economic, or cultural?

The Royal Culture of the Maya

The Classic Maya developed a complex and highly refined royal culture which was reflected in all areas of their art, architecture and writing. Rulers combined supreme political authority with a quasi-divine status that made them indispensable mediators between the mortal and supernatural realms. From ancient times they were especially identified with the youthful Maize God, whose bounty of corn underpinned all civilization in Mesoamerica. Each stage of life—from birth to death to resurrection—found its parallel in the cycle of the maize plant and the

Source: Simon Martin and Nikolai Grube, *Chronicle of the Maya Kings and Queens* (London: Thames & Hudson, 2008), 14–21.

myth that served as its metaphor. In this way, the interests of the humble farmer and high king were entwined and basic sustenance set at the heart of Maya religion.

The Path to Sacred Power

Royal succession was strongly patrilineal and the rule of queens arose only when the dynasty might otherwise be extinguished. As far as we can tell, primogeniture was the norm: eldest sons had preference. Princelings were termed *ch'ok*, originally meaning "unripe, youth," but later extended to the wider sense of "prince." The heir himself was distinguished as the *baah ch'ok* "head youth." Childhood was marked by a series of initiation rites, one of the more important being a bloodletting usually performed at the age of five or six. Although blood was their main claim to legitimacy, candidates still had to prove themselves in war. A bout of captive-taking often preceded elevation to office and the names of such prisoners were sometimes incorporated into the kings' name phrase, in the formula "Master/Guardian of so-and-so."

Kingly investitures were elaborate affairs made up of a series of separate acts. There was an enthronement, the heir's seating on a cushion of jaguar skin, and a crowning, as a white paper headband bearing a jade image of the "Jester God" (so called because of the leafy three-lobed top to its head and a patron of royal authority that stretches right back to Olmec times) was tied to the forehead. An elaborate headdress of jade and shell mosaic, trailing green iridescent plumes of the quetzal bird, would follow. A sceptre carved into an image of the snake-footed deity K'awiil was taken. The name carried in childhood was now joined by a *huun k'aba'* "headband name," usually taken from a predecessor, sometimes a grandparent (in modern Maya communities children are seen as reborn grandparents, a single word *mam* meaning both grandparent and grandchild).

The Rites of Kingship

From here on, the calendar dictated a lifelong regimen of ritual and performance. The most enduring relics of these rites are the multi-ton stelae the Maya called *lakamtuun* or "banner stones." Their engraved texts describe their own erection, the binding of the altar set before it and the scattering of blood or incense it received. These ceremonies replicated primeval acts that first set the universe in motion. Carved with the king's image, often shown standing on a bound captive or iconic location, their inscriptions go on to chronicle the major historical events that have occurred since the last stone was set up.

Most ceremonies were conducted in the guise of appropriate deities, identified by a full costume and usually a mask (almost always depicted in cutaway form to show the wearer's face). Some required specialized

Figure 8.1 Mayan Ruler Depicted on a Cylinder Vase.

In this "roll-out" photograph of a cylinder vase we see a ruler of Motul de San José relaxing in his palace surrounded by courtiers. A wooden model dwarf holds an obsidian mirror to his gaze, while musical entertainment is provided by a group of horn and conch-shell trumpeters outside.

Source: Photograph K1453 © Justin Kerr.

dance rituals, each identified by its own name and paraphernalia (one involved live snakes). The accompaniment would consist of singing, the blowing of trumpets and conch shells and the beating of drums and turtle carapaces. More privately, rulers and their families sought to enter the spirit world through vision and trance induced by hallucinogenic drinks and enemas. They also performed auto-sacrifice, drawing blood from their tongues and genitalia with the aid of thorns, stingray spines and blades of the volcanic glass obsidian.

Every major Maya city included at least one ballcourt. In the game itself two teams would attempt to keep a large (and very hard) rubber ball from touching the ground, scoring points by means of floor markers and wall-mounted rings. Equipment included padding for the knees and elbows and a wide waist belt or "yoke." Kings might style themselves *aj pitzal* "ballplayer," though their real interest lay in the game's mythic significance. The ballcourt of the Underworld was the place of sacrifice described in the Popol Vuh (the 16th-century creation epic of the K'iche' Maya) where the Maize God met his death, but from which he was ultimately reborn.

The Royal Court, Governance and War

Kings held court in palaces set in the heart of their capitals. Painted vessels show evocative scenes of courtly life, with enthroned lords surrounded by wives and retainers, often receiving the homage of vassals delivering mounds of tribute. Maya kings seem to have been polygamous, but marriage is not a topic much discussed in the inscriptions. Also in attendance were musicians and dwarves. The latter were more than simple jesters, they enjoyed a high status derived from their special association with caves and entries into the Underworld. Scenes showing the feasting and entertaining of both visiting lords and local nobility reflect not so much leisure activities as the operation of government and diplomacy.

A key responsibility of kingship was to lead one's forces into battle against rival kings. Although the timing of attacks was essentially a tactical decision, there can be no doubt that auguries[1] were strenuously examined in search of the most auspicious moment. To be taken captive was the greatest disaster to befall a Maya king. Public humiliation was obligatory and many seem to have been tortured before their execution by beheading, burning, or being tied into balls and cast down flights of steps. Occasionally, however, they appear to have survived their ordeals and even returned to their thrones as vassals of the victor.

Journeys to the Gods: Death and Burial

Advanced age was seen as especially prestigious, and long-lived kings would invariably carry titles stating how many K'atuns[2] they had seen. Death, when it came, was viewed as the beginning of a journey, a retracing of the Maize God's descent into the Underworld, where victory over the gods of decay and disease would lead to rebirth and apotheosis. In preparation for this odyssey, dead rulers were laid in well-built tomb chambers. Stretched out on a wooden bier, the corpse was dressed in the weighty jade jewelry worn in life, wrapped in textiles and jaguar pelts and given a heavy dusting of the blood-red minerals hematite and cinnabar. Accompanying offerings included: ceramic vessels holding foodstuffs and drinks made from kakaw (cocoa beans), shells and other marine "exotics," the effigies of gods in clay or wood, mirrors of polished hematite or pyrites, bark-paper books, musical instruments, items of furniture and, occasionally, human sacrifices. In many cases a steep pyramid would be raised above the tomb, its upper temple a shrine for the king's veneration as a deified ancestor. These temples were maintained over successive generations, forming a collective repository of dynastic power. In later years tombs might be ritually re-opened, their contents scattered about and the defleshed bones scorched with fire or removed as relics.

Classic Maya Politics

A fundamental question we ask of any ancient civilization is "how was it organized politically?" In the case of the Classic Maya we are fortunate in having both a strong archaeological record and, even more

---

[1] Signs in nature of the future. [Ed.]
[2] A Maya measurement of time equal to almost twenty years. [Ed.]

importantly, a unique collection of contemporary inscriptions. Their decipherment provides key insights into Maya conceptions of kingship and statehood, of political rhetoric and authority.

Though the significance of the Preclassic–Classic divide[3] can be overstated, the distinction does seem to reflect a transformation from one social and political order to another. The emerging Classic tradition certainly drew from existing practice, incorporating ideals of rulership—even specific forms of regalia—that can be traced back to Olmec times. But it also had a keen sense of itself as an innovation, as a break from the past. Authority in the Preclassic Maya lowlands was generally manifested in broad, impersonal terms, with huge architectural programmes emblazoned with god masks and cosmic symbols. The Classic, by contrast, emphasized the individual. The relationship between kingship and the cosmos was re-articulated, even reconceived. The monolithic stela, an ancient form, was now used to fix royal identity and life-history within a sacred order defined by the calendar. Ceremonial architecture underwent a similar development, as temple pyramids became mortuary shrines for the veneration of dead kings. These changes find explicit mention in the written histories, where Classic dynasties were established by named founders, sometimes on specific dates of "arrival.". . .

For the Maya, governance was invested in the rank of *ajaw* "lord, ruler." By the end of the 4th century, paramount rulers were distinguishing themselves from a larger lordly class by calling themselves *k'uhul ajaw*, "holy lord." Though this was initially confined to the most ancient and powerful centres in the form we know now as the "emblem glyph," it ultimately spread far and wide. Another title, *kaloomte'* (long known as "Batab") was of special importance and restricted to only the strongest dynasties during the Classic proper. When prefixed by *ochk'in*, "west," as is often the case, it asserts a legitimacy derived from the great Mexican city of Teotihuacan,* whose special role in the Maya area has still to be fully uncovered.

The dynastic system of the lowlands was initially slow to spread from the heart of the Central Area known as the Peten.[4] But after a phase of Teotihuacan intervention, towards the end of the 4th century, the pace quickened noticeably. New kingdoms, many of them established at existing Preclassic centres, ultimately filled most of the productive lands in the Maya area. Each was fiercely individual, adopting its own patron deities and mythic history, many doubtless drawn from existing Preclassic traditions. These polities were the largest stable

---

*tay OH tee hwah CAHN

[3] The difference between preclassical and classical culture; the degree of change from Olmec to Maya cultures in the third century. [Ed.]

[4] Modern northern Guatemala, including Tikal. [Ed.]

units to emerge over the six centuries of the Classic and, despite continual conflict, the Maya landscape was never unified under a single authority.

New Perspectives

Over the years scholars have differed both about the size of Maya polities, whether there were just a few regional-scale states or many small statelets; and their corresponding administrations, whether they had strong, centralized governments or weak, decentralized ones. . . . But the emergence of new information from the inscriptions, in which the Maya directly describe their political world, allows a re-assessment of the topic. Our own research—much of it summarized in this volume—points to a pervasive and enduring system of "overkingship" that shaped almost every facet of the Classic landscape. Such a scheme accords closely with wider Mesoamerican practice, while seeming to reconcile the most compelling features of the two existing views, namely the overwhelming evidence for multiple small kingdoms and the great disparities in the size of their capitals.

It has been known for some time that hierarchical relations appear in the texts, where they are expressed by the use of possession. Thus *sajal*, an office held by some of the leading nobility, becomes *usajal* or "the noble of," when linking such a lord to his king. The same structure can be seen with the kingly rank of *ajaw*, which becomes *yajaw* "the lord of." While this demonstrated that one king could be subordinated to another, the small number of examples made them seem, at first, ephemeral and of limited significance. But another kind of expression proves to be equally important, greatly expanding the number of such ties. Here, a normal statement of royal accession is appended by a second phrase headed *ukabjiiy* "he supervised it," followed by the name of a foreign king. This identifies the dominant "overking" to which the local king was beholden. Similar practices are documented across Mesoamerica and explicitly described for some Maya of the Postclassic. When combined with new examples of the *yajaw* relationship, and the ever growing bank of data on diplomacy and warfare, it is possible to construct an outline anatomy of interaction and political power for the Classic Maya Central Area.

As one would expect, relationships fluctuated over time, but long-lived patterns are also apparent. It should be emphasized that the Late Classic is much better represented in this kind of display than the Early Classic, for which fewer inscriptions are known and, in any case, political interaction is less discussed. The early influence of Tikal is under-represented as a result, while we get a much better picture of Calakmul's pre-eminence in the 7th century. While these were twin superpowers, . . . they were by no means the only polities to produce "overkings," and lesser hegemonies developed in every region.

Rule of the "Overkings"

How did this system work and what were the principles that lay behind it? Talk of states and kingdoms tends to bring borders and territories to mind, but these were not the primary ways in which Maya polities defined themselves. More important was the dynastic seat at their core, their ceremonial and commercial focus and the hub from which ties radiated to lesser lordships in their periphery.

Political expansion, where it occurred, was not an acquisition of territory per se, but rather an extension of these elite networks. The most powerful dynasties brought rival "holy lords" under their domination, with ties often reaching far outside their immediate region. The bonds between lords and their masters were highly personal and remained in effect even after the death of one party. But whether cemented by oaths of loyalty or marital unions they were, in practice, rather tenuous and more reliant on military threat and the benefits available to subject lords. Apart from direct gains, war victories would encourage new recruits to enter the sphere of a successful protector, while inspiring fear and respect among existing clients. With an intimidating reputation in place, diplomatic persuasion could exert influence without the need for fighting.

Where possible, dominant powers would operate through established local dynasties, but where these proved resistant, "overkings" were not above manipulating the local succession to their advantage. The degree of influence they exerted undoubtedly varied from case to case, but their involvement in internal affairs otherwise seems slight. Surprisingly perhaps, the great "overkings" rarely boasted of their possessions in their own inscriptions and we largely rely on vassal rulers to describe their subordinate status. Often such information only emerges when some subsequent event requires explanation or background, such as when patronage was overthrown by force. The fact that subordination could be suppressed on clients' monuments hints at how many more relationships of this kind remain to be discovered.

In common with all documented societies of Mesoamerica we can take it that an economic dimension was integral to the system—a flow of goods and services from lord to overlord that would account, at least in part, for the great differences in size and wealth between cities. Unfortunately, though scenes of tribute payment are very common on painted vases (where numbered sacks of cocoa beans, heaped textiles and feathers serve as iconic currency) carved inscriptions make very little mention of inter-kingdom arrangements. Indeed, our understanding of Maya economics in general, including the highly significant topic of long-distance trade, is frustratingly poor.

[Nevertheless, in] the political landscape of the Classic Maya . . . we see a complex world criss-crossed by numerous patron–client relationships and family ties, in which major centres vied with one another in enmities that could endure for centuries.

■ REFLECTIONS

Whatever particular period or region historians work on—in the
case of this chapter, medieval European, Islamic, Chinese, and Maya
civilizations—they also tend to specialize in particular kinds of documents and related aspects of life. They are political, social, economic,
or cultural historians. As a matter of fact, most of them would characterize their work even more precisely than that. A particular social
historian might prefer to be called a historian of gender or a historian
of the family. A political historian might be a diplomatic historian. A
cultural historian might be a historian of religion, or even of medieval
Christianity, or of Christian anti-Semitism. As in the sciences, historians are able to dig deeper and learn more by specializing. And, as in
any field, the more you specialize, the more you discover what you do
not know, the more questions you have, and the more you can learn.

All of this begins, however, with employing some basic categories,
like those we have used in this chapter. That is why you were asked
to think in terms of political, economic, social, and cultural history.

To pull together and compare some of the characterizations
you made from the selections in this chapter, make a chart: Write
the names of the four civilizations—European, Islamic, Chinese,
and Maya—across the top of the page, and the categories social,
economic, political, and cultural down the left margin, allowing a
quarter page for each. Try to fill in as many of the blocks as you
can. You might use more than one characterization for each. For
instance, in the box for social aspects of European civilization you
would, no doubt, write "feudalism." You might also write "nobles,"
"monasteries," "fealty and homage," "vassals defend," and "sons
inherit status." Or your style of observing and characterizing might
lead you to such notes as "churches can be landlords" and "contracts
with lots of witnesses." All of these descriptions are correct: Just
make sure your comments are about society, social behavior, social
relationships, social organization, or various social elements—class,
family, men and women, population, and age. Repeat this exercise
with the other three categories.

After you have filled in as many of the blanks as you can, you
can make comparisons in a number of interesting ways. (You have
already done some of this, but here you can be more systematic.)
First, compare how one category, say society, is different in Europe
and Islam, or Europe and China, or China and Islam. You might, for
example, say that European society was less centralized than Chinese
or Islamic society or that the extended family was more important
in China.

After doing the same for economics, politics, and culture, notice how the four categories of any civilization fit together. How does the type of society in medieval Europe, for instance, "fit" medieval Europe's economy? This interaction is what constitutes a civilization. See if you used a word repetitively in characterizing each of the four aspects of a particular civilization. Then try to categorize the civilization as a whole.

Now you are ready to compare each of these civilizations to another one. These characterizations may be general, or they may be qualified and later modified, but at the very least you now have a general starting point for more in-depth analysis of these great civilizations in future chapters.

9
....

Love, Sex, and Marriage

Medieval Europe and Asia, 400–1350

■ HISTORICAL CONTEXT

Most people in modern society share a common ideal about love, sex, and marriage. That ideal is that love, sex, and marriage are, and should be, a unified and exclusive experience. We might boil this down to a set of simple injunctions: You should marry the one you love, and love the one you marry; you should not love others more; you should have sex only with the one you love and marry. To say this is our ideal is not to say we always live up to it; rather, it is to say that we feel we ought to, and when we do not, we feel guilt, remorse, or disappointment with ourselves. In some parts of modern society, this ideal has recently been rejected, replaced by a culture of "hook-ups" or casual sex, but even then the rejected ideal casts a long shadow. A postlove culture is not a nonlove culture: It bears the marks of what it seeks to replace.

Historically, this love-culture ideal is relatively new. The idea that marriage should be based on love was hardly viable in societies where parents arranged marriages (as they did until very recently in most societies). Nor was sexual pleasure an intrinsic element. Most societies regulated women's sexual activity, but not men's. Patriarchal societies often made little association between sexuality and either marriage or love.

The modern idea of romantic love owes much to the idea of romance that developed in Europe in the Middle Ages. We have other ideas of love, to be sure: friendship, religious love, parental love, among others. But when we read love stories, watch romantic films or plays, or listen to love songs, we draw on the ideas and images of medieval romance. We begin this chapter by studying this European set of ideas because it is the origin of much of what we mean when

we use the word *love* today. We might be surprised, however, to see
how little such love had to do with marriage or even sex. Next we
look at two cultures of love—in India and Japan, about the same
time period—that are in some ways similar and in some ways different.
Finally, for another perspective, we read ideas about sex from a
Chinese visitor to medieval Cambodia.

■   THINKING HISTORICALLY

Analyzing Cultural Differences

In the previous chapter, we distinguished among the economic, social,
political, and cultural aspects of a society. In this chapter we will
examine cultural aspects alone. Actually, culture is never alone, any
more than is economics, politics, or social behavior. Culture is nothing less than all our thoughts and feelings and the way we express
them by the way we walk, talk, dream, and read history books. Every
culture encompasses a wide variety of ideas and behavior at any
one time, making it difficult to argue that a certain idea or behavior
defines the culture as a whole. Nevertheless, if there were no common-
alities there could be no culture.

Initially our focus is on love, the idea of romantic love or
courtly love, that was "cultivated" in medieval Europe (and perhaps
also in India and Japan). This is preeminently a cultural product.
Sex we think of as biological, and marriage is certainly a social
institution, but we will look at sex as driven as much by the psyche
as the body, and we will touch on the way people thought about
marriage. Therefore, we will be making cultural comparisons. We
will ask how each culture thought about love, sex, and marriage,
and how each culture did or did not put them together. You may
be struck by how varied cultures can be. For some, a conclusion of
human relativity is disconcerting; but it might also be seen as a testament to human invention and capacity. In any case, the exercise
in making comparisons is a fundamental skill in navigating any of
our worlds.

1

KEVIN REILLY

Love in Medieval Europe, India, and Japan

We hesitantly introduce this piece as a secondary source. It might
be better called a tertiary source because it is based so much on the
work of others and is part of a chapter in a college textbook. Nevertheless, it sets the stage for our discussion about love. The selection
begins with the classic argument that romantic love was a product of medieval Europe, originating in the troubadour tradition of
southern France around the twelfth century. The story of Ulrich von
Liechtenstein, although probably not typical, details all the facets of
the new idea of love, as well as the courts of chivalry that developed
its code of behavior. What, according to this interpretation, are the
elements of romantic love? How is it similar to, or different from,
other kinds of love? How does it relate to sex and marriage? How
is the medieval Indian tradition of *bhakti* different from European
romantic love? How were medieval Hindu ideas of sex different from
Christian ideas of sex? How was the Japanese idea of love during the
Heian* period (794–1185) different from European romantic love?
How was it similar?

THINKING HISTORICALLY

One way to understand what makes one culture different from
another is to discount the extreme behavior at the fringes and focus
on what most people think or do. But another way is to compare the
extremes of one culture with the extremes of another, on the assumption that the extremists of any culture will magnify the culture's
main trait. You might think of Ulrich von Liechtenstein as an extreme
example of medieval European ideas of romantic love. A question to
ask after you read about other societies is: Could there have been an
Ulrich elsewhere? Could medieval India or Japan have produced an
Ulrich? If not, why not?

Notice also that this selection highlights particular social classes
as well as particular cultures. How do cultures and classes interact to
form the ideal of romantic love in Europe and something both similar
and different in Japan?

* hay AHN

Source: Kevin Reilly, *The West and the World*, 3rd ed. (Princeton, NJ: Markus Wiener, 1997),
279–80, 282–83, 287–92.

In the Service of Woman

In the twelfth century the courtly love tradition of the troubadours traveled north into France and Germany, and it became a guide to behavior for many young knights.

We are lucky to have the autobiography of one of these romantic knights, a minor noble who was born in Austria about 1200. His name was Ulrich von Liechtenstein, and he called his autobiography, appropriately enough, *In the Service of Woman*.[1]

At an early age Ulrich learned that the greatest honor and happiness for a knight lay in the service of a beautiful and noble woman. He seems to have realized, at least subconsciously, that true love had to be full of obstacles and frustrations in order to be spiritually ennobling. So at the age of twelve Ulrich chose as the love of his life a princess. She was a perfect choice: Far above him socially, she was also older than Ulrich and already married. Ulrich managed to become a page in her court so that he could see her and touch the same things that she touched. Sometimes he was even able to steal away to his room with the very water that she had just washed her hands in, and he would secretly drink it.

By the age of seventeen Ulrich had become a knight and took to the countryside to joust in the tournaments wearing the lady's colors. Finally after a number of victories, Ulrich gained the courage to ask his niece to call on the lady and tell her that he wanted to be a distant, respectful admirer. The princess would have none of it. She told Ulrich's niece that she was repulsed by Ulrich's mere presence, that he was low class and ugly—especially with that harelip of his. On hearing her reply Ulrich was overjoyed that she had noticed him. He went to have his harelip removed, recuperated for six weeks, and wrote a song to the princess. When the lady heard of this she finally consented to let Ulrich attend a riding party she was having, suggesting even that he might exchange a word with her if the opportunity arose. Ulrich had his chance. He was next to her horse as she was about to dismount, but he was so tongue-tied that he couldn't say a word. The princess thought him such a boor that she pulled out a lock of his hair as she got off her horse.

Ulrich returned to the field for the next three years. Finally the lady allowed him to joust in her name, but she wouldn't part with as much as a ribbon for him to carry. He sent her passionate letters and songs that he had composed. She answered with insults and derision. In one letter the princess derided Ulrich for implying that he had lost a finger while fighting for her when he had actually only wounded it slightly. Ulrich responded by having a friend hack off the finger and send it to the lady in a green velvet case. The princess was evidently so impressed with the

---

[1] Paraphrased from Martin Hunt, *The National History of Love* (New York: Alfred A. Knopf, 1959), 132–39. Quotations from Hunt.

power that she had over Ulrich that she sent back a message that she would look at it every day—a message that Ulrich received as he had the others—"on his knees, with bowed head and folded hands."

More determined than ever to win his lady's love, Ulrich devised a plan for a spectacular series of jousts, in which he challenged all comers on a five-week trip. He broke eight lances a day in the service of his princess. After such a showing, the princess sent word that Ulrich might at last visit her, but that he was to come disguised as a leper and sit with the other lepers who would be there begging. The princess passed him, said nothing, and let him sleep that night out in the rain. The following day she sent a message to Ulrich that he could climb a rope to her bedroom window. There she told him that she would grant no favors until he waded across the lake; then she dropped the rope so that he fell into the stinking moat.

Finally, after all of this, the princess said that she would grant Ulrich her love if he went on a Crusade in her name. When she learned that he was making preparations to go, she called it off and offered her love. After almost fifteen years Ulrich had proved himself to the princess.

What was the love that she offered? Ulrich doesn't say, but it probably consisted of kisses, an embrace, and possibly even a certain amount of fondling. Possibly more, but probably not. That was not the point. Ulrich had not spent fifteen years for sex. In fact, Ulrich had not spent fifteen years to win. The quest is what kept him going. His real reward was in the suffering and yearning. Within two years Ulrich was after another perfect lady.

Oh yes. We forgot one thing. Ulrich mentions that in the middle of his spectacular five-week joust, he stopped off for three days to visit the wife and kids. He was married? He was married. He speaks of his wife with a certain amount of affection. She was evidently quite good at managing the estate and bringing up the children. But what were these mundane talents next to the raptures of serving the ideal woman? Love was certainly not a part of the "details of crops, and cattle, fleas and fireplaces, serfs and swamp drainage."[2] In fact, Ulrich might expect that his wife would be proud of him if she knew what he was up to. The love of the princess should make Ulrich so much more noble and esteemed in his wife's eyes.

Courtly Love

The behavior of Ulrich von Liechtenstein reflected in exaggerated form a new idea of love in the West. Historians have called it "courtly love" because it developed in the courts of Europe, where noble ladies and knights of "quality" came together. For the first time since the Greeks a man could idealize a woman, but only if he minimized her sexuality. The evidence is overwhelming that these spiritual affairs would ideally never be consummated.

[2] Martin Hunt.

It is difficult for us to understand how these mature lords and ladies could torture themselves with passionate oaths, feats of endurance, and fainting spells when they heard their lover's name or voice, in short the whole repertoire of romance, and then refrain from actually consummating that love. Why did they insist on an ideal of "pure love" that allowed even naked embraces but drew the line at intercourse, which they called "false love"? No doubt the Christian antipathy for sex was part of the problem. Earlier Christian monks had practiced a similar type of *agape*;[3] Christianity had always taught that there was a world of difference between love and lust. The tendency of these Christian men to think of their ladies as replicas of the Virgin Mother also made sex inappropriate, if not outright incestuous.

But these lords and ladies were also making a statement about their "class" or good breeding. They were saying (as did Sigmund Freud almost a thousand years later) that civilized people repress their animal lust. They were distinguishing themselves from the crude peasants and soldiers around them who knew only fornication and whoring and raping. They were cultivating their emotions and their sensitivity, and priding themselves on their self-control. They were privileged (as members of the upper class) to know that human beings were capable of loyalty and love and enjoying beauty without behaving like animals. They were telling each other that they were refined, that they had "class." . . .

Further, despite the new romanticized view of the woman (maybe because of it), wives were just as excluded as they had always been. Noble, uplifting love, genuine romantic love, could not be felt for someone who swept the floor any more than it could be felt *by* someone whose life was preoccupied with such trivia. The lords and one of their special ladies, Marie, the countess of Champagne, issued the following declaration in 1174:

> We declare and we hold as firmly established that love cannot exert its power between two people who are married to each other. For lovers give each other everything freely, under no compulsion of necessity, but married people are in duty bound to give in to each other's desires and deny themselves to each other in nothing.[4]

The Court of Love

The proclamation was one of many that were made by the "courts of love" that these lords and ladies established in order to settle lovers' quarrels — and to decide for themselves the specifics of the new morality. . . .

No one did more to formulate these rules than Andreas Capellanus. Andreas not only summarized the numerous cases that came before the

---

[3] Greek for a spiritual love. [Ed.]

[4] Andreas Capellanus, *Tractatus de Amore*, 1:6, 7th Dialogue. Quoted in Hunt, 143–44.

court, but he used these decisions to write a manual of polite, courtly love. He called his influential book *A Treatise on Love and Its Remedy*, a title that indicated his debt to Sappho and the Greek romantic idea of love as a sickness. Andreas, however, did not think that he was advocating a "romantic" idea of love. The word was not even used in his day. He considered himself to be a modern twelfth-century Ovid—merely updating the Roman's *Art of Love*. He called himself Andreas the Lover and, like Ovid, considered himself an expert on all aspects of love.

But Andreas only used the same word as Ovid. The similarity ended there. The "aspects" of love that Andreas taught concerned the loyalty of the lovers, courteous behavior, the spiritual benefits of "pure love," the importance of gentleness, the subservience of the man to his lover, and the duties of courtship. There is none of Ovid's preoccupation with the techniques of seduction. Andreas is not talking about sex. In fact, he clearly advises against consummating the relationship.

Ovid made fun of infatuation and silly emotional behavior, but urged his readers to imitate such sickness in order to get the woman in bed. Andreas valued the passionate emotional attachment that Ovid mocked. Sincerity and honesty were too important to Andreas to dream of trickery, deceit, or pretense. Love, for Andreas, was too noble an emotion, too worthy a pursuit, to be put on like a mask. In short, the Roman had been after sexual gratification; the Christian wanted to refine lives and cleanse souls. They both called it love, but Andreas never seemed to realize that they were not talking the same language.

A Medieval Indian Alternative: Mystical Eroticism

Sometimes the best way to understand our own traditions is to study those of a different culture. It is difficult, for instance, for us to see Christian sexual morality as unusual because it has shaped our culture to such a great extent.

There have been alternatives, however. One of the most remarkable was the Indian ecstatic religion of the Middle Ages. Some medieval temple sculpture was erotic. The temples at Khajuraho and Orissa are full of sexual imagery: sensuous nudes and embracing couples. Similarly, the popular story *Gita Govinda* of the twelfth century tells of the loves of the god Krishna. He is shown scandalizing young women, dancing deliriously, and bathing with scores of admirers. Krishna's erotic appeal is a testament to his charisma. He is

> divine in proportion to his superiority as a great lover. . . . Worshippers were encouraged to commit excesses during festivals as the surest way to achieve . . . ecstasy, the purging climax of the orgiastic feast, the surmounting of duality.[5]

[5] Richard Lannoy, *The Speaking Tree: A Study of Indian Culture and Society* (Oxford: Oxford University Press, 1971), 64.

Among the most popular forms of medieval Hindu worship were the *bhakti* cults, which originated in devotion to Krishna in the *Bhagavad Gita*. *Bhakti* cults underline the difference between Indian and European devotion. While the Christian church discouraged spiritual love that might easily lead to "carnal love," the Indian *bhakti* sects encouraged rituals of ecstasy and sensual love precisely because they obliterated moral distinctions. The ecstatic union with the divine Krishna, Vishnu, or Shiva enabled the worshiper to transcend the limitations of self and confining definitions of good and evil.

Thus, Indian ecstatic religion sought sexual expression as a path to spiritual fulfillment. It is interesting that the word *bhakti* meant sex as well as worship, while we use the word "devotion" to mean worship and love. Hindu eroticism had nothing to do with the private expression of romantic love. In fact, it was the opposite. While romantic love depended on the development of the individual personality and the cultivation of individual feelings, *bhakti* depended on the loss of self in the sexual act.

Bhakti cults differed from the European courtly love tradition in one other important respect. They were not expressions of upper-class control. They were popular expressions of religious feeling. In essence they were directed against the dominating *brahman* and *kshatriya* castes because they challenged the importance of caste distinctions altogether. The ecstatic communion with the deity that they preached was open to all, regardless of caste. They appealed even to women and untouchables, as well as to farmers and artisans.

As Christianity did in Europe, popular Hinduism of the Middle Ages replaced a classical formal tradition with a spiritual passion. Ovid's *Art of Love* and the *Kama Sutra* were mechanical, passionless exercises for tired ruling classes. Both India and Europe turned to more emotionally intense religious experiences in the Middle Ages. . . . But the differences between Christian courtly love and *bhakti* cults were also profound. In India, sexual passion was an avenue to spiritual salvation. In Christian Europe sexual passion was at best a dead end, and at worst a road to hell.

Polygamy, Sexuality, and Style: A Japanese Alternative

At the same time that feudal Europe was developing a code of chivalry that romanticized love and almost desexualized marriage, the aristocracy of feudal Japan was evolving a code of polygamous sexuality without chivalry and almost without passion. We know about the sexual lives of Japanese aristocrats between 950 and 1050—the apex of the Heian period—through a series of remarkable novels and diaries, almost all of which were written by women. These first classics of Japanese literature, like *The Tale of Genji* and *The Pillow Book*, were written by women because Japanese men were still writing the "more important" but less-informative laws and theological studies in Chinese (just as Europeans still wrote in a Latin that was very different from the everyday spoken language).

When well-born Japanese in the Heian court spoke of "the world" they were referring to a love affair, and the novels that aristocratic women like Murasaki Shikibu or Sei Shonagon had time to compose in the spoken language were full of stories of "the world."

In *The World of the Shining Prince* Ivan Morris distinguishes three types of sexual relationships between men and women of the Heian aristocracy. (Homosexuality among the court ladies was "probably quite common," he writes, "as in any society where women were obliged to live in continuous and close proximity," but male homosexuality among "warriors, priests, and actors" probably became prevalent in later centuries.) The first type of heterosexual relationship was between the male aristocrat and his "principal wife." She was often several years older than her boy-husband and frequently served more as a guardian than as a bride. She was always chosen for her social standing, usually to cement a political alliance between ruling families. Although the match must frequently have been loveless, her status was inviolate; it was strictly forbidden, for instance, for a prince to exalt a secondary wife to principal wife. Upon marriage the principal wife would normally continue to live with her family, visited by her husband at night, until he became the head of his own household on the death or retirement of his father. Then the principal wife would be installed with all of her servants and aides as the head of the north wing of her husband's residence. An aristocratic woman (but never a peasant woman) might also become a secondary wife or official concubine. If she were officially recognized as such (much to the pleasure of her family), she might be moved into another wing of the official residence (leading to inevitable conflicts with the principal wife and other past and future secondary wives), or she might be set up in her own house. The arrangements were virtually limitless. The third and most frequent type of sexual relationship between men and women was the simple (or complex) affair—with a lady at court, another man's wife or concubine, but usually with a woman of a far lower class than the man. Ivan Morris writes of this kind of relationship:

> Few cultured societies in history can have been as tolerant about sexual relations as was the world of *The Tale of Genji*. Whether or not a gentleman was married, it redounded to his prestige to have as many affairs as possible; and the palaces and great mansions were full of ladies who were only too ready to accommodate him if approached in the proper style. From reading the *Pillow Book* we can tell how extremely commonplace these casual affairs had become in court circles, the man usually visiting the girl at night behind her screen of state and leaving her at the crack of dawn.[6]

[6] Ivan Morris, *The World of the Shining Prince: Court Life in Ancient Japan* (Baltimore: Penguin Books, 1969), 237.

That emphasis on "the proper style" is what distinguishes the sexuality of medieval Japan from that of ancient Rome, and reminds us of the medieval European's display of form — the aristocracy's mark of "class." Perhaps because the sexuality of the Heian aristocracy was potentially more explosive than the repressed rituals of European chivalry, style was that much more important. Polygamous sexuality could be practiced without tearing the society apart (and destroying aristocratic dominance in the process) only if every attention were given to style. Listen, for instance, to what the lady of *The Pillow Book* expected from a good lover:

> A good lover will behave as elegantly at dawn as at any other time. He drags himself out of bed with a look of dismay on his face. The lady urges him on: "Come, my friend, it's getting light. You don't want anyone to find you here." He gives a deep sigh, as if to say that the night has not been nearly long enough and that it is agony to leave. Once up, he does not instantly pull on his trousers. Instead he comes close to the lady and whispers whatever was left unsaid during the night. Even when he is dressed, he still lingers, vaguely pretending to be fastening his sash.
>
> Presently he raises the lattice, and the two lovers stand together by the side door while he tells her how he dreads the coming day, which will keep them apart; then he slips away. The lady watches him go, and this moment of parting will remain among her most charming memories.
>
> Indeed, one's attachment to a man depends largely on the elegance of his leave-taking. When he jumps out of bed, scurries about the room, tightly fastens his trouser-sash, rolls up the sleeves of his Court cloak, over-robe, or hunting costume, stuffs his belongings into the breast of his robe and then briskly secures the outer sash — one really begins to hate him.[7]

The stylistic elegance of the lover's departure was one of the principal themes of Heian literature. Perhaps no situation better expressed the mood of the Japanese word *aware*** (a word that was used over a thousand times in *The Tale of Genji*), which meant the poignant or the stylishly, even artistically, sorrowful — a style of elegant resignation. The word also suggests the mood of "the lady in waiting" and even the underlying anguish and jealousy of a precariously polygamous existence for the women consorts and writers of the Japanese feudal age. . . .

---

* ah wa ray

[7] *The Pillow Book of Sei Shonagon*, trans. Ivan Morris (Baltimore: Penguin Books, 1971), 49–50.

Aristocracies have behaved in similar ways throughout the world, and throughout history. They demonstrate their "class" or "good breeding" with elaborate rituals that differentiate their world from the ordinary. But the example of aristocratic Heian Japan a thousand years ago points to some of the differences between Japanese and Christian culture. The Japanese developed rituals of courtship and seduction for the leisured few that were sexually satisfying and posed no threat to marriage. They were rituals that showed artistic refinement rather than sexual "purity" or chastity. They could be sexual because Japanese culture did not disparage sexuality. Rather it disparaged lack of "taste." The affair did not threaten marriage because the culture did not insist on monogamy. The new sexual interest could be carried on outside or inside the polygamous estate of the Japanese aristocrat. Perhaps the main difference, then, is that the Japanese aristocrat invented stylized sex rather than romantic love.

2

ULRICH VON LIECHTENSTEIN

The Service of Ladies

This selection is drawn from Ulrich von Liechtenstein's own account of his adventures. After over ten years of service, as a page and then a distant admirer, in 1226, von Liechtenstein undertook a spectacular series of jousts to impress and win his lady, the princess. In the course of a five-week itinerary in northern Italy and southern German-speaking areas in which he took on all comers, he claims to have broken 307 lances. In the first part of this selection he details his preparation for the traveling tournament. In the second part, he tells of a brief interruption in his jousting for a stop at home. What does this selection tell you about von Liechtenstein's ideas of love and marriage?

THINKING HISTORICALLY

Sometimes the best entry point for analyzing cultural differences is to begin with the surprising or incomprehensible. If we can refrain from merely dismissing what seems beyond the pale, this can be an opportunity to understand how cultures can be truly different from our own.

Source: Ulrich von Liechtenstein, *The Service of Ladies*, trans. J. W. Thomas (Suffolk, England and Rochester, NY: The Boydell Press, 2004; published by arrangement with University of North Carolina Press, Chapel Hill, 1969), 46–49, 85–86.

Even a moderately careful reading of the two selections from von Liechtenstein's autobiography should evoke some surprise. In the first selection, von Liechtenstein sketches a visual image of himself on horseback that is far from our expectations. Imagine what he must have looked like. Imagine how others must have seen him. Recognizing that this was not some Halloween prank, that others proceeded to joust with him rather than laugh him out of town, we are forced to rethink what his outfit and presentation meant to him and those in his society. The recognition that the meaning of an act (like donning women's clothing) could be vastly different in Europe of the thirteenth century from what it is today offers the entry to comparative analysis.

We may also note that there are many things in von Liechtenstein's description of love that are not at all surprising. This may be because they have become second nature to our own society. Certainly some of the elements of romantic love, which were fresh in von Liechtenstein's day, have become clichés in modern film and television. What do you make of the elements of this story that are familiar? What do you make of those that surprise you?

"My service must be God's command.
Now let me tell you what I've planned.
I'll take on woman's dress and name
and thus disguised will strive for fame.
Sweet God protect me and sustain!
I'll travel with a knightly train
up to Bohemia from the sea.
A host of knights shall fight with me.

"This very winter I shall steal
out of the land and shall conceal
my goal from everyone but you.
I'll travel as a pilgrim who
to honor God is bound for Rome
(no one will question this at home).
I'll stop in Venice and shall stay
in hiding till the first of May.

"I'll carefully remain unseen
but deck myself out like a queen;
it should be easy to acquire
some lovely feminine attire
which I'll put on — now hear this last —
and when St. George's day is past,
the morning afterwards, I'll ride
(I pray that God is on my side)

"from the sea to Mestre, near
by Venice. He who breaks a spear
with me to serve, by tourneying,
his lady fair will get a ring
of gold and it will be quite nice.
I'll give it to him with this advice,
that he present it to his love,
the one he's in the service of.

"Messenger, I'll make the trip
so there will never be a slip
and no one possibly can guess
whose form is hid beneath the dress.
For I'll be clad from head to toe
in woman's garb where'er I go,
fully concealed from people's eyes.
They'll see me only in disguise.

"If you would please me, messenger,
then travel once again to her.
Just tell her what I have in mind
and ask if she will be so kind
as to permit that I should fight
throughout this journey as her knight.
It's something she will not repent
and I'll be glad of her assent."

He rode at once to tell her this
and swore upon his hope of bliss
my loyalty would never falter,
that I was true and would not alter.
He told my plan in full detail
and said, "My lady, should you fail
to let him serve and show your trust
in him, it wouldn't seem quite just."

"Messenger," she spoke, "just let
him have this message, don't forget.
This trip, if I have understood
you right, will surely do him good
and he will win a rich reward
in praise from many a lady and lord.
Whether it helps with me or not,
from others he will gain a lot."

The messenger was pleased and sure.
He found me by the river Mur
at Liechtenstein where I was then.
'T was nice to have him there again.
I spoke, "O courtly youth, now tell
me if the lady's feeling well.
For, if my darling's doing fine,
then shall rejoice this heart of mine."

He spoke, "She's fair and happy too;
she bade me bring this word to you
about your journey. If you should
go through with it 't will do you good
and, whether it helps with her or not,
from others you will gain a lot.
She certainly supports your aim
and says that you'll be rich in fame."

. . .

I got to Venice without delay
and found a house in which to stay,
right on the edge of town, a place
where none would ever see my face
who might have recognized me there.
I was as cautious everywhere
and all the winter long I hid.
But let me tell you what I did:

I had some woman's clothing made
to wear throughout the masquerade.
They cut and sewed for me twelve skirts
and thirty fancy lady's shirts.
I bought two braids for my disguise,
the prettiest they could devise,
and wound them with some pearls I got
which didn't cost an awful lot.

I bade the tailors then prepare
three velvet cloaks for me to wear,
all white. The saddles too on which
the master labored, stitch by stitch,
were silver white. As for a king
was made the saddle covering,
long and broad and gleaming white.
The bridles all were rich and bright.

The tailors sewed for every squire
(there were a dozen) white attire.
A hundred spears were made for me
and all as white as they could be.
But I need not continue so,
for all I wore was white as snow
and everything the squires had on
was just as white as any swan.

My shield was white, the helmet too.
I had them make ere they were through
a velvet cover for each steed
as armor. These were white, indeed,
as was the battle cape which I
should wear for jousting by and by,
the cloth of which was very fine.
I was quite pleased to call it mine.

At last I had my horses sent
to me (none knew just where they went)
and got some servants, as I'd planned,
each native to a foreign land.
They carefully did not let slip
a thing about my coming trip
and I took heed that those who came
to serve me never learned my name.

. . .

They rode toward me with armor on;
I had not waited long to don
a rich and splendid battle dress.
Von Ringenberg with full success
broke off a spear on me. The one
I jousted with when this was done
I knocked down backwards off his horse,
which made him feel ashamed, of course.

The spears I broke then numbered four.
On the field had come no more
with armor on and lance in hand
and so I stopped. At my command
the servants gave six rings away.
I sought the inn where I should stay
and found a pretty hostel there;
I got some other things to wear.

I changed my clothing under guard,
and then the hostel door was barred.
I took with me a servant who
would not say anything, I knew.
We stole away without a sound
and rode with joy to where I found
my dearest wife whom I adore;
I could not ever love her more.

She greeted me just as a good
and loving woman always should
receive a husband she holds dear.
That I had come to see her here
had made her really very pleased.
My visit stilled her grief and eased
her loneliness. We shared our bliss,
my sweet and I, with many a kiss.

She was so glad to see her knight,
and I had comfort and delight
till finally the third day came;
to give me joy was her sole aim.
When dawn appeared it was the third.
I dressed, an early mass was heard,
I prayed God keep me from transgressing,
and then received a friendly blessing.

Right after that I took my leave,
lovingly, you may believe,
and rode with joyful heart to where
I'd left my servants unaware.
I entered Gloggnitz hastily
and found them waiting there for me,
prepared to journey on again.
At once we left the city then.

We rode to Neunkirchen gaily decked
and were received as I'd expect
of those whose manners are refined.
Each knight was courteous and kind
who waited there with spear and shield.
When I came riding on the field
I found them all prepared, adorned
with trappings no one would have scorned.

Nine waited there, not more nor less,
to joust with me, in battle dress.
I saw them and it wasn't long
till I'd donned armor, bright and strong.
The first to come I'd heard much of;
his great desire was ladies' love.
It was Sir Ortold von Graz, a name
already widely known to fame.

All that he wore was of the best.
The good man cut me in the chest
so strong and skilful was his joust;
through shield and armor went the thrust.
When I beheld the wound indeed
and saw that it began to bleed
I hid it quickly with my coat
before the other knights took note.

I broke nine lances there in haste
and found my inn. I dared not waste
much time before I got in bed.
I sent nine rings of golden red
to each of them who with his spear
had earned from me a present here.
My injuries were deftly bound
by a doctor whom my servants found.

3

ANDREAS CAPELLANUS

The Art of Courtly Love

Andreas Capellanus (Andreas the Chaplain) compiled this guide
to courtly love between 1184 and 1186. He probably intended his
book to update Ovid's *Art of Love*, as discussed in selection 1, but his
approach reflects many of the new ideas of love circulating among
the upper classes of Europe in the twelfth century. Andreas says that
love is suffering, but also that it is wonderful. What does he mean?

Source: Andreas Capellanus, *The Art of Courtly Love*, trans. John J. Parry (New York: Columbia University Press, 1990), 28–32, 159–86.

Compare his ideas about sex and marriage to those of Ulrich von Liechtenstein. The bishop of Paris condemned Andreas's ideas in 1277, but do they seem religious or Christian in any way? Notice the author's attention to passion and proper behavior. What does Andreas think is the proper relationship between passionate love and marriage? What is his attitude toward sexuality? Homosexuality?

THINKING HISTORICALLY

Compare this idea of "character" with that of the Japanese (discussed in the first selection). What does Andreas think of multiple partners? Compare this attitude with those of other cultures. How do the ideas of Andreas the Chaplain on love and marriage compare to those of a modern Christian chaplain?

Introduction to the Treatise on Love

We must first consider what love is, whence it gets its name, what the effect of love is, between what persons love may exist, how it may be acquired, retained, increased, decreased, and ended, what are the signs that one's love is returned, and what one of the lovers ought to do if the other is unfaithful.

What Love Is

Love is a certain inborn suffering derived from the sight of and excessive meditation upon the beauty of the opposite sex, which causes each one to wish above all things the embraces of the other and by common desire to carry out all of love's precepts in the other's embrace.

That love is suffering is easy to see, for before the love becomes equally balanced on both sides there is no torment greater, since the lover is always in fear that his love may not gain its desire and that he is wasting his efforts. He fears, too, that rumors of it may get abroad, and he fears everything that might harm it in any way, for before things are perfected a slight disturbance often spoils them. If he is a poor man, he also fears that the woman may scorn his poverty; if he is ugly, he fears that she may despise his lack of beauty or may give her love to a more handsome man; if he is rich, he fears that his parsimony in the past may stand in his way. To tell the truth, no one can number the fears of one single lover. This kind of love, then, is a suffering which is felt by only one of the persons and may be called "single love." But even after both are in love the fears that arise are just as great, for each of the lovers fears that what he has acquired with so much effort may be lost through the effort of someone else, which is certainly much worse for a man than if, having no hope, he sees that his efforts are accomplishing nothing, for it is worse to lose the things you are seeking than to be deprived of a gain you merely hope for. The lover fears, too, that he may offend his loved one in some way; indeed he fears so many things that it would be difficult to tell them.

That this suffering is inborn I shall show you clearly, because if you will look at the truth and distinguish carefully you will see that it does not arise out of any action; only from the reflection of the mind upon what it sees does this suffering come. For when a man sees some woman fit for love and shaped according to his taste, he begins at once to lust after her in his heart; then the more he thinks about her the more he burns with love, until he comes to a fuller meditation. Presently he begins to think about the fashioning of the woman and to differentiate her limbs, to think about what she does, and to pry into the secrets of her body, and he desires to put each part of it to the fullest use. Then after he has come to this complete meditation, love cannot hold the reins, but he proceeds at once to action; straightway he strives to get a helper to find an intermediary. He begins to plan how he may find favor with her, and he begins to seek a place and a time opportune for talking; he looks upon a brief hour as a very long year, because he cannot do anything fast enough to suit his eager mind. It is well known that many things happen to him in this manner. This inborn suffering comes, therefore, from seeing and meditating. Not every kind of meditation can be the cause of love, an excessive one is required; for a restrained thought does not, as a rule, return to the mind, and so love cannot arise from it.

Between What Persons Love May Exist

Now, in love you should note first of all that love cannot exist except between persons of opposite sexes. Between two men or two women love can find no place, for we see that two persons of the same sex are not at all fitted for giving each other the exchanges of love or for practicing the acts natural to it. Whatever nature forbids, love is ashamed to accept.

What the Effect of Love Is

Now it is the effect of love that a true lover cannot be degraded with any avarice. Love causes a rough and uncouth man to be distinguished for his handsomeness; it can endow a man even of the humblest birth with nobility of character; it blesses the proud with humility; and the man in love becomes accustomed to performing many services gracefully for everyone. O what a wonderful thing is love, which makes a man shine with so many virtues and teaches everyone, no matter who he is, so many good traits of character! There is another thing about love that we should not praise in few words: it adorns a man, so to speak, with the virtue of chastity, because he who shines with the light of one love can hardly think of embracing another woman, even a beautiful one. For when he thinks deeply of his beloved the sight of any other woman seems to his mind rough and rude.

If One of the Lovers Is Unfaithful to the Other

If one of the lovers should be unfaithful to the other, and the offender is the man, and he has an eye to a new love affair, he renders himself wholly unworthy of his former love, and she ought to deprive him completely of her embraces.

But what if he should be unfaithful to his beloved—not with the idea of finding a new love, but because he has been driven to it by an irresistible passion for another woman? What, for instance, if chance should present to him an unknown woman in a convenient place or what if at a time when Venus is urging him on to that which I am talking about he should meet with a little strumpet or somebody's servant girl? Should he, just because he played with her in the grass, lose the love of his beloved? We can say without fear of contradiction that just for this a lover is not considered unworthy of the love of his beloved unless he indulges in so many excesses with a number of women that we may conclude that he is overpassionate. But if whenever he becomes acquainted with a woman he pesters her to gain his end, or if he attains his object as a result of his efforts, then rightly he does deserve to be deprived of his former love, because there is strong presumption that he has acted in this way with an eye toward a new one, especially where he has strayed with a woman of the nobility or otherwise of an honorable estate.

I know that once when I sought advice I got the answer that a true lover can never desire a new love unless he knows that for some definite and sufficient reason the old love is dead; we know from our own experience that this rule is very true. We have fallen in love with a woman of the most admirable character, although we have never had, or hope to have, any fruit of this love. For we are compelled to pine away for love of a woman of such lofty station that we dare not say one word about it, nor dare we throw ourself upon her mercy, and so at length we are forced to find our body shipwrecked. But although rashly and without foresight we have fallen into such great waves in this tempest, still we cannot think about a new love or look for any other way to free ourself.

But since you are making a special study of the subject of love, you may well ask whether a man can have a pure love for one woman and a mixed or common love with another. We will show you, by an unanswerable argument, that no one can feel affection for two women in this fashion. For although pure love and mixed love may seem to be very different things, if you will look at the matter properly you will see that pure love, so far as its substance goes, is the same as mixed love and comes from the same feeling of the heart. The substance of the love is the same in each case, and only the manner and form of loving are different, as this illustration will make clear to you. Sometimes we see a man with a desire to drink his wine unmixed, and at another time his appetite prompts him to drink only water or wine and water mixed; although his appetite manifests itself differently, the substance of it is the same and unchanged. So likewise when two people have long been united by pure love and afterwards desire to practice mixed love, the substance of the love remains the same in them, although the manner and form and the way of practicing it are different. . . .

The Rules of Love

Let us come now to the rules of love, and I shall try to present to you very briefly those rules which the King of Love[1] is said to have proclaimed with his own mouth and to have given in writing to all lovers. . . .

I.	Marriage is no real excuse for not loving.
II.	He who is not jealous cannot love.
III.	No one can be bound by a double love.
IV.	It is well known that love is always increasing or decreasing.
V.	That which a lover takes against the will of his beloved has no relish.
VI.	Boys do not love until they arrive at the age of maturity.
VII.	When one lover dies, a widowhood of two years is required of the survivor.
VIII.	No one should be deprived of love without the very best of reasons.
IX.	No one can love unless he is impelled by the persuasion of love.
X.	Love is always a stranger in the home of avarice.
XI.	It is not proper to love any woman whom one should be ashamed to seek to marry.
XII.	A true lover does not desire to embrace in love anyone except his beloved.
XIII.	When made public love rarely endures.
XIV.	The easy attainment of love makes it of little value; difficulty of attainment makes it prized.
XV.	Every lover regularly turns pale in the presence of his beloved.
XVI.	When a lover suddenly catches sight of his beloved his heart palpitates.
XVII.	A new love puts to flight an old one.

[1] King Arthur of Britain. [Ed.]

XVIII. Good character alone makes any man worthy of love.

XIX. If love diminishes, it quickly fails and rarely revives.

XX. A man in love is always apprehensive.

XXI. Real jealousy always increases the feeling of love.

XXII. Jealousy, and therefore love, are increased when one suspects his beloved.

XXIII. He whom the thought of love vexes, eats and sleeps very little.

XXIV. Every act of a lover ends in the thought of his beloved.

XXV. A true lover considers nothing good except what he thinks will please his beloved.

XXVI. Love can deny nothing to love.

XXVII. A lover can never have enough of the solaces of his beloved.

XXVIII. A slight presumption causes a lover to suspect his beloved.

XXIX. A man who is vexed by too much passion usually does not love.

XXX. A true lover is constantly and without intermission possessed by the thought of his beloved.

XXXI. Nothing forbids one woman being loved by two men or one man by two women.

4

KALIDASA

Shakuntala

In addition to ideas of eroticized devotion discussed in the first selection, Indian culture even earlier developed an idea of love that resembled the European romantic idea. We see this idea in the plays of Kalidasa (c. 400 C.E.), one of the greatest Indian dramatists. His play *Shakuntala*, a classic of the Hindu literary tradition, tells the story of a love between a king and a hermit girl. The two fall passionately in love with each other although they have barely exchanged words. Despite their different stations in life, they are equally overcome by *kama*, one of the four great forces in the Hindu culture—the force of love and physical attraction.

Source: Kalidasa, *Shakuntala*, Act III, trans. Barbara Stoler Miller, in *Theater of Memory: The Plays of Kalidasa*, ed. Barbara Stoler Miller (New York: Columbia University Press, 1984), 114–18.

In this selection from Act 3 (of seven acts), Shakuntalā, who says she loves the king, is urged by her friends, Priyamvadā and Anasūyā, who say they "don't know what it is to be in love," to write a letter to the king, who overhears their conversation. The love of two people from radically different social backgrounds is a common theme in romantic stories. How is this theme developed here? How does such a "socially imbalanced" love threaten social stability? How does it raise questions about passion and power that help distinguish love from sex or marriage? How does an idea of propriety (proper behavior) balance the threat of passion?

THINKING HISTORICALLY

Compare the author's attention to physical signs of love with Ulrich's love story. In what ways is this story of love similar to European ideas of romantic love? In what ways is it different?

PRIYAMVADĀ   Compose a love letter and I'll hide it in a flower. I'll deliver it to his hand on the pretext of bringing a gift from our offering to the deity.

ANASŪYĀ   This subtle plan pleases me. What does Shakuntalā say?

SHAKUNTALĀ   I'll try my friend's plan.

PRIYAMVADĀ   Then compose a poem to declare your love!

SHAKUNTALĀ   I'm thinking, but my heart trembles with fear that he'll reject me.

KING [IN HIDING]   (*delighted*)
  The man whom you fear will reject you
  waits longing to love you, timid girl—
  a suitor may be lucky or cursed,
  but his goodness of fortune always wins.

BOTH FRIENDS   Why do you devalue your own virtues? Who would keep autumn moonlight from cooling the body by covering it with a bit of cloth?

SHAKUNTALĀ (*smiling*)   I'm following your advice. (*She sits thinking*)

KING   As I stare at her, my eyes forget to blink.
  She arches an eyebrow
  struggling to compose the verse—
  the down rises on her cheek,
  showing the passion she feels.

SHAKUNTALĀ   I have thought of a song, but there's nothing I can write it on.

PRIYAMVADĀ   Engrave the letters with your nails on this lotus leaf! It's as delicate as a parrot's breast.

SHAKUNTALĀ   (*miming what Priyamvadā described*) Listen and tell me if this makes sense!

BOTH FRIENDS   We're both paying attention.

SHAKUNTALĀ (*sings*)
> I don't know your heart,
> but day and night Love
> violently burns my limbs
> with desire for you, cruel man.

KING (*having been listening to them, entering suddenly*)
> Love torments you, slender girl,
> but he utterly consumes me —
> daylight makes the moon fade
> when it folds the white lotus.

BOTH FRIENDS (*looking, rising with delight*) Welcome to the swift success of love's desire! (*Shakuntalā tries to rise.*)

KING Don't strain yourself!
> Limbs on a couch of crushed flowers
> and fragrant tips of lotus stalks
> are too frail from suffering
> to perform ceremonial acts . . .

ANASŪYĀ We've heard that kings have many loves. Will our beloved friend become a sorrow to her relatives after you've spent your time with her?

KING Noble lady, enough of this! I may have many wives, but my royal line rests on two foundations: the sea-bound earth and this friend of yours!

BOTH FRIENDS We are assured.

PRIYAMVADĀ (*casting a glance*) Anasūyā this fawn is looking for its mother. Let's take it to her! (*They both begin to leave.*)

SHAKUNTALĀ Come back! Don't leave me unprotected!

BOTH FRIENDS The protector of the earth is at your side.

SHAKUNTALĀ Why have they gone?

KING Don't be alarmed! A servant worships at your side.
> Shall I set moist winds in motion
> with lotus-leaf fans to cool your pain,
> or put your pale red lotus feet on my lap
> and stroke them, voluptuous girl?

SHAKUNTALĀ I cannot sin against those I respect! (*standing as if she wants to leave*)

KING Beautiful Shakuntalā, the day is still hot.
> Why leave this couch of flowers
> and its shield of lotus leaves
> to venture into the heat
> with your frail wan limbs?
> (*Saying this, he forces her to turn around.*)

SHAKUNTALĀ Puru king, control yourself! Though I'm burning with love I'm not free to give myself to you.

KING Don't fear your elders! The father of your family knows the law. When he finds out, he will not fault you. Many kings' daughters first marry in secret and their fathers bless them.

SHAKUNTALĀ   Release me! I must ask my friends' advice!
KING   Yes, I shall release you.
SHAKUNTALĀ   When?
KING

> Only let my thirsting mouth
> gently drink from your lips,
> the way a bee sips nectar
> from a fragile virgin blossom.

5

MURASAKI SHIKIBU

The Tale of Genji

The *Tale of Genji* is, by some measures, the world's first novel. It was written by Murasaki Shikibu, a woman at the Japanese court, probably in the first decade after the year 1000. During the Heian period (794–1185) of Japanese history, women in the Japanese aristocracy differentiated their culture from the Chinese one that had dominated it since the seventh century.

In *The Tale of Genji* we also see signs of multiple marriages and numerous lovers, consorts, and courtesans among the Heian aristocracy. The emperor had been married but preferred a lower-class courtesan, Lady Kiritsubo, who died shortly after giving birth to Genji. Lady Kokiden, a more powerful mistress of the emperor, ensured that her son, Suzku, would outrank Genji as the next emperor. She forced the emperor to make Genji a commoner and go into exile. After Lady Kiritsubo's death, the despondent emperor met a princess, Fujitsubo, who reminded him of Kiritsubo. She became the emperor's favorite as well as the love of her stepson, Genji, who returned from exile. Fujitsubo bore the emperor a son whom everyone but she and Genji knew to be the emperor's, and that son became the Heir Apparent. Genji, cut off from intimate contact with Fujitsubo, and uninterested in his wife, played lover and patron to the young Murasaki, who bore him a future emperor, and carried out various affairs and liaisons—one of which is described in this selection. What does this relationship between Genji and one of the younger sisters of Kokiden tell you about sex, love, and marriage in upper-class Heian society?

Source: Murasaki Shikibu, *The Tale of Genji*, trans. Arthur Waley (1929; reprint, Garden City, NY: Anchor Books, 1955), 201–10.

This selection also reveals much about the culture of the Japanese court. Notice the cultivation of music, dance, and poetry among the court nobility. What, if anything, does this display of sensitivity have to do with ideas of love and marriage? What signs do you see here of the persistence of Chinese culture in Heian Japan?

Also, notice the absence of monogamy in the court. The emperor is married but has taken in turn three consorts: Kokiden, Kiritsubo, and now Fujitsubo. What is the relationship between marriage and sex in this society? What does that tell you about the mores of the time?

THINKING HISTORICALLY

Would you call this a story of romantic love? In what ways is the love Lady Murasaki describes similar to, or different from, the love Andreas Capellanus describes in selection 3? What aspects of Heian Japanese culture are different from the culture of medieval Europe? Is the dominant upper-class idea of love in Japan during this period different from that of Europe? How is this Japanese idea of love and marriage different from that of India?

About the twentieth day of the second month the Emperor gave a Chinese banquet under the great cherry-tree of the Southern Court. Both Fujitsubo and the Heir Apparent were to be there. Kokiden, although she knew that the mere presence of the Empress was sufficient to spoil her pleasure, could not bring herself to forgo so delightful an entertainment. After some promise of rain the day turned out magnificent; and in full sunshine, with the birds singing in every tree, the guests (royal princes, noblemen, and professional poets alike) were handed the rhyme words which the Emperor had drawn by lot, and set to work to compose their poems. It was with a clear and ringing voice that Genji read out the word "Spring" which he had received as the rhyme-sound of his poem. Next came To no Chujo who, feeling that all eyes were upon him and determined to impress himself favourably on his audience, moved with the greatest possible elegance and grace; and when on receiving his rhyme he announced his name, rank, and titles, he took great pains to speak pleasantly as well as audibly. Many of the other gentlemen were rather nervous and looked quite pale as they came forward, yet they acquitted themselves well enough. But the professional poets, particularly owing to the high standard of accomplishment which the Emperor's and Heir Apparent's lively interest in Chinese poetry had at that time diffused through the Court, were very ill at ease; as they crossed the long space of the garden on their way to receive their rhymes they felt utterly helpless. A simple Chinese verse is surely not much to ask of a professional poet; but they all wore an expression of the deepest gloom. . . .

Then the poems were opened and read aloud. The reading of Genji's verses was continually interrupted by loud murmurs of applause. Even the professional poets were deeply impressed, and it may well be imagined with what pride the Emperor, to whom at times Genji was a source of consolation and delight, watched him upon such an occasion as this. Fujitsubo, when she allowed herself to glance in his direction, marvelled that even Kokiden could find it in her heart to hate him. "It is because he is fond of me; there can be no other reason," she decided at last, and the verse, "Were I but a common mortal who now am gazing at the beauty of this flower, from its sweet petals not long should I withhold the dew of love," framed itself on her lips, though she dared not utter it aloud.

It was now very late and the banquet was over. The guests had scattered. The Empress and the Heir Apparent had both returned to the Palace—all was still. The moon had risen very bright and clear, and Genji, heated with wine, could not bear to quit so lovely a scene. The people at the Palace were probably all plunged in a heavy sleep. On such a night it was not impossible that some careless person might have left some door unfastened, some shutter unbarred. Cautiously and stealthily he crept towards Fujitsubo's apartments and inspected them. Every bolt was fast. He sighed; here there was evidently nothing to be done. He was passing the loggia of Kokiden's palace when he noted that the shutters of the third arch were not drawn. After the banquet Kokiden herself had gone straight to the Emperor's rooms. There did not seem to be anyone about. A door leading from the loggia into the house was standing open, but he could hear no sound within. "It is under just such circumstances as this that one is apt to drift into compromising situations," thought Genji. Nevertheless he climbed quietly on to the balustrade and peeped. Everyone must be asleep. But no; a very agreeable young voice with an intonation which was certainly not that of any waiting-woman or common person was softly humming the last two lines of the *Oborozuki-yo*.[1] Was not the voice coming towards him? It seemed so, and stretching out his hand he suddenly found that he was grasping a lady's sleeve. "Oh, how you frightened me!" she cried. "Who is it?" "Do not be alarmed," he whispered. "That both of us were not content to miss the beauty of this departing night is proof more clear than the half-clouded moon that we were meant to meet," and as he recited the words he took her gently by the hand and led her into the house, closing the door behind them. Her surprised and puzzled air fascinated him. "There is someone there," she whispered tremulously, pointing to the inner room. "Child," he answered, "I am allowed to go wherever I please and if you send for your friends they will only tell you that I have every right to be here. But if you will stay quietly here. . . ." It was Genji. She knew his voice and

---

[1] A famous poem by Oye no Chisato (ninth century): "What so lovely as a night when the moon though dimly clouded is never wholly lost to sight!"

the discovery somewhat reassured her. She thought his conduct rather strange, but she was determined that he should not think her prudish or stiff. And so because he on his side was still somewhat excited after the doings of the evening, while she was far too young and pliant to offer any serious resistance, he soon got his own way with her.

Suddenly they saw to their discomfiture that dawn was creeping into the sky. She looked, thought Genji, as though many disquieting reflections were crowding into her mind. "Tell me your name," he said. "How can I write you unless you do? Surely this is not going to be our only meeting?" She answered with a poem in which she said that names are of this world only and he would not care to know hers if he were resolved that their love should last till worlds to come. It was a mere quip and Genji, amused at her quickness, answered, "You are quite right. It was a mistake on my part to ask." And he recited the poem: "While still I seek to find on which blade dwells the dew, a great wind shakes the grasses of the level land." "If you did not repent of this meeting," he continued, "you would surely tell me who you are. I do not believe that you want. . . ." But here he was interrupted by the noise of people stirring in the next room. There was a great bustle and it was clear that they would soon be starting out to fetch Princess Kokiden back from the palace. There was just time to exchange fans in token of their new friendship before Genji was forced to fly precipitately from the room. In his own apartments he found many of his gentlemen waiting for him. Some were awake, and these nudged one another when he entered the room as though to say, "Will he never cease these disreputable excursions?" But discretion forbad them to show that they had seen him and they all pretended to be fast asleep. Genji too lay down, but he could not rest. He tried to recall the features of the lady with whom he had just spent so agreeable a time. Certainly she must be one of Kokiden's sisters. Perhaps the fifth or sixth daughter, both of whom were still unmarried. . . . But at present he could think of no way to make sure. She had not behaved at all as though she did not want to see him again. Why then had she refused to give him any chance of communicating with her? In fact he worried about the matter so much and turned it over in his mind with such endless persistency that it soon became evident he had fallen deeply in love with her. Nevertheless no sooner did the recollection of Fujitsubo's serious and reticent demeanour come back to his mind than he realized how incomparably more she meant to him than this light-hearted lady.

That day the after-banquet kept him occupied till late at night. At the Emperor's command he performed on the thirteen-stringed zithern and had an even greater success than with his dancing on the day before. At dawn Fujitsubo retired to the Emperor's rooms. Disappointed in his hope that the lady of last night would somewhere or somehow make her appearance on the scene, he sent for Yoshikiyo and Koremitsu with whom all his secrets were shared and bade them keep watch upon the lady's family. When he returned next day from duty at the Palace they reported that they had just witnessed the departure of several coaches which had been drawn up under shelter in the Courtyard of the Watch. "Among a group of persons who seemed to be the domestic attendants of those for whom the coaches were waiting two gentlemen came threading their way in a great hurry. These we recognized as Shii no Shosho and Uchuben, so there is little doubt that the carriages belonged to Princess Kokiden. For the rest we noted that the ladies were by no means ill-looking and that the whole party drove away in three carriages." Genji's heart beat fast. But he was no nearer than before to finding out which of the sisters it had been. Supposing her father, the Minister of the Right, should hear anything of this, what a to-do there would be! It would indeed mean his absolute ruin. It was a pity that while he was about it he did not stay with her till it was a little lighter. But there it was! He did not know her face, but yet he was determined to recognize her. How? . . . He still had her fan. It was a folding fan with ribs of hinoki-wood and tassels tied in a splice-knot. One side was covered with silver-leaf on which was painted a dim moon, giving the impression of a moon reflected in water. It was a device which he had seen many times before, but it had agreeable associations for him, and continuing the metaphor of the "grass on the moor" which she had used in her poem, he wrote on the fan—"Has mortal man ever puzzled his head with such a question before as to ask where the moon goes to when she leaves the sky at dawn?" And he put the fan safely away. . . .

Fugitive as their meeting had been, it had sufficed to plunge the lady whose identity Prince Genji was now seeking to establish into the depths of despair; for in the fourth month she was to become the Heir Apparent's wife. Turmoil filled her brain. Why had not Genji visited her again? He must surely know whose daughter she was. But how should he know which daughter? Besides, her sister Kokiden's house was not a place where, save under very strange circumstances, he was likely to feel at all at his ease. And so she waited in great impatience and distress; but of Genji there was no news.

About the twentieth day of the third month her father, the Minister of the Right, held an archery meeting in which most of the young noble-men and princes were present. It was followed by a wistaria feast. The cherry blossom was for the most part over, but two trees, which the Min-ister seemed somehow to have persuaded to flower later than all the rest, were still an enchanting sight. He had had his house rebuilt only a short time ago when celebrating the initiation of his granddaughters, the children of Kokiden. It was now a magnificent building and not a thing in it but was of the very latest fashion. He had invited Genji when he had met him at the Palace only a few days before and was extremely annoyed when he did not appear. . . . It was very late indeed when at last he [Genji] made his appearance at the party. He was dressed in a cloak of thin Chinese fabric, white outside but lined with yellow. His robe was of a deep wine-red colour with a very long train. The dignity and grace with which he carried this fancifully regal attire in a company where all were dressed in plain official robes were indeed remarkable, and in the end his presence perhaps contributed more to the success of the party than did the fragrance of the Minister's boasted flowers. His entry was followed by some very agreeable music. It was already fairly late when Genji, on the plea that the wine had given him a headache, left his seat and went for a walk. He knew that his two stepsisters, the daughters of Kokiden, were in the inner apartments of the palace. He went to the eastern portico and rested there. It was on this side of the house that the wistaria grew. The wooden blinds were raised and a number of ladies were leaning out of the window to enjoy the blossoms. They had hung bright-coloured robes and shawls over the windowsill just as is done at the time of the New Year dancing and other gala days and were behaving with a freedom of allure which contrasted very oddly with the sober decorum of Fujitsubo's household. "I am feeling rather overpowered by all the noise and bustle of the flowerparty," Genji explained. "I am very sorry to disturb my sisters, but I can think of nowhere else to seek refuge . . ." and advancing towards the main door of the women's apartments, he pushed back the curtain with his shoulder. . . . A scent of costly perfumes pervaded the room; silken skirts rustled in the darkness. There could be little doubt that these were Kokiden's sisters and their friends. Deeply absorbed, as indeed was the whole of his family, in the fashionable gaieties of the moment, they had flouted decorum and posted themselves at the window that they might see what little they could of the banquet which was proceeding outside. Little thinking that his plan could succeed, yet led on by delightful recollections of his previous encounter, he advanced towards them chanting in a careless undertone the song:

> At Ishikawa, Ishikawa
> A man from Koma [Korea] took my belt away . . .

But for "belt" he substituted "fan" and by this means he sought to discover which of the ladies was his friend. "Why, you have got it wrong! I never heard of *that* Korean," one of them cried. Certainly it was not she. But there was another who though she remained silent seemed to him to be sighing softly to herself. He stole towards the curtain-of-state behind which she was sitting and taking her hand in his at a venture he whispered the poem: "If on this day of shooting my arrow went astray, 'twas that in dim morning twilight only the mark had glimmered in my view." And she, unable any longer to hide that she knew him, answered with the verse: "Had it been with the arrows of the heart that you had shot, though from the moon's slim bow no brightness came, would you have missed your mark?" Yes, it was her voice. He was delighted, and yet . . .

ZHOU DAGUAN

Sex in the City of Angkor

Angkor, the great Kymer or Cambodian civilization of the Middle
Ages, originated in the early ninth century. At its zenith in the twelfth
and thirteenth centuries, its empire included the southern halves
of modern Laos and Thailand as well as all of modern Cambodia.
In 1296 Zhou Daguan was sent on a mission to Cambodia by the
Mongol emperor of China, Temur Khan, the grandson and successor
of Kubilai Khan. He stayed in the recently completed capital, which
still stands today as Angkor Thom, and wrote his record of the country and its people. This is a brief selection from what remains of that
account. What does it tell you about family life and attitudes toward
sex and sexuality in Angkor?

THINKING HISTORICALLY

Zhou Daguan makes no comparisons with other cultures, but implicit
in almost every statement is a comparison with his own Chinese culture. What surprises him? What does he find strange or even offensive? What do his responses tell us about the differences between
Chinese and Cambodian customs or ideas regarding sex and love?
Compare Cambodian ideas about sex with those in Europe, Japan,
and India. What do you think explains these differences? What seems
to be the impact of different religions on a culture's attitudes toward
sex and sexuality?

6
The People

The one thing people know about southern barbarians is that they are
coarse, ugly, and very black. I know nothing at all about those living on
islands in the sea or in remote villages, but this is certainly true of those
in the ordinary localities. When it comes to the women of the palace and
women from the *nanpeng*—that is, the great houses—there are many
who are as white as jade, but that is because they do not see the light of
the sun.

Generally, men and women alike wrap a cloth around their waist,
but apart from that they leave their smooth chests and breasts uncovered.

Source: Zhou Daguan, *A Record of Cambodia: The Land and Its People*, trans. Peter Harris
(Chiang Mai, Thailand: Silkworm Books, 2007), 54–59.

They wear their hair in a topknot and go barefoot. This is the case even with the wives of the king.

The king has five wives, one principal wife and one for each of the four cardinal points. Below them, I have heard, there are four or five thousand concubines and other women of the palace. They also divide themselves up by rank. They only go out of the palace on rare occasions.

Every time I went inside the palace to see the king, he always came out with his principal wife, and sat at the gold window in the main room. The palace women lined up by rank in two galleries below the window. They moved to and fro to steal looks at us, and I got a very full view of them. Any family with a female beauty is bound to have her summoned into the palace.

At the lower level there are also the so-called *chenjialan*, servant women who come and go providing services inside the palace and number at least a thousand or two. In their case they all have husbands and live mixed in among ordinary people. They shave back the hair on the top of their head, which gives them the look of northerners with their "open canal" partings.[1] They paint the area with vermilion, which they also paint on to either side of their temples. In this way they mark themselves out as being *chenjialan*. They are the only women who can go into the palace; no one else below them gets to go in. There is a continuous stream of them on the roads in front of and behind the inner palace.

Apart from wearing their hair in a topknot, ordinary women do not have ornaments in their hair like pins or combs. They just wear gold bracelets on their arms and gold rings on their fingers. The *chenjialan* and the women in the palace all wear them too. Men and women usually perfume themselves with scents made up of a mixture of sandalwood, musk, and other fragrances.

Every family practices Buddhism.

There are a lot of effeminate men in the country who go round the markets every day in groups of a dozen or so. They frequently solicit the attentions of Chinese in return for generous gifts. It is shameful and wicked.

7
Childbirth

As soon as they give birth the local women prepare some hot rice, mix it with salt, and put it into the entrance of the vagina. They usually take it out after a day and a night. Because of this, women do not fall

---

[1] Hair pulled back to show a wide part, which is then painted red. [Ed.]

sick when they are giving birth, and usually contract so as to be like young girls again.

When I first heard this I was surprised by it, and seriously doubted whether it was true. Then a girl in the family I was staying with gave birth to a child, and I got a full picture of what happened to her. The day after the birth, she took up the baby right away and went to bathe in the river with it. It was a truly amazing thing to see.

Then again, I have often heard people say that the local women are very lascivious, so that a day or two after giving birth they are immediately coupling with their husbands. If a husband doesn't meet his wife's wishes he will be abandoned right away, as Zhu Maichen[2] was. If the husband happens to have work to do far away, if it is only for a few nights that is all right, but if it is for more than ten nights or so the wife will say, "I'm not a ghost—why am I sleeping alone?" This is how strong their sexual feelings are. That said, I have heard that there are some who exercise self-restraint.

The women age very quickly indeed, the reason being that they marry and have children young. A twenty- or thirty-year-old woman is like a Chinese woman of forty or fifty.

8
Young Girls

When a family is bringing up a daughter, her father and mother are sure to wish her well by saying, "May you have what really matters—in future may you marry thousands and thousands of husbands!"

When they are seven to nine years old—if they are girls from wealthy homes—or only when they are eleven—if they come from the poorest families—girls have to get a Buddhist monk or a Daoist to take away their virginity, in what is called *zhentan*.

So every year, in the fourth month of the Chinese calendar, the authorities select a day and announce it countrywide. The families whose daughters should be ready for *zhentan* let the authorities know in advance. The authorities first give them a huge candle. They make a mark on it, and arrange for it to be lit at dusk on the day in question. When the mark is reached the time for *zhentan* has come.

A month, fifteen days, or ten days beforehand, the parents have to choose a Buddhist monk or a Daoist. This depends on where the Buddhist and Daoist temples are. The temples often also have their own clients. Officials' families and wealthy homes all get the good, saintly Buddhist monks in advance, while the poor do not have the leisure to choose.

---

[2] A Han dynasty folktale of a poor scholar, Zhu Maichen, whose wife left him for another man. [Ed.]

Wealthy and noble families give the monks wine, rice, silk and other cloth, betel nuts, silverware, and the like, goods weighing as much as a hundred piculs and worth two or three hundred ounces of Chinese silver. The smallest amount a family gives weighs ten to forty piculs, depending on how thrifty the family is.

The reason poor families only start dealing with the matter when their girls reach eleven is simply that it is hard for them to manage these things. Some wealthy families do also give money for poor girls' *zhentan*, which they call doing good work. Moreover in any one year a monk can only take charge of one girl, and once he has agreed to and accepted the benefits, he cannot make another commitment.

On the night in question a big banquet with drums and music is laid on for relatives and neighbors. A tall canopy is put up outside the entrance to the house, and various clay figurines of people and animals are laid out on top of it. There can be ten or more of these, or just three or four—or none at all in the case of poor families. They all have to do with events long ago, and they usually stay up for seven days before people start taking them down.

At dusk the monk is met with palanquin, parasol, drums, and music and brought back to the house. Two pavilions are put up, made of colorful silk. The girl sits inside one, and the monk inside the other. You can't understand what he's saying because the drums and music are making so much noise—on that night the night curfew is lifted. I have heard that when the time comes the monk goes into a room with the girl and takes away her virginity with his hand, which he then puts into some wine. Some say the parents, relatives and neighbors mark their foreheads with it, others say they all taste it. Some say the monk and the girl have sex together, others say they don't. They don't let Chinese see this, though, so I don't really know.

Toward dawn the monk is seen off again with palanquin, parasol, drums, and music. Afterward silk, cloth, and the like have to be given to the monk to redeem the body of the girl. If this is not done the girl will be the property of the monk for her whole life and won't be able to marry anyone else.

The instance of this that I saw took place early on the sixth night of the fourth month of the year *dingyou* in the Dade reign period (1297).

Before this happens, the parents always sleep together with their daughter; afterward, she is excluded from the room and goes wherever she wants without restraint or precaution. When it comes to marriage, there is a ceremony with the giving of gifts, but it is just a simple, easygoing affair. There are many who get married only after leading a dissolute life, something local custom regards as neither shameful nor odd.

On a *zhentan* night up to ten or more families from a single alley may be involved. On the city streets people are out meeting Buddhist monks and Daoists, going this way and that, and the sounds of drums and music are everywhere.

9
Slaves

Family slaves are all savages purchased to work as servants. Most families have a hundred or more of them; a few have ten or twenty; only the very poorest have none at all. The savages are people from the mountains. They have their own way of categorizing themselves, but are commonly called "thieving Zhuang." When they come to the city, none of them dares go in and out of people's homes. They are so despised that if there is a quarrel between two city dwellers, it only takes one of them to be called a Zhuang for hatred to enter into the marrow of his bones. . . .

The males and females mate together, but the master would never have reason to have intercourse with them. Sometimes a Chinese who comes to Cambodia and has long been single will act carelessly, but as soon as he has had relations with one of them the master will hear of it, and the following day he will refuse to sit with the Chinese, on the grounds that he has come into contact with a savage.

Sometimes one of them will have intercourse with an outsider, to the point of becoming pregnant and having a baby. But the master won't try and find out where it is from, since the mother has no status and he will profit from the child, who can eventually become his slave.

■ REFLECTIONS

Cultural comparisons, formerly a staple of historical studies, have come under harsh criticism in recent years, and for good reason. The ambitious general histories and philosophical anthropologies written at the beginning of the twentieth century were full of gross generalizations about the "essence" of various cultures and the advantages of one civilization over another. These grand overviews, predating serious empirical studies of African, Asian, and Latin American societies, invariably argued that such "premodern," or "traditional," societies lacked some critical cultural attribute honed in Europe that enabled Europeans to conquer the world after 1500. It goes without saying that these sweeping interpretations were written by Europeans and their North American descendants.

The comparative history of love got caught up in the academic whirlwind of historians and anthropologists, who, in seeking to explain European expansion, industrialization, and modernization, argued that conjugal love—the nonromantic familial variety—created family units in Europe and America that were different from those in other parts of the world. They saw the Western family as the stimulus of modern society. Some also found the Western practices of dating, mate choosing, and individual decision making unique.

Toward the end of the twentieth century, in a postcolonial age that had grown skeptical of Western claims of objectivity, cultural comparisons were seen for what they often were—thinly veiled exercises in self-aggrandizement and implicit rationales for Western domination. For example, Western scientific racism, in which some Western anthropologists and scientists divided the world by cranial sizes, nose width, or culture-bound intelligence tests (always putting themselves on top), lost favor after its rationale was exposed as the foundation for the horrific genocides of World War II. `

There is a growing debate about the strategy of explaining Western growth and dominance by looking for Western traits that non-Western cultures lacked. But whether or not such a strategy is wise, we would be foolish to stop trying to compare cultures. Cultures are rich repositories of human thought and behavior; they differ over time and across the globe; and the process of comparison is essential to learning and creating knowledge. In any case, historical comparisons should not be about establishing which culture is better or worse. Culture, almost by definition, is good for the particular society in which it arises. That people in different parts of the world have found different ways of dealing with the same human conditions should not surprise us. To call some better than others is meaningless.

What we can learn from cultural comparison is something about the malleability of human nature and the range of options available to us. We also learn much about ourselves when we peer at another face in the mirror. The differences leap out at us over time as well as space. In some ways, Ulrich's mirror is as foreign as Genji's. In other ways, it is not. In response to an age of prejudice and cultural stereotyping, many well-intentioned people choose to deny or celebrate cultural differences. A far wiser course is to understand what these differences reveal about our world and us.

10

The First Crusade

Muslims, Christians, and Jews during the First Crusade, 1095–1099

■ HISTORICAL CONTEXT

In the eleventh century the Seljuk Turks, recently converted to Islam, emerged from the grasslands of central Asia to conquer much of the land held by the weakened caliphate at Baghdad, the Egyptian Fatimid Caliphate, and the Byzantine Empire. By 1095 the Seljuks controlled the important cities of Baghdad and Jerusalem and threatened to take Constantinople.

Alexius, the Byzantine emperor, appealed to the Roman pope for help and found a receptive audience. Pope Urban II was continuing recent papal efforts to strengthen the Roman church's power over the scattered nobles and princes of European feudal society. He sought to free the church of abuses such as the sale of church offices and to bring peace to the fractious countryside, riddled with private armies of knights that fought each other or preyed on Christian peasants.

Urban II's efforts to revitalize Christendom found a mission in the Seljuk occupation of Jerusalem, and in 1095 the First Crusade began with his urgent call for Christians to rout the new Muslim occupiers of the Holy Land. (See Map 10.1.)

The Crusades were an important chapter in the religious and military history—or more broadly, the cultural and political history—of both European and Islamic civilizations. They brought large numbers of European Christians and Muslims into contact with each other in a struggle and dialogue that would last for centuries.

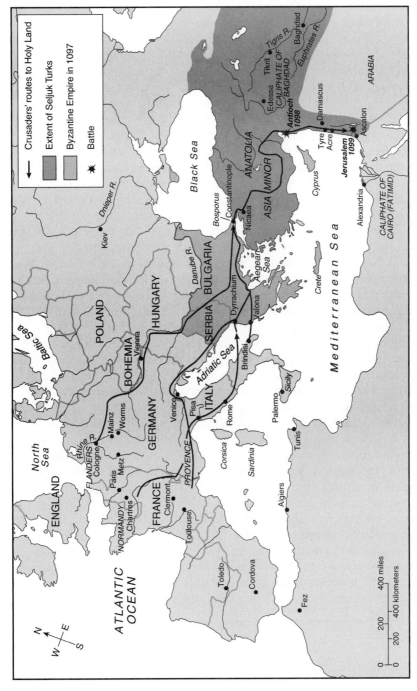

Map 10.1 The First Crusade, 1095–1099.

351

■ THINKING HISTORICALLY

Analyzing and Writing Narrative

When most people think of history, they think of narrative — the story itself. Narrative settles on specific details — one at a time — neither indiscriminately nor as examples of general laws, but usually chronologically, as they happen, woven in a chain of cause and effect. The "truth" of narrative is different from that of social science, which aspires to generality. The social scientist writes, "Holy wars among states are a dime a dozen." The narrative historian immerses us in the specific details of the battle: "The Duke's trumpets sounded, the shimmering line swayed forward, the long lances came down to point at the foe, their pennons shadowing the ground before them." A good narrative has the appeal of a good story.

The problem with narrative stems from the same factors that make it so appealing. By telling a believable story, narrative bypasses our critical faculties. It gives us little if any room to stop and question. We are carried along, sometimes enthralled, by a story that seems to build its truth one incontrovertible fact at a time. If we accept the legitimacy of the narrator, we have little basis for opening the story to analysis. Of course, not all narrators are interested in telling the truth, and even those who are may make mistakes. But even when they hope to be truthful and get their facts right (as do the authors in this chapter), they are invariably telling one truth out of many possible truths, and the one they tell has much to do with their own knowledge, assumptions, interests, and perspectives.

In this chapter you will read narratives from different perspectives. Consequently, you will gain greater awareness of other possible views the further you read. But there is always more to learn about any subject, and we will not presume any knowledge beyond this chapter. Therefore, we will only begin the process of analyzing narrative by asking you what questions you might ask about an author's point of view, bias, or interest. You should build on the attention to author, audience, and agenda developed in Chapter 5.

In addition to analyzing narratives, you will also be encouraged to write your own. In this way you will gain a better understanding of perhaps the most important, and certainly the most popular, form of historical presentation, both by examining its structure and by doing it yourself.

1

FULCHER OF CHARTRES
Pope Urban at Clermont

The Chronicle of Fulcher of Chartres is one of the few firsthand accounts of the First Crusade. Born in 1059, Fulcher was likely present at the Council of Clermont, where Pope Urban II issued his call for the First Crusade in 1095. In response to Urban's plea, Fulcher joined the army of Robert of Normandy, Stephen of Blois, and Robert of Flanders. He then joined Baldwin of Boulogne in Edessa (see Map 10.1, p. 351), the first of a number of feudal Crusader states along the eastern Mediterranean, and later visited Jerusalem after its capture by the Crusaders. In 1100, when Baldwin became king of Jerusalem, Fulcher returned to Jerusalem to continue as Baldwin's chaplain. There he wrote his history from 1101 until about 1128. The reliability of Fulcher's Chronicles, therefore, depends on his important contacts as well as his own observations. In addition, Fulcher had access to at least two important collections of letters and documents in Jerusalem.

Why, according to Fulcher, did Pope Urban II call the Council of Clermont? What did he hope to accomplish? How important among the pope's concerns was the capture of Jerusalem? How important was strengthening the church?

THINKING HISTORICALLY

What indications do you see in Urban's speech that the capture of Jerusalem was only part of his agenda, perhaps even an afterthought? Fulcher's account of the speech and his section on "events after the council" mainly address the issue of Jerusalem. That emphasis is appropriate in a history of the crusade, since historical narrative must follow a particular thread. If Fulcher had written a history of church reforms rather than of the First Crusade, what "events after the council" might he have included?

A narrative, or story, is different from an explanation. What do you think were the causes of the First Crusade, based on what you have read so far? How is your answer an explanation rather than a narrative? How would you make your answer more of a narrative?

Source: *The First Crusade: The Chronicle of Fulcher of Chartres and Other Source Materials*, 2nd ed., ed. Edward Peters (Philadelphia: University of Pennsylvania Press, 1998), 49–55.

I. The Council of Clermont

1. In the year 1095 from the Lord's Incarnation, with Henry reigning in Germany as so-called emperor,[1] and with Philip as king in France, manifold evils were growing in all parts of Europe because of wavering faith. In Rome ruled Pope Urban II, a man distinguished in life and character, who always strove wisely and actively to raise the status of the Holy Church above all things.

2. He saw that the faith of Christianity was being destroyed to excess by everybody, by the clergy as well as by the laity. He saw that peace was altogether discarded by the princes of the world, who were engaged in incessant warlike contention and quarreling among themselves. He saw the wealth of the land being pillaged continuously. He saw many of the vanquished, wrongfully taken prisoner and very cruelly thrown into foulest dungeons, either ransomed for a high price or, tortured by the triple torments of hunger, thirst, and cold, blotted out by a death hidden from the world. He saw holy places violated; monasteries and villas burned. He saw that no one was spared of any human suffering, and that things divine and human alike were held in derision.

3. He heard, too, that the interior regions of Romania, where the Turks ruled over the Christians, had been perniciously subjected in a savage attack.[2] Moved by long-suffering compassion and by love of God's will, he descended the mountains to Gaul, and in Auvergne he called for a council to congregate from all sides at a suitable time at a city called Clermont. Three hundred and ten bishops and abbots, who had been advised beforehand by messengers, were present.

4. Then, on the day set aside for it, he called them together to himself and, in an eloquent address, carefully made the cause of the meeting known to them. In the plaintive voice of an aggrieved Church, he expressed great lamentation, and held a long discourse with them about the raging tempests of the world, which have been mentioned, because faith was undermined.

5. One after another, he beseechingly exhorted them all, with renewed faith, to spur themselves in great earnestness to overcome the Devil's devices and to try to restore the Holy Church, most unmercifully weakened by the wicked, to its former honorable status.

---

[1] Henry IV (1056–1106). Fulcher uses the term "so-called emperor," since Henry was not recognized as rightful emperor by adherents of Gregory VII and Urban II.

[2] This refers to the Seljuk conquest of Anatolia, probably to Manzikert, 1071.

II. The Decree of Pope Urban in the Council

1. "Most beloved brethren," he said, "by God's permission placed over the whole world with the papal crown, I, Urban, as the messenger of divine admonition, have been compelled by an unavoidable occasion to come here to you servants of God. I desired those whom I judged to be stewards of God's ministries to be true stewards and faithful, with all hypocrisy rejected.

2. "But with temperance in reason and justice being remote, I, with divine aid, shall strive carefully to root out any crookedness or distortion which might obstruct God's law. For the Lord appointed you temporarily as stewards over His family to serve it nourishment seasoned with a modest savor. Moreover, blessed will you be if at last the Overseer find you faithful.

3. "You are also called shepherds; see that you are not occupied after the manner of mercenaries. Be true shepherds, always holding your crooks in your hands; and sleeping not, guard on every side the flock entrusted to you.

4. "For if through your carelessness or negligence, some wolf seizes a sheep, you doubtless will lose the reward prepared for you by our Lord. Nay, first most cruelly beaten by the whips of the lictors,[3] you afterwards will be angrily cast into the keeping of a deadly place.

5. "Likewise, according to the evangelical sermon, you are the 'salt of the earth.' But if you fail, it will be disputed wherewith it was salted. O how much saltiness, indeed, is necessary for you to salt the people in correcting them with the salt of wisdom, people who are ignorant and panting with desire after the wantonness of the world; so that, unsalted, they might not be rotten with sins and stink whenever the Lord might wish to exhort them.

6. "For if because of the sloth of your management, He should find in them worms, that is, sin, straightway, He will order that they, despised, be cast into the dungheap. And because you could not make restoration for such a great loss, He will banish you, utterly condemned in judgment, from the familiarity of His love.

7. "It behooves saltiness of this kind to be wise, provident, temperate, learned, peace-making, truth-seeking, pious, just, equitable, pure. For how will the unlearned be able to make men learned, the intemperate make temperate, the impure make them pure? If one despises peace, how will he appease? Or if one has dirty hands, how will he be able to wipe the filth off another one defiled? For it is read, 'If the blind lead the blind, both shall fall into a ditch.'[4]

---

[3] Enforcers. Latin term for imperial bodyguards. [Ed.]
[4] Matthew 15:14.

8. "Set yourselves right before you do others, so that you can blamelessly correct your subjects. If you wish to be friends of God, gladly practice those things which you feel will please Him.

9. "Especially establish ecclesiastical affairs firm in their own right, so that no simoniac⁵ heresy will take root among you. Take care lest the vendors and moneychangers, flayed by the scourges of the Lord, be miserably driven out into the narrow streets of destruction.

10. "Uphold the Church in its own ranks altogether free from all secular power. See that the tithes of all those who cultivate the earth are given faithfully to God; let them not be sold or held back.

11. "Let him who has seized a bishop be considered an outlaw. Let him who has seized or robbed monks, clerics, nuns and their servants, pilgrims, or merchants, be excommunicated. Let the robbers and burners of homes and their accomplices, banished from the Church, be smitten with excommunication.

12. "It must be considered very carefully, as Gregory says, by what penalty he must be punished who seizes other men's property, if he who does not bestow his own liberally is condemned to Hell. For so it happened to the rich man in the well-known Gospel, who on that account was not punished because he had taken away the property of others, but because he had misused that which he had received.

13. "And so by these iniquities, most beloved, you have seen the world disturbed too long; so long, as it was told to us by those reporting, that perhaps because of the weakness of your justice in some parts of your provinces, no one dares to walk in the streets with safety, lest he be kidnapped by robbers by day or thieves by night, either by force or trickery, at home or outside.

14. "Wherefore the Truce,⁶ as it is commonly called, now for a long time established by the Holy Fathers, must be renewed. In admonition, I entreat you to adhere to it most firmly in your own bishopric. But if anyone affected by avarice or pride breaks it of his own free will, let him be excommunicated by God's authority and by the sanction of the decrees of this Holy Council."

III. The Pope's Exhortation Concerning the Expedition to Jerusalem

1. These and many other things having been suitably disposed of, all those present, both clergy and people, at the words of Lord Urban, the Pope, voluntarily gave thanks to God and confirmed by a faithful

---

⁵ Buying or selling church offices. [Ed.]

⁶ Truce of God—Cessation of all feuds from Wednesday evening to Monday morning in every week and during church festivals, ordered by the Church in 1041. This was proclaimed anew at the Council of Clermont.

promise that his decrees would be well kept. But straightway he added that another thing not less than the tribulation already spoken of, but even greater and more oppressive, was injuring Christianity in another part of the world, saying:

2. "Now that you, O sons of God, have consecrated yourselves to God to maintain peace among yourselves more vigorously and to uphold the laws of the Church faithfully, there is work to do, for you must turn the strength of your sincerity, now that you are aroused by divine correction, to another affair that concerns you and God. Hastening to the way, you must help your brothers living in the Orient, who need your aid for which they have already cried out many times.

3. "For, as most of you have been told, the Turks, a race of Persians,[7] who have penetrated within the boundaries of Romania[8] even to the Mediterranean to that point which they call the Arm of Saint George[9] in occupying more and more of the lands of the Christians, have overcome them, already victims of seven battles, and have killed and captured them, have overthrown churches, and have laid waste God's kingdom. If you permit this supinely for very long, God's faithful ones will be still further subjected.

4. "Concerning this affair, I, with suppliant prayer—not I, but the Lord—exhort you, heralds of Christ, to persuade all of whatever class, both knights and footmen, both rich and poor, in numerous edicts, to strive to help expel that wicked race from our Christian lands before it is too late.

5. "I speak to those present, I send word to those not here; moreover, Christ commands it. Remission of sins will be granted for those going thither, if they end a shackled life either on land or in crossing the sea, or in struggling against the heathen. I, being vested with that gift from God, grant this to those who go.

6. "O what a shame, if a people, so despised, degenerate, and enslaved by demons would thus overcome a people endowed with the trust of almighty God, and shining in the name of Christ! O how many evils will be imputed to you by the Lord Himself, if you do not help those who, like you, profess Christianity!

7. "Let those," he said, "who are accustomed to wage private wars wastefully even against Believers, go forth against the Infidels in a battle worthy to be undertaken now and to be finished in victory. Now, let those, who until recently existed as plunderers, be soldiers of Christ; now, let those, who formerly contended against brothers and

---

[7] Really Seljuk Turks who conquered lands from east to west by way of Persia.

[8] Fulcher uses the term *Romania* to refer to the Anatolian as well as to the European provinces of the Byzantine Empire, but here, of course, he means the Anatolian. The Seljuks called the state which they founded here *Rum*.

[9] An eleventh-century term for the Bosphorus, since it ran by St. George's monastery near Byzantium. [Ed.]

relations, rightly fight barbarians; now, let those, who recently were hired for a few pieces of silver, win their eternal reward. Let those, who wearied themselves to the detriment of body and soul, labor for a twofold honor. Nay, more, the sorrowful here will be glad there, the poor here will be rich there, and the enemies of the Lord here will be His friends there.

8. "Let no delay postpone the journey of those about to go, but when they have collected the money owed to them and the expenses for the journey, and when winter has ended and spring has come, let them enter the crossroads courageously with the Lord going on before."

IV. The Bishop of Puy and the Events after the Council

1. After these words were spoken, the hearers were fervently inspired. Thinking nothing more worthy than such an undertaking, many in the audience solemnly promised to go, and to urge diligently those who were absent. There was among them one Bishop of Puy, Ademar by name, who afterwards, acting as vicar-apostolic, ruled the whole army of God wisely and thoughtfully, and spurred them to complete their undertaking vigorously.

2. So, the things that we have told you were well established and confirmed by everybody in the Council. With the blessing of absolution given, they departed; and after returning to their homes, they disclosed to those not knowing, what had taken place. As it was decreed far and wide throughout the provinces, they established the peace, which they call the Truce, to be upheld mutually by oath.

3. Many, one after another, of any and every occupation, after confession of their sins and with purified spirits, consecrated themselves to go where they were bidden.

4. Oh, how worthy and delightful to all of us who saw those beautiful crosses, either silken or woven of gold, or of any material, which the pilgrims sewed on the shoulders of their woolen cloaks or cassocks by the command of the Pope, after taking the vow to go. To be sure, God's soldiers, who were making themselves ready to battle for His honor, ought to have been marked and fortified with a sign of victory. And so by embroidering the symbol [of the cross] on their clothing in recognition of their faith, in the end they won the True Cross itself. They imprinted the ideal so that they might attain the reality of the ideal.

5. It is plain that good meditation leads to doing good work and that good work wins salvation of the soul. But, if it is good to mean well, it is better, after reflection, to carry out the good intention. So, it is best to win salvation through action worthy of the soul to be saved. Let each and everyone, therefore, reflect upon the good, that he makes better in fulfillment, so that, deserving it, he might finally receive the best, which does not diminish in eternity.

6. In such a manner Urban, a wise man and reverenced,
Meditated a labor, whereby the world florescenced.[10]

For he renewed peace and restored the laws of the Church to their former standards; also he tried with vigorous instigation to expel the heathen from the lands of the Christians. And since he strove to exalt all things of God in every way, almost everyone gladly surrendered in obedience to his paternal care.

[10] Blossomed. [Ed.]

2

Chronicle of Solomon bar Simson

Solomon bar Simson (who is known only from this chronicle) provides a Hebrew chronicle of the First Crusade that takes up the story after Pope Urban II's appeal. In early 1096, a few French and German crusaders led their followers in attacks on Jews in the cities of Speyer, Worms, and Mainz. Solomon bar Simson tells the story of these massacres from the viewpoint of the survivors. What seems to have been the reason for the attacks on Jews? What role was played by the common people, the officials of the church, and the government?

THINKING HISTORICALLY

Little is known about the author of this chronicle. Simson may have written this a generation after 1096: If so, he probably based it on earlier versions. Those who survived by converting to Christianity may have helped to shape the story, even if they later returned to Judaism. Some scholars see traces of Christian culture in the accounts of martyrdom, which was not a common theme in Hebrew writing until this time. What signs do you see of the Jewish author's knowledge of Christianity?

This narrative, like the previous selection, includes quotations from speeches. How can you tell that some of these quotations do not contain the exact words that were spoken?

Source: "Chronicle of Solomon bar Simson," in *The Jews and the Crusaders: The Hebrew Chronicles of the First and Second Crusades*, ed. and trans. Shlomo Eidelberg (Madison: University of Wisconsin Press, 1977), 21–26.

Solomon bar Simson's narrative contains another element that, although absent from modern histories, is found in other narratives of the Crusades and is especially pronounced here. This is not just a narrative of human action and intention, but also an interpretation of divine action and intention. Why is this narrative strategy necessary for this author? If you were writing a narrative of the Crusades today, would you want to tell both of these stories, or only the human one? Why?

I will now recount the event of this persecution in other martyred communities as well—the extent to which they clung to the Lord, God of their fathers, bearing witness to His Oneness to their last breath.

In the year four thousand eight hundred and fifty-six, the year one thousand twenty-eight of our exile, in the eleventh year of the cycle Ranu, the year in which we anticipated salvation and solace, in accordance with the prophecy of Jeremiah: "Sing with gladness for Jacob, and shout at the head of the nations," etc.—this year turned instead to sorrow and groaning, weeping and outcry. Inflicted upon the Jewish People were the many evils related in all the admonitions; those enumerated in Scripture as well as those unwritten were visited upon us.

At this time arrogant people, a people of strange speech, a nation bitter and impetuous, Frenchmen and Germans, set out for the Holy City, which had been desecrated by barbaric nations, there to seek their house of idolatry and banish the Ishmaelites and other denizens of the land and conquer the land for themselves. They decorated themselves prominently with their signs, placing a profane symbol—a horizontal line over a vertical one—on the vestments of every man and woman whose heart yearned to go on the stray path to the grave of their Messiah. Their ranks swelled until the number of men, women, and children exceeded a locust horde covering the earth; of them it was said: "The locusts have no king [yet go they forth all of them by bands]."[1] Now it came to pass that as they passed through the towns where Jews dwelled, they said to one another: "Look now, we are going a long way to seek out the profane shrine and to avenge ourselves on the Ishmaelites, when here, in our very midst, are the Jews—they whose forefathers murdered and crucified him for no reason. Let us first avenge ourselves on them and exterminate them from among the nations so that the name of Israel will no longer be remembered, or let them adopt our faith and acknowledge the offspring of promiscuity."

When the Jewish communities became aware of their intentions, they resorted to the custom of our ancestors, repentance, prayer, and charity. The hands of the Holy Nation turned faint at this time, their

---

[1] Proverbs 30:27. [Ed.]

hearts melted, and their strength flagged. They hid in their innermost rooms to escape the swirling sword. They subjected themselves to great endurance, abstaining from food and drink for three consecutive days and nights, and then fasting many days from sunrise to sunset, until their skin was shriveled and dry as wood upon their bones. And they cried out loudly and bitterly to God.

But their Father did not answer them; He obstructed their prayers, concealing Himself in a cloud through which their prayers could not pass, and He abhorred their tent, and He removed them out of His sight—all of this having been decreed by Him to take place "in the day when I visit"; and this was the generation that had been chosen by Him to be His portion, for they had the strength and the fortitude to stand in His Sanctuary, and fulfill His word, and sanctify His Great Name in His world. It is of such as these that King David said: "Bless the Lord, ye angels of His, ye almighty in strength, that fulfil His word," etc.

That year, Passover fell on Thursday, and the New Moon of the following month, Iyar, fell on Friday and the Sabbath. On the eighth day of Iyar, on the Sabbath, the foe attacked the community of Speyer and murdered eleven holy souls who sanctified their Creator on the holy Sabbath and refused to defile themselves by adopting the faith of their foe. There was a distinguished, pious woman there who slaughtered herself in sanctification of God's Name. She was the first among all the communities of those who were slaughtered. The remainder were saved by the local bishop without defilement [i.e., baptism], as described above.

On the twenty-third of Iyar they attacked the community of Worms.[2] The community was then divided into two groups; some remained in their homes and others fled to the local bishop seeking refuge. Those who remained in their homes were set upon by the steppe-wolves who pillaged men, women, and infants, children, and old people. They pulled down the stairways and destroyed the houses, looting and plundering; and they took the Torah Scroll, trampled it in the mud, and tore and burned it. The enemy devoured the children of Israel with open maw.

Seven days later, on the New Moon of Sivan—the very day on which the Children of Israel arrived at Mount Sinai to receive the Torah—those Jews who were still in the court of the bishop were subjected to great anguish. The enemy dealt them the same cruelty as the first group and put them to the sword. The Jews, inspired by the valor of their brethren, similarly chose to be slain in order to sanctify the Name before the eyes of all, and exposed their throats for their heads to be severed for the glory of the Creator. There were also those who took their own lives, thus fulfilling the verse: "The mother was dashed in pieces with her children."[3] Fathers fell upon their sons, being slaughtered upon one another, and

---

[2] Town in the Holy Roman Empire (now Germany). [Ed.]
[3] Hosea 10:14. [Ed.]

they slew one another—each man his kin, his wife and children; bride-grooms slew their betrothed, and merciful women their only children. They all accepted the divine decree wholeheartedly and, as they yielded up their souls to the Creator, cried out: "Hear, O Israel, the Lord is our God, the Lord is One." The enemy stripped them naked, dragged them along, and then cast them off, sparing only a small number whom they forcibly baptized in their profane waters. The number of those slain during the two days was approximately eight hundred—and they were all buried naked. It is of these that the Prophet Jeremiah lamented: "They that were brought up in scarlet embrace dunghills."[4] I have already cited their names above. May God remember them for good.

When the saints, the pious ones of the Most High, the holy community of Mainz, whose merit served as shield and protection for all the communities and whose fame had spread throughout the many provinces, heard that some of the community of Speyer had been slain and that the community of Worms had been attacked a second time, and that the sword would soon reach them, their hands became faint and their hearts melted and became as water. They cried out to the Lord with all their hearts, saying: "O Lord, God of Israel, will You completely annihilate the remnant of Israel? Where are all your wonders which our forefathers related to us, saying: 'Did You not bring us up from Egypt and from Babylonia and rescue us on numerous occasions?' How, then, have You now forsaken and abandoned us, O Lord, giving us over into the hands of evil Edom so that they may destroy us? Do not remove Yourself from us, for adversity is almost upon us and there is no one to aid us."

The leaders of the Jews gathered together and discussed various ways of saving themselves. They said: "Let us elect elders so that we may know how to act, for we are consumed by this great evil." The elders decided to ransom the community by generously giving of their money and bribing the various princes and deputies and bishops and governors. Then, the community leaders who were respected by the local bishop approached him and his officers and servants to negotiate this matter. They asked: "What shall we do about the news we have received regarding the slaughter of our brethren in Speyer and Worms?" They [the Gentiles] replied: "Heed our advice and bring all your money into our treasury. You, your wives, and your children, and all your belongings shall come into the courtyard of the bishop until the hordes have passed by. Thus will you be saved from the errant ones."

Actually, they gave this advice so as to herd us together and hold us like fish that are caught in an evil net, and then to turn us over to the enemy, while taking our money. This is what actually happened in the end, and "the outcome is proof of the intentions." The bishop assembled his ministers and courtiers—mighty ministers, the noblest in the

---

[4] Lamentations 4:5. [Ed.]

land—for the purpose of helping us; for at first it had been his desire to save us with all his might, since we had given him and his ministers and servants a large bribe in return for their promise to help us. Ultimately, however, all the bribes and entreaties were of no avail to protect us on the day of wrath and misfortune.

It was at this time that Duke Godfrey [of Bouillon], may his bones be ground to dust, arose in the hardness of his spirit, driven by a spirit of wantonness to go with those journeying to the profane shrine, vowing to go on this journey only after avenging the blood of the crucified one by shedding Jewish blood and completely eradicating any trace of those bearing the name "Jew," thus assuaging his own burning wrath. To be sure, there arose someone to repair the breach—a God-fearing man who had been bound to the most holy of altars—called Rabbi Kalonymos, the *Parnass*[5] of the community of Mainz. He dispatched a messenger to King Henry[6] in the kingdom of Pula, where the king had been dwelling during the past nine years, and related all that had happened.

The king was enraged and dispatched letters to all the ministers, bishops, and governors of all the provinces of his realm, as well as to Duke Godfrey, containing words of greeting and commanding them to do no bodily harm to the Jews and to provide them with help and refuge. The evil duke then swore that he had never intended to do them harm. The Jews of Cologne nevertheless bribed him with five hundred *zekukim* of silver, as did the Jews of Mainz. The duke assured them of his support and promised them peace.

However, God, the maker of peace, turned aside and averted His eyes from His people, and consigned them to the sword. No prophet, seer, or man of wise heart was able to comprehend how the sin of the people infinite in number was deemed so great as to cause the destruction of so many lives in the various Jewish communities. The martyrs endured the extreme penalty normally inflicted only upon one guilty of murder. Yet, it must be stated with certainty that God is a righteous judge, and we are to blame.

Then the evil waters prevailed. The enemy unjustly accused them of evil acts they did not do, declaring: "You are the children of those who killed our object of veneration, hanging him on a tree, and he himself had said: 'There will yet come a day when my children will come and avenge my blood.' We are his children and it is therefore obligatory for us to avenge him since you are the ones who rebel and disbelieve in him. Your God has never been at peace with you. Although He intended to deal kindly with you, you have conducted yourselves improperly before

---

[5] Reference to the Greek mountain Parnassus, perhaps meaning "mainstay" of the community. [Ed.]

[6] Henry IV was Holy Roman Emperor (1084–1105). [Ed.]

Him. God has forgotten you and is no longer desirous of you since you are a stubborn nation. Instead, He has departed from you and has taken us for His portion, casting His radiance upon us."

When we heard these words, our hearts trembled and moved out of their places. We were dumb with silence, abiding in darkness, like those long dead, waiting for the Lord to look forth and behold from heaven.

And Satan—the Pope of evil Rome—also came and proclaimed to all the nations believing in that stock of adultery—these are the stock of Seir[7]—that they should assemble and ascend to Jerusalem so as to conquer the city, and journey to the tomb of the superstition whom they call their god. Satan came and mingled with the nations, and they gathered as one man to fulfill the command, coming in great numbers like the grains of sand upon the seashore, the noise of them clamorous as a whirlwind and a storm. When the drops of the bucket had assembled, they took evil counsel against the people of the Lord and said: "Why should we concern ourselves with going to war against the Ishmaelites dwelling about Jerusalem, when in our midst is a people who disrespect our god—indeed, their ancestors are those who crucified him. Why should we let them live and tolerate their dwelling among us? Let us commence by using our swords against them and then proceed upon our stray path."

The heart of the people of our God grew faint and their spirit flagged, for many sore injuries had been inflicted upon them and they had been smitten repeatedly. They now came supplicating to God and fasting, and their hearts melted within them. But the Lord did as He declared, for we had sinned before Him, and He forsook the sanctuary of Shiloh—the Temple-in-Miniature[8]—which He had placed among His people who dwelt in the midst of alien nations. His wrath was kindled and He drew the sword against them, until they remained but as the flagstaff upon the mountaintop and as the ensign on the hill, and He gave over His nation into captivity and trampled them underfoot. See, O Lord, and consider to whom Thou hast done thus: to Israel, a nation despised and pillaged, Your chosen portion! Why have You uplifted the shield of its enemies, and why have they gained in strength? Let all hear, for I cry out in anguish; the ears of all that hear me shall be seared: How has the staff of might been broken, the rod of glory—the sainted community comparable to fine gold, the community of Mainz! It was caused by the Lord to test those that fear Him, to have them endure the yoke of His pure fear. . . .

---

[7] An enemy of ancient Israel.

[8] A model of Solomon's temple in Jerusalem. The point is that God abandoned his people. [Ed.]

3

ANNA COMNENA
The Alexiad

Anna Comnena was the daughter of Emperor Alexius
(r. 1081–1118) of Byzantium. Threatened on three sides — by the
Seljuk Turks to the east, the Norman kingdom of southern Italy
to the west, and rebellions to the north — Alexius appealed for
aid to Pope Urban II of Rome in 1095. He expected a mercenary
army, but because the pope saw a chance to send a massive force
against Muslim occupiers of Jerusalem as well as against those
threatening Constantinople, Alexius instead received an uncontrollable ragtag force of Christians and Crusaders that included his
Norman enemies, led by Bohemond.

Princess Anna recalled the story of the First Crusade's appearance
in Byzantium some forty years later in her history titled *The Alexiad*
after her father. According to Anna, how did Alexius respond to the
approach of the Crusader army? Did Alexius fear the Franks more
than he feared the Turks?

THINKING HISTORICALLY

This is a third perspective on the history of the First Crusade — the
view of a Christian ally of Rome, more directly threatened than the
Roman church by the Muslim armies. Yet, Byzantium and Rome were
also at odds. Since 1054, they had accepted a parting of the ways,
theologically and institutionally, with Byzantium now the center of
the Eastern Orthodox Church. And with the advancing Frankish
armies, Anna and Alexius were not sure whether they were facing
friend or foe. How does Anna view the Franks? How does Anna's
critical perspective change our idea of the Crusaders? How might
her idea of the Franks change our narrative of the early stage of
the crusade?

Notice how this narrative combines a sequence of events with
generalizations (often about the "race" or nature of the Franks) to
explain specific events. Does a narrative history have to include generalizations as well as a sequence of specific events? Can the events
alone provide sufficient explanation?

Source: Anna Comnena, *The Alexiad of the Princess Anna Comnena*, trans. Elizabeth A. S.
Dawes (London: Routledge & Kegan Paul Ltd., 1967), 247–52. Reprinted in William H.
McNeill and Schuyler O. Houser, *Medieval Europe* (Oxford: Oxford University Press, 1971),
135–40.

Before he [the Emperor Alexius] had enjoyed even a short rest, he heard a report of the approach of innumerable Frankish[1] armies. Now he dreaded their arrival for he knew their irresistible manner of attack, their unstable and mobile character and all the peculiar natural and concomitant characteristics which the Frank retains throughout; and he also knew that they were always agape for money, and seemed to disregard their truces readily for any reason that cropped up. For he had always heard this reported of them, and found it very true. However, he did not lose heart, but prepared himself in every way so that, when the occasion called, he would be ready for battle. And indeed the actual facts were far greater and more terrible than rumour made them. For the whole of the West and all the barbarian tribes which dwell between the further side of the Adriatic[2] and the pillars of Heracles,[3] had all migrated in a body and were marching into Asia through the intervening Europe, and were making the journey with all their household. The reason of this upheaval was more or less the following. A certain Frank, Peter by name, nicknamed Cucupeter,[4] had gone to worship at the Holy Sepulchre[5] and after suffering many things at the hands of the Turks and Saracens who were ravaging Asia, he got back to his own country with difficulty. But he was angry at having failed in his object, and wanted to undertake the same journey again. However, he saw that he ought not to make the journey to the Holy Sepulchre alone again, lest worse things befall him, so he worked out a cunning plan. This was to preach in all the Latin countries that "the voice of God bids me announce to all the Counts in France" that they should all leave their homes and set out to worship at the Holy Sepulchre, and to endeavour wholeheartedly with hand and mind to deliver Jerusalem from the hand of Hagarenes.[6] And he really succeeded. For after inspiring the souls of all with this quasi-divine command he contrived to assemble the Franks from all sides, one after the other, with arms, horses and all the other paraphernalia of war. And they were all so zealous and eager that every highroad was full of them. And those Frankish soldiers were accompanied by an unarmed host more numerous than the sand or the stars, carrying palms and crosses on their shoulders, women and children, too, came away from their countries and the sight of them was like many rivers streaming from all sides, and they were advancing towards us through Dacia[7] generally with all their hosts.

[1] Term generalizes from Franks (mainly French) to refer to all Western Europeans. [Ed.]

[2] Italy. [Ed.]

[3] Gibraltar, at the meeting of the Mediterranean and the Atlantic Ocean. [Ed.]

[4] Peter the Hermit, an effective lay preacher who raised an unruly army (far more peasants than knights) that Anna Comnena saw as the first army of Crusaders. [Ed.]

[5] The Church of the Holy Sepulchre in Jerusalem is said to hold the tomb where Jesus was buried. [Ed.]

[6] Muslims, who were considered "children of Hagar" (Gen. 16). [Ed.]

[7] Modern Romania.

Now the coming of these many peoples was preceded by a locust which did not touch the wheat, but made a terrible attack on the vines. This was really a presage as the diviners of the time interpreted it, and meant that this enormous Frankish army would, when it came, refrain from interference in Christian affairs, but fall very heavily upon the barbarian Ishmaelites[8] who were slaves to drunkenness, wine, and Dionysus.[9] For this race is under the sway of Dionysus and Eros,[10] rushes headlong into all kind of sexual intercourse, and is not circumcised either in the flesh or in their passions. It is nothing but a slave, nay triply enslaved, to the ills wrought by Aphrodite. For this reason they worship and adore Astarte and Ashtaroth[11] too and value above all the image of the moon, and the golden figure of Hobar[12] in their country. Now in these symbols Christianity was taken to be the corn because of its wineless and very nutritive qualities; in this manner the diviners interpreted the vines and the wheat. However let the matter of the prophecy rest.

The incidents of the barbarians' approach followed in the order I have described, and persons of intelligence could feel that they were witnessing a strange occurrence. The arrival of these multitudes did not take place at the same time nor by the same road (for how indeed could such masses starting from different places have crossed the straits of Lombardy all together?). Some first, some next, others after them and thus successively all accomplished the transit, and then marched through the Continent. Each army was preceded, as we said, by an unspeakable number of locusts; and all who saw this more than once recognized them as forerunners of the Frankish armies. When the first of them began crossing the straits of Lombardy sporadically the Emperor summoned certain leaders of the Roman forces, and sent them to the parts of Dyrrachium and Valona[13] with instructions to offer a courteous welcome to the Franks who had crossed, and to collect abundant supplies from all the countries along their route; then to follow and watch them covertly all the time, and if they saw them making any foraging-excursions, they were to come out from under cover and check them by light skirmishing. These captains were accompanied by some men who knew the Latin tongue, so that they might settle any disputes that arose between them.

---

[8] Muslims. Descended from Abraham's son Ishmael (and servant Hagar), whereas Jews were thought descended from Isaac, son of Abraham and wife Sarah. [Ed.]

[9] Anna's account of the beliefs of the Muslims was highly biased. Muhammad forbade his followers to drink intoxicating liquors.

[10] Dionysus was the Greek god associated with wine and revelry; Eros was the patron of lovers, and son of Aphrodite, goddess of love.

[11] Names of the Semitic goddess of fertility.

[12] I.e., Hathor, the Egyptian goddess of love, usually depicted with the head of a cow. (N.B. Idol worship was strictly forbidden by Islamic law.)

[13] Ports on the Adriatic, directly opposite the heel of Italy in modern Albania.

Let me, however, give an account of this subject more clearly and in due order. According to universal rumour Godfrey,[14] who sold his country, was the first to start on the appointed road; this man was very rich and very proud of his bravery, courage and conspicuous lineage; for every Frank is anxious to outdo the others. And such an upheaval of both men and women took place then as had never occurred within human memory, the simpler-minded were urged on by the real desire of worshipping at our Lord's Sepulchre, and visiting the sacred places; but the more astute, especially men like Bohemund and those of like mind, had another secret reason, namely, the hope that while on their travels they might by some means be able to seize the capital [Constantinople] itself,[15] looking upon this as a kind of corollary. And Bohemund disturbed the minds of many nobler men by thus cherishing his old grudge against the Emperor. Meanwhile Peter, after he had delivered his message, crossed the straits of Lombardy before anybody else with eighty thousand men on foot, and one hundred thousand on horseback, and reached the capital by way of Hungary.[16] For the Frankish race, as one may conjecture, is always very hotheaded and eager, but when once it has espoused a cause, it is uncontrollable.

The Emperor, knowing what Peter had suffered before from the Turks, advised him to wait for the arrival of the other Counts, but Peter would not listen for he trusted the multitude of his followers, so he crossed and pitched his camp near a small town called Helenopolis.[17] After him followed the Normans[18] numbering ten thousand, who separated themselves from the rest of the army and devastated the country round Nicaea, and behaved most cruelly to all. For they dismembered some of the children and fixed others on wooden spits and roasted them at the fire, and on persons advanced in age they inflicted every kind of torture. But when the inhabitants of Nicaea became aware of these doings, they threw open their gates and marched out upon them, and after a violent conflict had taken place they had to dash back inside their citadel as the Normans fought so bravely. And thus the latter recovered all the booty and returned to Helenopolis. Then a dispute arose between them and the others who had not gone out with them, as is usual in such cases, for the minds of those who stayed behind were aflame with envy, and thus caused a skirmish after which the headstrong Normans drew apart again, marched to

---

[14] Godfrey of Bouillon, the duke of Lower Lorraine (c. 1060–1100). To raise money for the Crusade, he sold two of his estates, and pledged his castle at Bouillon to the bishop of Liège.

[15] Bohemund and his father, Robert Guiscard, had already led Norman armies against Byzantium. [Ed.]

[16] Peter's contingent probably numbered about twenty thousand including noncombatants.

[17] I.e., Peter moved his forces across the Bosphorus and into Asia Minor.

[18] Bohemund's army. Normans, descended from Viking "Northmen" and Franks, had conquered Sicily and southern Italy. [Ed.]

Xerigordus[19] and took it by assault. When the Sultan[20] heard what had happened, he dispatched Elchanes[21] against them with a substantial force. He came, and recaptured Xerigordus and sacrificed some of the Normans to the sword, and took others captive, at the same time laid plans to catch those who had remained behind with Cucupeter. He placed ambushes in suitable spots so that any coming from the camp in the direction of Nicaea would fall into them unexpectedly and be killed. Besides this, as he knew the Franks' love of money, he sent for two active-minded men and ordered them to go to Cucupeter's camp and proclaim there that the Normans had gained possession of Nicaea, and were now dividing everything in it. When this report was circulated among Peter's followers, it upset them terribly. Directly [when] they heard the words "partition" and "money" they started in a disorderly crowd along the road to Nicaea, all but unmindful of their military experience and the discipline which is essential for those starting out to battle. For, as I remarked above, the Latin race is always very fond of money, but more especially when it is bent on raiding a country; it then loses its reason and gets beyond control. As they journeyed neither in ranks nor in squadrons, they fell foul of the Turkish ambuscades near the river Dracon and perished miserably. And such a large number of Franks and Normans were the victims of the Ishmaelite sword, that when they piled up the corpses of the slaughtered men which were lying on either side they formed, I say, not a very large hill or mound or a peak, but a high mountain as it were, of very considerable depth and breadth—so great was the pyramid of bones. And later men of the same tribe as the slaughtered barbarians built a wall and used the bones of the dead to fill the interstices as if they were pebbles, and thus made the city their tomb in a way. This fortified city is still standing today with its walls built of a mixture of stones and bones. When they had all in this way fallen prey to the sword, Peter alone with a few others escaped and reentered Helenopolis,[22] and the Turks who wanted to capture him, set fresh ambushes for him. But when the Emperor received reliable information of all this, and the terrible massacre, he was very worried lest Peter should have been captured. He therefore summoned Constantine Catacalon Euphorbenus (who has already been mentioned many times in this history), and gave him a large force which was embarked on ships of war and sent him across the straits to Peter's succour. Directly [when] the Turks saw him land they fled. Constantine, without the slightest delay, picked up Peter and his followers, who were but few, and brought them safe and sound to the Emperor. On the Emperor's reminding him of his original thoughtlessness and saying that it was due to his not having obeyed his,

---

[19] A castle held by the Turks.

[20] Qilij Arslan I, ruled 1092–1106.

[21] An important Turkish military commander.

[22] According to other accounts of the battle, Peter was in Constantinople at the time.

the Emperor's, advice that he had incurred such disasters, Peter, being a haughty Latin, would not admit that he himself was the cause of the trouble, but said it was the others who did not listen to him, but followed their own will, and he denounced them as robbers and plunderers who, for that reason, were not allowed by the Saviour to worship at His Holy Sepulchre. Others of the Latins, such as Bohemund and men of like mind, who had long cherished a desire for the Roman Empire,[23] and wished to win it for themselves, found a pretext in Peter's preaching, as I have said, deceived the more single-minded, caused this great upheaval and were selling their own estates under the pretence that they were marching against the Turks to redeem the Holy Sepulchre.

[23] Byzantine Empire. [Ed.]

4

FULCHER OF CHARTRES
The Siege of Antioch

We return here to Fulcher's Chronicles (Book I, Chapters 16 and 17). Antioch, in northern Syria, was the largest and most formidable Muslim-controlled city on the Crusaders' route to Jerusalem. After laying siege to the city for more than two years, the Crusader forces had suffered losses that seriously reduced their strength and morale. After their initial success, what events seem to have caused these reversals? What were the strengths and weaknesses of the Crusader armies?

THINKING HISTORICALLY

Like the narrative of Solomon bar Simson, this narrative operates on two levels: the human and the divine. Notice how Fulcher attempts to interpret both of these narrative lines, separately and in their interaction. How much of Fulcher's narrative recounts God's work? How much recounts the work of the Crusaders? How does he combine these two threads? Of course, modern historians are normally limited to the human thread. Try to write a narrative that shows how the human Crusaders conquered Antioch.

Source: *The First Crusade: The Chronicle of Fulcher of Chartres and Other Source Materials*, 2nd ed., ed. Edward Peters (Philadelphia: University of Pennsylvania Press, 1998), 73–75.

XVI. The Wretched Poverty of the Christians and the Flight of the Count of Blois

1. In the year of the Lord 1098, after the region all around Antioch had been wholly devastated by the multitude of our people, the strong as well as the weak were more and more harassed by famine.

2. At that time, the famished ate the shoots of beanseeds growing in the fields and many kinds of herbs unseasoned with salt; also thistles, which, being not well cooked because of the deficiency of firewood, pricked the tongues of those eating them; also horses, asses, and camels, and dogs and rats. The poorer ones ate even the skins of the beasts and seeds of grain found in manure.

3. They endured winter's cold, summer's heat, and heavy rains for God. Their tents became old and torn and rotten from the continuation of rains. Because of this, many of them were covered by only the sky.

4. So like gold thrice proved and purified sevenfold by fire, long predestined by God, I believe, and weighed by such a great calamity, they were cleansed of their sins. For even if the assassin's sword had not failed, many, long agonizing, would have voluntarily completed a martyr's course. Perhaps they borrowed the grace of such a great example from Saint Job, who, purifying his soul by the torments of his body, ever held God fast in mind. Those who fight with the heathen, labor because of God.

5. Granting that God—who creates everything, regulates everything created, sustains everything regulated, and rules by virtue—can destroy or renew whatsoever He wishes, I feel that He assented to the destruction of the heathen after the scourging of the Christians. He permitted it, and the people deserved it, because so many times they cheaply destroyed all things of God. He permitted the Christians to be killed by the Turks, so that the Christians would have the assurance of salvation; the Turks, the perdition of their souls. It pleased God that certain Turks, already predestined for salvation, were baptized by priests. "For those whom He predestined, He also called and glorified."

6. So what then? There were some of our men, as you heard before, who left the siege because it brought so much anguish; others, because of poverty; others, because of cowardice; others, because of fear of death; first the poor and then the rich.

7. Stephen, Count of Blois, withdrew from the siege and returned home to France by sea. Therefore all of us grieved, since he was a very noble man and valiant in arms. On the day following his departure, the city of Antioch was surrendered to the Franks. If he had persevered, he would have rejoiced much in the victory with the rest. This act disgraced him. For a good beginning is not beneficial to anyone unless it be well consummated. I shall cut short many things in the Lord's affairs lest I wander from the truth, because lying about them must be especially guarded against.

8. The siege lasted continuously from this same month of October, as it was mentioned, through the following winter and spring until June. The Turks and Franks alternately staged many attacks and counter-attacks; they overcame and were overcome. Our men, however, triumphed more often than theirs. Once it happened that many of the fleeing Turks fell into the Fernus River, and being submerged in it, they drowned. On the near side of the river, and on the far side, both forces often waged war alternately.

9. Our leaders constructed castles before the city, from which they often rushed forth vigorously to keep the Turks from coming out [of the city]. By this means, the Franks took the pastures from their animals. Nor did they get any help from Armenians outside the city, although these Armenians often did injury to our men.

XVII. The Surrender of the City of Antioch

1. When it pleased God that the labor of His people should be consummated, perhaps pleased by the prayers of those who daily poured out supplications and entreaties to Him, out of His compassion He granted that through a fraud of the Turks the city be returned to the Christians in a secret surrender. Hear, therefore, of a fraud, and yet not a fraud.

2. Our Lord appeared to a certain Turk, chosen beforehand by His grace, and said to him: "Arise, thou who sleepest! I command thee to return the city to the Christians." The astonished man concealed that vision in silence.

3. However, a second time, the Lord appeared to him: "Return the city to the Christians," He said, "for I am Christ who command this of thee." Meditating what to do, he went away to his ruler, the prince of Antioch, and made that vision known to him. To him the ruler responded: "You do not wish to obey the phantom, do you, stupid?" Returning, he was afterwards silent.

4. The Lord again appeared to him, saying: "Why hast thou not fulfilled what I ordered thee? Thou must not hesitate, for I, who command this, am Lord of all." No longer doubting, he discreetly negotiated with our men, so that by his zealous plotting they might receive the city.

5. He finished speaking, and gave his son as hostage to Lord Bohemond, to whom he first directed that discourse, and whom he first persuaded. On a certain night, he sent twenty of our men over the wall by means of ladders made of ropes. Without delay, the gate was opened. The Franks, already prepared, entered the city. Forty of our soldiers, who had previously entered by ropes, killed sixty Turks found there, guards of the tower. In a loud voice, altogether the Franks shouted:

"God wills it! God wills it!" For this was our signal cry, when we were about to press forward on any enterprise.

6. After hearing this, all the Turks were extremely terrified. Then, when the redness of dawn had paled, the Franks began to go forward to attack the city. When the Turks had first seen Bohemond's red banner on high, furling and unfurling, and the great tumult aroused on all sides, and the Franks running far and wide through the streets with their naked swords and wildly killing people, and had heard their horns sounding on the top of the wall, they began to flee here and there, bewildered. From this scene, many who were able fled into the citadel situated on a cliff.

7. Our rabble wildly seized everything that they found in the streets and houses. But the proved soldiers kept to warfare, in following and killing the Turks.

5

IBN AL-QALANISI
The Damascus Chronicle

Here we switch to a Muslim view of the events of 1098 and 1099: especially the battles of Antioch, Jerusalem, and Ascalon (modern Ashkelon, Israel). Ibn al-Qalanisi* (c. 1070–1160) was a scholar in Damascus, Syria. How does his account of the battle for Antioch differ from the previous selection by Fulcher of Chartres? How do you resolve these differences?

THINKING HISTORICALLY

We noticed how the medieval Christian historian provided two historical threads—the human and divine. How does this Muslim account integrate the threads of human action and divine will?

Modern historians restrict their accounts to human action but seek to include the views of both sides in a conflict. How do you integrate both sides into your narrative? Also, what signs do you see here of a possible second conflict, this one between Muslims?

* IH buhn   ahl kahl ah NEE see

Source: H. A. R. Gibb, *The Damascus Chronicle of the Crusades*, extracted and translated from the *Chronicle of Ibn al-Qalanisi* (Mineola, NY: Dover Publications, 2002), 44–49.

A.H. 491[1]

[9th December, 1097, to 27th November, 1098]

At the end of First Jumādā [beginning of June, 1098] the report arrived that certain of the men of Antioch among the armourers in the train of the amīr Yāghī Siyān had entered into a conspiracy against Antioch and had come to an agreement with the Franks to deliver the city up to them, because of some ill-usage and confiscations which they had formerly suffered at his hands. They found an opportunity of seizing one of the city bastions adjoining the Jabal, which they sold to the Franks, and thence admitted them into the city during the night. At daybreak they raised the battle cry, whereupon Yāghī Siyān took to flight and went out with a large body, but not one person amongst them escaped to safety. When he reached the neighbourhood of Armanāz, an estate near Ma'arrat Masrīn, he fell from his horse to the ground. One of his companions raised him up and remounted him, but he could not maintain his balance on the back of the horse, and after falling repeatedly he died. As for Antioch, the number of men, women, and children, killed, taken prisoner, and enslaved from its population is beyond computation. About three thousand men fled to the citadel and fortified themselves in it, and some few escaped for whom God had decreed escape.

In Sha'bān [July] news was received that al-Afdal, the commander-in-chief (amīr al-juyūsh), had come up from Egypt to Syria at the head of a strong 'askar.[2] He encamped before Jerusalem, where at that time were the two amīrs Sukmān and Il-Ghāzī, sons of Ortuq, together with a number of their kinsmen and followers and a large body of Turks, and sent letters to them, demanding that they should surrender Jerusalem to him without warfare or shedding of blood. When they refused his demand, he opened an attack on the town, and having set up mangonels[3] against it, which effected a breach in the wall, he captured it and received the surrender of the Sanctuary of David[4] from Sukmān. On his entry into it, he shewed kindness and generosity to the two amīrs, and set both them and their supporters free. They arrived in Damascus during the first ten days of Shawwāl [September], and al-Afdal returned with his 'askar to Egypt.

---

[1] "A.H." centers the Muslim calendar like B.C. and A.D. center the Christian calendar. A.H. means the year of the Hegira, the year Muhammad fled Mecca for Medina and established the first Muslim society there. This was in 622 of the Christian calendar. But the lunar years of the Muslim calendar are shorter than the Christian by about 1/20. Thus, the corresponding year to A.H. 491 is 1098. [Ed.]

[2] Small military force of slaves and freed men, under Muslim amirs. [Ed.]

[3] A catapult that could hurl large stones as far as four hundred feet to break down a wall. [Ed.]

[4] The Citadel of Jerusalem.

In this year also the Franks set out with all their forces to Ma'arrat al-Nu'mān,[5] and having encamped over against it on 29th Dhu'l-Hijja [27th November], they opened an attack on the town and brought up a tower and scaling-ladders against it.

Now after the Franks had captured the city of Antioch through the devices of the armourer, who was an Armenian named Fīrūz,[6] on the eve of Friday, 1st Rajab [night of Thursday 3rd June], and a series of reports were received confirming this news, the armies of Syria assembled in uncountable force and proceeded to the province of Antioch, in order to inflict a crushing blow upon the armies of the Franks. They besieged the Franks until their supplies of food were exhausted and they were reduced to eating carrion; but thereafter the Franks, though they were in the extremity of weakness, advanced in battle order against the armies of Islām, which were at the height of strength and numbers, and they broke the ranks of the Muslims and scattered their multitudes. The lords of the pedigree steeds[7] were put to flight, and the sword was unsheathed upon the footsoldiers who had volunteered for the cause of God, who had girt themselves for the Holy War, and were vehement in their desire to strike a blow for the Faith and for the protection of the Muslims. This befel on Tuesday, the [twenty] sixth of Rajab, in this year [29th June, 1098].

A.H. 492

[28th November, 1098, to 16th November, 1099]

In Muharram of this year [December, 1098], the Franks made an assault on the wall of Ma'arrat al-Nu'mān from the east and north. They pushed up the tower until it rested against the wall, and as it was higher, they deprived the Muslims of the shelter of the wall. The fighting raged round this point until sunset on 14th Muharram [11th December], when the Franks scaled the wall, and the townsfolk were driven off it and took to flight. Prior to this, messengers had repeatedly come to them from the Franks with proposals for a settlement by negotiation and the surrender of the city, promising in return security for their lives and property, and the establishment of a [Frankish] governor amongst them, but dissension among the citizens and the fore-ordained decree of God prevented

---

[5] Ma'arrat al-Numān or Ma'arat al-Numān: Syrian city south of Antioch. The conquest of Antioch did not provide enough food, so the Crusaders marched on to this next city on route to Jerusalem. There they massacred the population of 10,000–20,000 and by some accounts cannibalized some of them. [Ed.]

[6] In the text Nairūz.

[7] Literally "of the short-haired and swift-paced."

acceptance of these terms. So they captured the city after the hour of the sunset prayer, and a great number from both sides were killed in it. The townsfolk fled to the houses of al-Ma'arra, to defend themselves in them, and the Franks, after promising them safety, dealt treacherously with them. They erected crosses over the town, exacted indemnities from the townsfolk, and did not carry out any of the terms upon which they had agreed, but plundered everything that they found, and demanded of the people sums which they could not pay. On Thursday 17th Safar [13th January, 1099] they set out for Kafr Tāb.

Thereafter they proceeded towards Jerusalem, at the end of Rajab [middle of June] of this year, and the people fled in panic from their abodes before them. They descended first upon al-Ramla, and captured it after the ripening of the crops. Thence they marched to Jerusalem, the inhabitants of which they engaged and blockaded, and having set up the tower against the city they brought it forward to the wall. At length news reached them that al-Afdal was on his way from Egypt with a mighty army to engage in the Holy War against them, and to destroy them, and to succour and protect the city against them. They therefore attacked the city with increased vigour, and prolonged the battle that day until the daylight faded, then withdrew from it, after promising the inhabitants to renew the attack upon them on the morrow. The townsfolk descended from the wall at sunset, whereupon the Franks renewed their assault upon it, climbed up the tower, and gained a footing on the city wall. The defenders were driven down, and the Franks stormed the town and gained possession of it. A number of the townsfolk fled to the sanctuary [of David], and a great host were killed. The Jews assembled in the synagogue, and the Franks burned it over their heads. The sanctuary was surrendered to them on guarantee of safety on the 22nd of Sha'bān [14th July] of this year, and they destroyed the shrines and the tomb of Abraham. Al-Afdal arrived with the Egyptian armies, but found himself forestalled, and having been reinforced by the troops from the Sāhil,[8] encamped outside Ascalon on 14th Ramadān [4th August], to await the arrival of the fleet by sea and of the Arab levies. The army of the Franks advanced against him and attacked him in great force. The Egyptian army was thrown back towards Ascalon, al-Afdal himself taking refuge in the city. The swords of the Franks were given mastery over the Muslims, and death was meted out to the footmen, volunteers, and townsfolk, about ten thousand souls, and the camp was plundered. Al-Afdal set out for Egypt with his officers, and the Franks besieged Ascalon, until at length the townsmen agreed to pay them twenty thousand dinars as protection money, and to deliver this sum to them forthwith. They

---

[8] The Sāhil was the general name given to the coastal plain and the maritime towns, from Ascalon to Bairūt.

therefore set about collecting this amount from the inhabitants of the town, but it befel that a quarrel broke out between the [Frankish] leaders, and they retired without having received any of the money. It is said that the number of the people of Ascalon who were killed in this campaign—that is to say of the witnesses, men of substance, merchants, and youths, exclusive of the regular levies—amounted to two thousand seven hundred souls.

6

RAYMOND OF ST. GILES, COUNT OF TOULOUSE

The Capture of Jerusalem by the Crusaders

The author of this letter or proclamation was the secular military leader chosen by Pope Urban II to lead the crusade. By the time of the capture of Jerusalem in 1099, he was certainly—with the Norman Bohemond and a couple other nobles—among the top military leaders. How does he account for their capture of Jerusalem? How would you explain it? Raymond tells how immediately after conquering Jerusalem, the Crusaders went to meet an Egyptian army (mistakenly identified as Babylonian) at Ascalon. How does Raymond explain their success? How did Ibn al-Qalanisi explain it? How might you explain it?

THINKING HISTORICALLY

What seems to be the purpose of this letter? How might Raymond's purpose color what he says? A letter can read much like a historical narrative, as does this one by Raymond of St. Giles. The author clearly wants to tell his readers what has happened. But this letter addressed to the pope, his bishops, and "the whole Christian people" is as much a testament to God's work as it is a history. Why does this make it difficult to construct the human narrative? Which events could you confidently include in your history of the crusade?

Source: Raymond of St. Giles, Count of Toulouse, "The Capture of Jerusalem by the Crusaders," *Translations and Reprints from the Original Sources of European History*, 4th ed., ed. D. C. Munro, vol. 1, bk. 4 (New York: AMC Press, Inc., 1971), 8–12.

To lord Paschal, pope of the Roman church,[1] to all the bishops, and to the whole Christian people, from the archbishop of Pisa, duke Godfrey, now, by the grace of God, defender of the church of the Holy Sepulchre, Raymond, count of St. Giles, and the whole army of God, which is in the land of Israel, greeting.

Multiply your supplications and prayers in the sight of God with joy and thanksgiving, since God has manifested His mercy in fulfilling by our hands what He had promised in ancient times. For after the capture of Nicaea, the whole army, made up of more than three hundred thousand soldiers, departed thence. And, although this army was so great that it could have in a single day covered all Romania and drunk up all the rivers and eaten up all the growing things, yet the Lord conducted them amid so great abundance that a ram was sold for a penny and an ox for twelve pennies or less. Moreover, although the princes and kings of the Saracens rose up against us, yet, by God's will, they were easily conquered and overcome. Because, indeed, some were puffed up by these successes, God opposed to us Antioch, impregnable to human strength. And there He detained us for nine months and so humbled us in the siege that there were scarcely a hundred good horses in our whole army. God opened to us the abundance of His blessing and mercy and led us into the city, and delivered the Turks and all of their possessions into our power.

Inasmuch as we thought that these had been acquired by our own strength and did not worthily magnify God who had done this, we were beset by so great a multitude of Turks that no one dared to venture forth at any point from the city. Moreover, hunger so weakened us that some could scarcely refrain from eating human flesh. It would be tedious to narrate all the miseries which we suffered in that city. But God looked down upon His people whom He had so long chastised and mercifully consoled them. Therefore, He at first revealed to us, as a recompense for our tribulation and as a pledge of victory, His lance which had lain hidden since the days of the apostles. Next, He so fortified the hearts of the men, that they who from sickness or hunger had been unable to walk, now were endued with strength to seize their weapons and manfully to fight against the enemy.

After we had triumphed over the enemy, as our army was wasting away at Antioch from sickness and weariness and was especially hindered by the dissensions among the leaders, we proceeded into Syria, stormed Barra and Marra, cities of the Saracens, and captured the fortresses in that country. And while we were delaying there, there was so great a famine in the army that the Christian people now ate the putrid bodies of the Saracens.[2] Finally, by the divine admonition, we entered

---

[1] Pope Paschal II (r. 1099–1118). [Ed.]

[2] Radulph of Caen, another Crusader chronicler, wrote, "In Ma'arra our troops boiled pagan adults alive in cooking-pots; they impaled children on spits and devoured them grilled." [Ed.]

into the interior of Hispania,[3] and the most bountiful, merciful and victorious hand of the omnipotent Father was with us. For the cities and fortresses of the country through which we were proceeding sent ambassadors to us with many gifts and offered to aid us and to surrender their walled places. But because our army was not large and it was the unanimous wish to hasten to Jerusalem, we accepted their pledges and made them tributaries. One of the cities forsooth, which was on the sea-coast, had more men than there were in our whole army. And when those at Antioch and Laodicea and Archas heard how the hand of the Lord was with us, many from the army who had remained in those cities followed us to Tyre. Therefore, with the Lord's companionship and aid, we proceeded thus as far as Jerusalem.

And after the army had suffered greatly in the siege, especially on account of the lack of water, a council was held and the bishops and princes ordered that all with bare feet should march around the walls of the city, in order that He who entered it humbly in our behalf might be moved by our humility to open it to us and to exercise judgment upon His enemies. God was appeased by this humility and on the eighth day after the humiliation He delivered the city and His enemies to us. It was the day indeed on which the primitive church was driven thence, and on which the festival of the dispersion of the apostles is celebrated. And if you desire to know what was done with the enemy who were found there, know that in Solomon's Porch and in his temple our men rode in the blood of the Saracens up to the knees of their horses.

Then, when we were considering who ought to hold the city, and some moved by love for their country and kinsmen wished to return home, it was announced to us that the king of Babylon had come to Ascalon with an innumerable multitude of soldiers. His purpose was, as he said, to lead the Franks, who were in Jerusalem, into captivity, and to take Antioch by storm. But God had determined otherwise in regard to us.

Therefore, when we learned that the army of the Babylonians was at Ascalon, we went down to meet them, leaving our baggage and the sick in Jerusalem with a garrison. When our army was in sight of the enemy, upon our knees we invoked the aid of the Lord, that He who in our other adversities had strengthened the Christian faith, might in the present battle break the strength of the Saracens and of the devil and extend the kingdom of the church of Christ from sea to sea, over the whole world. There was no delay; God was present when we cried for His aid, and furnished us with so great boldness, that one who saw us rush upon the enemy would have taken us for a herd of deer hastening to quench their thirst in running water. It was wonderful, indeed, since there were

---

[3] Probably a metaphor for an extremely fertile Muslim land, as Muslim Spain was known to be. [Ed.]

in our army not more than 5,000 horsemen and 15,000 foot-soldiers, and there were probably in the enemy's army 100,000 horsemen and 400,000 foot-soldiers. Then God appeared wonderful to His servants. For before we engaged in fighting, by our very onset alone, He turned this multitude in flight and scattered all their weapons, so that if they wished afterwards to attack us, they did not have the weapons in which they trusted. There can be no question how great the spoils were, since the treasures of the king of Babylon were captured. More than 100,000 Moors perished there by the sword. Moreover, their panic was so great that about 2,000 were suffocated at the gate of the city. Those who perished in the sea were innumerable. Many were entangled in the thickets. The whole world was certainly fighting for us, and if many of ours had not been detained in plundering the camp, few of the great multitude of the enemy would have been able to escape from the battle.

And although it may be tedious, the following must not be omitted: On the day preceding the battle the army captured many thousands of camels, oxen, and sheep. By the command of the princes these were divided among the people. When we advanced to battle, wonderful to relate, the camels formed in many squadrons and the sheep and oxen did the same. Moreover, these animals accompanied us, halting when we halted, advancing when we advanced, and charging when we charged. The clouds protected us from the heat of the sun and cooled us.

Accordingly, after celebrating the victory, the army returned to Jerusalem. Duke Godfrey remained there; the count of St. Giles, Robert, count of Normandy, and Robert, count of Flanders, returned to Laodicea. There they found the fleet belonging to the Pisans and to Bohemond. After the archbishop of Pisa had established peace between Bohemond and our leaders, Raymond prepared to return to Jerusalem for the sake of God and his brethren.

Therefore, we call upon you of the Catholic Church of Christ and of the whole Latin church to exult in the so admirable bravery and devotion of your brethren, in the so glorious and very desirable retribution of the omnipotent God, and in the so devoutedly hoped-for remission of all our sins through the grace of God. And we pray that He may make you—namely, all bishops, clerks, and monks who are leading devout lives, and all the laity—to sit down at the right hand of God, who liveth and reigneth God for ever and ever. And we ask and beseech you in the name of our Lord Jesus, who has ever been with us and aided us and freed us from all our tribulations, to be mindful of your brethren who return to you, by doing them kindnesses and by paying their debts, in order that God may recompense you and absolve you from all your sins and grant you a share in all the blessings which either we or they have deserved in the sight of the Lord. Amen.

7

IBN AL-ATHIR

The Conquest of Jerusalem

Ibn al-Athir* (1160–1233) was an influential Arab historian who
wrote a history of the first three Crusades,[1] having witnessed the
third himself. The following selection, taken from his work *The Perfect
History*, is one of the most authoritative, roughly contemporaneous
histories of the First Crusade from the Muslim perspective. What
reason does al-Athir give for the Egyptian capture of Jerusalem from
the Turks? Why were the Franks successful in wresting Jerusalem and
other lands from Muslim control? What is the significance of the
poem at the end of the selection?

THINKING HISTORICALLY

There are always more than two sides to a story, but it is certainly
useful to have battle descriptions from two sides of a conflict. In
constructing your own narrative of the battle of Jerusalem, you might
first look for points of agreement. On what points does Ibn al-Athir
agree with other accounts you have read? How else would you decide
which elements from each account to include in your narrative?

Taj ad-Daula Tutūsh was the Lord of Jerusalem but had given it as a
feoff to the amīr Suqmān ibn Artūq the Turcoman. When the Franks
defeated the Turks at Antioch the massacre demoralized them, and the
Egyptians, who saw that the Turkish armies were being weakened by
desertion, besieged Jerusalem under the command of al-Afdal ibn Badr
al-Jamali. Inside the city were Artūq's sons, Suqmān and Ilghazi, their
cousin Sunij and their nephew Yaquti. The Egyptians brought more than
forty siege engines to attack Jerusalem and broke down the walls at several points. The inhabitants put up a defense, and the siege and fighting
went on for more than six weeks. In the end the Egyptians forced the
city to capitulate, in Sha'bān 489 [August 1096]. Suqmān, Ilghazi, and
their friends were well treated by al-Afdal, who gave them large gifts of
money and let them go free. They made for Damascus and then crossed

---

* IH buhn   ahl AH tuhr
[1] Second Crusade (1147–1149); Third Crusade (1189–1192).

Source: Francesco Gabrieli, ed., *Arab Historians of the Crusades: Selected and Translated
from the Arabic Sources*, ed. and trans. E. J. Costello. Islamic World Series (Berkeley:
University of California Press, 1969), 10–12.

the Euphrates. Suqmān settled in Edessa and Ilghazi went on into Iraq. The Egyptian governor of Jerusalem was a certain Iftikhār ad-Daula, who was still there at the time of which we are speaking.

After their vain attempt to take Acre by siege, the Franks moved on to Jerusalem and besieged it for more than six weeks. They built two towers, one of which, near Sion, the Muslims burnt down, killing everyone inside it. It had scarcely ceased to burn before a messenger arrived to ask for help and to bring the news that the other side of the city had fallen. In fact Jerusalem was taken from the north on the morning of Friday 22 Sha'bān 492 [July 15, 1099]. The population was put to the sword by the Franks, who pillaged the area for a week. A band of Muslims barricaded themselves into the Oratory of David and fought on for several days. They were granted their lives in return for surrendering. The Franks honoured their word, and the group left by night for Ascalon. In the Masjid al-Aqsa the Franks slaughtered more than 70,000 people, among them a large number of Imams and Muslim scholars, devout and ascetic men who had left their homelands to live lives of pious seclusion in the Holy Place. The Franks stripped the Dome of the Rock of more than forty silver candelabra, each of them weighing 3,600 drams, and a great silver lamp weighing forty-four Syrian pounds, as well as a hundred and fifty smaller silver candelabra and more than twenty gold ones, and a great deal more booty. Refugees from Syria reached Baghdād in Ramadan,[2] among them the qadi Abu Sa'd al-Hárawi. They told the Caliph's ministers a story that wrung their hearts and brought tears to their eyes. On Friday they went to the Cathedral Mosque and begged for help, weeping so that their hearers wept with them as they described the sufferings of the Muslims in that Holy City: the men killed, the women and children taken prisoner, the homes pillaged. Because of the terrible hardships they had suffered, they were allowed to break the fast. . . .

It was the discord between the Muslim princes, as we shall describe, that enabled the Franks to overrun the country. Abu l-Muzaffar al-Abiwardi composed several poems on this subject, in one of which he says:

> We have mingled blood with flowing tears, and there is no room
>   left in us for Pity.
> To shed tears is a man's worst weapon when the swords stir up the
>   embers of war.
> Sons of Islām, behind you are battles in which heads rolled at
>   your feet.
> Dare you slumber in the blessed shade of safety, where life is as
>   soft as an orchard flower?
> How can the eye sleep between the lids at a time of disasters that
>   would waken any sleeper?

[2] The holy month of Ramadan, the month of fasting. [Ed.]

While your Syrian brothers can only sleep on the backs of their
   chargers, or in vultures' bellies!
Must the foreigners feed on our ignominy, while you trail behind
   you the train of a pleasant life, like men whose world is at peace?
When blood has been spilt, when sweet girls must for shame hide
   their lovely faces in their hands!
When the white swords' points are red with blood, and the iron of
   the brown lances is stained with gore!
At the sound of sword hammering on lance young children's hair
   turns white.
This is war, and the man who shuns the whirlpool to save his life
   shall grind his teeth in penitence.
This is war, and the infidel's sword is naked in his hand, ready to
   be sheathed again in men's necks and skulls.
This is war, and he who lies in the tomb at Medina seems to raise
   his voice and cry: "O sons of Hashim!
I see my people slow to raise the lance against the enemy: I see the
   Faith resting on feeble pillars.
For fear of death the Muslims are evading the fire of battle, refus-
   ing to believe that death will surely strike them."
Must the Arab champions then suffer with resignation, while the
   gallant Persians shut their eyes to their dishonour?

8

Letter from a Jewish Pilgrim in Egypt

The following letter was written in 1100 by an anonymous Jewish
pilgrim from Alexandria, unable to make his pilgrimage to Jerusalem
because of the ongoing war. How does the letter's author regard the
Egyptian sultan? How does he view the struggle between the sultan
and the Franks? What does this suggest about the lives of Jews under
Muslim rule during this time period?

THINKING HISTORICALLY

What does this letter add to your understanding of the Crusaders' capture of Jerusalem? How would you write a narrative of the First Crusade
that took advantage of Christian, Muslim, and Jewish sources?

Source: S. D. Goitein, trans., "Contemporary Letters on the Capture of Jerusalem by the Crusaders," *Journal of Jewish Studies* 3, no. 4 (1952): 162–77.

In Your Name, You Merciful.

If I attempted to describe my longing for you, my Lord, my brother *and cousin*,—may God prolong your days and make permanent your honour, success, happiness, health, and welfare; and . . . subdue your enemies—all the paper in the world would not suffice. My longing will but increase and double, just as the days will grow and double. May *the Creator of the World* presently make us meet together in joy when I return under His guidance to my homeland *and to the inheritance of my Fathers* in complete happiness, *so that we rejoice and be happy through His great mercy and His vast bounty; and thus may be His will*!

You may remember, my Lord, that many years ago I left our country to seek God's mercy and help in my poverty, to behold Jerusalem and return thereupon. However, when I was in Alexandria God brought about circumstances which caused a slight delay. Afterwards, however, "the sea grew stormy," and many armed bands made their appearance in Palestine; "*and he who went forth and he who came had no peace*," so that hardly one survivor out of a whole group came back to us from Palestine and told us that scarcely anyone could save himself from those armed bands, since they were so numerous and were gathered round . . . every town. There was further the journey through the desert, among [the bedouins] and whoever escaped from the one, fell into the hands of the other. Moreover, mutinies [spread throughout the country and reached] even Alexandria, so that we ourselves were besieged several times and the city was ruined; . . . the end however *was good*, for the Sultan—may God bestow glory upon his victories—conquered the city and caused justice to abound in it in a manner unprecedented in the history of any king in the world; not even a dirham was looted from anyone. Thus I had come to hope that because of his justice and strength God would give the land into his hands, and I should thereupon go to Jerusalem in safety and tranquility. For this reason I proceeded from Alexandria to Cairo, in order to start [my journey] from there.

When, however, God had given Jerusalem, the blessed, into his hands this state of affairs continued for too short a time to allow for making a journey there. The Franks arrived and killed everybody in the city, whether of *Ishmael or of Israel*; and the few who survived the slaughter were made prisoners. Some of these have been ransomed since, while others are still in captivity in all parts of the world.

Now, all of us had anticipated that our Sultan—may God bestow glory upon his victories—would set out against them [the Franks] with his troops and chase them away. But time after time our hope failed. Yet, to this very present moment we do hope that God will give his [the Sultan's] enemies into his hands. For it is inevitable that the armies will join in battle this year; and, if God grants us victory through him [the Sultan] and he conquers Jerusalem—and so it may be, with God's will—I for one shall not be amongst those who will linger, but shall go there to behold the city; and shall afterwards return straight to you—if God wills it. My salvation is in God, for this [is unlike] the other previous occasions [of making a pilgrimage to Jerusalem]. God, indeed, will exonerate me, since at my age I cannot afford to delay and wait any longer; I want to return home under any circumstances, if I still remain alive—whether I shall have seen Jerusalem or have given up the hope of doing it—both of which are possible.

You know, of course, my Lord, what has happened to us in the course of the last five years: the plague, the illnesses, and ailments have continued unabated for four successive years. As a result of this the wealthy became impoverished and a great number of people died *of the plague*, so that entire families perished in it. I, too, was affected with a grave illness, from which I recovered only about a year ago; then I was taken ill the following year so that (on the margin) for four years I have remained. . . . He who has said: *The evil diseases of Egypt* . . . he who hiccups does not live . . . ailments and will die . . . otherwise . . . will remain alive.

■ REFLECTIONS

The First Crusade (1095–1099) only marks the beginning of a protracted conflict between Christians and Muslims that continued until, perhaps, the eighteenth century. In the Holy Land there were intermittent conflicts over the next forty years culminating in what was called the Second Crusade, from 1147 to 1149. Meanwhile, the conquest of Muslims in Spain, which had been equated with the crusade by Pope Urban II, continued, as did frequent crusades into Eastern Europe.

The establishment of Latin kingdoms in Palestine could not be maintained without continual reinforcements, and they were vulnerable to Muslim attack. It was the loss of the Crusader state of Edessa that launched the Second Crusade. Instead the Crusaders conquered formerly friendly Damascus. A Muslim power struggle resulted in the rise of Saladin (c. 1138–1193), who united Egypt, Syria, and Iraq and conquered Jerusalem. This led to the Third Crusade (1189–1192), in which the kings of England, France, and Germany attempted to recapture Jerusalem. Their failure led to a German Crusade (1197–1198) that took Beirut and Sidon on the Mediterranean coast but was otherwise a failure. Then a large, mainly French Fourth Crusade (1202–1204) was mounted from Venice, but it resulted in the sacking of Constantinople in 1204, dealing an irreparable blow to the Byzantine Empire. A Fifth Crusade (1217–1229) recovered Jerusalem, which was retaken by the Muslims in 1244, leading to crusades initiated by King Louis IX of France. Other crusading armies invaded Egypt, Tunisia, Muslim Spain, northwest Africa, southern France, Poland,

Latvia, Germany, Russia, the Mongol Empire, Finland, Bosnia, and Italy, against papal enemies and Eastern Orthodox Christians as well as Muslims. Recent histories of the Crusades have ended their narratives in 1521, 1560, 1588, and 1798, according to Jonathan Riley-Smith, who ends the recent *Oxford History of the Crusades* with images of the Crusades in twentieth-century wars. Does the imagery of the Crusades still animate our wars?

Americans like former president George W. Bush have learned the effects of using the term *crusade* in the context of American aspirations in the Middle East, and the interference of Western forces in the region has been a constant reminder to Muslims of a long history of Western intervention that began with the First Crusade. In Syria, Lebanon, Jordan, Palestine, and Israel, one can still see Crusader castles looming over the landscape and meet the descendants and coreligionists of the founders of Crusader states. From the perspective of many Muslims, unquestioned U.S. support of Israel, especially in Jerusalem, is a direct continuation of the Crusades. On more than one occasion, leaders of Middle Eastern countries have pictured themselves as a modern-day Saladin rising to battle invading Christian Crusaders.

Writing a narrative of the First Crusade is difficult enough given the many sides to the conflict. Anna Comnena and the Orthodox Christians of Byzantium had a very different perspective than the Franks or Roman Christian Crusaders of Western Europe. Nor were Muslims a single force of opposition. The Seljuk Turks had different interests than the caliph of Baghdad, and, contrary to the opinion of Raymond St. Giles, the Fatimid Egyptian forces at Ascalon were neither biblical Babylonians nor Abbasids from Baghdad. Then, too, there were Jews, and those in Germany may have had different interests than those in Egypt, despite an agreement about Christian crusading. There are more sources than we have been able to explore here, and more interpretations than we have been able to include.

After trying your hand at writing a narrative of the First Crusade, you might think of how narratives are constructed. Each story leaves out some information to include other information, lest it read like a phone book. How do you decide whose "numbers" to include? To stimulate your thoughts about narrative choices, you might choose a subject a little closer to home so that you have greater knowledge of the primary sources. Try a narrative of your own life up to now. If you dare, ask someone close to you to point out what you missed or overemphasized.

11

Raiders of Steppe and Sea: Vikings and Mongols

Eurasia and the Atlantic, 900–1350

■ HISTORICAL CONTEXT

Ever since the first urban settlements emerged five thousand years ago, they have been at risk of attack. The domestication of the horse and the development of sailing ships about four thousand years ago increased that risk. Much of ancient history is the story of the conflict between settled peoples and raiders on horseback or sailors on fleet ships. Eventually—between the third and fifth centuries C.E.—the great empires of Rome and Han dynasty China succumbed to raiding nomadic tribes from Central Asia. As nomadic peoples settled themselves, new waves of raiders appeared.

In the previous chapter, we explored the impact of the Seljuk Turks who conquered cities in the Middle East that had been taken hundreds of years earlier by Arab armies on horseback. At about the same time as the Turks emerged from Central Asia to threaten settlements south of the great Eurasian steppe grasslands, a new force from the north, Viking raiders on sailing ships, burst across the northern seas to attack the coastal enclaves and river cities of Europe and what came to be known in their wake as Russia. As generations oscillated between raiding and trading, new waves of Norsemen explored the edges of known waters to plant new settlements as far west as Iceland, Greenland, and North America. (See Map 11.1.) Who were these people? What did they hope to accomplish? How were they different from the land-raiders who preceded them?

At about the time that the Vikings were becoming farmers and settlers in their conquered lands, around the year 1200, the Eurasian steppe exploded with its last and largest force of nomadic tribesmen

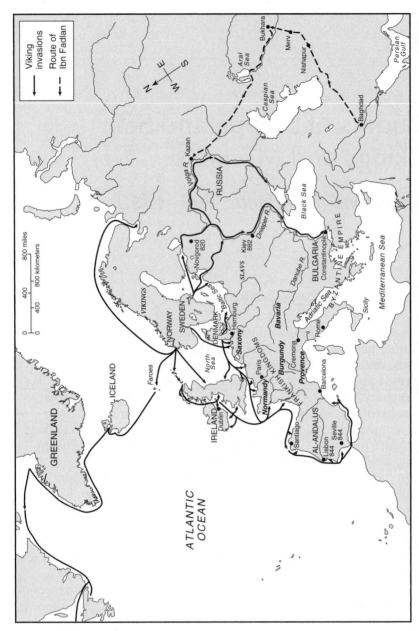

Map 11.1 Viking Invasions and Voyages of the Ninth and Tenth Centuries.

on horseback: the Mongols. Between the election of Chingis (or Genghis) Khan* (c. 1162–1227) as the Khan of Khans in 1206 and the pandemic plague known as the Black Death of 1346–1350 (or the end of the Mongol Yuan dynasty in China in 1368), the Mongols swept across Eurasia and created the largest empire the world had ever seen. (See Map 11.2.) Who were the Mongols? What made them so successful? How were they similar to, and different from, the Norsemen?

What was the impact of these raiding peoples on settled societies? How did they change each other? How did they change themselves? How did they create some of the conditions necessary for the modern world to come into being?

■ THINKING HISTORICALLY

Distinguishing Historical Understanding from Moral Judgments

The ancient Greeks called non-Greeks "barbarians" (because their languages contained "bar-bar"-like sounds that seemed foreign, untutored, and, thus, uncivilized). Since then the terms *barbarian* and *civilized* have been weighted with the same combination of descriptive and moral meaning. In the nineteenth century it was even fashionable among historians and anthropologists to use these terms to distinguish between nomadic peoples and settled, urban peoples. As our first reading (and perhaps modern common sense) makes clear, rural or nomadic people are not necessarily less "moral" than city people; technological development is hardly the same thing as moral development (or the opposite).

What connection, if any, is there between history and morality? Stories of the past are frequently used to celebrate or condemn past individuals or groups. Sometimes we find past behavior shocking or reprehensible. Is it logical or proper to make moral judgments about the past? Can historians find answers to moral questions by studying the past?

Perhaps the place to begin is by recognizing that just as the "is" is different from the "ought," so too the "was" is different from the "should have been." Historians must begin by finding out what was. Our own moral values may lead us to ask certain questions about the past, but the historian's job is only to find out what happened. We will see in the following selections how difficult it has been for past observers to keep their own moral judgments from coloring their descriptions of

* chihn GIHZ kahn

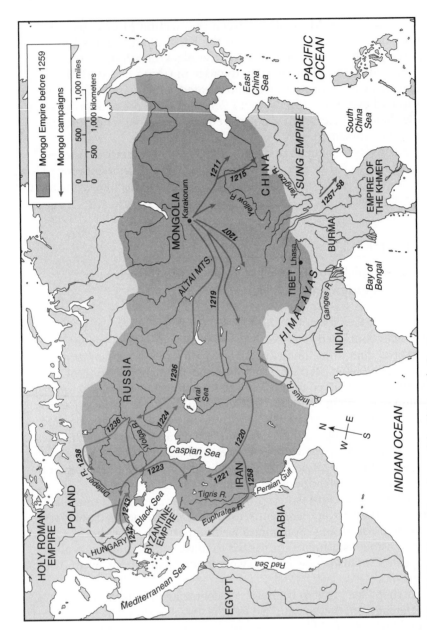

Map 11.2 Mongol Invasions of the Thirteenth Century.

peoples and events they found disagreeable. This part of our study may help us realize how our own moral feelings affect our responses.

Then, assuming we have established the facts fairly, can our moral sentiments legitimately come into play? As "consumers" of history, readers, and thinking people, we cannot avoid making judgments about the past. Under what conditions are such judgments fair, helpful, or appropriate? We will explore this much larger and more complex question in this chapter.

1

GREGORY GUZMAN

Were the Barbarians a Negative or Positive Factor in Ancient and Medieval History?

Gregory Guzman is a modern world historian. In this essay he asks some questions about the peoples who have been called "barbarians." How were the lives of pastoral nomads different from those of settled people? How did the horse shape life on the steppe? How effective were these herders as rulers of settled societies? What were the achievements of the pastoral nomads?

THINKING HISTORICALLY

Why, according to Guzman, have most histories of the barbarians made them look bad? How have city people or historians let their own prejudices block an appreciation of the achievements of pastoralists?

According to the general surveys of ancient and medieval history found in most textbooks, barbarian peoples and/or primitive savages repeatedly invaded the early Eurasian civilized centers in Europe, the Middle East, India, and China. All accounts of the early history of these four civilizations contain recurrent references to attacks by such familiar and famous barbarians as the Hittites, Hyksos, Kassites, Aryans, Scythians, Sarmatians, Hsiung-nu, Huns, Germans, Turks,

Source: Gregory Guzman, "Were the Barbarians a Negative or Positive Factor in Ancient and Medieval History?" *The Historian* 50 (August 1988): 558–72.

and Mongols, and they also record the absorption and assimilation of these Inner Asian barbarian hordes into the respective cultures and lifestyles of the more advanced coastal civilizations. The early sources generally equate the barbarians with chaos and destruction. The barbarians are presented as evil and despicable intruders, associated only with burning, pillaging, and slaughtering, while the civilized peoples are portrayed as the good and righteous forces of stability, order, and progress.

But it must be remembered that most of these early sources are not objective; they are blatantly one-sided, biased accounts written by members of the civilized societies. Thus, throughout recorded history, barbarians have consistently received bad press—bad PR to use the modern terminology. By definition, barbarians were illiterate, and thus they could not write their own version of events. All written records covering barbarian-civilized interaction came from the civilized peoples at war with the barbarians—often the sedentary peoples recently defeated and overwhelmed by those same barbarians. Irritated and angered coastal historians tended to record and emphasize only the negative aspects of their recent interaction with the barbarians. These authors tended to condemn and denigrate the way their barbarian opponents looked and to associate them with the devil and evil, rather than to report with objectivity what actually happened. For example, the Roman historian Ammianus Marcellinus, whose description is distorted by hatred and fear, described the barbarians as "two-footed beasts, seemingly chained to their horses from which they take their meat and drink, never touching a plough and having no houses." While living in Jerusalem, St. Jerome also left a vivid description of the Huns who ". . . filled the whole earth with slaughter and panic alike as they flittered hither and thither on their swift horses. . . . They were at hand everywhere before they were expected; by their speed they outstripped rumor, and they took pity neither upon religion nor rank nor age nor wailing childhood. Those who had just begun to live were compelled to die. . . ."

Such reports obviously made the barbarians look bad, while their nomadic habits and practices, which differed from those of the sedentary coastal peoples, were clearly portrayed as inferior and less advanced: the incarnation of evil itself. These horror-filled and biased descriptions were not the accounts of weak and defenseless peoples. Rather, they were written by the citizens of the most advanced and powerful states and empires in Europe, the Middle East, India, and China. The individual barbarian tribes were, nevertheless, able to attack and invade these strong and well-organized civilized states with relative impunity—pillaging and killing almost at will.

Several important questions, not addressed by the ancient and medieval historians, need to be answered here. Who were these barbarians? Why and how did they manage to repeatedly defeat and overwhelm so easily the wealthiest and most advanced civilizations of the day? And why were they so vehemently condemned and hated in recorded history, if these barbarian Davids were able to consistently defeat such mighty Goliath civilized centers? Since the rich and populous civilized states enjoyed tremendous advantages in the confrontations, why have the barbarians so often been denied the popular role of the underdog?

In the process of answering those questions, this study would like to suggest that maybe the barbarians were not really the "bad guys." While they may not deserve to be called the "good guys," they made a much more positive contribution to human civilization than presented in the grossly distorted written sources. The barbarians deserve much more credit than they have been given, for they created a complex pastoral lifestyle as an alternative to sedentary agriculture, and in that achievement they were not subhuman savages only out to loot, pillage, and destroy. As this study will show, the barbarians played a much more positive and constructive role in the development and diffusion of early human history than that with which they are usually credited.

Before proceeding further, it is necessary to identify these much-maligned barbarians and describe how their way of life and their basic practices differed from those of the sedentary coastal peoples in order to better evaluate the barbarian role and its impact on the history of humanity.

In terms of identity, the barbarians were the steppe nomads of Inner Asia or Central Eurasia. This area represents one of the toughest and most inhospitable places in the world in which to survive. The climate of the interior of the large Eurasian landmass is not moderated by the distant seas, resulting in extremes of climate, of hot and cold, wet and dry. It is an area of ice, forest, desert, and mountains—with bitter winds, dust, and poor soil. Unlike the coastal regions with their dependable moisture and warmth, the soil of Inner Asia was too cold, poor, and dry for agriculture; thus the sedentary urban lifestyle of the coastal civilized centers was not an option in the Eurasian heartland. The people living there had to be tough to endure such a hostile environment, where they constantly fought both nature and other people for survival.

Due to necessity, the people of Inner Asia were nomads, wandering in search of food and pasture, and they became herdsmen, shepherds, and warriors. These steppe nomads, the barbarians of recorded history, were frequently nothing more than migrants looking for new homes; these people needed little encouragement to seek safety, security, and better living conditions in the warm, rich, and fertile coastal civilization centers. Thus the steppe barbarians were not always savage marauders coming only to loot and pillage. Many of the so-called barbarian invaders constituted a surplus population which harsh Inner Asia could not support, or they represented whole tribes being pushed out of their ancestral homeland by stronger tribes behind them. At any rate, these repeated waves of nomadic peoples leaving the steppes soon encountered the coastal civilizations.

These Inner Asian barbarians were more or less harmless outsiders until the horse dramatically changed their lifestyle on the vast steppes. They adopted the pastoral system as the best way of providing for basic needs. The natural pasture provided by the steppe grassland proved ideal for grazing large herds and flocks of animals. Soon their whole life revolved around their animals; they became shepherds, herders, and keepers of beasts. . . .

The dominant feature of this emerging barbarian pastoralism was its mounted nature; it was essentially a horse culture by 1000 B.C. At first small horses were kept only for food and milk, but bigger horses eventually led to riding. Once an accomplished fact, mounted practices dramatically changed the lifestyle of the barbarian steppe peoples. Horseback riding made the tending of scattered herds faster and less tiring, and it enlarged the size of herds while increasing the range of pastoral movement. It also made possible, when necessary, the total migration of entire tribes and clans. Mastery of the horse reduced the vast expanses of steppe pasturage to more manageable proportions. Steppe nomads moved twice a year between traditional winter and summer pastures; the spring and fall were spent moving between the necessary grazing grounds. All peoples and possessions moved with regularity; the nomads became used to living in the saddle, so to speak.

The horse thus became the center of pastoral life on the steppes. The barbarian nomads could literally live off their animals which provided meat, milk, and hides for clothing, coverings, boots, etc. Tools and weapons were made from the bones and sinews, and dried dung was used as fuel. The barbarians ate, sold, negotiated, slept, and took care of body functions in the saddle. . . . These mounted practices led to the emergence of the centaur motif in Middle Eastern art, as the civilized people tended to view the horse and rider as one inseparable unit.

Military action also became an integral part of nomadic steppe life. Warfare was simply cavalry action by the pastoral herdsmen who served as soldiers for the duration of the conflict. Steppe military service differed little from the normal, on-the-move pastoral life. Large-scale steppe alliances were hard to organize and even harder to hold together among the independent nomads. Such temporary alliances, called hordes, rose swiftly to great strength and power, but they usually declined and disintegrated just as quickly.

At any rate, these barbarian nomads were tough and hardy warriors. The horse gave them speed and mobility over both the light and heavily armed infantry of the civilized centers, but for this speed and mobility the barbarians gave up any type of defensive armor. They learned to guide their horses with their knees, since both arms needed to be free for the bow and arrow, their primary offensive weapon. . . .

Early civilized armies had no cavalry. The famous Macedonian phalanx and the formidable Roman legions contained only light and heavily armed infantry. At first these brave foot soldiers had no tactical maneuvers to face and contain a barbarian cavalry charge. Even more devastating was the storm of arrows raining down upon them long before they could engage in the traditional hand-to-hand combat. The formidable steppe cavalry thus subjected civilized defenses to continuous pressure. Every nomad with a horse and bow was a potential front-line soldier who was tough, resourceful, and ferocious, whereas only a small percentage of the civilized population was equipped and trained for war. The nomadic lifestyle and the speed of the horse eliminated the need for expensive and heavy metal armor and its accompanying technological skills. Cavalry tactics gave an initial military advantage to the barbarians and the mounted horsemen won most of the early battles. The best defense against barbarian cavalry was an insurmountable obstacle, a wall. . . .

Since they had the military advantage of cavalry tactics, the steppe nomads attacked and conquered various coastal civilizations with regularity. In a typical conquest, the victorious barbarians were the new military/political rulers. These new rulers possessed strengths obvious to all. The barbarians had vigorous and dynamic leadership; good, able, and charismatic leadership had been needed to organize the independent nomads into an effective horde in the first place. The new rulers had the complete loyalty of their followers; their group identity based on common blood and ancestors resulted in an intense personal and individual allegiance and commitment.

The first century after the initial conquest was usually an era of dynamic leadership, good government, and economic prosperity, as nomadic strengths mixed with the local advances and practices of that civilization. The new ruling family was often a fusion of the best of both sides as the barbarian victors married into the previous ruling dynasty. This brought forth an age of powerful and successful rulers, and produced an era of energetic leadership, good government, low taxes, agricultural revival, and peace. . . .

After this early period of revitalized and dynamic rule, slow decline usually set in. Royal vigor and ability sank as the rulers became soft, both mentally and physically. Without physical exercise and self-discipline, the rulers became overindulgent, instantly acquiring everything they wanted—excessive amounts of food or drink, harems, puppets, and yes-men as advisers. At the same time court rivalries and internal divisiveness began to emerge once the strong unity required for the conquest was no longer needed. A rivalry that often arose was between the ruler and various groups of his followers. . . . His steppe horsemen began to give first loyalty to their new family land rather than to their individual leader who was now weak, impaired, and soft. Such internal rivalries weakened the central government and led to chaos and civil wars. Thus, a civilized center was ripe for the next series of invasions and conquest. . . .

The barbarians can and should be viewed as representing a dynamic and vital element in human history for they periodically revived many stagnating coastal civilizations. Many of these sedentary centers flourished, growing rich and powerful. In the process they also became conservative, settled into a fixed routine. Preferring the status quo, they tended to use old answers and ways to face new problems and issues, and as a consequence they lost the vitality and flexibility required for healthy and progressive growth.

The barbarians were active and dynamic. In their conquests of civilized centers, they frequently destroyed and eliminated the old and outdated and preserved and passed on only the good and useful elements. Sometimes, the mounted invaders also introduced new ideas and practices. Some of these new barbarian innovations (horseback riding, archery, trousers, and boots, etc.) fused with the good and useful practices of the sedentary peoples. . . . The ongoing encounters with barbarian strangers inevitably fostered innovation and progress in the civilized centers. . . .

It can be argued that barbarians also played a positive role in the spread and diffusion of civilization itself. The four major Eurasian civilization centers were separated from each other by deserts, mountains, and the vast expanses of the steppe heartland of Inner Asia. In its early stages each civilization was somewhat isolated from the others. Overland trade and contact was possible only through the barbarian steppe highway which stretched over five thousand miles across Eurasia, from Hungary to Manchuria. There was little early sea contact between the four sedentary centers, as naval travel was longer and more dangerous than the overland routes.

Thus the steppe barbarians were the chief agency through which the ideas and practices of one civilization were spread to another before 1500 A.D. According to [historian] William H. McNeill, there was much conceptual diffusion carried along the steppe highway by the barbarians. Writing originated in the ancient Middle East. The concept, not the form, of writing then spread eastward from the Middle East, as the Indian and Chinese forms and characters were significantly different than Middle Eastern cuneiform. The making and use of bronze and chariots also spread from the Middle East to Europe, India, and China. Chariots were introduced to China, on the eastern end of the steppe highway, a few centuries after their appearance in the Middle East. Needless to say, this type of early cultural diffusion is difficult to document with any degree of certainty, but enough evidence exists to make it highly probable, even if not scientifically provable.

The late medieval period provides even more examples of cultural diffusion via the movement of barbarians along the Inner Asian steppe highway. The great Eurasian *Pax Mongolica*[1] opened the way for much cultural cross-fertilization in the late-thirteenth and early-fourteenth centuries. Chinese inventions like gunpowder and printing made their way to the Middle East and Europe in this period. Records show that Chinese artillerymen accompanied the Mongol armies into the Middle East. Papal envoys like John of Plano Carpini and William of Rubruck traveled to the Mongol capital of Karakorum in the 1240s and 1250s. In the 1280s, Marco Polo brought with him from Kublai Khan's court in China a Mongol princess to be the bride of the Mongol Khan of Persia. . . .

This cultural interaction and exchange between Eurasian coastal civilizations ended with the collapse of the Mongol Khanates in Persia and China in the mid-fourteenth century. The barbarian Mongols, therefore, provided the last period of great cultural cross-fertilization before the modern age.

Historical evidence that exists enables one to argue that the barbarian nomads played an active and positive role in the history of mankind. The barbarian invaders revitalized stagnant and decaying civilizations and were responsible for a certain amount of cultural diffusion between emerging ancient and medieval civilizations. The traditional portrayal of barbarians as mere marauders and destroyers is misleading and incorrect. Unfortunately this is the usual role they are given when historians center their study of the past narrowly on the civilized centers and the biased written sources produced by those peoples. All too often historians tend to adopt and reflect the biases and values of their subjects under study, and thus continue to denigrate and condemn all barbarians without objectively evaluating their real contributions to human development. The study of the steppe nomads, the barbarians, is just as valid a topic for historical analysis as the traditional study of coastal sedentary civilizations. Only by knowing and understanding the pastoral barbarian can historians accurately evaluate the constant interaction between the two lifestyles and come to understand the full picture of humanity's early growth and development in the ancient and medieval periods of Eurasian history.

---

[1] Mongolian Peace, after the *Pax Romana*, or Roman Peace. [Ed.]

IBN FADLAN

The Viking Rus

In 921 the Muslim caliph of Baghdad sent Ibn Fadlan* on a mission to the king of the Bulgars.[1] The Muslim king of the Bulgars may have been looking for an alliance with the caliph of Baghdad against the Khazars, sandwiched between them just west of the Caspian Sea. North and west of the Bulgars was the area that became Ukraine and Russia. The Volga River, which had its source in the Ural Mountains, flowed north through this land into the Baltic Sea. In the eighth and ninth centuries this area was inhabited by various tribes, many of which spoke early Slavic languages. At some point these tribes were united under the command of a people called the Rus. The origins of the Rus are disputed, but most experts believe that they were either Vikings or the descendants of Vikings and Slavs.

Ibn Fadlan provides our earliest description of these Rus (or Northmen, as he calls them here), whom he encountered on the Volga near the modern city of Kazan during his trip to the Bulgar king. (See Map 11.1 on page 388 for his route.) They or their ancestors had sailed downriver from the Baltic Sea on raiding and trading expeditions. What does Ibn Fadlan tell us about these Scandinavian raiders who gave their name to Russia?

THINKING HISTORICALLY

Notice Ibn Fadlan's moral judgments about the Viking Rus. Notice your own moral judgments. How are Ibn Fadlan's judgments different from your own? What do you think accounts for those differences?

I saw how the Northmen had arrived with their wares, and pitched their camp beside the Volga. Never did I see people so gigantic; they are tall as palm trees, and florid and ruddy of complexion. They wear neither camisoles nor *chaftans*,[2] but the men among them wear a garment of

---

* IH buhn fahd LAHN

[1] These Bulgars, with a Muslim king, had recently been forced north of the Caspian Sea (while other Bulgars moved west to what is today Bulgaria where they were converted to Christianity by Byzantium).

[2] Probably means no fine or fitted tops or robes; but see later description of funeral. [Ed.]

Source: Albert Stanborough Cook, "Ibn Fadlan's Account of Scandinavian Merchants on the Volga in 922," *Journal of English and Germanic Philology* 22, no. 1 (1923): 56–63.

rough cloth, which is thrown over one side, so that one hand remains free. Every one carries an axe, a dagger, and a sword, and without these weapons they are never seen. Their swords are broad, with wavy lines, and of Frankish make. From the tip of the finger-nails to the neck, each man of them is tattooed with pictures of trees, living beings, and other things. The women carry, fastened to their breast, a little case of iron, copper, silver, or gold, according to the wealth and resources, of their husbands. Fastened to the case they wear a ring, and upon that a dagger, all attached to their breast. About their necks they wear gold and silver chains. If the husband possesses ten thousand dirhems, he has one chain made for his wife; if twenty thousand, two; and for every ten thousand, one is added. Hence it often happens that a Scandinavian woman has a large number of chains about her neck. Their most highly prized ornaments consist of small green shells, of one of the varieties which are found in [the bottoms of] ships. They make great efforts to obtain these, paying as much as a dirhem for such a shell, and stringing them as a necklace for their wives.

They are the filthiest race that God ever created. They do not wipe themselves after going to stool, nor wash themselves after a nocturnal pollution, any more than if they were wild asses.

They come from their own country, anchor their ships in the Volga, which is a great river, and build large wooden houses on its banks. In every such house there live ten or twenty, more or fewer. Each man has a couch, where he sits with the beautiful girls he has for sale. Here he is as likely as not to enjoy one of them while a friend looks on. At times several of them will be thus engaged at the same moment, each in full view of the others. Now and again a merchant will resort to a house to purchase a girl, and find her master thus embracing her, and not giving over until he has fully had his will.

Every morning a girl comes and brings a tub of water, and places it before her master. In this he proceeds to wash his face and hands, and then his hair, combing it out over the vessel. Thereupon he blows his nose, and spits into the tub, and, leaving no dirt behind, conveys it all into this water. When he has finished, the girl carries the tub to the man next [to] him, who does the same. Thus she continues carrying the tub from one to another till each of those who are in the house has blown his nose and spit into the tub, and washed his face and hair.

As soon as their ships have reached the anchorage, every one goes ashore, having at hand bread, meat, onions, milk, and strong drink, and betakes himself to a high, upright piece of wood, bearing the likeness of a human face; this is surrounded by smaller statues, and behind these there are still other tall pieces of wood driven into the ground. He advances to the large wooden figure, prostrates himself before it, and thus addresses it: "O my Lord, I am come from a far country, bringing with me so and so many girls, and so and so many pelts of sable" [or, marten]; and when he has thus enumerated all his merchandise, he continues, "I have brought thee this present," laying before the wooden statue what he has brought, and saying: "I desire thee to bestow upon me a purchaser who has gold and silver coins, who will buy from me to my heart's content, and who will refuse none of my demands." Having so said, he departs. If his trade then goes ill, he returns and brings a second, or even a third present. If he still continues to have difficulty in obtaining what he desires, he brings a present to one of the small statues, and implores its intercession, saying: "These are the wives and daughters of our lord." Continuing thus, he goes to each statue in turn, invokes it, beseeches its intercession, and bows humbly before it. If it then chances that his trade goes swimmingly, and he disposes of all his merchandise, he reports: "My lord has fulfilled my desire; now it is my duty to repay him." Upon this, he takes a number of cattle and sheep, slaughters them, gives a portion of the meat to the poor, and carries the rest before the large statue and the smaller ones that surround it, hanging the heads of the sheep and cattle on the large piece of wood which is planted in the earth. When night falls, dogs come and devour it all. Then he who has so placed it exclaims: "I am well pleasing to my lord; he has consumed my present."

If one of their number falls sick, they set up a tent at a distance, in which they place him, leaving bread and water at hand. Thereafter they never approach nor speak to him, nor visit him the whole time, especially if he is a poor person or a slave. If he recovers and rises from his sick bed, he returns to his own. If he dies, they cremate him; but if he is a slave they leave him as he is till at length he becomes the food of dogs and birds of prey.

If they catch a thief or a robber, they lead him to a thick and lofty tree, fasten a strong rope round him, string him up, and let him hang until he drops to pieces by the action of wind and rain.

I was told that the least of what they do for their chiefs when they die, is to consume them with fire. When I was finally informed of the death of one of their magnates, I sought to witness what befell. First they laid him in his grave—over which a roof was erected—for the space of ten days, until they had completed the cutting and sewing of his clothes. In the case of a poor man, however, they merely build for him a boat, in which they place him, and consume it with fire. At the death of a rich man, they bring together his goods, and divide them into three parts. The first of these is for his family; the second is expended for the garments they make; and with the third they purchase strong drink, against the day when the girl resigns herself to death, and is burned with her master. To the use of wine they abandon themselves in mad fashion, drinking it day and night; and not seldom does one die with the cup in his hand.

When one of their chiefs dies, his family asks his girls and pages: "Which one of you will die with him?" Then one of them answers, "I."

From the time that he [or she] utters this word, he is no longer free: should he wish to draw back, he is not permitted. For the most part, however, it is the girls that offer themselves. So, when the man of whom I spoke had died, they asked his girls, "Who will die with him?" One of them answered, "I." She was then committed to two girls, who were to keep watch over her, accompany her wherever she went, and even, on occasion, wash her feet. The people now began to occupy themselves with the dead man — to cut out the clothes for him, and to prepare whatever else was needful. During the whole of this period, the girl gave herself over to drinking and singing, and was cheerful and gay.

When the day was now come that the dead man and the girl were to be committed to the flames, I went to the river in which his ship lay, but found that it had already been drawn ashore. Four corner-blocks of birch and other woods had been placed in position for it, while around were stationed large wooden figures in the semblance of human beings. Thereupon the ship was brought up, and placed on the timbers above mentioned. In the mean time the people began to walk to and fro, uttering words which I did not understand. The dead man, meanwhile, lay at a distance in his grave, from which they had not yet removed him. Next they brought a couch, placed it in the ship, and covered it with Greek cloth of gold, wadded and quilted, with pillows of the same material. There came an old crone, whom they call the angel of death, and spread the articles mentioned on the couch. It was she who attended to the sewing of the garments, and to all the equipment; it was she, also, who was to slay the girl. I saw her; she was dark, . . . thickset, with a lowering countenance.

When they came to the grave, they removed the earth from the wooden roof, set the latter aside, and drew out the dead man in the loose wrapper in which he had died. Then I saw that he had turned quite black, by reason of the coldness of that country. Near him in the grave they had placed strong drink, fruits, and a lute; and these they now took out. Except for his color, the dead man had not changed. They now clothed him in drawers, leggings, boots, and a *kurtak* and *chaftan* of cloth of gold, with golden buttons, placing on his head a cap made of cloth of gold, trimmed with sable! Then they carried him into a tent placed in the ship, seated him on the wadded and quilted covering, supported him with the pillows, and, bringing strong drink, fruits, and basil, placed them all beside him. Then they brought a dog, which they cut in two, and threw into the ship; laid all his weapons beside him; and led up two horses which they chased until they were dripping with sweat, whereupon they cut them in pieces with their swords, and threw the flesh into the ship. Two oxen were then brought forward, cut in pieces, and flung into the ship. Finally they brought a cock and a hen, killed them, and threw them in also.

The girl who had devoted herself to death meanwhile walked to and fro, entering one after another of the tents which they had there. The occupant of each tent lay with her, saying, "Tell your master, 'I [the man] did this only for love of you.'"

When it was now Friday afternoon, they led the girl to an object which they had constructed, and which looked like the framework of a door. She then placed her feet on the extended hands of the men, was raised up above the framework, and uttered something in her language, whereupon they let her down. Then again they raised her, and she did as at first. Once more they let her down, and then lifted her a third time, while she did as at the previous times. They then handed her a hen, whose head she cut off and threw away; but the hen itself they cast into the ship. I inquired of the interpreter what it was that she had done. He replied: "The first time she said, 'Lo, I see here my father and mother'; the second time, 'Lo, now I see all my deceased relatives sitting'; the third time, 'Lo, there is my master, who is sitting in Paradise. Paradise is so beautiful, so green. With him are his men and boys. He calls me, so bring me to him.'" Then they led her away to the ship.

Here she took off her two bracelets, and gave them to the old woman who was called the angel of death, and who was to murder her. She also drew off her two anklets, and passed them to the two servingmaids, who were the daughters of the so-called angel of death. Then they lifted her into the ship, but did not yet admit her to the tent. Now men came up with shields and staves, and handed her a cup of strong drink. This she took, sang over it, and emptied it. "With this," so the interpreter told me, "she is taking leave of those who are dear to her." Then another cup was handed her, which she also took, and began a lengthy song. The crone admonished her to drain the cup without lingering, and to enter the tent where her master lay. By this time, as it seemed to me, the girl had become dazed [or, possibly, crazed]; she made as though she would enter the tent, and had brought her head forward between the tent and the ship, when the hag seized her by the head, and dragged her in. At this moment the men began to beat upon their shields with the staves, in order to drown the noise of her outcries, which might have terrified the other girls, and deterred them from seeking death with their masters in the future. Then six men followed into the tent, and each and every one had carnal companionship with her. Then they laid her down by her master's side, while two of the men seized her by the feet and two by the hands. The old woman known as the angel of death now knotted a rope around her neck, and handed the ends to two of the men to pull. Then with a broad-bladed dagger she smote her between the ribs, and drew the blade forth while the two men strangled her with the rope till she died.

The next of kin to the dead man now drew near, and, taking a piece of wood, lighted it, and walked backwards toward the ship holding the stick in one hand, with the other placed upon his buttocks (he being naked), until the wood which had been piled under the ship was ignited. Then the others came up with staves and firewood, each one carrying a stick already lighted at the upper end, and threw it all on the pyre. The pile was soon aflame, then the ship, finally the tent, the man, and the girl, and everything else in the ship. A terrible storm began to blow up, and thus intensified the flames, and gave wings to the blaze.

At my side stood one of the Northmen, and I heard him talking with the interpreter, who stood near him. I asked the interpreter what the Northman had said, and received this answer: "'You Arabs,' he said, 'must be a stupid set! You take him who is to you the most revered and beloved of men, and cast him into the ground, to be devoured by creeping things and worms. We, on the other hand, burn him in a twinkling, so that he instantly, without a moment's delay, enters into Paradise.' At this he burst out into uncontrollable laughter, and then continued: 'It is the love of the Master [God] that causes the wind to blow and snatch him away in an instant.'" And, in very truth, before an hour had passed, ship, wood, and girl had with the man, turned to ashes.

Thereupon they heaped over the place where the ship had stood something like a rounded hill, and erecting on the centre of it a large birchen post, wrote on it the name of the deceased, along with that of the king of the Northmen. Having done this, they left the spot.

3

BARRY CUNLIFFE

The Western Vikings

The Vikings who sailed down the rivers of Russia to raid, trade, and settle came mainly from eastern Scandinavia — what is today Sweden and Finland. Their cousins in western Scandinavia sailed to the south and west. In this selection from a wide-ranging history of the European Atlantic world, the author, a modern archaeologist, discusses the expansion of Western Vikings — mainly Danes and Norwegians — into the Atlantic. How would you compare the expansion of the Western Vikings with that of the Eastern Vikings into what became Russia?

Source: Barry Cunliffe, *Facing the Ocean: The Atlantic and Its Peoples* (Oxford: Oxford University Press, 2001), 482–83, 488–95, 499, 514–16.

THINKING HISTORICALLY

The modern historian lets us hear enough from the medieval victims of the Vikings for us to feel their fear, and his list of destroyed cities and massacred peoples registers the horror they must have unleashed in their era. But Cunliffe also puts the Viking attacks in a longer-term historical perspective. How does that longer-term perspective change your reaction to the Viking raids?

The Coming of the Northmen

About 790 Beaduheard, the king's reeve[1] at Dorchester in southern Britain, got news that three foreign ships had landed at Portland and, assuming them to be traders, he went to welcome them. He was wrong. They were raiders from Scandinavia and he died for his mistake. The Dorset landing was a foretaste. A few years later, in 793, the raiding began in earnest with the attack on the monastery of St. Cuthbert on Lindisfarne:[2] "Never before has such terror appeared in Britain as we have now suffered from a pagan race, nor was it thought that such an inroad from the sea could be made. Behold, the church of St. Cuthbert spattered with the blood of the priests of God, despoiled of all its ornaments; a place more venerable than all in Britain is given as prey to pagan people." So wrote the English cleric Alcuin at the court of Charlemagne. Many more raids followed around the coasts of Britain and Ireland. The Franks were soon to suffer, so too the Bretons.[3] By the 840s Viking war bands were exploring further south along the Atlantic coasts. A vast fleet of 150 ships sailed up the Garonne and plundered almost to Toulouse.[4] Then it moved onwards to attack Galicia and Lisbon before sailing into the Guadalquivir.[5] Here, from their base on the Isla Menor, the Vikings pillaged Seville but were severely mauled by the Moors. Those captured were hanged from the city's palm trees, and two hundred Viking heads were sent by the Emir to his allies in Tangier as an effective witness to his military prowess. Undeterred, the Viking force continued through the Straits of Gibraltar harassing the coasts as they sailed to the mouth of the Rhône where, on an island in the Camargue,[6] a base was established for raiding upriver into the heart of France and across the sea to the coasts of Italy. In 861 they returned to their base on the Loire. The expedition had been "at once profitable and honourable."

[1] Representative. [Ed.]
[2] Island off the northwest coast of Britain. [Ed.]
[3] People of Brittany, northwest France. [Ed.]
[4] City in south central France. [Ed.]
[5] River in southern Spain. [Ed.]
[6] Marshland in Rhône River delta. [Ed.]

The Mediterranean venture, while a notable feat, was of little lasting consequence. But meanwhile, in the north, raids and settlement had reached significant proportions. Some indication of what was going on is given by the pained lamentation of Ermentarius, a monk at Noirmoutier,[7] writing in the 860s:

> The number of ships increases, the endless flood of Vikings never ceases to grow bigger. Everywhere Christ's people are the victims of massacre, burning, and plunder. The Vikings overrun all that lies before them, and no one can withstand them. They seize Bordeaux, Périgueux, Limoges, Angoulême, Toulouse; Angers, Tours, and Orleans are made deserts. Ships past counting voyage up the Seine . . . Rouen is laid waste, looted, and burnt; Paris, Beauvais, Meaux are taken, Melun's stronghold is razed to the ground, Chartres occupied, Evreux and Bayeux looted, and every town invested. . . .

Why the Raids of the Northmen Began

The raids of the Danes and Norwegians began in the last decade of the eighth century, and over the next seventy years rose to a devastating crescendo. No single factor was responsible for unleashing the fury, but there can be little doubt that the overseas ventures became possible only after the longship had reached its peak of excellence by the middle of the eighth century. The Scandinavian landscape demanded good shipping. The long Atlantic coastline of Norway, with its deeply indented fjords, was accessible with ease only by sea, while the sounds and islands of Denmark had, for millennia, been bound together by boat. The Baltic, too, was a cradle for navigation—a great inland sea providing ease of access between the extensive littorals[8] and their productive hinterlands, and to the river routes penetrating far south across the North European Plain. Throughout Scandinavia settlements favoured the sea coasts and the inland lakes and waterways. They faced the open water and kept their backs to the forest. Thus communities depended upon ships for their livelihood, their rulers able to maintain their power only by command of the sea. In such a world it is easy to see how the ship became a symbol of authority, honed to perfection to reflect the status of the elite. A ship, either real or symbolic, might also accompany its owner in his burial. . . . By the early years of the ninth century, all the features characteristic of the classic Viking ship had been brought together, creating fast and highly efficient seagoing vessels suitable for carrying men across the ocean in search of land and plunder.

---

[7] Atlantic island off France. [Ed.]
[8] Coasts. [Ed.]

. . . In the course of the eighth century, trade between continental Europe and England developed apace, with well-established links leading northwards to the Baltic. In this way the volume of mercantile traffic in the southern North Sea increased dramatically, while the rulers of Denmark became increasingly aware of the wealth to be had to the south. Through the various traders who visited the Scandinavian ports they would also have learnt the political geography of western Europe— most notably the whereabouts of its rich, isolated monasteries and the distracting factional disputes endemic among its ruling households. To the Scandinavian elite there was much prestige to be had in leading a successful raid: the spoils would enrich the begetters and would bind followers closer to their leader. In the competitive emulation which accompanied the early raiding expeditions the number, intensity, and duration of the raids inevitably escalated.

Another, quite different, factor at work was the desire for new land to settle. With a growing population the narrow coastal zone of Norway was too restricted a territory to provide the social space needed for enterprising sons to establish themselves. The only solution was to find new territories overseas in Britain and Ireland, and further afield on the more remote islands of the north Atlantic. For the most part what was sought was new farmland, like the home territories, where families could set up new farms with plenty of space around for expansion by successive generations. It was this that the north Atlantic could supply in plenty. What England had to offer was rather different but no less acceptable—well-run estates which new Scandinavian lords could leave largely undisturbed, simply taking the profits.

Another incentive to moving overseas was the possibility of setting up merchant colonies emulating those that were so successful in the Baltic and along the eastern coasts of the North Sea. York, already a developing English market, was taken over by the Northmen in 866 and rapidly expanded to become the principal entrepôt[9] in northern Britain, while an entirely new port-of-trade was established at Dublin and soon became a centre for Irish Sea commerce. In all of these ventures the ship was vital.

It would be wrong to give the impression that overseas activities were narrowly focused: trading could soon turn into raiding, while raiding could dissipate itself into settlement. One was never exclusive of the other. This is evocatively summed up in an account of the lifestyle of Svein Asleifarson recorded in the twelfth-century *Orkneyinga Saga*, no doubt referring wistfully to a long-gone era when Vikings behaved like Vikings:

> In the spring he had more than enough to occupy him, with a great deal of seed to sow which he saw to carefully himself. Then when the job was done, he would go off plundering in the Hebrides and

---

[9] Storage site for trade goods. [Ed.]

in Ireland on what he called his "spring-trip," then back home just after midsummer where he stayed till the cornfields had been reaped and the grain was safely in. After that he would go off raiding again, and never came back till the first month of winter was ended. This he used to call his "autumn trip."

The Vikings in the West: A Brief Progress

. . . *Viking* is the word frequently used by the English sources to describe raiders and settlers from Scandinavia, while the Carolingian sources prefer *Northmen*. Both words include, without differentiation, Danes and Norwegians. Until the mid-ninth century it is possible to make a broad distinction between Norwegians, who settled northern and western Scotland and the Northern and Western Isles and were active in the Irish Sea, and Danes, who raided the North Sea and Channel coasts, but thereafter the distinction becomes blurred.

The progress of the settlement of north-western Britain by the Norwegians is unrecorded, but contact began as early as the seventh century and it is quite likely that the colonization was largely completed during the course of the eighth century. The newly settled areas provided the springboard for attacks on Ireland and the Irish Sea coasts, becoming increasingly widespread and frequent in the period 795–840. The rich and unprotected monasteries were the target. Iona[10] was attacked three times, in 795, 802, and 806, in the first flush of activity. Thereafter raids thrust further and further south—821 Wexford, 822 Cork, and 824 the isolated monastery of Skelling Michael in the Atlantic off the Kerry coast.[11] Having picked off the vulnerable coastal communities the attacks then began to penetrate inland, but usually no more than 30 kilometres or so from the safety of navigable water. These early attacks were opportunistic hit-and-run affairs, meeting no significant organized opposition.

Meanwhile in the North Sea the Danes adopted similar tactics. In 820 a massive Danish fleet of two hundred vessels threatened Saxony, and in three successive years, beginning in 834, the great trading port of Dorestad[12] was devastated. Frisia[13] became the immediate focus of contention. In 838 the Danish king Harik demanded of the Frankish king Louis that "The Frisians be given over to him"—a request that was roundly refused. The vulnerability of the coast was vividly brought

---

[10] Island off Scotland. [Ed.]

[11] These are places in modern Ireland. [Ed.]

[12] City in modern Netherlands. [Ed.]

[13] North Sea coast from modern Netherlands to Germany; people spoke Frisian (close to English). [Ed.]

home when, in 835, the monastery of St. Philibert on the island of Noir-moutier south of the Loire estuary was attacked. England suffered only sporadic raids at first, but these intensified in the 830s. . . .

The events of 840–865 saw the Scandinavians working the full length of the Atlantic zone from the Rhine to Gibraltar and beyond, but they were at their most active and most persistent along the major rivers—the Seine, the Thames, the Loire, and the Garonne—feeding off the cities that owed their wealth and well-being to their command of the river routes. The rivers that brought them their commercial advantage through access to the sea now brought men who sought to take it for themselves.

The 860s saw a change of pace from raid to settlement, accompa-nied by intensified and co-ordinated opposition by those whose land the Northmen were intent on taking. The Franks were the first to come to terms with the new reality by building fortified bridges across the rivers Seine and Loire, by fortifying towns and monasteries, and by paying tribute to groups of Vikings in return for protection or military services. These tactics protected the heart of the kingdom while leaving the lower reaches of the two rivers to the roving bands of invaders who had now taken up residence in the areas. The strategy kept Frankia free from fur-ther incursions until a new wave of attacks began on Paris in 885. . . .

Towards the end of the tenth century, with the rise of a strong dynasty in Denmark under Harald Bluetooth and his son, Sven Forkbeard, a new phase of Viking raiding was initiated, and once more it was the Atlantic coastal regions as far south as Iberia that took the brunt of the attack. England was particularly vulnerable. In 991 Sven Forkbeard led his first raid against the English, his activities culminating in the conquest of the kingdom in 1013. Three years later, after his death, his son Knut was formally recognized as king of England. Dynastic squabbles and claims and counter-claims to the English throne rumbled on through-out the eleventh century, but the failure of the threatened Danish con-quest of England to materialize in 1085 was the effective end of the Viking episode. Occasional Norwegian expeditions to the Northern and Western Isles were the last ripples, three centuries after the Viking wave first struck.

The Northmen and the Atlantic Communities

That the impact of the Scandinavians on the Atlantic communities was profound and lasting there can be no doubt, but sufficient will have been said to show that it varied significantly from region to region.

In lightly inhabited or empty lands like the Northern and Western Isles, the Faroes, Iceland, and Greenland, Scandinavian culture was directly transplanted in its entirety and flourished much in the style of the Norwegian homeland, but elsewhere the Scandinavian component fused with indigenous culture. In regions where the local systems were well established and comparatively stable, as in eastern England and the maritime region of France (soon to become Normandy), the new order emerged imperceptibly from the old with little disruption to the social or economic balance, but in other areas, like Ireland, where warfare between rival factions of the elite was endemic, the Scandinavian presence was a catalyst for widespread change. Here the ferocity of the Irish warlords matched their own. For this reason the small enclaves established at harbours around the coast remained small, developing as isolated trading colonies in an otherwise hostile landscape. Apart from certain areas of the north-east, large-scale land-taking and settlement was not possible. Much the same pattern can be seen in south-west Wales.

The Scandinavian settlements of the Irish Sea zone chose good docking facilities, initially to serve as protected anchorages for the vessels of the early raiders, but these quickly developed as trading centres, making the Irish Sea the major focus of exchange in the Scandinavian maritime system. From here ships might go south to Andalucía, north to Iceland and beyond, or around Britain eastwards to the Baltic. In this way the Irish Sea became the hub of a complex network of communications built upon the long-distance exchange systems which had already been established in the preceding centuries.

In Brittany a rather different pattern of interaction emerged. Here the long-term hostility between the Bretons and the Franks provided a situation in which raiding and mercenary activity could profitably be maintained, while the internecine warfare that broke out in both kingdoms in the painful periods when succession was being contested offered the raiders further opportunities for easy intervention. Throughout this time the Loire formed the focus of Scandinavian activity and Nantes was often in their control, but there is, as yet, little evidence that a major trading enclave developed here. It may simply have been that the political turmoil in the region allowed warfare in its various modes to provide the necessary economic underpinning to sustain Viking society. From the Breton point of view the Scandinavian presence, disruptive though it was, was an important factor in helping to maintain their independence from the Franks.

South of the Loire, Viking military activity was sporadic and superficial, at least in so far as the historical record allows us to judge, but given their interest in trade it is difficult to believe that there were not regular visits by merchants to the Gironde and Garonne and along the Atlantic seaboard of Iberia. In this they would simply have been following the routes plied by their predecessors.

Some measure of the integration of the multifaceted maritime system that emerged is provided by a wreck excavated at Skuldelev in the Danish fjord of Roskilde. It was one of six that had been sunk to block the fjord from seaward attack some time in the late eleventh or early twelfth century. The vessel was a typical Viking longship suitable for carrying fifty to sixty warriors. Dendrochronology has shown that the ship had been built about 1060 at, or in the vicinity of, Dublin. What service it saw as a raiding vessel in the seas around Britain and France we will never know, but its final resting place 2,200 kilometres from the yard in which it had been built is a vivid reminder of the capacity of the sea in bringing the communities of Atlantic Europe ever closer together.

4

Eirik's Saga

Scandinavian seafarers spread out in all directions in the tenth century. While Swedes and Finns sailed down the rivers of Russia to the Black and Caspian seas, Danes conquered and colonized from England down the coast of France into the Mediterranean as far as Italy, North Africa, and Arabia. The Vikings of Norway sailed mainly westward, colonizing Iceland, Greenland, and North America (certainly Newfoundland but likely further south). The Norsemen discovered Iceland in about 860 and began settlement some fourteen years later. By 930, Iceland contained the families and retainers of many lords who fled western Norway to escape the conquering Harald Fairhair.

Eirik the Red (950–1003) came to Iceland with his family in 960 after his father had to flee Norway because of "some killings." In turn, Eirik was exiled from Iceland in 982 after he committed murder in the heat of two quarrels. Exile meant searching for a settlement even further west, leading Eirik to Greenland. Although not the first to see or land in Greenland, Eirik established the first colony there.

Insofar as it captures the oral tradition, this excerpt from "Eirik's Saga," written about 1260, gives us an idea of Viking thought in the tenth century. What kind of world does it portray? How does it contribute to your understanding of the Viking expansion?

THINKING HISTORICALLY

How does this internal view of Viking society inevitably change our moral perspective from that of an outsider? How might the differences between Ibn Fadlan and this author lead to different moral perspectives?

Source: "Eirik's Saga," in *The Vinland Sagas: The Norse Discovery of America*, trans. and introduction by Magnus Magnusson and Hermann Palsson (Harmondsworth, Middlesex, England: Penguin Books, 1965), 75–78.

There was a warrior king called Olaf the White, who was the son of King Ingjald. Olaf went on a Viking expedition to the British Isles, where he conquered Dublin and the adjoining territory and made himself king over them. He married Aud the Deep-Minded, the daughter of Ketil Flat-Nose; they had a son called Thorstein the Red.

Olaf was killed in battle in Ireland, and Aud and Thorstein the Red then went to the Hebrides. There Thorstein married Thurid, the daughter of Eyvind the Easterner; they had many children.

Thorstein the Red became a warrior king, and joined forces with Earl Sigurd the Powerful, together they conquered Caithness, Sutherland, Ross, and Moray, and more than half of Argyll. Thorstein ruled over these territories as king until he was betrayed by the Scots and killed in battle.

Aud the Deep-Minded was in Caithness when she learned of Thorstein's death; she had a ship built secretly in a forest, and when it was ready she sailed away to Orkney. There she gave away in marriage Groa, daughter of Thorstein the Red.

After that, Aud set out for Iceland; she had twenty freeborn men aboard her ship. She reached Iceland and spent the first winter with her brother Bjorn at Bjarnarhaven. Then she took possession of the entire Dales district between Dogurdar River and Skraumuhlaups River, and made her home at Hvamm. She used to say prayers at Kross Hills; she had crosses erected there, for she had been baptized and was a devout Christian.

Many well-born men, who had been taken captive in the British Isles by Vikings and were now slaves, came to Iceland with her. One of them was called Vifil; he was of noble descent. He had been taken prisoner in the British Isles and was a slave until Aud gave him his freedom.

When Aud gave land to members of her crew, Vifil asked her why she did not give him some land like the others. Aud replied that it was of no importance, and said that he would be considered a man of quality wherever he was. She gave him Vifilsdale, and he settled there. He married, and had two sons called Thorbjorn and Thorgeir; they were both promising men, and grew up with their father.

Eirik Explores Greenland

There was a man called Thorvald, who was the father of Eirik the Red. He and Eirik left their home in Jaederen because of some killings and went to Iceland. They took possession of land in Hornstrands, and made their home at Drangar. Thorvald died there, and Eirik the Red then married Thjodhild, and moved south to Haukadale; he cleared land there and made his home at Eirikstead, near Vatnshorn.

Eirik's slaves started a landslide that destroyed the farm of a man called Valthjof, at Valthjofstead; so Eyjolf Saur, one of Valthjof's kinsmen, killed the slaves at Skeidsbrekkur, above Vatnshorn. For this, Eirik killed Eyjolf Saur; he also killed Hrafn the Dueller, at Leikskalar. Geirstein and Odd of Jorvi, who were Eyjolf's kinsmen, took action over his killing, and Eirik was banished from Haukadale.

Eirik then took possession of Brok Island and Oxen Island, and spent the first winter at Tradir, in South Island. He lent his benchboards to Thorgest of Breidabolstead. After that, Eirik moved to Oxen Island, and made his home at Eirikstead. He then asked for his benchboards back, but they were not returned; so Eirik went to Breidabolstead and seized them. Thorgest pursued him, and they fought a battle near the farmstead at Drangar. Two of Thorgest's sons and several other men were killed there.

After this, both Eirik and Thorgest maintained a force of fighting-men at home. Eirik was supported by Styr Thorgrimsson, Eyjolf of Svin Island, Thorbjorn Vifilsson, and the sons of Thorbrand of Alptafjord; Thorgest was supported by Thorgeir of Hitardale, Aslak of Langadale and his son Illugi, and the sons of Thord Gellir.

Eirik and his men were sentenced to outlawry at the Thorsness Assembly. He made his ship ready in Eiriksbay, and Eyjolf of Svin Island hid him in Dimunarbay while Thorgest and his men were scouring the islands for him.

Thorbjorn Vifilsson and Styr and Eyjolf accompanied Eirik out beyond the islands, and they parted in great friendship; Eirik said he would return their help as far as it lay within his power, if ever they had need of it. He told them he was going to search for the land that Gunnbjorn, the son of Ulf Crow, had sighted when he was driven westwards off course and discovered the Gunnbjarnar Skerries; he added that he would come back to visit his friends if he found this country.

Eirik put out to sea past Snæfells Glacier, and made land near the glacier that is known as Blaserk. From there he sailed south to find out if the country were habitable there. He spent the first winter on Eiriks Island, which lies near the middle of the Eastern Settlement. In the spring he went to Eiriksfjord, where he decided to make his home. That summer he explored the wilderness to the west and gave names to many landmarks there. He spent the second winter on Eiriks Holms, off Hvarfs Peak. The third summer he sailed all the way north to Snæfell and into Hrafnsfjord, where he reckoned he was farther inland than the head of Eiriksfjord. Then he turned back and spent the third winter on Eiriks Island, off the mouth of Eiriksfjord.

He sailed back to Iceland the following summer and put in at Breidafjord. He stayed the winter with Ingolf of Holmlatur. In the spring he fought a battle with Thorgest of Breidabolstead and was defeated. After that a reconciliation was arranged between them.

That summer Eirik set off to colonize the country he had discovered; he named it *Greenland*, for he said that people would be much more tempted to go there if it had an attractive name.

5

YVO OF NARBONA

The Mongols

Within a couple of generations after 1206, a nomadic tribe of herders from the grasslands of Central Asia created a mounted army that conquered an expanse from the Pacific coast of Asia to Eastern Europe. With the conquest of the Islamic caliphate at Baghdad in 1258 and Song dynasty China by 1276, Mongols ruled about a hundred million people, having killed about thirty million others. They ruled almost a third of the human population and the largest land empire the world had ever known. Who were they? How did they manage such a feat? What were its costs?

To help answer some of those questions, we have a selection from a letter written in 1243 from one Yvo of Narbona[1] (we know nothing else about him) to the archbishop of Bordeaux, France. Yvo has just witnessed the conquest of Hungary by a Mongol army. He describes what he saw and also relates the account of an Englishmen (also unknown, even by name) who worked for the Mongols as an interpreter before he escaped amidst the Mongol withdrawal from Hungary. What does this document tell us about the Mongols? What does it suggest about the reasons for their rapid expansion? What does it suggest about their impact?

THINKING HISTORICALLY

No people before modern times received greater condemnation than the Mongols. Their negative reputation originated in the writings of their victims almost immediately after Chingis Khan expanded

---

[1] Narbona, or Narbonne, was a Mediterranean port city in what is today southern France.

Source: Samuel Purchas, *Hakluytus Posthumus or Purchas His Pilgrimes: Contayning a History of the World, in Sea voyages & lande-Trauells, by Englishmen & others [with Purchas his Pilgrimage or Relations of the world]* (London: William Stanley for Henrie Featherstone 1625–26) 5 vols., 183–87. Spelling modernized and Americanized.

Mongol power into China and Central Asia in the 1210s and 1220s. The second-generation Mongol onslaught on Russia and Europe had a similar impact. Here we get an eyewitness account of the Mongol invasion of Hungary in 1241. Actually, we have two accounts: the tale of an Englishman who served as interpreter for the Mongols is contained within the letter of Yvo, who was also a witness. Which of these two witnesses is more objective, or less moralistic? What examples do you see of either witness judging rather than describing? What descriptions do not seem factually based? What examples do you see of either witness interpreting Mongol behavior in a favorable light?

Part of an Epistle written by one Yvo of Narbona unto the Archbishop of Bordeaux, containing the confession of an Englishman as touching the barbarous demeanor of the Tartars,[2] which had lived long among them, and was drawn along perforce with them in their expedition against Hungary: Recorded by Mathew Paris in the year of our Lord 1243.

The Lord therefore being provoked to indignation, by reason of this and other sins committed among us Christians, is become, as it were, a destroying enemy, and a dreadful avenger.[3] This I may justly affirm to be true, because a huge nation, and a barbarous and inhumane people, whose law is lawless, whose wrath is furious, even the rod of Gods anger, overruns and utterly wastes infinite countries, cruelly abolishing all things where they come, with fire and sword. And this present summer, the foresaid nation, being called Tartars, departing out of Hungary,[4] which they had surprised by treason, laid siege unto the very same town, wherein I myself abode, with many thousands of soldiers: neither were there in the said town on our part above 50 men of war, whom, together with 20 crossbows, the captain had left in garrison. All these, out of certain high places, beholding the enemies vast army, and abhorring the beastly cruelty of Anti-Christ his accomplices, signified forthwith unto their governor, the hideous lamentations of his Christian subjects, who suddenly being surprised in all the province adjoining, without any difference or respect of condition, fortune, sex, or age, were by manifold

---

[2] The Mongols were misidentified as "Tatars" (another central Asian people), which then became "Tartars," probably to suggest people of "Tartarus," the underground place of punishment in Greek mythology, that is, devils. [Ed.]

[3] Like the prophets of ancient Israel, Christians interpreted invasions as God's punishment for their sins. [Ed.]

[4] The Mongols invaded Hungary in 1241 under Batu Khan, the grandson of Chingis Khan. They withdrew in the spring of 1242 because of the death of Ogodei, the successor to Chingis, to return to Mongolia to choose the next Great Khan. [Ed.]

cruelties, all of them destroyed[5]: with whose carcasses, the Tartarian chieftains, and their brutish and savage followers, glutting themselves, as with delicious cakes, left nothing for vultures but the bare bones. And a strange thing it is to consider, that the greedy and ravenous vultures disdained to prey upon any of the relics, which remained. Old and deformed women they gave, as it were for daily sustenance, unto their Cannibals[6]: the beautiful devoured they not, but smothered them lamenting and scratching, with forced and unnatural ravishments. Like barbarous miscreants, they quelled virgins unto death, and cutting off their tender paps[7] to present for dainties unto their magistrates, they engorged themselves with their bodies.[8]

. . . In the meantime crying from the top of a high mountain, the Duke of Austria, the King of Bohemia, the Patriarch of Aquileia, the Duke of Carinthia, and (as some report) the Earl of Baden, with a mighty power, and in battle array, approaching towards them, that accursed crew immediately vanished,[9] and all those Tartarian vagabonds retired themselves into the distressed and vanquished land of Hungary; who as they came suddenly, so they departed also on the sudden: which their celerity[10] caused all men to stand in horror and astonishment of them. But of the said fugitives, the prince of Dalmatia took eight: one of which number the Duke of Austria knew to be an English man, who was perpetually banished out of the Realm of England, in regard of certain notorious crimes by him committed. This fellow, on the behalf of the most tyrannical king of the Tartars, had been twice, as a messenger and interpreter, with the king of Hungary, menacing and plainly foretelling the mischief which afterward happened, unless he would submit himself and his kingdom unto the Tartars yoke. Well, being allured by our Princes to confess the truth, he made such oaths and protestations, as (I think) the devil himself would have been trusted for. First therefore he reported of himself, that presently after the time of his banishment, namely about the 30th year of his age, having lost all that he had in the city of Acon[11] at dice, even in the midst of Winter, being compelled by ignominious hunger, wearing nothing about him but a shirt of sack, a

[5] The Mongols normally spared women and children. In this case they killed all the captives before returning to Mongolia. [Ed.]

[6] The charge of cannibalism is contested by modern historians. The Mongols would sometimes eat horse meat, mice, lice, and the afterbirth of foals, but the eating of human flesh was a rare occurrence, confined to threats of starvation. [Ed.]

[7] Breasts. [Ed.]

[8] Rape was common among all medieval armies, as was the selection of young women for slaves or harems, but the charges of cutting off their breasts are almost certainly fictional since that would make captured women less valuable. [Ed.]

[9] A classic Mongol tactic was a pretended retreat followed by an ambush, but this may refer to the return to Mongolia. [Ed.]

[10] Speed. [Ed.]

[11] Acre, in modern north-coastal Israel. Captured by the Crusaders in 1104 and again in 1191. Stronghold of Crusader state until 1291 fall to Mamluks. [Ed.]

pair of shoes, and a hair cap only, being shaven like a fool, and uttering an uncouth noise as if he had been dumb, he took his journey, and so travelling many countries, and finding in divers places friendly entertainment, he prolonged his life in this manner for a season, albeit every day by rashness of speech, and inconstancy of heart, he endangered himself to the devil. At length, by reason of extreme travail, and continual change of air and of meats in Chaldea,[12] he fell into a grievous sickness insomuch that he was weary of his life. Not being able therefore to go forward or backward, and staying there a while to refresh himself, he began (being somewhat learned) to commend to writing those words which he heard spoken, and within a short space, so aptly to pronounce, and to utter them himself, that he was reputed for a native member of that country: and by the same dexterity he attained to many languages. This man the Tartars having intelligence of by their spies, drew him perforce into their society: and being admonished by an oracle or vision, to challenge dominion over the whole earth, they allured him by many rewards to their faithful service, by reason that they wanted Interpreters. But concerning their manners and superstitions, of the disposition and stature of their bodies, of their country and manner of fighting etc., he protested the particulars following to be true: namely, that they were above all men, covetous, hasty, deceitful, and merciless: notwithstanding, by reason of the rigor and extremity of punishments to be inflicted upon them by their superiors, they are restrained from brawling, and from mutual strife and contention. The ancient founders and fathers of their tribes, they call by the name of gods,[13] and at certain set times they do celebrate solemn feasts unto them, many of them being particular, and but four only general. They think that all things are created for themselves alone. They esteem it no offense to exercise cruelty against rebels. They are hardy and strong in the breast, lean and pale-faced, rough and hug-shouldered, having flat and short noses, long and sharp chins, their upper jaws are low and declining, their teeth long and thin, their eye-brows extending from their foreheads down to their noses, their eyes inconstant and black, their countenances writhen and terrible, their extreme joints strong with bones and sinews, having thick and great thighs, and short legs, and yet being equal unto us in stature: for that length which is wanting in their legs, is supplied in the upper parts of their bodies. Their country in old time was a land utterly desert and waste,[14] situated far beyond Chaldea, from whence they have expelled lions, bears, and such like untamed beasts, with their bows, and other engines. Of the hides of beasts being tanned,

---

[12] Mesopotamia; modern Iraq. [Ed.]

[13] Might refer to elements of ancestor worship in traditional Mongol belief system of Tengriism, which also included elements of shamanism, anamism, and totenism, but Chingis Khan recognized the numerous religions of Central Asia (including Christianity, Buddhism, and Islam) and so maintained religious tolerance. [Ed.]

[14] Bordered by desert in the south and forests in the north, the steppe is relatively treeless and dry but with ample grass for grazing. [Ed.]

they use to shape for themselves light but yet impenetrable armor. They ride fast bound unto their horses, which are not very great in stature, but exceedingly strong, and maintained with little provender.[15] They used to fight constantly and valiantly with javelins, maces, battle-axes, and swords. But especially they are excellent archers, and cunning warriors with their bows. Their backs are slightly armed, that they may not flee. They withdraw not themselves from the combat till they see the chief standard of their general give back. Vanquished, they ask no favor, and vanquishing, they show no compassion. They all persist in their purpose of subduing the whole world under their own subjection, as if they were but one man, and yet they are more than millions in number.[16] They have 60,000 couriers, who being sent before upon light horses to prepare a place for the army to encamp in, will in the space of one night gallop three days journey. And suddenly diffusing themselves over a whole province, and surprising all the people thereof unarmed, unprovided, dispersed, they make such horrible slaughters, that the king or prince of the land invaded, cannot find people sufficient to wage battle against them, and to withstand them. They delude all people and princes of regions in time of peace, pretending that for a cause, which indeed is no cause. Sometimes they say that they will make a voyage to Cologne to fetch home the three wise kings into their own country;[17] sometimes to punish the avarice and pride of the Romans,[18] who oppressed them in times past;[19] sometimes to conquer barbarous and Northern nations; sometimes to moderate the fury of the Germans[20] with their own meek mildness; sometimes to learn warlike feats and stratagems of the French; sometimes for the finding out of fertile ground to suffice their huge multitudes; sometimes again in derision they say that they intend to go on pilgrimage to St. James of Galicia.[21] In regard of which slights and collusions certain indiscreet governors concluding a league with them, have granted them free passage through their territories, which leagues notwithstanding being violated, were an occasion of ruin and destruction unto the governors, etc.

---

[15] Food. [Ed.]

[16] A likely exaggeration. Probably more like a million. Individual armies like Batu's probably numbered something like 30,000. Total forces of 500,000 might have been possible. All Mongol men rode in battle. All enemies were killed or enslaved. At its height the Mongol Empire might have ruled 100 million people. On the other hand, Mongol rule depleted the population of that empire by tens of millions. [Ed.]

[17] Cologne, in modern Germany. A medieval legend told of how the three kings who visited Jesus were reburied together in St. Peter's church in Cologne. [Ed.]

[18] "Romans" is a general term for Christians of Western Europe. [Ed.]

[19] May refer to the Roman Empire or to Christian Crusades, or it may conflate both. [Ed.]

[20] The German Teutonic Knights fought Crusades to Christianize the Baltic, Poland, and Hungary in the thirteenth century. [Ed.]

[21] Santiago De Compostela, in northwest Spain; a pilgrimage site, said to be the burial place of St. James. [Ed.]

The Secret History of the Mongols

This Mongol account records the early years of Mongol expansion under Chingis Khan, the founder of the empire. Born Temujin in 1155 or 1167, this son of a minor tribal chieftain attracted the support of Mongol princes in the years between 1187 and 1206 through a series of decisive military victories over other tribes and competing Mongol claimants to the title of Great Khan.

The Mongols were illiterate before the time of Chingis Khan, who adopted the script of the Uighurs,* one of the more literate peoples of the steppe. Thus *The Secret History* was written in Mongolian with Uighur letters. The only surviving version is a fourteenth-century Chinese translation. The author is unknown, but the book provides detailed accounts of the early years of Temujin and ends with the reign of his son and successor, Ogodei, in 1228 — only a year after his father's death.

Because so much about the Mongols was written by their literate enemies, *The Secret History* is an invaluable resource: It is clearly an "insider's" account of the early years of Mongol expansion. Although it includes mythic elements — it begins with the augury of the birth of a blue wolf to introduce Chingis Khan — *The Secret History* is, without doubt, an authentic representation of a Mongol point of view.

In this selection, you will read the Mongol account of an important Mongol victory over the Naiman, a neighboring Turkic- or Mongol-speaking people, in 1204. What does the account tell you about the lives of steppe nomads like the Naiman and Mongols? What does this selection tell you about the sources of Mongol military strength?

THINKING HISTORICALLY

What moral values does this selection reveal? Do the Mongols think of themselves as "moral" people? Is the author-historian interested in describing what happened objectively or in presenting an unblemished, sanitized view?

In what ways does this written Mongol history make you more sympathetic to the Mongols? Notice that the selection begins with

* WEE gurs

Source: Adapted by K. Reilly from R. P. Lister, *Genghis Khan* (New York: Barnes & Noble, 1993), 166–76. While this volume is a retelling of the almost indecipherable *The Secret History of the Mongols* in Lister's own words, the selections that follow simplify without contextualizing or explaining the original work. More scholarly editions, trans. and ed. Francis Woodman Cleaves (Cambridge, MA: Harvard University Press, 1982) and Paul Kahn (San Francisco: North Point Press, 1984), are less accessible.

an "inside" view of the Mongol's enemy, the Naiman. How informed and fair does the Mongol author seem to be toward the Naiman? Do you think the Mongol authors described the Naiman more accurately than Chinese or Europeans described the Mongols?

Tayang Khan of the Naiman

When the news was brought to [the Naiman] Tayang Khan that someone claiming to be Ong Khan had been slain at the Neikun watercourse, his mother, Gurbesu, said: "Ong Khan was the great Khan of former days. Bring his head here! If it is really he, we will sacrifice to him."

She sent a message to Khorisu, commanding him to cut the head off and bring it in. When it was brought to her, she recognised it as that of Ong Khan. She placed it on a white cloth, and her daughter-in-law carried out the appropriate rites. . . . A wine-feast was held and stringed instruments were played. Gurbesu, taking up a drinking-bowl, made an offering to the head of Ong Khan.

When the sacrifice was made to it, the head grinned.

"He laughs!" Tayang Khan cried. Overcome by religious awe, he flung the head on the floor and trampled on it until it was mangled beyond recognition.

The great general Kokse'u Sabrakh was present at these ceremonies, and observed them without enthusiasm. It was he who had been the only Naiman general to offer resistance to Temujin and Ong Khan on their expedition against Tayang Khan's brother Buyiruk.

"First of all," he remarked, "you cut off the head of a dead ruler, and then you trample it into the dust. What kind of behaviour is this? Listen to the baying of those dogs: It has an evil sound. The Khan your father, Inancha Bilgei, once said: 'My wife is young, and I, her husband, am old. Only the power of prayer has enabled me to beget my son, this same Tayang. But will my son, born a weakling, be able to guard and hold fast my common and evil-minded people?'

"Now the baying of the dogs seems to announce that some disaster is at hand. The rule of our queen, Gurbesu, is firm; but you, my Khan, Torlukh Tayang, are weak. It is truly said of you that you have no thought for anything but the two activities of hawking and driving game, and no capacity for anything but these."

Tayang Khan was accustomed to the disrespect of his powerful general, but he was stung into making a rash decision.

"There are a few Mongols in the east. From the earliest days this old and great Ong Khan feared them, with their quivers; now they have made war on him and driven him to death. No doubt they would like to be rulers themselves. There are indeed in Heaven two shining lights, the sun and the moon, and both can exist there; but how can there be two rulers here on earth? Let us go and gather those Mongols in."

His mother Gurbesu said: "Why should we start making trouble with them? The Mongols have a bad smell; they wear black clothes. They are far away, out there; let them stay there. Though it is true," she added, "that we could have the daughters of their chieftains brought here; when we had washed their hands and feet, they could milk our cows and sheep for us."

Tayang Khan said: "What is there so terrible about them? Let us go to these Mongols and take away their quivers."

"What big words you are speaking," Kokse'u Sabrakh said. "Is Tayang Khan the right man for it? Let us keep the peace."

Despite these warnings, Tayang Khan decided to attack the Mongols. It was a justifiable decision; his armies were stronger, but time was on Temujin's side. Tayang sought allies, sending a messenger to Alakhu Shidigichuri of the Onggut, in the south, the guardians of the ramparts between Qashin and the Khingan. "I am told that there are a few Mongols in the east," he said. "Be my right hand! I will ride against them from here, and we will take their quivers away from them."

Alakhu's reply was brief: "I cannot be your right hand." He in his turn sent a message to Temujin. "Tayang Khan of the Naiman wants to come and take away your quivers. He sent to me and asked me to be his right hand. I refused. I make you aware of this, so that when he comes your quivers will not be taken away."[1]

War against the Naiman

When he received Alakhu's message Temujin, having wintered near Guralgu, was holding one of his immense roundups of game on the camel-steppes of Tulkinche'ut, in the east. The beasts had been encircled by the clansmen and warriors; the chieftains were gathered together, about to begin the great hunt.

"What shall we do now?" some of them said to each other. "Our horses are lean at this season."

. . . The snow had only lately left the steppe; the horses had found nothing to graze on during these recent months. Their ribs stuck out and they lacked strength.

The Khan's youngest brother, Temuga, spoke up. . . .

"How can that serve as an excuse," he said, "that the horses are lean? My horses are quite fat enough. How can we stay sitting here, when we receive a message like that?"

---

[1] Temujin, grateful for this warning, sent him five hundred horses and a thousand sheep. His friendship with Alakhu was valuable to him at a later time.

Prince Belgutai spoke. . . .

"If a man allows his quivers to be taken away during his lifetime, what kind of an existence does he have? For a man who is born a man, it is a good enough end to be slain by another man, and lie on the steppe with his quiver and bow beside him. The Naiman make fine speeches, with their many men and their great kingdom. But suppose, having heard their fine speeches, we ride against them, would it be so difficult to take their quivers away from them? We must mount and ride; it is the only thing to do."

Temujin was wholly disposed to agree with these sentiments. He broke off the hunt, set the army in motion, and camped near Ornu'u on the Khalkha. Here he paused for a time while he carried out a swift reorganization of the army. A count was held of the people; they were divided up into thousands, hundreds, and tens, and commanders of these units were appointed. Also at this time he chose his personal body-guards, the seventy day-guards and eighty night-guards.

Having reorganised the army, he marched away from the mountainside of Ornu'u on the Khalkha, and took the way of war against the Naiman.

The spring of the Year of the Rat [1204] was by now well advanced. During this westward march came the Day of the Red Disc, the sixteenth day of the first moon of summer. On this day, the moon being at the full, the Khan caused the great yak's-tail banner to be consecrated, letting it be sprinkled with fermented mare's milk, with the proper observances.

They continued the march up the Kerulen, with Jebe and Khubilai in the van. When they came on to the Saari steppes, they met with the first scouts of the Naiman. There were a few skirmishes between the Naiman and Mongol scouts; in one of these, a Mongol scout was captured, a man riding a grey horse with a worn saddle. The Naiman studied this horse with critical eyes, and thought little of it. "The Mongols' horses are inordinately lean," they said to each other.

The Mongol army rode out on to the Saari steppes, and began to deploy themselves for the forthcoming battle. . . . Dodai Cherbi, one of the newly appointed captains, put a proposal before the Khan.

"We are short in numbers compared to the enemy; besides this, we are exhausted after the long march, our horses in particular. It would be a good idea to settle in this camp, so that our horses can graze on the steppe, until they have had as much to eat as they need. Meanwhile, we can deceive the enemy by making puppets and lighting innumerable fires. For every man, we will make at least one puppet, and we will burn fires in five places. It is said that the Naiman people are very numerous, but it is rumored also that their king is a weakling, who has never left his tents. If we keep them in a state of uncertainty about our numbers, with our puppets and our fires, our geldings can stuff themselves till they are fat."

The suggestion pleased Temujin, who had the order passed on to the soldiers to light fires immediately. Puppets were constructed and placed all over the steppe, some sitting or lying by the fires, some of them even mounted on horses.

At night, the watchers of the Naiman saw, from the flanks of the mountain, fires twinkling all over the steppe. They said to each other: "Did they not say that the Mongols were very few? Yet they have more fires than there are stars in Heaven."

Having previously sent to Tayang Khan news of the lean grey horse with the shabby saddle, they now sent him the message: "The warriors of the Mongols are camped out all over the Saari steppes. They seem to grow more numerous every day; their fires outnumber the stars."

When this news was brought to him from the scouts, Tayang Khan was at the watercourse of Khachir. He sent a message to his son Guchuluk.

"I am told that the geldings of the Mongols are lean, but the Mongols are, it seems, numerous. Once we start fighting them, it will be difficult to draw back. They are such hard warriors that when several men at once come up against one of them, he does not move an eyelid; even if he is wounded, so that the black blood flows out, he does not flinch. I do not know whether it is a good thing to come up against such men.

"I suggest that we should assemble our people and lead them back to the west, across the Altai; and all the time, during this retreat, we will fight off the Mongols as dogs do, by running in on them from either side as they advance. Our geldings are too fat; in this march we shall make them lean and fit. But the Mongols' lean geldings will be brought to such a state of exhaustion they will vomit in the Mongols' faces."

On receiving this message, Guchuluk Khan, who was more warlike than his father, said: "That woman Tayang has lost all his courage, to speak such words. Where does this great multitude of Mongols come from? Most of the Mongols are with Jamukha, who is here with us. Tayang speaks like this because fear has overcome him. He has never been farther from his tent than his pregnant wife goes to urinate. He has never dared to go so far as the inner pastures where the knee-high calves are kept." So he expressed himself on the subject of his father, in the most injurious and wounding terms.

When he heard these words, Tayang Khan said: "I hope the pride of this powerful Guchuluk will not weaken on the day when the clash of arms is heard and the slaughter begins. Because once we are committed to battle against the foe, it will be hard to disengage again."

Khorisu Beki, a general who commanded under Tayang Khan, said: "Your father, Inancha Bilgei, never showed the back of a man or the haunch of a horse to opponents who were just as worthy as these. How can you lose your courage so early in the day? We would have done better to summon your mother Gurbesu to command over us. It is a pity that Kokse'u Sabrakh has grown too old to lead us. Our army's discipline has become lax. For the Mongols, their hour has come. It is finished! Tayang, you have failed us." He belted on his quiver and galloped off.

Tayang Khan grew angry. "All men must die," he said. "Their bodies must suffer. It is the same for all men. Let us fight, then."

So, having created doubt and dismay, and lost the support of some of his best leaders, he decided to give battle. He broke away from the watercourse of Khachir, marched down the Tamir, crossed the Orkhon and skirted the eastern flanks of the mountain Nakhu. When they came to Chakirma'ut, Temujin's scouts caught sight of them and brought back the message: "The Naiman are coming!"

The Battle of Chakirma'ut

When the news was brought to Temujin he said: "Sometimes too many men are just as big a handicap as too few."

Then he issued his general battle orders. "We will march in the order 'thick grass,' take up positions in the 'lake' battle order, and fight in the manner called 'gimlet.'"[2] He gave Kasar the command of the main army, and appointed Prince Otchigin to the command of the reserve horses, a special formation of great importance in Mongol warfare.

The Naiman, having advanced as far as Chakirma'ut, drew themselves up in a defensive position on the foothills of Nakhu, with the mountain behind them. . . . The Mongols forced their scouts back on to the forward lines, and then their forward lines back on to the main army, and drove tightly knit formations of horsemen again and again into the Naiman ranks. The Naiman, pressed back on themselves, could do nothing but retreat gradually up the mountain. Many of their men . . . hardly had the chance to fight at all, but were cut down in an immobile mass of men as soon as the Mongols reached them.

Tayang Khan, with his advisers, also retreated up the mountain as the day advanced. From the successive spurs to which they climbed, each one higher than the last, they could see the whole of this dreadful disaster as it took place below them.

Jamukha was with Tayang Khan. . . .

"Who are those people over there," Tayang Khan asked him, "who throw my warriors back as if they were sheep frightened by a wolf, who come huddling back to the sheepfold?"

Jamukha said: "My *anda*[3] Temujin has four hounds whom he brought up on human flesh, and kept in chains. They have brows of copper, snouts like chisels, tongues like bradawls, hearts of iron, and

---

[2] These were the names of various tactical disciplines in which he had drilled his army.
[3] Sworn brother, blood brother, declared ally.

tails that cut like swords. They can live on dew, and ride like the wind. On the day of battle they eat the flesh of men. You see how, being set loose, they come forward slavering for joy. Those two are Jebe and Khubilai; those two are Jelmei and Subetai. That is who those four hounds are.". . .

"Who is it coming up there in the rear," Tayang Khan asked him, "who swoops down on our troops like a ravening falcon?"

"That is my *anda* Temujin. His entire body is made of sounding copper; there is no gap through which even a bodkin could penetrate. There he is, you see him? He advances like an eagle about to seize his prey. You said formerly that if you once set eyes on the Mongols you would not leave so much of them as the skin of a lamb's foot. What do you think of them now?"

By this time the chieftains were standing on a high spur. Below them, the great army of the Naiman, Jamukha's men with them, were retreating in confusion, fighting desperately as the Mongols hemmed them in.

"Who is that other chieftain," Tayang asked Jamukha, "who draws ever nearer us, in a dense crowd of men?"

"Mother Hoelun brought up one of her own sons on human flesh. He is nine feet tall; he eats a three-year-old cow every day. If he swallows an armed man whole, it makes no difference to his appetite. When he is roused to anger, and lets fly with one of his *angqu'a* [forked] arrows, it will go through ten or twenty men. His normal range is a thousand yards; when he draws his bow to its fullest extent, he shoots over eighteen hundred yards. He is mortal, but he is not like other mortals; he is more than a match for the serpents of Guralgu. He is called Kasar."

They were climbing high up the mountain now, to regroup below its summit. Tayang Khan saw a new figure among the Mongols.

"Who is that coming up from the rear?" he asked Jamukha.

"That is the youngest son of Mother Hoelun. He is called Otchigin [Odeigin] the Phlegmatic. He is one of those people who go to bed early and get up late. But when he is behind the army, with the reserves, he does not linger; he never comes too late to the battle lines."

"We will climb to the peak of the mountain," Tayang Khan said.

Jamukha, seeing that the battle was lost, slipped away to the rear and descended the mountain, with a small body of men. One of these he sent to Temujin with a message. "Say this to my *anda*. Tayang Khan, terrified by what I have told him, has completely lost his senses. He has retreated up the mountain as far as he can. He could be killed by one harsh word. Let my *anda* take note of this: They have climbed to the top of the mountain, and are in no state to defend themselves any more. I myself have left the Naiman."

Since the evening was drawing on, Temujin commanded his troops in the forefront of the attack to draw back. Bodies of men were sent forward on the wings, east and west, to encircle the summit of Mount Nakhu.

There they stood to arms during the night. During the night, the Naiman army tried to break out of the encircling ring. Bodies of horsemen plunged down the mountainside in desperate charges; many fell and were trampled to death, the others were slain. In the first light they were seen lying about the mountain in droves, like fallen trees. Few were left defending the peak; they put up little resistance to the force sent up against them.

7

JOHN OF PLANO CARPINI

History of the Mongols

Chingis Khan united the tribes of the steppe and conquered northern China, capturing Peking by 1215. He then turned his armies against the West, conquering the tribes of Turkestan and the Khorezmian Empire, the great Muslim power of Central Asia, by 1222 and sending an army around the Caspian Sea into Russia. In 1226, he turned again to the East, subduing and destroying the kingdom of Tibet before he died in 1227. One historian, Christopher Dawson, summarizes the career of Chingis Khan this way:

> In spite of the primitive means at his disposal, it is possible that [Chingis Khan] succeeded in destroying a larger portion of the human race than any modern expert in total warfare. Within a dozen years from the opening of his campaign against China, the Mongol armies had reached the Pacific, the Indus, and the Black Sea, and had destroyed many of the great cities in India. For Europe especially, the shock was overwhelming.[1]

European fears intensified in 1237 as the principal Mongol armies under Batu Khan systematically destroyed one Russian city after another. In April 1241, one Mongol army destroyed a combined force of Polish and German armies, while another defeated the Hungarian army and threatened Austria. In 1245, desperate to learn as much as

[1] From Christopher Dawson, ed., *Mission to Asia*, p. xii.

Source: John of Plano Carpini, "History of the Mongols," in *Mission to Asia: Narratives and Letters of the Franciscan Missionaries in Mongolia and China in the Thirteenth and Fourteenth Centuries*, trans. a nun of Stanbrook Abbey, ed. Christopher Dawson (1955; reprint, New York: Harper & Row, 1966), 60–69.

possible about Mongol intentions, Pope Innocent IV sent a mission to the Mongols. For this important task, he sent two Franciscan monks — one of whom was John of Plano Carpini — with two letters addressed to the Emperor of the Tartars (a compounded error that changed the Tatars, the Mongols' enemy, into the denizens of Tartarus, or Hell).

In May, the barefoot sixty-five-year-old Friar John reached Batu's camp on the Volga River, from which he was relayed to Mongolia by five fresh horses a day in order to reach the capital at Karakorum in time for the installation of the third Great Khan, Guyuk (r. 1246–1248) in July and August.

In this selection from his *History of the Mongols*, John writes of his arrival in Mongolia for the installation of Guyuk (here written as Cuyuc). In what ways does John's account change or expand your understanding of the Mongols? Was John a good observer? How does he compensate for his ignorance (as an outside observer) of Mongol society and culture? In what ways does he remain a victim of his outsider status?

How was Mongol society similar to, and different from, Viking society? Compare the role of women in Mongol and Viking societies.

THINKING HISTORICALLY

How would you characterize John's moral stance toward the Mongols? How is his judgment of the Mongols different from that of Yvo of Narbona, and what might account for that difference? Consider your own moral judgment, if any, of the Mongols. How is it related to your historical understanding?

. . . On our arrival Cuyuc had us given a tent and provisions, such as it is the custom for the Tartars to give, but they treated us better than other envoys. Nevertheless we were not invited to visit him for he had not yet been elected, nor did he yet concern himself with the government. The translation of the Lord Pope's letter, however, and the things I had said had been sent to him by Bati. After we had stayed there for five or six days he sent us to his mother where the solemn court was assembling. By the time we got there a large pavilion had already been put up made of white velvet, and in my opinion it was so big that more than two thousand men could have got into it. Around it had been erected a wooden palisade, on which various designs were painted. On the second or third day we went with the Tartars who had been appointed to look after us and there all the chiefs were assembled and each one was riding with his followers among the hills and over the plains round about.

On the first day they were all clothed in white velvet, on the second in red—that day Cuyuc came to the tent—on the third day they were all in blue velvet, and on the fourth in the finest brocade. In the palisade round the pavilion were two large gates, through one of which the Emperor alone had the right to enter and there were no guards placed at it although it was open, for no one dare enter or leave by it; through the other gate all those who were granted admittance entered and there were guards there with swords and bows and arrows. . . . The chiefs went about everywhere armed and accompanied by a number of their men, but none, unless their group of ten was complete, could go as far as the horses; indeed those who attempted to do so were severely beaten. There were many of them who had, as far as I could judge, about twenty marks' worth of gold on their bits, breastplates, saddles, and cruppers. The chiefs held their conference inside the tent and, so I believe, conducted the election. All the other people however were a long way away outside the aforementioned palisade. There they remained until almost midday and then they began to drink mare's milk and they drank until the evening, so much that it was amazing to see. We were invited inside and they gave us mead as we would not take mare's milk. They did this to show us great honour, but they kept on plying us with drinks to such an extent that we could not possibly stand it, not being used to it, so we gave them to understand that it was disagreeable to us and they left off pressing us.

Outside were Duke Jerozlaus of Susdal in Russia and several chiefs of the Kitayans and Solangi, also two sons of the King of Georgia, the ambassador of the Caliph of Baghdad, who was a Sultan, and more than ten other Sultans of the Saracens, so I believe and so we were told by the stewards. There were more than four thousand envoys there, counting those who were carrying tribute, those who were bringing gifts, the Sultans and other chiefs who were coming to submit to them, those summoned by the Tartars and the governors of territories. All these were put together outside the palisade and they were given drinks at the same time, but when we were outside with them we and Duke Jerozlaus were always given the best places. I think, if I remember rightly, that we had been there a good four weeks when, as I believe, the election took place; the result however was not made public at that time; the chief ground for my supposition was that whenever Cuyuc left the tent they sang before him and as long as he remained outside they dipped to him beautiful rods on the top of which was scarlet wool, which they did not do for any of the other chiefs. They call this court the Sira Orda.

Leaving there we rode all together for three or four leagues to another place, where on a pleasant plain near a river among the mountains another tent had been set up, which is called by them the Golden Orda, it was here that Cuyuc was to be enthroned on the feast of the Assumption of Our Lady. . . .

At that place we were summoned into the presence of the Emperor, and Chingay the protonotary wrote down our names and the names of those who had sent us, also the names of the chief of the Solangi and of others, and then calling out in a loud voice he recited them before the Emperor and all the chiefs. When this was finished each one of us genuflected four times on the left knee and they warned us not to touch the lower part of the threshold. After we had been most thoroughly searched for knives and they had found nothing at all, we entered by a door on the east side, for no one dare enter from the west with the sole exception of the Emperor or, if it is a chief's tent, the chief; those of lower rank do not pay much attention to such things. This was the first time since Cuyuc had been made Emperor that we had entered his tent in his presence. He also received all the envoys in that place, but very few entered his tent.

So many gifts were bestowed by the envoys there that it was marvellous to behold—gifts of silk, samite, velvet, brocade, girdles of silk threaded with gold, choice furs, and other presents. The Emperor was also given a sunshade or little awning such as is carried over his head, and it was all decorated with precious stones. . . .

Leaving there we went to another place where a wonderful tent had been set up all of red velvet, and this had been given by the Kitayans; there also we were taken inside. Whenever we went in we were given mead and wine to drink, and cooked meat was offered us if we wished to have it. A lofty platform of boards had been erected, on which the Emperor's throne was placed. The throne, which was of ivory, was wonderfully carved and there was also gold on it, and precious stones, if I remember rightly, and pearls. Steps led up to it and it was rounded behind. Benches were also placed round the throne, and here the ladies sat in their seats on the left; nobody, however, sat on the right, but the chiefs were on benches in the middle and the rest of the people sat beyond them. Every day a great crowd of ladies came.

Finally, after some time, John was to be brought again before the Emperor. When he heard from them that we had come to him he ordered us to go back to his mother, the reason being that he wished on the following day to raise his banner against the whole of the Western world—we were told this definitely by men who knew . . .—and he wanted us to be kept in ignorance of this. On our return we stayed for a few days, then we went back to him again and remained with him for a good month, enduring such hunger and thirst that we could scarcely keep alive, for the food provided for four was barely sufficient for one, moreover, we were unable to find anything to buy, for the market was a very long way off. If the Lord had not sent us a certain Russian, by name Cosmas, a goldsmith and a great favourite of the Emperor, who supported us to some extent, we would, I believe, have died, unless the Lord had helped us in some other way. . . .

After this the Emperor sent for us, and through Chingay his protonotary told us to write down what we had to say and our business, and give it to him. We did this and wrote out for him all that we said earlier to Bati. . . . A few days passed by; then he had us summoned again and told us through Kadac, the procurator of the whole empire, in the presence of Bala and Chingay his protonotaries and many other scribes, to say all we had to say: We did this willingly and gladly. Our interpreter on this as on the previous occasion was Temer, a knight of Jerozlaus': and there were also present a cleric who was with him and another cleric who was with the Emperor. On this occasion we were asked if there were any people with the Lord Pope who understood the writing of the Russians or Saracens or even of the Tartars. We gave answer that we used neither the Ruthenian nor Saracen writing; there were however Saracens in the country but they were a long way from the Lord Pope; but we said that it seemed to us that the most expedient course would be for them to write in Tartar and translate it for us, and we would write it down carefully in our own script and we would take both the letter and the translation to the Lord Pope. Thereupon they left us to go to the Emperor.

On St. Martin's day we were again summoned, and Kadac, Chingay, and Bala, the aforementioned secretaries, came to us and translated the letter for us word by word. When we had written it in Latin, they had it translated so that they might hear a phrase at a time, for they wanted to know if we had made a mistake in any word. When both letters were written, they made us read it once and a second time in case we had left out anything. . . .

It is the custom for the Emperor of the Tartars never to speak to a foreigner, however important he may be, except through an intermediary, and he listens and gives his answer, also through the intermediary. Whenever his subjects have any business to bring before Kadac, or while they are listening to the Emperor's reply, they stay on their knees until the end of the conversation, however important they may be. It is not possible nor indeed is it the custom for anyone to say anything about any matter after the Emperor has declared his decision. This Emperor not only has a procurator and protonotaries and secretaries, but all officials for dealing with both public and private matters, except that he has no advocates, for everything is settled according to the decision of the Emperor without the turmoil of legal trials. The other princes of the Tartars do the same in those matters concerning them.

The present Emperor may be forty or forty-five years old or more; he is of medium height, very intelligent, and extremely shrewd, and most serious and grave in his manner. He is never seen to laugh for a slight cause nor to indulge in any frivolity, so we were told by the Christians who are constantly with him. The Christians of his household also told us that they firmly believed he was about to become a Christian, and they have clear evidence of this, for he maintains Christian clerics and provides them with supplies of Christian things; in addition he always has a chapel before his chief tent and they sing openly and in public and beat the board for services after the Greek fashion like other Christians, however big a crowd of Tartars or other men be there. The other chiefs do not behave like this.

. . . on the feast of St. Brice [November 13th], they gave us a permit to depart and a letter sealed with the Emperor's seal, and sent us to the Emperor's mother. She gave each of us a fox-skin cloak, which had the fur outside and was lined inside, and a length of velvet; our Tartars stole a good yard from each of the pieces of velvet and from the piece given to our servant they stole more than half. This did not escape our notice, but we preferred not to make a fuss about it.

We then set out on the return journey.

■ REFLECTIONS

The great Chinese artist Cheng Ssu-hsaio (1241–1318) continued to paint his delicate Chinese orchids in the years after the Mongol defeat of the Sung dynasty, under the alien rule of Khubilai Khan (r. 1260–1294), the fifth Great Khan and the founder of the Mongol Yuan dynasty of China. But when Cheng was asked why he always painted the orchids without earth around their roots, he replied that the earth had been stolen by the barbarians.

Just as it would be a mistake to see a fifth-generation Mongol ruler like Khubilai as a barbarian, it would also be a mistake to assume that Cheng's hardened resistance remained the norm. In fact, a younger generation of artists found opportunity and even freedom in Khubilai's China. Khubilai appointed some of the most famous Chinese painters of his era to positions of government—Ministries of War, Public Works, Justice, Personnel, Imperial Sacrifices—actively recruiting the bright young men, artists and intellectuals, for his government. While some painters catered to the Mongol elite's inclination for paintings of horses, others relished the wider range of subjects allowed by a regime free of highly cultivated prejudices.

If conquest invariably brings charges of barbarism, it also eventually turns to issues of government and administration. Administrators need officials. Though Khubilai Khan abolished the Chinese civil service examination system because it would have forced him to rely on Chinese officials, the Chinese language, and an educational system based on the Chinese classics, he actively sought ways of governing that were neither too Chinese nor too Mongolian. Typically, he promulgated a Chinese alphabet that was based on Tibetan, hoping that its phonetic symbols would make communication easier and less

classical. Many of his achievements were unintended. While his officials continued to use Chinese characters and the Uighur script, the
Yuan dynasty witnessed a flowering of literary culture, including theater and novels. For some, no doubt, the wind from the steppe blew
away the dust and cobwebs that had accumulated for too long.

Our judgment of the Mongols depends to a great extent on the
period of Mongol history we consider. But while it is easy to condemn
Chingis Khan and the initial conquests and praise the later enlightened
governance, two considerations come to mind. First, in the great sweep
of history, many "barbarians" became benign, even indulgent, administrators. Second, the Mongols were not unique in making that transition.

Before the Mongols, the Vikings had already made the transition
from raiding to trading and from conquering to colonizing. In fact, as
Cunliffe points out, the Vikings had always been farmer-sailors who
were as hungry for land as for plunder. Unlike the Mongols who were
born on horses, continually picking up and remaking camp in new pas-
tureland, the Vikings became nomadic in emergencies when a search
for new settlements was necessary.

The memory of Viking assaults also faded faster than that of the
Mongols. The Viking Rus had the Mongols to thank. The Rus of
Viking cities like Novgorod became the national heroes of anti-Mongol
Russian legend, eventually becoming the Russians. In Europe, too, the
descendants of Vikings helped establish new national identities. The
last great Viking king, Harald the Hard Ruler, "Thunderbolt of the
North," won back his father's crown as king of Norway in 1047, after
preparing himself in Russian trading cities and Byzantine courts. He
had married a Russian princess and fought for the Byzantines in Asia
Minor, Jerusalem, and the Caucasus Mountains. In 1066, this king of
Norway lost his control of England when he was killed by an English
earl. A few days later the new English king was killed by William Duke
of Normandy, a Viking son who had previously conquered much of
France. Norman rule was to last over a hundred years, from 1066 to
1215, and create a new English identity.

At the end of the day, history is neither moral nor immoral. History is what happened, for better or worse, and moralistic history is
generally bad history. The Vikings and Mongols of our period were
no more morally frozen in time than were the Christian and Muslim
Crusaders of the same era who visited such violence upon each other.

Just as the role of nomads and settlers changes over time, so does
the degree to which a people are particularly aggressive or peaceful. It is
hard to imagine a more fearful people than the Mongols of the thirteenth
century or the Vikings of the tenth century. Yet modern Scandinavia,
Iceland, and Mongolia are among the most peaceful places on the planet.

12

The Black Death

Afro-Eurasia, 1346–1350

The Mongol peace that made the Persian Ilkhanid dynasty (1256–1353) and the Chinese Yuan dynasty (1279–1368) sister empires nurtured a level of economic exchange and artistic communication greater than in the most cosmopolitan days of the early Roman/Han Silk Road. But the new caravan routes that spanned Central Asia could carry microbes as well as people. The plague that had long been endemic in country rats spread by fleas to city rats and other animals, including humans. As early as 1346, travelers reported millions killed in China, Central Asia, and the Middle East. In Europe and Egypt, approximately a third of the population perished. In some cities, the death toll was greater than half. This pandemic plague of 1346–1350 is sometimes called the Black Death, after the discolored wounds it caused.

■ THINKING HISTORICALLY

Considering Cause and Effect

The study of history, like the practice of medicine, is a process of understanding the causes of certain effects. In medicine the effects are diseases or good health; in history they are more varied events. Nevertheless, understanding the causes of things is central to both disciplines. For medical specialists the goal of understanding causes is implicitly a part of the process of improving health or finding a cure. Historians rarely envision "cures" for social ills, but many believe that an understanding of cause and effect can improve society's chances of avoiding undesirable outcomes in favor of more helpful ones.

Still, the most hopeful medical researcher or historian would agree that the process of relating cause and effect, of finding causes and explaining effects, is fraught with difficulties. There is first the problem of precisely defining the effect to be explained. Next there is the need to find possible causes in past events (though medical specialists often have the advantage of replicating the past by experiment). Then there is the need to establish a connection between the past event and the current condition (avoiding the logical fallacy *post hoc ergo propter hoc:* "after this, therefore because of this"). We will explore some of those difficulties in this chapter.

1

MARK WHEELIS

Biological Warfare at the 1346 Siege of Caffa

We are used to thinking of biological warfare as a recently developed threat. This article, published in a journal for public health professionals, suggests a longer history. According to the author, how and where did the Black Death originate? What was the significance of the Mongol siege of the northern Black Sea port of Caffa in 1346? The author draws on the contemporary account of the Black Death by Gabriele de' Mussis. On what points does he agree and disagree with de' Mussis?

THINKING HISTORICALLY

The author of this selection, a professor of microbiology at the University of California, was trained as a bacterial physiologist and geneticist, but for more than the last ten years his research has concentrated on the history and control of biological weapons. Notice how he uses both medical and historical ways of explaining causes. In medicine and science, the study of causes is called etiology. Give an example from the reading of an etiological explanation of the Black Death. The author also offers historical explanations of causes. Give examples of these. How are the etiological and historical similar and different?

Source: Mark Wheelis, "Biological Warfare at the 1346 Siege of Caffa," *Emerging Infectious Diseases* 8, no. 9 (September 2002): 971–75. The journal is published by the U.S. Centers for Disease Control and Prevention (C.D.C.), Atlanta, and is also available online at http://www.cdc.gov/ncidod/EID/vol8no9/01-0536.htm.

The Black Death, which swept through Europe, the Near East, and North Africa in the mid-fourteenth century, was probably the greatest public health disaster in recorded history and one of the most dramatic examples ever of emerging or reemerging disease. Europe lost an estimated one-quarter to one-third of its population, and the mortality in North Africa and the Near East was comparable. China, India, and the rest of the Far East are commonly believed to have also been severely affected, but little evidence supports that belief.

A principal source on the origin of the Black Death is a memoir by the Italian Gabriele de' Mussis. This memoir has been published several times in its original Latin and has recently been translated into English (although brief passages have been previously published in translation). This narrative contains some startling assertions: that the Mongol army hurled plague-infected cadavers into the besieged Crimean city of Caffa, thereby transmitting the disease to the inhabitants; and that fleeing survivors of the siege spread plague from Caffa to the Mediterranean Basin. If this account is correct, Caffa should be recognized as the site of the most spectacular incident of biological warfare ever, with the Black Death as its disastrous consequence. After analyzing these claims, I have concluded that it is plausible that the biological attack took place as described and was responsible for infecting the inhabitants of Caffa; however, the event was unimportant in the spread of the plague pandemic.

Origin of the Fourteenth-Century Pandemic

The disease that caused this catastrophic pandemic has, since Hecker,[1] generally been considered to have been a plague, a zoonotic disease caused by the gram-negative bacterium *Yersinia pestis*, the principal reservoir for which is wild rodents. The ultimate origin of the Black Death is uncertain—China, Mongolia, India, central Asia, and southern Russia have all been suggested. Known fourteenth-century sources are of little help; they refer repeatedly to an eastern origin, but none of the reports is firsthand. Historians generally agree that the outbreak moved west out of the steppes north of the Black and Caspian Seas, and its spread through Europe and the Middle East is fairly well documented (see Map 12.1). However, despite more than a century of speculation about an ultimate origin further east, the requisite scholarship using Chinese and central Asian sources has yet to be done. In any event, the Crimea[2] clearly played a pivotal role as the proximal source from which the Mediterranean Basin was infected.

---

[1] Justus Friedrich Karl Hecker (1795–1850), German physician who founded the study of disease in history. See *The Black Death: The Dancing Mania*. [Ed.]

[2] The peninsula that juts into the Black Sea from the north (modern Ukraine); Caffa was one of its port cities. [Ed.]

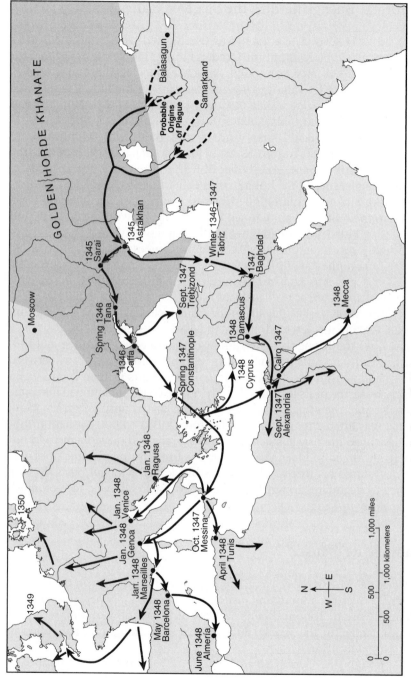

Map 12.1 Tentative Chronology of the Initial Spread of Plague in the Mid-Fourteenth Century.

Historical Background to the Siege of Caffa

Caffa (now Feodosija, Ukraine) was established by Genoa in 1266 by agreement with the Kahn of the Golden Horde. It was the main port for the great Genoese merchant ships, which connected there to a coastal shipping industry to Tana (now Azov, Russia) on the Don River. Trade along the Don connected Tana to Central Russia, and overland caravan routes linked it to Sarai and thence to the Far East.

Relations between Italian traders and their Mongol hosts were uneasy, and in 1307 Toqtai, Kahn of the Golden Horde, arrested the Italian residents of Sarai, and besieged Caffa. The cause was apparently Toqtai's displeasure at the Italian trade in Turkic slaves (sold for soldiers to the Mameluke Sultanate). The Genoese resisted for a year, but in 1308 set fire to their city and abandoned it. Relations between the Italians and the Golden Horde remained tense until Toqtai's death in 1312.

Toqtai's successor, Özbeg, welcomed the Genoese back, and also ceded land at Tana to the Italians for the expansion of their trading enterprise. By the 1340s, Caffa was again a thriving city, heavily fortified within two concentric walls. The inner wall enclosed 6,000 houses, the outer 11,000. The city's population was highly cosmopolitan, including Genoese, Venetian, Greeks, Armenians, Jews, Mongols, and Turkic peoples.

In 1343 the Mongols under Janibeg (who succeeded Özbeg in 1340) besieged Caffa and the Italian enclave at Tana following a brawl between Italians and Muslims in Tana. The Italian merchants in Tana fled to Caffa (which, by virtue of its location directly on the coast, maintained maritime access despite the siege). The siege of Caffa lasted until February 1344, when it was lifted after an Italian relief force killed 15,000 Mongol troops and destroyed their siege machines. Janibeg renewed the siege in 1345 but was again forced to lift it after a year, this time by an epidemic of plague that devastated his forces. The Italians blockaded Mongol ports, forcing Janibeg to negotiate, and in 1347 the Italians were allowed to reestablish their colony in Tana.

Gabriele de' Mussis

Gabriele de' Mussis, born circa 1280, practiced as a notary in the town of Piacenza, over the mountains just north of Genoa. [Nineteenth-century Italian historian] Tononi summarizes the little we know of him. His practice was active in the years 1300–1349. He is thought to have died in approximately 1356.

Although [the German historian] Henschel thought de' Mussis was present at the siege of Caffa, Tononi asserts that the Piacenza archives contain deeds signed by de' Mussis spanning the period 1344 through the first half of 1346. While this does not rule out travel to Caffa in late 1346, textual evidence suggests that he did not. He does not claim to have witnessed any of the Asian events he describes and often uses a passive voice for descriptions. After describing the siege of Caffa, de' Mussis goes on to say, "Now it is time that we passed from east to west to discuss all the things which we ourselves have seen. . . ."

The Narrative of Gabriele de' Mussis

The de' Mussis account is presumed to have been written in 1348 or early 1349 because of its immediacy and the narrow time period described. The original is lost, but a copy is included in a compilation of historical and geographic accounts by various authors, dating from approximately 1367. The account begins with an introductory comment by the scribe who copied the documents: "In the name of God, Amen. Here begins an account of the disease or mortality which occurred in 1348, put together by Gabrielem de Mussis of Piacenza."

The narrative begins with an apocalyptic speech by God, lamenting the depravity into which humanity has fallen and describing the retribution intended. It goes on:

". . . In 1346, in the countries of the East, countless numbers of Tartars and Saracens were struck down by a mysterious illness which brought sudden death. Within these countries broad regions, far-spreading provinces, magnificent kingdoms, cities, towns and settlements, ground down by illness and devoured by dreadful death, were soon stripped of their inhabitants. An eastern settlement under the rule of the Tartars called Tana, which lay to the north of Constantinople and was much frequented by Italian merchants, was totally abandoned after an incident there which led to its being besieged and attacked by hordes of Tartars who gathered in a short space of time. The Christian merchants, who had been driven out by force, were so terrified of the power of the Tartars that, to save themselves and their belongings, they fled in an armed ship to Caffa, a settlement in the same part of the world which had been founded long ago by the Genoese.

"Oh God! See how the heathen Tartar races, pouring together from all sides, suddenly invested the city of Caffa and besieged the trapped Christians there for almost three years. There, hemmed in by an immense army, they could hardly draw breath, although food could be shipped in, which offered them some hope. But behold, the whole army was affected by a disease which overran the Tartars and killed thousands upon thousands every day. It was as though arrows were raining down from heaven to strike and crush the Tartars' arrogance. All medical advice and attention was useless; the Tartars died as soon as the signs of disease appeared on their bodies: swellings in the armpit or groin caused by coagulating humours, followed by a putrid fever.

"The dying Tartars, stunned and stupefied by the immensity of the disaster brought about by the disease, and realizing that they had no hope of escape, lost interest in the siege. But they ordered corpses to be placed in catapults[3] and lobbed into the city in the hope that the intolerable stench would kill everyone inside.[4] What seemed like mountains of dead were thrown into the city, and the Christians could not hide or flee or escape from them, although they dumped as many of the bodies as they could in the sea. And soon the rotting corpses tainted the air and poisoned the water supply, and the stench was so overwhelming that hardly one in several thousand was in a position to flee the remains of the Tartar army. Moreover one infected man could carry the poison to others, and infect people and places with the disease by look alone. No one knew, or could discover, a means of defense.

"Thus almost everyone who had been in the East, or in the regions to the south and north, fell victim to sudden death after contracting this pestilential disease, as if struck by a lethal arrow which raised a tumor on their bodies. The scale of the mortality and the form which it took persuaded those who lived, weeping and lamenting, through the bitter events of 1346 to 1348—the Chinese, Indians, Persians, Medes, Kurds, Armenians, Cilicians, Georgians, Mesopotamians, Nubians, Ethiopians, Turks, Egyptians, Arabs, Saracens, and Greeks (for almost all the East has been affected)—that the last judgement had come.

". . . As it happened, among those who escaped from Caffa by boat were a few sailors who had been infected with the poisonous disease. Some boats were bound for Genoa, others went to Venice and to other Christian areas. When the sailors reached these places and mixed with the people there, it was as if they had brought evil spirits with them: every city, every settlement, every place was poisoned by the contagious pestilence, and their inhabitants, both men and women, died suddenly. And when one person had contracted the illness, he poisoned his whole family even as he fell and died, so that those preparing to bury his body were seized by death in the same way. Thus death entered through the windows, and as cities and towns were depopulated their inhabitants mourned their dead neighbours."

The account closes with an extended description of the plague in Piacenza, and a reprise of the apocalyptic vision with which it begins.

---

[3] Technically trebuchets, not catapults. Catapults hurl objects by the release of tension on twisted cordage; they are not capable of hurling loads over a few dozen kilograms. Trebuchets are counter-weight-driven hurling machines, very effective for throwing ammunition weighing a hundred kilos or more.

[4] Medieval society lacked a coherent theory of disease causation. Three notions coexisted in a somewhat contradictory mixture: 1) disease was a divine punishment for individual or collective transgression; 2) disease was the result of "miasma," or the stench of decay; and 3) disease was the result of person-to-person contagion.

Commentary

In this narrative, de' Mussis makes two important claims about the siege of Caffa and the Black Death: that plague was transmitted to Europeans by the hurling of diseased cadavers into the besieged city of Caffa and that Italians fleeing from Caffa brought it to the Mediterranean ports.

Biological Warfare at Caffa

De' Mussis's account is probably secondhand and is uncorroborated; however, he seems, in general, to be a reliable source, and as a Piacenzian he would have had access to eyewitnesses of the siege. Several considerations incline me to trust his account: this was probably not the only, nor the first, instance of apparent attempts to transmit disease by hurling biological material into besieged cities; it was within the technical capabilities of besieging armies of the time; and it is consistent with medieval notions of disease causality.

Tentatively accepting that the attack took place as described, we can consider two principal hypotheses for the entry of plague into the city: it might, as de' Mussis asserts, have been transmitted by the hurling of plague cadavers; or it might have entered by rodent-to-rodent transmission from the Mongol encampments into the city.

Diseased cadavers hurled into the city could easily have transmitted plague, as defenders handled the cadavers during disposal. Contact with infected material is a known mechanism of transmission; for instance, among 284 cases of plague in the United States in 1970–1995 for which a mechanism of transmission could be reasonably inferred, 20 percent were thought to be by direct contact. Such transmission would have been especially likely at Caffa, where cadavers would have been badly mangled by being hurled, and many of the defenders probably had cut or abraded hands from coping with the bombardment. Very large numbers of cadavers were possibly involved, greatly increasing the opportunity for disease transmission. Since disposal of the bodies of victims in a major outbreak of lethal disease is always a problem, the Mongol forces may have used their hurling machines as a solution to their mortuary problem, in which case many thousands of cadavers could have been involved. De' Mussis's description of "mountains of dead" might have been quite literally true.

Thus it seems plausible that the events recounted by de' Mussis could have been an effective means of transmission of plague into the city. The alternative, rodent-to-rodent transmission from the Mongol encampments into the city, is less likely. Besieging forces must have camped at least a kilometer away from the city walls. This distance is necessary to have a healthy margin of safety from arrows and artillery and to provide space for logistical support and other military activities between the encampments and the front lines. Front-line location must have been approximately 250–300 m from the walls; trebuchets are known from modern reconstruction to be capable of hurling 100 kg more than 200 m, and historical sources claim 300 m as the working range of large machines. Thus, the bulk of rodent nests associated with the besieging armies would have been located a kilometer or more away from the cities, and none would have likely been closer than 250 m. Rats are quite sedentary and rarely venture more than a few tens of meters from their nest. It is thus unlikely that there was any contact between the rat populations within and outside the walls.

Given the many uncertainties, any conclusion must remain tentative. However, the considerations above suggest that the hurling of plague cadavers might well have occurred as de' Mussis claimed, and if so, that this biological attack was probably responsible for the transmission of the disease from the besiegers to the besieged. Thus, this early act of biological warfare, if such it were, appears to have been spectacularly successful in producing casualties, although of no strategic importance (the city remained in Italian hands, and the Mongols abandoned the siege).

Crimea as the Source of European and Near Eastern Plague

There has never been any doubt that plague entered the Mediterranean from the Crimea, following established maritime trade routes. Rat infestations in the holds of cargo ships would have been highly susceptible to the rapid spread of plague, and even if most rats died during the voyage, they would have left abundant hungry fleas that would infect humans unpacking the holds. Shore rats foraging on board recently arrived ships would also become infected, transmitting plague to city rat populations.

Plague appears to have been spread in a stepwise fashion, on many ships rather than on a few [see Map 12.1], taking over a year to reach Europe from the Crimea. This conclusion seems fairly firm, as the dates for the arrival of plague in Constantinople and more westerly cities are reasonably certain. Thus de' Mussis was probably mistaken in attributing the Black Death to fleeing survivors of Caffa, who should not have needed more than a few months to return to Italy.

Furthermore, a number of other Crimean ports were under Mongol control, making it unlikely that Caffa was the only source of infected ships heading west. And the overland caravan routes to the Middle East from Serai and Astrakhan insured that plague was also spreading south (Map 12.1), whence it would have entered Europe in any case. The siege of Caffa and its gruesome finale thus are unlikely to have been seriously implicated in the transmission of plague from the Black Sea to Europe.

Conclusion

Gabriele de' Mussis's account of the origin and spread of plague appears to be consistent with most known facts, although mistaken in its claim that plague arrived in Italy directly from the Crimea. His account of biological attack is plausible, consistent with the technology of the time, and it provides the best explanation of disease transmission into besieged Caffa. This thus appears to be one of the first biological attacks recorded and among the most successful of all time.

However, it is unlikely that the attack had a decisive role in the spread of plague to Europe. Much maritime commerce probably continued throughout this period from other Crimean ports. Overland caravan routes to the Middle East were also unaffected. Thus, refugees from Caffa would most likely have constituted only one of several streams of infected ships and caravans leaving the region. The siege of Caffa, for all of its dramatic appeal, probably had no more than anecdotal importance in the spread of plague, a macabre incident in terrifying times.

Despite its historical unimportance, the siege of Caffa is a powerful reminder of the horrific consequences when disease is successfully used as a weapon. The Japanese use of plague as a weapon in World War II and the huge Soviet stockpiles of *Y. pestis* prepared for use in an all-out war further remind us that plague remains a very real problem for modern arms control, six and a half centuries later.

2

GABRIELE DE' MUSSIS

Origins of the Black Death

Gabriele de' Mussis (d. 1356) was a lawyer who lived in the northern Italian city of Piacenza. The previous reading introduced you to de' Mussis and the importance of his history of the Black Death. Since Wheelis quoted abundantly from the story of the siege of Caffa, we pick up the story in de' Mussis's words regarding the spread of the plague to Europe, where, as he wrote, he had direct evidence. How would you rate de' Mussis as an eyewitness observer? According to his evidence, how did the Black Death spread in Italy? How deadly was it?

Source: *The Black Death*, trans. and ed. Rosemary Horrox (Manchester, England: Manchester University Press, 1994), 18–26.

THINKING HISTORICALLY

As in the previous selection, there are two causal chains in this account, but in this case they are not medical and historical. Rather, reminiscent of the readings on the First Crusade, they are divine and human chains of causation. What, according to the author, were the divine or religious causes of the Black Death? What were the human, physical, or scientific causes? What remedies does each type of cause call for?

Now it is time that we passed from east to west, to discuss all the things which we ourselves have seen, or known, or consider likely on the basis of the evidence, and, by so doing, to show forth the terrifying judgements of God. Listen everybody, and it will set tears pouring from your eyes. For the Almighty has said: "I shall wipe man, whom I created, off the face of the earth. Because he is flesh and blood, let him be turned to dust and ashes. My spirit shall not remain among man."

— "What are you thinking of, merciful God, thus to destroy your creation and the human race; to order and command its sudden annihilation in this way? What has become of your mercy; the faith of our fathers; the blessed virgin, who holds sinners in her lap; the precious blood of the martyrs; the worthy army of confessors and virgins; the whole host of paradise, who pray ceaselessly for sinners; the most precious death of Christ on the cross and our wonderful redemption? Kind God, I beg that your anger may cease, that you do not destroy sinners in this way, and, because you desire mercy rather than sacrifice, that you turn away all evil from the penitent, and do not allow the just to be condemned with the unjust."

— "I hear you, sinner, dropping words into my ears. I bid you weep. The time for mercy has passed. I, God, am called to vengeance. It is my pleasure to take revenge on sin and wickedness. I shall give my signs to the dying, let them take steps to provide for the health of their souls."

As it happened, among those who escaped from Caffa by boat were a few sailors who had been infected with the poisonous disease. Some boats were bound for Genoa, others went to Venice and to other Christian areas. . . .

— "We Genoese and Venetians bear the responsibility for revealing the judgements of God. Alas, once our ships had brought us to port we went to our homes. And because we had been delayed by tragic events, and because among us there were scarcely ten survivors from a thousand sailors, relations, kinsmen and neighbours flocked to us from all sides. But, to our anguish, we were carrying the darts of death. While they hugged and kissed us we were spreading poison from our lips even as we spoke."

When they returned to their own folk, these people speedily poisoned the whole family, and within three days the afflicted family would succumb to the dart of death. Mass funerals had to be held and there was not enough room to bury the growing numbers of dead. Priests and doctors, upon whom most of the care of the sick devolved, had their hands full in visiting the sick and, alas, by the time they left they too had been infected and followed the dead immediately to the grave. Oh fathers! Oh mothers! Oh children and wives! For a long time prosperity preserved you from harm, but one grave now covers you and the unfortunate alike. You who enjoyed the world and upon whom pleasure and prosperity smiled, who mingled joys with follies, the same tomb receives you and you are handed over as food for worms. Oh hard death, impious death, bitter death, cruel death, who divides parents, divorces spouses, parts children, separates brothers and sisters. We bewail our wretched plight. The past has devoured us, the present is gnawing our entrails, the future threatens yet greater dangers. What we laboured to amass with feverish activity, we have lost in one hour.

Where are the fine clothes of gilded youth? Where is nobility and the courage of fighters, where the mature wisdom of elders and the regal throng of great ladies, where the piles of treasure and precious stones? Alas! All have been destroyed; thrust aside by death. To whom shall we turn, who can help us? To flee is impossible, to hide futile. Cities, fortresses, fields, woods, highways and rivers are ringed by thieves—which is to say by evil spirits, the executioners of the supreme Judge, preparing endless punishments for us all.

We can unfold a terrifying event which happened when an army was camped near Genoa. Four of the soldiers left the force in search of plunder and made their way to Rivarolo on the coast, where the disease had killed all the inhabitants. Finding the houses shut up, and no one about, they broke into one of the houses and stole a fleece which they found on a bed. They then rejoined the army and on the following night the four of them bedded down under the fleece. When morning comes it finds them dead. As a result everyone panicked, and thereafter nobody would use the goods and clothes of the dead, or even handle them, but rejected them outright.

Scarcely one in seven of the Genoese survived. In Venice, where an inquiry was held into the mortality, it was found that more than 70 percent of the people had died, and that within a short period 20 out of 24 excellent physicians had died. The rest of Italy, Sicily, and Apulia and the neighbouring regions maintain that they have been virtually emptied of inhabitants. The people of Florence, Pisa, and Lucca, finding themselves bereft of their fellow residents, emphasise their losses. The Roman Curia at Avignon, the provinces on both sides of the Rhône, Spain, France, and the Empire cry up their griefs and disasters—all of which makes it extraordinarily difficult for me to give an accurate picture.

By contrast, what befell the Saracens can be established from trustworthy accounts. In the city of Babylon alone (the heart of the Sultan's power), 480,000 of his subjects are said to have been carried off by disease in less than three months in 1348—and this is known from the Sultan's register which records the names of the dead, because he receives a gold bezant for each person buried. I am silent about Damascus and his other cities, where the number of dead was infinite. In the other countries of the East, which are so vast that it takes three years to ride across them and which have a population of 10,000 for every one inhabitant of the west, it is credibly reported that countless people have died.

Everyone has a responsibility to keep some record of the disease and the deaths, and because I am myself from Piacenza I have been urged to write more about what happened there in 1348. . . .

I don't know where to begin. Cries and laments arise on all sides. Day after day one sees the Cross and the Host[1] being carried about the city, and countless dead being buried. The ensuing mortality was so great that people could scarcely snatch breath. The living made preparations for their burial, and because there was not enough room for individual graves, pits had to be dug in colonnades and piazzas, where nobody had ever been buried before. It often happened that man and wife, father and son, mother and daughter, and soon the whole household and many neighbours, were buried together in one place. The same thing happened in Castell' Arquato and Viguzzolo and in the other towns, villages, cities, and settlements, and last of all in the Val Tidone, where they had hitherto escaped the plague.

Very many people died. One Oberto de Sasso, who had come from the infected neighbourhood around the church of the Franciscans, wished to make his will and accordingly summoned a notary and his neighbours as witnesses, all of whom, more than sixty of them, died soon after. At this time the Dominican friar Syfredo de Bardis, a man of prudence and great learning who had visited the Holy Sepulchre, also died, along with 23 brothers of the same house. There also died within a short time the Franciscan friar Bertolino Coxadocha of Piacenza, renowned for his learning and many virtues, along with 24 brothers of the same house, nine of them on one day; seven of the Augustinians; the Carmelite friar Francesco Todischi with six of his brethren; four of the order of Mary; more than sixty prelates and parish priests from the city and district of Piacenza; many nobles; countless young people; numberless women, particularly those who were pregnant. It is too distressing to recite any more, or to lay bare the wounds inflicted by so great a disaster.

---

[1] The consecrated Eucharistic wafer. The reference is to priests taking the last sacrament to the dying. [Ed.]

Let all creation tremble with fear before the judgement of God. Let human frailty submit to its creator. May a greater grief be kindled in all hearts, and tears well up in all eyes as future ages hear what happened in this disaster. When one person lay sick in a house no one would come near. Even dear friends would hide themselves away, weeping. The physician would not visit. The priest, panic-stricken, administered the sacraments with fear and trembling.

Listen to the tearful voices of the sick: "Have pity, have pity, my friends. At least say something, now that the hand of God has touched me."

"Oh father, why have you abandoned me? Do you forget that I am your child?"

"Mother, where have you gone? Why are you now so cruel to me when only yesterday you were so kind? You fed me at your breast and carried me within your womb for nine months."

"My children, whom I brought up with toil and sweat, why have you run away?"

Man and wife reached out to each other, "Alas, once we slept happily together but now are separated and wretched."

And when the sick were in the throes of death, they still called out piteously to their family and neighbours, "Come here. I'm thirsty, bring me a drink of water. I'm still alive. Don't be frightened. Perhaps I won't die. Please hold me tight, hug my wasted body. You ought to be holding me in your arms."

At this, as everyone else kept their distance, somebody might take pity and leave a candle burning by the bed head as he fled. And when the victim had breathed his last, it was often the mother who shrouded her son and placed him in the coffin, or the husband who did the same for his wife, for everybody else refused to touch the dead body. . . .

I am overwhelmed, I can't go on. Everywhere one turns there is death and bitterness to be described. The hand of the Almighty strikes repeatedly, to greater and greater effect. The terrible judgement gains in power as time goes by.

—What shall we do? Kind Jesus, receive the souls of the dead, avert your gaze from our sins and blot out all our iniquities.

We know that whatever we suffer is the just reward of our sins. Now, therefore, when the Lord is enraged, embrace acts of penance, so that you do not stray from the right path and perish. Let the proud be humbled. Let misers, who withheld alms from the poor, blush for shame. Let the envious become zealous in almsgiving. Let lechers put aside their filthy habits and distinguish themselves in honest living. Let the raging and wrathful restrain themselves from violence. Let gluttons temper their appetites by fasting. Let the slaves of sloth arise and dress themselves in good works. Let adolescents and youths abandon their present delight in following fashion. Let there be good faith and equity among judges, and respect for the law among merchants. Let pettifogging lawyers study and grow wise before they put pen to paper. Let members of religious orders abandon hypocrisy. Let the dignity of prelates be put to better use. Let all of you hurry to set your feet on the way of salvation. And let the over-weening vanity of great ladies, which so easily turns into voluptuousness, be bridled. It was against their arrogance that Isaiah inveighed: "Because the daughters of Sion are haughty, and have walked with stretched out necks and wanton glances of their eyes, and made a noise as they walked with their feet, and moved in a set pace. . . . Thy fairest men also shall fall by the sword: and thy valiant ones in battle. And her gates shall lament and mourn: and she shall sit desolate on the ground" [Isaiah 3.16–26]. This was directed against the pride of ladies and young people.

For the rest, so that the conditions, causes, and symptoms of this pestilential disease should be made plain to all, I have decided to set them out in writing. Those of both sexes who were in health, and in no fear of death, were struck by four savage blows to the flesh. First, out of the blue, a kind of chilly stiffness troubled their bodies. They felt a tingling sensation, as if they were being pricked by the points of arrows. The next stage was a fearsome attack which took the form of an extremely hard, solid boil. In some people this developed under the armpit and in others in the groin between the scrotum and the body. As it grew more solid, its burning heat caused the patients to fall into an acute and putrid fever, with severe headaches. As it intensified its extreme bitterness could have various effects. In some cases it gave rise to an intolerable stench. In others it brought vomiting of blood, or swellings near the place from which the corrupt humour arose: on the back, across the chest, near the thigh. Some people lay as if in a drunken stupor and could not be roused. Behold the swellings, the warning signs sent by the Lord.[2] All these people were in danger of dying. Some died on the very day the illness took possession of them, others on the next day, others—the majority—between the third and fifth day. There was no known remedy for the vomiting of blood. Those who fell into a coma, or suffered a swelling or the stink of corruption very rarely escaped. But from the fever it was sometimes possible to make a recovery. . . .

Truly, then was a time of bitterness and grief, which served to turn men to the Lord. I shall recount what happened. A warning was given by a certain holy person, who received it in a vision, that in cities, towns and other settlements, everyone, male and female alike, should gather in their parish church on three consecutive days and, each with a lighted candle in their hand, hear with great devotion the mass of the Blessed Anastasia, which is normally performed at dawn on Christmas day, and they should humbly beg for mercy, so that they might be delivered from the disease through the merits of the holy mass. Other people sought deliverance

---

[2] A pun: *bulla* is a swelling, but it is also the word for the papal seal, and hence for a papal document (or bull). De' Mussis is playing on the idea of the swelling characteristic of the plague being God's seal, notifying the victim of his imminent fate. [Ed.]

through the mediation of a blessed martyr; and others humbly turned to other saints, so that they might escape the abomination of disease. For among the aforesaid martyrs, some, as stories relate, are said to have died from repeated blows, and it was therefore the general opinion that they would be able to protect people against the arrows of death. Finally, in 1350, the most holy Pope Clement ordained a general indulgence, to be valid for a year, which remitted penance and guilt to all who were truly penitent and confessed. And as a result a numberless multitude of people made the pilgrimage to Rome, to visit with great reverence and devotion the basilicas of the blessed apostles Peter and Paul and St John.

Oh, most dearly beloved, let us therefore not be like vipers, growing ever more wicked, but let us rather hold up our hands to heaven to beg for mercy on us all, for who but God shall have mercy on us? With this, I make an end. May the heavenly physician heal our wounds — our spiritual rather than our bodily wounds. To whom be the blessing and the praise and the glory for ever and ever, Amen.

3

GIOVANNI BOCCACCIO

The Plague in Florence: *From* the Decameron

Giovanni Boccaccio* (1313–1375) was a poet in Florence, Italy, when the plague struck in 1348. His *Decameron*† is a collection of a hundred tales based on his experiences during the plague years. This selection is drawn from the Introduction. What does Boccaccio add to your understanding of the Black Death?

THINKING HISTORICALLY

Compare Boccaccio's treatment of divine and human causes of the plague. Boccaccio not only muses on the causes of the plague; he also sees the plague as the cause of new forms of behavior. What were the behavioral effects of the plague according to Boccaccio?

* boh KAH chee oh
† deh KAM uh rahn

Source: Giovanni Boccaccio, *Decameron*, trans. G. H. McWilliam (Harmondsworth, England: Penguin, 1972), 50–58.

I say, then, that the sum of thirteen hundred and forty-eight years had elapsed since the fruitful Incarnation of the Son of God, when the noble city of Florence, which for its great beauty excels all others in Italy, was visited by the deadly pestilence. Some say that it descended upon the human race through the influence of the heavenly bodies, others that it was a punishment signifying God's righteous anger at our iniquitous way of life. But whatever its cause, it had originated some years earlier in the East, where it had claimed countless lives before it unhappily spread westward, growing in strength as it swept relentlessly on from one place to the next.

In the face of its onrush, all the wisdom and ingenuity of man were unavailing. Large quantities of refuse were cleared out of the city by officials specially appointed for the purpose, all sick persons were forbidden entry, and numerous instructions were issued for safeguarding the people's health, but all to no avail. Nor were the countless petitions humbly directed to God by the pious, whether by means of formal processions or in any other guise, any less ineffectual. For in the early spring of the year we have mentioned, the plague began, in a terrifying and extraordinary manner, to make its disastrous effects apparent. It did not take the form it had assumed in the East, where if anyone bled from the nose it was an obvious portent of certain death. On the contrary, its earliest symptom, in men and women alike, was the appearance of certain swellings in the groin or the armpit, some of which were egg-shaped whilst others were roughly the size of the common apple. Sometimes the swellings were large, sometimes not so large, and they were referred to by the populace as *gavòccioli*. From the two areas already mentioned, this deadly *gavòcciolo* would begin to spread, and within a short time it would appear at random all over the body. Later on, the symptoms of the disease changed, and many people began to find dark blotches and bruises on their arms, thighs, and other parts of the body, sometimes large and few in number, at other times tiny and closely spaced. These, to anyone unfortunate enough to contract them, were just as infallible a sign that he would die as the *gavòcciolo* had been earlier, and as indeed it still was.

Against these maladies, it seemed that all the advice of physicians and all the power of medicine were profitless and unavailing. Perhaps the nature of the illness was such that it allowed no remedy; or perhaps those people who were treating the illness (whose numbers had increased enormously because the ranks of the qualified were invaded by people, both men and women, who had never received any training in medicine), being ignorant of its causes, were not prescribing the appropriate cure. At all events, few of those who caught it ever recovered, and in most cases death occurred within three days from the appearance of the symptoms we have described, some people dying more rapidly than others, the majority without any fever or other complications.

But what made this pestilence even more severe was that whenever those suffering from it mixed with people who were still unaffected, it would rush upon these with the speed of a fire racing through dry or oily substances that happened to be placed within its reach. Nor was this the full extent of its evil, for not only did it infect healthy persons who conversed or had any dealings with the sick, making them ill or visiting an equally horrible death upon them, but it also seemed to transfer the sickness to anyone touching the clothes or other objects which had been handled or used by its victims. . . .

Some people were of the opinion that a sober and abstemious mode of living considerably reduced the risk of infection. They therefore formed themselves into groups and lived in isolation from everyone else. Having withdrawn to a comfortable abode where there were no sick persons, they locked themselves in and settled down to a peaceable existence, consuming modest quantities of delicate foods and precious wines and avoiding all excesses. They refrained from speaking to outsiders, refused to receive news of the dead or sick, and entertained themselves with music and whatever other amusements they were able to devise.

Others took the opposite view, and maintained that an infallible way of warding off this appalling evil was to drink heavily, enjoy life to the full, go round singing and merrymaking, gratify all of one's cravings whenever the opportunity offered, and shrug the whole thing off as one enormous joke. Moreover, they practised what they preached to the best of their ability, for they would visit one tavern after another, drinking all day and night to immoderate excess; or alternatively (and this was their more frequent custom), they would do their drinking in various private houses, but only in the ones where the conversation was restricted to subjects that were pleasant or entertaining. Such places were easy to find, for people behaved as though their days were numbered, and treated their belongings and their own persons with equal abandon. Hence most houses had become common property, and any passing stranger could make himself at home as naturally as though he were the rightful owner. But for all their riotous manner of living, these people always took good care to avoid any contact with the sick.

In the face of so much affliction and misery, all respect for the laws of God and man had virtually broken down and been extinguished in our city. For like everybody else, those ministers and executors of the laws who were not either dead or ill were left with so few subordinates that they were unable to discharge any of their duties. Hence everyone was free to behave as he pleased.

There were many other people who steered a middle course between the two already mentioned, neither restricting their diet to the same degree as the first group, nor indulging so freely as the second in drinking and other forms of wantonness, but simply doing no more than satisfy their appetite. Instead of incarcerating themselves, these people moved about freely, holding in their hands a posy of flowers, or fragrant herbs, or one of a wide range of spices, which they applied at frequent intervals to their nostrils, thinking it an excellent idea to fortify the brain with smells of that particular sort; for the stench of dead bodies, sickness, and medicines seemed to fill and pollute the whole of the atmosphere.

Some people, pursuing what was possibly the safer alternative, callously maintained that there was no better or more efficacious remedy against a plague than to run away from it. Swayed by this argument, and sparing no thought for anyone but themselves, large numbers of men and women abandoned their city, their homes, their relatives, their estates, and their belongings, and headed for the countryside, either in Florentine territory or, better still, abroad. It was as though they imagined that the wrath of God would not unleash this plague against men for their iniquities irrespective of where they happened to be, but would only be aroused against those who found themselves within the city walls; or possibly they assumed that the whole of the population would be exterminated and that the city's last hour had come.

Of the people who held these various opinions, not all of them died. Nor, however, did they all survive. On the contrary, many of each different persuasion fell ill here, there, and everywhere, and having themselves, when they were fit and well, set an example to those who were as yet unaffected, they languished away with virtually no one to nurse them. It was not merely a question of one citizen avoiding another, and of people almost invariably neglecting their neighbours and rarely or never visiting their relatives, addressing them only from a distance; this scourge had implanted so great a terror in the hearts of men and women that brothers abandoned brothers, uncles their nephews, sisters their brothers, and in many cases wives deserted their husbands. But even worse, and almost incredible, was the fact that fathers and mothers refused to nurse and assist their own children, as though they did not belong to them.

Hence the countless numbers of people who fell ill, both male and female, were entirely dependent upon either the charity of friends (who were few and far between) or the greed of servants, who remained in short supply despite the attraction of high wages out of all proportion to the services they performed. Furthermore, these latter were men and women of coarse intellect and the majority were unused to such duties, and they did little more than hand things to the invalid when asked to do so and watch over him when he was dying. And in performing this kind of service, they frequently lost their lives as well as their earnings.

As a result of this wholesale desertion of the sick by neighbours, relatives, and friends, and in view of the scarcity of servants, there grew up a practice almost never previously heard of, whereby when a woman fell ill, no matter how gracious or beautiful or gently bred she might be, she raised no objection to being attended by a male servant, whether he was young or not. Nor did she have any scruples about showing him every part of her body as freely as she would have displayed it to a woman, provided that the nature of her infirmity required her to do so; and this explains why those women who recovered were possibly less chaste in the period that followed.

Moreover a great many people died who would perhaps have survived had they received some assistance. And hence, what with the lack of appropriate means for tending the sick, and the virulence of the plague, the number of deaths reported in the city whether by day or night was so enormous that it astonished all who heard tell of it, to say nothing of the people who actually witnessed the carnage. . . .

As for the common people and a large proportion of the bourgeoisie, they presented a much more pathetic spectacle, for the majority of them were constrained, either by their poverty or the hope of survival, to remain in their houses. Being confined to their own parts of the city, they fell ill daily in their thousands, and since they had no one to assist them or attend to their needs, they inevitably perished almost without exception. Many dropped dead in the open streets, both by day and by night, whilst a great many others, though dying in their own houses, drew their neighbours' attention to the fact more by the smell of their rotting corpses than by any other means. And what with these, and the others who were dying all over the city, bodies were here, there, and everywhere. . . .

[T]here were no tears or candles or mourners to honour the dead; in fact, no more respect was accorded to dead people than would nowadays be shown towards dead goats. For it was quite apparent that the one thing which, in normal times, no wise man had ever learned to accept with patient resignation (even though it struck so seldom and unobtrusively), had now been brought home to the feeble-minded as well, but the scale of the calamity caused them to regard it with indifference.

Such was the multitude of corpses (of which further consignments were arriving every day and almost by the hour at each of the churches), that there was not sufficient consecrated ground for them to be buried in, especially if each was to have its own plot in accordance with long-established custom. So when all the graves were full, huge trenches were excavated in the churchyards, into which new arrivals were placed in their hundreds, stowed tier upon tier like ships' cargo, each layer of corpses being covered over with a thin layer of soil till the trench was filled to the top.

But rather than describe in elaborate detail the calamities we experienced in the city at that time, I must mention that, whilst an ill wind was blowing through Florence itself, the surrounding region was no less badly affected. In the fortified towns, conditions were similar to those in the city itself on a minor scale; but in the scattered hamlets and the countryside proper, the poor unfortunate peasants and their families had no physicians or servants whatever to assist them, and collapsed by the wayside, in their fields, and in their cottages at all hours of the day and night, dying more like animals than human beings. Like the townspeople, they too grew apathetic in their ways, disregarded their affairs, and neglected their possessions. Moreover, they all behaved as though each day was to be their last, and far from making provision for the future by tilling their lands, tending their flocks, and adding to their previous labours, they tried in every way they could think of to squander the assets already in their possession. Thus it came about that oxen, asses, sheep, goats, pigs, chickens, and even dogs (for all their deep fidelity to man) were driven away and allowed to roam freely through the fields, where the crops lay abandoned and had not even been reaped, let alone gathered in. And after a whole day's feasting, many of these animals, as though possessing the power of reason, would return glutted in the evening to their own quarters without any shepherd to guide them.

But let us leave the countryside and return to the city. What more remains to be said, except that the cruelty of heaven (and possibly, in some measure, also that of man) was so immense and so devastating that between March and July of the year in question, what with the fury of the pestilence and the fact that so many of the sick were inadequately cared for or abandoned in their hour of need because the healthy were too terrified to approach them, it is reliably thought that over a hundred thousand human lives were extinguished within the walls of the city of Florence? Yet before this lethal catastrophe fell upon the city, it is doubtful whether anyone would have guessed it contained so many inhabitants.

4

Images of the Black Death

Contemporary accounts testify to the plague's terrifying physical, social, and psychological impact. Images from the period document the ravages of the epidemic as well, sometimes in gruesome detail. The engraving in Figure 12.1, for example, shows a plague victim covered in the dark blotches characteristic of the disease. The town in the background appears to be going up in flames while lightning flares in the sky above. What else do you think is going on in this image?

Figure 12.1 The Black Death, 1348.

Source: The Bridgeman Art Library International.

Figures 12.2 and 12.3 show two well-documented phenomena of the plague years: The first depicts a group of flagellants, members of a movement who wandered from town to town beating themselves with whips studded with iron nails in an effort to do penance for the sins they believed had brought on the plague. Written accounts confirm many elements in this picture: Flagellants usually carried crosses or banners with crosses on them, wore long pleated skirts, and went around bare-chested, the better to make their scourging as painful as possible. Figure 12.3 illustrates a similar impulse toward punishment as a means of coping with the plague, but this time the violence is directed outward, against Jews, so often the scapegoats in troubled times. Baseless accusations that Jews poisoned wells to spread the plague resulted in many such attacks against them during the period.

Figure 12.2 Flagellants, from a Fifteenth-Century Chronicle from Constance, Switzerland.

Source: © Bettmann/CORBIS.

Figure 12.3 The Burning of Jews in an Early Printed Woodcut.

Source: © Christel Gerstenberg/CORBIS.

Figure 12.4 François de la Sarra, Tomb at La Sarraz, Switzerland, c. 1390.
Source: Musée de l'Elysée, Lausanne.

The final image, Figure 12.4, is one of a transi tomb from 1390. Transi tombs, which emerged during and after the plague era, were a major departure from standard funerary monuments that typically offered an idealized depiction of the deceased. Instead these tombs showed decaying or skeletal corpses covered with worms and other emblems of bodily corruption. Scholars differ over their meaning. How might you explain them?

THINKING HISTORICALLY

What can these images tell us about fourteenth-century people's beliefs about the possible causes — medical or religious — of the plague? Do the images suggest a greater belief in medical or religious causes? Think about the social and religious changes wrought by the plague recounted in the de' Mussis and Boccaccio readings. What evidence, if any, do you see in these images of these changes?

5

AHMAD AL-MAQRIZI
The Plague in Cairo

Ahmad al-Maqrizi* (1364–1442) became a historian after pursuing a career as an administrator in postplague Cairo. Although he wrote his history of the plague period more than fifty years after the event, he probably had access to contemporary sources that are now lost to us. Compare al-Maqrizi's account of the plague in Cairo with the prior accounts of the plague in Italy. How was the experience of the Black Death in Cairo similar to, and different from, the experience in Florence?

THINKING HISTORICALLY

Like Boccaccio, al-Maqrizi devotes more attention to the effects than to the causes of the Black Death. What effects were similar in Florence and Cairo? Al-Maqrizi discusses certain effects that were not mentioned in the Italian accounts. Which, if any, of these effects do you think also probably occurred in Italy?

In January 1349, there appeared new symptoms that consisted of spitting up of blood. The disease caused one to experience an internal fever, followed by an uncontrollable desire to vomit; then one spat up blood and died. The inhabitants of a house were stricken one after the other, and in one night or two, the dwelling became deserted. Each individual lived with this fixed idea that he was going to die in this way. He prepared for himself a good death by distributing alms; he arranged for scenes of reconciliation and his acts of devotion multiplied. . . .

By January 21, Cairo had become an abandoned desert, and one did not see anyone walking along the streets. A man could go from the Port Zuwayla to Bāb al-Nasr[1] without encountering a living soul. The dead were very numerous, and all the world could think of nothing else. Debris piled up in the streets. People went around with worried faces. Everywhere one heard lamentations, and one could not pass by any house without being overwhelmed by the howling. Cadavers formed

*ahk MAHD ahl mah KREE zee
[1] This was apparently the busiest boulevard in medieval Cairo.

Source: John Aberth, *The Black Death: The Great Mortality of 1348–1350, A Brief History with Documents* (Boston: Bedford/St. Martin's, 2005), 84–87.

a heap on the public highway, funeral processions were so many that they could not file past without bumping into each other, and the dead were transported in some confusion. . . .

One began to have to search for readers of the Koran for funeral ceremonies, and a number of individuals quit their usual occupations in order to recite prayers at the head of funeral processions. In the same way, some people devoted themselves to smearing crypts with plaster; others presented themselves as volunteers to wash the dead or carry them. These latter folk earned substantial salaries. For example, a reader of the Koran took ten *dirhams*.[2] Also, hardly had he reached the oratory when he slipped away very quickly in order to go officiate at a new [funeral]. Porters demanded 6 *dirhams* at the time they were engaged, and then it was necessary to match it [at the grave]. The gravedigger demanded fifty *dirhams* per grave. Most of the rest of these people died without having taken any profit from their gains. . . . Also families kept their dead on the bare ground, due to the impossibility of having them interred. The inhabitants of a house died by the tens and, since there wasn't a litter ready to hand, one had to carry them away in stages. Moreover, some people appropriated for themselves without scruple the immovable and movable goods and cash of their former owners after their demise. But very few lived long enough to profit thereby, and those who remained alive would have been able to do without. . . .

Family festivities and weddings had no more place [in life]. No one issued an invitation to a feast during the whole time of the epidemic, and one did not hear any concert. The *vizier*[3] lifted a third of what he was owed from the woman responsible [for collecting] the tax on singers. The call to prayer was canceled in various places, and in the exact same way, those places [where prayer] was most frequent subsisted on a *muezzin*[4] alone. . . .

The men of the [military] troop and the cultivators took a world of trouble to finish their sowing [of fields]. The plague emerged at the end of the season when the fields were becoming green. How many times did one see a laborer, at Gaza, at Ramleh, and along other points of the Syrian littoral,[5] guide his plow being pulled by oxen suddenly fall down dead, still holding in his hands his plow, while the oxen stood at their place without a conductor.

It was the same in Egypt: When the harvest time came, there remained only a very small number of *fellahs*.[6] The soldiers and their valets left for

---

[2] A silver coin used in the Muslim world.

[3] The chief minister of the caliph, or leader of the Muslim community.

[4] An official of the mosque who called the faithful to prayer from the minaret.

[5] The coastal plain of southern Palestine, where the most fertile land was located.

[6] Arabic word for ploughman or tiller, which also denoted the peasantry of Egypt and is the origin of the modern term, *fellahin*.

the harvest and attempted to hire workers, promising them half of the crop, but they could not find anyone to help them reap it. They loaded the grain on their horses, did the mowing themselves, but, being powerless to carry out the greatest portion of the work, they abandoned this enterprise.

The endowments[7] passed rapidly from hand to hand as a consequence of the multiplicity of deaths in the army. Such a concession passed from one to the other until the seventh or eighth holder, to fall finally [into the hands] of artisans, such as tailors, shoemakers, or public criers, and these mounted the horse, donned the [military] headdress, and dressed in military tunics.

Actually, no one collected the whole revenue of his endowment, and a number of holders harvested absolutely nothing. During the flooding of the Nile[8] and the time of the sprouting of vegetation, one could procure a laborer only with difficulty: On half the lands only did the harvest reach maturity. Moreover, there was no one to buy the green clover [as feed] and no one sent their horses to graze over the field. This was the ruin of royal properties in the suburbs of Cairo, like Matarieh, Hums, Siryaqus, and Bahtit. In the canton [administrative district] of Nay and Tanan, 1,500 *feddans*[9] of clover were abandoned where it stood: No one came to buy it, either to pasture their beasts on the place or to gather it into barns and use it as fodder.

The province of Upper Egypt was deserted, in spite of the vast abundance of cultivable terrain. It used to be that, after the land surface was cultivated in the territory of Asyūt,[10] 6,000 individuals were subject to payment of the property tax; now, in the year of the epidemic [1348–1349], one could not count on more than 106 contributors. Nevertheless, during this period, the price of wheat did not rise past fifteen *dirhams* per *ardeb*.[11]

Most of the trades disappeared, for a number of artisans devoted themselves to handling the dead, while the others, no less numerous, occupied themselves in selling off to bidders [the dead's] movable goods and clothing, so well that the price of linen and similar objects fell by a fifth of their real value, at the very least, and still further until one found customers. . . .

Thus the trades disappeared: One could no longer find either a water carrier, or a laundress, or a domestic. The monthly salary of a groom rose from thirty *dirhams* to eighty. A proclamation made in Cairo invited the artisans to take up their old trades, and some of the recalcitrants reformed themselves. Because of the shortage of men and camels, a goatskin of water reached the price of eight *dirhams*, and in order to grind an *ardeb* of wheat, one paid fifteen *dirhams*.

---

[7] Mamluk commanders and elite soldiers, like their Ayyubid predecessors, were paid out of the revenues of land grants, known as *iqtas* (similar to fiefs in Europe). With the dearth of labor caused by the Black Death, it became far more difficult to extract income from these estates.

[8] This usually took place between September and November of every year.

[9] A *feddan* is equivalent to 1.038 acres.

[10] Located along the Nile in Upper Egypt, about midway between Cairo and Aswan.

[11] An *ardeb* is equivalent to 5.62 bushels.

6

MICHAEL W. DOLS

The Comparative Communal Responses to the Black Death in Muslim and Christian Societies

Here a modern historian compares the impact of the Black Death in Christian Europe and the Muslim Middle East. He is particularly interested in how Christian and Muslim communities had different group responses. What similarities or differences does he see in the actual disease and its death toll? How is his description of the disease similar to, or different from, those in the previous selections? How might you account for any differences in the descriptions? How would you summarize the author's thesis or argument? How were the responses to the plague different in Christian and Muslim societies? What is his explanation for these differences?

THINKING HISTORICALLY

In modern society, we tend to give greater credence to scientific and medical explanations of disease. We are even inclined to dismiss the religious explanations of our medieval forbears. But Dols suggests that the religious ideas of the fourteenth century caused the different responses to the plague. Thus, the consequences of the Black Death were different in Europe and the Middle East. What sort of argument could be made to dispute Dols's idea of causes and consequences?

In the middle of the fourteenth century a devastating pandemic of plague, commonly known in European history as the Black Death, swept through the entire Mediterranean world. This cataclysmic event caused a dramatic demographic decline in Muslim and Christian countries and provoked definable communal responses. . . .

The pandemic was transmitted from central Asia and spread throughout the Middle East, North Africa, and Europe. Based on contemporary Arabic and Latin sources, we can be certain of the existence of the

Source: Michael W. Dols, "The Comparative Communal Responses to the Black Death in Muslim and Christian Societies," *Viator* 5(1974): 269–87.

three major forms of plague (bubonic, pneumonic, and septicaemic)[1] in these regions. In any historical comparison of the role of the pandemic in Muslim and Christian societies we can assume as a constant the medical nature of the disease itself. In addition, almost all of the medieval physicians believed that the immediate cause of this disease was a pestilential miasma or corruption of the air; this belief was broadly accepted in both societies due to their common reliance on the theory of epidemics found in Hippocrates and elaborated by Galen and Ibn Sina (Avicenna), the greatest medical authorities for the fourteenth century physicians. Therefore, in the Oriental and Western plague treatises there is similar advice for improving or changing the air in a plague-stricken community. . . .

The Black Death was variously interpreted by contemporary European writers. The pandemic was considered, however, by most European observers to result directly from the pestilential miasma, and it was believed that the disease was contagious, which accounts for the important protective measures taken by the Italian cities and the widespread advocacy of flight as the best means of escaping the epidemic. The physicians mention natural causations of the disease (such as an unfavorable conjunction of the planets, or earthquakes) among the remote causes of the miasma. Yet only one European treatise gives a concrete remedy against the astrological causes of plague; the customary recommendations were flight and prayer.

The most commonly held opinion about the ultimate cause of the plague pandemic was religious: the European Christian viewed the Black Death as an overwhelming punishment from God for his sins and those of his fellow Christians. Despite the other interpretations of the disease, this view is the only one that satisfactorily explains the extraordinary forms of communal behavior that took place in many parts of Europe during the Black Death. This supernatural solution was propagated by the Church and is reflected in contemporary European art and literature. The chronicles of the fourteenth century almost always attribute the affliction to divine retribution for the wickedness of European society. [William] Langland[2] summarizes the common view succinctly: "These pestilences were for pure sin."

Based directly on biblical and classical precedents, a conviction of personal guilt and a need for individual and collective expiation were engendered in the faithful Christian. His attitude to the Black Death is well illustrated by the European communal response. This response took the forms of the flagellant movement, the persecution of alien groups (particularly the Jews), and a pessimistic preoccupation with imminent death.[3]

---

[1] All three are produced by the virus *Yersinia pestis*; *bubonic* is named for "buboes" or lesions on the skin (see Figure 12.1), *pneumonic* (like pneumonia) is in the lungs, and *septicaemic* is in the blood. [Ed.]

[2] Contemporary author (c. 1330–c. 1400). [Ed.]

[3] See Figures 12.2, 12.3, and 12.4. [Ed.]

The flagellant movement was based on a belief in the mortification of the flesh as suitable penance for men's sins. Beginning in mid-thirteenth-century Italy, a series of natural disasters convinced many that God's wrath was visiting men as a punishment for their sinfulness. This concept was acted out in expiatory pilgrimages and processions in an attempt to divert or allay God's chastisement. The processions recurred continually during the later Middle Ages. From their inception, an implicit element of the flagellant movement was its participation in the millennial ideas that Professor Cohn[4] has shown to be a significant theme of late medieval Christendom, stemming especially from the millennial scheme of Joachim of Fiore.[5] Self-flagellation was "a collective *imitatio Christi*,[6] a redemptive sacrifice which protected the world from final overwhelming catastrophe, and by virtue of which they themselves [the flagellants] became a holy elite.". . .

The flagellant movement was a complex social phenomenon. Its apocalyptic ambitions proved to be an incentive to personal mysticism, anticlericalism, and social revolutionary ideas such as the destruction of private wealth. The flagellants were also intimately associated with the second major feature of the European reaction to the pandemic: the persecution of the Jews.

The massacres of the Jews during the Black Death were unprecedented in their extent and ferocity until the twentieth century. The first attacks on the Jews resulted from the accusation that this inassimilable community had caused the pestilence by poisoning wells; this was neither new (Jews had been accused and massacred in southern France and Spain during the . . . epidemics of 1320 and 1333), nor confined to the Jews alone. Lepers, gravediggers and other social outcasts, Muslims in Spain, or any foreigners were liable to attack. . . . But in September 1348 the forced confessions from ten Jews in Chillon[7] were adduced to support this fantasy and to implicate all European Jews. A second wave of massacres from the middle of 1349 was instigated by the propaganda of the flagellants. In many cities of Germany and the Low Countries (Frankfort, Maine, Cologne, Brussels) the destruction of the Jewish population was led by the flagellants, aided by the masses of the poor. Pope Clement VI finally condemned the flagellants in 1349 after two bulls in the same year against the persecution of the Jews had been ineffectual. . . .

In the complex psychological response to the Black Death, the natural preoccupation with death was therefore not inconsistent with

---

[4] Norman Cohn, *The Pursuit of the Millennium.* [Ed.]

[5] Twelfth-century theologian; predicted New Age of universal harmony based on Book of Revelations. [Ed.]

[6] Imitation of Christ, in suffering. [Ed.]

[7] A castle on Lake Geneva in modern Switzerland. [Ed.]

a vision of the biblical Apocalypse.[8] Many believed that the end of the world had come, plague being the apocalyptic rider on the white horse. In an account of the island of Cyprus during the pandemic, an Arabic chronicler testifies to the Christian belief by his remark that the Christian Cypriots "feared that it was the end of the world." The Black Death did not create these forms of reaction or the ideology that lay behind them; it was a stimulus, despite its irregularity of attack, which exposed the nerve system of late medieval Christian society.

The Middle Eastern interpretations of the Black Death display a diversity of opinions similar to that of the European accounts. Yet, the dominant Muslim view of plague was set forth in the formulation of three religio-legal principles, which directly affected communal behavior: (1) plague was a mercy from God and a martyrdom for the faithful Muslim; (2) a Muslim should not enter nor flee from a plague-stricken land; and (3) there was no contagion of plague since disease came directly from God. . . .

All three traditions were attributed to the Prophet. Muhammad was reputed to have prohibited flight from a plague-stricken community. . . . Accordingly, Muhammad was understood to have denied the pre-Islamic Arab belief in contagion. Consistent with this idea that plague was a divine selection is the principle that plague was a mercy from God for the faithful Muslim but a punishment for the infidel. . . .

The importance of these three principles to Muslim society was in what they did *not* affirm: they did not declare that plague was God's punishment; they did not encourage flight; and they did not support a belief in the contagious nature of plague—all of which were prevalent in Christian Europe. These principles appear to be borne out by the reports of the general communal responses to the Black Death in the major cities in the Middle East.

The Muslim reaction to the Black Death was characterized by organized communal supplication that included processions through the cities and mass funerals in the mosques. There is no indication of the abandonment of religious rites and services for the dead but rather an increased emphasis on personal piety and ritual purity. . . .

It is reported that pious men were stationed at various places of worship in Cairo and Fustat[9] in order to recite the funeral prayers. Many men left their normal occupations to profit from the funerals, as by chanting the funeral prayers at the head of processions. These processions from the mosques or homes to the cemeteries filled the streets of Cairo during the Black Death. They were so numerous that they could not pass in the roadways without disturbing one another. Moreover, there were

---

[8]The end of the world. See Chapter 6, Book of Daniel, for origins of idea. Also see Book of Revelations. [Ed.]

[9]Old Cairo. [Ed.]

pious visitations to the graves in the common belief that the souls of the deceased resided in the tombs. . . .

An important part of urban activity in response to the Black Death was the communal prayers for the lifting of the disease. During the greatest severity of the pandemic, orders were given in Cairo to assemble in the mosques and to recite the recommended prayers in common. Fasting and processions took place in the cities during the Black Death and later plague epidemics; the supplicatory[10] processions followed the traditional form of prayer for rain. . . . As the Black Death worsened, a proclamation was made in Damascus inviting the population to fast for three days and to go out on the fourth day (Friday) to the Mosque of the Foot, in order to supplicate God for the removing of this scourge. Most of the Damascenes were reported to have fasted, and several spent the night in the Umayyad Mosque[11] performing the acts of faith as in the ritual during Ramadan and reading al-Bukhari.[12] On Friday morning the inhabitants of Damascus came out from all sides, including Jews, Christians, Samaritans, old men and women, young infants, the poor, amirs, notables, and magistrates. Before the morning prayer, they marched from the Umayyad Mosque to the Mosque of the Foot and did not cease chanting the prayers throughout the day. . . .

The plague treatises also attest to a large number of popular magical beliefs and practices concerning plague, which should be interpreted as a significant element in the total religious response of Muslim society. The amulets and talismans, incantations, and magical inscriptions that were directed against plague were not unique phenomena; they were only part of a vast body of magical beliefs and practices that are more familiarly associated with the "evil eye." . . .

The comparison of Christian and Muslim societies during the Black Death points to the significant disparity in their general communal responses. . . . [In Christian Europe] mass communal funeral services, processions, and journeys to the cemeteries were greatly limited by the common European belief in contagion. . . . Conversely, the Arabic sources do not attest to the "striking manifestations of abnormal collective psychology, of dissociation of the group mind," which occurred in Christian Europe. Fear and trepidation of the Black Death in Europe activated what Professor Trevor-Roper has called, in a different context,[13] a European "stereotype of fear"; the collective emotion played upon a mythology of messianism, anti-Semitism, and man's culpability for his sins.

---

[10] Pleading, begging. [Ed.]
[11] The great mosque in Damascus, the capital of the Umayyad Caliphate. [Ed.]
[12] Compiler of *hadiths* (sayings of the Prophet). [Ed.]
[13] *The European Witch-Craze of the Sixteenth and Seventeenth Centuries* (1978). [Ed.]

Why are the corresponding phenomena not found in the Muslim reaction to the Black Death? The stereotypes did not exist. There is no evidence for the appearance of messianic movements in Muslim society at this time which might have associated the Black Death with an apocalypse. . . . Furthermore, the fact that there was no certainty that plague was a divine punishment for sin removed the impetus for a cohesive puritanical and revivalist popular movement.

The impact of the Black Death poses the question of the Muslim attitude toward minorities. The unassimilated communities were tolerated in medieval Muslim society and, in this instance, were not held responsible for the ravages of the pandemic. However theoretical, the legal tenet against contagion of plague would have militated against the accusation of the minorities. In no case is there a direct causal relationship to be found between the Black Death (and subsequent plague epidemics) and the active persecution of minorities as in Europe.

The Christian belief in plague as a divine punishment for men's sins was preached by clergymen deeply committed to the idea of original sin and man's guilt arising from his essential depravity, as well as to a fundamental contempt—both Christian and Stoic—for this world. The Black Death was the occasion for the vigorous realization of these ideas. However, there is no doctrine of original sin and of man's insuperable guilt in Islamic theology. The Muslim writers on plague did not dwell on the guilt of their co-religionists even if they did admit that plague was a divine warning against sin. Prayer was supplication and not expiation.

In contrast, the general reaction of Muslim society to the Black Death was governed by its interpretation as only another common natural disaster. . . . Further, obedience to the decision of the communal leader (*mukhldr*) with regard to moving away or remaining must be preserved. If changing the air by flight cannot be undertaken because: (1) the epidemic is universal; (2) the fear that the plague victims would be neglected; or (3) the need to preserve the commonweal of the community (which is an essential tenet of Islam) from disruption and disorder, the people are simply to remain and improve their circumstances by cleaning their houses and fumigating the air with various scents and fresh fruits.

The prescriptions . . . for a Muslim community at the time of a plague epidemic bring into focus the contrasting orientations of the two religions. The Black Death touched upon the central theme of Christian teaching concerning evil and human suffering; Western man took the plague epidemic as an individual trial more than a collective, social calamity. The Islamic tradition, however, has not concerned itself to the same degree with personal suffering; the central problem for the Muslim is the solemn responsibility for his decisions that affect other men's lives and fortunes within a purposeful creation. The cosmic settings of the two faiths are wide apart in their emphasis: where the Muslim's primary duty was toward the correct behavior of the total community based on the sacred law, the Christian's was with personal redemption. Where the Qur'an supplied guidance, the Bible furnished consolation. For the Muslim the Black Death was part of a God-ordered, natural universe; for the Christian it was an irruption of the profane world of sin and misery.

In sum, it would be as great an error to discount the religious interpretations of plague as motives and limits to communal behavior as to discount the classical medical theories of plague which underlay most of the medical remedies and treatments in both the East and West. Taken together, the medieval Christian ideas of punishment and guilt, militancy toward alien communities, and millennialism are raised to crucial significance in contrast to the Muslim understanding of the Black Death. The operative European Christian concepts were lacking in Muslim society as were their unattractive consequences of religious fanaticism, persecution, and desperation. The predominant theological views of the two societies set the framework for normative attitudes and the prescriptions for communal behavior in which human nature found expression and form when confronted by the Black Death.

■ REFLECTIONS

It might seem that there would be little more we could learn about a plague that occurred over 650 years ago. But that is not the case. Historians are constantly asking new questions about the past, sometimes armed with new sources of information or new techniques of investigation. One recent line of inquiry has centered on the causes of the disease. In *The Black Death and the Transformation of the West* (Harvard University Press, 1997), David Herlihy questions whether the Black Death was in fact the plague. His student, Samuel K. Cohn Jr., answers a vigorous "no." Cohn's *The Black Death Transformed: Disease and Culture in Early Renaissance Europe* (Arnold, 2003) argues that the disease resembled a viral infection rather than the bacterium *Yersinia pestis* that causes the plague. Cohn writes that the Black Death, like the flu pandemic of 1918, was highly contagious, moved very rapidly, apparently on droplets in the air, taking enormous casualties. By contrast, the last wave of plague, which originated in Hong Kong in 1894 (and from which *Y. pestis* was identified), traveled slowly as it was transferred by fleas from rats to humans, infecting only those who were bitten, and killing only about 3 percent of those exposed. Further, Cohen points out, we do not hear of rats and fleas in the accounts of the Black Death. He adds that twentieth-century plague deaths in India and Manchuria continued year after year, providing no immunity from exposure, whereas the Black Death occurred only in the summer of 1348 (when incidentally the hot, dry weather meant few fleas) and then again for about one year every decade, causing fewer and fewer fatalities, except for children—who had no immunity. This would seem to be a good case for DNA testing. In fact, a disputed test of a bone from a possible Black Death victim in France revealed the existence of *Y. pestis*, but other samples have not, leaving the issue still in doubt.

Scholars have also explored the dimensions of the Black Death beyond Europe. Until recently, the subject was a virtual monopoly of European historians, but we can now ask about the Black Death in Egypt and the Middle East, as we do here with Michael W. Dols's comparison of the consequences of Christian and Muslim beliefs. Stuart J. Borsch, in *The Black Death in Egypt and England: A Comparative Study* (University of Texas Press, 2005), asks about longer-term consequences: Why did Europe recover and thrive after 1350 whereas the economy of Egypt began a long decline? He finds the answer in the differences between the landholding systems of English peasants, who prospered as their numbers declined, and the disinterested absentee landlords of the Egyptian Mamluk regime (1250–1517), who just cut their losses and left. Other factors may account for the long-term economic decline of Egypt and other Muslim regimes in contrast to the revival of Christian Europe. Whereas Michael Dols emphasizes the role of religious ideas, others have commented on the changing balance of religious and secular explanations in both cultures. Religious explanations were, in fact, more common in Christian Europe in 1348 than they were in Muslim Egypt, where secular explanations outnumbered religious ones. Yet this imbalance was reversed in later years. After 1350 Europeans increasingly described the event in secular terms, crediting individual doctors and medical treatments rather than supernatural factors for their survival. The Islamic world of the Middle East moved in the opposite direction after 1350, becoming less secular and more religious. Cohn offers the rise of secular humanism in the European Renaissance as further evidence that the Black Death was like a flu that abated as people developed immunity and therefore felt more confident about human effort; but a similar response to the same disease did not occur in Egypt or the Middle East, more generally.

We still do not know how global the Black Death was. We trace its origins to Central Asia because we have no anecdotal or literary evidence for China or India. But we know that the population of China declined drastically from about 1200 to 1400[1] and that India was part of the Eurasian zone of shared diseases and immunities. We also do not know if the Black Death penetrated beyond the Sahara or up the Nile to sub-Saharan Africa. So there is still a lot more to learn, even to answer today's questions.

---

[1] In 1400 the Chinese population was actually about the same as it had been in 1200, but in both the previous and the subsequent 200-year period, it increased by 40–50 percent. A continuous population increase between 1200 and 1400 would have added about 150 million people. But this was also the period of the Mongol conquest and the revolt against the Mongols that issued in the Ming dynasty, both extraordinary killers.

13

On Cities

European, Chinese, Islamic, and Mexican Cities, 1000–1550

During the last five thousand years, cities have grown and multiplied, with the world becoming increasingly urbanized. There have been interruptions in this process, however: the period of the Mongol invasions in the first half of the thirteenth century and the era of the Black Death, the plague that wiped out urban populations in the middle of the fourteenth century, for instance. But, by and large, the general course of world history has promoted the rise and expansion of cities and of urban over rural populations.

In this chapter, we ask what this increasing urbanization meant for those who lived in the cities and for those who did not. We compare cities in various parts of the world between 1000 and 1550. We will study primary and secondary sources, and you will be asked to note the ways in which these cities are similar and different.

■ THINKING HISTORICALLY

Evaluating a Comparative Thesis

Many of the chapters, even individual readings, in this volume have been comparative. Making comparisons is a critical skill in any disciplined thinking process. In the study of world history, comparisons are particularly important and potentially fruitful, since until recently the historical profession tended to study different nations' histories somewhat in isolation from each other or without reference to a broader comparative context.

However, comparisons are not useful in and of themselves. They are merely a first step toward a thesis that attempts to explain the differences or similarities noticed. To say that something is bigger or smaller, hotter or colder, than something else, that one country is more densely populated or more religious than another, may be obvious or interesting, but the observation takes on meaning with the application of a theory or thesis that explains the difference. In history, there are many comparative theses. An example of one might run something like this: Canada has a more universal health care system than the United States because it has a longer tradition of mutual aid and trust in government. Now, one might agree or disagree with either the comparison or the explanation. If one disagrees with the comparison there is no need to go further. But if one agrees with the comparison, then one has to evaluate the comparative thesis.

In this chapter you will be asked to consider a comparative thesis about cities that is offered in the first reading. The other readings in the chapter will enable you to consider what evidence they offer for or against the initial comparison and its explanatory thesis.

1

FERNAND BRAUDEL

Towns and Cities

Fernand Braudel* (1902–1985) was one of the great historians of the twentieth century, and the following selection, which provides a broad overview of medieval towns and cities throughout the world, is from one of his interpretative works of world history. According to Braudel, what were some of the distinctive characteristics of Western, or European, towns? Why did Western towns acquire these characteristics? How does Braudel describe Chinese and Islamic cities? Why and how did these towns develop differently?

THINKING HISTORICALLY

Braudel begins with a comparative judgment — that European towns "were marked by an unparalleled freedom." How does he explain this supposed difference between European towns and those of

* broh DELL

Source: Fernand Braudel, *The Structures of Everyday Life: The Limits of the Possible* (London: Collins, 1983), 509–15, 518–25.

other societies? He offers a thesis about the development of European towns. He says that because the European state was weak, these towns developed autonomous, self-governing bodies of largely middle-class citizens who thought of themselves as a community. They were not governed by a king, emperor, or territorial state, but, rather, governed themselves through a number of organizations. In addition to governing councils and militaries, these organizations included guilds, church groups, and various other voluntary societies in which citizens exercised real power over their lives. Braudel attributes these differences to the long history of European feudalism and weak states, and to the rise of capitalism and a middle class in these independent towns.

As you read Braudel, try to weigh his evidence for both the comparison and his explanation. Does it appear from the reading that inhabitants of European towns had greater freedom than the people of other towns? If you agree with his comparison, try to evaluate his explanation. Was there a complex of features in Western society that did not occur elsewhere? What is his evidence for that comparative thesis? What else would you want to learn to challenge or confirm his thesis?

The Originality of Western Towns

. . . What were Europe's differences and original features? Its towns were marked by an unparalleled freedom. They had developed as autonomous worlds and according to their own propensities. They had outwitted the territorial state, which was established slowly and then only grew with their interested co-operation—and was moreover only an enlarged and often insipid copy of their development. They ruled their countrysides autocratically, regarding them exactly as later powers regarded their colonies, and treating them as such. They pursued an economic policy of their own via their satellites and the nervous system of urban relay points; they were capable of breaking down obstacles and creating or recreating protective privileges. Imagine what would happen if modern states were suppressed so that the Chambers of Commerce of the large towns were free to act as they pleased!

Even without resort to doubtful comparisons these long-standing realities leap to the eye. And they lead us to a key problem which can be formulated in two or three different ways: What stopped the other cities of the world from enjoying the same relative freedom? Or to take another aspect of the same problem, why was change a striking feature of the destiny of Western towns (even their physical existence was transformed) while the other cities have no history by comparison and seem to have been shut in long periods of immobility? Why were some cities like steam-engines while the others were like clocks, to parody Lévi-Strauss?[1] Comparative history compels us to look for the reason for these differences and to attempt to establish a dynamic "model" of the turbulent urban evolution of the West, whereas a model representing city life in the rest of the world would run in a straight and scarcely broken line across time.

Free Worlds

Urban freedom in Europe is a classic and fairly well documented subject; let us start with it.

In a simplified form we can say:

1. The West well and truly lost its urban framework with the end of the Roman Empire. Moreover the towns in the Empire had been gradually declining since before the arrival of the barbarians. The very relative animation of the Merovingian period[2] was followed, slightly earlier in some places, slightly later in others, by a complete halt.

2. The urban renaissance from the eleventh century was precipitated by and superimposed on a rise in rural vigour, a growth of fields, vineyards, and orchards. Towns grew in harmony with villages and clearly outlined urban law often emerged from the communal privileges of village groups. The town was often simply the country revived and remodeled. . . .

This rural rearrangement naturally brought to the nascent city the representatives of political and social authority: nobles, lay princes, and ecclesiastics.

3. None of this would have been possible without a general return to health and a growing monetary economy.[3] . . .

Thousands of towns were founded at this time, but few of them went on to brilliant futures. Only certain regions, therefore, were urbanized in depth, thus distinguishing themselves from the rest and playing a vitalizing role: such was the region between the Loire and the Rhine, for instance, or northern and central Italy, and certain key points on Mediterranean coasts. Merchants, craft guilds, industries, long-distance trade, and banks were quick to appear there, as well as a certain kind of bourgeoisie[4] and

---

[1] Claude Lévi-Strauss (1908–2009), anthropologist who in 1962 compared primitive societies to clocks (controlled change returning to order) and modern societies to steam engines (dynamic, unpredictable change). [Ed.]

[2] 450–751. [Ed.]

[3] He means the reappearance of money and markets, especially in towns. [Ed.]

[4] A middle class in the sense that they were in the middle between aristocrats and peasants. A property-owning city-based class who made their living in the new money economy (from bankers and lawyers to merchants, store owners, and writers). [Ed.]

even some sort of capitalism.[5] The destinies of these very special cities were linked not only to the progress of the surrounding countryside but to international trade. Indeed, they often broke free of rural society and former political ties. The break might be achieved violently or amicably, but it was always a sign of strength, plentiful money, and real power.

Soon there were no states around these privileged towns. This was the case in Italy and Germany, with the political collapses of the thirteenth century. The hare beat the tortoise for once. Elsewhere—in France, England, Castile, even in Aragon—the earlier rebirth of the territorial state restricted the development of the towns, which in addition were not situated in particularly lively economic areas. They grew less rapidly than elsewhere. . . .

In fact the miracle in the West was not so much that everything sprang up again from the eleventh century, after having been almost annihilated with the disaster of the fifth. History is full of examples of secular revivals, of urban expansion, of births and rebirths: Greece from the fifth to the second century B.C.E.; Rome perhaps; Islam from the ninth century; China under the Sungs. But these revivals always featured two runners, the state and the city. The state usually won and the city then remained subject and under a heavy yoke. The miracle of the first great urban centuries in Europe was that the city won hands down, at least in Italy, Flanders, and Germany. It was able to try the experiment of leading a completely separate life for quite a long time. This was a colossal event. Its genesis cannot be pinpointed with certainty, but its enormous consequences are visible.

Towns as Outposts of Modernity

It was on the basis of this liberty that the great Western cities, and other towns they influenced and to which they served as examples, built up a distinctive civilization and spread techniques which were new, or had been revived or rediscovered after centuries—it matters little which. The important thing is that these cities had the rare privilege of following through an unusual political, social, and economic experience.

In the financial sphere, the towns organized taxation, finances, public credit, customs, and excise. They invented public loans: the first issues of the Monte Vecchio[6] in Venice could be said to go back to 1167, the first formulation of the Casa di San Giorgio[7] to 1407. One after another,

---

[5] There are many definitions of capitalism: a money-based economic system; a system where everything (land, labor, and capital) is for sale; the modern economic system in which society is based on the market; a system in which capital (productive resources, money, companies) is privately rather than publicly owned. [Ed.]

[6] The Republic of Venice's first bonds. [Ed.]

[7] Genoa's first public bank. In 1407 Genoa was bankrupt after wars with Venice. The governing Council of Ancients authorized the House of St. George to raise money by selling city debt (at 7 percent interest) and collecting taxes and custom duties owed to the city. [Ed.]

they [the towns] reinvented gold money, following Genoa which may have minted the *genovino* as early as the late twelfth century. They organized industry and the guilds; they invented long-distance trade, bills of exchange, the first forms of trading companies and accountancy. They also quickly became the scene of class struggles: . . . nobles against bourgeois; poor against rich ("thin people" *popolo magro* against "fat people" *popolo grosso*). . . .

This society divided from within also faced enemies from without— . . . everybody who was not a citizen. The cities were the West's first focus for patriotism—and the patriotism they inspired was long to be more coherent and much more conscious than the territorial kind, which emerged only slowly in the first states. . . .

A new state of mind was established, broadly that of an early, still faltering, Western capitalism—a collection of rules, possibilities, calculations, the art both of getting rich and of living. It also included gambling and risk: the key words of commercial language, *fortuna, ventura, ragione, prudenza, sicurta*,[8] define the risks to be guarded against. No question now of living from day to day as noblemen did, always putting up their revenues to try to meet the level of their expenditure, which invariably came first—and letting the future take care of itself. The merchant was economical with his money, calculated his expenditure according to his returns, his investments according to their yield. . . . He would also be economical with his time: . . . "time is money."

Capitalism and towns were basically the same thing in the West. Lewis Mumford humorously claimed that capitalism was the cuckoo's egg laid in the confined nests of the medieval towns. By this he meant to convey that the bird was destined to grow inordinately and burst its tight framework (which was true), and then link up with the state, the conqueror of towns but heir to their institutions and way of thinking and completely incapable of dispensing with them. The important thing was that even when it had declined as a city the town continued to rule the roost all the time it was passing into the actual or apparent service of the prince. The wealth of the state would still be the wealth of the town: Portugal converged on Lisbon, the Netherlands on Amsterdam, and English primacy was London's primacy (the capital modelled England in its own image after the peaceful revolution of 1688). The latent defect in the Spanish imperial economy was that it was based on Seville—a controlled town rotten with dishonest officials and long dominated by foreign capitalists—and not on a powerful free town capable of producing and carrying through a really individual economic policy. . . .

---

[8] Luck, business venture, reason, prudence, security. [Ed.]

Urban Patterns

Let us imagine we are looking at a comprehensive history of the towns of Europe covering the complete series of their forms from the Greek city-state to an eighteenth-century town—everything Europe was able to build at home and overseas, from Muscovy in the East to America in the West. . . .

Simplifying, one could say that the West has had three basic types of town in the course of its evolution: open towns, that is to say not differentiated from their hinterland, even blending into it (A); towns closed in on themselves in every sense, their walls marking the boundaries of an individual way of life more than a territory (B); finally towns held in subjection, by which is meant the whole range of known controls by prince or state (C).

Roughly, A preceded B, and B preceded C. But there is no suggestion of strict succession about this order. It is rather a question of directions and dimensions shaping the complicated careers of the Western towns. They did not all develop at the same time or in the same way. Later we will see if this "grid" is valid for classifying all the towns of the world.

Type A: the ancient Greek or Roman city was open to the surrounding countryside and on terms of equality with it. Athens accepted inside its walls as rightful citizens the Eupatrid[9] horse-breeders as well as the vine-growing peasants so dear to Aristophanes. As soon as the smoke rose above the Pnyx,[10] the peasant responded to the signal and attended the Assembly of the People, where he sat among his equals. At the beginning of the Peloponnesian war,[11] the entire population of the Attic countryside evacuated itself to Athens where it took refuge while the Spartans ravaged the fields, olive groves, and houses. When the Spartans fell back at the approach of winter, the country people returned to their homes. The Greek city was in fact the sum of the town and its surrounding countryside. . . . Likewise, if one explores the ruins of Roman cities, one is in open country immediately outside the gates: There are no suburbs, which is as good as saying no industry or active and organized trades in their duly allotted place.

Type B: the closed city: the medieval town was the classic example of a closed city, a self-sufficient unit, an exclusive, Lilliputian[12] empire. Entering its gates was like crossing one of the serious frontiers of the world today. You were free to thumb your nose at your neighbour from the

[9] Old rural nobility near Athens. [Ed.]

[10] A hill in central Athens near the Acropolis. [Ed.]

[11] War between Athens and Sparta (431–404 B.C.E.). [Ed.]

[12] A small empire. In Jonathan Swift's novel, *Gulliver's Travels* (1726), the inhabitants of Lilliput were "not six inches high." [Ed.]

other side of the barrier. He could not touch you. The peasant who uprooted himself from his land and arrived in the town was immediately another man. He was free—or rather he had abandoned a known and hated servitude for another, not always guessing the extent of it beforehand. But this mattered little. If the town had adopted him, he could snap his fingers when his lord called for him.[13] And though obsolete elsewhere, such calls were still frequently to be heard in Silesia in the eighteenth century and in Muscovy up to the nineteenth.

Though the towns opened their gates easily it was not enough to walk through them to be immediately and really part of them. Full citizens were a jealous minority, a small town inside the town itself. A citadel of the rich was built up in Venice in 1297 thanks to the *serrata*, the closing of the Great Council to new members. The *nobili* of Venice became a closed class for centuries. Very rarely did anyone force its gates. The category of ordinary *cittadini*—at a lower level—was probably more hospitable. But the Signoria[14] very soon created two types of citizen, one *de intus*, the other *de intus et extra*, the latter full, the former partial. Fifteen years' residence were still required to be allowed to apply for the first, twenty-five years for the second. A decree by the Senate in 1386 even forbade new citizens (including those who were full citizens) from trading directly in Venice with German merchants at the Fondego dei Todeschi or outside it. The ordinary townspeople were no less mistrustful or hostile to newcomers. According to Marin Sanudo, in June 1520, the street people attacked the peasants who had arrived from the mainland as recruits for the galleys or the army, crying *"Poltroni ande arar!"* "Back to the plough, shirkers!"

Of course Venice was an extreme example. Moreover, it owed the preservation of its own constitution until 1797 to an aristocratic and extremely reactionary regime, as well as to the conquest at the beginning of the fifteenth century of the Terra Firma,[15] which extended its authority as far as the Alps and Brescia. It was the last *polis*[16] in the West. But citizenship was also parsimoniously granted in Marseilles in the sixteenth century; it was necessary to have "ten years of domicile, to possess property, to have married a local girl." Otherwise the man remained amongst the masses of non-citizens of the town. This limited conception of citizenship was the general rule everywhere.

---

[13] "Thumb his nose at" or ignore common responsibilities of peasants, serfs, and country dwellers, like submission to the lord's courts, feudal dues, required work days, and military service. [Ed.]

[14] One of the governing councils of Venice; ten people who oversaw the larger Senate and the still larger Great Council. [Ed.]

[15] Mainland areas controlled by Venice. [Ed.]

[16] City-state. One of many in the fourteenth century; the last in 1797 maybe, though there is still today San Marino in Italy, Andorra between Spain and France, and small states like Monaco and Luxembourg, in Europe. [Ed.]

The main source of contention can be glimpsed throughout this vast process: to whom did industry and craft, their privileges and profits, belong? In fact they belonged to the town, to its authorities and to its merchant entrepreneurs. They decided if it were necessary to deprive, or to try to deprive, the rural area of the city of the right to spin, weave, and dye, or if on the contrary it would be advantageous to grant it these rights. Everything was possible in these interchanges, as the history of each individual town shows.

As far as work inside the walls was concerned (we can hardly call it industry without qualification), everything was arranged for the benefit of the craft guilds. They enjoyed exclusive contiguous monopolies, fiercely defended along the imprecise frontiers that so easily led to absurd conflicts. The urban authorities did not always have the situation under control. Sooner or later, with the help of money, they were to allow obvious, acknowledged, honorary superiorities, consecrated by money or power, to become apparent. The "Six Corps" (drapers, grocers, haberdashers, furriers, hosiers, goldsmiths) were the commercial aristocracy of Paris from 1625. In Florence it was the *arte dela lana* and the *Arte di Calimala* (engaged in dyeing fabric imported from the north, unbleached). . . .

An even more telling example was the City of London and its annexes (running along its walls) in the eighteenth century, still the domain of fussy, obsolete, and powerful guilds. If Westminster and the suburbs were growing continually, noted a well-informed economist (1754), it was for obvious reasons: "These suburbs are free and present a clear field for every industrious citizen, while in its bosom London nourishes ninety-two of all sorts of those exclusive companies [guilds], whose numerous members can be seen adorning the Lord Mayor's Show every year with immoderate pomp." . . .

Type C: subjugated towns, of early modern times. Everywhere in Europe, as soon as the state was firmly established it disciplined the towns with instinctive relentlessness, whether or not it used violence. The Habsburgs did so just as much as the Popes, the German princes as much as the Medicis or the kings of France. Except in the Netherlands and England, obedience was imposed.

Take Florence as an example: The Medicis had slowly subjugated it, almost elegantly in Lorenzo's time. But after 1532 and the return of the Medicis to power the process accelerated. Florence in the seventeenth century was no more than the Grand Duke's court. He had seized everything—money, the right to govern, and to distribute honours. . . .

Different Types of Development

But we know, of course, that urban development does not happen of its own accord. . . . It is always the expression of a society which controls it from within, but also from without, and in this respect, our classification is, I repeat, too simple. That said, how does it work when applied out-side the narrow confines of Western Europe?

1. *Towns in colonial America.* We should say "in Latin America," because the English towns remained a separate case. They had to live by their own resources and emerge from their wilderness to find a place in the vast world; the real parallel for them is the medieval city. The towns in Iberian America had a much simpler and more limited career. Built like Roman camps inside four earth walls, they were garrisons lost in the midst of vast hostile expanses, linked together by communications which were slow because they stretched across enormous empty spaces. Curiously, at a period when the privileged medieval town had spread over practically the whole of Europe, the ancient rule prevailed in all Hispano-Portuguese America, apart from the large towns of the vice-roys: Mexico City, Lima, Santiago de Chile, San Salvador (Bahia)—that is to say the official, already parasitical organisms.[17]

There were scarcely any purely commercial towns in this part of America, or if there were they were of minor importance. For example, Recife—the merchants' town—stood next to aristocratic Olinda, town of great plantation owners, *senhores de engenbos,*[18] and slave owners. . . . Buenos Aires after its second foundation (the successful one in 1580) was still a small market village. . . . It had the misfortune to have nothing but Indian *bravos*[19] round about, and its inhabitants complained of being forced to earn "their bread by the sweat of their brow" in this America where the whites were *rentiers.*[20] But caravans of mules or large wooden carts arrived there from the Andes, from Lima, which was a way of acquiring Potosi silver. Sugar, and soon gold, came by sailing ship from Brazil. And contact with Portugal and Africa was maintained through the smuggling carried on by sailing ships bringing black slaves. But Buenos Aires remained an excep-tion amidst the "barbarism" of nascent Argentina.

The American town was generally tiny, without these gifts from abroad. It governed itself. No one was really concerned with its fate. Its masters were the landowners who had their houses in the town. . . . These were the "men of property," *os homes bons* of the municipalities of Brazil, or the *hacendados* of the Spanish *cabildos.*[21] . . . Naturally there was no separa-tion between the towns and the hinterland and there was no industry to be

---

[17] Parasitic in the sense that they were European government centers that exploited the countryside and the indigenous population. In the case of Mexico City, this had been true even before European colonization. [Ed.]

[18] Men of talent. Olinda sits on a hill above Recife. [Ed.]

[19] Actually Spanish and mixed Indian-Spanish gauchos as well as Indian horsemen, but the dry pampas or plains south and west of Buenos Aires were, and still are, lightly populated. [Ed.]

[20] Property owners. [Ed.]

[21] Town councils. [Ed.]

shared out. Wherever industry appeared—in Mexico City, for example—it was carried on by slaves or semi-slaves. The medieval European town would not have been conceivable if its artisans had been serfs.

2. *How should Russian towns be classified?* One can tell at a glance that the towns that survived or grew up again in Muscovy after the terrible catastrophes of the Mongol invasion no longer lived according to the Western pattern. Although there were great cities among them, like Moscow or Novgorod, they were kept in hand sometimes brutally. . . . [Novgorod, for example,] was harshly brought to heel in 1427 and again in 1477 (it had to deliver 300 cartloads of gold). Executions, deportations, confiscations followed in quick succession. Above all, these towns were caught up in the slow circulation of traffic over an immense, already Asiatic, still wild expanse. In 1650, as in the past, transport on the rivers or overland by sledge or by convoys of carts moved with an enormous loss of time. It was often dangerous even to go near villages, and a halt had to be called every evening in open country—as on the Balkan roads—deploying the carriages in a circle, with everyone on the alert to defend himself.

For all these reasons the Muscovy towns did not impose themselves on the vast surrounding countryside; quite the reverse. They were unable to dictate their wishes to a peasant world which was biologically extraordinarily strong, although poverty-stricken, restless, and perpetually on the move. The important fact was that "harvests per hectare in the European countries of the East remained constant on average, from the sixteenth to the nineteenth century"—at a low level. There was no healthy rural surplus and therefore no really prosperous town. Nor did the Russian towns have serving them those secondary towns that were a characteristic of the West and its lively trade.

Consequently, there were innumerable peasant serfs practically without land, insolvent in the eyes of their lords and even the state. It was of no importance whether they went to towns or to work in the houses of rich peasants. In the town they became beggars, porters, craftsmen, poor tradesmen, or very rarely merchants who got rich quickly. They might also stay put and become craftsmen in their own villages, or seek the necessary supplement to their earnings by becoming carriers or travelling peddlers. This irresistible tide of mendicancy could not be stemmed, and indeed it often served the interests of the landlord who gave it his blessing: All such artisans and traders remained his serfs whatever they did and however great their social success; they still owed him their dues.

These examples and others indicate a fate resembling what may after all have happened at the beginning of Western urbanization. Though a clearer case, it is comparable to the caesura[22] between the eleventh and thirteenth centuries, that interlude when almost everything was born of

---

[22] Pause. [Ed.]

the villages and peasant vitality. We might call it an intermediate position between A and C, without the B type (the independent city) ever having arisen. The prince appeared too quickly, like the ogre in a fairy tale.

3. *Imperial towns in the East and Far East.* The same problems and ambiguities—only deeper—arise when we leave Europe and move east.

Towns similar to those in medieval Europe—masters of their fate for a brief moment—only arose in Islam when the empires collapsed. They marked some outstanding moments in Islamic civilization. But they only lasted for a time and the main beneficiaries were certain marginal towns like Cordoba, or the cities which were urban republics by the fifteenth century, like Ceuta before the Portuguese occupation in 1415, or Oran before the Spanish occupation in 1509. The usual pattern was the huge city under the rule of a prince or a Caliph: a Baghdad or a Cairo.

Towns in distant Asia were of the same type: imperial or royal cities, enormous, parasitical, soft, and luxurious—Delhi and Vijayanagar, Peking and to some extent Nanking, though this was rather different. The great prestige enjoyed by the prince comes as no surprise to us. And if one ruler was swallowed up by the city or more likely by his palace, another immediately took his place and the subjection continued. Neither will it surprise us to learn that these towns were incapable of taking over the artisanal trades from the countryside: They were both open towns and subject towns simultaneously. Besides, in India as in China, social structures already existing hampered the free movement of the towns. If the town did not win its independence, it was not only because of the bastinadoes[23] ordered by the mandarins[24] or the cruelty of the prince to merchants and ordinary citizens. It was because society was prematurely fixed, crystallized in a certain mould.

In India, the caste system automatically divided and broke up every urban community. In China, the cult of the *gentes*[25] on the one hand was confronted on the other by a mixture comparable to that which created the Western town: Like the latter it acted as a melting-pot, breaking old bonds and placing individuals on the same level. The arrival of immigrants created an "American" environment, where those already settled set the tone and the way of life. In addition, there was no independent authority representing the Chinese town as a unit, in its dealings with the State or with the very powerful countryside. The rural areas were the real heart of living, active, and thinking China.

---

[23] Beatings (often on the soles of the feet). [Ed.]
[24] Chinese bureaucrats. [Ed.]
[25] People. [Ed.]

The town, residence of officials and nobles, was not the property of either guilds or merchants. There was no gradual "rise of the bourgeoisie" here. No sooner did a bourgeoisie appear than it was tempted by class betrayal, fascinated by the luxurious life of the mandarins. The towns might have lived their own lives, filled in the contours of their own destiny, if individual initiative and capitalism had had a clear field. But the tutelary State hardly lent itself to this. . . .

Only the West swung completely over in favor of its towns. The towns caused the West to advance. It was, let us repeat, an enormous event, but the deep-seated reasons behind it are still inadequately explained. What would the Chinese towns have become if the junks[26] had discovered the Cape of Good Hope at the beginning of the fifteenth century, and had made full use of such a chance of world conquest?

[26] Chinese flat-bottomed ships with battened sails. [Ed.]

2

GREGORIO DATI

Corporations and Community in Florence

This is an account of the Italian city of Florence and its inhabitants from 1380 to 1405. While family identity was primary, residents of Florence were also members of many corporate organizations that served to channel their loyalty to the larger urban community. Among these were guilds and parish churches, as well as political, welfare, and religious organizations. On public holidays like the feast day of St. John the Baptist, the patron saint of Florence, these various groups would come together in a display of communal solidarity that was often more fraternal than the deliberations in the political arena. What seems to motivate people to participate in public acts and parades in Florence?

THINKING HISTORICALLY

Are events like those described here signs of urban autonomy, or are they likely to encourage it? What aspects of this account support Braudel's thesis?

Source: Gregorio Dati, "*Istoria di Firenze dall'anno MCCCLXXX all'anno MCCCCV*" (History of Florence from 1380 to 1405) (Florence, 1735), in *The Society of Renaissance Florence*, ed. and trans. Gene Brucker (New York: Harper & Row, 1971), 75–78.

When springtime comes and the whole world rejoices, every Florentine begins to think about organizing a magnificent celebration on the feast day of St. John the Baptist [June 24]. . . . For two months in advance, everyone is planning marriage feasts or other celebrations in honor of the day. There are preparations for the horse races, the costumes of the retinues, the flags, and the trumpets; there are the pennants and the wax candles and other things which the subject territories offer to the Commune. Messengers are sent to obtain provisions for the banquets, and horses come from everywhere to run in the races. The whole city is engaged in preparing for the feast, and the spirits of the young people and the women [are animated] by these preparations. . . . Everyone is filled with gaiety; there are dances and concerts and songfests and tournaments and other joyous activities. Up to the eve of the holiday, no one thinks about anything else.

Early on the morning of the day before the holiday, each guild has a display outside of its shops of its fine wares, its ornaments, and jewels. There are cloths of gold and silk sufficient to adorn ten kingdoms. . . . Then at the third hour, there is a solemn procession of clerics, priests, monks, and friars, and there are so many [religious] orders, and so many relics of saints, that the procession seems endless. [It is a manifestation] of great devotion, on account of the marvelous richness of the adornments . . . and clothing of gold and silk with embroidered figures. There are many confraternities of men who assemble at the place where their meetings are held, dressed as angels, and with musical instruments of every kind and marvelous singing. They stage the most beautiful representations of the saints, and of those relics in whose honor they perform. They leave from S. Maria del Fiore [the cathedral] and march through the city and then return.

Then, after midday, when the heat has abated before sunset, all of the citizens assemble under [the banner of] their district, of which there are sixteen. Each goes in the procession in turn, the first, then the second, and so on with one district following the other, and in each group the citizens march two by two, with the oldest and most distinguished at the head, and proceeding down to the young men in rich garments. They march to the church of St. John [the Baptistery] to offer, one by one, a wax candle weighing one pound. . . . The walls along the streets through which they pass are all decorated, and there are . . . benches on which are seated young ladies and girls dressed in silk and adorned with jewels, pearls, and precious stones. This procession continues until sunset, and after each citizen has made his offering, he returns home with his wife to prepare for the next morning.

Whoever goes to the Piazza della Signoria on the morning of St. John's Day witnesses a magnificent, marvelous, and triumphant sight, which the mind can scarcely grasp. Around the great piazza are a hundred towers which appear to be made of gold. Some were brought on carts and others by porters. . . . [These towers] are made of wood, paper, and wax [and decorated] with gold, colored paints, and with figures. . . . Next to the rostrum of the palace [of the Signoria] are standards . . . which belong to the most important towns which are subject to the Commune: Pisa, Arezzo, Pistoia, Volterra, Cortona, Lucignano. . . .

First to present their offering, in the morning, are the captains of the Parte Guelfa, together with all of the knights, lords, ambassadors, and foreign knights. They are accompanied by a large number of the most honorable citizens, and before them, riding on a charger covered with a cloth . . . is one of their pages carrying a banner with the insignia of the Parte Guelfa. Then there follow the above-mentioned standards, each one carried by men on horseback . . . and they all go to make their offerings at the Baptistery. And these standards are given a tribute by the districts which have been acquired by the Commune of Florence. . . . The wax candles, which have the appearance of golden towers, are the tribute of the regions which in most ancient times were subject to the Florentines. In order of dignity, they are brought, one by one, to be offered to St. John, and on the following day, they are hung inside the church and there they remain for the entire year until the next feast day. . . . Then come . . . an infinite number of large wax candles, some weighing one hundred pounds and others fifty, some more and some less . . . carried by the residents of the villages [in the *contado*[1]] which offer them. . . .

Then the lord priors and their colleges come to make their offerings, accompanied by their rectors, that is, the podestà, the captain [of the *popolo*[2]], and the executor. . . . And after the lord [priors] come those who are participating in the horse race, and they are followed by the Flemings and the residents of Brabant who are weavers of woolen cloth in Florence. Then there are offerings by twelve prisoners who, as an act of mercy, have been released from prison . . . in honor of St. John, and these are poor people. . . . After all of these offerings have been made, men and women return home to dine. . . .

[1] Countryside. [Ed.]
[2] People. [Ed.]

3

MARCO POLO

On the City of Hangchou

In *The Travels of Marco Polo*, the Venetian merchant recounted his travels across the Silk Road to Mongolia and China. According to his account, he stayed in China from 1275 to 1292 before returning to Venice. In 1275, the Chinese Southern Song capital of Hangchou had just been conquered by Kubilai Khan, the grandson of Chingis Khan.

Source: Marco Polo, *The Travels of Marco Polo*, the Complete Yule-Currier ed. (New York: Dover, 1993), 2:185–206.

The Mongols were able to conquer China, but they could not radically change it. The structure and organization of towns and cities
remained very much the way it had been under the Song. In addition to
Hangchou, which Marco Polo calls Kinsay, he had been to the Mongol
capital at Karakorum and to the Chinese cities of Peking and Changan.
Why does he consider the city of Hangchou "the finest and the noblest
in the world"? How does his description support that characterization?

THINKING HISTORICALLY

In what ways does the Hangchou that emerges from this document
resemble Florence? In what ways was Hangchou significantly different? Does Marco Polo's description show signs that Chinese cities were
autonomous or that they were not? What do you see in this account of
Hangchou that supports or challenges Braudel's comparison and thesis?

When you have left the city of Changan and have travelled for three
days through a splendid country, passing a number of towns and villages,
you arrive at the most noble city of Kinsay,[1] a name which is as much as
to say in our tongue "The City of Heaven," as I told you before.

And since we have got thither I will enter into particulars about its
magnificence; and these are well worth the telling, for the city is beyond
dispute the finest and the noblest in the world. In this we shall speak
according to the written statement which the Queen of this Realm sent
to Bayan the conqueror of the country for transmission to the Great
Kaan, in order that he might be aware of the surpassing grandeur of the
city and might be moved to save it from destruction or injury. I will tell
you all the truth as it was set down in that document. For truth it was,
as the said Messer Marco Polo at a later date was able to witness with
his own eyes. And now we shall rehearse those particulars.

First and foremost, then, the document stated the city of Kinsay to
be so great that it hath an hundred miles of compass. And there are in it
twelve thousand bridges of stone,[2] for the most part so lofty that a great
fleet could pass beneath them. And let no man marvel that there are so
many bridges, for you see the whole city stands as it were in the water and
surrounded by water, so that a great many bridges are required to give
free passage about it. [And though the bridges be so high, the approaches
are so well contrived that carts and horses do cross them.]

The document aforesaid also went on to state that there were in this city
twelve guilds of the different crafts, and that each guild had twelve thousand
houses in the occupation of its workmen. Each of these houses contains at

[1] *Kinsay* simply means "capital." The current name is Hangchou. [Ed.]
[2] Generally assumed to be an exaggeration; one thousand would have been a lot. [Ed.]

least twelve men, whilst some contain twenty and some forty,—not that these are all masters, but inclusive of the journeymen who work under the masters. And yet all these craftsmen had full occupation, for many other cities of the kingdom are supplied from this city with what they require.

The document aforesaid also stated that the number and wealth of the merchants, and the amount of goods that passed through their hands, was so enormous that no man could form a just estimate thereof. And I should have told you with regard to those masters of the different crafts who are at the head of such houses as I have mentioned, that neither they nor their wives ever touch a piece of work with their own hands, but live as nicely and delicately as if they were kings and queens. The wives indeed are most dainty and angelical creatures! Moreover it was an ordinance laid down by the King that every man should follow his father's business and no other, no matter if he possessed 100,000 bezants.[3]

Inside the city there is a Lake which has a compass of some thirty miles[4]: and all round it are erected beautiful palaces and mansions, of the richest and most exquisite structure that you can imagine, belonging to the nobles of the city. There are also on its shores many abbeys and churches of the Idolaters. In the middle of the Lake are two Islands, on each of which stands a rich, beautiful, and spacious edifice, furnished in such style as to seem fit for the palace of an Emperor. And when any one of the citizens desired to hold a marriage feast, or to give any other entertainment, it used to be done at one of these palaces. And everything would be found there ready to order, such as silver plate, trenchers, and dishes [napkins and tablecloths], and whatever else was needful. The King made this provision for the gratification of his people, and the place was open to every one who desired to give an entertainment. . . .

The people are Idolaters; and since they were conquered by the Great Kaan they use paper money. [Both men and women are fair and comely, and for the most part clothe themselves in silk, so vast is the supply of that material, both from the whole district of Kinsay, and from the imports by traders from other provinces.] And you must know they eat every kind of flesh, even that of dogs and other unclean beasts, which nothing would induce a Christian to eat.

Since the Great Kaan occupied the city he has ordained that each of the twelve thousand bridges should be provided with a guard of ten men, in case of any disturbance, or of any being so rash as to plot treason or insurrection against him. [Each guard is provided with a hollow instrument of wood and with a metal basin, and with a timekeeper to enable them to know the hour of the day or night. . . .

[3] A gold coin struck at Byzantium (or Constantinople) and used throughout Europe from the ninth century on. [Ed.]

[4] The circumference of the lake was more probably 30 li. A li was about a third of a mile, but it was sometimes used to mean a hundredth of a day's march. The entire circumference of the city could not have been more than 100 li. [Ed.]

Part of the watch patrols the quarter, to see if any light or fire is burning after the lawful hours; if they find any they mark the door, and in the morning the owner is summoned before the magistrates, and unless he can plead a good excuse he is punished. Also if they find any one going about the streets at unlawful hours they arrest him, and in the morning they bring him before the magistrates. Likewise if in the daytime they find any poor cripple unable to work for his livelihood, they take him to one of the hospitals, of which there are many, founded by the ancient kings, and endowed with great revenues. Or if he be capable of work they oblige him to take up some trade. . . .

The Kaan watches this city with especial diligence because it forms the head of all Manzi[5]; and because he has an immense revenue from the duties levied on the transactions of trade therein, the amount of which is such that no one would credit it on mere hearsay.

All the streets of the city are paved with stone or brick, as indeed are all the highways throughout Manzi, so that you ride and travel in every direction without inconvenience. . . .

You must know also that the city of Kinsay has some three thousand baths, the water of which is supplied by springs. They are hot baths, and the people take great delight in them, frequenting them several times a month, for they are very cleanly in their persons. They are the finest and largest baths in the world; large enough for one hundred persons to bathe together.

And the Ocean Sea comes within twenty-five miles of the city at a place called Ganfu, where there is a town and an excellent haven, with a vast amount of shipping which is engaged in the traffic to and from India and other foreign parts, exporting and importing many kinds of wares, by which the city benefits. And a great river flows from the city of Kinsay to that sea-haven, by which vessels can come up to the city itself. This river extends also to other places further inland.

Know also that the Great Kaan hath distributed the territory of Manzi into nine parts, which he hath constituted into nine kingdoms. To each of these kingdoms a king is appointed who is subordinate to the Great Kaan, and every year renders the accounts of his kingdom to the fiscal office at the capital. This city of Kinsay is the seat of one of these kings, who rules over one hundred forty great and wealthy cities. For in the whole of this vast country of Manzi there are more than twelve hundred great and wealthy cities, without counting the towns and villages, which are in great numbers. And you may receive it for certain that in each of those twelve hundred cities the Great Kaan has a garrison, and that the smallest of such garrisons musters one thousand men; whilst there are some of ten thousand, twenty thousand, and thirty thousand; so that the total number of troops is something scarcely calculable. . . . And all of them belong to the army of the Great Kaan.

[5] China. [Ed.]

I repeat that everything appertaining to this city is on so vast a scale, and the Great Kaan's yearly revenues therefrom are so immense, that it is not easy even to put it in writing, and it seems past belief to one who merely hears it told. But I *will* write it down for you. . . .

I must tell you that in this city there are 160 *tomans*[6] of fires, or in other words 160 *tomans* of houses. Now I should tell you that the *toman* is 10,000, so that you can reckon the total as altogether 1,600,000 houses, among which are a great number of rich palaces. There is one church only, belonging to the Nestorian Christians.

There is another thing I must tell you. It is the custom for every burgess of this city, and in fact for every description of person in it, to write over his door his own name, the name of his wife, and those of his children, his slaves, and all the inmates of his house, and also the number of animals that he keeps. And if any one dies in the house then the name of that person is erased, and if any child is born its name is added. So in this way the sovereign is able to know exactly the population of the city. And this is the practice also throughout all Manzi and Cathay.

And I must tell you that every hosteler who keeps an hostel for travellers is bound to register their names and surnames, as well as the day and month of their arrival and departure. And thus the sovereign hath the means of knowing, whenever it pleases him, who come and go throughout his dominions. And certes this is a wise order and a provident [one].

The position of the city is such that it has on one side a lake of fresh and exquisitely clear water (already spoken of), and on the other a very large river. The waters of the latter fill a number of canals of all sizes which run through the different quarters of the city, carry away all impurities, and then enter the Lake; whence they issue again and flow to the Ocean, thus producing a most excellent atmosphere. By means of these channels, as well as by the streets, you can go all about the city. Both streets and canals are so wide and spacious that carts on the one and boats on the other can readily pass to and fro, conveying necessary supplies to the inhabitants.

At the opposite side the city is shut in by a channel, perhaps forty miles in length, very wide, and full of water derived from the river aforesaid, which was made by the ancient kings of the country in order to relieve the river when flooding its banks. This serves also as a defence to the city, and the earth dug from it has been thrown inward, forming a kind of mound enclosing the city.

In this part are the ten principal markets, though besides these there are a vast number of others in the different parts of the town. The former are all squares of half a mile to the side, and along their front passes the main street, which is forty paces in width, and runs straight from end to end of the city, crossing many bridges of easy and commodious approach. At every four miles of its length comes one of those great squares of

[6] A *toman* is a Mongol measurement of ten thousand. [Ed.]

two miles (as we have mentioned) in compass. So also parallel to this great street, but at the back of the marketplaces, there runs a very large canal, on the bank of which toward the squares are built great houses of stone, in which the merchants from India and other foreign parts store their wares, to be handy for the markets. In each of the squares is held a market three days in the week, frequented by forty thousand or fifty thousand persons, who bring thither for sale every possible necessary of life, so that there is always an ample supply of every kind of meat and game, as of roebuck, red-deer, fallow-deer, hares, rabbits, partridges, pheasants, francolins, quails, fowls, capons, and of ducks and geese an infinite quantity; for so many are bred on the Lake that for a Venice groat of silver[7] you can have a couple of geese and two couple of ducks. Then there are the shambles where the larger animals are slaughtered, such as calves, beeves, kids, and lambs, the flesh of which is eaten by the rich and the great dignitaries.

Those markets make a daily display of every kind of vegetables and fruits; and among the latter there are in particular certain pears of enormous size, weighing as much as ten pounds apiece, and the pulp of which is white and fragrant like a confection; besides peaches in their season both yellow and white, of every delicate flavour. . . .

All the ten marketplaces are encompassed by lofty houses, and below these are shops where all sorts of crafts are carried on, and all sorts of wares are on sale, including spices and jewels and pearls. Some of these shops are entirely devoted to the sale of wine made from rice and spices, which is constantly made fresh, and is sold very cheap.

Certain of the streets are occupied by the women of the town, who are in such a number that I dare not say what it is. They are found not only in the vicinity of the marketplaces, where usually a quarter is assigned to them, but all over the city. They exhibit themselves splendidly attired and abundantly perfumed, in finely garnished houses, with trains of waiting-women. These women are extremely accomplished in all the arts of allurement, and readily adapt their conversation to all sorts of persons, insomuch that strangers who have once tasted their attractions seem to get bewitched, and are so taken with their blandishments and their fascinating ways that they never can get these out of their heads. Hence it comes to pass that when they return home they say they have been to Kinsay or the City of Heaven, and their only desire is to get back thither as soon as possible.

Other streets are occupied by the Physicians, and by the Astrologers, who are also teachers of reading and writing; and an infinity of other professions have their places round about those squares. In each of the squares there are two great palaces facing one another, in which are established the officers appointed by the King to decide differences arising between merchants, or other inhabitants of the quarter. It is the daily duty of these officers to see that the guards are at their posts on the neighbouring bridges, and to punish them at their discretion if they are absent. . . .

[7] A small coin. Point is that because there are so many, they are very cheap. [Ed.]

The natives of the city are men of peaceful character, both from education and from the example of their kings, whose disposition was the same. They know nothing of handling arms, and keep none in their houses. You hear of no feuds or noisy quarrels or dissensions of any kind among them. Both in their commercial dealings and in their manufactures they are thoroughly honest and truthful, and there is such a degree of good will and neighbourly attachment among both men and women that you would take the people who live in the same street to be all one family.

And this familiar intimacy is free from all jealousy or suspicion of the conduct of their women. These they treat with the greatest respect, and a man who should presume to make loose proposals to a married woman would be regarded as an infamous rascal. They also treat the foreigners who visit them for the sake of trade with great cordiality, and entertain them in the most winning manner, affording them every help and advice on their business. But on the other hand they hate to see soldiers, and not least those of the Great Kaan's garrisons, regarding them as the cause of their having lost their native kings and lords.

4

S. D. GOITEIN

Cairo: An Islamic City in Light of the Geniza

The author of this selection provides an especially detailed picture of medieval Cairo due to an unusual discovery of documents. "The Geniza" refers to a treasure trove of documents maintained by a Jewish synagogue in Cairo from the tenth to thirteenth centuries. It contains correspondence, legal documents, receipts, inventories, prescriptions, and notes—written in Hebrew characters in the Arabic language—and offers a rare opportunity to review virtually everything a community wrote over a long period of time. It is an extremely valuable resource that can answer most questions about medieval society in Cairo.

In this selection, S. D. Goitein studies the documents for the insight they provide into city life in Cairo. What do the Geniza documents tell us about city life in Cairo? What would it have been like to live in medieval Cairo? In what ways would life in medieval Cairo have been similar to, or different from, life in a city

Source: S. D. Goitein, "Cairo: An Islamic City in Light of the Geniza," in *Middle Eastern Cities*, ed. Ira M. Lapidus (Berkeley and Los Angeles: University of California Press, 1969), 90–95.

of medieval Europe or medieval China? What is the significance of the lack of public buildings and guilds in Cairo? In what ways was the Muslim identity larger or more cosmopolitan than European urban identities?

THINKING HISTORICALLY

How does this support or challenge Braudel's thesis? Which of Braudel's city models does Cairo most closely resemble?

. . . It is astounding how rarely government buildings are mentioned in the Geniza documents. There were the local police stations and prisons, as well as the offices where one received the licenses occasionally needed, but even these are seldom referred to. The Mint and the Exchange are frequently referred to, but at least the latter was only semi-public in character, since the persons working there were not on the government payroll. Taxes were normally collected by tax farmers.[1] Thus there was little direct contact between the government and the populace and consequently not much need for public buildings. The imperial palace and its barracks formed a city by itself, occasionally mentioned in Ayyūbid times, but almost never in the Fāṭimid period.

Government, although not conspicuous by many public buildings, was present in the city in many other ways. A city was governed by a military commander called *amīr*, who was assisted by the *wālī* or superintendent of the police. Smaller towns had only a *wālī* and no *amīr*. Very powerful, sometimes more powerful than the *amīr*, was the *qāḍī*, or judge, who had administrative duties in addition to his substantial judicial functions. The chief *qāḍī* often held other functions such as the control of the taxes or of a port, as we read with regard to Alexandria or Tyre. The city was divided into small administrative units called *rab'* (which is not the classical *rub*, meaning quarter, but instead designates an area, or rather a compound). Each *rab'* had a superintendent called *ṣāḥib rab'* (pronounced rub), very often referred to in the Geniza papers. In addition to regular and mounted police there were plain clothesmen, or secret service men, called *aṣḥāb al-khabar*, "informants" who formed a government agency independent even of the *qāḍī*, a state of affairs for which there seem to exist parallels in more modern times.

An ancient source tells us that the vizier[2] al-Ma'mūn, mentioned above, instructed the two superintendents of the police of Fusṭāṭ[3] and

---

[1] Private collectors who bought or were given authority to collect taxes and keep all or a percentage of proceeds. Common practice in ancient world. [Ed.]

[2] Prime minister. [Ed.]

[3] Old Cairo. [Ed.]

Cairo, respectively, to draw up exact lists of the inhabitants showing their occupations and other circumstances and to permit no one to move from one house to another without notification of the police. This is described as an extraordinary measure aimed at locating any would-be assassins who might have been sent to the Egyptian capital by the Bāṭiniyya, an Ismāʿīlī group using murder as a political weapon. Such lists, probably with fewer details, no doubt were in regular use for the needs of taxation. In a letter from Sicily, either from its capital Palermo or from Mazara on its southwestern tip, the writer, an immigrant from Tunisia around 1063, informs his business friend in Egypt that he is going to buy a house and that he has already registered for the purpose in the *qānūn* (Greek *canon*) which must have designated an official list of inhabitants. With regard to non-Muslims, a differentiation was made between permanent residents and newcomers. Whether the same practice existed with respect to Muslims is not evident from the Geniza papers.

What were the dues that a town dweller had to pay to the government in his capacity as the inhabitant of a city, and what were the benefits that he derived from such payments? By right of conquest, the ground on which Fusṭāṭ stood belonged to the Muslims, that is, to the government (the same was the case in many other Islamic cities), and a ground rent, called *ḥikr*, had to be paid for each building. A great many deeds of sale, gift, and rent refer to this imposition. . . .

Besides the ground rent, every month a *ḥarāsa*, or "due for protection," had to be paid to the government. The protection was partly in the hands of a police force, partly in those of the superintendents of the compounds, and partly was entrusted to nightwatchmen, usually referred to as *ṭawwāfūn*, literally, "those that make the round," but known also by other designations. As we learn expressly from a Geniza source, the nightwatchmen, like the regular police, were appointed by the government (and not by a municipality or local body which did not exist). The amounts of the *ḥarāsa* in the communal accounts cannot be related to the value of the properties for which they were paid, but it is evident that they were moderate.

In a responsum[4] written around 1165, Rabbi Maimon, the father of Moses Maimonides,[5] states that the markets of Fusṭāṭ used to remain open during the nights, in contrast of course to what the writer was accustomed from having lived in other Islamic cities. In Fusṭāṭ, too, this had not been always the case. In a description of the festival of Epiphany from the year 941 in which all parts of the population took part, it is mentioned as exceptional that the streets were not closed during that particular night.

[4] A legal document. [Ed.]
[5] (1135–1204), a Jewish rabbi, physician, and philosopher in Spain and Egypt. [Ed.]

Sanitation must have been another great concern of the government, for the items "removal of rubbish" (called "throwing out of dust") and "cleaning of pipes" appear with great regularity in the monthly accounts preserved in the Geniza. One gets the impression that these hygienic measures were not left to the discretion of each individual proprietor of a house. The clay tubes bringing water (for washing purposes) to a house and those connecting it with a cesspool constantly needed clearing, and there are also many references to their construction. The amounts paid for both operations were considerable. The Geniza has preserved an autograph note by Maimonides permitting a beadle[6] to spend a certain sum on "throwing out of dust" (presumably from a synagogue). This may serve as an illustration for the fact that landlords may have found the payment of these dues not always easy.

In this context we may also draw attention to the new insights gained through the study of the documents from the Geniza about the social life of Cairo. Massignon[7] had asserted, and he was followed by many, that the life-unit in the Islamic city was the professional corporation, the guilds of the merchants, artisans, and scholars which had professional, as well as social and religious functions. No one would deny that this was true to a large extent for the sixteenth through the nineteenth centuries. However, there is not a shred of evidence that this was true for the ninth through the thirteenth centuries. . . .

Further, we have stated before that no formal citizenship existed. The question is, however, how far did people feel a personal attachment to their native towns. "Homesickness," says Professor Gibb in his translation of the famous traveler Ibn Baṭṭūṭa, "was hardly to be expected in a society so cosmopolitan as that of medieval Islam." Indeed the extent of travel and migration reflected in the Geniza is astounding. No less remarkable, however, is the frequency of expressions of longing for one's native city and the wish to return to it, as well as the fervor with which compatriots stuck together when they were abroad. On the other hand, I cannot find much of neighborhood factionalism or professional *esprit de corps*, both of which were so prominent in the later Middle Ages. Under an ever more oppressive military feudalism and government-regimented economy, life became miserable and insecure, and people looked for protection and assistance in their immediate neighborhood. In an earlier period, in a free-enterprise, competitive society, there was no place for such factionalism. A man felt himself to be the son of a city which provided him with the security, the economic possibilities, and the spiritual amenities which he needed.

---

[6] A minor official. [Ed.]

[7] Louis Massignon (1883–1962), a French scholar of Islam. [Ed.]

5

BERNAL DÍAZ

Cities of Mexico

Bernal Díaz (1492–1580) accompanied Hernando Cortés* and
the band of Spanish conquistadors who were the first Europeans
to see the cities of the central Mexican plateau, dominated by the
Aztec capital of Tenochtitlan,† or Mexico, in 1519. Later in life,
he recalled what he saw in this account of *The Conquest of New
Spain*. The cities of Mexico provide the best example of how much
cities could differ. Unlike the cities of Eurasia, or even Islamic
Africa, the development of Mexican cities was entirely separate
from and uninfluenced by the other cultures we have studied.
Therefore, this description of Mexico, and the other cities of the
Mexican plateau, like Iztapalapa and Coyoacan, is enormously
useful to us.

What impressed Díaz about the cities of Mexico? How, according
to Díaz, were they different from the cities of Europe?

THINKING HISTORICALLY

In what respects were these cities different from others you have
read about? What other cities do they most resemble? How
does this selection support or challenge Braudel's comparison
and thesis?

Next morning, we came to a broad causeway[1] and continued our march
towards Iztapalapa. And when we saw all those cities and villages built in
the water, and other great towns on dry land, and that straight and level
causeway leading to Mexico, we were astounded. These great towns and
cues[2] and buildings rising from the water, all made of stone, seemed like
an enchanted vision from the tale of Amadis. Indeed, some of our soldiers
asked whether it was not all a dream. It is not surprising therefore that I
should write in this vein. It was all so wonderful that I do not know how
to describe this first glimpse of things never heard of, seen, or dreamed
of before.

---

* kohr TEHZ
† the NOHCH teet LAHN
[1] The causeway of Cuitlahuac, which separated the lakes of Chalco and Xochimilco. [Ed.]
[2] Spanish for temple; probably refers to pyramids. [Ed.]

Source: Bernal Díaz, *The Conquest of New Spain*, trans. J. M. Cohen (London: Penguin
Books, 1963), 214–20, 230–35.

When we arrived near Iztapalapa we beheld the splendour of the other *Caciques*[3] who came out to meet us, the lord of that city whose name was Cuitlahuac, and the lord of Culuacan, both of them close relations of Montezuma. And when we entered the city of Iztapalapa, the sight of the palaces in which they lodged us! They were very spacious and well built, of magnificent stone, cedar wood, and the wood of other sweet-smelling trees, with great rooms and courts, which were a wonderful sight, and all covered with awnings of woven cotton.

When we had taken a good look at all this, we went to the orchard and garden, which was a marvelous place both to see and walk in. I was never tired of noticing the diversity of trees and the various scents given off by each, and the paths choked with roses and other flowers, and the many local fruit-trees and rose-bushes, and the pond of fresh water. Another remarkable thing was that large canoes could come into the garden from the lake, through a channel they had cut, and their crews did not have to disembark. Everything was shining with lime and decorated with different kinds of stonework and paintings which were a marvel to gaze on. Then there were birds of many breeds and varieties which came to the pond. I say again that I stood looking at it, and thought that no land like it would ever be discovered in the whole world, because at that time Peru was neither known nor thought of.[4] But today all that I then saw is overthrown and destroyed; nothing is left standing.

The Entrance into Mexico

Early next day we left Iztapalapa with a large escort of these great *Caciques*, and followed the causeway, which is eight yards wide and goes so straight to the city of Mexico that I do not think it curves at all. Wide though it was, it was so crowded with people that there was hardly room for them all. Some were going to Mexico and others coming away, besides those who had come out to see us, and we could hardly get through the crowds that were there. For the towers and the *cues* were full, and they came in canoes from all parts of the lake. No wonder, since they had never seen horses or men like us before!

With such wonderful sights to gaze on we did not know what to say, or if this was real that we saw before our eyes. On the land side there were great cities, and on the lake many more. The lake was crowded

---

[3] ka SEEK ehs   Word for rulers in the language of the Taino, a Native American people of the Carribean. [Ed.]

[4] Spanish arrived about 1527; Díaz began writing of 1521 conquest of Mexico in 1568. [Ed.]

with canoes. At intervals along the causeway there were many bridges, and before us was the great city of Mexico [Tenochtitlan]. . . .

We marched along our causeway to a point where another small causeway branches off to another city called Coyoacan, and there, beside some towerlike buildings, which were their shrines, we were met by many more *Caciques* and dignitaries in very rich cloaks. The different chieftains wore different brilliant liveries, and the causeways were full of them. Montezuma[5] had sent these great *Caciques* in advance to receive us, and as soon as they came before Cortes they told him in their language that we were welcome, and as a sign of peace they touched the ground with their hands and kissed it. . . .

They led us to our quarters, which were in some large houses capable of accommodating us all and had formerly belonged to the great Montezuma's father, who was called Axayacatl. Here Montezuma now kept the great shrines of his gods, and a secret chamber containing gold bars and jewels. This was the treasure he had inherited from his father, which he never touched. Perhaps their reason for lodging us here was that, since they called us *Teules*[6] and considered us as such, they wished to have us near their idols. In any case they took us to this place, where there were many great halls, and a dais hung with the cloth of their country for our Captain, and matting beds with canopies over them for each of us.

On our arrival we entered the large court, where the great Montezuma was awaiting our Captain. Taking him by the hand, the prince led him to his apartment in the hall where he was to lodge, which was very richly furnished in their manner. . . .

We divided our lodgings by companies, and placed our artillery in a convenient spot. Then the order we were to keep was clearly explained to us, and we were warned to be very much on the alert, both the horsemen and the rest of us soldiers. We then ate a sumptuous dinner which they had prepared for us in their native style.

So, with luck on our side, we boldly entered the city of Tenochtitlan or Mexico on 8 November in the year of our Lord 1519. . . .

I must now speak of the skilled workmen whom Montezuma employed in all the crafts they practised, beginning with the jewellers and workers in silver and gold and various kinds of hollowed objects, which excited the admiration of our great silversmiths at home. Many of the best of them lived in a town called Atzcapotzalco, three miles from Mexico. There were other skilled craftsmen who worked with precious stones and *chalchihuites*,* and specialists in feather-work, and very fine painters and carvers. We can form some judgement of

---

* chal chee WEE tes
[5] Montezuma or Moctezuma II (c. 1480–1520), the Aztec emperor. [Ed.]
[6] Gods. [Ed.]

what they did then from what we can see of their work today. There are three Indians now living in the city of Mexico, named Marcos de Aquino, Juan de la Cruz, and El Crespillo, who are such magnificent painters and carvers that, had they lived in the age of the Apelles of old,[7] or of Michael Angelo,[8] or Berruguete[9] in our own day, they would be counted in the same rank.

Let us go on to the women, the weavers and sempstresses, who made such a huge quantity of fine robes with very elaborate feather designs. These things were generally brought from some towns in the province of Cotaxtla, which is on the north coast, quite near San Juan de Ulua. In Montezuma's own palaces very fine cloths were woven by those chieftains' daughters whom he kept as mistresses; and the daughters of other dignitaries, who lived in a kind of retirement like nuns in some houses close to the great *cue* of Huichilobos,[10] wore robes entirely of featherwork. Out of devotion for that god and a female deity who was said to preside over marriage, their fathers would place them in religious retirement until they found husbands. They would then take them out to be married.

Now to speak of the great number of performers whom Montezuma kept to entertain him. There were dancers and stilt-walkers, and some who seemed to fly as they leapt through the air, and men rather like clowns to make him laugh. There was a whole quarter full of these people who had no other occupation. He had as many workmen as he needed, too, stonecutters, masons, and carpenters, to keep his houses in repair. . . .

When we had already been in Mexico for four days, . . . Cortés said it would be a good thing to visit the large square of Tlatelolco and see the great *cue* of Huichilobos. So he sent Aguilar, Doña Marina,[11] and his own young page Orteguilla, who by now knew something of the language, to ask for Montezuma's approval of this plan. On receiving his request, the prince replied that we were welcome to go, but for fear that we might offer some offence to his idols he would himself accompany us with many of his chieftains. Leaving the palace in his fine litter, when he had gone about half way, he

---

[7] Famous Ancient Greek painter. [Ed.]

[8] Michelangelo (1476–1564), Renaissance master painter and sculptor. [Ed.]

[9] Berruguete is either Pedro (1450–1504) or his son, Alonso (1488–1561), both famous Spanish painters. [Ed.]

[10] Huitzilopochtli, Aztec god of sun and war; required human sacrifice. [Ed.]

[11] Also known as Malinche (mah LEEN cheh). According to Díaz, she was the daughter of a cacique, who was given away after her mother remarried. She had learned Nahuatl as a youth and Yucatec Mayan as a slave. Thus, with the help of a Spanish sailor who learned Mayan, Cortéz could translate between Nahuatl and Spanish. Dona Marina also learned Spanish and became Cortéz's translator and mistress, eventually giving birth to Cortéz's son, Martin. [Ed.]

dismounted beside some shrines, since he considered it an insult to his gods to visit their dwelling in a litter. Some of the great chieftains then supported him by the arms, and his principal vassals walked before him, carrying two staves, like sceptres raised on high as a sign that the great Montezuma was approaching. When riding in his litter he had carried a rod, partly of gold and partly of wood, held up like a wand of justice. The prince now climbed the steps of the great *cue*, escorted by many *papas*,[12] and began to burn incense and perform other ceremonies for Huichilobos. . . .

On reaching the market-place, escorted by the many *Caciques* whom Montezuma had assigned to us, we were astounded at the great number of people and the quantities of merchandise, and at the orderliness and good arrangements that prevailed, for we had never seen such a thing before. The chieftains who accompanied us pointed everything out. Every kind of merchandise was kept separate and had its fixed place marked for it.

Let us begin with the dealers in gold, silver, and precious stones, feathers, cloaks, and embroidered goods, and male and female slaves who are also sold there. They bring as many slaves to be sold in that market as the Portuguese bring Negroes from Guinea. Some are brought there attached to long poles by means of collars round their necks to prevent them from escaping, but others are left loose. Next there were those who sold coarser cloth, and cotton goods and fabrics made of twisted thread, and there were chocolate merchants with their chocolate. In this way you could see every kind of merchandise to be found anywhere in New Spain, laid out in the same way as goods are laid out in my own district of Medina del Campo, a centre for fairs, where each line of stalls has its own particular sort. So it was in this great market. There were those who sold sisal cloth and ropes and the sandals they wear on their feet, which are made from the same plant. All these were kept in one part of the market, in the place assigned to them, and in another part were skins of tigers and lions, otters, jackals, and deer, badgers, mountain cats, and other wild animals, some tanned and some untanned, and other classes of merchandise.

There were sellers of kidney-beans and sage and other vegetables and herbs in another place, and in yet another they were selling fowls, and birds with great dewlaps,[13] also rabbits, hares, deer, young ducks, little dogs, and other such creatures. Then there were the fruiterers; and the women who sold cooked food, flour and honey cake, and

---

[12] Aztec priests. [Ed.]
[13] Turkeys.

tripe, had their part of the market. Then came pottery of all kinds, from big water-jars to little jugs, displayed in its own place, also honey, honeypaste, and other sweets like nougat. Elsewhere they sold timber too, boards, cradles, beams, blocks, and benches, all in a quarter of their own.

Then there were the sellers of pitch-pine for torches, and other things of that kind, and I must also mention, with all apologies, that they sold many canoe-loads of human excrement, which they kept in the creeks near the market. This was for the manufacture of salt and the curing of skins, which they say cannot be done without it. I know that many gentlemen will laugh at this, but I assure them it is true. I may add that on all the roads they have shelters made of reeds or straw or grass so that they can retire when they wish to do so, and purge their bowels unseen by passers-by, and also in order that their excrement shall not be lost. . . .

We went on to the great *cue*, and as we approached its wide courts, before leaving the market-place itself, we saw many more merchants who, so I was told, brought gold to sell in grains, just as they extract it from the mines. This gold is placed in the thin quills of the large geese of that country, which are so white as to be transparent. They used to reckon their accounts with one another by the length and thickness of these little quills, how much so many cloaks or so many gourds of chocolate or so many slaves were worth, or anything else they were bartering.

Now let us leave the market, having given it a final glance, and come to the courts and enclosures in which their great *cue* stood. Before reaching it you passed through a series of large courts, bigger I think than the Plaza at Salamanca. These courts were surrounded by a double masonry wall and paved, like the whole place, with very large smooth white flagstones. Where these stones were absent everything was whitened and polished, indeed the whole place was so clean that there was not a straw or a grain of dust to be found there.

When we arrived near the great temple and before we had climbed a single step, the great Montezuma sent six *papas* and two chieftains down from the top, where he was making his sacrifices, to escort our Captain; and as he climbed the steps, of which there were one hundred and fourteen, they tried to take him by the arms to help him up in the same way as they helped Montezuma, thinking he might be tired, but he would not let them near him.

The top of the *cue* formed an open square on which stood something like a platform, and it was here that the great stones stood on which they placed the poor Indians for sacrifice. Here also was a massive image like a dragon, and other hideous figures, and a great deal of blood that had been spilled that day. Emerging in the company of two *papas* from the shrine which houses his accursed images,

Montezuma made a deep bow to us all and said: "My lord Malinche, you must be tired after climbing this great *cue* of ours." And Cortés replied that none of us was ever exhausted by anything. Then Montezuma took him by the hand, and told him to look at his great city and all the other cities standing in the water, and the many others on the land round the lake; and he said that if Cortés had not had a good view of the great market-place he could see it better from where he now was. So we stood there looking, because that huge accursed *cue* stood so high that it dominated everything. We saw the three causeways that led into Mexico: the causeway of Iztapalapa by which we had entered four days before. . . . We saw the fresh water which came from Chapultepec to supply the city, and the bridges that were constructed at intervals on the causeways so that the water could flow in and out from one part of the lake to another. We saw a great number of canoes, some coming with provisions and others returning with cargo and merchandise; and we saw too that one could not pass from one house to another of that great city and the other cities that were built on the water except over wooden drawbridges or by canoe. We saw *cues* and shrines in these cities that looked like gleaming white towers and castles: a marvellous sight. All the houses had flat roofs, and on the causeways were other small towers and shrines built like fortresses.

Having examined and considered all that we had seen, we turned back to the great market and the swarm of people buying and selling. The mere murmur of their voices talking was loud enough to be heard more than three miles away. Some of our soldiers who had been in many parts of the world, in Constantinople, in Rome, and all over Italy, said that they had never seen a market so well laid out, so large, so orderly, and so full of people.

6

Images of Medieval Cities

The first two images, of Florence and Cairo, are bird's-eye illustrations that might function as maps. They are both done by European artists. In what ways were the two cities similar? In what ways were they different? The second set of images shows a Chinese city (probably Kaifeng, capital of the Song dynasty), attributed to the Chinese artist Zhang Zeduan (1085–1145) and the Italian city of Siena about 1339. In what ways are the Italian and Chinese cities similar and different?

Figure 13.1 *City View of Florence, 1482* by Lucantonio degli Uberti.

Source: The Granger Collection, New York.

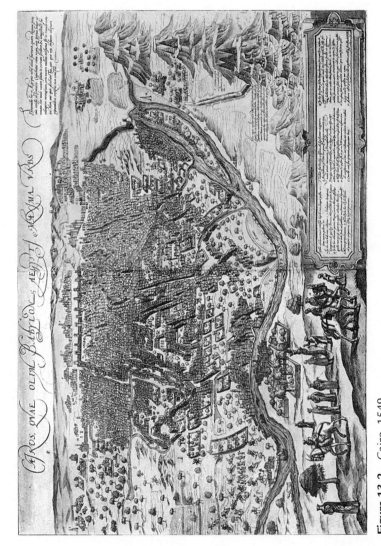

Figure 13.2 Cairo, 1549.

Source: Map created by Matteo Pagano, 1549.

Figure 13.3 A Chinese City in *Along the River during the Qingming Festival* by Zhang Zeduan.

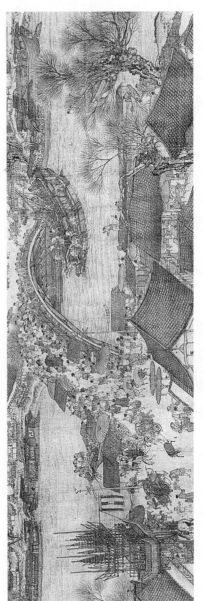

Figure 13.4 Siena in *Effects of Good Government* by Ambrogio Lorenzetti. Fresco in Hall of Nine, Siena.

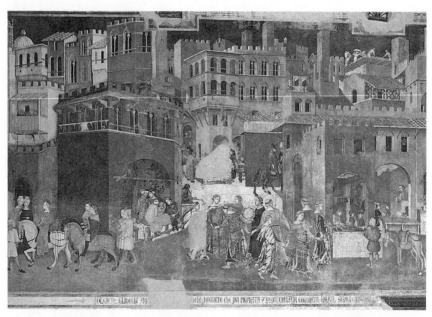

Source: *Good Government in the City*, 1338–40 (detail) (fresco), Lorenzetti, Ambrogio (1285–c. 1348)/Palazzo Pubblico, Siena, Italy/The Bridgeman Art Library.

Source: *Effects of Good Government*, c. 1338 (fresco), Lorenzetti, Ambrogio (1285–c. 1348)/ Palazzo Pubblico, Siena, Italy/Alinari/The Bridgeman Art Library.

THINKING HISTORICALLY

Relate the similarities and differences you noted to Braudel's thesis about the differences between European and non-European cities. Which, if any, of the differences you noted provide support for Braudel's thesis? Which of the similarities or differences you noted undermine his thesis?

■ REFLECTIONS

Our selections certainly offer support for Braudel's thesis on the European city. The chartering of cities as independent corporations with their own laws, courts, and independent citizenry was a phenomenon repeated throughout Europe, especially in the West and the Mediterranean from the eleventh to the fifteenth centuries. The Florentine festival demonstrates how citizens came together in so many groups to celebrate their collective identity as citizens. Europe was a world without emperors, in which kings and lords were forced to bargain freedoms for favors.

Marco Polo unwittingly points to the power of the emperor, Song or Mongol, in imperial China. The capital city especially is designed and maintained according to his specifications. City life may be vibrant. There may even be enormous markets and wealthy merchants, but it is the emperor's city, not the merchants'. Rich merchants might train their sons to govern, but only as officials of the emperor.

Neither Chinese nor Muslim urban dwellers find their primary identities as citizens or even as residents of a particular city. They may be Cairenes, but they are Muslims first. Muslims had no need for self-governing cities when they could travel and work anywhere in the vast world of Islam.

Braudel struggled with American cities. North American towns, he thought, were re-creations of European towns. In Latin America, he classified Mexico City as similar to the imperial capitals of other parts of the world. Like Hangchou, Mexico City could be astonishingly rich, but it was not an autonomous entity under Aztecs or Spaniards. The readings were selected not to stack the deck, but to show what Braudel meant. Consequently, some qualifications of Braudel's thesis might be in order.

First, we should not assume that autonomous or communal cities were limited to Europe. Rather, they were a product of a feudal, or politically weak and decentralized, society, where urban populations could bargain for special privileges. We could find similar examples of urban autonomy among, for example, Japanese port cities during the Japanese feudal era of the fourteenth to sixteenth centuries. One of these, Sakai, was called the Venice of Japan. Not until after 1600 and the recentral-ization of Japan under the Tokugawa administration were these inde-pendent cities brought to heel. In many ways, Tokugawa developments paralleled those of Europe, where centralized states also subordinated the independence of commercial cities after 1700.

Second, the absence of a movement for urban autonomy in Islamic and Chinese cities — important as it was in the time and places dis-cussed in this chapter — was not universal. Chinese cities before the Mongol Yuan dynasty, especially in the earlier Sung dynasty, had developed an extremely prosperous commercial class. And while it is true that they did not gain (or seek) urban independence, they were content to exercise sufficient influence on the local representatives of the emperor. No appointed official could think lightly of ignoring the advice of Chinese merchants, the uniquely Chinese class of civil-service exam graduates, and the many Chinese guilds (one of the more impor-tant forces for self-government in Europe).

Third, while medieval Muslim cities encouraged little urban autonomy or identity, a prosperous class of merchants — always at the core of Islam — were nourished by more enlightened sultans and emirs. The Turkish historian Halil Inalcik writes that it was "the deliberate policy" of the Ottoman government, as it founded its successive capi-tals at Bursa in 1326, Edirne in 1402, and Istanbul in 1453, to cre-ate commercial and industrial centers, and that it consequently used every means — from tax exemptions to force — to attract and settle merchants and artisans in the new capitals. With the same end in view, Mehmed II encouraged the Jews of Europe to migrate to his new capi-tal at Istanbul as they were being expelled from Spain and Portugal.

Braudel's thesis emphasizes the differences among cities, but as he well knew, one could emphasize the similarities as well. All cities distinguished themselves from the countryside which they controlled and exploited. All cities built and concentrated the wealth, achieve-ments, and opportunities of the culture within their walls. All cities were greater engines of change than were villages, farms, and pastures. And some have argued that all cities promote patriarchy and class stratification.

Today about half the world's people live in cities. In 1800 only 3 percent of the world's population lived in cities. It is expected that by 2030, 60 percent of the world's population will be urban. Does that mean the lives of so many people will change in a similar way? Does it mean increasing patriarchy? Increasing exploitation of the countryside? Increasing inequality? Do significant choices need to be made about the types of cities we inhabit? Can we find ways to make our cities of the future our own?

14

Ecology, Technology, and Science

Europe, Asia, and Oceania, 500–1550

■ HISTORICAL CONTEXT

Everyone knows that the world has changed drastically since the
Middle Ages. And most people would agree that the most important
and far-reaching changes have occurred in the fields of ecology, technology, and science. Global population has grown tenfold. The world
has become a single ecological unit where microbes, migrants, and
money travel everywhere at jet speed. In most parts of the world, average life expectancy has doubled; cities have mushroomed, supplanting
farm and pasture. Machines have replaced the labor of humans and
animals. Powers that were only imagined in the Middle Ages—elixirs
to cure disease, energy to harness rivers, machines that could fly—are
now commonplace. Other aspects of life—among them religion, political behavior, music, and art—have also evolved, but even these were
affected significantly by advances in modern science and technology.

Have the changes been for good or ill? The signs of environmental
stress are visible everywhere. The North Pole floats in the summer. Ten-
thousand-year-old glaciers are disappearing. The oceans are rising two
to four inches every ten years. Our atmosphere contains more carbon
gasses than it has for at least 650,000 years. The stored energy of millions of years burns to service the richest members of a couple of generations. Ancient aquifers are drained to water the lawns of desert cities.

Precisely what change or changes occurred? When did the cycle
of change begin, and what caused it? We will examine these questions
here. You will read three substantial answers. These explanations of
long-term change differ most markedly in how they explain the roots
of the transformation. Lynn White Jr. defines the transformation to
modernity in largely technological and ecological terms but emphasizes
the role of cultural causes. Though a historian of medieval European

technology, he focuses on the role of medieval European religion: Christianity. Lynda Shaffer discusses technological and scientific changes as spreading through contact and trade. As a world historian, she underscores the role of medieval India and South Asia in creating modern technology. Jared Diamond writes of cultural failures to meet new natural and technological crises. Diamond, a professor of geography with numerous specializations in fields like physiology, evolutionary biology, and biogeography, warns that our contemporary ecological problems are very similar to earlier tragedies that ended in a failure of will.

■ THINKING HISTORICALLY

Evaluating Grand Theories

Big questions deserve big answers—or at least grand theories. Here we consider three grand theories about the origins of our technological transformation and ecological difficulties, the links between environmental decline and the growth of technology and science, and the role of Western (European and American) economic growth in undermining the environment. Grand theories are especially speculative. They give us much to question and challenge. But their scope and freshness can often suggest new insights. Grand theories almost inevitably have elements that seem partly wrong and partly right. You will be encouraged to weigh some of the many elements in these theories. After reading the first essay, you will also view visual sources. Then you can evaluate the theories, decide where you agree and disagree, and, perhaps, begin to develop your own grand theory as well.

1

LYNN WHITE JR.

The Historical Roots of Our Ecological Crisis

This classic essay first appeared in the magazine *Science* in 1967 and has since been reprinted and commented on many times. What do you think of White's linkage of ecological crisis and Christianity? Which of White's arguments and evidence do you find most persuasive? Which do you find least convincing? Imagine a continuum that includes all of the world's people, from the most ecologically minded "tree-huggers"

Source: Lynn White Jr., "The Historical Roots of Our Ecological Crisis," *Science* 155 (March 1967): 1203–7.

on one end to the most damaging polluters and destroyers of the environment on the other end. Where on that continuum would you place the historical majority of Christians? Buddhists? Why?

THINKING HISTORICALLY

A grand theory like this—that Christianity is responsible for our environmental problems—argues far more than can be proven in such a brief essay. White concentrates on making certain kinds of connections and marshaling certain kinds of evidence. In addition to weighing the arguments he makes, consider the gaps in his argument. What sorts of evidence would you seek to make White's theory more convincing?

A conversation with Aldous Huxley[1] not infrequently put one at the receiving end of an unforgettable monologue. About a year before his lamented death he was discoursing on a favorite topic: man's unnatural treatment of nature and its sad results. To illustrate his point he told how, during the previous summer, he had returned to a little valley in England where he had spent many happy months as a child. Once it had been composed of delightful grassy glades; now it was becoming overgrown with unsightly brush because the rabbits that formerly kept such growth under control had largely succumbed to a disease, myxomatosis, that was deliberately introduced by the local farmers to reduce the rabbits' destruction of crops. Being something of a Philistine,[2] I could be silent no longer, even in the interests of great rhetoric. I interrupted to point out that the rabbit itself had been brought as a domestic animal to England in 1176, presumably to improve the protein diet of the peasantry.

All forms of life modify their contexts. The most spectacular and benign instance is doubtless the coral polyp. By serving its own ends, it has created a vast undersea world favorable to thousands of other kinds of animals and plants. Ever since man became a numerous species he has affected his environment notably. The hypothesis that his firedrive[3] method of hunting created the world's great grasslands and helped to exterminate the monster mammals of the Pleistocene from much of the globe is plausible, if not proved. For six millennia at least, the banks of the lower Nile have been a human artifact rather than the swampy African jungle which nature, apart from man, would have

---

[1] Aldous Huxley (1894–1963), British author of novels, short stories, travel books, biography, and essays. Best known for *Brave New World* (1932). [Ed.]

[2] An anti-intellectual (though obviously White is not; he was only impatient with Huxley's pedantry). [Ed.]

[3] Paleolithic hunters used fires to drive animals to their deaths. [Ed.]

made it. The Aswan Dam, flooding five thousand square miles, is only the latest stage in a long process. In many regions terracing or irrigation, overgrazing, and the cutting of forests by Romans to build ships to fight Carthaginians or by Crusaders to solve the logistics problems of their expeditions have profoundly changed some ecologies. Observation that the French landscape falls into two basic types, the open fields of the north and the *bocage*[4] of the south and west, inspired Marc Bloch to undertake his classic study of medieval agricultural methods. Quite unintentionally, changes in human ways often affect nonhuman nature. It has been noted, for example, that the advent of the automobile eliminated huge flocks of sparrows that once fed on the horse manure littering every street.

The history of ecologic change is still so rudimentary that we know little about what really happened, or what the results were. The extinction of the European aurochs[5] as late as 1627 would seem to have been a simple case of overenthusiastic hunting. On more intricate matters it often is impossible to find solid information. For a thousand years or more the Frisians and Hollanders have been pushing back the North Sea, and the process is culminating in our own time in the reclamation of the Zuider Zee.[6] What, if any, species of animals, birds, fish, shore life, or plants have died out in the process? In their epic combat with Neptune have the Netherlanders overlooked ecological values in such a way that the quality of human life in the Netherlands has suffered? I cannot discover that the questions have ever been asked, much less answered.

People, then, have often been a dynamic element in their own environment, but in the present state of historical scholarship we usually do not know exactly when, where, or with what effects man-induced changes came. . . . But it was not until about four generations ago that Western Europe and North America arranged a marriage between science and technology, a union of the theoretical and the empirical approaches to our natural environment. The emergence in widespread practice of the Baconian creed that scientific knowledge means technological power over nature can scarcely be dated before about 1850, save in the chemical industries, where it is anticipated in the eighteenth century. Its acceptance as a normal pattern of action may mark the greatest event in human history since the invention of agriculture, and perhaps in nonhuman terrestrial history as well.

[4] Full of groves or woodlands. Marc Bloch reasoned that the open fields north of the Loire River in France must have been plowed by teams of oxen and heavy plows because of the hard soil. In the south farmers could use scratch plows on the softer soil and therefore did not clear large fields, preserving more woodlands. [Ed.]

[5] A now extinct European wild ox believed to be the ancestor of European domestic cattle. [Ed.]

[6] Once a Dutch lake, it was joined to the North Sea by a flood in the thirteenth century but has since been reclaimed by the building of a dam. [Ed.]

Almost at once the new situation forced the crystallization of the novel concept of ecology; indeed, the word *ecology* first appeared in the English language in 1873. Today, less than a century later, the impact of our race upon the environment has so increased in force that it has changed in essence. When the first cannons were fired, in the early fourteenth century, they affected ecology by sending workers scrambling to the forests and mountains for more potash, sulfur, iron ore, and charcoal, with some resulting erosion and deforestation. Hydrogen bombs are of a different order: A war fought with them might alter the genetics of all life on this planet. By 1285 London had a smog problem arising from the burning of soft coal, but our present combustion of fossil fuels threatens to change the chemistry of the globe's atmosphere as a whole, with consequences which we are only beginning to guess. With the population explosion, the carcinoma of planless urbanism, the now geological deposits of sewage and garbage, surely no creature other than man has ever managed to foul its nest in such short order. . . .

What shall we do? No one yet knows. Unless we think about fundamentals, our specific measures may produce new backlashes more serious than those they are designed to remedy.

As a beginning we should try to clarify our thinking by looking, in some historical depth, at the presuppositions that underlie modern technology and science. Science was traditionally aristocratic, speculative, intellectual in intent; technology was lower-class, empirical, action-oriented. The quite sudden fusion of these two, toward the middle of the nineteenth century, is surely related to the slightly prior and contemporary democratic revolutions which, by reducing social barriers, tended to assert a functional unity of brain and hand. Our ecologic crisis is the product of an emerging, entirely novel, democratic culture. The issue is whether a democratized world can survive its own implications. Presumably we cannot unless we rethink our axioms.

The Western Traditions of Technology and Science

One thing is so certain that it seems stupid to verbalize it: Both modern technology and modern science are distinctively *Occidental*. Our technology has absorbed elements from all over the world, notably from China; yet everywhere today, whether in Japan or in Nigeria, successful technology is Western. Our science is the heir to all the sciences of the past, especially perhaps to the work of the great Islamic scientists of the Middle Ages, who so often outdid the ancient Greeks in skill and perspicacity: al-Rāzī in medicine, for example; or ibn-al-Haytham in optics; or Omar Khayyám in mathematics. . . .

The leadership of the West, both in technology and in science, is far older than the so-called Scientific Revolution of the seventeenth century or the so-called Industrial Revolution of the eighteenth century. These terms are in fact outmoded and obscure the true nature of what they try to describe—significant stages in two long and separate developments. By A.D. 1000 at the latest—and perhaps, feebly, as much as two hundred years earlier—the West began to apply water power to industrial processes other than milling grain. This was followed in the late twelfth century by the harnessing of wind power. From simple beginnings, but with remarkable consistency of style, the West rapidly expanded its skills in the development of power machinery, labor-saving devices, and automation. Those who doubt should contemplate that most monumental achievement in the history of automation: the weight-driven mechanical clock, which appeared in two forms in the early fourteenth century. Not in craftsmanship but in basic technological capacity, the Latin West of the later Middle Ages far outstripped its elaborate, sophisticated, and esthetically magnificent sister cultures, Byzantium and Islam. In 1444 a great Greek ecclesiastic, Bessarion, who had gone to Italy, wrote a letter to a prince in Greece. He is amazed by the superiority of Western ships, arms, textiles, glass. But above all he is astonished by the spectacle of waterwheels sawing timbers and pumping the bellows of blast furnaces. Clearly, he had seen nothing of the sort in the Near East.

By the end of the fifteenth century the technological superiority of Europe was such that its small, mutually hostile nations could spill out over all the rest of the world, conquering, looting, and colonizing. The symbol of this technological superiority is the fact that Portugal, one of the weakest states of the Occident, was able to become, and to remain for a century, mistress of the East Indies. . . .

In the present-day vernacular understanding, modern science is supposed to have begun in 1543, when both Copernicus and Vesalius published their great works. It is no derogation of their accomplishments, however, to point out that such structures as the *Fabrica*[7] and the *De revolutionibus*[8] do not appear overnight. The distinctive Western tradition of science, in fact, began in the late eleventh century with a massive movement of translation of Arabic and Greek scientific works into Latin. . . . [W]ithin less than two hundred years effectively the entire corpus of Greek and Muslim science was available in Latin, and was

---

[7] *De Humani Corporis Fabrica* (1543), an illustrated work on human anatomy based on dissections, was produced by Andreas Vesalius (1514–1564), a Flemish anatomist, at the University of Padua in Italy. [Ed.]

[8] *De revolutionibus orbium coelestium* (1543; On the Revolution of Heavenly Bodies) was published by Nicolas Copernicus (1473–1543); it showed the sun as the center of a system around which the Earth revolved. [Ed.]

being eagerly read and criticized in the new European universities. Out of criticism arose new observation, speculation, and increasing distrust of ancient authorities. By the late thirteenth century Europe had seized global scientific leadership from the faltering hands of Islam. . . .

Since both our technological and our scientific movements got their start, acquired their character, and achieved world dominance in the Middle Ages, it would seem that we cannot understand their nature or their present impact upon ecology without examining fundamental medieval assumptions and developments.

Medieval View of Man and Nature

Until recently, agriculture has been the chief occupation even in "advanced" societies; hence, any change in methods of tillage has much importance. Early plows, drawn by two oxen, did not normally turn the sod but merely scratched it. Thus, cross-plowing was needed and fields tended to be squarish. In the fairly light soils and semiarid climates of the Near East and Mediterranean, this worked well. But such a plow was inappropriate to the wet climate and often sticky soils of northern Europe. By the latter part of the seventh century after Christ, however, following obscure beginnings, certain northern peasants were using an entirely new kind of plow, equipped with a vertical knife to cut the line of the furrow, a horizontal share to slice under the sod, and a moldboard to turn it over. The friction of this plow with the soil was so great that it normally required not two but eight oxen. It attacked the land with such violence that cross-plowing was not needed, and fields tended to be shaped in long strips.

In the days of the scratch-plow, fields were distributed generally in units capable of supporting a single family. Subsistence farming was the presupposition. But no peasant owned eight oxen: to use the new and more efficient plow, peasants pooled their oxen to form large plowteams, originally receiving (it would appear) plowed strips in proportion to their contribution. Thus, distribution of land was based no longer on the needs of a family but, rather, on the capacity of a power machine to till the earth. Man's relation to the soil was profoundly changed. Formerly man had been part of nature; now he was the exploiter of nature. Nowhere else in the world did farmers develop any analogous agricultural implement. Is it coincidence that modern technology, with its ruthlessness toward nature, has so largely been produced by descendants of these peasants of northern Europe?

This same exploitive attitude appears slightly before A.D. 830 in Western illustrated calendars. In older calendars the months were shown as passive personifications. The new Frankish calendars, which set the style for the Middle Ages, are very different: They show men coercing the world around them—plowing, harvesting, chopping trees, butchering pigs. Man and nature are two things, and man is master.

These novelties seem to be in harmony with larger intellectual patterns. What people do about their ecology depends on what they think about themselves in relation to things around them. Human ecology is deeply conditioned by beliefs about our nature and destiny—that is, by religion. . . .

The victory of Christianity over paganism was the greatest psychic revolution in the history of our culture. It has become fashionable today to say that, for better or worse, we live in "the post-Christian age." Certainly the forms of our thinking and language have largely ceased to be Christian, but to my eye the substance often remains amazingly akin to that of the past. Our daily habits of action, for example, are dominated by an implicit faith in perpetual progress which was unknown either to Greco-Roman antiquity or to the Orient. It is rooted in, and is indefensible apart from, Judeo-Christian teleology.[9] The fact that Communists share it merely helps to show what can be demonstrated on many other grounds: that Marxism, like Islam, is a Judeo-Christian heresy. We continue today to live, as we have lived for about seventeen hundred years, very largely in a context of Christian axioms.

What did Christianity tell people about their relations with the environment?

. . . Christianity inherited from Judaism not only a concept of time as nonrepetitive and linear but also a striking story of creation. By gradual stages a loving and all-powerful God had created light and darkness, the heavenly bodies, the earth and all its plants, animals, birds, and fishes. Finally, God had created Adam and, as an afterthought, Eve to keep man from being lonely. Man named all the animals, thus establishing his dominance over them. God planned all of this explicitly for man's benefit and rule: No item in the physical creation had any purpose save to serve man's purposes. And, although man's body is made of clay, he is not simply part of nature: He is made in God's image.

Especially in its Western form, Christianity is the most anthropocentric religion the world has seen. As early as the second century both Tertullian and Saint Irenaeus of Lyons were insisting that when God shaped Adam he was foreshadowing the image of the incarnate Christ, the Second Adam. Man shares, in great measure, God's transcendence of nature. Christianity, in absolute contrast to ancient paganism and Asia's religions (except, perhaps, Zoroastrianism), not only established

[9] The biblical idea that God's purpose is revealed in his creation, that human history can be seen as the result of God's intentions. [Ed.]

a dualism of man and nature but also insisted that it is God's will that man exploit nature for his proper ends.

At the level of the common people this worked out in an interesting way. In Antiquity every tree, every spring, every stream, every hill had its own *genius loci*, its guardian spirit. These spirits were accessible to men, but were very unlike men; centaurs, fauns, and mermaids show their ambivalence. Before one cut a tree, mined a mountain, or dammed a brook, it was important to placate the spirit in charge of that particular situation, and to keep it placated. By destroying pagan animism, Christianity made it possible to exploit nature in a mood of indifference to the feelings of natural objects. . . .

When one speaks in such sweeping terms, a note of caution is in order. Christianity is a complex faith, and its consequences differ in differing contexts. What I have said may well apply to the medieval West, where in fact technology made spectacular advances. But the Greek East, a highly civilized realm of equal Christian devotion, seems to have produced no marked technological innovation after the late seventh century, when Greek fire[10] was invented. The key to the contrast may perhaps be found in a difference in the tonality of piety and thought which students of comparative theology find between the Greek and the Latin Churches. The Greeks believed that sin was intellectual blindness, and that salvation was found in illumination, orthodoxy — that is, clear thinking. The Latins, on the other hand, felt that sin was moral evil, and that salvation was to be found in right conduct. Eastern theology has been intellectualist. Western theology has been voluntarist. The Greek saint contemplates; the Western saint acts. The implications of Christianity for the conquest of nature would emerge more easily in the Western atmosphere.

The Christian dogma of creation, which is found in the first clause of all the Creeds, has another meaning for our comprehension of today's ecologic crisis. By revelation, God had given man the Bible, the Book of Scripture. But since God had made nature, nature also must reveal the divine mentality. The religious study of nature for the better understanding of God was known as natural theology. In the early Church, and always in the Greek East, nature was conceived primarily as a symbolic system through which God speaks to men: The ant is a sermon to sluggards; rising flames are the symbol of the soul's aspiration. This view of nature was essentially artistic rather than scientific. . . .

However, in the Latin West by the early thirteenth century natural theology was following a very different bent. It was ceasing to

---

[10]Byzantine incendiary weapon developed about seventh century. Siphon tube spewed fire on enemy. Used especially against Arab ships (material continued to burn on water). [Ed.]

be the decoding of the physical symbols of God's communication with man and was becoming the effort to understand God's mind by discovering how his creation operates. The rainbow was no longer simply a symbol of hope first sent to Noah after the Deluge: Robert Grosseteste, Friar Roger Bacon, and Theodoric of Freiberg produced startlingly sophisticated work on the optics of the rainbow, but they did it as a venture in religious understanding. From the thirteenth century onward, up to and including Leibnitz and Newton, every major scientist, in effect, explained his motivations in religious terms. Indeed, if Galileo had not been so expert an amateur theologian he would have got into far less trouble: The professionals resented his intrusion. And Newton seems to have regarded himself more as a theologian than as a scientist. It was not until the late eighteenth century that the hypothesis of God became unnecessary to many scientists.

It is often hard for the historian to judge, when men explain why they are doing what they want to do, whether they are offering real reasons or merely culturally acceptable reasons. The consistency with which scientists during the long formative centuries of Western science said that the task and the reward of the scientist was "to think God's thoughts after him" leads one to believe that this was their real motivation. If so, then modern Western science was cast in a matrix of Christian theology. The dynamism of religious devotion, shaped by the Judeo-Christian dogma of creation, gave it impetus.

An Alternative Christian View

We would seem to be headed toward conclusions unpalatable to many Christians. Since both *science* and *technology* are blessed words in our contemporary vocabulary, some may be happy at the notions, first, that, viewed historically, modern science is an extrapolation of natural theology and, second, that modern technology is at least partly to be explained as an Occidental, voluntarist realization of the Christian dogma of man's transcendence of, and rightful mastery over, nature. But, as we now recognize, somewhat over a century ago science and technology—hitherto quite separate activities—joined to give mankind powers which, to judge by many of the ecologic effects, are out of control. If so, Christianity bears a huge burden of guilt.

I personally doubt that disastrous ecologic backlash can be avoided simply by applying to our problems more science and more technology. Our science and technology have grown out of Christian attitudes toward man's relation to nature which are almost universally held not only by Christians and neo-Christians but also by those who fondly regard themselves as post-Christians. Despite Copernicus, all the cosmos rotates around our little globe. Despite Darwin, we are *not*, in our hearts, part of the natural process. We are superior to nature, contemptuous of it, willing to use it for our slightest whim. . . .

What we do about ecology depends on our ideas of the man-nature relationship. More science and more technology are not going to get us out of the present ecologic crisis until we find a new religion, or rethink our old one. . . .

Possibly we should ponder the greatest radical in Christian history since Christ: Saint Francis of Assisi. The prime miracle of Saint Francis is the fact that he did not end at the stake, as many of his left-wing followers did. He was so clearly heretical that a General of the Franciscan Order, Saint Bonaventura, a great and perceptive Christian, tried to suppress the early accounts of Franciscanism. The key to an understanding of Francis is his belief in the virtue of humility—not merely for the individual but for man as a species. Francis tried to depose man from his monarchy over creation and set up a democracy of all God's creatures. With him the ant is no longer simply a homily for the lazy, flames a sign of the thrust of the soul toward union with God; now they are Brother Ant and Sister Fire, praising the Creator in their own ways as Brother Man does in his.

Later commentators have said that Francis preached to the birds as a rebuke to men who would not listen. The records do not read so: He urged the little birds to praise God, and in spiritual ecstasy they flapped their wings and chirped rejoicing. Legends of saints, especially the Irish saints, had long told of their dealings with animals but always, I believe, to show their human dominance over creatures. With Francis it is different. The land around Gubbio in the Apennines was being ravaged by a fierce wolf. Saint Francis, says the legend, talked to the wolf and persuaded him of the error of his ways. The wolf repented, died in the odor of sanctity, and was buried in consecrated ground.

What Sir Steven Ruciman calls "the Franciscan doctrine of the animal soul" was quickly stamped out. . . . [St. Francis's] view of nature and of man rested on a unique sort of pan-psychism of all things animate and inanimate, designed for the glorification of their transcendent Creator, who, in the ultimate gesture of cosmic humility, assumed flesh, lay helpless in a manger, and hung dying on a scaffold.

I am not suggesting that many contemporary Americans who are concerned about our ecologic crisis will be either able or willing to counsel with wolves or exhort birds. However, the present increasing disruption of the global environment is the product of a dynamic technology and science which were originating in the Western medieval world against which Saint Francis was rebelling in so original a way. Their growth cannot be understood historically apart from distinctive attitudes toward nature which are deeply grounded in Christian dogma. The fact that most people do not think of these attitudes as Christian is irrelevant. No new set of basic values has been accepted in our society to displace those of Christianity. Hence we shall continue to have a worsening ecologic crisis until we reject the Christian axiom that nature has no reason for existence save to serve man.

The greatest spiritual revolutionary in Western history, Saint Francis, proposed what he thought was an alternative Christian view of nature and man's relation to it: He tried to substitute the idea of the equality of all creatures, including man, for the idea of man's limitless rule of creation. He failed. Both our present science and our present technology are so tinctured with orthodox Christian arrogance toward nature that no solution for our ecologic crisis can be expected from them alone. Since the roots of our trouble are so largely religious, the remedy must also be essentially religious, whether we call it that or not. We must rethink and refeel our nature and destiny. The profoundly religious, but heretical, sense of the primitive Franciscans for the spiritual autonomy of all parts of nature may point a direction. I propose Francis as a patron saint for ecologists.

2

Image from a Cistercian Manuscript, Twelfth Century

This image of a Christian monk chopping down a tree while his lay servant prunes the branches is from a manuscript of the Cistercian order of monks, from the twelfth century. The Cistercians, more than other orders, spoke out in favor of conserving forest resources, but they also celebrated manual labor. Does this image indicate that the monks were in favor of forest clearance?

THINKING HISTORICALLY

Does this image lend support to White's argument? Why or why not? If there were many such images, would visual evidence like this

Source: Image from a Cistercian manuscript, twelfth century, monk chopping tree (Dijon, Bibliothèque municipale, MS 173), duplicated in *Cambridge Illustrated History of the Middle Ages*, ed. Robert Fossier (Cambridge: Cambridge University Press, 1997), 72.

Figure 14.1 Twelfth-Century Manuscript.

convince you of White's argument? Would it be more convincing if almost all European images of trees showed someone chopping them down and virtually no Chinese tree images showed that? In other words, how much visual evidence would convince you of White's interpretation?

3

Image from a French Calendar, Fifteenth Century

This French calendar scene for March is from the early fifteenth century. What sorts of activities does it show? How does it relate specifically to White's argument about the changing images of European calendars? (See pp. 511–12.) The top half of the calendar shows an astrological zodiac. In what ways are these images of nature different from those in the bottom half?

THINKING HISTORICALLY

What technologies are shown here? Were any of these technologies particularly recent or European? Does this image merely illustrate White's argument, or does it support it to some extent? What other visual evidence would you want to see to be persuaded by White's argument?

Source: From *Les trés riches heures du duc de Berry*, Giraudon, Musée de Condé.

Figure 14.2 French Calendar Scene.

Source: Bridgeman-Giraudon/Art Resource, N.Y.

4

Image of a Chinese *Feng-Shui* Master

Although the Chinese celebrated the natural landscape in their paintings, they also created drawings that showcased their advanced technologies. The Chinese made and used the compass (as well as paper, printing, and gunpowder) long before Europeans. Instead of using it to subdue the natural world, however, they used it to find harmony with nature, specifically through the practice of *feng-shui*.* *Feng-shui*, which literally means wind over water, is the Chinese art of determining the best position and placement of structures such as houses within the natural environment. In the following image we see a type of compass used in the work of a Chinese *feng-shui* master. Before building, the *feng-shui* master would use instruments like this to ascertain the flow of energy (*chi*) on the site, resulting in new buildings that would be in harmony with, rather than obstruct, this flow. How might a compass detect energy? How was the Chinese use of a compass-like device different from the modern scientific use of the compass?

THINKING HISTORICALLY

An image has many elements to read. What information is revealed about Chinese society in this image, in addition to the scientific devices? What significance do you attach to the artist's depiction of humans and the natural setting? In what ways does this image support Lynn White Jr.'s argument? In what ways does it challenge his interpretation? On balance, do you find it more supportive or critical of White's position?

* fung SHWEE

Source: Joseph Needham, *Science and Civilization in China* (Cambridge: Cambridge University Press, 1956), 2:362.

Figure 14.3 Chinese *Feng-Shui* Master.

5

Image of European Surveying Instruments

Europeans used a wide range of instruments for surveying and gunnery by 1600. Here we see various instruments for figuring the height or depth of an object by making it the third side of a triangle. What does this image show us about European ideas of the Earth and the heavens? How would this knowledge be useful in war as well as surveying? What does it suggest about European ideas of nature?

THINKING HISTORICALLY

Compare this European image with the previous Chinese image. If these images are at all representative of their cultures, what does the comparison suggest about European and Chinese attitudes toward nature? How do these images support or challenge Lynn White Jr.'s thesis?

Figure 14.4   European Surveying, c. 1600.
Source: The Granger Collection, New York.

Source: Kevin Reilly, *The West and the World: A History of Civilization*, 2nd ed. (New York: Harper & Row, 1989), 344.

6

LYNDA NORENE SHAFFER

Southernization

The author of this selection began her career as a historian of China, but she is currently a world historian, having published books on Native American, Southeast Asian, and Chinese history. Shaffer coins the term *Southernization* to suggest that *Westernization* was preceded by an earlier "southern" process of technological expansion that eventually made Westernization possible. Which of her examples of Southernization do you find most important in changing the world? Which least significant? Did India and Indian Ocean societies of the early Middle Ages play a role like that of the West today?

THINKING HISTORICALLY

Shaffer did not write this essay to criticize Lynn White Jr., nor does her essay address precisely the same issues. Our exercise here is not the relatively simple task of weighing two debaters on a single issue. Rather, Shaffer's essay challenges some of the assumptions and arguments made by White and many other historians when they discuss the history of technology. What are some of the assumptions and arguments of White that Shaffer challenges? How might you use Shaffer to challenge White's grand theory? Which essay provides a more satisfying explanation of the origins of modern science and technology?

The term *Southernization* is a new one. It is used here to refer to a multifaceted process that began in Southern Asia and spread from there to various other places around the globe. The process included so many interrelated strands of development that it is impossible to do more here than sketch out the general outlines of a few of them. Among the most important that will be omitted from this discussion are the metallurgical, the medical, and the literary. Those included are the development of mathematics; the production and marketing of subtropical or tropical spices; the pioneering of new trade routes; the cultivation, processing, and marketing of southern crops such as sugar and cotton; and the development of various related technologies.

The term *Southernization* is meant to be analogous to *Westernization*. Westernization refers to certain developments that first occurred in western Europe. Those developments changed Europe and eventually

Source: Lynda Norene Shaffer, "Southernization," *Journal of World History* 5 (Spring 1994): 1–21.

spread to other places and changed them as well. In the same way, southernization changed Southern Asia and later spread to other areas, which then underwent a process of change.

Southernization was well under way in Southern Asia by the fifth century C.E., during the reign of India's Gupta kings (320–535 C.E.). It was by that time already spreading to China. In the eighth century various elements characteristic of Southernization began spreading through the lands of the Muslim caliphates. Both in China and in the lands of the caliphate, the process led to dramatic changes, and by the year 1200 it was beginning to have an impact on the Christian Mediterranean. One could argue that within the Northern Hemisphere, by this time the process of Southernization had created an Eastern Hemisphere characterized by a rich south and a north that was poor in comparison. And one might even go so far as to suggest that in Europe and its colonies, the process of Southernization laid the foundation for Westernization.

The Indian Beginning

Southernization was the result of developments that took place in many parts of southern Asia, both on the Indian subcontinent and in Southeast Asia. By the time of the Gupta kings, several of its constituent parts already had a long history in India. Perhaps the oldest strand in the process was the cultivation of cotton and the production of cotton textiles for export. Cotton was first domesticated in the Indus River valley some time between 2300 and 1760 B.C.E., and by the second millennium B.C.E., the Indians had begun to develop sophisticated dyeing techniques. During these early millennia Indus River valley merchants are known to have lived in Mesopotamia, where they sold cotton textiles.

In the first century C.E. Egypt became an important overseas market for Indian cottons. By the next century there was a strong demand for these textiles both in the Mediterranean and in East Africa, and by the fifth century they were being traded in Southeast Asia. The Indian textile trade continued to grow throughout the next millennium. Even after the arrival of European ships in Asian ports at the turn of the sixteenth century, it continued unscathed. According to one textile expert, "India virtually clothed the world" by the mid-eighteenth century. The subcontinent's position was not undermined until Britain's Industrial Revolution, when steam engines began to power the production of cotton textiles.

Another strand in the process of Southernization, the search for new sources of bullion, can be traced back in India to the end of the Mauryan Empire (321–185 B.C.E.). During Mauryan rule Siberia had been India's main source of gold, but nomadic disturbances in Central Asia disrupted the traffic between Siberia and India at about the time that the Mauryans fell. Indian sailors then began to travel to the Malay peninsula and the islands of Indonesia in search of an alternative source, which they most likely "discovered" with the help of local peoples who knew the sites. (This is generally the case with bullion discoveries, including those made by Arabs and Europeans.) What the Indians (and others later on) did do was introduce this gold to international trade routes.

The Indians' search for gold may also have led them to the shores of Africa. Although its interpretation is controversial, some archaeological evidence suggests the existence of Indian influence on parts of East Africa as early as 300 C.E. There is also one report that gold was being sought in East Africa by Ethiopian merchants, who were among India's most important trading partners.

The sixth-century Byzantine geographer Cosmas Indicopleustes described Ethiopian merchants who went to some location inland from the East African coast to obtain gold. "Every other year they would sail far to the south, then march inland, and in return for various made-up articles they would come back laden with ingots of gold." The fact that the expeditions left every other year suggests that it took two years to get to their destination and return. If so, their destination, even at this early date, may have been Zimbabwe. The wind patterns are such that sailors who ride the monsoon south as far as Kilwa can catch the return monsoon to the Red Sea area within the same year. But if they go beyond Kilwa to the Zambezi River, from which they might go inland to Zimbabwe, they cannot return until the following year.

Indian voyages on the Indian Ocean were part of a more general development, more or less contemporary with the Mauryan Empire, in which sailors of various nationalities began to knit together the shores of the "Southern Ocean," a Chinese term referring to all the waters from the South China Sea to the eastern coast of Africa. During this period there is no doubt that the most intrepid sailors were the Malays, peoples who lived in what is now Malaysia, Indonesia, the southeastern coast of Vietnam, and the Philippines.

Sometime before 300 B.C.E. Malay sailors began to ride the monsoons, the seasonal winds that blow off the continent of Asia in the colder months and onto its shores in the warmer months. Chinese records indicate that by the third century B.C.E. "Kunlun" sailors, the Chinese term for the Malay seamen, were sailing north to the southern coasts of China. They may also have been sailing west to India, through the straits now called Malacca and Sunda. If so they may have been the first to establish contact between India and Southeast Asia.

Malay sailors had reached the eastern coast of Africa at least by the first century B.C.E., if not earlier. Their presence in East African waters is testified to by the peoples of Madagascar, who still speak a Malayo-Polynesian language. Some evidence also suggests that Malay sailors had settled in the Red Sea area. Indeed, it appears that they were the first to develop a long-distance trade in a southern spice. In the last centuries B.C.E., if not earlier, Malay sailors were delivering cinnamon from South China Sea ports to East Africa and the Red Sea.

By about 400 C.E. Malay sailors could be found two-thirds of the way around the world, from Easter Island to East Africa. They rode the monsoons without a compass, out of sight of land, and often at latitudes below the equator where the northern pole star cannot be seen. They navigated by the wind and the stars, by cloud formations, the color of the water, and swell and wave patterns on the ocean's surface. They could discern the presence of an island some thirty miles from its shores by noting the behavior of birds, the animal and plant life in the water, and the swell and wave patterns. Given their manner of sailing, their most likely route to Africa and the Red Sea would have been by way of the island clusters, the Maldives, the Chagos, the Seychelles, and the Comoros.

Malay ships used balance lug sails, which were square in shape and mounted so that they could pivot. This made it possible for sailors to tack against the wind, that is, to sail into the wind by going diagonally against it, first one way and then the other. Due to the way the sails were mounted, they appeared somewhat triangular in shape, and thus the Malays' balance lug sail may well be the prototype of the triangular lateen, which can also be used to tack against the wind. The latter was invented by both the Polynesians to the Malays' east and by the Arabs to their west, both of whom had ample opportunity to see the Malays' ships in action.

It appears that the pepper trade developed after the cinnamon trade. In the first century C.E. Southern India began supplying the Mediterranean with large quantities of pepper. Thereafter, Indian merchants could be found living on the island of Socotra, near the mouth of the Red Sea, and Greek-speaking sailors, including the anonymous author of the *Periplus of the Erythraean Sea*,[1] could be found sailing in the Red Sea and riding the monsoons from there to India.

Indian traders and shippers and Malay sailors were also responsible for opening up an all-sea route to China. The traders' desire for silk drew them out into dangerous waters in search of a more direct way to its source. By the second century C.E. Indian merchants could make the trip by sea, but the route was slow, and it took at least two years to make a round trip. Merchants leaving from India's eastern coast rounded the shores of the Bay of Bengal. When they came to the Isthmus of Kra, the narrowest part of the Malay peninsula, the ships were unloaded, and the goods were portaged across to the Gulf of Thailand. The cargo was then reloaded on ships that rounded the gulf until they reached Funan, a kingdom on what is now the Kampuchea [Cambodia]-Vietnam

---

[1] Written about 60 C.E. [Ed.]

border. There they had to wait for the winds to shift, before embarking upon a ship that rode the monsoon to China.

Some time before 400 C.E. travelers began to use a new all-sea route to China, a route that went around the Malay peninsula and thus avoided the Isthmus of Kra portage. The ships left from Sri Lanka and sailed before the monsoon, far from any coasts, through either the Strait of Malacca or the Strait of Sunda into the Java Sea. After waiting in the Java Sea port for the winds to shift, they rode the monsoon to southern China. The most likely developers of this route were Malay sailors, since the new stopover ports were located within their territories.

Not until the latter part of the fourth century, at about the same time as the new all-sea route began to direct commercial traffic through the Java Sea, did the fine spices—cloves, nutmeg, and mace—begin to assume importance on international markets. These rare and expensive spices came from the Moluccas, several island groups about a thousand miles east of Java. Cloves were produced on about five minuscule islands off the western coast of Halmahera; nutmeg and mace came from only a few of the Banda Islands, some ten islands with a total area of seventeen square miles, located in the middle of the Banda Sea. Until 1621 these Moluccan islands were the only places in the world able to produce cloves, nutmeg, and mace in commercial quantities. The Moluccan producers themselves brought their spices to the international markets of the Java Sea ports and created the market for them.

It was also during the time of the Gupta kings, around 350 C.E., that the Indians discovered how to crystallize sugar. There is considerable disagreement about where sugar was first domesticated. Some believe that the plant was native to New Guinea and domesticated there, and others argue that it was domesticated by Southeast Asian peoples living in what is now southern China. In any case, sugar cultivation spread to the Indian subcontinent. Sugar, however, did not become an important item of trade until the Indians discovered how to turn sugarcane juice into granulated crystals that could be easily stored and transported. This was a momentous development, and it may have been encouraged by Indian sailing, for sugar and clarified butter (ghee) were among the dietary mainstays of Indian sailors.

The Indians also laid the foundation for modern mathematics during the time of the Guptas. Western numerals, which the Europeans called Arabic since they acquired them from the Arabs, actually come from India. (The Arabs call them Hindi numbers.) The most significant feature of the Indian system was the invention of the zero as a number concept. The oldest extant treatise that uses the zero in the modern way is a mathematical appendix attached to Aryabhata's text on astronomy, which is dated 499 C.E.

The Indian zero made the place-value system of writing numbers superior to all others. Without it, the use of this system, base ten or otherwise, was fraught with difficulties and did not seem any better than alternative systems. With the zero the Indians were able to perform calculations rapidly and accurately, to perform much more complicated calculations, and to discern mathematical relationships more aptly. These numerals and the mathematics that the Indians developed with them are now universal—just one indication of the global significance of Southernization.

As a result of these developments India acquired a reputation as a place of marvels, a reputation that was maintained for many centuries after the Gupta dynasty fell. As late as the ninth century Amr ibn Bahr al Jahiz (c. 776–868), one of the most influential writers of Arabic, had the following to say about India:

> As regards the Indians, they are among the leaders in astronomy, mathematics—in particular, they have Indian numerals—and medicine; they alone possess the secrets of the latter, and use them to practice some remarkable forms of treatment. They have the art of carving statues and painted figures. They possess the game of chess, which is the noblest of games and requires more judgment and intelligence than any other. They make Kedah swords, and excel in their use. They have splendid music. . . . They possess a script capable of expressing the sounds of all languages, as well as many numerals. They have a great deal of poetry, many long treatises, and a deep understanding of philosophy and letters; the book *Kalila wa-Dimna* originated with them. They are intelligent and courageous. . . . Their sound judgment and sensible habits led them to invent pins, cork, toothpicks, the drape of clothes, and the dyeing of hair. They are handsome, attractive, and forbearing; their women are proverbial; and their country produces the matchless Indian aloes which are supplied to kings. They were the originators of the science of *fikr*, by which a poison can be counteracted after it has been used, and of astronomical reckoning, subsequently adopted by the rest of the world. When Adam descended from Paradise, it was to their land that he made his way.

The Southernization of China

These Southern Asian developments began to have a significant impact on China after 350 C.E. The Han dynasty had fallen in 221 C.E., and for more than 350 years thereafter China was ruled by an ever-changing collection of regional kingdoms. During these centuries Buddhism became increasingly important in China, Buddhist monasteries spread throughout the disunited realm, and cultural exchange between India and China grew accordingly. By 581, when the Sui dynasty reunited the empire, processes associated with Southernization had already had a major impact on China. The influence of Southernization continued during the T'ang (618–906) and Sung (960–1279) dynasties. One might even go so far as to suggest that the process of Southernization underlay the revolutionary social, political, economic, and technological developments of the T'ang and Sung.

The Chinese reformed their mathematics, incorporating the advantages of the Indian system, even though they did not adopt the Indian numerals at that time. They then went on to develop an advanced mathematics, which was flourishing by the time of the Sung dynasty. Cotton and indigo became well established, giving rise to the blueblack peasant garb that is still omnipresent in China. Also in the Sung period the Chinese first developed cotton canvas, which they used to make a more efficient sail for ocean-going ships.

Although sugar had long been grown in some parts of southern China it did not become an important crop in this region until the process of Southernization was well under way. The process also introduced new varieties of rice. The most important of these was what the Chinese called Champa rice, since it came to China from Champa, a Malay kingdom located on what is now the southeastern coast of Vietnam. Champa rice was a drought-resistant, early ripening variety that made it possible to extend cultivation up well-watered hillsides, thereby doubling the area of rice cultivation in China. . . .

In southern China the further development of rice production brought significant changes in the landscape. Before the introduction of Champa rice, rice cultivation had been confined to lowlands, deltas, basins, and river valleys. Once Champa rice was introduced and rice cultivation spread up the hillsides, the Chinese began systematic terracing and made use of sophisticated techniques of water control on mountain slopes. Between the mid-eighth and the early twelfth century the population of southern China tripled, and the total Chinese population doubled. According to Sung dynasty household registration figures for 1102 and 1110—figures that Sung dynasty specialists have shown to be reliable—there were 100 million people in China by the first decade of the twelfth century.

Before the process of Southernization, northern China had always been predominant, intellectually, socially, and politically. The imperial center of gravity was clearly in the north, and the southern part of China was perceived as a frontier area. But Southernization changed this situation dramatically. By 600, southern China was well on its way to becoming the most prosperous and most commercial part of the empire. The most telling evidence for this is the construction of the Grand Canal, which was completed around 610, during the Sui dynasty. Even though the rulers of the Sui had managed to put the pieces of the empire back together in 581 and rule the whole of China again from a single northern capital, they were dependent on the new southern crops. Thus it is no coincidence that this dynasty felt the need to build a canal that could deliver southern rice to northern cities.

The T'ang dynasty, when Buddhist influence in China was especially strong, saw two exceedingly important technological innovations—the invention of printing and gunpowder. These developments may also be linked to Southernization. Printing seems to have developed within the walls of Buddhist monasteries between 700 and 750, and subtropical Sichuan was one of the earliest centers of the art. The invention of gunpowder in China by Taoist alchemists in the ninth century may also be related to the linkages between India and China created by Buddhism. In 644 an Indian monk identified soils in China that contained saltpeter and demonstrated the purple flame that results from its ignition. As early as 919 C.E. gunpowder was used as an igniter in a flamethrower, and the tenth century also saw the use of flaming arrows, rockets, and bombs thrown by catapults. The earliest evidence of a cannon or bombard (1127) has been found in Sichuan, quite near the Tibetan border, across the Himalayas from India.

By the time of the Sung the Chinese also had perfected the "south-pointing needle," otherwise known as the compass. Various prototypes of the compass had existed in China from the third century B.C.E., but the new version developed during the Sung was particularly well suited for navigation. Soon Chinese mariners were using the south-pointing needle on the oceans, publishing "needle charts" for the benefit of sea captains, and following "needle routes" on the Southern Ocean.

Once the Chinese had the compass they, like Columbus, set out to find a direct route to the spice markets of Java and ultimately to the Spice Islands in the Moluccas. Unlike Columbus, they found them. They did not bump into an obstacle, now known as the Western Hemisphere, on their way, since it was not located between China and the Spice Islands. If it had been so situated, the Chinese would have found it some 500 years before Columbus.

Cities on China's southern coasts became centers of overseas commerce. Silk remained an important export, and by the T'ang dynasty it had been joined by a true porcelain, which was developed in China sometime before 400 C.E. China and its East Asian neighbors had a monopoly on the manufacture of true porcelain until the early eighteenth century. Many attempts were made to imitate it, and some of the resulting imitations were economically and stylistically important. China's southern ports were also exporting to Southeast Asia large quantities of ordinary consumer goods, including iron hardware, such as needles, scissors, and cooking pots. Although iron manufacturing was concentrated in the north, the large quantity of goods produced was a direct result of the size of the market in southern China and overseas. Until the British Industrial Revolution of the eighteenth century, no other place ever equaled the iron production of Sung China.

The Muslim Caliphates

In the seventh century C.E., Arab cavalries, recently converted to the new religion of Islam, conquered eastern and southern Mediterranean shores that had been Byzantine (and Christian), as well as the Sassanian empire (Zoroastrian) in what is now Iraq and Iran. In the eighth century they went on to conquer Spain and Turko-Iranian areas of Central Asia, as well as northwestern India. Once established on the Indian frontier, they became acquainted with many of the elements of Southernization.

The Arabs were responsible for the spread of many important crops, developed or improved in India, to the Middle East, North Africa, and Islamic Spain. Among the most important were sugar, cotton, and citrus fruits. Although sugarcane and cotton cultivation may have spread to Iraq and Ethiopia before the Arab conquests, only after the establishment of the caliphates did these southern crops have a major impact throughout the Middle East and North Africa.

The Arabs were the first to import large numbers of enslaved Africans in order to produce sugar. Fields in the vicinity of Basra, at the northern end of the Persian Gulf, were the most important sugar-producing areas within the caliphates, but before this land could be used, it had to be desalinated. To accomplish this task, the Arabs imported East African (Zanj) slaves. This African community remained in the area, where they worked as agricultural laborers. The famous writer al Jahiz, whose essay on India was quoted earlier, was a descendant of Zanj slaves. In 869, one year after his death, the Zanj slaves in Iraq rebelled. It took the caliphate fifteen years of hard fighting to defeat them, and thereafter Muslim owners rarely used slaves for purposes that would require their concentration in large numbers.

The Arabs were responsible for moving sugarcane cultivation and sugar manufacturing westward from southern Iraq into other relatively arid lands. Growers had to adapt the plant to new conditions, and they had to develop more efficient irrigation technologies. By 1000 or so sugarcane had become an important crop in the Yemen; in Arabian oases; in irrigated areas of Syria, Lebanon, Palestine, Egypt, and the Mahgrib; in Spain; and on Mediterranean islands controlled by Muslims. By the tenth century cotton also had become a major crop in the lands of the caliphate, from Iran and Central Asia to Spain and the Mediterranean islands. Cotton industries sprang up wherever the plant was cultivated, producing for both local and distant markets. . . .

Under Arab auspices, Indian mathematics followed the same routes as the crops. Al-Kharazmi (c. 780–847) introduced Indian mathematics to the Arabic-reading world in his *Treatise on Calculation with the Hindu Numerals*, written around 825. Mathematicians within the caliphates then could draw upon the Indian tradition, as well as the Greek and Persian. On this foundation Muslim scientists of many nationalities, including al-Battani (d. 929), who came from the northern reaches of the Mesopotamian plain, and the Persian Omar Khayyám (d. 1123), made remarkable advances in both algebra and trigonometry.

The Arab conquests also led to an increase in long-distance commerce and the "discovery" of new sources of bullion. Soon after the Abbasid caliphate established its capital at Baghdad, the caliph al-Mansur (r. 745–75) reportedly remarked, "This is the Tigris; there is no obstacle between us and China; everything on the sea can come to us." By this time Arab ships were plying the maritime routes from the Persian Gulf to China, and they soon outnumbered all others using these routes. By the ninth century they had acquired the compass (in China, most likely), and they may well have been the first to use it for marine navigation, since the Chinese do not seem to have used it for this purpose until after the tenth century.

. . . [Similarly,] the Arabs "pioneered" or improved an existing long-distance route across the Sahara, an ocean of sand rather than water. Routes across this desert had always existed, and trade and other contacts between West Africa and the Mediterranean date back at least to the Phoenician period. Still, the numbers of people and animals crossing this great ocean of sand were limited until the eighth century when Arabs, desiring to go directly to the source of the gold,[2] prompted an expansion of trade across the Sahara. Also during the eighth century Abdul al-Rahman, an Arab ruler of Morocco, sponsored the construction of wells on the trans-Saharan route from Sijilmasa to Wadidara to facilitate this traffic. This Arab "discovery" of West African gold eventually doubled the amount of gold in international circulation. East Africa, too, became a source of gold for the Arabs. By the tenth century Kilwa had become an important source of Zimbabwean gold.

Developments after 1200: The Mongolian Conquest and the Southernization of the European Mediterranean

By 1200 the process of Southernization had created a prosperous south from China to the Muslim Mediterranean. Although mathematics, the pioneering of new ocean routes, and "discoveries" of bullion are not inextricably connected to locations within forty degrees of the equator, several crucial elements in the process of Southernization were closely linked to latitude. Cotton generally does not grow above the fortieth parallel. Sugar, cinnamon, and pepper are tropical or subtropical crops, and the fine spices will grow only on particular tropical islands. Thus for many centuries the more southern parts of Asia

---

[2] One of the sources of gold was the area called the "gold coast" of Africa, south of the Sahara centered in what is today Ghana. [Ed.]

and the Muslim Mediterranean enjoyed the profits that these developments brought, while locations that were too far north to grow these southern crops were unable to participate in such lucrative agricultural enterprises.

The process of Southernization reached its zenith after 1200, in large part because of the tumultuous events of the thirteenth century. During that century in both hemispheres there were major transformations in the distribution of power, wealth, and prestige. In the Western Hemisphere several great powers went down. Cahokia (near East St. Louis, Illinois), which for three centuries had been the largest and most influential of the Mississippian mound-building centers, declined after 1200, and in Mexico Toltec power collapsed. In the Mediterranean the prestige of the Byzantine empire was destroyed when Venetians seized its capital in 1204. From 1212 to 1270 the Christians conquered southern Spain, except for Granada. In West Africa, Ghana fell to Sosso, and so did Mali, one of Ghana's allies. But by about 1230 Mali, in the process of seeking its own revenge, had created an empire even larger than Ghana's. At the same time Zimbabwe was also becoming a major power in southern Africa.

The grandest conquerors of the thirteenth century were the Central Asians. Turkish invaders established the Delhi sultanate in India. Mongolian cavalries devastated Baghdad, the seat of the Abbasid caliphate since the eighth century, and they captured Kiev, further weakening Byzantium. By the end of the century they had captured China, Korea, and parts of mainland Southeast Asia as well.

Because the Mongols were pagans at the time of their conquests, the western Europeans cheered them on as they laid waste to one after another Muslim center of power in the Middle East. The Mongols were stopped only when they encountered the Mamluks of Egypt at Damascus. In East Asia and Southeast Asia only the Japanese and the Javanese were able to defeat them. The victors in Java went on to found Majapahit, whose power and prestige then spread through maritime Southeast Asia.

Both hemispheres were reorganized profoundly during this turmoil. Many places that had flourished were toppled, and power gravitated to new locales. In the Eastern Hemisphere the Central Asian conquerors had done great damage to traditional southern centers just about everywhere, except in Africa, southern China, southern India, and maritime Southeast Asia. At the same time the Mongols' control of overland routes between Europe and Asia in the thirteenth and early fourteenth centuries fostered unprecedented contacts between Europeans and peoples from those areas that had long been southernized. Marco Polo's long sojourn in Yüan Dynasty China is just one example of such interaction.

Under the Mongols overland trade routes in Asia shifted north and converged on the Black Sea. After the Genoese helped the Byzantines to retake Constantinople from the Venetians in 1261, the Genoese were granted special privileges of trade in the Black Sea. Italy then became directly linked to the Mongolian routes. Genoese traders were among the first and were certainly the most numerous to open up trade with the Mongolian states in southern Russia and Iran. In the words of one Western historian, in their Black Sea colonies they "admitted to citizenship" people of many nationalities, including those of "strange background and questionable belief," and they "wound up christening children of the best ancestry with such uncanny names as Saladin, Hethum, or Hulugu."

Such contacts contributed to the Southernization of the Christian Mediterranean during this period of Mongolian hegemony. Although European conquerors sometimes had taken over sugar and cotton lands in the Middle East during the Crusades, not until some time after 1200 did the European-held Mediterranean islands become important exporters. Also after 1200 Indian mathematics began to have a significant impact in Europe. Before that time a few western European scholars had become acquainted with Indian numerals in Spain, where the works of al-Kharazmi, al-Battani, and other mathematicians had been translated into Latin. Nevertheless, Indian numerals and mathematics did not become important in western Europe until the thirteenth century after the book *Liber abaci* (1202), written by Leonardo Fibonacci of Pisa (c. 1170–1250), introduced them to the commercial centers of Italy. Leonardo had grown up in North Africa (in what is now Bejala, Algeria), where his father, consul over the Pisan merchants in that port, had sent him to study calculation with an Arab master.

In the seventeenth century, when Francis Bacon observed the "force and virtue and consequences of discoveries," he singled out three technologies in particular that "have changed the whole face and state of things throughout the world." These were all Chinese inventions—the compass, printing, and gunpowder. All three were first acquired by Europeans during this time of hemispheric reorganization.

It was most likely the Arabs who introduced the compass to Mediterranean waters, either at the end of the twelfth or in the thirteenth century. Block printing, gunpowder, and cannon appeared first in Italy in the fourteenth century, apparently after making a single great leap from Mongolian-held regions of East Asia to Italy. How this great leap was accomplished is not known, but the most likely scenario is one suggested by Lynn White Jr., in an article concerning how various other Southern (rather than Eastern) Asian technologies reached western Europe at about this time. He thought it most likely that they were introduced by "Tatar" slaves, Lama Buddhists from the frontiers of China whom the Genoese purchased in Black Sea marts and delivered to Italy. By 1450 when this trade reached its peak, there were thousands of these Asian slaves in every major Italian city. . . .

The Rise of Europe's North

The rise of the north, or more precisely, the rise of Europe's northwest, began with the appropriation of those elements of Southernization that were not confined by geography. In the wake of their southern European neighbors, they became partially southernized, but they could not engage in all aspects of the process due to their distance from the equator. Full Southernization and the wealth that we now associate with northwestern Europe came about only after their outright seizure of tropical and subtropical territories and their rounding of Africa and participation in Southern Ocean trade. . . .

Even though the significance of indigenous developments in the rise of northwestern Europe should not be minimized, it should be emphasized that many of the most important causes of the rise of the West are not to be found within the bounds of Europe. Rather, they are the result of the transformation of western Europe's relationships with other regions of the Eastern Hemisphere. Europe began its rise only after the thirteenth-century reorganization of the Eastern Hemisphere facilitated its Southernization, and Europe's northwest did not rise until it too was reaping the profits of Southernization. Thus the rise of the North Atlantic powers should not be oversimplified so that it appears to be an isolated and solely European phenomenon, with roots that spread no farther afield than Greece. Rather, it should be portrayed as one part of a hemisphere-wide process, in which a northwestern Europe ran to catch up with a more developed south—a race not completed until the eighteenth century.

7

JARED DIAMOND
Easter Island's End

In comparison with the grand theories of White and Shaffer, an essay on a small island in the Pacific might seem to be an exercise in the recent vogue of small-bore "micro-history." It is not. Jared Diamond, author of *Guns, Germs, and Steel*, uses small examples to big effect. In this selection and in his larger book-length treatment, *Collapse: How Societies Choose to Fail or Succeed*, Diamond teases a global lesson from the history of tiny Easter Island. What is that lesson? What does

---

Source: Jared Diamond, "Easter Island's End," *Discover* 16, no. 8 (August 1995).

Diamond's essay suggest about the causes of environmental decline?
Are we in danger of duplicating the fate of Easter Island? How can we
avoid the fate of Easter Island?

THINKING HISTORICALLY

How does Diamond's essay challenge the thesis of Lynn White Jr.? Do
you see in this essay an alternative grand theory for understanding
our environmental problems? If so, what is that theory? Do you agree
or disagree with it? Why or why not?

In just a few centuries, the people of Easter Island wiped out their
forest, drove their plants and animals to extinction, and saw their complex society spiral into chaos and cannibalism. Are we about to follow
their lead?

Among the most riveting mysteries of human history are those posed
by vanished civilizations. Everyone who has seen the abandoned buildings of the Khmer, the Maya, or the Anasazi is immediately moved to
ask the same question: Why did the societies that erected those structures disappear? . . .

Among all such vanished civilizations, that of the former Polynesian
society on Easter Island remains unsurpassed in mystery and isolation.
The mystery stems especially from the island's gigantic stone statues and
its impoverished landscape, but it is enhanced by our associations with
the specific people involved: Polynesians represent for us the ultimate in
exotic romance. . . .

But my interest has been revived recently by . . . painstaking research
and analysis. My friend David Steadman, a paleontologist, has been
working with a number of other researchers who are carrying out the
first systematic excavations on Easter intended to identify the animals
and plants that once lived there. Their work is contributing to a new
interpretation of the island's history that makes it a tale not only of
wonder but of warning as well.

Easter Island, with an area of only 64 square miles, is the world's most
isolated scrap of habitable land. It lies in the Pacific Ocean more than
2,000 miles west of the nearest continent (South America), 1,400 miles
from even the nearest habitable island (Pitcairn). Its subtropical location
and latitude—at 27 degrees south, it is approximately as far below the
equator as Houston is north of it—help give it a rather mild climate,
while its volcanic origins make its soil fertile. In theory, this combination
of blessings should have made Easter a miniature paradise, remote from
problems that beset the rest of the world.

The island derives its name from its "discovery" by the Dutch explorer Jacob Roggeveen, on Easter (April 5) in 1722. Roggeveen's first impression was not of a paradise but of a wasteland: "We originally, from a further distance, have considered the said Easter Island as sandy; the reason for that is this, that we counted as sand the withered grass, hay, or other scorched and burnt vegetation, because its wasted appearance could give no other impression than of a singular poverty and barrenness."

The island Roggeveen saw was a grassland without a single tree or bush over ten feet high. Modern botanists have identified only 47 species of higher plants native to Easter, most of them grasses, sedges, and ferns. The list includes just two species of small trees and two of woody shrubs. With such flora, the islanders Roggeveen encountered had no source of real firewood to warm themselves during Easter's cool, wet, windy winters. Their native animals included nothing larger than insects, not even a single species of native bat, land bird, land snail, or lizard. For domestic animals, they had only chickens. European visitors throughout the eighteenth and early nineteenth centuries estimated Easter's human population at about 2,000, a modest number considering the island's fertility. As Captain James Cook recognized during his brief visit in 1774, the islanders were Polynesians (a Tahitian man accompanying Cook was able to converse with them). Yet despite the Polynesians' well-deserved fame as a great seafaring people, the Easter Islanders who came out to Roggeveen's and Cook's ships did so by swimming or paddling canoes that Roggeveen described as "bad and frail." Their craft, he wrote, were "put together with manifold small planks and light inner timbers, which they cleverly stitched together with very fine twisted threads. . . . But as they lack the knowledge and particularly the materials for caulking and making tight the great number of seams of the canoes, these are accordingly very leaky, for which reason they are compelled to spend half the time in bailing." The canoes, only ten feet long, held at most two people, and only three or four canoes were observed on the entire island.

With such flimsy craft, Polynesians could never have colonized Easter from even the nearest island, nor could they have traveled far offshore to fish. The islanders Roggeveen met were totally isolated, unaware that other people existed. Investigators in all the years since his visit have discovered no trace of the islanders' having any outside contacts: not a single Easter Island rock or product has turned up elsewhere, nor has anything been found on the island that could have been brought by anyone other than the original settlers or the Europeans. Yet the people living on Easter claimed memories of visiting the uninhabited Sala y Gomez reef 260 miles away, far beyond the range of the leaky canoes seen by Roggeveen. How did the islanders' ancestors reach that reef from Easter, or reach Easter from anywhere else?

Figure 14.5   Easter Island Statues.
Source: © Westend61/Alamy.

Easter Island's most famous feature is its huge stone statues, more than 200 of which once stood on massive stone platforms lining the coast. [See Figure 14.5.] At least 700 more, in all stages of completion, were abandoned in quarries or on ancient roads between the quarries and the coast, as if the carvers and moving crews had thrown down their tools and walked off the job. Most of the erected statues were carved in a single quarry and then somehow transported as far as six miles—despite heights as great as 33 feet and weights up to 82 tons. The abandoned statues, meanwhile, were as much as 65 feet tall and weighed up to 270 tons. The stone platforms were equally gigantic: up to 500 feet long and 10 feet high, with facing slabs weighing up to 10 tons.

Roggeveen himself quickly recognized the problem the statues posed: "The stone images at first caused us to be struck with astonishment," he wrote, "because we could not comprehend how it was possible that these people, who are devoid of heavy thick timber for making any machines, as well as strong ropes, nevertheless had been able to erect such images." Roggeveen might have added that the islanders had no wheels, no draft animals, and no source of power except their own muscles. How did they transport the giant statues for miles, even before erecting them? To deepen the mystery, the statues were still standing in 1770, but by 1864 all of them had been pulled down, by the islanders themselves. Why then did they carve them in the first place? And why did they stop?

The statues imply a society very different from the one Roggeveen saw in 1722. Their sheer number and size suggest a population much larger than 2,000 people. What became of everyone? Furthermore, that society must have been highly organized. Easter's resources were scattered across the island: the best stone for the statues was quarried at Rano Raraku near Easter's northeast end; red stone, used for large crowns adorning some of the statues, was quarried at Puna Pau, inland in the southwest; stone carving tools came mostly from Aroi in the northwest. Meanwhile, the best farmland lay in the south and east, and the best fishing grounds on the north and west coasts. Extracting and redistributing all those goods required complex political organization. What happened to that organization, and how could it ever have arisen in such a barren landscape? . . .

[There is] overwhelming evidence that the Easter Islanders were typical Polynesians derived from Asia rather than from the Americas and that their culture (including their statues) grew out of Polynesian culture. Their language was Polynesian, as Cook had already concluded. Specifically, they spoke an eastern Polynesian dialect related to Hawaiian and Marquesan, a dialect isolated since about A.D. 400, as estimated from slight differences in vocabulary. Their fishhooks and stone adzes resembled early Marquesan models. Last year DNA extracted from 12 Easter Island skeletons was also shown to be Polynesian. The islanders grew bananas, taro, sweet potatoes, sugarcane, and paper mulberry—typical Polynesian crops, mostly of Southeast Asian origin. Their sole domestic animal, the chicken, was also typically Polynesian and ultimately Asian, as were the rats that arrived as stowaways in the canoes of the first settlers.

What happened to those settlers? The fanciful theories of the past must give way to evidence gathered by hardworking practitioners in three fields: archeology, pollen analysis, and paleontology. Modern archeological excavations on Easter have continued since Heyerdahl's 1955 expedition. The earliest radiocarbon dates associated with human activities are around A.D. 400 to 700, in reasonable agreement with the approximate settlement date of 400 estimated by linguists. The period of statue construction peaked around 1200 to 1500, with few if any statues erected thereafter. Densities of archeological sites suggest a large population; an estimate of 7,000 people is widely quoted by archeologists, but other estimates range up to 20,000, which does not seem implausible for an island of Easter's area and fertility.

Archeologists have also enlisted surviving islanders in experiments aimed at figuring out how the statues might have been carved and erected. Twenty people, using only stone chisels, could have carved even the largest completed statue within a year. Given enough timber and fiber for making ropes, teams of at most a few hundred people could have loaded the statues onto wooden sleds, dragged them over lubricated wooden tracks or rollers, and used logs as levers to maneuver them into a standing position. Rope could have been made from the fiber of a small native tree, related to the linden, called the hauhau. However, that tree is now extremely scarce on Easter, and hauling one statue would have required hundreds of yards of rope. Did Easter's now barren landscape once support the necessary trees? . . .

. . . [Pollen analysis reveals that for] at least 30,000 years before human arrival and during the early years of Polynesian settlement, Easter was not a wasteland at all. Instead, a subtropical forest of trees and woody bushes towered over a ground layer of shrubs, herbs, ferns, and grasses. . . . The tall, unbranched trunks of the Easter Island palm would have been ideal for transporting and erecting statues and constructing large canoes. The palm would also have been a valuable food source, since its [still-surviving] Chilean relative yields edible nuts as well as sap from which Chileans make sugar, syrup, honey, and wine.

What did the first settlers of Easter Island eat when they were not glutting themselves on the local equivalent of maple syrup? Recent excavations by David Steadman, of the New York State Museum at Albany, have yielded a picture of Easter's original animal world as surprising as Flenley and King's picture of its plant world. . . . Less than a quarter of the bones in its early garbage heaps (from the period 900 to 1300) belonged to fish; instead, nearly one-third of all bones came from porpoises.

Nowhere else in Polynesia do porpoises account for even 1 percent of discarded food bones. But most other Polynesian islands offered animal food in the form of birds and mammals. . . . The porpoise species identified at Easter, the common dolphin, weighs up to 165 pounds. It generally lives out at sea, so it could not have been hunted by line fishing or spearfishing from shore. Instead, it must have been harpooned far offshore, in big seaworthy canoes built from the extinct palm tree.

In addition to porpoise meat, Steadman found, the early Polynesian settlers were feasting on seabirds. For those birds, Easter's remoteness and lack of predators made it an ideal haven as a breeding site, at least until humans arrived. Among the prodigious numbers of seabirds that bred on Easter were albatross, boobies, frigate birds, fulmars, petrels, prions, shearwaters, storm petrels, terns, and tropic birds. With at least 25 nesting species, Easter was the richest seabird breeding site in Polynesia and probably in the whole Pacific. Land birds as well went into early Easter Island cooking pots. . . .

Porpoises, seabirds, land birds, and rats did not complete the list of meat sources formerly available on Easter. A few bones hint at the possibility of breeding seal colonies as well. All these delicacies were cooked in ovens fired by wood from the island's forests.

Such evidence lets us imagine the island onto which Easter's first Polynesian colonists stepped ashore some 1,600 years ago, after a long canoe voyage from eastern Polynesia. They found themselves in a pristine paradise. What then happened to it? The pollen grains and the bones yield a grim answer.

Pollen records show that destruction of Easter's forests was well under way by the year 800, just a few centuries after the start of human settlement. Then charcoal from wood fires came to fill the sediment cores, while pollen of palms and other trees and woody shrubs decreased or disappeared, and pollen of the grasses that replaced the forest became more abundant. Not long after 1400 the palm finally became extinct, not only as a result of being chopped down but also because the now ubiquitous rats prevented its regeneration: of the dozens of preserved palm nuts discovered in caves on Easter, all had been chewed by rats and could no longer germinate. While the hauhau tree did not become extinct in Polynesian times, its numbers declined drastically until there weren't enough left to make ropes from. By the time Heyerdahl visited Easter, only a single, nearly dead toromiro tree remained on the island, and even that lone survivor has now disappeared. (Fortunately, the toromiro still grows in botanical gardens elsewhere.)

The fifteenth century marked the end not only for Easter's palm but for the forest itself. Its doom had been approaching as people cleared land to plant gardens; as they felled trees to build canoes, to transport and erect statues, and to burn; as rats devoured seeds; and probably as the native birds died out that had pollinated the trees' flowers and dispersed their fruit. The overall picture is among the most extreme examples of forest destruction anywhere in the world: the whole forest gone, and most of its tree species extinct.

The destruction of the island's animals was as extreme as that of the forest: without exception, every species of native land bird became extinct. Even shellfish were overexploited, until people had to settle for small sea snails instead of larger cowries. Porpoise bones disappeared abruptly from garbage heaps around 1500; no one could harpoon porpoises anymore, since the trees used for constructing the big seagoing canoes no longer existed. The colonies of more than half of the seabird species breeding on Easter or on its offshore islets were wiped out.

In place of these meat supplies, the Easter Islanders intensified their production of chickens, which had been only an occasional food item. They also turned to the largest remaining meat source available: humans, whose bones became common in late Easter Island garbage heaps. Oral traditions of the islanders are rife with cannibalism; the most inflammatory taunt that could be snarled at an enemy was "The flesh of your mother sticks between my teeth." With no wood available to cook these new goodies, the islanders resorted to sugarcane scraps, grass, and sedges to fuel their fires.

All these strands of evidence can be wound into a coherent narrative of a society's decline and fall. The first Polynesian colonists found themselves on an island with fertile soil, abundant food, bountiful building materials, ample lebensraum,[1] and all the prerequisites for comfortable living. They prospered and multiplied.

[1] Room to live. [Ed.]

After a few centuries, they began erecting stone statues on platforms, like the ones their Polynesian forebears had carved. With passing years, the statues and platforms became larger and larger, and the statues began sporting ten-ton red crowns—probably in an escalating spiral of one-upmanship, as rival clans tried to surpass each other with shows of wealth and power. . . .

Eventually Easter's growing population was cutting the forest more rapidly than the forest was regenerating. The people used the land for gardens and the wood for fuel, canoes, and houses—and, of course, for lugging statues. As forest disappeared, the islanders ran out of timber and rope to transport and erect their statues. Life became more uncomfortable—springs and streams dried up, and wood was no longer available for fires.

People also found it harder to fill their stomachs, as land birds, large sea snails, and many seabirds disappeared. Because timber for building seagoing canoes vanished, fish catches declined and porpoises disappeared from the table. Crop yields also declined, since deforestation allowed the soil to be eroded by rain and wind, dried by the sun, and its nutrients to be leeched from it. Intensified chicken production and cannibalism replaced only part of all those lost foods. Preserved statuettes with sunken cheeks and visible ribs suggest that people were starving.

With the disappearance of food surpluses, Easter Island could no longer feed the chiefs, bureaucrats, and priests who had kept a complex society running. Surviving islanders described to early European visitors how local chaos replaced centralized government and a warrior class took over from the hereditary chiefs. The stone points of spears and daggers, made by the warriors during their heyday in the 1600s and 1700s, still litter the ground of Easter today. By around 1700, the population began to crash toward between one-quarter and one-tenth of its former number. People took to living in caves for protection against their enemies. Around 1770 rival clans started to topple each other's statues, breaking the heads off. By 1864 the last statue had been thrown down and desecrated.

As we try to imagine the decline of Easter's civilization, we ask ourselves, "Why didn't they look around, realize what they were doing, and stop before it was too late? What were they thinking when they cut down the last palm tree?"

I suspect, though, that the disaster happened not with a bang but with a whimper. After all, there are those hundreds of abandoned statues to consider. The forest the islanders depended on for rollers and rope didn't simply disappear one day—it vanished slowly, over decades. Perhaps war interrupted the moving teams; perhaps by the time the carvers had finished their work, the last rope snapped. In the meantime, any islander who tried to warn about the dangers of progressive deforestation would have been overridden by vested interests of carvers, bureaucrats, and chiefs, whose jobs depended on continued deforestation. Our Pacific Northwest loggers are only the latest in a long line of loggers to cry, "Jobs over trees!" The changes in forest cover from year to year would have been hard to detect: yes, this year we cleared those woods over there, but trees are starting to grow back again on this abandoned garden site here. . . .

Gradually trees became fewer, smaller, and less important. By the time the last fruit-bearing adult palm tree was cut, palms had long since ceased to be of economic significance. That left only smaller and smaller palm saplings to clear each year, along with other bushes and treelets. No one would have noticed the felling of the last small palm.

By now the meaning of Easter Island for us should be chillingly obvious. Easter Island is Earth writ small. Today, again, a rising population confronts shrinking resources. We too have no emigration valve, because all human societies are linked by international transport, and we can no more escape into space than the Easter Islanders could flee into the ocean. If we continue to follow our present course, we shall have exhausted the world's major fisheries, tropical rain forests, fossil fuels, and much of our soil by the time my sons reach my current age.

. . . Our risk now is of winding down, slowly, in a whimper. Corrective action is blocked by vested interests, by well-intentioned political and business leaders, and by their electorates, all of whom are perfectly correct in not noticing big changes from year to year. Instead, each year there are just somewhat more people, and somewhat fewer resources, on Earth. It would be easy to close our eyes or to give up in despair. If mere thousands of Easter Islanders with only stone tools and their own muscle power sufficed to destroy their society, how can billions of people with metal tools and machine power fail to do worse? But there is one crucial difference. The Easter Islanders had no books and no histories of other doomed societies. Unlike the Easter Islanders, we have histories of the past—information that can save us. My main hope for my sons' generation is that we may now choose to learn from the fates of societies like Easter's.

■ REFLECTIONS

Grand theories are difficult to evaluate, as are these. In part the difficulty is that they cover so much. How many images or primary sources could ever establish that a particular set of Christian ideas affected the way Christians actually behaved? And yet we know, or believe, that ideas matter. How many South Asian crops, tools, skills, and ideas constitute a global technological, let alone a scientific, revolution? And yet we know that past historians have overemphasized the impact of

European independence and Westernization. How many histories of societal collapse do we need to understand the threats to our own? And yet, we know that the more knowledge of how others have struggled and failed or succeeded we possess, the better our own chances for survival.

At least two issues lie beneath the surface of the debate in this chapter. One is the issue of culture, specifically the importance of cultural or religious ideas in shaping human behavior. White argues that religious ideas have a profound impact on how societies behave. Shaffer's study of material things rather than ideas, and even of ideas as things, offers a different view. By her account economic growth and technological development proceed with little regard to religions, ideologies, or belief systems. For Diamond too, not only are Christian or monotheistic ideas irrelevant, but historical processes leave precious little room for thoughtful intervention.

Historians are always working between ideas and things. Historians of ideas may have a tendency to see ideas shaping history, and historians of things (economic historians, for instance) may see ideas as mere rationalizations. But good historians are not predictable. Lynn White Jr. is perhaps best known for his book *Medieval Technology and Social Change* in which he argued, among other things, that the introduction of the stirrup into medieval Europe was the cause of the society and culture we call feudalism. While this idea is much debated today, one would have a hard time finding an example of a stronger argument of how a thing created a culture. Nor does Diamond, a professor of geography and physiology, ignore the role of ideas. In addition to the case of Easter Island, he surveys the example of Viking collapse in Greenland in his recent book, *Collapse: How Societies Choose to Fail or Succeed* (a title that suggests the power of will and ideas). The Vikings, he suggests, failed in Greenland because they were unable to change their culture in ways necessary to adapt to the new environment. For Diamond, ideas and political will offer the only hope against the blind destructiveness of entrenched interests and seemingly unstoppable historical processes.

Another issue below the surface of this debate is the relationship between ecology and economic development. We tend to think that one comes at the expense of the other. White criticizes Western (Christian) environmental behavior with the same lens that has allowed others to celebrate Western (Christian) economic development. This is a reason, by the way, why many contemporary world historians find both views too centered on the West or Europe. Lynda Shaffer's article on "Southernization" is in good part an effort to counter Europe-centered history with a more global version. But if Europe was not the source of modern technology, it was also not a source of our modern ecological predicament. Diamond is also critical of approaches that start and end in Europe. (His area of specialty is New Guinea.) Since he eliminated religious or cultural motives, his story of Easter Island can be read as an indictment of economic growth as the cause of ecological collapse. But the villain in Diamond's essay is not any kind of economic growth; it is the competitive economic exploitation of different tribes without any common plan or restraint. His message for our own predicament is to correct the anarchy of competing greedy corporations and interest groups with a common agenda and control.

Are not genuine economic growth and ecological balance mutually supportive? It is difficult to imagine long-term, healthy economic growth continuing while wrecking the environment. Similarly with environmental movements: White has us imagine that the true environmentalists are Buddhist mendicants and Hindu tree-huggers. But Buddhist monks might be content to cultivate their own gardens and ignore the rest of the world. After all, modern ecological political movements are largely products of rich societies with threatened environments. Might the most precarious ecologies display—by necessity—the greatest ecological concern? If that is the case, is the renewed popularity of environmental movements in our own age at least a sign of hope?

Acknowledgments

Chapter 1

1   Natalie Angier. "Furs for Evening, But Cloth Was the Stone Age Standby." From *The New York Times,* December 15, 1999. Copyright © 1999 by The New York Times Company. All rights reserved. Used by permission and protected by the Copyright Laws of the United States. The printing, copying, redistribution, or retransmission of the Material without express written permission is prohibited.

2   Marjorie Shostak. Excerpt from *Nisa: The Life and Words of a !Kung Woman.* Copyright © 1981 by Marjorie Shostak. Reprinted with the permission of Harvard University Press.

3   Margaret Ehrenberg. "The First Farmers." From *Women in Prehistory.* Copyright © 1989. Reprinted with the permission of University of Oklahoma Press.

4   Ramon A. Gutierrez. "The Pueblo Indian World in the Sixteenth Century." From *When Jesus Came, the Corn Mothers Went Away: Marriage, Sexuality and Power in New Mexico, 1500–1846.* Copyright © 1991. Reprinted with the permission of Stanford University Press.

5   Catherine Clay, Chandrika Paul, and Christine Senecal. "Women in the First Urban Communities." From *Envisioning Women in World History.* Copyright © 2009. Reprinted with the permission of McGraw-Hill, Inc.

6   Martha T. Roth. Excerpts from *Law Collections from Mesopotamia and Asia Minor,* Second Edition. Copyright © 1997. Reprinted with the permission of the Society of Biblical Literature.

Chapter 2

1   Kevin Reilly. "Cities and Civilization." From *The West and the World: A History of Civilization,* Second Edition. Copyright © 1988 by Kevin Reilly. Reprinted by permission of Pearson Education, Inc., Upper Saddle River, NJ.

2   Anonymous. Excerpt from *The Epic of Gilgamesh,* translated by N. K. Sandars. Copyright © 1972 by N. K. Sandars. Reprinted with the permission of Penguin Books, Ltd.

3   Martha T. Roth. Excerpt from *Law Collections from Mesopotamia and Asia Minor,* Second Edition. Copyright © 1997. Reprinted with the permission of the Society of Biblical Literature.

4   Miriam Lichtheim. "Advice to the Young Egyptian: 'Be a Scribe.'" From *Ancient Egyptian Literature: A Book of Readings, Volume 2: The New Kingdom.* Copyright © 1976 by the University of California Press Books. Reproduced with permission of University of California Press Books via Copyright Clearance Center.

5   Richard Hooker. Excerpts from *Book of the Dead*, Chapter 125, http://www. wsu.edu/~dee/EGYPT/BOD125.HTM. Copyright © 1996 by Richard Hooker. Reprinted with the permission of Richard Hines, Washington State University.

7   John Noble Wilford. "Mother Culture, or Only a Sister?" From *The New York Times*, March 15, 2005. Copyright © 2005 by The New York Times Company. All rights reserved. Used by permission and protected by the Copyright Laws of the United States. The printing, copying, redistribution, or retransmission of the Material without express written permission is prohibited.

Chapter 3

1   William H. McNeill. "Greek and Indian Civilization." From *A World History*, Second Edition. Copyright © 1971 by Oxford University Press. Reprinted by permission of the author.

2   Ainslie T. Embree. Excerpt from "The Rig Veda: Sacrifice as Creation." From *Sources of Indian Tradition*, Second Edition. Copyright © 1988 by Columbia University Press. Reprinted with permission of the publisher.

3   Ainslie T. Embree. Excerpt from "The Upanishads: Karma and Reincarnation." From *The Hindu Tradition: Readings in Oriental Thought*. Copyright © 1966 by Random House, Inc. Used by permission of Modern Library, a division of Random House, Inc.

4   Anonymous. Excerpt from "The Upanishads: Brahman and Atman." From "Chandogya Upanishad" in *The Upanishads*, translated by Juan Mascaro. Copyright © 1965 by Juan Mascaro. Reprinted with Permission of Penguin Books, Ltd.

5   Barbara Stoler Miller. "The Bhagavad Gita: Caste and Self." From *Bhagavad Gita*, translated by Barbara Stoler Miller. Translation copyright © 1986 by Barbara Stoler Miller. Used by permission of Bantam Books, a division of Random House, Inc.

6   Aristotle. "The Athenian Constitution: Territorial Sovereignty." From *Aristotle, Politics, and the Athenian Constitution*, translated by John Warrington. Copyright © 1959 by John Warrington. Reprinted with the permission of David Campbell Publishers, Ltd.

Chapter 4

1   Valerie Hansen. "The Creation of the Chinese Empire." From *The Open Empire: A History of China to 1600*. Copyright © 2000 by W. W. Norton & Company, Inc. Used by permission of W. W. Norton & Company, Inc.

2   Sima Qian. "The First Emperor." Excerpts from *Historical Records*, translated by Raymond Dawson. Copyright © 1994. Reprinted with the permission of Oxford University Press.

3   Confucius. Excerpts from *The Analects of Confucius*, translated by Arthur Waley. Copyright © 1958 by Arthur Waley. Reprinted with the permission of George Allen & Unwin and HarperCollins UK.

4   Han Fei. "Legalism." Excerpt from *Sources of Chinese Tradition, Volume 1: From Earliest Times to 1600*, edited by William Theodore de Bary. Copyright © 1963. Reprinted with the permission of Columbia University Press.

5   Laozi. "Taoism." Excerpts translated by Arthur Waley, from *The Way and Its Power: A Study of the* Tao Te Ching *and Its Place in Chinese Thought*. Reprinted with the permission of The Estate of Arthur Waley.

6   Rebecca Fleming. "Knowledge and Empire." From *Cambridge Illustrated History of the Roman World*, edited by Greg Woolf. Copyright © 2003. Reprinted with the permission of Cambridge University Press.

Chapter 5

1   Sarah Shaver Hughes and Brady Hughes. "Women in Ancient Civilizations." From *Women's History in Global Perspective, Volume II*, edited by Bonnie G. Smith. Copyright © 2005. Reprinted with the permission of the American Historical Association.

2   Ban Zhao. "Lessons for Women." Excerpt from *Pan Chao: Foremost Woman Scholar of China, First Century A.D.: Background, Ancestry, Life and Writings of the Most Celebrated Chinese Woman of Letters*, translated by Nancy Lee Swann. Copyright © East Asian Library and the Gest Collection, Princeton University.

5   Ovid. "The Art of Love." Translated by A. S. Kline. Reprinted with permission.

Chapter 6

1   Anonymous. "Svetasvatara Upanishad." From *The Upanishads: The Breath of the Eternal*, translated by Swami Prabhavananda and Frederick Manchester. Copyright 1948, © 1957 by The Vedanta Society of Southern California. Reprinted by permission.

2   E. H. Brewster (translator). "Buddhism: Gotama's Discovery." Excerpt from "The Life of Gotama the Buddha" in *Buddhism* by Clarence H. Hamilton (1926).

3   William Theodore de Bary (editor). "Buddhism and Caste." From *The Buddhist Tradition in India, China, and Japan*. Copyright © 1969 by William Theodore de Bary, renewed 1997. Used by permission of Random House, Inc.

4   The Buddhist Text Translation Society. Excerpts from "The Lotus Sutra." Reprinted by permission.

5   Judaism and the Bible: History, Laws, and Psalms. Scripture taken from the HOLY BIBLE, New International Version ®. Copyright © 1973, 1978, 1984 by Biblica, Inc. Used by permission of Zondervan. All rights reserved.

6   Judaism and the Bible: Prophecy and the Apocalypse. Scripture taken from the HOLY BIBLE, New International Version ®. Copyright © 1973, 1978, 1984 by Biblica, Inc. Used by permission of Zondervan. All rights reserved.

7   The Christian Bible: Jesus According to Matthew. Scripture taken from the HOLY BIBLE, New International Version ®. Copyright © 1973, 1978, 1984 by Biblica, Inc. Used by permission of Zondervan. All rights reserved.

8   Paul, Letters. Scripture taken from the HOLY BIBLE, New International Version ®. Copyright © 1973, 1978, 1984 by Biblica, Inc. Used by permission of Zondervan. All rights reserved.

Chapter 7

1   Ofri Ilani. "Shattering a National Mythology." From *Haaretz,* March 21, 2008. Copyright © 2008. Reprinted with permission.

2   Pliny the Younger. "Pliny Consults the Emperor Trajan." Excerpt from *Pliny the Younger: Volume II*, Loeb Classical Library, translated by Betty Radice. Copyright © 1969 by the President and Fellows of Harvard College. The Loeb Classical Library ® is a registered trademark of the President and Fellows of Harvard College. Reprinted by permission of the publishers and the Trustees of the Loeb Classical Library.

3   Eusebius, Life of Constantine.

4   Christianity in China: The Nestorian Monument. Excerpt from *The Sacred Books and Early Literature of the East,* by Charles F. Horne, ed. (New York: Parke, Austin & Lipscomb, 1917), Vol. XII, *Medieval China,* pp. 381–92.

5   William Theodore de Bary (editor). "Buddhism in China: The Disposition of Error." From *The Buddhist Tradition in India, China, and Japan.* Copyright © 1969. Used by permission of Random House, Inc.

6   Michael Sells (translator), selections from the Koran, Chapters 1, 91, 109, and 112, excerpt from *Approaching the Qu'ran: The Early Revelations.* Copyright © 1999. Published by White Cloud Press. Reprinted by permission of White Cloud Press in the format Textbook via Copyright Clearance Center. Chapters 2, 4 from The Koran from *The New On-Line Translation of the Qur'an* (The Noor Foundation), www.islamusa.org.

7   Alexander Stille. "Scholars Are Quietly Offering New Theories of the Koran." From *The New York Times,* March 2, 2002. Copyright © 2002 by The New York Times Company. All rights reserved. Used by permission and protected by the Copyright Laws of the United States. The printing, copying, redistribution, or retransmission of the Material without express written permission is prohibited.

8   "Peace Terms with Jerusalem" from *Islam from the Prophet Muhammad to the Conquest of Constantinople,* edited and translated by Bernard Lewis. Reprinted by permission of Oxford University Press, Ltd.

9   "The Epic of Sundiata" (excerpts) from *Sundiata: A West African Epic of the Mande Peoples,* translated by David C. Conrad and narrated by Djanka Tassey Condé. Copyright © 2004. Reprinted with the permission of Hackett Publishing Company, Inc.

Chapter 8

2   The Magna Carta. From *Translations and Reprints from the Original Sources of European History,* translated by E. P. Cheney and edited by D. C. Munro,

volume I, book 6 (Philadelphia: University of Pennsylvania Press, 1897), 6–15, passim.

3   Islam: Sayings Ascribed to the Prophet. Excerpt from *Kanz al'Ummal*, Al-Muttaqi, quoted in *Islam from the Prophet Muhammad to the Capture of Constantinople*, ed. and trans. Bernard Lewis, vol. I (New York: Harper, 1974), 150–51.

4   "Hadith: Muhammad's Night Journey" from "Miracle of Al-Isra and Al-Miraj," www.geocities.com/islamicmiracles/miracle_of_al.htm. Reprinted with permission.

5   Al-Tanukhi. A Government Job. Excerpt from "Resurrections of Loquacity or Table-talk (10th century)" in *Muhammad's People: A Tale by Anthology* by Eric Schroeder (Portland, ME: Bond Wheelwright Company, 1955), 566–68.

6   Ichisada Miyazaki. "The Chinese Civil Service Exam." Excerpt from *China's Examination Hell*, translated by Conrad Schirokauer (New York: Weatherhill, 1976), 13–17, 111–16, passim.

7   Liu Tsung-yuan. "Camel Kuo the Gardener." From *Anthology of Chinese Literature*, edited and translated by Cyril Birch. Copyright © 1965 by Grove Press. Used by permission of Grove/Atlantic, Inc.

8   Simon Martin and Nikolai Grube. Excerpt from *Chronicle of the Maya Kings and Queens*. Copyright © 2008 by Simon Martin and Nikolai Grube. Reprinted by kind permission of Thames & Hudson, Ltd.

Chapter 9

1   Kevin Reilly. "Love in Medieval Europe, India, and Japan." From *The West and the World,* Third Edition. Copyright © 1997 by Kevin Reilly. Reprinted with the permission of Markus Wiener Publishers.

2   Ulrich von Liechtenstein. Excerpt from *The Service of Ladies*, translated by J. W. Thomas. Copyright © 1969 by the University of North Carolina Press. Used by permission of the publisher, www.uncpress.unc.edu.

3   Andreas Capellanus. Excerpt from *The Art of Courtly Love*, translated by John J. Parry. Copyright © 1990 by John J. Parry. Reprinted with the permission of Columbia University Press.

4   Kalidasa. Excerpt from "Shakuntala," translated by Barbara Stoler Miller, from *Theater of Memory: The Plays of Kalidasa*, edited by Barbara Stoler Miller. Copyright © 1984 by Barbara Stoler Miller. Reprinted with the permission of Columbia University Press.

5   Murasaki Shikibu. Excerpt from *The Tale of Genji*, translated by Arthur Waley. Copyright 1929 by Arthur Waley. Reprinted with the permission of The Estate of Arthur Waley.

6   Zhou Daguan. "Sex in the City of Angkor." Excerpt from *A Record of Cambodia: The Land and Its People*, translated by Peter Harris. Copyright © 2007 by Peter Harris. Reprinted with the permission of Silkworm Books.

Chapter 10

1 Fulcher of Chartres. "Pope Urban at Clermont." From *The First Crusade: The Chronicle of Fulcher of Chartres and Other Source Materials*, edited by Edward Peters. Copyright © 1998. Reprinted by permission of the University of Pennsylvania Press.

2 Solomon bar Simson. "Chronicle of Solomon bar Simson." From *The Jews and the Crusaders: The Hebrew Chronicles of the First and Second Crusades*, edited and translated by Shlomo Eidelberg. Copyright © 1977. Reprinted with the permission of Shlomo Eidelberg.

3 Anna Comnena. "The Alexiad." Excerpt from *The Alexiad of Princess Anna Comnena*, translated by Elizabeth A. S. Dawes. Reprinted with permission of Barnes and Noble Books, Totowa, New Jersey 07512.

4 Fulcher of Chartres. "The Siege of Antioch." From *The First Crusade: The Chronicle of Fulcher of Chartres and Other Source Materials*, edited by Edward Peters. Copyright © 1998. Reprinted by permission of the University of Pennsylvania Press.

7 Ibn al-Athir. "The Conquest of Jerusalem." From *Arab Historians of the Crusades: Selected and Translated from the Arabic Sources*, edited and translated by E. J. Costello and Francesco Gabrieli. Copyright © 1969 by The Regents of the University of California. Reprinted with permission of the University of California Press via Copyright Clearance Center.

8 S. D. Goitein (translator). "Letter from a Jewish Pilgrim in Egypt." From "Contemporary Letters on the Capture of Jerusalem by the Crusaders" in *Journal of Jewish Studies* 3, No. 4 (1952). Copyright 1952 by S. D. Goitein. Reprinted with the permission of the *Journal of Jewish Studies*.

Chapter 11

1 Gregory Guzman. Excerpt from "Were the Barbarians a Negative or Positive Factor in Ancient and Medieval History?" From *The Historian* 50 (August 1988): 558–72. Copyright © 1988. Reprinted with the permission of Blackwell Publishers, Ltd.

2 Ibn Fadlan. "The Viking Rus." From Albert Stanborough Cook, "Ibn Fadlan's Account of Scandinavian Merchants on the Volga in 922" from *Journal of English and Germanic Philology*, vol. 22, no. 1 (1923): 56–63. Copyright 1923 by the Board of Trustees of the University of Illinois. Used with permission of the author and the University of Illinois Press.

3 Barry Cunliffe. "The Western Vikings." From *Facing the Ocean: The Atlantic and Its Peoples*. Copyright © 2001 by Barry Cunliffe. Reprinted with the permission of Oxford University Press, Ltd.

4 Magnus Magnusson and Hermann Palsson (translators). "Eirik's Saga." From *The Vinland Sagas: The Norse Discovery of America*. Copyright © 1965 by Magnus Magnusson and Hermann Palsson. Reprinted with the permission of Penguin Books Ltd.

6   Kevin Reilly. "The Secret History of the Mongols." Adapted from R. P. Lister, *Genghis Khan*. Copyright © 1993. Reprinted with the permission of Cooper Square Press.

7   John of Plano Carpini. "History of the Mongols." From *Mission to Asia: Narratives and Letters of the Franciscan Missionaries in Mongolia and China in the Thirteenth and Fourteenth Centuries*, translated by a nun of Stanbrook Abbey, edited by Christopher Dawson. Copyright © 1955. Reprinted with permission.

Chapter 12

1   Mark Wheelis. "Biological Warfare at the 1346 Siege of Caffa." From *Emerging Infectious Diseases* 8, no. 9 (September 2002): 971–75, www.cdc.gov/ncidod/EID/vol8no9/01-0536.html.

2   Gabriele de' Mussis. "Origins of the Black Death." From *The Black Death*, translated and edited by Rosemary Horrox. Copyright © 1994 by Rosemary Horrox. Reprinted with the permission of Manchester University Press.

3   Giovanni Boccaccio. "The Plague in Florence." From *The Decameron*, translated by G. H. McWilliam. Copyright © 1972 by G. H. McWilliam. Reprinted with the permission of Penguin Books, Ltd.

6   Michael W. Dols. Excerpt from "The Comparative Communal Responses to the Black Death in Muslim and Christian Societies" from *Viator* 5 (1974): 269–87. Copyright © 1974. Reprinted with the permission of Brepols Publishers.

Chapter 13

1   Fernand Braudel. "Towns and Cities." From *The Structures of Everyday Life: The Limits of the Possible*. Copyright © 1983 by Fernand Braudel. Reprinted with the permission of HarperCollins Publishers, Ltd.

2   Gregorio Dati. "Corporations and Community in Florence." From "Istoria di Firenze dall'anno MCCCLXXX all'anno MCCCCV" (History of Florence from 1380 to 1405) from *The Society of Renaissance Florence*, edited and translated by Gene Brucker. Copyright © 1971 by Gene Brucker. Reprinted with the permission of the translator.

3   Marco Polo. "On the City of Hangchou." From *The Travels of Marco Polo*, the Complete Yule-Currier ed., volume 2 (New York: Dover, 1993), 185–206.

4   S. D. Goitein. "Cairo: An Islamic City in Light of the Geniza." From *Middle Eastern Cities*, edited by Ira M. Lapidus. Copyright © 1969 by The Regents of the University of California. Reprinted with permission of the University of California Press via Copyright Clearance Center.

5   Bernal Díaz. "Cities of Mexico." From *The Conquest of New Spain*, translated by J. M. Cohen. Copyright © 1963 by J. M. Cohen. Reprinted with the permission of Penguin Books, Ltd.

Chapter 14

1   Lynn White Jr. "The Historical Roots of Our Ecological Crisis." From *Science* 155 (March 1967): 1203–7. Copyright © 1967 by the American Association for the Advancement of Science. Reprinted by permission.

6   Lynda Norene Shaffer. "Southernization." From *Journal of World History* 5 (Spring 1994): 1–21. Copyright © 1994. Reprinted with the permission of University of Hawai'i Press.

7   Jared Diamond. Excerpt from "Easter Island's End." From *Discover* 16, no. 8 (August 1995). Copyright © 1995 by Jared Diamond. Reprinted with the permission of the author.

Popular value packages from Bedford/St. Martin's

For information on **free items for packaging** and **discounts up to 50%,** visit **bedfordstmartins.com/reilly/catalog** or contact your local Bedford/St. Martin's sales representative.

Textbooks

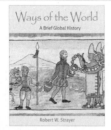

Guides

The Bedford Series in History and Culture

Trade Books   bedfordstmartins.com/tradeup

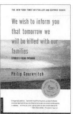

For a complete list of titles, visit **bedfordstmartins.com/history**.